SARAJEVO
A BIOGRAPHY

ROBERT J. DONIA

Sarajevo
A Biography

HURST & COMPANY, LONDON

First published in the United Kingdom by
C. Hurst & Co. (Publishers) Ltd,
41 Great Russell Street, London WC1B 3PL
© Robert J. Donia, 2006
All rights reserved.
Printed in India

A catalogue record for this volume is available
from the British Library.

ISBN 1–85065–765–3

To my father, Robert A. Donia,
and for the people of Sarajevo

Contents

Preface and Acknowledgements

What follows is, in several respects, an intimate history. Such an approach befits a city that is a compact, crowded, and intimate place. On the spectrum between experience and imagination expounded by Benedict Anderson,[1] Sarajevo is more an experienced than an imagined community. Crowded by hills to the north and south into a narrow east-west valley, the city boasts a public life that is largely concentrated in a kilometer-long stretch of land on either side of the Miljacka River. People know one another, greet one another on the street, and share the evening *korzo*, or stroll, on east-west walkways and streets in the heart of the Old City.

This history of Sarajevo is also intimate by virtue of my reliance on personal experiences and communications, as well as academic research, in preparing it. Over the past three decades, I have conducted research in archives and libraries in the city and spent, all told, about three years there. I first visited Sarajevo briefly as an undergraduate student in 1965, and in 1974–5 I lived there while conducting research in the city's archives and libraries for a dissertation on Bosnian history. After an absence of almost a decade, I have returned several times a year since 1994 to do research in its archives, to walk its streets, to seek out old friends, and to make new acquaintances. I have delighted in the hospitality of its people and no longer feel like an outsider. In this account I have drawn on my experiences and observations during those many visits and on information and insights provided by friends, acquaintances, and colleagues during my stays in the city.

My experience testifying before the International Criminal Tribunal for the Former Yugoslavia at The Hague informs parts of the following account. Chapters Eight and Nine owe much to my investigations into the complex antecedents of the siege of 1992–5 in preparation for that testimony and the written submission made to the court. The account that follows cites many documents admitted into evidence in conjunction with my testimony in 2002.

The work is a political history titled as a biography. It is a cumulative biography of those who have most influenced Sarajevo. At any given time a city is the aggregation of the individuals who live there, influence its development, and leave behind their achievements, both physical and intangible. In the following pages I identify the major actors who influenced Sarajevo and describe their achievements and legacy. My selection of the city's leading lights inevitably omits many individuals who merit that designation, but considerations of length and consistency have forced me to make difficult choices.

The book proceeds chronologically, as do individual chapters. Most of the following account is devoted to the late nineteenth and twentieth centuries, when the pace of change accelerated and the twin tragedies of fascist occupation in the 1940s and siege in the 1990s wrought the greatest destruction on the town. I have concentrated on transitional times, when the ragged edges of historical change often allowed local leaders to exercise considerable control over the city's destiny before more powerful forces coerced conformity with broader trends.

Despite its focus on the city of Sarajevo, this book is also intended as a contribution to the history of Bosnia-Herzegovina. I have concluded that it is both impractical and unwise to disentangle completely the experiences of from Sarajevans from the history of the country. To extract the "national" urban life would be to strip away Sarajevans' leading role in shaping the character of Bosnia-Herzegovina, and to risk presenting the city's history as a collection of parochialisms. More often than not, Sarajevans led the movements and trends in their homeland, and their roles as leaders constitute an illuminating part of the city's history.

The sum of my historical research and personal experience has compelled one overriding conclusion: much remains untold, and more yet undiscovered, in the informational catacombs of the city's past. Sarajevo only slowly and reluctantly gives up its secrets (unlike its myths, which are readily available and propagated indiscriminately to insiders and visitors alike) when it gives them up at all. To conclude that one has reached the bottom of any historical issue in Sarajevo almost guarantees the eventual discovery of additional material that stirs doubt and compels further inquiry.

Acknowledgements

In my journey of discovery I have been aided by hundreds of Sarajevans and friends of the city, far too many to mention here. But among the many I want to thank my good friend and colleague Husnija Kamberović, Director of the Institute for History in Sarajevo, and Institute associates Seka Brkljača, Vera Kac, and Senija Milišić. In the 1970s, when I first delved into the history of Bosnia-Herzegovina, Dževad Juzbašić and Nusret Šehić were also associates at the Institute, and they helped me immensely. Through the many changes in our lives over the past three decades, they have continued to be confidants and colleagues, and I thank them for enriching my understanding. For his help in exploring Sarajevo and in many other ways, I am thankful to Kemal Bakaršić, Professor of Library Science at the University of Sarajevo and tireless devotee of new and interesting discoveries.

This study has been aided in important ways by four former directors of the Institute for History: Ibrahim Karabegović, Tomislav Išek, the late Boris Nilević, and Enver Redžić. To Tomo Kraljačić and Ibrahim Tepić, both deceased, and to Iljas Hadžibegović I owe insights gained in many hours over coffee in the 1970s when we were all conducting doctoral research, and to Iljas my thanks for his steady support and guidance over the past decade. I value the many insights and the friendship of Mirko Pejanović over the past several years. I appreciate the ever-helpful directors and staff of the Archive of Bosnia-Herzegovina, the Historical Archive of Sarajevo (*Istorijski arhiv Sarajevo*), the Historical Museum of Bosnia-Herzegovina (*Historijski muzej Bosne i Hercegovine*), the Soros Media Center, and the National and University Library. My thanks to Messrs Suljo Džamalija and Mahir Esad at the Geodetic Institute of Bosnia-Herzegovina (*Geodetski zavod Bosne i Hercegovine*) for assistance in compiling information for the maps. And I thank the members of the Hondo family for making me feel I have a home in Sarajevo.

I also acknowledge several co-discoverers of the city who have raised provocative questions and joined me in seeking answers. First among them are John Fine, tireless historian and lifelong friend, and his wife Gena. I also thank Victor Jackovich, the first US Ambassador to Bosnia-Herzegovina and a friend of Sarajevo since the 1970s; and Sinan Alić, Tuzlan by residence and journalist by passion, and his wife Sonja, both of whom have helped me with my understanding of all things Bosnian. Mary Murrell provided an invaluable editorial review of the manuscript. Chris Brest prepared the maps. I am indebted to each of them for their professionalism, patience, provocative questions, and careful attention to the details of their crafts. To the publishers—Christopher Hurst and Michael Dwyer in London and James Reische in Ann Arbor, Michigan—my thanks for their encouragement and commitment to seeing this work through to publication.

These faithful friends and colleagues bear no responsibility for any errors or omissions in the following pages.

Portions of chapters 2 and 3 appeared in Robert J. Donia, "Fin-de-Siècle Sarajevo: The Habsburg Transformation of an Ottoman Town," *Austrian History Yearbook*, 32 (2002), pp. 43–76, and are reprinted with the permission of the Center for Austrian Studies at the University of Minnesota.

La Jolla, California   R.J.D.
September 2005

Illustrations

Illustrations

COLOR
between pages 202 and 203

Maps

Tables

Abbreviations

ABH	*Arhiv Bosne i Hercegovine* (Archive of Bosnia-Herzegovina)
ARBiH	*Armija Republike Bosne i Hercegovine* (Army of the Republic of Bosnia-Herzegovina
AVNOJ	*Antifašističko vijeće narodnog oslobodjenja Jugoslavije* (Anti-Fascist Council of People's Liberation of Yugoslavia)
BCS	Bosnian-Croatian-Serbian (language)
BiH	Bosnia-Herzegovina
ERN	Evidence Registration Number
GFM	*Gemeinsam Finanzministerium* (Joint Ministry of Finance)
HDZ	*Hrvatska demokratska zajednica* (Croat Democratic Union)
HHSA	*Haus, Hof und Staatsarchiv* (House, Court, and State Archive) (Vienna)
HSS	*Hrvatska seljačka stranka* (Croat Republican Peasant Party)
IAS	*Istorijski arhiv Sarajevo* (Historical Archive, Sarajevo)
ICTY	International Criminal Tribunal for the Former Yugoslavia
IFOR	Implementation Force (NATO-led, 1996–7)
JMO	*Jugoslovenska muslimanska organizacija* (Yugoslav Muslim Organization)
JNA	*Jugoslavenska narodna armija* (Yugoslav People's Army)
KP	*Komunistička partija* (Communist Party)
LR	*Landesregierung* (Regional Government)
MUP	*Ministarstvo unutrašnjih poslova* (Ministry of Internal Affairs)
NDH	*Nezavisna Država Hrvatska* (Independent State of Croatia)
OMRI	Open Media Research Institute
PrBH	*Präsidial Register* (in Archive of Bosnia-Herzegovina)
PRO	Public Records Office (London)
SDA	*Stranka demokratske akcije* (Party of Democratic Action)
SDS	*Srpska demokratska stranka* (Serb Democratic Party)
SDP	*Socijaldemokratska partija* (Social Democratic Party)
SGV	*Sarajevo gradsko vijeće* (Sarajevo City Council)
SK	*Savez Komunista* (League of Communists)
SUR	Publication entitled *Sarajevo u revoluciji* (Sarajevo in revolution)
SUSJ	Publication entitled *Sarajevo u socijalističkoj Jugoslaviji* (Sarajevo in socialist Yugoslavia)

UNPROFOR United Nations Protection Force
VRS *Vojska Republike Srpske* (Army of Republika Srpska)
ZAVNOBiH *Zemaljsko antifašističko vijeće narodnog oslobodjenja Bosne i Hercegovine* (Regional Antifascist Council for the People's Liberation of Bosnia-Herzegovina)
ZNOR *Zbornik dokumenata i podataka o narodnooslobodilačkom ratu jugoslovenskih naroda* (Collection of documents and data on the People's Liberation War of the Yugoslav Peoples)

Pronunciation and Foreign Terms

The language known until about 1991 as Serbo-Croatian has since trifur-cated into three closely related and mutually intelligible languages: Bosnian, Croatian, and Serbian, often referred to conveniently by foreigners as the "local language." Serbian is most frequently rendered in the Cyrillic alphabet (although use of the Latin alphabet is becoming more common), whereas Bosnian and Croatian are written exclusively in the Latin alphabet. I use the Latin alphabet here, with diacritical marks over letters as appropriate. On occasion, as many as five consonants follow one another without an inter-vening vowel; in such cases, the trilled letter "r" assumes the role of a vowel, and all letters are pronounced in the order in which they appear. Vowels and consonants that are pronounced differently from English and consonants with diacritics are listed below.

a	*a*, as in far
c	*ts*, as in tbats
č	*ch*, as in touch
ć	*ch*, softer than *č*, between *ch* in chew and the first *t* in astute
dž	a hard *j*, as in judge
dj	a bit softer than *dž*, between the *j* in judge and *d* in duplex
e	*a*, as in bay
h	guttural, as the *ch* in Scottish loch
i	*ee*, as in cheese
j	*y*, as in young (Jugoslavija equals Yugoslavia)
o	*o* (long), as in open
r	is trilled
š	*sh*, as in shush
u	*u* (long), as in lute
ž	*zh*, as in leisure

The group known through most of its history as the Bosnian Muslims changed its name in September 1993 to the Bosniaks. Therefore I use the term Muslims, or Bosnian Muslims, in chapters 1 through 8 but Bosniaks from chapter 9 forward in accord with the group's preferred name. Bosniaks, however, are to be distinguished from Bosnians, a term that refers to people of all nationalities and religions who are citizens or residents of Bosnia-Herzegovina. I employ the adjectival forms Serb, Croat, and Bosniak (or Muslim) in reference to those of Serb, Croat, and Bosniak (Muslim) nationality regardless of where they live. As used here, the adjectival forms Bosnian, Serbian, and Croatian are reserved for the specific polities known today as Bosnia-Herzegovina (or Bosnia and Herzegovina), the Republic of Serbia, the Republic of Croatia, their respective predecessor polities, inhabitants, and citizens; and for the languages of the Bosniaks, Serbs, and Croats. Serbian is also used in reference to the Serbian Orthodox Church.

Terms from Arabic, Turkish, German, English, and other languages have found their way into Sarajevo's local language over the centuries. When a term is used in English (such as pasha, Chetnik, and Ustasha), I have rendered it in its common English form. Less familiar terms I have either translated into English or transliterated, after first mention in their original form.

Introduction

In the 1990s Sarajevo became synonymous with human agony. Millions of television viewers around the globe observed daily the death, injury, and deprivation inflicted on Sarajevans by the protracted siege of their city. The images were particularly inexplicable to those who had come to know the city as the idyllic backdrop to the Winter Olympic Games in 1984. To others, however, the siege brought to mind the city's notoriety as the site of the assassination of the Habsburg Archduke Franz Ferdinand in 1914, an act that set off a chain of events culminating in the First World War. Some observers hastily transformed Sarajevo into a metaphor for the times, portraying the 1914 assassination and the 1990s siege as two signature events that symbolically and chronologically bracketed Europe's violent twentieth century.

Walking the city's streets gives an impression that contradicts these popular media images of spectacular violence. In the course of a short east-west walk (about half an hour from the city's eastern end to the Marindvor square), one sees houses of worship of several faiths in close proximity to one another, Sarajevans greeting one another on the streets, and people gathered in cafés. A rich variety of architectural styles from several different eras attests to the respect of each new regime's visionaries for the achievements of their predecessors. In the city's eastern end, monumental Islamic institutions and reconstructed artisan shops testify to over four hundred years of Ottoman rule. Next, a sector of historicist and Secession structures bears witness to a briefer but growth-filled period of Habsburg administration. And to the west of Marindvor, high-rises and modernist public buildings from the era of socialism stretch for several miles to the western suburb of Ilidža. Buildings from one era stand next to those from another. The brief transversal of the city's core reveals a city of intimate diversity and vibrant human activity.

The city's physical layout has a counterpart in historical experience. In the past six centuries, six different governments have ruled the city, five of them in the twentieth century alone. Today's Sarajevo was almost entirely

1

built in three major eras of expansion: the first 140 years of Ottoman rule (approximately 1460–1600), the peacetime years of Austro-Hungarian administration (1883–1914), and the formative years of socialist rule (1945 until the 1984 Olympic Games.) Three of Sarajevo's six governing polities were great city-builders with distinct visions that structured or restructured society in an urban context. In each era, the new power-holders held a unifying vision of urban life that reflected their values and goals, and they implemented that vision to govern the contours of growth. Except for eliminating sworn enemies, these three governments sponsored Sarajevo's growth while facilitating the participation of multiple groups in molding Sarajevo's urban environment.

Human diversity has been Sarajevo's hallmark since it was founded in the fifteenth century. Outsiders have long marveled at its mixture of religions, peoples, and influences and have shared with its residents a certain incredulity that anyone would want to destroy it. The relative size of the city's major groups has changed many times through its history, and so have the designations by which they were known. In the city's early centuries, distinctions among groups were primarily religious, but in the twentieth century the differences were mainly among national groups.

Contemporary Sarajevo and Bosnia-Herzegovina are populated overwhelmingly by members of three major national groups: Bosniaks, Croats, and Serbs. Members of each group hold tenaciously to their secular identity, but they also invoke a distinctive religious heritage. Bosnia's Croats hark back to their Catholic heritage; Bosnia's Serbs call upon their Serbian Orthodox background; and Bosniaks see the Islamic faith and Muslim culture as their most formative influences. Today's Serbs were previously called Orthodox, Serbian Orthodox, or even Greek Orthodox Christians; Croats were referred to as Catholics or (less frequently) Latins; and Bosniaks were known until the late twentieth century as Bosnian Muslims or simply as Muslims. In addition, Jews have been a significant group in Bosnia-Herzegovina since their arrival in the sixteenth century. The tragedy of their near-total annihilation in the Second World War has meant that their role has diminished since then, but they nonetheless play a substantial role in Bosnia's public life.

Identities are never a simple matter, and rarely are they as complex as in Bosnia-Herzegovina. Some Sarajevans, feeling no primary loyalty to any of the above groups, declared themselves Yugoslavs (literally meaning South Slavs), particularly during the socialist era. About 5 percent of all Bosnians declared Yugoslav identity in the 1991 census, but about 10 percent in Sarajevo and several other towns claimed that identity. This group included many born of mixed marriages and others who found it a refuge from all national identities, as well as those who thought of themselves first and foremost as citizens of Yugoslavia. Some advocates believed that the separate nations in Yugoslavia might merge into an overarching Yugoslav identity, but the notion increasingly lost its appeal as the fortunes of socialist Yugoslavia waned in the 1980s. Yugoslav identity became a refuge, a census category for those seeking an alternative to the major national identities of the twentieth century.

Ironically group identities become more complex as the degree of magnification increases and the units of historical analysis become smaller, as evident in the period between the First and Second World Wars. During that time, leaders of the newly formed Yugoslav royal state recognized only three "named tribes" of the Yugoslav nation: Serbs, Croats, and Slovenes. But at the next level down in political organization, decisions made in Bosnia-Herzegovina took into account another group, the Bosnian Muslims, as well as the Serbs and Croats. In the city of Sarajevo, meanwhile, *four* groups were routinely recognized as collective actors: Catholics (Croats), Orthodox (Serbs), Muslims, and Jews. To establish their parity in public life, these four groups were normally identified as religious communities, even though Croats and Serbs advanced claims to a national identity and were recognized as nations by the royal government. Thus, upon closer examination, the number of political actors increased while the role of ideology correspondingly diminished as a criterion for recognizing group actors.

But just how "separate" were these groups in Sarajevo, and how did they get along? The siege and war of the 1990s ignited fierce polemics on these issues. In contrast to those who argued that Sarajevans had engaged in centuries of violent strife against one another, the United Nations Security Council hailed the "unique character of the city of Sarajevo, as a multi-cultural, multi-ethnic and pluri-religious center" in Resolution 824 of May 1993 and declared that the city (along with five others in Bosnia-Herzegovina) should be treated as a "safe area."[1] I argue not only that the Security Council's characterization is closer to the truth than the contentions of pundits who saw only perpetual savagery, but also that the relative demographic and social position of each group varied substantially with historical changes over the centuries.

Before the early 1990s Sarajevans would not have described their city using any of the "multi" terms embedded in Resolution 824. Instead, they referred approvingly to their "common life" (*zajednički život*). They envisioned their ethnically diverse city as a "neighborhood" (*komšiluk*), spoke of those from other ethnonational groups as "neighbors" (*komšije*), and valued their association with others as "neighborly relations" (*komšijski odnosi*).[2] These expressions more aptly capture Sarajevo's uniqueness and the traits that Sarajevans themselves value in their city's history. The prefix multi-, meaning "composed of many parts," affirms the existence of distinct cultural, ethnic, and religious communities that do not necessarily overlap and commingle. Common life, on the other hand, necessarily includes tolerance, defined as "a fair and permissive attitude toward those whose race, religion, nationality, etc., differ from one's own."[3] Like tolerance, common life presupposes that people belong to different groups and are unlikely to assimilate into an undifferentiated, homogenous whole. Sarajevans have long used the concept of neighborliness to express their respect for those of different faiths and nationalities, manifest in the practices of mutual visitations and well-wishing on holidays as well as everyday cordial relations. Common life is neighborliness writ large. It embodies those values, experiences, institutions, and aspirations *shared* by Sarajevans of different identities, and it has been treasured by most Sarajevans since the city's founding.

Common life has not been the same in each historical era, and at no time was it either easily constructed or effortlessly maintained. Relations among groups within the city have never been static, and the changes in relations among those of various groups have been anything but linear. Common life was fostered, under considerably varying policies and in quite different ways, by the Ottoman, Habsburg, and socialist regimes. But at other times, those who believed in a common life had to defend it against their rulers with all available means. Large-scale intergroup violence occurred on several occasions in the twentieth century. The Second World War and the prolonged siege of the early 1990s profoundly endangered common life. Its continuation is by no means assured as of this writing. But most Sarajevans, at most times and in widely varying circumstances, have held dear the traditions and practices of their common life.

Is Sarajevo unique for having experienced changes in its composition over time and as a home to diverse peoples? The populations of many other cities have been diverse, and most have experienced changes over time. But in major cities throughout Europe and the Mediterranean region, pluralism based on religious identity has not fared well at the hands of the modern nation-state. In a recent study of Salonica, the historian Mark Mazower shows how that city, richly diverse in Ottoman times, became an almost exclusively Greek city as a result of the internationally-sanctioned expulsion of its Muslims (1923–4), the extermination of its Jews (1943), and a Greek nationalist cultural campaign.[4] Residents of Istanbul and Jerusalem have also experienced political divisions, population shifts, and ethnonational conflict that resulted from the powerful onslaughts of modern nationalism and the aspiring nation-state.[5] Western European capital cities likewise have a history of diverse populations, and in the twentieth century many former capitals of empire, such as London, Amsterdam, Paris, and Vienna have become home to hundreds of thousands of émigrés from their former imperial lands. But they, too, have been profoundly changed by nationalist pressures. In those cities (including Sarajevo) that experienced Nazi occupation in the Second World War, the Holocaust constituted an unparalleled catastrophe for their Jews and a tragic change for the cities themselves in permanently altering their composition and quality of life.

Although Sarajevo has not been alone in experiencing diversity and major historical changes, the city's path through history has indeed been unique. Sarajevo benefited from the relatively benign environment of multinational empires until 1941. Most important, it experienced a Habsburg interregnum (1878–1918) between four centuries of Ottoman rule and inclusion in the royal Yugoslav state. During those forty years, Sarajevans became Europeans, and the city absorbed western influences that mixed and blended with its Ottoman past. Driven by the goals of pacifying Bosnians and impressing Europeans with their administrative aptitude, Habsburg administrators implemented a European vision of expansive construction without displacing either peoples or major monuments. In a little-noted achievement of a much-maligned bureaucracy, Habsburg rulers buffered Sarajevo (and Bosnia-Herzegovina) against the harsh gales of nationalist rage during the late nineteenth and early twentieth centuries. Sarajevo was thus spared the ruinous expulsions of peoples and the destruction of Ottoman-era Islamic structures that often accompanied nation-states' conquests of other cities. Furthermore, during royal Yugoslav governance (1918–41), Sarajevo's diversity likewise remained largely intact, despite the regime's tilt toward Serb national aspirations and its malign neglect of the city's economic condition.

In the twentieth century Sarajevo's diversity and tradition of tolerance suffered greatly in two great paroxysms of violence: occupation during the Second World War (1941–5) and siege during the Bosnian War (1992–5). In both instances many Sarajevans fought back, rising to defend their city and their neighbors against the extreme nationalisms that aimed to eradicate, in whole or in part, certain groups in the city. The city's history in these two eras reveals that the damage to diversity and pluralism was done by an alliance of neighboring nationalist polities and local nationalist political formations. In the absence of a strong national state in Bosnia-Herzegovina, nationalist political parties acquired some of the trappings, and performed some of the functions, of a sovereign state. Furthermore, in their successive incarnations during the century, nationalist Serb and Croat parties became more closely aligned with neighboring polities, coming by 1992 under the influence or control of the republics of Serbia and Croatia. It was not an indigenous nation-state that nearly wiped out Sarajevo's pluralism, it was the political parties that acted as surrogates for the interests of neighboring states.

This study is an inquiry into how the city's development was affected by the major historical transitions that accompanied changing regimes. My central thesis is that the city and its people became more prosperous, diverse, and tolerant in eras governed by a single inclusive vision, regardless of the particularities of the political system that sponsored or oversaw the realization of those aspirations. On the other hand, the city became less prosperous and less diverse in times of sectarian rule, extended contention, and noninclusive conceptions of urban life. In short, leadership mattered. Those leaders who projected a compelling inclusive vision and engaged a large portion of the population to participate actively in its realization made the city a better place and gave its inhabitants a more satisfying life. Leaders whose vision excluded members of major groups polarized the population and ultimately diminished the position even of those in whose name they claimed to have acted.

Numerous other studies have extensively examined the various regimes that governed the region, but these works have rarely focused on the role of a single community in the changing political landscape. A city's history offers the opportunity to capture human experience at the local level in a way that is necessarily elusive in a history of larger spaces. To examine a city's history is to view life up close. The particular emerges more conspicuously than the panoramic, individuals and events loom large, and facts stubbornly refuse to blur to accommodate generalizations. As the English historian Jay Winter stated in a recent manifesto for studying capital cities in wartime, "The best way to penetrate behind the illusory veil of a unitary 'national experience' is to describe the character of community life."[6]

No group of people has experienced more poignantly the depths and peaks of recent historical change than the Sarajevans, and no city's history better illuminates the far-reaching changes that have enveloped the region. In their aspirations, achievements, perseverance, and survival, Sarajevans over the centuries have come to exemplify the indomitable human spirit. What follows is their story.

1. Sarajevo's Founders and Foundations

Authorities of the Ottoman Empire founded Sarajevo as a new city in the middle of the fifteenth century, intending it to be an expression of Ottoman Islamic civilization.[1] The city's first major structures were built to advance the empire's strategic interests and promote its philosophy of governance, and many early residents earned their livelihoods supporting Ottoman military advances into Europe. Although the Ottomans envisioned Sarajevo as a "city in the service of Islamic ideology,"[2] their plans accommodated neighborhoods and places of worship for Catholic, Orthodox, and (by the mid-sixteenth century) Jewish residents. Its founding in the era of Ottoman imperial expansion has given Sarajevo an aura of the East that contributes to its uniqueness among cities in the region.

Site and circumstance

Sarajevo arose in the eastern end of a flat alluvial valley where the Miljacka River emerges from its twisting mountainous course. Hills rise to the south and north like tiered bleachers of an amphitheater, while rocky hills and cliffs form the amphitheater's eastern end, parting just enough to allow the river to enter the valley. Surrounding the valley are the forested highlands of east-central Bosnia and four major mountains: Romanija, Bjelašnica, Igman, and Trebević. With the exception of Mount Trebević, these mountains are rounded rather than high-peaked, but they are rugged and have historically posed a serious challenge to anyone seeking to cross them. But the surrounding mountains have also provided natural beauty, recreational opportunities, and Sarajevo's trademark image of a bustling urban enclave nestled within pristine mountains. At the same time, the city's lowland site has made it virtually indefensible against attack from the surrounding hills.

Sarajevo acquired its name from a Slavic contraction of the Turkish words *saraj* (court) and *ovaši* (field), a reference to the expansive fields west of the administrative buildings established to house the area's government. The

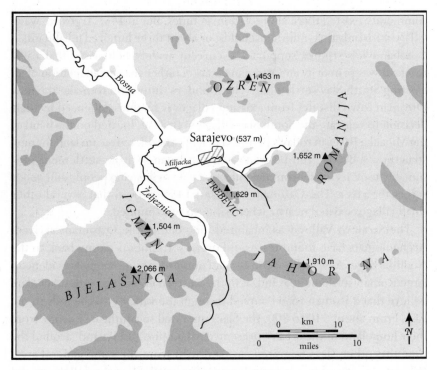

1.1. Sarajevo and the mountains of East-Central Bosnia.

town's name had several variants, especially as used by foreigners, including
Bosna Serai (court of Bosnia) and Serai Bosna, but the component parts of
the name were invariably recognizable. The first document to mention a
variant of the name "Sarajevo" dates from 1455, so a court or government
building very likely existed by that time.[3] For many years, historians maintained that Sarajevo was built on the site of an earlier town called Vrhbosna
(Summit Bosnia), a name that occurs on many early modern European
maps. But after examining Ottoman censuses, Sarajevo historian Hazim
Šabanović demonstrated in 1960 that Vrhbosna was the name of an administrative region, not a town, and that the fortified town of Hodidjed, the only
sizeable settlement in the vicinity of Sarajevo, was further east and upstream
on the Miljacka River.[4] Traveling Dubrovnik merchants used the name
Vrhbosna to refer to the marketplace of a village called Trgovište (or Stara
Varoš), situated along a small stream that flows into the Miljacka River about
a kilometer west of the valley's eastern end. The merchants spread the name
Vrhbosna to other parts of Europe, creating the impression that a sizeable

community existed there in pre-Ottoman times. But in 1455 Trgovište was a village with only fifty-nine households, or about three hundred inhabitants.[5]

Šabanović's studies support the current widely held view that early Sarajevo was primarily an Ottoman creation rather than an adaptation of an existing South Slav settlement. The founders' intention to make the new Ottoman town distinct from existing villages is further evidenced by their decision to relocate the South Slav village of Brodac, located on the bend of the Miljacka River in today's Bembaša neighborhood, to free up land for new structures.[6] Brodac can be translated "boatman," so the settlement presumably took its name from the villagers' role in ferrying people and goods across the river. The Ottoman census of 1455 showed that several other small villages existed nearby when Sarajevo was founded.

The Sarajevo Valley was inhabited long before the Ottomans arrived. Archeologists have found traces of human settlements dating back to the Neolithic Age. A large floor mosaic and numerous stone capitals evidence a large Roman settlement at Ilidža, in the western end of the valley. Scholars believe that a Roman road coursed through the valley into the hills to the east. From about 540 to 800, the Slavs migrated to southeast Europe from their homeland in the area of present-day Ukraine and Poland, around the time that other Slavs migrated east and west from the same general area. When they arrived in southeast Europe, the South Slavs were illiterate and held largely animist beliefs. They had been organized as tribes in their previous homeland, and most scholars believe they maintained the tribal structure during migration. Most Serbs and Croats trace their group names to two tribes that migrated to the Balkan Peninsula, but it is not known if either tribe moved to the area of present-day Bosnia-Herzegovina.

Bosnia lies at the center of a large area of the Balkan Peninsula where the South Slavs settled. In the centuries after they arrived, South Slavs in the Sarajevo area were ruled by a succession of states or empires, including Croatia, Serbia, Bulgaria, Byzantium, and Hungary.[7] Missionaries from Rome to the west and from Constantinople to the east gradually converted the South Slavs to Christianity. From the time of these competing conversions, Bosnia has been home to rival variants of Christianity.

Late in the twelfth century a medieval Bosnian state arose in the winding north-south river valley occupied by the present-day towns of Sarajevo, Visoko, and Zenica. Its rulers acknowledged the suzerainty of the Kingdom of Hungary throughout the Middle Ages, but after 1180 gradually achieved de facto independence. Medieval Bosnia was a feudal state riven by armed contention among its leading noble families, particularly in its later years. In the fifteenth century the armies of the Ottoman Empire defeated the medieval Bosnian kingdom in a series of battles and gained control of most of Bosnia, ending years of chaotic struggle among noble families in the medieval state.

At the time of the Ottoman conquest in the 1430s, Catholics who had accepted the jurisdiction of the Pope inhabited the Sarajevo area. The area had seen considerable rivalry among various Christian churches in the centuries preceding the conquest, and conversions from one faith to another were not uncommon. Members of two other Christian churches, the independent Bosnian Church and the Serbian Orthodox Church, lived in neighboring lands. Most villagers in the Sarajevo area were feudal wards of the Serbian Orthodox Pavlović family. Many Slavs mingled their Christian faith with holdover pagan practices, and the church probably had little doctrinal sophistication. The absence of a well-organized church structure meant that the Christian Slavs of Bosnia had little institutional support for their religious beliefs and practices. The environment of religious heterodoxy and syncretism made many South Slavs receptive to Islam when the Ottomans conquered the area in the fifteenth century.

Sarajevo and the Ottoman urban ideal

Ottoman officials saw urbanization as an integral part of the empire's mission to Islamicize and civilize the lands that it conquered. Owing to a dearth of documentation and distinctly Ottoman methods of data collection, many questions remain unanswered regarding both the theory and practice of Ottoman urbanization,[8] but the basic distinctions in urban planning, and their application to Sarajevo, are clear enough. The Ottoman vision of urban space awarded centrality to Islamic religious, cultural, educational, and governmental institutions, but it also provided ample space for non-Muslims, their houses of worship, and institutions providing for their economic livelihood. The Ottoman approach to the urban population was highly prescriptive, expressed in a large number of regulations and practices that distinguished urban residents by religious affiliation, class, and gender. The legal distinctions faded only in the mid-nineteenth century in the era of reform; their passing was lamented and combated by conservative Bosnian Muslims who felt that such reforms disenfranchised them from their traditional privileges.

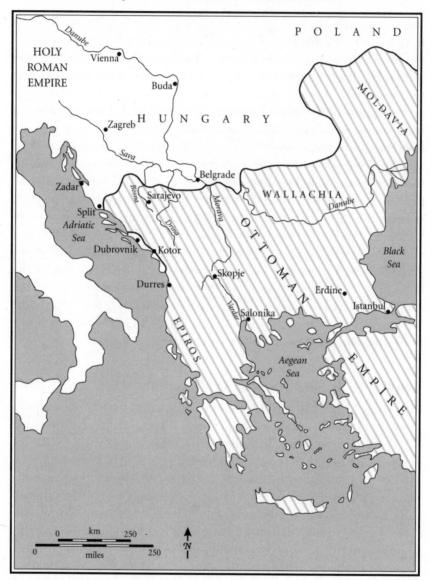

1.2. Sarajevo in the Ottoman Empire, 1512.

The Ottomans distinguished between towns and cities on the basis of their size and function. In Ottoman documents, a small town is typically referred to as a *kasaba*, an unfortified settlement larger than a village but lacking the size, appearance, and internal differentiation of a city.[9] Sarajevo was founded as a kasaba in about 1462, and Ottoman authorities recognized it as a city (*šeher*) early in the sixteenth century. Following a common Ottoman practice, Sarajevo was unfortified (except for a hilltop citadel overlooking the city) until the early eighteenth century. Also in accord with Ottoman conceptions of urban space, institutions of imperial importance were concentrated in the city center, spatially and functionally discrete from residential areas. Towering above all other structures were minarets of mosques named after the sultans, generals, and administrators who donated and endowed them. Other structures such as educational institutions, homes for dervish orders, administrative headquarters, inns, and shops gathered in the shadows of the minarets. The various buildings in the city center stood at the nexus of Islamic faith, conquest, administration, and prosperity that defined the Ottoman theocratic state ideal.

The central zone in Sarajevo has been known for centuries as the *Baščaršija*, or Main Market, but economic activities took place in a much larger area known generally as the *čaršija* (market), parallel to and on both sides of the Miljacka River. Non-Muslims as well as Muslims conducted many of their economic activities in the čaršija. Many structures devoted to economic activities were made of wood or other less durable and cheaper materials. The čaršija also became a social center, the focal point of the city's common life in Ottoman times, where those of all faiths and classes mingled in front of shops and on the streets. Neither the activities conducted in the city's market area nor its appearance, with predominantly small shops crowded next to one another, changed very much from the city's founding until after the Second World War.

Like most Ottoman cities, Sarajevo was divided into residential neighborhoods known as *mahalas*. Each mahala was typically home to members of only one religious community, and each was anchored by a house of worship, so the mahala system meant that, with some exceptions, residences were segregated by religion. Mahalas were named after the person who donated and endowed the religious structure. In a Muslim mahala, the structure was either a mosque or a *mesdžid*. (A mesdžid is a Muslim place of worship without a minaret, smaller than most mosques, where prayers are offered daily except on Fridays and certain holidays.)[10] The number of mahalas grew steadily and peaked at just over one hundred at the end of the sixteenth century. All but three or four of Sarajevo's mahalas were Muslim. The city thus came to be dotted with mosques. Monumental mosques were concentrated in the *čaršija*, and modest-sized mosques were spread throughout the city's residential quarters.

Small, crowded shops in Sarajevo's marketplace (*čaršija*), c. 1914. (Courtesy of Historical Museum, Sarajevo)

Visitors from abroad often commented upon the extraordinary beauty and rich vegetation of Sarajevo's mahalas. Evlija Čelebi, visiting in 1660, called Sarajevo "progressive, beautiful, and lively" and reported that "unlimited fresh water flows everywhere," making possible "numerous gardens that look like rose gardens or enclosed paradise gardens."[11] Most private residences were inward-oriented, with a large outer gate leading to an inner courtyard that often included a central fountain, fruit trees, and a vegetable garden. Fruits, vegetables, and flowers grew in the spacious areas between residences. Water was readily available, either at one of over two hundred public fountains or from a host of fountains in local mosques or residences.[12] Residences were built to accommodate gender segregation.

The largest non-Muslim mahala was inhabited primarily by Catholics from Dubrovnik who were either craftsmen in the building trades or representatives of Dubrovnik's commercial interests. The Latin Quarter, distinguished by a small Catholic church, contained sixty-six houses in the mid-1500s. By the end of the century, some native Sarajevo Catholics and representatives from other mercantile cities also lived there. An Orthodox mahala, established about a hundred meters from the city's eastern end, was anchored by a Serbian Orthodox church built sometime between 1520 and 1539.[13] The church still stands, albeit with substantial modifications that have enlarged the structure over the years.

Jews were already living in Sarajevo as early as 1565, adding a fourth religious group to the city's already diverse population of Muslims, Orthodox, and Catholics.[14] Expelled from Spain by the religiously intolerant monarchs Ferdinand and Isabella in 1492, many Sephardim subsequently made their way to the more hospitable Ottoman Empire and took up residence in its cities.[15] Speaking Ladino, a language closely related to Spanish, Sephardim established a Jewish mahala with a small synagogue in 1580–1.[16] But unlike the Catholics and Orthodox, the Sephardim established residences outside the Jewish mahala as well. The first Ashkenazim arrived from Buda over a century later, after the Ottomans had lost much of their Hungarian territory. Most Ashkenazim spoke German or Hungarian as a first language. After their arrival the Ashkenazim and Sephardim existed as distinct communities, each with its own house of worship and preferred language. The number of Ashkenazim remained relatively small until the onset of Austro-Hungarian rule in 1878.

Except for the greater dispersion of Jews, the mahala system's religion-based residential segregation persisted into the 1940s. The Ottoman Empire tolerated and even provided for adherents of monotheistic faiths other than Islam, but non-Muslims were subject to discriminatory regulations. They were forbidden to wear brightly colored clothing (although that regulation was largely ignored in Sarajevo), to ride a horse, or to enter certain professions without converting to Islam. Although non-Muslim life was regulated, Christians in the cities enjoyed advantages unavailable in the countryside. Like their Muslim neighbors, urban non-Muslims were exempt from various tax burdens imposed on the peasantry. At first non-Muslims were banned from practicing crafts, but that restriction eased over time. Several crafts became multiconfessional, and a few came to be dominated by Jews and Orthodox. Muslim women, the most restricted of any social group in the city, were permitted in public only when veiled. They spent most of their time in the family home, viewing life outside from the quarters to which they were confined.

The location and size of the various houses of worship in Sarajevo reveal much about interconfessional relationships. Non-Muslim houses of worship

Sephardic Jewish couple in traditional attire,
c. 1900. (Courtesy of Historical Archive,
Sarajevo)

were not allowed to exceed the height of the tallest Islamic mosque, and they
could only be built with government permission. Christian structures were
forbidden to have bells. The first Catholic, Orthodox, and Jewish structures
in Sarajevo were diminutive compared to the towering minarets and monumental mosques of the inner city. But they were by no means inconspicuous,
each having approximately the dimensions of mosques and mesdžids in
Muslim mahalas. The visiting Evlija Čelebi summarized what he saw in
1660: "All the churches are small; no church has bells. The churches of the
Serbian and Latin Christians are in good condition. Europeans, Frenchmen,
and Greeks also conduct their religious rites in them. There is one Jewish
synagogue."[17] Non-Muslim houses of worship and their mahalas were
situated on the periphery of the central market area, near some of the largest
mosques and Islamic cultural institutions in the city. Their location and size

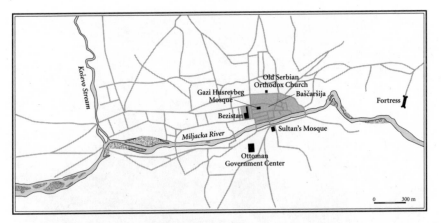

1.3. Urban development of Sarajevo, *c.* 1600.

are evidence of the complex combination of tolerance and discrimination that prevailed in the first several centuries of the Ottoman state.

Founders

Isabeg Ishaković is generally accepted as Sarajevo's founder.[18] Like his father, he was both a conquerer and administrator. Ishaković served the Ottoman Empire as governor of the Skopje district, which included the newly conquered territory of Bosnia, and in the 1460s he became the governor of Bosnia.[19] Sometime before 1462 Ishaković donated funds to build the first large buildings along the Miljacka River where it emerges from the hills to the east. Among the first structures on the south side of the river was a court (*saraj*) that served as administrative headquarters. On the north side of the river he built a home for an order of dervishes (*tekija*), several water-powered mills, a public bath, commercial structures, and several other mosques. He also built bridges spanning the river. On instructions from the sultan dated 1470, he oversaw the building of a mosque on the south bank of the Miljacka in front of his administrative court building. Named the Sultan's Mosque (*Careva džamija*), it served over the next several centuries as the central structure for religious and political gatherings.

Sarajevo historians consider the sixteenth century to have been the city's Golden Age. Gazi Husrevbeg, another Ottoman official who combined careers as conquering general and provincial administrator, contributed to making it so. The city's principal benefactor in the early decades of that

The Sultan's Mosque, built in 1566 replacing a structure of the same name erected on the same site some time before 1462. (Postcard, *c*. 1914, courtesy of Historical Museum, Sarajevo)

century, Husrevbeg was born to a father from a Christian family who had converted to Islam and married a Muslim woman. Along with the sultan himself, he was credited with defeating an alliance of Christian powers at the Battle of Mohacs in 1526, allowing Ottoman forces to besiege Vienna in

1529. He acquired great wealth in conquering various parts of Hungary, Croatia, and Slavonia. He served as governor of Bosnia from 1521–41, interrupted by three absences to lead military campaigns elsewhere.

He is best remembered for founding three institutions that bear his name: a mosque, a library, and an Islamic institution of higher learning (*medresa*). The Gazi Husrevbeg mosque, a monumental but elegantly simple achievement of sixteenth-century Ottoman architecture, remains the largest house of worship in the central city. Like Ishaković before him, Husrevbeg donated facilities for civic economic activity, including a lodge for traveling merchants and facilities for hundreds of craft and mercantile establishments. Under his patronage the city continued to expand, and it met the criteria to be designated a city (*šeher*) during his tenure. When Husrevbeg died in 1541, he was interred in a large classical mausoleum in the courtyard of his eponymous mosque.[20]

Both Ishaković and Husrevbeg garnered laurels and wealth in warfare. Their careers attest to the close relationship between Ottoman military

Gazi Husrevbeg Mosque, 1530. (Postcard, c. 1900, courtesy of Historical Museum, Sarajevo)

Gazi Husrevbeg Mosque, 1530, interior courtyard. (Postcard, *c.* 1900, courtesy of Historical Museum, Sarajevo)

conquests and Sarajevo's early prosperity. Never far from the empire's shifting boundaries with Venice and the Habsburg Monarchy, Sarajevo became the staging area for major Ottoman offensives to the north and west and served as the principal supplier to Ottoman military forces campaigning in the area.

From half a dozen scattered villages in the 1450s, Sarajevo's population grew to about 23,500 by 1600, making it the third largest city in the European lands of the Ottoman Empire, after Salonica and Edirne.[21] The growth stemmed largely from South Slav immigration from nearby villages and other areas of Bosnia; Ottoman census records show that few Sarajevans immigrated from elsewhere in the Ottoman Empire. Local officials controlled migration into the city. Although Turkish was the official language in Sarajevo's early centuries, almost all inhabitants were native Slavic speakers. Turkish, Arabic, and Persian were languages of official function and literary culture.

Religious affiliation was the most significant determinant of residence, social position, and political status in Sarajevo's early years. Most early residents were Slavic speakers who had converted to Islam either before or shortly after they immigrated into the city. Non-Muslims of monotheistic faiths were also welcomed, and some became indispensable to the city's development. Although they were subject to certain limitations on behavior and attire, these practices appear not to have created major contention between Muslims and non-Muslims in the city under Ottoman adminis- tration. (There is evidence that some sumptuary laws were widely disre- garded in Sarajevo, but the extent of noncompliance has not been systematically examined by historians of the city.) The notion that non- Muslims suffered grinding oppression under the Ottoman yoke, an idea lib- erally promulgated by Serb and Croat nationalists in the nineteenth and twentieth centuries, finds no support in historical accounts of life in the city under Ottoman rule.

Most scholars agree that Islamization in Bosnia was gradual and generally voluntary. Through conversions of local Slavic-speakers to Islam, Sarajevo's urban population changed from being about 73 percent Christian and 27 percent Muslim in 1485, to about 97 percent Muslim in 1530.[22] Census records show that conversions occurred at about the same pace in nearby rural settlements as in the city itself.

Much as in Western European cities, urban society was a hierarchy in which a combination of wealth, rank, privilege, and religion determined status. In the early Ottoman state, feudal warriors were at the top of Sarajevo's social hierarchy. Most prominent were cavalrymen (*spahis*), who received income from certain lands as payment for their military services. Most cavalrymen were Muslim, but religion was not a barrier to such service; there were Christian cavalrymen as well. Members of the Janissary Corps, an elite border unit that also served as the sultan's retinue, enjoyed a status comparable to cavalrymen. Islamic religious functionaries and admin- istrative officials were also among prominent early Sarajevans.

Founding institutions

The central financial institution in the city's dynamic Ottoman-era growth was called the *vakuf* (the Bosnian spelling of the Arabic *wakf*), or charitable endowment. A vakuf provided for the operation and maintenance of religious, cultural, and economic institutions. Typically, a wealthy individual would donate funds for a new structure. He (or, very rarely, she) would dedicate certain income-producing properties, usually agricultural land or urban shops, for the structure's perpetual upkeep and maintenance. Each vakuf was established by a founding charter (*vakufnama*), identifying the institution to be endowed and specifying the properties dedicated to its upkeep. Most early benefactors were successful military commanders who acquired great wealth in their exploits and then devoted that wealth— clearly with the approval or encouragement of the central authorities—to the empire's key urban institutions. By 1604 the city had more than one hundred vakufs, and a considerable portion of the city's economic life revolved around the maintenance and upkeep of its religious and educational structures. The largest vakufs sustained both the city's major Islamic institutions and the smaller mahala mosques and schools.

Continuing Ottoman conquests to the west and north fueled the city's economy. Ottoman forces encamped in the Sarajevo area and prepared for the extended campaigns that made up sixteenth-century warfare. Early benefactors donated the infrastructure for Sarajevo's craft production and mercantile exchanges to ensure that the Ottoman cavalryman was fully equipped for war. Most workshops and small stores were clustered in the Baščaršija amid the monumental mosques of the city center. Ishaković and Husrevbeg each established a long, narrow, covered commercial structure (*bezistan*) with shops lining each side of a central passageway. The shops in these structures typically sold imports from other parts of the empire.

Both Ishaković and Husrevbeg built inns (*karavan-saraj* or *han*) to provide overnight accommodation for caravans and traders. Such inns were found throughout the Ottoman world, and most shared a common functional design. The ground floor consisted of horse stalls and storage areas surrounding a central courtyard. On the second floor were quarters to accommodate visitors. Ishaković's inn contained forty rooms and could accommodate twenty-five horses in its courtyard.[23] Traveling merchants were granted three days of free food and lodging in the inns. Such hospitality welcomed visitors while simultaneously discouraging them from exploiting the host's generosity.

Craft workshops were organized according to the goods they produced. Shops specializing in a particular product lined a single street that bore the name of the goods produced there. Craftsmen organized themselves in guilds (*esnafi*), much as in medieval European cities. As was customary in Ottoman towns, the guilds enjoyed broad autonomy. Many craft shops would develop a relationship with an individual cavalryman, who then served as patron and protector of the shop. The early ties between military officers and guilds helped to link the fortunes of craftsmen with the privileged feudal military class. As the first signal of a protest, merchants and craftsmen in Sarajevo and other towns would simultaneously shutter their shops in the Baščaršija and then retire to coffee shops to grouse about their grievances.

Ottoman officials founded Sarajevo as a seat of regional government, and for much of the Ottoman era it served as a regional capital.[24] Even when the authorities transferred the governor's residence to Banja Luka (1553–1639) or Travnik (1699–1850), newly appointed Bosnian governors acknowledged the primacy of Sarajevo by ceremonially asking permission to enter the city. Its role as a regional political center not only brought economic benefits to the city, but also elevated the importance of relations between the governor and the city's elite. These relations, harmonious during Sarajevo's Golden Age, began to become contentious at the first signs of Ottoman weakness on the battlefield after 1600.

Sarajevo's prosperity rested on preparing men for war, but as an unfortified city its very survival depended on peace. It flourished and grew as long as the Ottoman Empire expanded. But when the expansion gradually halted and the empire began to suffer territorial losses, Sarajevo's physical location and economic foundations made it vulnerable to invaders arriving on the high hills around the town. With initial indications that the Ottoman conquests were coming to an end, the city entered a sustained decline lasting into the middle of the nineteenth century.

Reversal of Ottoman fortunes and the burning of the city

The Ottoman Empire had reached the farthest extent of its conquests and the pinnacle of its internal vitality in the late sixteenth century. The major defeats it suffered in the naval battle of Lepanto (1571) and the land battle for Sisak (1593) signaled the end of its territorial expansion into Europe. The English historian Noel Malcolm has suggested the twin events of coins minted with reduced silver content (1585) and the revolt of Janissaries (1589), who were paid in these debased coins, as the beginning of the extended Ottoman decline.[25] At about the same time members of the military feudal elite began to transform their revocable landholdings into hereditary holdings. As described by Sarajevo historian Ahmed Aličić, the Muslim elite of Sarajevo (and of Bosnia) became a "lasting, numerically limited domestic military nobility that, owing to inheritance, acquired with time the character of a blood nobility."[26]

Over many years the empire's military losses and internal weaknesses fueled each other. Central officials labored in vain to increase tax revenues, causing soldiers to go unpaid and be inadequately equipped. Segments of the feudal military elite rebelled against the central government, which was unable to pay them and guarantee their privileges. Regional challengers arose to assert their interests against appointed Ottoman officials. These changes proceeded slowly, and energetic central leaders reversed them on several occasions, but the two dominant trends in the empire from 1600 to the first half of the 1800s were military setbacks and internal decline.

Territorial losses and the empire's internal crisis were ominous portents for Sarajevo. The city's conspicuously vulnerable location made it a prime target for the Austrian army, which sought to wreak vengeance on inhabitants of Ottoman lands. Prince Eugene of Savoy, a conquering general in the service of the Austrian Empire, commanded an army that seized territory from the Ottomans in Dalmatia, Slavonia, and Hungary after breaking the siege of Vienna in 1683. After his offensive against northwestern Bosnia stalled in the summer of 1697, he led his troops across the Sava River into northern Bosnia at Brod and followed the Bosna River south to Sarajevo.

Encamped on the city's outskirts, Prince Eugene promised to "destroy everything with sword and fire" unless the city capitulated. The city leaders remained defiant, and soon Eugene fulfilled his promise. The Habsburg army entered Sarajevo and burned most of the city on the night of October 23–4, 1697.[27] Most wooden structures were destroyed, and some of the city's stone mosques and other religious buildings were damaged. An anonymous Sarajevo writer suggested that desecration of Islamic institutions and practices was a deliberate part of the destruction:

Austrian infidels came with an army, they burned books and mosques, ravaged mihrabs [the niche in a mosque in the direction of prayer] and the beautiful Šeher-Sarajevo, from one end to the other. They herded men like sheep, shed bloody tears from their eyes, imprisoned and ruined many a man, and even girls, heavenly beauties with faces that saw neither sun nor moon, were driven barefoot and bareheaded from their happy lives and sent as a present to the king, for an infidel came and seized their belongings and food while ten thousand imprisoned people cried.[28]

Within a few years, most of the mosques were repaired and being used for worship or calls to prayer, and eventually most of the burned structures were replaced. But Sarajevo's population and prosperity did not return to its pre-fire levels until the early 1900s, ironically, under the administration of the same Habsburg Monarchy that had nearly destroyed it in 1697. In the aftermath of the fire, the city lost its status as the seat of the Bosnian government, which was transferred in 1699 from Sarajevo to nearby Travnik, where it remained until 1850. Ottoman officials made the change in hopes that the governor would not face the constant obstruction of the Sarajevo Muslims. Nevertheless, Sarajevo remained Bosnia's most politically active city, and its warrior elite remained the most influential political element in the land.

The city's decline in the aftermath of its Golden Age had deeper and more sustained causes than a single punitive Habsburg raid. Generally Sarajevo's fortunes fell with defeats of the Ottoman armies no less than they had risen with their victories. The soldiers' seemingly insatiable needs abated, and craft production and commerce declined in the 1600s. Even more significant was the gradual change in the social structure and political behavior of the Sarajevo Muslims, a process that lasted at least 200 years (approximately 1600 to 1800). The dominant military class continued to provide martial services to the Ottoman central government, but its members also resisted the authority of governors dispatched from Istanbul to rule Bosnia. Leading Sarajevo Muslims exercised the autonomous rights given to the city in its early days, refusing to recognize the authority of some arriving government officials. The Muslims of Sarajevo and Banja Luka first rose militarily to challenge a newly dispatched governor in 1603.[29]

Members of the Janissary Corps made up the vanguard of the Sarajevo Muslim resistance to central Ottoman rule. Conceived as elite border troops and a guard unit at the sultan's personal disposal, Janissaries held a privileged position within the empire. Janissaries gathered in towns and cities in the 1600s and 1700s and advanced their political demands under the cover of urban autonomy. In Sarajevo the Janissaries became a part of the domestic hereditary Muslim elite. Many became protectors of individual craft shops or were themselves engaged as craftsmen, and the Janissary Corps became synonymous with guild organizations in the city.[30] With their claims to privilege and in close alliance with the guilds, they became the dominant political force in the city by the late 1700s.

As the Sarajevo Muslims gradually became irrelevant in their economic and social roles, they asserted demands to restore the traditional practices and privileges that they claimed the central authorities had usurped. They opposed reforms advocated by various Ottoman grand viziers to re-centralize the state, rationalize the tax structure, and modernize the empire's military forces. Although their demands for autonomy did not formally crystallize into a political program until the 1830s, the Sarajevo elite increasingly sought local autonomy for the city and for Bosnia as a whole.

For over two centuries the Ottoman central authorities and the leading Sarajevo Muslims were regularly at odds and occasionally in armed conflict. A downward spiral of events unfolded with the dispatch of each new governor to Bosnia. Whenever he appointed a new governor, the grand vizier would typically dispatch a punitive expedition to impose the new appointee on the recalcitrant Sarajevans. The military force would then subdue the rebels, and a few Sarajevo leaders would be neutralized by execution or exile. But the financially strapped Ottoman central government would then withdraw its punitive force, leaving the local Muslims to their own devices. The cycle replayed when local Muslims renewed their resistance to the governor's authority, and the governor was either co-opted by the city's Muslims, removed by central directive, or forced to flee in the face of intractable opposition. Repeated with many variations in the 1600s and 1700s, this pattern of events further weakened the city's economy and exacerbated the internal bickering among leading Sarajevo Muslims.

Beginning in 1729, Sarajevans responded to growing insecurity by constructing a complex of walls, towers, and gates. These fortifications consisted of about three hundred meters of walls and four towers.[31] Two gates and a portion of the wall survive to this day. Since approaching conquerors could use the high ground of the surrounding hills to attack the city, the fortifications were of limited military value, but the gates enabled city officials to regulate routine entry into the city, and the walls prevented much unauthorized economic activity.

Although they regularly contested the authority of appointed governors, Sarajevo's Muslims never raised the flag of rebellion against the sultan himself. The city's institutions remained Ottoman in character, and the city was administratively as much as ever a part of the empire.[32] The city's Muslims remained among the empire's loyal fighting forces, and many of them died for the sultan on battlefields near and far. Sarajevo Muslims responded to the Ottoman call-up of forces for the war against the Persian Empire in 1727.[33] Of 5,200 officers and men from Bosnia, only 500 returned from the battlefield. In 1737, a contingent of 10,000 Bosnians was part of the Ottoman force that fought the Russian Empire. Only a handful returned, straggling back in the fall and winter of 1737.

In addition to serving on remote battlefields, Bosnian Muslim forces were periodically engaged to keep nearby territory under the sultan's rule. In 1712, Bosnian forces fought Montenegrin tribesmen who were making periodic raids into Herzegovina. Although the Montenegrins were driven back, many Muslims in the recaptured areas chose to leave with the Bosnian forces. Muslims from contested areas fled their homes and became refugees in the sanctuary of Sarajevo.

Bosnian Muslims provided much of the sultan's manpower in continual wars with the Habsburg Monarchy along Bosnia's northern and western frontiers. Members of the Bosnian Muslim warrior class provided almost all the forces that successfully defended the city of Banja Luka in a major battle in 1738, leading some historians to cite that battle as a pivotal event in the development of Muslim and Bosniak identity distinct from other Muslims in the Ottoman Empire.[34] Recently the American historian Michael Hickok has argued that the Bosnians were not self-sufficient, and he has characterized the undertaking as an effective joint effort of Bosnia's Ottoman governor and the Bosnian warriors.[35] Although the sources of victory in the Banja Luka battle remain in dispute, there is little doubt that the Ottomans' ability to retain Bosnia until 1878 owed much to the military prowess of the Bosnian Muslim warrior elite with its primary center in Sarajevo.

The grand vizier called upon the Bosnian Muslim warriors to put down the 1804 rebellion of Serbs in the Belgrade region. For the next several years, the Bosnians constituted the bulk of forces deployed against the incipient Serb national uprising, which was supported by the Russian tsar and volunteers from the pan-Slavic movement in Russia. By 1830 international negotiations and Ottoman losses combined to produce outcomes generally favorable for the Serbs.

Many Sarajevo Muslim warriors opposed reforms for fear of losing the right to collect certain state-sanctioned levies from peasants. The progressive weakening of Ottoman authority gave them considerable latitude to gather those levies in cash and in kind, and many landlords retained some or all of the proceeds for themselves. As such abuses grew, peasants became increasingly restive. Both Christian and Muslim peasants were burdened by tax abuse, but the plight of Christian peasants became an international issue, with France, Russia, and Britain asserting themselves as protectors of the empire's Christian residents. As unrelenting opponents of reform, the Sarajevo Muslim elite came to see the Ottoman reform movement as a response to the unwanted and unwarranted intrusion of foreign infidel powers into the empire's affairs, as well as inimical to their traditional prerogatives. On both accounts the Muslims of Sarajevo and other Bosnian towns were struggling against both the central Ottoman government and the empire's primary international adversaries among the European powers.

The movement for Bosnian autonomy

Following the Napoleonic Wars, rulers of the Ottoman Empire renewed their campaign to reform the government and the military. They acted under considerable international pressure, but they also realized that the empire's survival depended upon reversing the trend of military defeat and internal decay. In May 1826 the sultan dissolved the Janissary Corps, and a month later he ordered the dissolution of the Bektashi order of dervishes. [36] Ottoman troops stormed the Janissary stronghold in Istanbul and killed or imprisoned thousands, effectively ending the challenge to central rule in the capital city. It proved much more difficult to eliminate their influence in the provinces.

In Bosnia the sultan's order dissolving the Janissaries was first proclaimed at a public reading in Travnik on July 12, 1826. [37] The Travnik Janissaries meekly accepted the order. The Sarajevo Janissaries, on the other hand, immediately rejected the order when it was read in Sarajevo three days later. The čaršija was closed, and those who had delivered the proclamation were expelled from Sarajevo. The Sarajevo Janissaries organized a delegation to Travnik and persuaded the Janissaries there to recant their acceptance of the order. They dispatched a delegation to Istanbul to protest the sultan's decision. The Sarajevo group initially won widespread support from other Bosnian Muslims for resisting the order, but the sympathy from other towns largely evaporated when Sarajevans brutally murdered a local Muslim supporter of the sultan in January 1827. When the central authorities dispatched a punitive expedition and a new governor to subdue the Sarajevans, Muslim leaders in most other towns kept their forces at home. The punitive force easily defeated the Sarajevans and restored order, but few Janissaries left the city. With many of their number well integrated into guild organizations, they remained and joined others in the Sarajevo Muslim elite to challenge central Ottoman rule.

Shortly after the suppression of the Janissaries, international events again roused the Sarajevo Muslim elite to action. Preparing for the Ottoman Empire's war with Russia in 1827, the Bosnian governor called upon Sarajevo's Muslims to supply troops. The Sarajevans and other Bosnian Muslims complied, but the war went against the Ottoman Empire. As part of the settlement, the Ottoman authorities agreed to cede six historically Bosnian administrative districts (*nahije*) to neighboring Serbia. This was particularly offensive to Bosnian Muslim warriors, who had fought against the Serbian insurgency at various times over the preceding twenty-five years. The

Sarajevo Muslims, enraged, again prepared to resist the will of the central authorities. This time they found themselves among the followers of an able military commander and administrator from the northern Bosnian town of Gradačac, Husein-kapetan Gradaščević.

Husein-kapetan emerged as the consensus choice to lead the movement of 1831–2. In the last few decades Bosniaks have lionized him as the Dragon of Bosnia (*Zmaj od Bosne*). He was, and remains, an enigmatic figure; historians have debated his role for many decades.[38] He evidently had not supported those Sarajevans resisting the dissolution of the Janissaries in 1826–7. At least twice he traveled to Sarajevo at the governor's behest to help mobilize forces for the war with Russia, so he was not averse to helping Ottoman rulers. But in December 1830 he nonetheless invited Muslim leaders from all over Bosnia to his lands near Gradačac to plot resistance against Ottoman central rule.

Following successive assemblies in Tuzla and Travnik during early 1831, Husein-kapetan led a force of more than twenty thousand on a two-week march to Kosovo. There his forces did battle with Ottoman regulars sent by the grand vizier to extinguish simultaneous Muslim uprisings in Kosovo and Bosnia.[39] Husein-kapetan's forces handed the imperial troops a major defeat, but he failed to follow up the victory, instead leading his troops back to Bosnia. On September 12, 1831, Muslims from Sarajevo and other Bosnian towns installed him as governor of Bosnia at a ceremony in the Sultan's Mosque in Sarajevo. He moved his headquarters to Travnik and governed from there. He dispatched emissaries to Istanbul in hopes of gaining the sultan's recognition of his election.

The sultan, beset by various separatist movements that were gradually dismembering the empire, refused to recognize Husein-kapetan as Bosnia's governor. Instead, the grand vizier himself headed a punitive expedition to subdue the rebellious Bosnians. He dispatched two major forces, one on a southern route and one along a northern route, to converge on Sarajevo. After initial skirmishes, the decisive battle for Bosnia was fought on June 4, 1832, at Stup, a few kilometers west of the Sarajevo center, near the location of the present-day airport. The superior Ottoman forces and allied units of Muslims from Herzegovina routed Husein-kapetan's troops. Husein-kapetan escaped and fled to Habsburg territory. Eventually he was allowed into the Ottoman Empire's eastern territories, on condition that he never again set foot on the empire's European lands. He died in Istanbul in 1834 at the age of thirty-two.

The movement of 1831–2 joined regional, class, and religious currents under a single charismatic leader. Most Sarajevo Muslims made common cause with those from other towns, and together the movement's leaders first articulated the previously inchoate strivings for Bosnian autonomy in a formal political program. Their discontent was fueled by the Ottoman government's willingness to cede traditionally Bosnian territory to Serbia. The leaders believed autonomy would restore privileges that the urban elites had either once held or imagined they had once held. However, some Bosnian Christians joined the military forces, often fighting in the retinues of the landlords to whom they paid taxes. The movement was therefore not exclusively a revolt of reactionary Muslims, but Islamic religious conservatism no doubt motivated many participants.

The defeat of the Gradaščević movement failed to end the protracted struggle between the Ottoman central government and the recalcitrant Sarajevo Muslim elite. In 1833, only a year after the battle of Stup, leading Sarajevo Muslims refused orders to join the refashioned Ottoman military, which required them to wear new uniforms and don the fez.[40] (The fez, later synonymous with conservative Islam in the Balkans, was staunchly resisted at the time by conservative Muslims, who traditionally wore turbans.) The Ottoman governor bombarded the town, and the Sarajevo Muslims feigned assent to serve in the new force. The cycle of Sarajevo's resistance and Ottoman suppression thus continued.

Despite the resistance of many conservative Muslims, the movement for Ottoman reform gained strength and urgency in the 1830s. Shortly after assuming the throne in 1839, Sultan Abdul Medžid promulgated the first comprehensive, empirewide reforms (*Tanzimat*). This sweeping decree pronounced all inhabitants of the empire equal subjects of the sultan, regardless of religion or class. It introduced a tax system based on wealth rather than privilege, and it sought to modernize the army through direct levies and mandatory modern uniforms.[41]

Most Sarajevo Muslims saw the decree as further grounds for resisting central authority. They particularly objected to the provisions for military reform. In 1840 Ahmet Munib Glodjo, a Sarajevo Muslim, led an armed movement to resist enrollment in the modernized Ottoman army.[42] His force, estimated at some twenty thousand men, was defeated by units loyal to the sultan. After their victory the Ottoman governor's forces entered Sarajevo, arrested forty-one of the movement's leaders, and exiled them to Istanbul.

Although many Sarajevans fought with Glodjo to resist central authority, the promulgation of the Tanzimat won the support of a few prominent Sarajevo Muslims who were prepared to reconcile themselves to empire-wide changes. Among the forces that defeated Glodjo's movement was a contingent under the command of the Sarajevo Muslim Fazli Šerifović.[43] In aiding the suppression of his fellow Sarajevans, Šerifović pioneered the strategy of cautious cooperation with the central government while seeking to maintain ties with antireform forces. In reward for helping to suppress Glodjo's uprising, the Ottomans appointed him the head of local administration in the Sarajevo area. Despite being exiled from Sarajevo for several years in the 1850s, Šerifović consistently sought accommodation with Ottoman central authorities. He carefully balanced allegiance to the Ottoman regime with attention to the needs of his fellow Sarajevo Muslims. He remained in this position of calculated ambiguity until Ottoman rule ended in 1878, and thereafter his two sons, Mustajbeg and Mahmudbeg Fadilpašić, adopted a similar posture toward the new Austro-Hungarian rulers.[44] The father and two sons became the most politically influential Sarajevans until the end of the nineteenth century, spanning the transition from Ottoman to Habsburg control.

The Ottoman government's repression met persistent resistance. Further uprisings occurred in the late 1840s. Rebellious Muslims in northwestern Bosnia frustrated the efforts of an energetic Bosnian governor to implement the reforms promulgated a decade earlier. Impatient, the sultan in 1849 designated Omer-paša Latas as his special envoy to implement the reforms in Bosnia. Latas was given a mandate to bring the obstreperous Sarajevans firmly under Ottoman control.

Repression and transformation of the Sarajevo Muslim elite

Latas employed harsh measures to end armed resistance to Ottoman reforms. Most members of the Sarajevo Muslim elite were removed by execution, imprisonment, or exile. Even the regime's major ally, Fazli-paša Šerifović, was exiled to Istanbul. In a major step to reform the economy and end the sanctuary enjoyed by rebellious former Janissaries, Latas dissolved the powerful guild organizations in 1851. The implementation of reforms alienated not only the Muslims but also the Christian peasants, who found themselves subjected to additional burdens under the new tax system. In addition to suppressing Muslim uprisings, Latas was forced to quell revolts by Christian (mainly Serbian Orthodox) peasants.

The harsh repression effectively ended the sporadic armed rebellions of the Sarajevo Muslims. A new group of Muslim leaders gradually emerged, principally from the same families that had been prominent before the repression. Šerifović epitomized the reconstituted Sarajevo Muslim elite. With vast landholdings in the Posavina region of northern Bosnia and a cozy relationship with Ottoman officials, he survived and ultimately thrived in the relatively tranquil Sarajevo of the 1860s and early 1870s. The spirit of conservative Islamic resistance to reforms remained alive, but it was increasingly limited to the Muslim lower classes. With Latas's purges of those inclined to resist Ottoman reforms by force of arms, the Sarajevo Muslims moved from being disenfranchised warriors to landholders living on the fruits of peasant labor in the relative luxury of urban Sarajevo.

Thereafter, Ottoman governors courted a new breed of loyalist land-owning Muslims. By the mid-1870s the wealthiest and most powerful Muslim landowners were joined at the hip with Ottoman administration. In 1875 the Austro-Hungarian consul prepared a list of the most prominent and influential Muslims. "It is not necessary to separate the Muslim officials from the landowners," he wrote, "since all significant landowners serve in some administrative branch without compensation."[45]

Despite changes in the composition and political posture of the Muslim elite, Sarajevo's gradual economic and demographic decline continued in the late Ottoman years. From a peak of about 24,000 inhabitants in the early seventeenth century, the city's population declined to about 20,000 or fewer in the 1860s. Except for repairs and maintenance, the cityscape was little changed from 1697 when Eugene of Savoy's forces wrought havoc on the town's main structures. Indications of widespread revitalization first appeared in the 1860s.

New entrepreneurs

Two major changes in the third quarter of the nineteenth century brought about a new alignment of population and political forces in the city. First, the expansion of the Serb merchant class, made possible by the improved legal status of the empire's non-Muslim citizens, added demographic diversity to the city. Second, the city's Muslim elite lost its intransigence and propensity for armed rebellion following Omer Pasha Latas's conquest and repression of the 1850s. These changes would become major factors in developments during the last days of Ottoman rule in 1878.

The Muslim elite, obsessed with resisting reform and wielding political influence, gradually lost its monopoly over important areas of craft production and commerce. With a shift in military methods and technology, foot soldiers replaced the traditional privileged cavalrymen, and powerful artillery batteries superseded the lance and rifle. Some craftsmen faced obsolescence as the market for their traditional products declined or disappeared completely. Additionally, Ottoman reforms implemented in the 1850s opened many doors for non-Muslim entrepreneurs by revoking regulations that discriminated against them and enabling them to acquire property in urban areas.[46] Ottoman reformers abolished guilds in 1851, leaving Muslim craftsmen without the influential organizations that had helped ensure their economic dominance. Serb and Jewish entrepreneurs enjoyed close ties with those in neighboring lands of their faith and ethnicity, and they excelled in importing cheap manufactured goods from abroad that challenged the more expensive locally produced handicrafts. The Bosnian historian Iljas Hadžibegovic summarized the process: "As early as the second half of the eighteenth century, many Serb craftsmen expanded into commerce and, together with Jews, took almost all external trade into their own hands, while the Muslims retained a dominant role in crafts and domestic retail trade."[47]

With growing numbers and increasing affluence, Serbs organized Serbian Orthodox communes in major Bosnian towns to support their church and promote the education of Serb youth. Acting in part through the commune, Serb merchants helped fund the first permanent Serb school in Sarajevo in 1850–1.[48] Each commune was governed by a council of prominent local Serb laymen. The Serbian Orthodox communes built and subsidized schools for Serbs during Ottoman times when no public education system existed, and they were in the forefront of increasing literacy and practical skills required in business and commerce. To the dismay of both Ottoman officials and the Habsburg authorities who superseded them, the communes also brought together nationally conscious Serbs who promoted their identity and closer ties with neighboring Serbia.

The most enduring achievement of Sarajevo's Serbian Orthodox commune was the monumental Assembly Church (*Saborna crkva*), begun in 1863 and dedicated in 1872.[49] Known locally as the New Serbian Orthodox Church to distinguish it from the sixteenth-century church a few hundred meters to the east, it was the first building to break the Muslim monopoly on monumental edifices in Sarajevo's central city. Built with the approval of

Ottoman officials, it was dedicated under the protection of Ottoman troops. Financing and constructing the church was a multiconfessional and international success story of its time. Most of the 36,000 dukat cost was borne by Sarajevo's Serb merchants, led by Manojlo Jeftanović with a donation of 2,000 dukats. In a symbolic act of equality, the Ottoman sultan and the prince of Serbia each donated 500 dukats. Russia's Tsar Aleksandar II sent expert craftsmen to construct the iconostasis. The church remains Sarajevo's most prominent structure from the Ottoman reform era.

But the church tower rose above many mosques in town, offending conservative Muslims who wanted traditional limitations respected. The same group objected to a small bell that was installed in the old Serbian Orthodox church at about the same time. In May 1871, a group of forty lower-class Muslims, led by a Sarajevo imam named Salih Vilajetović, sought to block dedication of the church. Vilajetović, known also by the pseudonym Hadži Lojo, was a man of great size and strength (Lojo refers to tallow, the fat from which candles were made). He had made the pilgrimage to Mecca sometime before 1871 (hence the name Hadži, meaning pilgrim) and returned to serve as imam at a small mosque and teach religion at a trade school.[50] A conservative Muslim from an established Sarajevo family, he detested the Ottoman reforms and considered the time before the abolition of the Janissaries in 1829 as a lost golden age.

The Ottoman governor, notified of the intended obstruction, ordered the police to arrest Vilajetović and his followers. Six were arrested, but the others fled when police arrived. Led by Jeftanović, members of the Serbian Orthodox commune in Sarajevo lodged a protest with the Russian consul, and Russian diplomats shortly thereafter protested the episode to the Ottoman sultan. The ceremony was postponed for a year, but in summer 1872, Ottoman officials dispatched a new military commander with twelve hundred men to provide security for the church dedication. Sarajevo's loyalist Muslims, led by Šerifović, supported the Ottoman governor and distanced themselves from the vandals' attack on the church. "We have always lived in harmony with the Serbs and helped one another," Šerifović told the governor, "but we don't have power over Hadži Lojo and his (gang of) homeless."[51] Thereupon the Ottoman commander, in a show of force, positioned cannon to bombard the city and deployed troops to guard the ceremony. The festive dedication, attended by high Ottoman officials and by the young Austro-Hungarian ambassador to Belgrade, Benjamin von Kállay, proceeded flawlessly. Vilajetović subsequently fled the city and became the leader of a band of brigands in the final years of Ottoman rule. The episode revealed that members of the reconstituted Sarajevo Muslim elite shared with Serbian Orthodox merchants and Ottoman officials an interest in facilitating religious coexistence in the city.

Economic development and administrative reform

Topal Šerif Osman Pasha, Bosnia's governor from 1861–9, introduced major changes in transportation, communications, industry, and government.[52] He oversaw the founding of the Sarajevo Brewery in 1864 and the building of a telegraph line to connect Sarajevo and Istanbul. His administration developed an ambitious plan to build a railway connecting Sarajevo with Bosanski Novi to the northwest and Mitrovica (in present-day Kosovo) to the southeast, but only a fraction of the projected track was completed under Ottoman rule. In 1866 the first printing press was established in Sarajevo, publishing *Bosanski Vjestnik* and *Bosna*, the official publication of the Bosnian regional government, in both Turkish and in Cyrillic Bosnian.[53] Ottoman officials erected a European-style building known as the Konak (lodge), completed in 1869, as their headquarters in Bosnia. Although these innovations were later dwarfed by building activity and economic expansion in the Austro-Hungarian era, they first made their appearance in Sarajevo in the late Ottoman years during Topal's tenure as governor.

In a major administrative reform undertaken in 1865, the Ottoman Empire introduced councils at all levels of government. Seats were allocated based on confession. In the regional council (Bosnian: *Opće vilajetsko vijeće*; Turkish: *medžlisi umumii vilayet*) for Bosnia, each of seven districts was entitled to four seats, two for Muslims and two for non-Muslims.[54] Members were selected in a complex process in which a government-appointed electoral commission played the dominant role. Many non-Muslim delegates were religious leaders, while Muslim delegates were both religious functionaries and wealthy landowners. In Sarajevo, the regional council took over the functions of lower levels of government in 1872, so a single council served both the city and the rest of Bosnia (including Herzegovina, one of the seven districts). By 1878, wealthy Sarajevo landlords dominated the regional council. The council brought a certain amount of popular opinion into Ottoman governance, but it was far from being a democratically elected representative body. Most significantly, the embryonic Ottoman representative bodies of the 1860s adopted a confessional key in allocating delegate seats. That practice would be followed, with many variations, by city governments under subsequent regimes.

New sources of unrest

Latas had eradicated the principal opponents of reform, but had not fully implemented several key reform measures. Bosnia was among the provinces in which creation of a modernized full-time military had been postponed. Instead, a force of volunteers known as *bašibozuks* was created, and it engaged in some of the same misconduct and corruption as the antiquated Bosnian forces before military reforms. Members of the traditional Muslim elites continued to collect most taxes, so the tax collection system was likewise subject to the abuses that were commonplace before the reforms.

Peasant grievances came to a head in 1875. In the volatile region of eastern Herzegovina, peasants in the Nevesinje district began a rebellion in the spring of 1875. It soon spread to the Bosnian Krajina region of northwestern Bosnia and to other parts of Bosnia–Herzegovina. Its participants were encouraged by Great Power rivalry, pan-Slav agitators from Russia, clandestine aid to the rebels from Serbia and Montenegro, and implicit support from the Habsburg Emperor Franz Joseph on a visit to Dalmatia in 1875. The failure of the Ottoman state over many decades to alleviate the burdens on the peasantry molded the rebels' social demands and made the uprising a matter of international concern. It would eventually lead to the end of Ottoman rule in Bosnia and the beginning of vast changes in the demographic composition and physical appearance of Sarajevo.

2. The Sarajevo Uprising and the Advent of Habsburg Rule

The Habsburg Monarchy succeeded the Ottoman Empire as the ruler of Sarajevo and of Bosnia-Herzegovina in the summer of 1878.[1] Some Sarajevans accepted or even welcomed a prospective change of governments, but many others detested the notion of rule by Austria-Hungary, perceiving the monarchy as a bastion of Catholicism and the centuries-long archrival of the Ottoman Empire. Opponents organized a resistance movement that delayed for many months the monarchy's complete takeover of the province. But before the opponents could freely organize to resist the Habsburg forces, they moved to eliminate the few vestigial institutions of Ottoman authority. Consequently, well before the pitched battles between armed Bosnians and Habsburg troops, Sarajevo experienced agitation, violence, revolution, and military mobilization.[2] During these tumultuous events, Sarajevans proved able and willing to engage in armed conflict with opposition forces but were disinclined for intergroup violence.

The Eastern Crisis

The Eastern Crisis began in 1875 when Christian peasants in Herzegovina rose up against the abuses of their Muslim landlords.[3] When the rebellion spread to other rural areas of Bosnia-Herzegovina and Ottoman authorities moved to suppress the outbreaks, Serbia and Montenegro declared war on the Ottoman Empire in sympathy with their fellow South Slavs. But Ottoman forces readily defeated the two allied South Slav states, leading Russia to come to the rescue of its fellow Slavs and attack the Ottoman Empire. Together, the forces of Russia, Serbia, and Montenegro inflicted a crushing defeat on the Ottomans in 1877–8. The Montenegrin capture of Nikšić from Ottoman forces occasioned the flight of about three thousand of its Muslim inhabitants, most of them seeking refuge in Sarajevo.

37

In the spring of 1878 a Russian force advanced to the outskirts of Istanbul, where Russian diplomats dictated the Treaty of San Stefano to the humbled Ottoman Empire on March 3, 1878. Among other provisions, the treaty provided that Bosnia-Herzegovina was to become an autonomous province within the Ottoman Empire. San Stefano's provisions alarmed the British and French, who feared expanded Russian hegemony in the Balkans. To avert further armed conflict, the German Chancellor Otto von Bismarck invited the major European powers (France, Britain, Russia, Austria-Hungary, Germany, and Italy) to the Congress of Berlin (June 13 to July 13, 1878). After a month of talks, the powers signed the Treaty of Berlin, rolling back many Russian battlefield gains and redrawing the map of southeast Europe. Article 25 of the Treaty of Berlin gave Austria-Hungary the right to "occupy and administer" Bosnia-Herzegovina but not to annex it.[4] The Treaty of Berlin thus nullified the provision of the San Stefano treaty that foresaw autonomy for Bosnia-Herzegovina, but it allowed the sultan to retain de jure sovereignty over Bosnia-Herzegovina. The inherent ambiguity left an opening for Bosnian dissidents to appeal to the sultan against Habsburg repression, an opportunity seized many times during Austro-Hungarian administration. But despite de jure Ottoman sovereignty, the Habsburg Monarchy eagerly assumed full control starting in 1878 and excluded Ottoman officials from any further role in the province.

In the three decades before the Eastern Crisis, several European powers had posted consuls to Sarajevo. Representing five European powers (Britain, France, Germany, Italy, and Austria-Hungary) and reporting in four different languages, the consuls regularly shared information and exchanged insights.[5] During the crisis of 1878 they constituted an embryonic international community, occasionally acting together as well as reporting to their respective governments. The Austro-Hungarian Consul Konrad von Wassitsch, in addition to reporting on local events, became the on-the-scene representative of the designated successor government once the Berlin Congress approved the Habsburg occupation in early July. Many Bosnians, particularly those hoping to retain privileges under the new regime, sought to curry his favor. But to Bosnians who opposed Austro-Hungarian occupation, his presence in Sarajevo posed a threat. He fled with his staff and belongings on August 4 after receiving a written directive from the revolutionary government to leave the city. But until his departure in early August, he was the best informed and most insightful of the foreign consuls in the city.

Consul Wassitsch reported on the decline in Ottoman authority in Bosnia-Herzegovina following the Russian, Serbian, and Montenegrin victories over Ottoman troops. In January 1878 he noted that Ottoman "administrative bodies have no authority, and the population has lost its confidence in the government."[6] The government's dwindling authority rested increasingly on its armed garrisons, and the loyalty of its units in Bosnia was very much in doubt. Of the nineteen divisions stationed in the province, all but two consisted of local Bosnian Muslim conscripts. Most Ottoman troops were tied to the local population by blood and friendship, and they were less likely than other forces to side against their kin and neighbors in the event of local unrest. Their loyalty was further undermined by the Ottoman government's inability to feed and clothe its soldiers. By the spring of 1878 an estimated three thousand deserters were roaming the countryside in small bands, frequently terrorizing peasants. Bands of outlaws, both Serbian Orthodox and Muslim, operated with impunity in many rural areas and seized control of significant territories.

Discontent and intrigue on the eve of occupation

The Eastern Crisis of 1875–8 echoed resoundingly in Sarajevo. In the aftermath of Ottoman defeat in the spring of 1878, Sarajevans discussed possible alternatives to Ottoman rule. The San Stefano Treaty rekindled among many Bosnian Muslims long-subdued aspirations for an autonomous Bosnia-Herzegovina, but these hopes faded rapidly when Bismarck's plan for a conference in Berlin was announced. Rumors of imminent Austro-Hungarian occupation circulated in Sarajevo as early as April 1878 (well before the Berlin Congress) and evoked different responses from various confessions and classes. Many Bosnian Catholics in Sarajevo welcomed the notion of occupation by coreligionists. Many Serbian Orthodox Bosnians, on the other hand, were disappointed that neither Serbia nor Montenegro was given any role in Bosnia, and they found little reason to cheer an impending invasion by Serbia's nemesis, the Habsburg Monarchy.

The prospect of Austro-Hungarian rule divided Bosnian Muslims along social lines. Wealthy and influential landowners, closely tied to officials of the waning Ottoman regime, supported the change. They hoped that a smooth transfer of power would enhance their value to the new rulers and help preserve their privileged status and property rights. Many religious authorities and urban lower-class Muslims, centered in the marketplaces of

Sarajevo and other towns, were stridently opposed. They viewed the prospect of Habsburg rule as a triple threat, combining the liabilities of occupation by a foreign power, rule by the dreaded Christian infidel, and the end of hopes for Bosnian autonomy.

Members of Sarajevo's landowning elite, at a meeting in April 1878 at the Sultan's Mosque, showed support for the Austro-Hungarian occupation.[7] One Islamic religious official noted that the San Stefano treaty had left the situation in Bosnia-Herzegovina unresolved, and it was evident that the Ottoman Empire had neither the power nor the support to rule the land. He asserted that a ruler who cannot control his lands also loses claim to his subjects' obedience. Living under a non-Muslim government did not violate religious law, he argued. No Muslim would want to be a subject of Serbia or Montenegro, he reasoned, so Austria-Hungary was the only viable alternative. Its officials would protect all confessions and nationalities. The assembled leaders expressed their hope that Catholics, Serbian Orthodox, and Muslims would unite in urging the Habsburg emperor to occupy the land.

The first evidence of lower-class Muslim hostility to Habsburg rule appeared in April and May 1878 in a petition discreetly circulated in the marketplace by two conservative Sarajevo Muslim religious officials of institutions that carried the Gazi Husrevbeg name. Both later became leaders in the summer uprising against Ottoman rule. Abdulah Kaukčija, a noted religious conservative, was an imam of the Gazi Husrevbeg Mosque. Muhamed Hadžijamaković was a highly regarded preacher and scholar and headmaster of the dervish quarters. Although both men were native Sarajevans who had received most of their education there, each had also studied in Istanbul and served as a religious functionary outside the city. Their leadership ensured that the lower-class discontent bore the imprint of Islamic religious conservatism.

The petition, known as the Allied Appeal, urged all Bosnians to unite in opposition to Austro-Hungarian rule. It advocated making the *sheriat* (canon law of Islam; Arabic: *shari'a*, Turkish: *sheriat*, Bosnian: *šerijat*) the exclusive law of the land; demanded the dismissal of all Christian officials in Ottoman service; and appealed for formation of an assembly to control the government. The British Consul Edward Freeman reported that the petition also requested the removal of bells from the New Orthodox Church (a request that the same group had made five years earlier when the church was dedicated) and the demobilization of certain Ottoman troops.[8] The petition reportedly included about five hundred signatures. Most Muslim landowners, however, refused to sign.

Austrian Consul Wassitsch subsequently learned that political intrigue was behind the petition. The Ottoman governor, Ahmed Mazhar Pasha, had assumed his post only a year earlier (June 1877) and hoped to keep his position in the event Bosnia-Herzegovina acquired autonomy as specified in the Treaty of San Stefano. He planned to use the petition to gain popular support in his bid to oust Konstan Pasha, his deputy and principal rival. Konstan was a Greek of Orthodox faith and the only Christian (as the consuls uniformly described him) to hold high office in the Ottoman civil administration in Bosnia. The petitioners' demand to eliminate Christian officials would thus have removed Konstan from office and secured the Muslim Mazhar's advantage had the San Stefano agreement been implemented. Rivalry among local Ottoman officials was nothing new in Sarajevo, but the isolation into which Ottoman officials were thrust in summer 1878 contributed to an endemic division in their ranks. They disagreed among themselves about whether to encourage or dampen the local population's impulse to resist Habsburg rule.

When some upper-class Muslims and Serbian Orthodox leaders learned of the petition, they urged that it be redrafted without its explicitly anti-Christian demands. The original petition was withdrawn and a new version, written by an Ottoman official, was circulated. Through negotiation and revision, the leading Muslim landowners successfully purged the petition of its anti-Christian and antireform provisions. Formally submitted to the Governor Mazhar on June 2, the revised appeal contained only two points. It asked that a popular assembly rule the land and urged all groups to unite in opposition to Austro-Hungarian occupation.

The People's Assembly

Members of Sarajevo's Muslim elite undertook further mediation over the next few days to build consensus among the factionalized local actors. They persuaded representatives of lower-class Muslims, including religious leaders, to join a single all-Muslim assembly. Having achieved a united front, the Muslim landowners persuaded Mazhar to allow the assembly to meet in the government headquarters building, the Konak.

The People's Assembly met for the first time on June 5. Originally it was an all-Muslim body, consisting of thirty "notables" (Wassitsch's term for members of the Muslim landowning elite) and thirty "imams and merchants" (as he called the alliance of Muslim religious functionaries, artisans, and shopkeepers). In its first week, the assembly underwent four changes in composition as elite Muslims sought a formula that would include all factions yet preserve their own dominance. On June 8, the all-Muslim assembly appealed to Ottoman authorities to recognize a representative body of twelve Muslims, two Catholics, two Orthodox, and one Jew, all from Sarajevo, plus one Muslim and one Christian delegate from each of the six administrative districts in Bosnia-Herzegovina. According to the proposal, matters affecting a single confession were to be handled by delegates from that group, and common matters would be decided in plenary sessions. The assembly's proposed composition approximated the makeup of the regional council, the consultative body formed in the 1860s that had governed Sarajevo since 1872. Mazhar approved the assembly's new composition after consulting with the regional council.

The elite Muslims successfully preserved the fragile unity of Sarajevo's various local groups and Ottoman officials through the remainder of June 1878. The reconstituted multireligious People's Assembly first met on June 10 in the Konak. Serbian Orthodox nominees originally balked at participating, claiming that the scheduled meeting fell on an Orthodox religious holiday. After the date was changed, they agreed to participate but declined to take an active role.[9] At the first meeting, Serbian Orthodox representatives claimed they were underrepresented. The assembly honored their request and invited the Sarajevo Serbian Orthodox Commune to name three more delegates.[10] The three subsequently took their seats in the People's Assembly, which became more representative and more diverse simply by adding more members.

The Muslim lower classes were represented in the assembly, but most members from all confessions were drawn from the small coterie of upper-class local leaders who enjoyed honorary Ottoman titles and close ties to the government.[11] The assembly chose Sunulah Sokolović, a wealthy Muslim landowner and member of the regional council, as its president.[12] Other members included Mustajbeg Fadilpašić, son of the Ottoman-era wealthy landowner and political leader Šerifović; and Mehmedbeg Kapetanović, a Herzegovinian with perpetual difficulty being accepted as a true Sarajevan; two Serbian Orthodox representatives, Dimitrije Jeftanović and Petraki Petrović; Father Grga Martić, the Catholic representative; and Salomon Salom, the Jewish member, a merchant who sold provisions to Ottoman troops.

In its first days the assembly institutionalized earlier informal arrangements whereby the landowners claimed to speak on behalf of all Sarajevo

Mustajbeg Fadilpašić.
(Photograph, c. 1885,
from Vladislav Skarić,
Sarajevo i njegova okolina od
najstarijih vremena do austro-
ugarske okupacije, Sarajevo:
Opština grada Sarajevo,
1937, p. 263)

classes and confessions. Bosnian Muslim landowners adeptly steered the
deliberations to avoid divisive demands such as the adoption of the sheriat,
the dismissal of Christian officials, and a ban on bells in Christian church
towers. In an appeal to the central Ottoman government approved on June 5,
when the assembly was still an all-Muslim body, Bosnia's woes were blamed
on Istanbul's mismanagement and the government's failure to respond to
individual complaints. The address claimed that the distant government had
driven Bosnians to form their own representative body to address local
needs with local officials, and it warned that Bosnians would defend their
homeland with their lives in the event of war. It was unnecessary, the appeal
went on, to retain permanent garrisons of Ottoman troops in Bosnia, and in
any case the government could neither feed nor clothe its own troops. The
appeal further protested the punishment of deserters and their families.[13]
With this list of complaints, the elite Muslims voiced the general dissatis-

faction of all Muslim classes, excluding those grievances that might jeop-
ardize the fragile united front. Despite token efforts to include members
from other regions, the assembly remained Sarajevan both in composition
and influence. The six seats reserved for delegates from other parts of
Bosnia-Herzegovina remained empty, and the Sarajevo Muslims reportedly
believed that no one from the outlying areas could afford the burden of
travel expenses and a stay in Sarajevo.[14]

Uprising

The cobbled-together consensus among upper- and lower-class Muslims
began to unravel in early July as rumors of an imminent Habsburg occupation were confirmed. The monarchy asserted its intent to occupy Bosnia-
Herzegovina in a telegram from the Foreign Ministry received by Consul
Wassitsch on July 3, 1878.[15] By the morning of July 4, Sarajevo's hyperactive
rumor mill was abuzz with news of the Berlin decision, and Ottoman
officials in the Konak learned of the impending occupation from telegrams
that arrived shortly after Wassitsch's. That morning, Wassitsch met with
upper-class landowners and political activists Kapetanović, Sokolović, and
Fadilpašić to remind them of the generous benefits that would accrue to
those loyal to the new regime. The three promised to work toward a
peaceful reception for Habsburg troops, but they expressed fears, soon
proven well founded, of a lower-class uprising to oppose the new occupiers.

Wassitsch called on Mazhar on July 4. The governor told Wassitsch that
he would support armed resistance to Austro-Hungarian rule unless he
received orders to the contrary. At a meeting of the regional council later
that day, Mazhar exhorted its members to support a resistance movement.
Sokolović, president of the People's Assembly and a member of the regional
council, took the unusual step of opposing the governor's recommendation
by advocating a peaceful transition of power to Habsburg officials. Fadilpašić
and Kapetanović agreed with him. They, too, were unwilling to encourage
armed resistance.[16] Finally, on July 7, the Ottoman governor heard from his
superiors, but he received only vague instructions to retain public order
pending conclusion of negotiations with Austria-Hungary. Lacking firm
direction, he continued to take a permissive stance toward possible locally
organized resistance to Habsburg rule.

Popular demand for resistance was not long in coming. Shops in the marketplace were closed on July 4, and a large green flag was hoisted in the

courtyard of the Gazi Husrevbeg Mosque. On July 5 Muslim worshippers lingered in the mosque courtyard after noontime prayers, and the crowd spilled into the surrounding streets. A stirring speech was delivered by Salih Vilajetović, who had returned home to Sarajevo after three years of living as a brigand. He proposed that Wassitsch and his entourage in the Austro-Hungarian consulate be expelled from the city. He then led the all-Muslim crowd from the Gazi Husrevbeg Mosque across the river to confront the governor, Mazhar, and other Ottoman officials in the Konak. When the governor's appeal from the Konak balcony failed to disperse the crowd, the governor hastened to negotiate with the crowd's leaders. He agreed to dismiss the incumbent Ottoman military commander, long an unpopular figure, on condition that he be replaced with a Sarajevo-born commander appointed by the governor. Satisfied for the moment, the Muslims dispersed at dusk.

Although its leaders incited the crowd to resist Habsburg occupation and expel the Austro-Hungarian consul, the disgruntled Muslim crowd took no overt action against members of other confessions or against their cultural and religious institutions. Christians and Jews, out of concern for their safety if they defied the business closures in the marketplace, retired to their homes when the demonstrations began. Sisters of Mercy, who had resided in Sarajevo for only four years and had established a school, applied to Wassitsch for refuge in the Austro-Hungarian consulate, but he concluded there was no imminent danger and rejected the request.

Crowds of Muslim men continued to gather and demonstrate in the courtyards of Gazi Husrevbeg Mosque and the Sultan's Mosque over the next several days. They wanted Christians and Jews to join them in resisting the impending occupation. On July 10 the crowd demanded a change in the composition of the People's Assembly. The assembly proved flexible regarding its own composition and expanded the number of seats to accommodate groups claiming to be underrepresented. Wassitsch reported that the change was instigated by pan-Slav activists who encouraged armed resistance to any Habsburg invasion; indeed, the number of Serbian Orthodox members increased in the reconstituted assembly. The new body consisted of thirty Muslims, fifteen Serbian Orthodox, three Jews, and two Catholics. Most Muslim landlords abandoned the assembly within days, but Mustajbeg Fadilpašić was persuaded to remain and was elected president.

On July 9 the assembly relocated from the Konak, south of the Miljacka River, to the Morića Han, a hostelry directly across from the Gazi Husrevbeg Mosque on the Miljacka's north side. The new meeting place symbolized the assembly's transition from a nascent representative body under elite Muslim leadership to a group of activists under the influence of the conservative religious establishment and lower-class Muslims. The assembly, in its new location, changed from being a deliberative body into organizing resistance to Habsburg rule. The assembly divided into two committees, one to assemble troops and the other to secure provisions and funds. With most elite Muslims gone from the assembly, it came increasingly under Vilajetović's sway. In a quest for respectability, Vilajetović assembled an armed retinue and called upon Mazhar in the Konak. He sought immunity for his past misdeeds as a bandit. He demanded and received a token cash payment from the humiliated governor in recognition of his name being cleared.

On July 12 fading Ottoman authority was temporarily restored by the arrival of four battalions of troops dispatched from Istanbul under Hafiz Pasha's command. Hafiz was the last of a decades-long succession of military commanders and governors sent to subdue the restless Sarajevans under nearly impossible circumstances. With him arrived Mehmed Nurudin Vehbi Šemsekadić, mufti of Pljevlje (in the Sandžak region southeast of Sarajevo) and a learned Islamic scholar educated in Sarajevo. Šemsekadić subsequently proved an able and courageous military leader as well as a dynamic orator. But rather than occasioning a common Ottoman strategy to deal with the populace, the two men's simultaneous arrival further fractured the small community of Ottoman officials.

Hafiz hoped that the imminent Austro-Hungarian occupation would proceed peaceably. Showing the assembly his orders to welcome the Habsburg Monarchy's troops, he urged the Bosnians to lay down their arms and accept the occupation. But Hafiz sat in enigmatic silence at subsequent meetings of the regional council, leaving the consuls to ponder his personal attitude toward possible resistance as the invasion drew near.[17] Although his predecessor had on July 9 banned further meetings of the People's Assembly, Hafiz did not interfere when meetings resumed on July 18. For the next two weeks, Sarajevo settled into a stalemate. The People's Assembly feverishly prepared for armed resistance, while Ottoman troops under Hafiz did little but patrol the streets and keep their distance from the assembly's preparations.

Revolution

As rumors of an imminent Austro-Hungarian military incursion swirled through Sarajevo during much of July 1878, the consuls fretted that the imperial army's delay was increasing the likelihood of Bosnian armed resistance. Although the People's Assembly organized its forces unimpeded by the new Ottoman commander, Ottoman forces retained control of weapons and ammunition of potentially great value against Austro-Hungarian forces. On July 25 Vilajetović led a demonstration in front of the Konak demanding that the Ottoman officials turn over their weapons to the crowd.[18] The military commander Hafiz, now the only Ottoman official in Sarajevo with even a shred of credible authority, told the crowd that although he had no authorization to distribute arms, he would wire the central government and seek approval to do so. That promise won him another forty-eight hours.

The final assault on Ottoman authority began on July 27.[19] Like the demonstrations that brought the People's Assembly under the crowd's influence only three weeks earlier, further evidence of an imminent Austro-Hungarian invasion sparked unrest. That morning, Wassitsch distributed copies of the Habsburg emperor's proclamation of the occupation. Returning from visits to his fellow consuls just before noon, Wassitsch noted that shops were closing and that shopkeepers were hurrying home to get weapons.

Led by the charismatic Vilajetović, the Muslim crowd gathered around noon in front of the Konak, where Ottoman officials and members of the local Muslim elite had fled for protection. Bosnian conscripts from the nearby barracks deserted their units and joined the crowd. Around 4 p.m. Hafiz's remaining loyal Ottoman force tried to clear the street next to the Konak. Swelled by defecting soldiers, the crowd fought back. The two groups exchanged gunfire at close quarters. The street was cleared, but more Bosnian soldiers deserted the Ottoman ranks in the course of the battle. The French consul estimated that fewer than twenty Ottoman soldiers and members of the crowd died in the firefight.[20] Hafiz and his dwindling forces returned to the barracks, where Bosnian deserters had seized control of the arsenal. Yielding to the returning troops under Hafiz's command, the Bosnian deserters left the barracks. They rejoined the resurgent crowd, which cut water lines to the barracks and blocked the delivery of further provisions.[21] That evening the crowd also cut telegraph wires, hoping to isolate the city and prevent Ottoman officials from summoning reinforcements.

On the night of July 27–8 members of the People's Assembly conferred till well past midnight. They had again moved the assembly's meeting place, this time from the Morića Han to the Sultan's Mosque, in an apparent effort to intimidate those in the last bastion of Ottoman authority, the Konak. The assembly demanded the departure of Ottoman officials and their local allies from Sarajevo. At daybreak on July 28, Hafiz made one last attempt to assert Ottoman control. He led his loyalists to the fortress high above the city, but there he encountered Bosnian members of the Ottoman unit prepared to defy their commander. The Sarajevo crowd prevailed. Troops in the fortress seized Hafiz, escorted him back to the city, and turned him over to the movement's leaders at the Sultan's Mosque. Hearing of Hafiz's capture, other Ottoman officials resigned. By 9 a.m. on July 28, Ottoman arsenals were at the disposal of those planning all-out resistance to Austro-Hungarian rule. "The worst classes have the upper hand," British Consul Freeman reported.[22] Wassitsch, fearing that the crowd might harm others in Sarajevo, wired his fellow Austro-Hungarian consul in Mostar, "The position of officials, Turkish troops, the consulates, the Christian population, and even the Muslim notables of Bosnia is dangerous, since the fanatical mob has the most decisive influence over their fate."[23]

Later that day the crowd's leaders, led by members of the People's Assembly, met at the Gazi Husrevbeg Mosque and proclaimed the People's Government. Although sentiment favored the election of native Bosnians, the leaders persuaded the crowd to elect the imprisoned Hafiz as governor, providing a thread of continuity with the previous regime. One of the April petition instigators, Muhamed Hadžijamaković, was made Commander of the People's Army, the highest ranking military post in the People's Government. The government dispatched an emissary to Wassitsch to assure him that no harm would come to him, to others in his consulate, or to other consuls in the city. He responded, "I fully trust the good intentions of the Bosnians," but within hours he received another visit from assembly leaders, who asked if he wished to depart for the Adriatic coast along with the party of deposed Ottoman officials. Undeterred, he opted to stay. The other consuls followed suit and remained at their posts. "It appears to me that we in Sarajevo still enjoy the greatest possible security," Wassitsch wired his government, but added, "If we all leave Sarajevo together, we will be more secure than if we travel alone."[24]

The situation changed rapidly. Ottoman officials who opposed the coup came within minutes of losing their lives. The two former rivals and top Ottoman officials, Mazhar and Konstan, were stopped by the crowd as they were departing for Istanbul via Mostar. While in the hands of the crowd, they were robbed of all their possessions and their lives were threatened.

This caused great concern among the foreign consuls. Wassitsch proposed that all five consuls appear together at the Konak to ask that the two pashas and other prisoners be delivered to them. The four other consuls, meeting without Wassitsch because troops loyal to the crowd ringed the Austro-Hungarian consulate, felt that any *démarche* involving Wassitsch was bound to inflame the crowd. They agreed instead to send a conciliatory letter asking that the lives of the two captive Ottoman officials be spared. Just in time, Vilajetović personally intervened to rescue the two officials. They both eventually reached Istanbul and returned to unremarkable careers in the Ottoman bureaucracy.

In the meantime, the People's Government decided it was time to expel Wassitsch from the city. After receiving a written request on August 4 to depart, Wassitsch led a convoy of about one hundred consular employees and Austro-Hungarian citizens on the road to Mostar. The government provided armed escorts to ward off the dangers posed by Muslim irregulars along the way.[25] Wassitsch and his entourage safely reached Metković on the Dalmatian Coast some days later.

Resistance

On July 29, 1878, the day after the People's Government was proclaimed in Sarajevo, Austro-Hungarian troops under the command of Field-Marshal Josip Philippovich entered Bosnia-Herzegovina at four different crossings. Philippovich wanted first to secure the major transportation arteries and the largest towns. Approaching from the south, west, and north, the imperial forces planned to suppress the incipient resistance by conquering Sarajevo, its organizing center.

In Sarajevo, the People's Government prepared full-scale military resistance. On August 2, the first units were dispatched with flags to the battlefront, and others followed within days. Muslim, Orthodox, and Catholic volunteers assembled in the courtyard of the Konak for a celebratory send-off. These units were segregated by confession: each unit drew its volunteers from a single religious community, and units subsequently dispatched from the city were likewise segregated. Foreign consuls marveled at the lack of logistical support and the decentralized nature of the forces. "There is no organization of any kind, no arrangement for regular and continuing provisioning of the men, no plan of operation and, above all, no one in whom is vested the supreme command," reported British Consul Freeman. "Every little band of men acts entirely on its own responsibility."[26]

Field-Marshal Josip Philippovich, who led the Habsburg army which invaded Bosnia–Herzegovina in 1878. (Photograph, c. 1880, courtesy of Historical Archive, Sarajevo)

Although neither Serbian Orthodox nor Muslim leaders put forward a formal ideology, their appeals for volunteers expressed their ideals and objectives. The appeals, taken together with several discussions they held with foreign consuls, reveal that the leaders of various faiths served a common cause but for quite different reasons. Religious leaders were the most influential among all confessional communities in the city. Muslim and Serbian Orthodox leaders exhorted their followers to take up arms. But

Catholics found no encouragement to join, and few did. Jews were exempt from service in the resistance detachments, but were ordered to pay a special "war tax" of one million grosche. The French Consul Louis Patin, asserting that only six hundred Jews and perhaps twenty wealthy Jewish families lived in town, viewed this as a minor contribution to the overall effort. The levy was mandated by a large gathering of Muslims at the Gazi Husrevbeg Mosque on August 3 and approved by the People's Government in the Konak a few hours later. The same gathering levied a war tax of 150,000 grosche on Mustajbeg Fadilpašić, believed to be the wealthiest of the local Muslim landowners.

Muslim leaders invoked both precedent and the imminent Habsburg threat to mobilize volunteers and foment armed opposition to Austro-Hungarian occupation.[27] Vilajetović repeatedly cited the Koran and emphasized that its mandates motivated all his actions.[28] The Koran, he said, obligated him to fight anyone who took up arms to invade Muslim lands, regardless of the odds. Vilajetović told Consul Wassitsch that the Koran required that he provide security for the foreign consuls, just as he was then protecting the former governor Mazhar, once his sworn enemy. Pljevlje Mufti Šemsekadić argued that the Koran obligated the faithful to fight the infidel and that those who refused to fight should be banished and their houses burned.[29] Similarly, the public appeal of August 7 placed the struggle against the invading Austrians in the tradition of "warriors and martyrs" (*gazija i šehita*) who had fought for their homeland generations before. Those sacrifices obligated their descendents to defend against those "seeking to conquer the graves of our mothers and fathers." The enemy can be defeated with God's help, intoned the appeal.

Vilajetović wanted to make Koranic law the exclusive governing code, and he wished to abolish a standing army in favor of mobilizing all Muslims when confronted with a specific threat. The Koran and sheriat were invoked principally to mobilize Muslims for the armed struggle against Austria-Hungary. Freeman, the British Consul, reported that the sheriat was declared on August 3, that Muslim women were required to wear the veil, and that Christians who had previously worn European attire were now wearing "national" costumes. He also noted that no actions were taken to implement other measures. His displeasure suggests that at least some Muslim women were not veiled before the proclamation and that many of Sarajevo's Christians wore Western-style attire.

The final objective of the Muslim movement's leaders was to restore a perceived golden age, a time in which they believed that Bosnians enjoyed self-rule under institutions that followed Koranic dictates. Freeman noted that the leaders wanted to restore the situation before the reform era, before enactment of the Tanzimat when "allegiance to the Porte was merely nominal" and the native landowners were the sole power in the land.[30]

In their nostalgia for Bosnian autonomy, the Muslim leaders foresaw no role for the Ottoman government. The appeal of August 7 mentioned neither the Ottoman Empire nor its officials. The rebels' slogan proclaimed that Bosnia was their homeland. The sultan could give away Istanbul if he wished, but he had no authority to give away Bosnia. On the other hand, there was surprisingly little effort to vilify the Austro-Hungarians either as a German or Christian power, although Josef Koetschet reports that the word *Švabe* first entered Sarajevans' vocabulary as a pejorative term in the summer of 1878. The appeal of August 7 noted, "the Austrians are known for their cowardice, and those who read history know how our forefathers defeated them."[31] The Bosnian Muslim commander invited Orthodox and Catholics to join the resistance out of patriotism: "You fellow Bosnians, Christians, and Latins (*Hristjani i Latini*), for the honor of the homeland in which you have experienced centuries of tranquility, go with your Islamic countrymen into battle and expel the enemy. ... Defending the homeland is the duty of all peoples who live in it."[32]

Serbian Orthodox leaders mobilized their followers with their own distinctive appeals. Serbian Orthodox volunteers received a rousing send-off from Stevo Petranović, a merchant from Dalmatia and noted supporter of the pan-Slav movement.[33] The French Consul, Patin, identified him as second only to Vilajetović as influential in the resistance movement.[34] Sending off a unit of Orthodox troops to the front, Petranović cited with hope several articles from Serbian papers regarding Serbia's intent to conquer Bosnia. "Brothers! We are all of one blood!" he proclaimed, echoing a slogan of the pan-Slavic promoters of the revolution against Ottoman rule.[35] The highest Serbian Orthodox church official in Sarajevo, Metropolitan Antimos, blessed the battle flag and led the Serbian Orthodox volunteers to the outskirts of town. Arhimadrit Sava Kosanović and another priest, dressed as bandit leaders with pistols and daggers in their belts, led parades of singing young enthusiasts through the streets and declared brotherhood with the Muslims.

Slavic brotherhood and defense of the homeland were the essential components of Serbian Orthodox participation in the resistance, but they referred to a pan-Slavic brotherhood and a Slavic homeland rather than the explicitly Bosnian patriotism articulated in the Muslim leaders' appeal. Although they had not responded to earlier calls from Serb supporters of the peasant rebellion, the Serbian Orthodox followed their local Sarajevo leaders in mobilizing against the Habsburg occupation.

The battle for Sarajevo

Volunteers streamed out of Sarajevo in small units to repel the Habsburg forces, but they experienced a series of defeats in pitched battles with imperial troops in the first two weeks of August 1878. Equally demoralizing to leaders of the People's Government were telegrams from the Porte that deplored the Bosnian resistance and reported that the Ottomans were nearing an agreement with the Austro-Hungarian government regarding its occupation and administration of Bosnia. Ottoman Governor Hafiz, having returned to Sarajevo on August 13, pleaded with the People's Assembly and the crowd to end their futile resistance to the occupation. On August 15, he was shouted down by a vocal minority that opposed the peaceful surrender favored by most Muslims. But two days later, with reports of further defeats streaming in, the People's Assembly met in the Konak and voted unanimously to cease resistance and allow the city to be taken by Habsburg troops. The decision to capitulate coincided with the public humiliation of the movement's chief charismatic leader, Vilajetović.

The former bandit proved to be more of an inspirational crowd-pleaser than a warrior. On August 7, he had led his personal retinue out of Sarajevo to the northeast, but he and his entourage soon reported that they were mysteriously unable to locate the omnipresent Habsburg troops. Rumors spread in Sarajevo that he had robbed peasants, killed a young Muslim in Kiseljak, and killed a Christian near Sarajevo. He returned on August 14 to Sarajevo and was summoned before the People's Assembly. Condemned for his unauthorized flight from the front lines and fearful of being sent back into battle, he disabled himself by shooting himself in the leg. He was carried home by his entourage, disgraced among those who had made him an icon of resistance only a few days before. Three days later, he was reported to have fled to the hills around Sarajevo where he had previously lived as a brigand. He remained in a village there until early October 1878, protected by a Serbian Orthodox host from neighbors who threatened his life.

As Austro-Hungarian forces reached Sarajevo's outskirts from the north and the west on the evening of the eighteenth, they placed cannon on high ground at various points around the city. Sarajevans abandoned several vulnerable neighborhoods and found shelter with relatives and acquaintances in Vratnik, in the shadow of the Ottoman fortress on the hill above. At dawn on August 19, the invading troops began an overpowering artillery bombardment of the city. The Sarajevans fought back, using cannon seized from Ottoman arsenals, but the eight-hour battle ended with Sarajevo's defenders completely vanquished. Heavy street fighting accompanied the troops' entry into the city, and snipers firing from homes were answered by troops burning houses with the inhabitants inside. At 2 p.m. the yellow and black imperial flag was hoisted over Sarajevo, and Field-Marshal Philippovich entered the city at 5 p.m., to be greeted as a liberator by small groups of hastily assembled Sarajevans. The four consuls called on him in the Konak that evening, and the era of Habsburg rule had begun.

But the battle for Bosnia was far from over. Although the organizational nerve center in Sarajevo was extinguished on August 19, forces of Bosnian Muslims and Serbian Orthodox put up a determined resistance.[36] Frustrated Habsburg officials eventually committed 285,000 troops to a campaign that lasted well into the fall. They incurred some five thousand casualties and were criticized by foreigners and several groups within the monarchy for underestimating the scope of resistance to imperial rule.

The role of Salih Vilajetović

The movement and its leaders were widely disparaged by contemporaries and have since been further demonized by historians. To the consuls, movement leaders were religious fanatics, driven to irrational behavior by their hatred of non-Muslims. One Habsburg sympathizer called it a "mutiny of a socialist character."[37] Behind these assessments lay an orientalist predisposition to attribute fanaticism to Muslims and the hope that the chaotic, uncivilized Ottoman Empire would soon be superseded by an enlightened Christian power. But the movement was not socialist, and the objectives of the leaders as conveyed to the consuls could not have been clearer. Conservative religious beliefs motivated both Muslims and Serbian Orthodox to oppose the Habsburg military occupation, but those same beliefs restrained Muslim participants from violence against Christian Sarajevans.

The greatest scorn has been heaped upon Salih Vilajetović, the movement's first charismatic leader. The consuls consistently derided Vilajetović as an outlaw and brigand, and they reinforced their pejorative terminology by using his pseudonym, Hadži Lojo. Writing in the 1970s, the historian Rade Petrović noted that authors of prior studies had been "very critical in their assessment of the personality and role of Hadži Lojo, proceeding in their analysis on the basis of sources available to them."[38] In fact, Vilajetović was born a Sarajevan and had worked for years as one of the many religious functionaries in the city's mosques and Islamic educational institutions. He shared both his vocation and educational background with the two charismatic Muslim leaders who succeeded him, the April petition circulators and later military leaders Muhamed Hadžijamaković and Abdulah Kaukčija.

Vilajetović turned to brigandage only after being expelled from Sarajevo and for only about three years before returning to the city in 1878. Far from being irrational, he understood the political culture in which he was operating and skillfully exploited it to galvanize the crowd to action. The Italian consular representative, confessing that he had misjudged the man, noted that Vilajetović exercised a moderating influence and prevented some acts of violence despite his reputation as a bandit. He saved the lives of the two fleeing Ottoman officials, one Christian and one Muslim, on July 30. But his urban upbringing ill prepared him for military command, and he proved every bit the coward in evading imperial troops in August 1878. When Vilajetović was accused of murdering a Christian and a Muslim outside Sarajevo, the People's Assembly, despite having fallen under his sway the previous month, promptly condemned him to death (a sentence never carried out).

Popular perceptions of Vilajetović have changed over time. The socialist regime, enamored of his background as a bandit and champion of lower-class rebellion, gave the name Hadži Lojo to a Sarajevo street in the Bjelave neighborhood. With the fall of socialism, Vilajetović's stature as a Muslim hero was tarnished by his reputation as a populist rabble-rouser and bandit, practices too closely akin to the rural primitivism that many Sarajevans attributed to Serb nationalists. In 1991, Hadži Lojo Street was renamed Bardakčija Street, and the name Hadži Lojo was conferred on an even smaller street elsewhere in the city.

Austro-Hungarian retribution

Neither the People's Assembly nor many of its members survived the Austro-Hungarian occupation. Habsburg retribution was swift and ruthless in the first days after they conquered the city. On August 23, four days after his victory, Field-Marshal Philippovich impaneled a special court with summary judgment authority. In the next several days nine Sarajevo Muslims were hanged for instigating the uprising or leading resistance forces against Austro-Hungarian troops.

The first condemned to death was Muhamed Hadžijamaković, the commander of resistance forces who had roused Sarajevans to resistance on August 18. While approaching the Konak to give himself up to Philippovich, he was captured. He was tried the same day, condemned to hang by mid-afternoon, and led to a makeshift gallows around 4 p.m. where a rope had been strung from an oak tree branch. Over sixty years old at the time, Hadžijamaković was nonetheless a powerful man. As the execution party approached the gallows, he wrested a revolver from one of his captors and fired twice. The ensuing struggle left several guards injured, and the doomed prisoner lay bloodied and unconscious from a knife wound. After sunset the mortally wounded Hadžijamaković was carried the rest of the way to the gallows and hanged.[39] Abdulah Kaukčija, who in April 1878 had circulated the first protest petition under the influence of Ottoman Governor Mazhar, was the next to be condemned to die. His brief hearing took place on August 24, and he was sentenced and hanged the same day. Seven others were hanged in the first days of the occupation, at a time when resistance was still gaining strength in areas outside Sarajevo.

Besides the summary court-martial executions, imperial troops arrested hundreds of Sarajevans of all confessions in the first few days of their conquest. Prisoners were herded into a makeshift camp on the western edge of the city. Women and children were released, leaving about six hundred prisoners in the army's charge. Over the next several days, the prisoners were forced to march to the Sava River town of Brod. From there they were transported by train to Vienna and then marched across the city from one railway station to another, berated by Viennese whose friends and relatives had been mobilized for the Bosnian campaign. They were then shipped to the prison at Olomuc (in the present-day Czech Republic) and confined in conditions that gradually improved.

After a general amnesty was proclaimed on November 15, 1878, the prisoners were allowed to return to Sarajevo but forced to walk home from Brod. No accommodations could be found for them on one wintry December night of the march, and some ten to fifteen froze to death. When these deaths are added to those who perished on the gallows, Austria-Hungary's vituperative campaign of retribution claimed more victims than had the entire revolutionary movement in Sarajevo during the preceding two months.

An Austro-Hungarian patrol captured Vilajetović, still hiding in a small village, on October 2, 1878, and brought him to the military hospital in Sarajevo, where doctors amputated his leg. Immediately after attempting escape in June 1879, he was tried before a military court and sentenced to death, but his sentence was simultaneously commuted to five years in jail by order of the emperor. He spent those five years in the Theresienstadt prison and was released in 1884 on condition that he would never return to Bosnia-Herzegovina. He did not. He went to Trieste, then a part of the Habsburg Monarchy, where his wife and children were allowed to join him, and together they took up exile in Ottoman lands east of Bosnia-Herzegovina. Vilajetović died in Mecca in 1887.[40] Although they visited Sarajevo occasionally, members of his immediate family spent the rest of their lives in various towns of the Ottoman Empire.

Reconsidering the movement of 1878

The Sarajevo movement of 1878 was a bona fide revolution. Although it was short-lived, local, and ultimately futile, the movement led to a complete transfer of power from the legal government of the Ottoman Empire to the People's Government in late July. The successful revolutionaries were then free to organize and lead the widespread resistance to the Austro-Hungarian invasion. The revolutionaries were guided by no formally articulated ideology, and the modest changes they made in the local situation did not survive the vengeance of the Austro-Hungarian occupying forces.

The various local actors in the 1878 Sarajevo revolution were leaders and members of religious communities, and their religious affiliations and loyalties governed much of their behavior. The primary meeting locations were religious structures, the Sultan's Mosque and the Gazi Husrevbeg Mosque. The movement's most important leaders were religious functionaries from each of the major faiths in the city. Emblematic of the indivisibility of secular and religious functions, the Serbian Orthodox Commune elected the three delegates that were added to the People's Assembly in early June. The movements of 1878 were primarily those of religious communities, under local leaders, with only traces of loyalty to outside ideologies or secular identities.

The events of 1878 reveal an urban society that had evolved substantially since the 1840s under the influence of Ottoman reforms. The revolutionary movement laid bare the rifts among the city's various communities. The course of the struggle sharply divided the Muslims. Religious functionaries, including Vilajetović, inspired and guided the lower-class crowd to over-throw the Ottoman government and resist the Austro-Hungarian troops. They had adopted in whole the ideology, symbols, and program of auto-nomy and resistance to reform that the affluent classes of a generation before had advocated. In the verbal treatise he delivered to Consul Wassitsch, Vila-jetović reiterated the complaints and demands that leaders of the resistance to Ottoman centralization had set forth from the 1820s to 1850.

Members of the Muslim landowning elite and affluent Serb merchants fared best in the aftermath of the revolution. Most had either stood aside or joined late in the movement, and Austro-Hungarian rulers subsequently cultivated their cooperation to restore order and establish a new regime. Many became government advisors and members of the Sarajevo city coun-cil organized by the new imperial authorities. The new generation of upper-class Sarajevo Muslims had a vested interest in maintaining tranquility. Members of the new elite sought a nonviolent transition to Austro-Hun-garian rule, a stance for which they would be handsomely rewarded by the new authorities. The new elite was neither progressive nor reformist but conciliatory to the core, committed to using political influence rather than armed resistance to achieve its aims.

The revolution began as an exclusively Muslim affair, but by the time it reached the level of armed resistance, it brought together Muslim and Serbian Orthodox volunteers. There is no evidence to suggest divisions among the Serbian Orthodox comparable to those experienced by the Mus-lims. But like the Muslims, they responded primarily to religious leaders urging them to mobilize militarily, as well as to the appeal of a pan-Slav activist. At the same time, the mobilization had the support of important leaders among the wealthy Serb merchant class that had grown substantially in Sarajevo during the Ottoman reform era. The appeals to them blended the secular and the religious, revealing a group in the process of moving beyond religious identity into part of a broader Slavic and Serb community.

The revolution was not bloodless, but it cost relatively few lives before the armed conflict with Austro-Hungarian troops.[41] Most loss of life occur-red in the armed confrontation between loyalist forces and the crowd on July 27. This was a fight among Muslims; it is unlikely, although not wholly impossible, that Christians participated on either side. If one accepts the French consul's estimate that "fewer than 20" dead and wounded resulted from that confrontation, the number is small indeed. On these occasions, the crowd was prepared to use violence against those obstructing the resistance campaign, but not against individuals based on their religious affiliation or identity. The crowd's accommodating and protective treatment of other Sarajevans contrasted starkly with the bitter and ferocious resistance to Austro-Hungarian troops. Women and children as well as forces under various commanders participated in house-to-house fighting on August 19, and after the conquest, Philippovich's forces reciprocated the rancor with summary executions and the forced transfer of hundreds of prisoners to Vienna and back.

A low level of violence, however, should not be confused with the absence of intimidation. The crowd and its leaders threatened coercion to acquire the critical resources needed to mount the campaign. The People's Government levied a war tax on wealthy Jews and the leading Muslim landowner, and it exempted Jews from military service only because they believed that the sheriat forbade such compulsory service. The consuls repeatedly wrote of feeling intimidated, and they reported that Christians and Jews retreated to their homes as armed Muslims roamed the streets when the movement gained momentum in early June. The British Consul, Freeman, was particularly dismayed that Christians were intimidated into wearing traditional garb and that Muslim women were forced to wear veils. But in the sources these are the only instances of the crowd enforcing cultural norms on members of entire groups. Authorities of the Habsburg Monarchy were shocked and dismayed by the revolution in Sarajevo and the widespread armed resistance that followed it. Their first response after conquering the city was revenge, exacted in summary executions and imprisonments. It would fall to more thoughtful and experienced leaders to craft a policy that would eventually revitalize Sarajevo as a city that accepted European cultural influences while retaining much of its Ottoman heritage.

3. The Making of *Fin de Siècle* Sarajevo

Sarajevo entered the twentieth century larger, more developed, and more European than it had been when Austro-Hungarian troops took control of Bosnia-Herzegovina in 1878.[1] With the implementation of an imperial vision of urban spatial design based on Western models and Viennese precedents, the city acquired a Western-oriented face to accompany its previous profile as a classical Ottoman town. Accompanying this physical transformation were major changes in demography, political organization, cultural life, and social practices in the city. Taken together, these changes may be characterized broadly as "modernization" or "Westernization," but they reached Sarajevo mediated through the filters of Habsburg and Viennese experience and often mixed unpredictably with local culture and traditions. By 1900 Sarajevo found itself in the overlap of two cultural orbits: one largely traditional, centered in Istanbul; and the other European and "modern," emanating from Vienna. During forty years of Habsburg rule Sarajevo became unique among major cities in southeast Europe in blending the cultural influences brought from Vienna with those preserved from its four hundred years in the Ottoman Empire.

Austro-Hungarian approaches to Sarajevo

In their forty years of governing, authorities of the Habsburg Monarchy shifted their policies toward Bosnia-Herzegovina several times. Although deriving their approach to Sarajevo from broader policies, at all times they treated Sarajevo as the first city of the land and sought to mold it into a shining example of Habsburg administrative success. As a result, the monarchy bestowed a disproportionate amount of attention in Bosnia-Herzegovina on the city of Sarajevo.

The first impulse of the new authorities was to favor and cultivate the Catholic population while issuing harsh warnings to Muslims, Jews, and Serbian Orthodox about the need for loyalty to the empire. On August 21, the second day of occupation, Field-Marshal Philippovich received representatives of all four confessions in audience at the Konak, the Ottoman-era government headquarters commandeered by the new rulers. Father Grga Martić, a Franciscan priest who led Sarajevo's Catholic community, arranged the meeting and selected the delegates. Philippovich directed that the representatives come in two groups, and he received first those of the Jewish, Serbian Orthodox, and Muslim communities. Arhimadrit Sava Kosanović, the ranking Orthodox clergyman in Sarajevo, greeted Philippovich on behalf of the other members of the delegation.[2] Philippovich responded with a torrent of condemnation and insults directed primarily at the Muslims, whom he denounced for confronting imperial troops with armed resistance rather than greeting them in gratitude. He then abruptly terminated the meeting and left the room. Minutes later, he greeted Father Martić with warmth and appreciation.

Following the two audiences, one of Philippovich's aides invited two members of the Muslim delegation to join Martić in a private meeting. The two Muslims were asked to identify the primary instigators of the Sarajevo-based military opposition to Austro-Hungarian rule. They named Muhamed Hadžijamaković, Abdullah Kaukčija, and Salih Vilajetović.[3] Not coincidentally (as discussed in the previous chapter), Hadžijamaković and Kaukčija were the first two Muslims executed in the next few days; Vilajetović had already fled the city and was not found for several months.

Favoring the Catholic population proved to be a costly strategy for the new authorities, and a policy of treating the major religious communities equally eventually superseded it. The change in course followed a serious challenge to Habsburg authority in 1881–2, when Serb peasants in eastern Herzegovina rose in opposition to the monarchy's imposition of military conscription.[4] After another major military campaign to suppress the peasant revolt, imperial officials in Vienna realized they needed a comprehensive, long-term approach if the province was to become a showplace of Austro-Hungarian administration. For that task they turned to Benjamin von Kállay, a promising youthful diplomat with extensive knowledge of the South Slav lands and a singular vision for Bosnia-Herzegovina's future.

An imperial vision

Benjamin Kállay von Nagy-Kálló (1839–1903) orchestrated many of Sarajevo's changes from 1882 until 1903 from his post as joint minister of finance.[5] Many of Kállay's ideals and aspirations for Bosnia predated him and were shared by other imperial officials, but he was the most influential in translating general ideals into specific policies and programs. His ideas were based on extensive personal experience in the region and an avid determination to implement Habsburg imperial values in Bosnia-Herzegovina and its capital city, Sarajevo. Kállay brought vast knowledge and careful preparation to the task of governing Bosnia.[6] Born in Pest in 1839, he was an avid student of languages who became an expert on Serbia while attending Budapest University. In 1865 he launched an unsuccessful campaign to win a seat in the Hungarian parliament, hoping to win the votes of local Serbs by advertising his knowledge of their language and history. He served as Austro-Hungarian consul in Belgrade in 1868–75 and in 1872 traveled extensively in Bosnia, taking copious notes on local customs and the political situation. He wrote a well-regarded history of Serbia, published in Hungarian in 1877 and in German a year later.[7]

Kállay believed that the masses should be showered with benefits but deprived of rights. Although other imperial officials of his generation and background had begrudgingly reached accommodation with ascendant liberalism as early as the 1860s, he approached his task as an unrepentant apostle of neoabsolutism.[8] Authoritarian ancient Rome, rather than democratic ancient Greece, served as his prototype of an ideal polity.[9] In Rome's classical era, Kállay saw a vast empire bound by a uniform legal code, a far-flung system of roads, and allegiance to the person of the emperor. He felt that the best antidote to popular unrest was a rational, fair, and generous government. He vigorously combated all but the most superficial institutions of democracy and sought to bolster the influence of a narrow circle of allies carefully selected from local elites.

Along with many other imperial civil servants, Kállay believed the Habsburg Monarchy had a mission to civilize Bosnia-Herzegovina, and for two decades he worked to mold Bosnia and Sarajevo into his vision of enlightened European state and society. He aggressively promoted economic development, Westernization, Bosnian cultural awareness, and modern administration of the monarchy's new territory. Such innovations, he believed, would result in a docile, contented, and grateful population. At the same time, Kállay came to share the view of many Habsburg officials that neighboring Serbia and Montenegro might incite the Serbian Orthodox population of Bosnia-Herzegovina to rebellion. To combat the infiltration of nationalism from neighboring states, his administration fostered a regional patriotism called *bošnjaštvo*, a multiconfessional Bosnian nationalism that he hoped would prevail over the Serb and Croat nationalist waves then lapping at the province's boundaries. In Sarajevo particularly he instigated a major makeover of the central city to highlight the importance of religion and to divert popular attention from potentially divisive nationalism.

Kállay oversaw a rearrangement of central urban space. Under his direction the major religious, cultural, and educational institutions of each religious community were clustered around a downtown square, and these small neighborhoods were placed in close proximity to one another. He therefore continued the policy, implicit in the building of the new Serbian Orthodox church in the Ottoman reform period, of divesting Muslims of their monopoly on monumental structures in the city center, but he encountered no opposition from the docile Sarajevo Muslim leaders in this substantial change. He was careful to see that all major Muslim structures were maintained and new ones built as well, some of them monumental in character. Kállay and his fellow Austro-Hungarian administrators are most responsible for the present-day proximity and relative parity of large religious structures in the Sarajevo city center.

Sources of demographic growth

Between the first and last population censuses taken during Habsburg rule (1879 and 1910), the city's population more than doubled, a growth rate that outpaced all other Bosnian municipalities and Bosnia-Herzegovina as a whole (see Table 3.1).[10] Growth in the Roman Catholic population accounted for well over half of the numerical increase (Table 3.2). Numbers of Jews and Serbian Orthodox also increased substantially, owing largely to their participation in the expanding entrepreneurial and mercantile sectors of the economy. The centuries-old community of Sephardim, numbering approximately 2,000 in 1879, grew to 4,985 as reported in the 1910 census.[11] Most spoke Ladino and were known locally as "*Špagnioli*." A community of Ashkenazim grew to 1,412 in 1910. Most Ashkenazim spoke German as their first language and came to Sarajevo from elsewhere in the monarchy.[12] Sarajevo's Muslims, who had enjoyed a demographic majority for the previous four hundred years, grew only modestly in numbers but preserved their leading social and political stature with the aid of Kállay's new policies.

The tree of Habsburg administrative centralization was planted and grew dominant in Sarajevo, and its fruit fell near the tree, nourishing the city's

Table 3.1. POPULATION GROWTH IN CITIES OF BOSNIA-HERZEGOVINA, 1879–1910

	1879	1885	1895	1910	Increase 1879–1910 (%)
Sarajevo	21,377	26,268	38,083	51,919	143
Travnik	5,887	5,933	6,261	6,647	13
Mostar	10,848	12,665	14,370	16,392	51
Banja Luka	9,560	11,357	13,566	14,800	55
Bihać	3,097	3,506	3,943	6,201	100
Bosnia-Herzegovina	1,158,440	1,336,091	1,568,092	1,898,044	64

Source: Bosnia-Herzegovina, Landesregierung, *Die Ergebnisse der Volkszählung in Bosnien und der Hercegovina vom 10 Oktober 1910* (Results of the census in Bosnia-Herzegovina), Sarajevo: Landesdruckerei, 1912.

growth but distributing its benefits differentially among various groups. Although Sarajevo's population growth was driven in part by the need for skilled labor in the city's new and expanded factories, much of the increase came from the burgeoning corps of civil servants and government contractors. The influx of civil servants, professionals, merchants, and government suppliers from other Habsburg lands consisted primarily of Catholics, accounting for much of that group's exponential growth. According to the 1910 census, 16,786 Sarajevo residents, 32 percent of the total, claimed citizenship in either Austria or Hungary.[13] These immigrants from the Habsburg Monarchy often brought with them ideas and habits new to Sarajevo, and they functioned as a vanguard of innovation in the city during Habsburg rule.

Table 3.2. SARAJEVO POPULATION BY CONFESSION, 1879–1910

	1879	1885	1895	1910	Numerical increase	Increase %
Muslims	14,848	15,787	17,158	18,603	3,755	25
Serbian Orthodox	3,747	4,431	5,858	8,450	4,703	126
Catholics	698	3,326	10,672	17,922	17,224	2468
Sephardic Jews	2,077	2,618	3,159	4,985	2,908	140
Other Jews	*n.a.*	*n.a.*	899	1,412	*n.a.*	*n.a.*
Evangelicals	*n.a.*	*n.a.*	337	547	*n.a.*	*n.a.*
Other	7	106	—	—	*n.a.*	*n.a.*
Total	21,377	26,268	38,083	51,919	30,542	143

Source: Bosnia-Herzegovina Landesregierung, *Die Ergebnisse der Volkszählung in Bosnien und der Hercegovina vom 10 Oktober 1910* (Results of the census in Bosnia-Herzegovina), Sarajevo: Landesdruckerei, 1912.

Industrialization and infrastructure

Industrialization was seen by Kállay as a measure of a society's modernity, and he worked actively to industrialize Bosnia-Herzegovina in a way that would advance the monarchy's strategic interests in the region. The government set out to exploit Bosnia's timber, ores, and minerals and to build the roads and railroads necessary to facilitate that exploitation.[14] Making one's way through the country's mountains and winding river valleys presented many challenges, as invading imperial forces had discovered to their dismay in 1878, and building railroads into Sarajevo was even more daunting. The authorities opted to lay narrow-gauge track to save time and money, and as a result rail travel within Bosnia-Herzegovina was mainly on narrow-gauge tracks until well into the socialist era. Habsburg officials, largely following a plan drawn up by Ottoman officials in the 1860s, oversaw the completion of track from Sarajevo northward to Zenica in 1879 and to the Sava River town of Brod in 1882. That same year a railway station was built at the city's western end to accommodate trains using narrow-gauge rails. The line south to Metković on the Adriatic coast was completed in 1892,[15] and in 1906 a line was completed to the east. Much of the track in Bosnia-Herzegovina was laid by private investors, principally timber companies needing to transport lumber to markets within the monarchy.[16]

Sarajevo became the center of railroad building and maintenance in Bosnia-Herzegovina, and in turn the railroads became a mainstay of the city's economy. Austro-Hungarian authorities made the Main Railway Workshop the centerpiece of state-owned enterprises in Sarajevo. Located to the west of the railroad station, the workshop specialized in repairing and servicing equipment for narrow-gauge rail travel. It employed about a thousand people in Austro-Hungarian times. Because the city's first railroad station was three kilometers from downtown, a horse-drawn carriage began operating in 1882 to transport passengers and luggage from the station to the inner city. The first tracks were laid for a horse-drawn tram in 1894, making the trip easier for both man and beast.[17] In 1895 electrical power replaced horses and the tram tracks were extended along the banks of the Miljacka River. The new tram cars were divided into two compartments, the smaller compartment reserved for nonsmokers.

Most exploitation of natural resources took place outside Sarajevo, but many of the firms conducting that exploitation were headquartered in the city. Additionally, the authorities assiduously cultivated the growth of industry in Sarajevo, principally in the city's relatively undeveloped western end.[18] Habsburg administrators inherited from the Ottomans several Western-style embryonic manufacturing enterprises, most significantly the Sarajevo Brewery built in 1864. The state built, owned, and operated some of these facilities; others were built by private investors from outside Bosnia-Herzegovina; and still others were joint ventures between the state and private entrepreneurs. Additionally several installations that provided utility services to the city were owned and operated by the municipal government.

The government, cash-strapped after having been denied direct allocations from the monarchy's budget, declared state monopolies over salt and tobacco in April 1880 to enhance revenues. In 1881 the regime began construction of a state-owned factory that provided a manufacturing outlet for tobacco grown in western Herzegovina. The tobacco factory, in the city's western end beside the Miljacka River, employed between five and nine hundred people in the Habsburg years and remained a staple of Sarajevo's economy until the 1990s. In the late 1880s various private investors built a complex of textile facilities. Textile factories took advantage of expertise from an Ottoman-era cottage industry in carpet weaving and clothing production, carried out almost exclusively by women. In 1888 the Viennese firm of Philipp Haas and Sons built a factory that produced carpets featuring traditional motifs used in the cottage crafts of the time. A factory for thread, embroidery, and needlepoint was built shortly thereafter, and a workshop for artistic crafts was founded in 1892. Together these production facilities employed about a thousand workers, mostly women, throughout Austro-Hungarian rule. The carpet factory was later refurbished and modernized in the socialist era and continued to be a mainstay of Sarajevo's economy.

Supplying the construction and infrastructure needs of fast-growing Sarajevo was both a government imperative and an inviting business opportunity. August Braun built a brick factory in 1880, and by 1904 nine brick factories were operating in the city. Several sawmills were built in various parts of Sarajevo, all privately owned. The city and provincial governments built and operated facilities to provide running water, electricity, public transportation, and essential foodstuffs. A reservoir was established at Moščanica on a hill above the northeastern Vratnik neighborhood to supply the fast-growing public water system.[19] An up-to-date electrical generation plant was built in 1910 along the Miljacka River. A city slaughterhouse was built in the western end of town in 1881.[20] The slaughterhouse fulfilled part

Women working in a Sarajevo textile factory, *c*. 1910. (Courtesy of Historical Museum, Sarajevo)

of the city council's perceived obligation to ensure that the city had adequate food and also produced tax revenue. Stone walls were built along most of the Miljacka River to channel its flow through the city and contain its springtime and autumn torrents.[21]

A second face

In the twenty-one years of Kállay's rule, the Sarajevo cityscape was reshaped to correspond to his ideals. By 1900 an east-west axis was defined by two new secular administrative buildings at either end of the city: the Regional Government Building in the west, and the Sarajevo City Hall in the east. Along the east-west axis two clusters of religious structures were built, one each for Catholics and for Serbian Orthodox (built around the existing new Serbian Orthodox church), in close proximity to each other. The central Christian houses of worship were thereby divorced from the residential neighborhoods and located in positions of parity with those of Muslims. This ended the Muslim monopoly in the central city, but houses of worship for Muslims and most Islamic cultural institutions were undisturbed except for the addition of structures to advance education. The newly configured

Sarajevo embodied Kállay's belief that enlightened secular administration mandated that all confessional communities be treated equally. In fostering the growth of clusters of religious and educational structures, Kállay hoped to bolster the prestige of authorities from all religious communities and enhance their influence to oppose the rise of secular Croat and Serb nationalism.

The principal inspiration for Sarajevo's physical transformation was Vienna's Ringstrasse, the vast undertaking that replaced medieval walled fortifications with dozens of monumental structures built from 1859 to 1900. Sarajevo, crowded into an east-west valley, had few medieval fortifications in 1878 and therefore could never be encircled by a Ringstrasse, but Vienna's trends were copied in Sarajevo on a more modest scale in hundreds of buildings erected during imperial rule. Vienna's Ringstrasse project was conceived and carried out in the spirit of romantic historicism: Each building's design was chosen to evoke the particular bygone era deemed most appropriate for its function.[22] The Ringstrasse's first structure, the towering Votivkirche erected from 1856 to 1879, was a monumental neo-Gothic structure that, in the words of Carl Schorske, "expressed the unbreakable unity of throne and altar" in the Habsburg Monarchy.[23]

Ringstrasse styles were exported from Vienna to Sarajevo by a handful of able architects, all of whom were educated or had practiced in Vienna. Josip Vancaš (1859–1932) became the most influential among them.[24] After completing secondary school in Zagreb, he studied architecture in Vienna and was recommended to Kállay by his mentor, Friedrich Schmidt, a specialist in medieval architecture. Kállay promptly invited Vancaš to Sarajevo to design

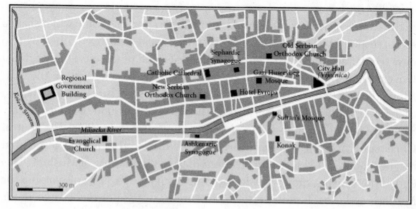

3.1 Key structures in Sarajevo, 1914.

a new Catholic cathedral. Vancaš arrived in 1884 as a precocious young
innovator with the potential to remake the entire city. Loyal to a fault to the
Habsburg emperor, he remained in the city for thirty-seven years. He eventually became the city's most important architect, a member of the first
Bosnian Parliament in 1910, and deputy mayor of Sarajevo.[25] Throughout his
career Vancaš remained an admirer of Viennese architectural trends and
often brought them to expression in his Sarajevo projects. But he was no
slavish imitator. By adapting Viennese models to Bosnian conditions, he
aspired to valorize all Bosnian religious communities to encourage religion
as an alternative to secular nationalism. The Catholic, Muslim, Serbian Orthodox, and Jewish faithful had to be accommodated with new structures, so
the historic unity of throne and altar forged in Vienna had to find separate
expression in individual structures. Vancaš would serve both God and Mam-
mon in Sarajevo, but he would serve them separately.

Josip Vancaš, Sarajevo's principal architect during
Austro-Hungarian rule. (Photograph, c. 1900,
courtesy of Historical Museum, Sarajevo)

The new Catholic cathedral became the central structure in a square just west of the city's older Ottoman-era center. Vancaš followed the central motif of the Votivkirche in adopting a neo-Gothic form, but with limitations on available space and funding, he incorporated many neo-Romanesque features. As a result, the cathedral invites favorable comparison to small-town Catholic churches rather than to the grand cathedrals of Europe's major metropolitan centers. Within a few years of its completion and dedication in 1889, the church's square was bounded on three sides by other romantic historicist structures, and the linear approach street to its south was similarly lined with facades derived from various architectural eras. The cathedral square and its approach street remain, at the beginning of the twenty-first century, perhaps the most symmetrical and architecturally harmonious part of the city.

Vancaš next designed the Regional Government Building, headquarters of the Austro-Hungarian Regional Government and known today as the Presidency Building.[26] A massive three-story block with thick walls and high interior ceilings, it features a modest and rigorously proportional neo-Renaissance facade.[27] Vancaš's design established another trend of incorporating features from the Italian Renaissance, known for its secular values and urban political centers, in Sarajevo structures "with provincewide significance."[28] The new government headquarters was situated at the far western end of the city's developed urban core, across the Miljacka River and about as far removed as possible from the old Ottoman government headquarters at the Konak. Location, mass, and architecture combined in the Regional Government Building to proclaim the importance of new authorities, who were eager to replicate European models and distance themselves from the Ottoman past.[29]

In subsequent projects Vancaš displayed considerable versatility and increasing understanding of the city's diverse religious traditions and cultures. In his most prolific period under Kállay's tutelage, he designed three structures in the late 1880s that incorporated architectural features of the Islamic East: a hall for the Muslim Reading Society (destroyed before the Second World War), the Hotel Central, and a Turkish-style bath named after Sarajevo's founder, Isabeg Isaković. Each had decorative motifs that are often called pseudo-Moorish but might better be classified as neo-Oriental, a variant of romantic historicism deriving its inspiration from Islamic architectural motifs rather than European historical eras. Like its cousins in the European panoply of romantic historicism, neo-Orientalism synthesized and simplified the architecture that it sought to evoke, leading the Bosnian architectural historian Nedžad Kurto to note that such architecture was a "generalized expression of the Oriental building heritage" not traceable to any specific source.[30]

Vijećnica (City Hall), completed 1894, interior stairway. (From the periodical
Nada (Hope), Sarajevo, December 1, 1897)

Neo-Orientalism won favor with Kállay and his subordinates, who believed it fostered a sense of local identity by evoking the elusive, exotic spirit of the Muslim population. Sarajevo's most distinctive neo-Orientalist monument, the *Vijećnica* (City Hall) was designed by another Viennese architect, Karl Wittek, under close supervision of officials acting on Kállay's directives. Located on the north bank of the Miljacka River near the first Islamic religious structures built in the fifteenth century, the Vijećnica is a marvel of both design and engineering. Stained glass windows, a large dome admitting generous exterior light, and a stately six-sided central interior vestibule combine to recall the Alhambra built by the Moorish rulers of Granada in the fifteenth century.[31]

Romantic historicism influenced the appearance of the many buildings that served the Austro-Hungarian government, Sarajevo's confessional communities, and several cultural societies. Neo-Orientalist designs were employed in the design of Islamic religious and cultural facilities, most notably in the schools of Islamic theology and sheriat. Schools and seminaries for Catholics and Serbian Orthodox were built in neo-Romanesque styles, and the Ashkenazim and Evangelicals constructed new houses of worship in the historicist style.

The Secession movement influenced many designs in Vienna in the 1890s, and Sarajevo's resident Viennese architects soon adopted the style.

New Ashkenazic synagogue, completed 1902, and the Appel Quay. (Postcard, *c.* 1914, courtesy of Historical Museum, Sarajevo)

The authorities, however, deemed Secessionist architecture lacking in the solemnity and traditionalism required for official buildings, so it flourished primarily in the design of family residences. Vancaš, the adaptable architectural pioneer, spearheaded the introduction of Secessionist style in the city.[32] By the turn of the century, it had become dominant, although the historicist tradition continued to inform the design of many new structures, particularly those created for government use.

Capital primacy

Austro-Hungarian officials turned to local elites to help them rule Bosnia-Herzegovina. Prominent Bosnians of all confessions were appointed to local posts if they were politically loyal and enjoyed the confidence of the local population. József Szlávy von Okány, Joint Finance Minister in 1880–2 and Kállay's immediate predecessor, wrote that he sought "personalities who appear able to influence their coreligionists because of their integrity, education, irreproachable conduct, and social status."[33]

In the first two decades of their rule, the authorities chose Sarajevans for most of their major appointments in Bosnia-Herzegovina. The most avid supporters of Austria-Hungary were the leading members of the loyalist Muslim elite from the late Ottoman era, but the regime found many willing and able allies in each of Sarajevo's confessional communities. Rising economic prosperity had brought many Serbian Orthodox merchants and entrepreneurs into leading positions in the city. Although many of them would have preferred a greater role for Serbia in Bosnian matters, most also found reasons to ally with the new regime. Catholic and Jewish Sarajevans also proved willing to accept appointments in the new regional and local governments.

Officials encouraged loyal Muslim and Serbian Orthodox Sarajevans to establish progovernment newspapers and provided generous subsidies for their publication.[34] This policy had considerably more success with Muslims than with Serbs. In 1891 Mehmedbeg Kapetanović launched *Bošnjak*, a publication devoted to trumpeting Kállay's multiconfessional bošnjaštvo. The paper gradually abandoned bošnjaštvo when that concept failed to gain popular support, but it continued publication as the voice of progovernment Muslims until 1902. Government supporter Risto Besarović obtained approval to publish a Cyrillic progovernment Serb newspaper, *Prosvjeta*, but a Serb from Vojvodina became its editor after Besarović declined further involvement. Both *Prosvjeta* and *Napredak* were published for some years as proregime Serbian Orthodox papers but failed to achieve the government's aim of creating a "loyal, conservative current among Serbs."[35] Kállay abandoned an initiative to launch another progovernment paper in 1897, after both Besarović and Petro Petrović declined to participate under pressure from Serb nationalists.[36]

City government

A few days after Habsburg troops conquered Sarajevo in August 1878, Field-Marshal Philippovich promulgated a statute creating the Sarajevo city council. The statute was styled "provisional," but its basic principles changed little during the subsequent four decades of Habsburg rule. Following the Ottoman-era precedent, Sarajevo council members were to be chosen according to confessional affiliation. The new body was to consist of six Serbian Orthodox (*Nichtunirte Christen*), five Muslims (*Mohamedaner*), four Jews (*Israeliten*), and three Catholics (*Katholiken*).[37] Mustajbeg Fadilpašić, from Ottoman times a leading supporter of the Austro-Hungarian occupation, was appointed the first mayor when the statute was proclaimed. Although not required by law, in practice all five Habsburg-era Sarajevo mayors were Muslims, as were the mayors of most Bosnian towns. Fadilpašić's successor, Mehmedbeg Kapetanović, another Sarajevo resident who had served the Ottomans, remained in office until becoming seriously ill in 1899.

A permanent city council statute was promulgated in 1884. Drawn up under the direction of the newly appointed Kállay, it expanded the council to twenty-seven members while following the principle of a confessional key. The composition was changed to twelve Muslims, six Serbian Orthodox, three Catholics, and three Jews. One-third of the members were to be appointed by the government, and they were routinely selected from the ranks of esteemed, prominent, and wealthy Sarajevans. Two-thirds of the members were to be elected, but the corpus of eligible voters was defined so narrowly as to ensure continued government control of the council. Male Sarajevo citizens aged twenty-four and over could vote only if they paid taxes at a specified level. All Austro-Hungarian civil servants, on the other hand, had the right to vote regardless of taxes paid. The civil servant votes were sufficient to swamp the candidacy of any unwelcome challenger, and government bureaucrats voted in full strength on several occasions to ensure the election of favored candidates.

In its first few years the council was assigned some of the more odious tasks required to secure imperial control of the city. The provisional statute of 1878 held the council responsible for feeding and quartering the monarchy's troops, for aiding in the collection of taxes, for publicizing all laws, and for the usual array of public services such as sanitation, schools, fire protection, and public health. In its first month the council provided wagons to transport wounded soldiers to hospitals and to move provisions to distribution points. Its members provided grain, straw, and 150 head of cattle per day to meet the needs of the newly arrived occupation forces. Muslim council members requisitioned mosques to store military provisions and commandeered private homes to house imperial army officers.

The council's role as the army's supplier was short-lived. Many of the council's activities had been mandated when imperial forces were campaigning in the countryside to subdue resistance. After Habsburg forces prevailed in October 1878, some army units were withdrawn from the province. The army built its own facilities for the remaining troops, and its officers procured supplies from local markets or imported them from elsewhere in the monarchy. By the end of 1879 most of the requisitioned mosques had returned to serving Islamic religious needs, in most cases without lasting damage.[38]

Having met the occupiers' most urgent needs, the council became the government's handmaiden in building local institutions and creating an urban infrastructure based on European models. The city's twin scourges, fire and flood, recurred often in the early occupation years, reminding both the new regime and Sarajevans of many badly needed changes. In August 1879 a fire in the Catholic mahala, north of the Miljacka River, destroyed several blocks of buildings. In March 1880 the City Commissioner, Kosta Hörmann, proposed to the council a comprehensive plan to repair or replace burned structures and to build walls to channel the Miljacka River over a short stretch to protect the most threatened areas. The council responded eagerly, approving a project to erect walls along the river for the entire central city area. Permanent walls were completed in 1896.

Religious communities

When imperial troops entered the province in 1878, the Roman Catholic, Serbian Orthodox, and Muslim religious communities each owed allegiance to leaders beyond the borders of Bosnia-Herzegovina. Before Kállay's

Panoramic view of the Miljacka River and the Appel Quay, with completed river wall, a row of historicist structures, and tram line. (Photograph, *c.* 1914, courtesy of Historical Museum, Sarajevo)

appointment in 1882, his predecessors had secured control over the personnel appointments and budgets of the Catholic and Serbian Orthodox communities. Officials hoped that able, energetic clerical leaders would help counteract the appeal of Serb and Croat nationalism, since secular nationalism threatened the primacy of religious leaders no less than it endangered the monarchy's political goals.

Under the concordat between the Vatican and the Habsburg Monarchy reached on June 8, 1881, an archbishopric was created in Sarajevo with jurisdiction over all bishoprics in Bosnia-Herzegovina.[39] The newly created post required additional facilities, including a parish church, an archbishop's residence, and a monastery, all to be built in Sarajevo. Vancaš, as already noted, was first engaged to design the cathedral, and he won the favor of other Habsburg officials and church authorities for further projects. He designed the archbishop's residence and several buildings to house a Catholic seminary and school to be located on the northern periphery of the cathedral square. With the completion of these projects, Sarajevo had a center of Catholic religious and educational life in the heart of the old city. The monarchy's control over the Serbian Orthodox hierarchy was secured by a convention concluded with the patriarch of Constantinople on March

28, 1880. The agreement provided that the three existing metropolitans, based in Tuzla, Mostar, and Sarajevo, be retained in their posts for the time being, but the emperor acquired the right to dismiss them at will and to appoint their successors. He first exercised that right in 1891, replacing Sarajevo's metropolitan with Sava Kosanović, believed (wrongly) to be a reliable government supporter.

The government faced a more complex task in restructuring the Islamic religious hierarchy than with either the Serbian Orthodox or Roman Catholic organizations. Secular and religious authority shaded uncertainly into one another in Islamic legal theory and in Ottoman practice. In addition to regulating the religious hierarchy, Habsburg officials had to deal with vakufs, sheriat courts (to administer traditional Islamic law), and an educational system that was structured quite differently from those of the other faiths.[40] Once Kállay came into office, the authorities lent their support to a group of Sarajevo Muslims who were pleading for a leading role in the province's Islamic affairs. Several weeks after the Habsburgs arrived in 1878, Sarajevo Muslims petitioned for a Bosnian to be appointed to head the province's Islamic hierarchy. When this appeal went unheeded, Sarajevo Muslims repeated their request in a second petition in November 1881. Shortly after he took office, Kállay responded favorably and sent the emperor a proposal to establish the office of *Reis-ul-ulema* as the supreme Islamic religious authority in Bosnia-Herzegovina. The emperor concurred, and Mustafa Hilmi Omerović, the Ottoman-appointed mufti of Bosnia and a recognized leader among Sarajevo Muslims, was named as the first holder of the office.

After four centuries of Ottoman rule, large parts of Sarajevo and considerable rural land had fallen under vakuf administration. Typically the administrators were scions of donor families who often used their positions to prolong familial control of property in addition to supporting charitable causes. In 1883 Kállay ordered the creation of a provisional vakuf commission to inventory and oversee the vakuf administrative system. Sarajevo Mayor Mustajbeg Fadilpašić was named its president, and many members were recognized leaders among the Sarajevo Muslims. In 1894 this temporary arrangement was replaced with a permanent commission of twenty-one members, including two representing each of the six administrative districts in Bosnia-Herzegovina. The broadened membership weakened but did not end the leading role of Sarajevo Muslims in regulating vakufs provincewide.

These new organizations required quarters, of course, but Sarajevo already had many Islamic places of worship. Buildings constructed for the

Islamic community in fin-de-siècle Sarajevo were not clustered around any single square but were generally located in the eastern end of the city, the hub of political and social life in Ottoman times. In encouraging the design and use of these structures, the regime's leaders hoped to modernize and Westernize the Bosnian Muslim community. Vancaš designed a neo-Oriental building for the Sarajevo Muslim Reading Society, an association formed under government auspices. The authorities hoped that both the society and the building would not only encourage a progressive, modern outlook among Sarajevo Muslims but also foster the unity of all groups in the spirit of bošnjaštvo. At the dedication ceremony for the new building in 1888, one imperial official voiced the hope that the society would "decisively influence the progressive and enlightened urban residents of all confessions to achieve harmonious reciprocal influence."[41]

Committed to retaining the loyalty of the Sarajevo elites, the authorities generally refrained from tearing down mosques, churches, and other local religious institutions that were valued by religious leaders. The Ottoman-era religious monuments of Sarajevo were largely preserved, unlike those of many other cities that passed from Ottoman control to the Habsburg Monarchy or were conquered by Balkan national successor states. Only in promoting public parks did the authorities evoke concern from Muslim leaders opposed to removing the Muslim grave markers that were scattered about open spaces in the old city.[42] After Muslim leaders protested, officials agreed that the grave markers could be fenced off and preserved with private funds. The weathered Muslim gravestones have remained a distinctive feature of many Sarajevo parks.

During the Habsburg era Evangelicals and Ashkenazim grew in numbers to make up new religious communities in Sarajevo. Houses of worship for both faiths were built on the south bank of the Miljacka River, and both were designed by Karl Parik, a Viennese architect of Czech origin. Parik designed a new Jewish synagogue, giving the city's fourteen hundred Ashkenazim a place of worship separate from the Sephardic synagogue. Dedicated in 1902, the new synagogue shows Secessionist influence, but its primary motifs reflect Jewish history and religious symbols in the tradition of romantic historicism. Parik also designed the Evangelical church, a wide neo-Baroque edifice, beside the Miljacka River. When completed in 1899 it was the largest Christian church in Sarajevo even though, according to the 1910 census, only 547 Evangelicals lived in the city. Most of them had moved there to work as administrators or to exploit emerging commercial opportunities.

The Habsburg authorities strengthened the prestige and visibility of Sarajevo's religious leaders in hopes of bolstering religious loyalties to forestall the growth of secular nationalism. In constructing houses of worship for Catholics, Evangelicals, and Ashkenazim, the authorities provided religious leaders with visual affirmation of their importance in Kállay's plans for a loyal, docile Bosnian population. Habsburg authorities and Viennese architects created several monumental religious structures within a few blocks of one another, adding to diversity and diluting Muslim dominance in the central city. Non-Muslim houses of worship were no longer restricted to individual mahalas and arose instead in the central city where monumental structures had once been an Islamic monopoly. The Habsburg authorities' visual remake of the cityscape persists as a reminder of Sarajevans' propensity to live, work, and worship in the city center with respect for one another's affiliations and allegiances.

Private parties and public manifestations

Through four decades of Austro-Hungarian administration, Sarajevo's leaders were routinely expected to lead deputations of thanks to appropriate officials and to attend elaborate welcoming ceremonies for visiting dignitaries from the monarchy. These events were something new for the Bosnians. In Ottoman times Sarajevo's leaders had regularly assembled at the city's eastern approach to greet newly appointed pashas dispatched from Istanbul. However, repeated ostentatious deputations of thanks to local officials began with Habsburg rule.

On Kállay's appointment as joint finance minister, top imperial officials invited prominent Sarajevans to social events in their urban villas. Baron Feodor Nikolić, Ziviladlatus[43] in 1882–6, grew famous for his weekly parties that drew 100 to 240 guests from the ranks of both Habsburg officialdom and local dignitaries. These gatherings featured theatrical acts, songs, and games. Such gatherings were out of character for some of Sarajevo's conservative Muslims, who attended but, according to one observer, remained stolidly aloof from the surrounding levity: "They normally sat quietly next to one another and looked with suspicion as German officers and young officials flirted with the young women of wealthy Sarajevo families. ... They scornfully condemned these [activities] as Western luxuries that would bring both the young girl's house and her family to ruin."[44] Other local leaders mimicked Western practices and hosted various social

events. Sarajevo's Muslim Mayor Mustajbeg Fadilpašić and Serbian Orthodox Vice-Mayor Dimitrije Jeftanović each reciprocated with large parties at
their residences. Mehmedbeg Kapetanović hosted a party to welcome
Kállay to Sarajevo in 1882. Although Kállay was unable to attend because of
illness, *Landeschef* Johann Freiherr von Appel expressed in the "local language" his pleasure at seeing such a fine gathering of Muslims in one of their
homes.[45]

Such staged gatherings were only one component of the effort to introduce Western practices into the leisure time of Sarajevans. Social gatherings
in homes and religious establishments, the prevailing pattern in Ottoman
times, were gradually supplemented with secular public activities that
included evening café life, theater performances, concerts, and the evening
stroll known as the *korzo*. Each of these institutions at first served primarily
as entertainment for imperial officials, army officers, and other immigrants
from the monarchy, but local participation increased over the years. Vocal
concerts grew in popularity, particularly as the regime sanctioned singing
societies made up of members of a single religious community. The korzo
began each evening about dusk and proceeded east-west in the city's
Ottoman core, with informal gatherings taking place in the squares in front
of the Catholic cathedral and the new Serbian Orthodox church.

In parallel with the city's architectural orientation to Vienna, festivals and
holidays came to reflect practices in the imperial capital and elsewhere in the
monarchy. These were carefully organized to supplement the myriad religious holidays that had been a part of Bosnian life for centuries. Anniversaries of major events in Emperor Franz Joseph's life were occasions for
major public celebrations. (Because Franz Joseph assumed the throne in
1848 and remained emperor until his death in 1916, he was the only
Habsburg emperor most Sarajevans experienced.) Habsburg authorities,
following practices in the monarchy, sponsored celebrations on the emperor's birthday, coronation date, saint's name day, and wedding anniversary. Field-Marshal Philippovich understood the importance of these
anniversaries. On the outskirts of Sarajevo in mid-August 1878, he had
planned to conquer the city in time to offer it as a gift for the emperor's
fortieth-eighth birthday on August 17. Tactical considerations forced him to
delay his assault by a day, robbing him of the glory that would have followed
such a birthday gift to His Imperial Highness.

The tenth, twenty-fifth, and fiftieth anniversaries of major events were
marked for special festivities and full public participation. The first oppor-

tunity to celebrate such a milestone in newly occupied Sarajevo arose on April 24, 1879, the silver anniversary of Franz Joseph's wedding to Empress Elisabeth. The city council, clearly coached by imperial authorities, went to extraordinary lengths to detail the nature of events that would take place. The council directed that festivities commence the evening of April 23 and feature light and fire from a variety of sources.[46] It ordered that candles be lit in churches, mosques, the Jewish synagogue, shops, public buildings, walls, and city gates.[47] That evening, each private home was required to burn at least two candles in the windows. A column of at least five hundred singers was to be transported together in wagons to a departure point, where they were to divide into two processional columns, one on each side of the Miljacka River. Their musical parade was to proceed to the military barracks near the Konak, where the two columns would reunite. Another twenty to thirty Sarajevans, mounted on horseback, were to follow the same route.

The next morning religious services and audiences were mandated for each religious community and the town's leading citizens. In early morning a bonfire was to be lit on each of the major hills surrounding the city, fed by five cubic meters of firewood to be assembled on the summit of each hill. When signaled by cannon fired from the fortress at the city's eastern end, tenders were to light these bonfires. All religious houses of worship were ordered to hold services between 7 and 8:30 a.m., or earlier if that was the established custom. Following these services, at 9 a.m., the highest ranking Habsburg official in town, Baron Jovanović, was to receive the obligatory delegation of local dignitaries in the Konak. On the evening of April 24, all participants and citizens were to travel, either on horseback or by carriage, to the military barracks for recreation organized by the citizenry.

In common with practices elsewhere in the monarchy, the Sarajevo council was expected to allocate charitable assistance to the poor on holidays honoring the emperor. The council voted to assist victims of a recent flood as part of its plan for the emperor's silver wedding anniversary in 1879. This practice received ongoing financial support in 1888 on the fortieth anniversary of the emperor's coronation. Council member Risto Besarović proposed establishing a city lottery to aid the poor, an alternative preferred over a special tax or permanent board to gather voluntary contributions. He voiced pleasant surprise that citizens "regardless of faith, social standing, and wealth have exercised their civil duty toward the poor and ... expressed patriotic feelings toward their exalted ruler" on the fortieth anniversary of the coronation.[48] Besarović crafted his proposal, which passed unanimously, to express the council's gratitude to the emperor and concern for the poor in the city.

Political controls

Austro-Hungarian officials approached all local initiatives with a combination of intense scrutiny, cautious containment, and selective co-optation. They sponsored or tolerated initiatives likely to promote the monarchy's interests and goals, but they were acutely aware that local initiatives might find provincewide followings and become broad challenges to Habsburg authority. As with the religious hierarchies, Kállay was determined that secular societies and associations not become forward outposts of political agitation that originated beyond Bosnia's borders. The administration adopted a concession system modeled on practices in Austria during the neoabsolutist era of Alexander Bach (leading minister, 1852–9).[49] The authorities found many advantages in the great latitude they could exercise in denying or modifying concession requests. The aspiring founders of any society were required to submit a proposed statute for government review, and the statute's contents were typically the subject of protracted negotiations between the founders and authorities. Statute language was approved only if it included provisions for a society to engage in cultural, educational, and entertainment activities rather than anything that hinted of politics. Statutes were further required to specify that the government could dissolve the society if its activities exceeded those authorized in its statute. This system equipped government overseers with both belt and suspenders— having dictated the statute, they could disband a group at will for violating statute provisions.

Using its discretionary authority in approving statutes and overseeing the activities of all societies, Habsburg officials aggressively sought to contain the activities of each society within the boundaries of a single Bosnian city or town. They also monitored many activities beyond Bosnia's borders. Associations were permitted to carry only the names of historical personalities whose careers were limited to Bosnia-Herzegovina.[50] Kállay's extensive network of spies and informants reported all cross-border visits by outsiders and by Bosnians traveling to neighboring lands. The regime carefully monitored the 1889 Sarajevo visit of Josip Strossmayer, the Bishop of Djakovo and a figure admired by many in neighboring Croatia, to attend the consecration of the Catholic cathedral. Fears that Strossmayer might use the visit to promote Yugoslavism or pan-Slavism proved unfounded, for he became acutely aware of the official scrutiny and scrupulously avoided inflammatory statements.[51]

Administrative restrictions were brought to bear most heavily upon nascent national movements. The national names "Serb" and "Croat" were prohibited in association names and in public speeches. Some draft statutes were returned with instructions that only the term "Orthodox" should be used in society titles. Later, the regime relented slightly and approved the use of the word "Serb" but only if it was used in tandem with the word "Orthodox."

With these tightly woven constraints, associational life in Sarajevo under Kállay was principally recreational and educational. Societies were formed by mountain climbers, hunters, beekeepers, and promoters of modern agricultural practices. In 1892 the city's Jews founded La Benevolencija to aid the poor and to award scholarships that enabled Sephardic youth to attend secondary school and universities in Vienna, Graz, and Prague.[52] Serbs formed a singing society called Sloga in 1889, and Croats established one called Trebević in 1894. The activities of these nationality-based societies were carefully monitored. Sloga, formally called the Sarajevo Serbian Orthodox Church Singing Society, proposed to stage a play entitled Nemanje in 1894. The reviewing censor ordered changes to the play's text, finding that it alluded to the unity of all Serbs regardless of where they lived.[53] Trebević received its charter as the National Singing Society only after the government rejected the founders' proposed name, Croat Singing Society.

In the early 1890s some Sarajevans began honoring holidays associated with leaders or events outside Bosnia-Herzegovina. Muslims celebrated the sultan's birthday as a reminder of his de jure sovereignty over Bosnia-Herzegovina. Sloga, the Serbian Orthodox singing society, planned to celebrate Vidovdan (anniversary of the 1389 battle at Kosovo Polje) in 1892. Government censors prohibited a speech that implicitly called for the unity of all Serbs by attributing the 1389 defeat at Kosovo to Serb national disunity. They also forbade the singing of a song in praise of the gusle (a national folk stringed instrument) and demanded changes in the text of the invitation, which was to read, "We invite to this event all Serb brothers and sisters and all friends of the Serb nation." With these limitations and changes, the event went forward, and Vidovdan thereafter became a staple among anniversaries honored by Sarajevo's Serbs. By the turn of the century Sarajevans could participate in a variety of holidays, some scheduled by the government and others organized by various citizen groups.

Molding a new intelligentsia: Sarajevo's schools

To fulfill its civilizing mission the monarchy required a secular native intelligentsia that shared the imperial vision. To develop an educated elite, officials founded hundreds of public elementary and secondary schools during Austro-Hungarian rule. These schools supplemented but never wholly supplanted the parochial schools that predated the Habsburg occupation, but by the turn of the twentieth century over two-thirds of all students were in public rather than parochial institutions. Officials hoped that the public schools would foster loyalty to the monarchy and, in Kállay's time, impart to students a Bosnian identity rather than the Serb and Croat alternatives. Since the training of a loyal intelligentsia was a priority of the Habsburg administrators, they concentrated many of the new secular schools in the province's capital city, Sarajevo.

Parochial educational institutions coexisted uneasily with public schools throughout the Habsburg period. Muslim, Serbian Orthodox, Catholic, and Jewish confessional communities had founded parochial schools at different times with the goal of inculcating religious belief and imparting basic skills to their youth. Students of other confessions were not barred from parochial schools, but their numbers at any time were miniscule. After taking over in 1878, the authorities subjected nonpublic institutions as well as public schools to close supervision, political controls, and periodic inspections by dreaded school inspectors. Habsburg officials found that some parochial schools were useful in advancing their imperial vision, and those schools often received substantial government subsidies. Other schools represented political tendencies that posed grave dangers to the monarchy's Balkan ambitions. But because Bosnians of all faiths clung doggedly to their confessional schools, a diverse assortment of parochial schools survived and even thrived during Habsburg rule, remaining a feature of the city's educational life.

The new rulers had lofty ambitions for education but lacked the financial means to realize them. Early in the years of occupation they were forced by budgetary constraints to defer indefinitely their hopes for rapid expansion of public education. They therefore concentrated on creating a loyal elite at the expense of more ambitious goals such as universal literacy. The authorities fell short of realizing their goal of having no child be more than four kilometers from an elementary school. They also faced political challenges in promoting public education. Hungarian politicians in the monarchy, concerned that Bosnian schools might become a medium for spreading Croat identity, favored financial support and close supervision of parochial schools rather than building a system of free public schools. Only a handful of teachers in Bosnia-Herzegovina were trained in Western instructional methods, so nearly all teachers had to be imported from the monarchy. Compulsory elementary school attendance, impractical in the early occupation years, did not become law until 1911.

Determined from the beginning to stimulate growth of modern local elites through secular education, the authorities in 1879 opened a public high school (*gimnazija*) and three public elementary schools.[54] The schools were multiconfessional but segregated by gender, with two elementary schools for boys and one for girls. The Sarajevo high school (for male students only) was the only one in Bosnia-Herzegovina until 1893. The government offered scholarships for poorer students, making upward social movement possible if not commonplace. Of the forty-two students enrolled in the first year, eighteen were drawn from outside Sarajevo.[55] By 1904–5 enrollment in the high school had increased to 630 students of all confessions, but Catholics (232 students), Serbian Orthodox (233 students), and Jews (66 students) were proportionally more represented than Muslims (95 students).

In subsequent decades, three more public elementary schools were opened in Sarajevo for boys of all confessions. In 1882 a teacher preparation course was offered in Sarajevo, and in 1886 it was expanded to a three year teachers' preparatory school. In 1904–5 its enrollment consisted of thirty-nine Catholics, thirty-three Serbian Orthodox, twenty-one Muslims, and one Jew.[56] Several technical secondary schools were established in Sarajevo to prepare students for work in Bosnia's primary industries, including a school for business opened in 1886 and another for construction trades opened in 1893.

The authorities encouraged women's education, although they spent less on facilities for women. A public four-year multiconfessional secondary school for women was founded in Sarajevo in 1882. The curriculum centered on handicrafts and domestic tasks, supplemented with courses in general education. Attendance was modest and stratified by confession. Of 187 students enrolled in 1904–5, 84 were Catholics, 67 were Jews, and 36 were Serbian Orthodox. Not a single Muslim attended, as the life of a Muslim girl was largely confined to her parents' home. To encourage formal education for Muslim girls, the government in 1897 opened a public elementary school solely for Muslim girls and drew sixty-four enrollees in its first year, but most Muslim girls received no formal education during

Austro-Hungarian times. As a sad consequence, the literacy rate for Sara-jevo's Muslim women in 1910 was reportedly only 2.2 percent.

Authorities believed that the Muslim parochial schools were backward and inadequate. For Muslim boys, *mektebs* (Islamic elementary schools) had, since early Ottoman times, provided a basic education centered on religious instruction and memorization of passages from the Koran. Imperial autho-rities derided these schools for their lack of discipline and unsystematic approach to instruction:

In these mektebs, the students receive instruction in reading the Koran and other religious books in Arabic and Turkish. ... The students can come and go as they please ... and there is no division into classes. ... The instruction is totally unsys-tematic and takes place at the discretion of the *hodža*. He recites a text and the students repeat it loudly and in unison. ... With these unsystematic instructional methods of the pedagogically uneducated hodžas, these mektebs produce no practical results.[57]

In an effort to introduce European practices into the education of Muslim boys, authorities opened seven reformed mektebs (*iptidaija*) in Sarajevo in the 1890s, five for boys and two for girls. Officials attributed the initiative for reformed mektebs to "more intelligent circles of Muslims," but the schools failed to draw significant numbers of Muslims boys, most of whom continued to receive their sole educational experience in traditional mek-tebs. Although some Muslims boys attended public elementary and sec-ondary schools, they did so in proportionally fewer numbers than did Jewish, Catholic, and Serbian Orthodox youth.

Serb schools evoked the greatest concern among the authorities. By the late Ottoman years, affluent Serb merchants and traders had established Serb church and school communes in most towns of Bosnia-Herzegovina. The communes financed schools to impart basic literacy and business skills to Serbian Orthodox youth. The schools were also expected to foster Serb national awareness. They bore the adjective Serb in their names, taught the Cyrillic script, and imported textbooks and many of their teachers from the Kingdom of Serbia. Upon taking over in 1878, the Habsburg authorities were profoundly suspicious that these schools would become centers of Serb nationalist agitation. In November 1878 they fired two teachers at the Serb secondary school (*realka*) and expelled them from Sarajevo.[58] The Serb secondary school in Sarajevo operated for another five years but closed in 1883 owing to a host of problems stemming from lack of government support. As with the Muslim mektebs, Serb elementary schools coexisted with public elementary schools until the First World War, and their numbers gradually increased.

Serb girls predominated in Sarajevo's most unusual elementary school. In 1866 the English benefactor and schoolteacher Elizabeth Irby opened a school that operated until her death in 1911. Appalled by the inadequacy of educational establishments for girls, Irby devoted her wealth and her energies to the school. After first erroneously suspecting Miss Irby of proselytizing for the Protestant faith, Sarajevo's Serbian Orthodox community accepted and supported the school. Miss Irby herself is etched in the city's memory for her work, memorialized in a street name near the Presidency Building where her school once stood.

After securing control over the three major confessional institutions in the early 1880s, the government lavished support on their religious training institutions. Such visible manifestations of support were intended to boost the prestige of the loyal confessional leaders in the eyes of the populace. A sheriat law school received an elaborate neo-Orientalist structure designed by Vancaš. Catholic schools were built north of the cathedral, physical monuments to the newly acquired preeminence of the secular clerical establishment over Franciscan traditions. The government built and supported the Serbian Orthodox seminary at Reljevo and a Serb elementary school adjacent to the new Serbian Orthodox church.

New educational institutions did not extend to founding a university, but Habsburg officials encouraged selected high school graduates to attend university in Vienna. Students were discouraged or forbidden to study in Zagreb, Prague, and, above all, Belgrade, where authorities deemed them likely to be infected by the dreaded nationalism virus. Students were steered to Vienna by offers of scholarships and a special student dormitory for Bosnians. After 1911, when Zagreb University degrees gained recognition throughout the monarchy, some students enrolled there as well, but until the monarchy's demise Vienna continued to host the greatest number of Bosnian students.

The government experienced considerable success in raising the educational level among Sarajevans, but the results differed substantially along ethnonational lines and were considerably less satisfactory in the countryside. Literacy rates in the final years of Austro-Hungarian administration reflected both Sarajevo's primacy as an educational center and the relative participation of the youth of each confession in the public school system. In 1910, Sarajevo's population was 57 percent literate compared to 12 percent for Bosnia-Herzegovina.[59] Literacy was most widespread among Catholics, many of whom had come to Sarajevo from the monarchy. Eighty-nine percent of Catholic men were literate, as were 82 percent of Catholic women. The Serbian Orthodox ranked next in literacy; 74 percent of men and 51 percent of women could read and write. Thirty percent of Muslim men were literate. There were only 154 literate Muslim women in Sarajevo in 1910, 107 of them under the age of twenty-one.

The modest success of Habsburg authorities in building a secular public educational system turned into something of a Pyrrhic victory. Austro-Hungarian administrators were to share with colonial administrators elsewhere the realization that secular education, far from churning out loyal followers of the regime, incubated resentment of colonialism and spawned revolutionary intellectuals who turned to radical European ideologies for their inspiration. Sarajevo's schools became the institutional epicenter of a protracted struggle to mold the future Bosnian intelligentsia. Through the halls of Sarajevo's secular public schools passed many who would become the empire's most passionate critics, including a few who would hatch a conspiracy to assassinate the heir apparent to the imperial throne.

Making history: the Regional Museum

As part of his grand vision of bringing Bosnia-Herzegovina into the orbit of Western secular values and scientific practices, Kállay supported the formation of the Regional Museum, conceived as a premier institution of academic inquiry, collection, and dissemination. Following the pattern of the Court Museum in Vienna and the Hungarian National Museum in Budapest, Sarajevo's Regional Museum was much more than its name implied. It was founded as an institutional conglomerate that combined the facilities and activities of a museum, library, archive, and research institute. Like its parent institutions in the monarchy's capitals, the Regional Museum consisted of two divisions, one for the natural sciences and a second for humanities.

In fulfilling Kállay's mission, the museum had a tripartite role. In the broadest sense, it advanced scientific research and learning in accord with the Western civilizing mission that was central to his plans. Second, it sought to advance Austro-Hungarian geopolitical interests in the region by proving that the monarchy could advance and disseminate knowledge in its newly acquired territory. And finally, in support of Kállay's promotion of bošnjaštvo and negation of Serb and Croat territorial claims, the museum was created to build the case for the distinctiveness of Bosnia-Herzegovina and its people. Habsburg officials anticipated that the museum staff would discover prolific evidence of Bosnian distinctiveness and refute rival claims that Bosnians were Serbs or Croats.

The museum was founded in 1884 by a group of Sarajevans led by Dr. Julije Makanec, who formed a committee to establish a *Landesmuseum* or *Zemaljski muzej* (translated here as Regional Museum.)[60] The museum was first housed in two offices of Vancaš's Regional Government Building (symbolically confirming its status as an arm of imperial officials) but soon moved to the Pension Fund Building opposite the Catholic cathedral. These quarters also proved inadequate after some years, and in 1908 a new building was begun in the far western end of the city to house the museum and its burgeoning holdings.

The museum's new quarters were a testament to the ingenuity of Sarajevo's architects and to their devotion to Viennese precedents. Spare neoclassicism is the dominant motif of the museum's four pavilions, reflecting the general trend of Sarajevo structures to capture major Viennese trends but to conform to provincial proportions through simplification and austerity. The inspiration of the Ringstrasse's Imperial Museum is unmistakable. Like the two Imperial Museum structures on the Ringstrasse in Vienna, the four pavilions of the Regional Museum in Sarajevo face one another around a central courtyard. Like the Vienna buildings, each pavilion serves either the natural or the human sciences.

The first issue of the museum's journal, *Glasnik Zemaljskog muzeja*, reflected the museum's mission to promote a Bosnian identity.[61] Truhelka, who later became the museum's second director, praised Bosnia's rich cultural heritage. He argued that *Bosančica*, a script very similar to Cyrillic, was a cultural treasure unique to Bosnia-Herzegovina. In contrast to the widely held view that "bosančica" was used in Bosnia-Herzegovina only to distinguish the Cyrillic script from Turkish, Truhelka argued that bosančica was a uniquely Bosnian script that shared a common historical origin with the Cyrillic in which most Serbs wrote. "Both are of the same origin: Greek," he wrote. "One developed in the eastern Balkans, and the other in the western Balkans; each development was independent."[62] Taking the argument further, he contended that the western Balkan variant—that used in Bosnia—was closer to original Greek, whereas the Slavic purity of its eastern counterpart had been corrupted by Latin accretions.

In the museum's early years, prehistoric sites received substantial funding and attention, imitating the late nineteenth-century European fascination with sites and artifacts of ancient civilizations. The museum conducted archeological digs of Roman settlements (the civilization most admired by Kállay) and discovered a spectacular mosaic floor at Butmir, a few kilometers west of Sarajevo. Bosnia's Ottoman-era heritage, on the other hand, was largely neglected. The museum had no full-time Ottoman specialist during the early years of Austro-Hungarian administration, although it did preserve in its nascent archives the provincial records of Bosnia's Ottoman administrators and reports of Austro-Hungarian consuls during Ottoman rule. The museum staff largely followed scientific principles in its findings, but skewed its programs toward showing that Bosnia-Herzegovina had a Western cultural heritage.

At the heart of the museum's political agenda was the belief that a dualist religious heresy known as Bogomilism had been widespread among members of the medieval Bosnian church. After the Ottoman conquest, Bogomils were believed to have converted en masse to Islam to preserve their privileged social status and retain their large landholdings. In the view promoted by museum researchers, Bogomils were proto-Muslims unique to Bosnia-Herzegovina and the forefathers of its contemporary population. Bosnians could trace their origins to identifiable antecedents that long preceded the arrival of Islam. Throughout Bosnia-Herzegovina, the museum's scientific investigators encountered thousands of distinctive medieval burial markers, some decorated with architectural, floral, and human motifs. Museum researchers saw in these tombstones, known as *stećci* (singular: *stećak*), the sculptural evidentiary remains of vanished Bogomilism. They argued that the primary sculptural motifs found on the tombstones were unique to Bogomil beliefs and practices. Subsequent research has established that the stećci were used in pre-Ottoman Bosnia by believers of all faiths and incorporated an eclectic mixture of motifs favored by the Dubrovnik stonemasons who crafted many of them.[63] Some of the largest and most elaborately carved stećci were transported to the Regional Museum for display on the grounds, where they remain as of this writing in the open air, gradually deteriorating from weather and pollution.

The Bogomil hypothesis was not without supporting empirical evidence. During the medieval period, the papacy received many reports of a dualist heresy in Bosnia, both from lands neighboring Bosnia and from emissaries dispatched to investigate the charges. The alarming reports conveniently coincided with Hungary's plans to advance its geopolitical ambitions in Bosnia under cover of a religious crusade to extirpate the alleged heresy. Reliable information was difficult to come by, but museum investigators mustered all collaborating evidence, obscured countervailing discoveries, and stretched arguments in support of the Bogomil hypothesis. In the first edition of *Glasnik*, Truhelka reported on inscriptions identified at the church of Herceg Stjepan near Goražde and pronounced them to be Bogomil. Herceg Stjepan (after whom Herzegovina was named) was unambiguously proclaimed to have been a Bogomil and thus outside the fold of the Serbian Orthodox church to which he more probably belonged. Various motifs on stećci were interpreted as evidence of heretical beliefs found in dualist heresies elsewhere in Europe.

Belief in the Bogomils has been one of the most enduring legacies of the Regional Museum's early decades. The Bogomil myth has far outrun its flimsy evidentiary foundations and been amplified and simplified for popular consumption. It found new life in the 1960s and 1970s in the assertion of a secular Bosnian Muslim (Bosniak) national identity. Most Bosniaks now believe that the Bogomils were forerunners of their national group, even as persuasive academic studies have cast serious doubts on the importance and even the existence of a Bogomil heresy in Bosnia-Herzegovina.[64]

Like many of Kállay's projects, the Regional Museum's permanent legacy enriched the city's cultural life while failing to achieve its specific political goal of inculcating loyalty to the Habsburg Monarchy. During socialist years, many of its omnibus functions were taken over by newly formed institutions including the State Archives of Bosnia-Herzegovina, the National and University Library, and the Oriental Institute. But both before and after the divestiture of some of its roles, the museum fostered hundreds of research projects during the twentieth century and employed some of Sarajevo's most noted intellectuals.

Sarajevo's Habsburg legacy

Benjamin von Kállay's vision of urban space was hardly revolutionary, but for Sarajevo it proved to be transformational. Habsburg officials incorporated both rational secularism and religious institutions in their redesign of Sarajevo's urban space in the last two decades of the nineteenth century. With their pluralist conception of urban space, they bequeathed to the city its trademark secular historicist buildings and its contiguous clusters of religious structures in the city center. Their urban plan reflected and encouraged Sarajevans' propensity to live together and to worship in close proximity to one another in the central city.

The specific model for the city's dynamic development in the late nineteenth century may be traced to Vienna, but influences from the imperial capital often mutated into distinctively Sarajevan variants. The cityscape bore the imprint of a Sarajevo version of romantic historicism that evoked architectural precedents from both the West and East. Sarajevans were devoting more leisure time to a variety of secular public practices, performances, and observances that supplemented the intimate religious and family gatherings of Ottoman times. The Secession's growing popularity in the waning years of the old century coincided with the government's adoption of greater flexibility in dealing with political movements. By the turn of the century, Sarajevo manifested a unique diversity that affirmed the city's capacity to blend Western influences with Eastern traditions and local culture.

In addition to their imprint on Sarajevo's physical appearance, Habsburg officials created many institutions that have endured to the present, albeit in altered form. These were founded with the intention of spreading European practices, advancing Habsburg imperial aims, and fostering an urban elite loyal to the monarchy. Although officials failed to inculcate enduring loyalty to the empire in founding European institutions in Sarajevo, they endowed the city and Bosnia-Herzegovina with a lasting legacy of educational, cultural, and research institutions.

4. The New Nationalism, Assassination, and War

The dawn of the twentieth century in Sarajevo coincided with the development of industrialization, socialism, and nationalism and the founding of a host of new indigenous institutions. Primarily the home of Habsburg administrative institutions in the 1890s, the city by 1910 had evolved into the locus of all major movements and organizations in Bosnia-Herzegovina and into the capital city for all Bosnians. At the same time, Sarajevo's traditional ethnonational elites gradually lost their informal influence with the authorities, becoming instead equals within the geographically diversified structure of provincewide Bosnian organizations. But what the city lost from the erosion of its leaders' relationships with the state, it more than gained as the uncontested center of institutional life in Bosnia-Herzegovina. After the turn of the century, both conservative local elites and their imperial rulers found themselves challenged by restive, youthful nationalists prepared to use violence to draw attention to their causes. The Serb nationalist assassination of the Habsburg heir apparent Franz Ferdinand and his wife in 1914 contributed mightily to the monarchy's demise.

The new nationalism in the South Slav lands

Major social movements achieved organizational cohesion in Bosnia-Herzegovina somewhat later than comparable movements elsewhere in Europe, including neighboring Croatia and Serbia. The Bosnian movements typically followed their European predecessors in ideology and organization. Much as in the colonial societies of Africa and Asia in the nineteenth and twentieth centuries, European practices and technologies became instruments in Bosnian hands. As the leaders of these new organizations found ways to circumvent the harassment and intermittent repression by neoabsolutist rulers, political life gradually grew beyond the monarchy's control. In addition, industrialization spawned the growth of a working class, and the

93

Habsburg-sponsored educational system produced a generation of radi-
calized nationalist intellectuals.

Behind many of the changes in Sarajevo was a growing group consciousness among members of all ethnoconfessional communities. By the turn of
the century, most Sarajevans of Serbian Orthodox faith felt themselves to be
Serbs, members of a nationality whose members lived in several polities in
the region. Most Catholics came to view themselves as Croats, although this
process advanced more slowly than among the Serbs. Muslims scrupulously
avoided proclaiming their group to be a nation, but they too acquired a
stronger sense of cohesion and shared membership in a distinct community.
City dwellers, as a rule, became nationally conscious before peasants because of their higher literacy rates, education, and greater awareness of
events outside their immediate area of residence. Teachers, scholars, journalists, and some clergymen were the missionaries of the new secular
nationalism. They were most numerous and most influential in the cities,
particularly in Sarajevo, the principal administrative and intellectual center
of Bosnia-Herzegovina.

Intellectuals and politicians in neighboring lands led the effort to build
national consciousness. Nationalist Serbs and Croats saw Bosnia-Herzegovina as a key battleground in their conflicting claims to territorial expansion. Each claimed the territory, basing their claims on historical precedent
and ethnic composition, but neither group could set forth a compelling
claim without including the Bosnian Muslims. With Muslim leaders claiming that they comprised a religious community but not a separate nation, the
door was open for Serb and Croat nationalists to persuade Muslims to declare themselves Serbs or Croats. In the first half of the twentieth century,
many prominent Muslims declared such an identity at one time or another,
but few abandoned their identity as Muslims in doing so. To the frustration
of Serb and Croat nationalists, the vast majority of Bosnian Muslims ultimately rejected both Serb and Croat identity, but not until the 1960s did
they assert themselves as a separate nation distinguished from both Serbs and
Croats by their culture, history, and religious heritage. Until then, the national
identity and loyalty of Bosnia's Muslims hung in the balance in the fierce
debate between Serbs and Croats staking claims in Bosnia-Herzegovina.

At the beginning of the century, the new nationalists initiated political
movements and parties to advance their cause. Factional conflict plagued
these national movements, keynoted by ideological differences but in fact
often produced by rivalries among competing leaders and social groups.

The campaigns of the new nationalists in Bosnia-Herzegovina were fundamentally struggles among rising new elites to marginalize the aristocrats and
bureaucrats who governed on behalf of the Habsburg Monarchy. Their
conationalists in neighboring Serbia and Croatia, however, had a different
goal: inclusion of Bosnia-Herzegovina in their respective states. The nationalist Serb and Croat drives for territorial expansion came to be known by the
expressions "Great Serbia" (*velika Srbija*) and "Great Croatia" (*velika Hrvatska*). Individual nationalists in both Serbia and Croatia had set forth early
versions of these goals no later than 1850, and the campaigns to achieve
them intensified during the Eastern Crisis of 1875–8 and thereafter. Additionally, some Croat nationalists promoted trialism, a variant of the Great
Croat ideal that favored dividing the Habsburg Monarchy into three parts
(Austrian, Hungarian, and South Slavic) and adding additional South Slavs to
the monarchy. Although most imperial officials rejected trialist ideas,
Archduke Franz Ferdinand, the heir apparent to Emperor Franz Joseph, was
associated with the idea and therefore valorized by many Croats and some
Muslims in Bosnia-Herzegovina. Although the concept of trialism died with
the Habsburg Monarchy in 1918, Great Serb and Great Croat ideals
survived throughout the century to serve as rationales for Serb and Croat
nationalists to pursue the acquisition or division of Bosnia-Herzegovina.

The Serb and Muslim movements for autonomy

In the late 1880s and 1890s, Habsburg administrators were increasingly
challenged by small groups of Bosnians whose aspirations clashed with the
monarchy's aims. For over a decade, Kállay's determined repression prevented such aspirants from mounting provincewide challenges to imperial
policies. But in the final years of the nineteenth century and the first decade
of the twentieth, autonomy movements launched by Serbs and Muslims successfully challenged the government's prohibitions on provincewide organizations. Originating in inchoate and scattered local protests in the 1890s,
the movements consolidated under the unified leadership of conservative
elites. Each movement triggered the formation of organizations that
gathered local protesters into a provincewide structure.

Both autonomy movements began not in Sarajevo but in Mostar. Sarajevans joined only after those movements had garnered widespread popular
support. The outbreak of dissatisfaction in Mostar stemmed in part from the
authorities' relative neglect of regional leaders in favor of Sarajevans as their

preferred allies in governing the province. As beneficiaries of that favoritism, prominent Sarajevans held prized government appointments and were reluctant to risk them by opposing the regime. But although the city's leaders were at first followers rather than leaders in organized dissent, their eventual adherence proved pivotal to the success of each movement in forcing the regime to enter into negotiations.

The Serb and Muslim autonomy movements were limited and conservative in character, but they comprised an essential first step in the development of large-scale, provincewide political organizations. By adopting formal programs and institutional structures, the autonomy movement leaders harnessed popular dissatisfaction to form organizations that were political parties in all but name. They developed mechanisms to select leaders, ensured equal participation from each of the six administrative regions of Bosnia-Herzegovina, elaborated a common set of objectives, and mobilized widespread popular support. Bosnians were eventually allowed to form political parties after the turn of the century because the well-organized autonomy movements overwhelmed the regime's ability to suppress political expression.

Serb leaders enjoyed an advantage over those of other Bosnian ethno-confessional communities in having formed Serbian Orthodox communes in the late Ottoman years to promote education and the Serbian Orthodox Church. Made up mainly of successful merchants and entrepreneurs rather than clergymen, the communes gained lay members and garnered additional financial support in the first decades of Habsburg rule. The authorities moved cautiously in regulating these existing bodies, hoping not to alienate commune leaders. In this they failed. The Mostar Serbian Orthodox Church and School Commune was deemed by one scholar the "initiator and organizer of resistance to the policies of the occupying administration."[1] In 1881 the leaders of the Mostar commune, speaking in the name of the Serbian Orthodox population of Herzegovina, objected to a military draft law promulgated by the regime. The commune's public condemnation helped spark a major peasant uprising in Herzegovina in 1881–2. Thereafter, Serbs in the Mostar commune periodically contested the authority of the progovernment Mostar metropolitan (*mitropolit*) and otherwise annoyed the authorities with demands and protests.

In contrast to the tradition of dissent in Mostar, the Sarajevo Serbian Orthodox commune was headed in the early occupation years by Petro Petrović, a government loyalist and member of the first Sarajevo city

council.² The regime deferred to Petrović by waiving the formal requirement that officials receive advance notice of meetings scheduled by the
Sarajevo commune. But in the 1890s a faction supporting Gligorije Jeftanović, the wealthy owner of the Hotel Evropa, challenged Petrović's leadership. In late 1895 Petrović resigned as commune president and was
replaced by Jeftanović. Officials at first viewed this change with detachment, believing that Sarajevo Serb leaders such as Jeftanović were sufficiently dependent on government loans and concessions to intimidate them
from organizing opposition. But in January 1896 the city commissioner (the
officially appointed city manager) informed the leaders that prior notification of meetings would thenceforth be required of the Sarajevo commune
as well as those in other towns.

The commune leaders flatly refused. They made successive appeals to the
city commissioner and the provincial government, arguing that the waiver
of notification was part of their commune's traditional autonomy. In short
order Jeftanović convened two meetings of the commune's executive board
without informing the authorities, for which he was fined and reprimanded.
He resolved to take his case to Vienna and protest directly to Kállay and, if
that failed, to the Habsburg emperor. His decision set the leaders of
Sarajevo's Serbs on a path parallel to that of their brethren in Mostar.

The funeral of Sarajevo Metropolitan Nikolajević in February 1896
provided an occasion for the representatives of Serb communes in Mostar,
Sarajevo, and other towns to meet discreetly and concoct a plan of common
action. But it proved difficult for the emerging opposition leaders to communicate under the scrutiny of officials and informants in Bosnia-Herzegovina. In November 1896 Mostar Serb delegates headed by Vojislav Šola,
president of the Mostar Church and School Commune, traveled to Vienna
to present their case to the emperor. Jeftanović led a delegation of Sarajevo
Serbs that departed for Vienna about the same time. Once there, they
formed a central committee that included representatives from thirteen
other Serb communes, drew up a common platform, and agreed on a united
strategy. By forming the committee to coordinate their efforts, the Serb
activists defeated the regime's efforts to keep all politics local. The government could no longer dismiss the Serb protests as episodic and incon-
sequental outbursts of a few isolated malcontents. The Serb success evoked a
sharp response, as the government set out to eradicate the agitation at its
source. Kállay enlisted the newly appointed Serbian Orthodox metropolitan of Sarajevo to counter the influence of the commune leaders, but the

metropolitan's efforts failed to impede the movement's continued growth. Shortly after the Vienna meetings, government authorities in Sarajevo and Mostar dissolved the Serbian Orthodox Church and School Communes in their respective cities.

The authorities also retaliated with economic measures directed against members of the Vienna delegation. The authorities held considerable economic leverage over Sarajevo's Serbs, but they erred in concluding they could deter further protests. The movement's leaders added each threat and repressive measure to their litany of grievances, which came to include the dissolution of the Mostar and Sarajevo communes. They presented additional petitions to the emperor in 1897 and 1900, each signed by representatives of a growing number of communes. Each delegation was headed jointly by Jeftanović, the dissolved Sarajevo commune's last president, and Šola, who had held the same post in the Mostar commune. Each delegation included representatives from all six administrative regions of Bosnia-Herzegovina.

Having unsuccessfully enlisted the full force of his administration and the Serbian Orthodox church hierarchy against the movement, Kállay relented. In February 1902 he directed his subordinates to negotiate with leaders of the provincewide movement.[3] Negotiations did not yield results during Kállay's lifetime, but his successor reached an agreement with movement leaders. On August 13, 1905, Emperor Franz Joseph promulgated a statute establishing autonomous Serb educational and cultural institutions, thereby granting most demands of those in the moderate wing of the autonomy movement.[4]

The Muslim movement for autonomy, like its Serb counterpart, first gained momentum from discontent in Mostar. Sarajevo's leading Muslims had a great deal to lose by joining any opposition movement. Their privileged ties with imperial officials enabled them to advance their concerns informally and achieve most of their goals without mobilizing followers in meetings, petitions, or protests. What finally forced them into action was their desire to limit or end conversions from Islam to Christianity. They linked the conversion issue with their ongoing efforts to acquire a greater say in the appointment of officials making up the Islamic religious hierarchy, to achieve increased control over the administration of vakufs, and to protect Muslim gravemarkers in public parks.

Religious conversions of any kind were already rare in Bosnia-Herzegovina by the late nineteenth century. The government recorded fewer than two hundred conversions during the Habsburg period, and most of the converts were young women who accepted the faith of a suitor on the eve of a wedding. But conversions became flashpoints of contention between religious communities and the Habsburg authorities, and conversions to Catholicism frequently roiled the Orthodox and Muslim populations. Stoking the controversy was the widespread belief that Sarajevo Archbishop Josip Stadler and the Roman Catholic Church were promoting conversions as part of a political plan to increase the Catholic population of Bosnia-Herzegovina. Although there is no evidence of such a systematic plan, converts were welcomed by the Catholic Church. Stadler often went to extremes to protect the convert and to defend her right to remain Catholic. It was Stadler's aggressive defense of a single convert that roused the Sarajevo Muslims to action.

As was common practice in the households of prominent Muslims, Sarajevo city council member Esad Kulović retained a young Muslim woman, Uzeifa Deliahmetović from Kreševo, as a servant in his family home. In the summer of 1890 Deliahmetović sought shelter in a Catholic monastery in her hometown and expressed a desire to convert to Catholicism.[5] Clerics in Sarajevo rushed to take her under their protection. They sequestered her in the home of Archbishop Stadler and refused to allow Muslims to visit her. When the government refused to intervene, leading Sarajevo Muslims gathered in the Reading Society hall and organized a delegation to complain of Stadler's behavior to Austro-Hungarian authorities.

Despite their outrage, Sarajevo's leading Muslims were loath to threaten their cozy and beneficial relationship with the Habsburg authorities. The authorities were equally eager to avoid a breach of confidence with their Sarajevo allies and to stem the discontent. They quickly abandoned their long-standing policy of dealing with conversions on a case-by-case basis,[6] and they expeditiously drafted a conversion statute that included provisions for all parties to gain direct access to a potential convert. The Sarajevo Muslims were not immediately appeased, but after extensive talks and threats to carry their protest to Vienna, they resolved their differences with the authorities. In 1891 the authorities promulgated the final conversion statute. Leading Sarajevo Muslims declared themselves satisfied and reinstated their symbiotic relationship with the authorities, despite continued dissatisfaction among Muslim religious leaders in other communities.

The propensity for dissent ran deeper among Muslims in Mostar than in Sarajevo.[7] In 1899 members of a Catholic suitor's family abducted Fata

Omanović, a Muslim girl from a village near Mostar, and spirited her away to Dalmatia with the help of Catholic priests. Her conversion led Muslims in her village to appeal to Mufti Ali Džabić of Mostar. Known to the government for his strict adherence to Islamic law and his opposition to the 1891 conversion statute, Džabić readily embraced the campaign against religious conversions. He met with other Mostar Muslims in the reading society to formulate a unified protest strategy. In this respect, the Mostar and Sarajevo reading societies provided institutional forums to launch the Muslim movement much as the church and school communes did for the Serbs. The Mostar-led movement eventually drew in many Muslim landowners, who added their own demands to the list of grievances with the intent of strengthening their land ownership rights and class position.

Despite government efforts to stem the protest, Mostar Muslims in October 1899 dispatched delegations to Vienna to present their grievances to the emperor, and the leaders lengthened their list of grievances in successive petitions. In response, the authorities dissolved the Mostar Muslim Reading Society in February 1900, and in April of that year dismissed Džabić from his post as mufti. He subsequently led a small group of followers to exile in Istanbul, where the Ottoman government, with some discomfort, accommodated his continued criticism of Austro-Hungarian rule while keeping him under close surveillance.

Sarajevo's leading Muslim landowners remained aloof from the autonomy movement in its early months, no doubt sensing a threat to the regime's belief that they could reliably speak on behalf of all Bosnian Muslims. They were not eager to join a movement in which they could hope for nothing better than being one of six regional groups vying for influence in the provincewide Muslim organization. But in 1900, with the evident shift in public sentiment toward the dissidents, Sarjevo's leading Muslim landlords belatedly and reluctantly joined the movement. With their adherence, the Muslim autonomy movement overcame the regime's campaign to limit protests to local communities. But the Sarajevo Muslims, many of whom continued to prefer close cooperation with the authorities over organized opposition, remained underrepresented in provincewide Bosnian Muslim political activities for the next decade. Overwhelmed by the widespread opposition, Kállay opened negotiations with the movement's leaders in early 1901. In initiating talks, he hoped to slow the movement's momentum and allow police spies to sow dissent among the leaders. These negotiations yielded little and were adjourned in April 1901, not to be resumed until 1907, long after Kállay had passed from the scene.

Liberalization and provincewide organizations

By 1901 Kállay had lost his sustained struggle to repress the autonomy movements and the provincewide political organizations they spawned. Along with the failure of his Bosnian nationality project in prior decades, the durability of the autonomy movements exposed the futility of Kállay's archaic neoabsolutism. His blend of limited democracy, elite cultivation, strict controls, and close surveillance proved insufficiently flexible to accommodate the dynamic changes that he himself had promoted in Sarajevo and Bosnia-Herzegovina. Acquiescing to these failures without acknowledging them, Kállay permitted a modest relaxation of the regime's policies in the first few years of the new century.

In a change of policy with long-lasting consequences, Kállay permitted members of the three largest ethnoconfessional communities to form provincewide cultural societies. Orthodox Serbs founded the cultural society *Prosvjeta* (Enlightenment) in 1902,[8] Muslims formed a similar organization named *Gajret* (Zeal, from Turkish) in 1903,[9] and in 1904 Catholic Croats established *Napredak* (Progress),[10] all with official approval. For the four decades after their founding, these societies became the central institutions promoting national consciousness throughout Bosnia-Herzegovina. Their stated objective was to promote culture and education among its constituents, but their activities were aimed more specifically at creating an indigenous intelligentsia loyal to the national ideals of the sponsoring group. In their early years, the societies functioned mainly as providers of scholarships to students from their respective ethnoreligious communities. Since the government was also awarding stipends to needy students, the cultural societies were competing directly with the government to garner the loyalty of Bosnia's future intellectuals.

The cultural societies, with their headquarters in Sarajevo and branches throughout Bosnia-Herzegovina, worked to strengthen the identities of all ethnoconfessional communities. Built in highly visible locations in demonstrative architectural styles and bright coloration, their headquarters buildings reflected their key role. These striking buildings, representative of the new, secular, and indigenous national movements, complemented the administrative and religious structures built by the authorities and announced Sarajevo's new role as host to organizations with branches in other towns of Bosnia-Herzegovina. Two of these structures (those of Napredak and Prosvjeta) have survived into the twenty-first century.

Following Kállay's death in office in 1903, his successor as joint finance minister, István von Burián, further liberalized the government's policy toward Bosnian political activities. Although the authorities retained full discretion to approve proposed organizations and to review charter drafts, they readily sanctioned a host of new associations and publications. The elaborate surveillance apparatus created by Kállay became less intrusive after 1903. In 1910 the newly convened Bosnian parliament formalized the liberalization by enacting a law establishing guidelines for granting charters to new organizations.

For politically engaged Serbs and Muslims, forming political parties from 1906 to 1910 merely entailed renaming the organizations that had successfully led their struggles for religious and cultural autonomy. However, each group had to bridge internal factional differences in order to create a single dominant party.[11] The formation of parties revealed that Sarajevo's elites had indeed lost their monopoly on key positions, as officials from various parts of Bosnia-Herzegovina were elected to leading party posts. Clashes over local interests persisted within each group, and often one political disposition would predominate in a single city, such as Mostar (the center of Serb intellectual dissidents) and Sarajevo (home of many supporters of the regime).

Before forming a political party, leaders of the Muslim autonomy movement sought to end the rift between former Mostar Mufti Džabić, then in exile in Istanbul, and the landowner wing of the autonomy movement led by Alibeg Firdus.[12] In February 1906 a delegation of Muslim activists traveled to Istanbul and secured Džabić's authorization for autonomy movement leaders to represent the interests of Bosnia's Muslims. With Džabić's endorsement in hand, Firdus invited Muslim representatives from all Bosnian administrative regions to meet in Slavonski Brod, a town in Croatia just across the Sava River from Bosnian territory. On December 6, 1906, the delegates formed the Muslim People's Organization (*Muslimanska narodna organizacija*). They designated Budapest as the party's headquarters, following the autonomy movement leaders' practice of basing their activities there. The Muslim People's Organization, as the successor of the autonomy movement's ad hoc institutions, bore the mantle of Islamic orthodoxy and the social conservatism of its predecessor movement.

Only among Sarajevo's Muslims did a significant number of activists withhold their support from the newly formed party. In August 1908 some Muslim intellectuals and government employees, led by Sarajevo Mayor

Esad Kulović, formed the Muslim Progressive Party (*Muslimanska napredna stranka*) as a rival to the Muslim People's Organization.[13] Kulović and his supporters were the last vestiges of the Sarajevo landowners and their urban allies who favored informal accommodation with the province's rulers over organized dissent. The party acquired significant support only in Sarajevo, revealing the paucity of support for cooperation with the government in all but the capital city. Government subsidies and favors kept the party alive until August 1911. Then, in a rebuff to government officials, the progressives merged with the Muslim People's Organization and adopted its program.[14] With the merger, the last organizational basis for the Sarajevo Muslims' close cooperation with the government vanished from the Bosnian political scene.

Like the Muslims, Serb political leaders faced the challenge of bridging regional and ideological divisions among politically active Serbs. Most Serbs favored the nationalist policies advocated in the newspaper *Srpska riječ* (The Serb Word), but a large second group favored Yugoslavism and identified with the Mostar newspaper *Narod* (the People)[15] In Banja Luka, urban intellectuals led by Petar Kočić constituted a third faction; they formed the newspaper *Otadžbina* (Homeland). A fourth and much smaller faction, led by Lazo Dimitrijević, was overtly and fawningly complimentary of the regime and covertly supported by it. The Dimitrijević faction gathered around the Sarajevo publication, *Dan* (Day).

A young Serb attorney, Milan Srškić (1880–1937), became the bridgebuilder between the two largest factions among the Serbs. Srškić was a devoted nationalist by family background, conviction, experience, and even by marriage. He was born in the Serbian capital of Belgrade, where his father, a Sarajevo Serb shopkeeper, had fled in fear of Austro-Hungarian reprisals following the occupation in 1878. After his family returned to Sarajevo, Srškić attended a Serb parochial elementary school, where he learned the Cyrillic alphabet and received instruction on the glorious achievements of the Serb people and the Serbian Orthodox Church. He then attended a Habsburg-sponsored public high school, where he and his fellow students grew increasingly resentful of the nonnationalist instructional program. By the time he completed his formal education studying law in Vienna, he was a convinced Serb nationalist devoted to realizing the political aspirations of his people.

On returning to Sarajevo in 1905, Srškić married Kruna Jeftanović, daughter of Serb autonomy movement leader Gligorije Jeftanović. He opened a law practice and dove headlong into Serb national causes. In 1905 he helped form the Serb athletic society *Dušan silni* (Dušan the almighty), later named *Sokol* (Falcon), and in 1906 he was elected vice president of the Serb singing society Sloga. Although his background suggested he should become a radical nationalist student-turned-intellectual, he abjured extreme methods of protest and joined Gligorije Jeftanović (his father-in-law) and Mostar's Vojislav Šola in founding the newspaper *Srpska riječ* in Sarajevo in 1905. In opting to ally with his father-in-law, Srškić successfully transcended the differences that separated his fellow intellectuals from the older, socially conservative generation of mercantile leaders.

In May 1907 a group of Serb leaders met in hopes of uniting the squabbling factions. Most came from outside Sarajevo, but they held their meeting in the capital city. Srškić, bridging the generational gap between the young intellectuals and the older mercantile autonomy leaders, was the sole Sarajevan to participate. The Serb leaders adopted the Sarajevo Resolution, in which they advocated "complete autonomy for our homeland, which can only be won by civil liberties and constitutional life."[16] In October 1907 the leaders convened a provincewide assembly of Bosnian Serbs and proclaimed the Serb People's Organization (*Srpska narodna organizacija*). Although the formation of the Serb People's Organization did not end factional disputes among Serb leaders, the party soon became the dominant political force representing the views of politically articulate Bosnian Serbs. The new party was headquartered in Sarajevo.

Another young Sarajevo attorney, Nikola Mandić, became the leader of the largest Croat political party, the Croat People's Union (*Hrvatska narodna zajednica*). Drawing support principally from Croat urban professionals and merchants, the party received government approval in November 1907.[17] In January 1908 the Sarajevo chapter of the party held its organizing assembly, with over four hundred Croats attending. Mandić, who was then serving as deputy mayor of Sarajevo, was elected president at the founding assembly of the provincewide party in February 1908. Aware that Croats were the least numerous of the three major groups in Bosnia, the party placed great stock in winning over the Bosnian Muslims. Its leaders abjured Catholicism as essential to national identity and defined the Croat nation in secular terms. Aware that the Croats could achieve a demographic majority in the province if enough Muslims adopted Croat identity, they hoped Bosnia's Muslims would become "Croats of the Muslim faith."

Sarajevo Archbishop Stadler wanted none of this. To him, Muslims could enter the Croat fold only through conversion to Catholicism. Croat identity, he believed, should rest first and foremost on a Catholic moral foundation. Short of converting, in his view, Muslims could cooperate with Croats only by first organizing on their own and then cooperating as partners with a purely Catholic Croat organization. Stadler combated the Croat People's Union's secular ideology with all the means at his disposal. In newspapers that he controlled, he attacked the party for failing to take a stand on the agrarian question—a conciliatory precondition for any cooperation with Muslim leaders—and advocated full and immediate transfer of land ownership to Catholic peasant cultivators.

From December 1908 until May 1909 Stadler undertook an unsuccessful campaign to take over the Croat People's Union, seeking to unseat party leaders and replace them with Catholic loyalists. When that failed, he reached an agreement with leaders of the Croat People's Union to alter their program, but the accord was rejected by a vote of party members.[18] Following these failures, Catholic clergymen advocated the formation of clerical political party to rival the Croat People's Union. With elections to the new Bosnian Parliament imminent, Stadler convened a meeting of clerics in his office in July 1909 and formally launched the Croat Catholic Association (*Hrvatska katolička udruga*) at a founding assembly in January 1910. The two Croat parties vied for votes in the 1910 election for the Bosnian Parliament and in elections for the Sarajevo city council. Stadler's clerical party won delegates in each but ran a distant second to the secular Croat People's Union among Croats enfranchised to vote in each election. For the remainder of the Habsburg era, the secular variant of Croat nationalism predominated in representative bodies in Bosnia-Herzegovina and in Sarajevo, but some clericalists also held seats.

The dominant party in each of the three ethnoconfessional communities represented primarily the interests of conservative urban elites. The pivotal issue of the time was how to alleviate the burden of dues that the mainly Serbian Orthodox and Croat Catholic peasants paid to their mainly Muslim landlords. The Muslim People's Organization, dominated by landlords, opposed mandatory abolition of peasant dues. But the leading Serb and Croat parties did not press the issue. They treasured an alliance with the Muslim leaders more than they valued the interests of lower-class members of their own national groups who were excluded from voting by franchise restrictions. Their reluctance to support their own peasants made these conservative leaders the target of bitter criticism by youthful nationalists among the students and teachers in the Habsburg-sponsored public school system.

In contrast to the traditional elites that dominated the first political formations of the city's ethnoconfessional communities, the Social Democratic Party (SDP; *Socijaldemokratska partija*) arose from a new class of workers created by the industrialization of Bosnia-Herzegovina.[19] Workers were drawn from all of Sarajevo's ethnoconfessional communities and from elsewhere in the monarchy. With surplus labor available and few legal constraints on employment practices, working conditions in most factories were deplorable. Wages were barely sufficient to sustain a worker, let alone a family, and housing was overcrowded and unhealthy. Workers' grievances gave rise to organizations to advance their interests. In August 1905 the first workers' organization, the Main Workers' Alliance (*Glavni radnički savez*), was founded at a rally in Sarajevo.[20] Its statute was approved by the provincial government in September 1906 when the government legalized labor unions. In May 1906 workers in the tobacco factory organized a strike that soon spread to other industries and other towns. In June 1909 the SDP of Bosnia-Herzegovina was founded at a two-day meeting in Sarajevo. The SDP initially operated in the spirit of Austrian social democracy and abjured the overt revolutionary ideology of the Russian Bolsheviks. The party played little role in the organized political life of the province owing to the limited electoral franchise, but it effectively advanced worker demands and organized public protests. Both the working class and its political outgrowth, the SDP, grew increasingly important over the next forty years.

Sarajevo and the annexation of Bosnia-Herzegovina

The prospect of formally annexing Bosnia-Herzegovina was never far from the minds of the monarchy's policymakers, but in 1908 external circumstances came together to create a propitious moment for the move. The Young Turk revolution of July 1908 shook the Ottoman Empire to its foundations, leaving it vulnerable to further dismemberment of its lands in southeast Europe. Upon coming to power, the Young Turks restored the long-suspended Ottoman constitution of 1876, whetting Bosnians' appetites for a constitution of their own. Seizing the moment, the Habsburg emperor unilaterally declared the annexation of Bosnia-Herzegovina on October 5, and the king of Bulgaria declared that country's independence of nominal Ottoman overlordship on the same day.

The emperor's declaration was carefully crafted, printed well in advance, and rushed to Sarajevo in thousands of copies for posting throughout

Bosnia-Herzegovina. In the proclamation, the emperor justified the annexation in part by endorsing a constitution for Bosnia-Herzegovina, something impossible (so the emperor argued) as long as the province remained under the sultan's nominal sovereignty. Officials hoped that Serb and Muslim political leaders would be swayed by the emperor's stated intent to promulgate a constitution and establish a central representative body. Had they succeeded in winning approval from leaders of the recently formed Serb People's Organization and the Muslim People's Organization, Habsburg officials might have been able to convince critics of the annexation to accept the unilateral act. Instead, Serbs and Muslims continued to agitate against the annexation until all the major European powers had formally accepted it.

Sarajevans first responded to the annexation with celebratory glee, inaugurated by loyalist mayor Kulović's declaration of a three-day holiday.[21] Officials feted the annexation in Sarajevo as though it were the creation of a new state, replete with displays of light and sound that were the hallmark of imperial anniversaries. The city council held a special session of recognition on October 7, followed by delegates attending congratulatory audiences with Habsburg authorities. Respecting the Muslim holiday of Ramadan, officials waited until evening hours, a time "when the entire public is out and about," to fire a 101-gun salute from atop surrounding hills on October 7.[22] But the triumphant celebrations were accompanied by a government embargo on telephone and telegraph communication with the outside world, presumably out of fear that adverse reactions elsewhere might be communicated to the city's celebrants.

In the ensuing weeks, delegations of government loyalists trooped en masse from Sarajevo to Vienna to express thanks and acknowledge the emperor's newly declared sovereignty over Bosnia-Herzegovina.[23] On November 9, 1908, Sarajevo Mayor Kulović led a delegation of thirteen mayors and 51 other prominent Muslims in calling on the emperor. That same day, the emperor received in audience twenty-four members of the Sarajevo city council. Lazo Dimitrijević, head of the tiny proregime Serb Independent Party (Srpska samostalna stranka), led a delegation consisting of eighteen Serb peasants in thanking the emperor for the annexation. Sarajevo Jews sent one delegation consisting of Sephardim and a second of Ashkenazim. The largest delegation, 430 Bosnian Catholics led by Archbishop Stadler, required two chartered trains for transportation to Vienna and back. While in Vienna, some of the delegations also called on Archduke Franz Ferdinand, widely seen at the time as the champion of adding more Slavs to the Habsburg Monarchy.

Only part of Sarajevo's population was drawn into the ostentatious expressions of gratitude. Leaders of the primary Serb and Muslim parties, the Serb People's Organization and the Muslim People's Organization, stridently opposed the annexation. Tipped off in advance to the impending proclamation, the leaders were on a train en route to Budapest when the annexation was announced. They adopted a resolution while on the train, bitterly denouncing the Habsburg negation of the sultan's sovereignty and appealing to the signatories of the Berlin Treaty to reverse the annexation. For the next several months, they refused invitations to participate in planning for the constitution, fearing that their cooperation might be interpreted as de facto acceptance of the annexation.

Meanwhile, a six-month diplomatic drama was playing out among the European powers.[24] Leaders in Bosnia-Herzegovina's neighbor Serbia reacted to the annexation with anger and alarm. They mobilized army reserves and sought support from their Russian ally. Germany, although upset at not having been part of the annexation decision, backed the Habsburg Monarchy and brought persuasion and pressure to bear on the recalcitrant British, French, Russians, and Ottomans to accept the fait accompli. After months of brinksmanship diplomacy, aversion to war overcame the outrage over Austria-Hungary's defiance of the Berlin Treaty. The Ottoman Empire, motivated in part by hefty compensation from the Austro-Hungarian government, signed an agreement accepting the annexation on February 26, 1909. Russia rebuffed Serbia's pleas for support. A joint démarche by the British, French, Russian, and Italian foreign ministers on March 30, 1909, was accepted by the Serbian government, and the Serbian army stood down. The Habsburg Monarchy had accomplished the annexation without a shot being fired, but the episode left many Serbs in Bosnia-Herzegovina and in the Kingdom of Serbia sullen and resentful of Habsburg rule.

The resolution of the diplomatic crisis doomed the protests of Bosnian malcontents. The Serbs gave up first. On May 3, 1909, old guard Serb leaders including Jeftanović, Šola, and Srškić called on the emperor in Vienna, pledged their loyalty, and promised to desist from further carping.[25] Although the Serb People's Organization never formally embraced the position set forth by Jeftanović's old guard faction, the party effectively ceased public opposition after the audience with the emperor. Muslim leaders held out longer. Although the Ottoman Empire's capitulation in February 1909 robbed Bosnian dissidents of their last prospective foreign ally, Muslim leaders sent a delegation to the Ottoman capital in search of support. But Ottoman officials gave them only lectures on the need to avoid disturbing peace in the region. Having been abandoned by the empire whose sovereignty they sought to preserve, leaders of the Muslim National Organization declared their loyalty to the emperor on February 10, 1910, and recognized the new circumstances of Austro-Hungarian sovereignty. With their reluctant acquiescence, the turmoil touched off by the annexation came to an end.

Constitutionalism and the new nationalism in Sarajevo

The annexation, despite being opposed by many Muslims and Serbs, cleared the way for the government to grant some of their most pressing demands. In the spring of 1909 Habsburg officials promulgated a statute granting the religious and educational autonomy sought by the Muslims. In 1910 the Habsburg officials fulfilled their promise and promulgated a constitution. The document created a central representative body, the Parliament (*Sabor*) of Bosnia-Herzegovina, although that body's powers were carefully circumscribed. Its members were elected on the basis of a limited franchise, electoral districts were segregated by confession, and ethnonational quotas were built into the parliament's composition. The new constitutional order allowed for political parties to operate in full legality, constrained only by increasingly dysfunctional government limitations on the content of print publications and public discourse. The headquarters of the Muslim People's Organization moved from Budapest, joining other major parties in locating within blocks of the Bosnian Parliament. Thenceforth, Sarajevo was the true capital city not only of Bosnia-Herzegovina's government but of all Bosnians.

The new constitution of Bosnia-Herzegovina ensured domination by traditional elites in the Bosnian Parliament and made it most unlikely that the festering agrarian crisis would be resolved by mandatory land transfers to the peasants. The constitutional order thus deepened the rift between traditional elites and the embryonic groups of discontented intellectuals forming in the monarchy's educational institutions. In addition to becoming the headquarters of administrative institutions and all major cultural and political associations, Sarajevo became the center of contention between old and new generations of Bosnians and the scene of strife between Bosnians and the Habsburg regime.

Leading politicians from all the major parties were elected to seats in the parliament. Josip Vancaš won a seat, as did Nikola Mandić and Milan Srškić. The festive first day of the assembly's deliberations were marred by an attempt on the life of Bosnia's governor, Marijan Varešanin, by a Bosnian Serb student named Bogdan Žerajić.[26] Žerajić fired five errant shots at Varešanin before committing suicide with the sixth shot. He was later lionized by other radical students, including several who participated in the assassination of Franz Ferdinand in 1914. The attempt on Varešanin's life foreshadowed further student violence directed against high officials of the Habsburg Monarchy in the next several years.

The brief constitutional era in Bosnia-Herzegovina (1910–14) was also marked by greater freedom of travel and increasing contact between Bosnians and those in other South Slav lands. Through his father-in-law, Srškić became acquainted with Nikola Pašić, leader of the Serb Radical Party (*Srpska radikalna stranka*) and Prime Minister of Serbia from 1891–2 and again 1903–18. Pašić later confirmed that Srškić had coordinated his political activities with the Radicals in Serbia during Bosnia's short-lived constitutional era.[27] Srškić's political skills and contacts with leaders in Serbia were indispensable in making him the most influential Bosnian Serb politician for the next quarter century.

The era of party politics brought heightened acrimony in the Sarajevo city council. Elections to the council were heatedly contested in 1910 and 1913, and growing nationalism echoed in the council chambers. In 1910 the city council rejected a proposal by the proregime mayor, Esad Kulović, to give all Austrian and Hungarian citizens the right to vote in municipal elections.[28] Kulović, who could count on such voters for support, resigned to protest the defeat of his proposal. The council was prorogued pending new elections. In a bitter electoral campaign, Kulović allied with Archbishop Stadler's Croat Catholic Association, while his primary opponent Mustajbeg Halibašić made common cause with the Serb People's Organization and the Croat People's Union. Kulović prevailed in the election with 1,275 out of 1,831 votes cast, but he declined to serve as mayor after failing to secure the government's agreement to appoint persons of his choice to city positions. Fehim Ćurčić, appointed in his place, served as mayor until the city administration was reorganized during the First World War. But Kulović remained on the city council as a delegate and continued to be a major factor in

Sarajevo politics, leading a slate of candidates that did well in the fiercely contested city council election of December 11, 1913.

In January 1914 Kulović resigned and was replaced at the next meeting by a young Muslim attorney, Mehmed Spaho. Spaho would become the undisputed political leader of the Bosnian Muslims after the First World War, but he earned his first political experience in the Sarajevo city council as an ardent critic of city government and an opponent of Mayor Čurčić. He became a one-person opposition and challenged nearly every decision reached in the course of the council's meetings in 1914. He championed the "upper mahalas," as he characterized the Muslim neighborhoods on the hills rising above the city center. They had been neglected, and the central city had been developed at their expense, he argued.

Spaho first challenged the appointment of Josip Vancaš as vice mayor, contending that as an official in the government of Bosnia-Herzegovina (he was a delegate in the Bosnian Parliament), Vancaš should not hold two positions at once. Mayor Čurčić responded that Spaho's complaints should not be directed to the council but to the chief of the Regional Government. Spaho, his complaint dismissed, thereafter made Vancaš the principal target of his criticism. Spaho and Vancaš sparred repeatedly at meetings in the first six months of 1914.[29] Spaho demanded that the city extend running water service to the upper mahalas, pointing out that the water came from Moščanica reservoir, located in one of the upper mahalas in Vratnik. Spaho opposed plans for paving several streets, arguing instead for a comprehensive plan that included paving roads to the outlying areas. He spoke out against new taxes and criticized the proposal to seek a major loan to keep the city government operating. He criticized cost overruns on building projects such as the new fire station. Along with another Muslim delegate, he declined to vote for establishing an eighth pharmacy in the city until he received assurances that the ninth one would be owned and operated by a Muslim. And he demanded to know why new barracks could not be built so that soldiers no longer had to be billeted in schools. Spaho criticized city leaders on behalf of Muslim residents while party leaders in the Bosnian Parliament (1910–14) were vocally promoting the interests of their ethnonational groups. His critique was distinctly secular and practical. Although he was frequently the lone voice of dissent in a body packed with government supporters, he broke new ground in articulating Muslim interests without resorting to principles of the sheriat.

Young Bosnia and the assassination of June 1914

There is no more controversial event in European history than the assassination of Archduke Franz Ferdinand in Sarajevo on June 28, 1914. But for all
its impact on world history, the assassination had local roots in nationalist
student movements that flourished in Sarajevo after 1910. Like similar
movements in colonial societies, Sarajevo's student movements arose in
schools the government had built to promote secular education. The very
social group fostered by imperial authorities spawned the most virulent
opposition to imperial rule. Particularly inclined to political activism, the
youthful intellectuals founded newspapers, wrote articles and pamphlets,
read widely, and discussed politics among themselves. Many were passionately preoccupied with ideologies of the time, drinking deeply at the
well of ideologies such as romantic nationalism, racism, anarchism, communism, socialism, and nihilism. The obsession with ideology led many to
conclude that their convictions demanded individual action. In their world,
theory demanded practice. The engaged student radicals of the time
practiced the "propaganda of the deed," an apt phrase the Habsburg prosecutors used at the assassins' trial in October 1914.[30]

Serb student nationalists lionized Bogdan Žerajić for his effort to kill the
Bosnian governor in 1910. Žerajić came to epitomize the ideal of self-sac-
rifice in the service of striking down the Serbs' enemies. Vladimir Gaćino-
vić, who later conspired to assassinate Franz Ferdinand, lionized Žerajić in
an article entitled "Death of a Hero" (Smrt jednog heroja) in the Belgrade publication Pijemont (Piedmont, a reference to that region's role as the kernel of
Italian national consolidation). Although that article was banned in Bosnia-
Herzegovina, Serb youth in Sarajevo visited Žerajić's grave in the Serbian
Orthodox graveyard in Koševo and honored for the next four years the anniversaries of his attempted assassination. Gavrilo Princip was among those
who put flowers on the grave.

After the assassination, Bosnian student movements of the early twentieth
century became labeled as "Young Bosnia." It is something of a misnomer.
No single organization carried the name Young Bosnia, and the term was
rarely used by contemporaries. The prewar Bosnian student movements
were diverse, amorphous, and transient. Their participants embraced no
common ideology, had no unified view of appropriate strategy or tactics,
and did not coalesce into a united organization. Some organizations operated openly, registered with and overseen by the authorities. Others were
spontaneous and clandestine. Even to later investigators, the secret organi-

zations were elusive. Writing nearly thirty years later (albeit without access to archival sources), revolutionary activist Veselin Masleša noted a reason for the lack of concrete evidence: "[There is a] shortage of sources about Young Bosnia itself. Memoirs are weak, incomplete, and unreliable. All the participants of that movement who have written about it have fallen into one basic error: They have devoted more attention to their views at the time they were writing than to the movement itself."[31] Despite their lack of ideological cohesion, most Bosnian students professed devotion to some form of Yugoslavism, the belief that the Serbs, Croats, and Slovenes should unite and form their own South Slav state. That ideology was inherently revolutionary to Habsburg officials, for its implementation would dictate realigning state boundaries and an end to the monarchy's existing political arrangements. But while the student activists professed admiration for Yugoslavism, the meaning of that ideal was the source of division within their movement. Despite efforts to leave the concept sufficiently vague to accommodate divergent interpretations, Serb and Croat societies disagreed fundamentally on its meaning.[32] Croat students, acting under the aegis of student groups in Zagreb, formed societies that looked to Croatia as the center of a future South Slav polity. Serb students formed organizations devoted to the idea that a future Yugoslavia would be an extension of the Serbian kingdom. Not until after Serbian victories in the two Balkan Wars of 1912 and 1913 did Serb youth come to believe that the pendulum was swinging in favor of a Serbia-centered variant of Yugoslavism.

The young intellectuals were organizationally divided into Serb and Croat societies. In his classic study of the assassination, Vladimir Dedijer argued that these organizations united in the few years before it took place.[33] But the evidence from various government reports suggests that although the students cooperated tactically and often supported one another's initiatives, they declined to fuse. As one scholar concluded in a study of the Bosnian student movements:

[Students] organized primarily according to religious or national affiliation and most frequently separately, for one set of events motivated Serb students and others [motivated] Croat students. There were common undertakings, but rarely and with few participants. ... [Other authors] have exaggerated cooperation between students of various nationalities and emphasized general Yugoslav ideas in the work of student societies where there were none.[34]

What of the Bosnian Muslim students? No evidence of separate Muslim student societies was found in the exhaustive inquiry undertaken by the

Regional Government after the assassination. A few Muslims were found in both the Croat and Serb student organizations, and one of the Sarajevo assassins, Muhamed Mehmedbašić, was a Muslim. Both Croat and Serb students worked hard to recruit Muslims into their ranks, imitating the behavior of senior Serb and Croat politicians to persuade Muslims to declare themselves as Serbs or Croats. The efforts of the student leaders, like those of their elders, achieved only modest success, but Muslims who adopted "national coloration" (as it was called at the time) were among the most ardent advocates of the Serb and Croat national causes.

The soon-to-be assassins remained on the periphery of these movements. No student society organized the assassination. The ties binding the assassins were interpersonal and impromptu. The Sarajevo assassins imbibed the ideological ferment of Sarajevo's student movements and participated in some of the resulting political upheavals, but they were not among the leaders of Sarajevo's student organizations. They were, however, confirmed urbanites. Although most deplored the backward state of the peasantry, they were not "primitive rebels," as Vladimir Dedijer portrayed them, but alienated and transient intellectuals who rarely returned to the small towns and villages from whence they came.

Croat student protests

In 1910 the director of Sarajevo High School made a disturbing discovery. According to documents he had obtained, some Bosnian Croat youth considered themselves "Young Croats" and had organized chapters of the "Organization of Starčević Middle School Youth" in Sarajevo, Banja Luka, Travnik, Tuzla, and Mostar.[35] Sarajevo schools had the most members, with twenty-seven in the secondary school and eighteen in the teachers' preparatory school. Each chapter held regular meetings, maintained a library with a few hundred volumes, and charged membership dues to support operating expenses. The groups offered regular lectures on topics such as "How Bosnia Fell under the Habsburgs," "The Status of Croat Affairs across our Homeland," and "The Death of Zrinjski and Frankopan." The groups idolized the ultranationalist Croat Party of Rights and its founder, Ante Starčević. "These are not literary societies; they are purely political," wrote the high school director. He further wrote that "the Serb students have something similar. ... Among the students of various nationalities, these societies spread separatism and great hatred of one toward others."

The director proposed immediate, firm measures. Concerned that teachers were losing their authority, he urged the government to use the police to "take drastic measures to suppress this dangerous movement." But the government's view of political activities had changed since the years of Kállay's vigilant repression. Higher officials, unconcerned with the reported student activism, told the director that "the introduction of police measures will probably be unsuccessful and unnecessarily accentuate the very concerns that drove these students to create secret societies in the first place."[36] Higher authorities agreed with the director that officially sponsored literary and sports societies might channel some student activism into more constructive directions and noted that such groups had already been formed in other Bosnian schools. "It should be expected that under such circumstances the youth will abandon secret associations of their own accord," wrote the director's superior.

Less than two years after the director's discovery, a growing political crisis in Croatia roused Bosnian Croat students to direct political action. In January 1912 the Hungarian government appointed Count Slavko Cuvaj as Governor (*Ban*) of Croatia, ignoring the victory of the Croat-Serb coalition in parliamentary elections of December 1911. Cuvaj's appointment has been characterized by Croat historians as a "return to open absolutism" in Croatia.[37] Student groups at Zagreb University scheduled protests and dispatched emissaries to encourage sympathy demonstrations in other Habsburg South Slav cities. In 1910 some 139 Bosnian students were pursuing their degrees at Zagreb University, a number that had grown rapidly after the university's degrees were recognized in other lands of the monarchy in 1904.[38] A Bosnian Croat law student in Zagreb, Luka Jukić traveled with a colleague in mid-February 1912 to Sarajevo to organize an anti-Hungarian demonstration.[39] The organizers made plans to burn a Hungarian flag in downtown Sarajevo on Sunday, February 18.

Upon receiving informants' reports of the planned demonstration, Habsburg authorities in Sarajevo dispatched sixty extra police officers to center city locations as a precautionary measure. Just before 6 p.m., as the streets were filling with Sarajevans taking their evening stroll, several hundred demonstrators gathered at the Cathedral Square and began to sing Croat national songs.[40] Mounted police charged the crowd with sabers drawn, leaving many demonstrators with minor wounds, torn clothing, and some injuries from being trampled by the horses. Later, demonstrators alleged that this assault had been unprovoked, but the government reported that seven police officers had been hit by stones hurled by the demonstrators. In the midst of the resulting disorder, several shots rang out. A Muslim student, identified in reports only by his last name of Šahinagić, was severely wounded and taken immediately to a hospital in the western end of town. After being dispersed by mounted police in the Cathedral Square, the demonstrators regrouped and attempted to burn the Hungarian flag. Two companies of mounted army troops finally dispersed them.

The next morning, the students gathered again to march westward to visit Šahinagić in the hospital. The column was accompanied by two Bosnian Croat members of the Bosnian Parliament, who pleaded for last-minute official approval of the spontaneous parade. But when government approval was denied, the student marchers followed the instructions of their parliamentary champions and dispersed. That evening the students rallied again at the Cathedral Square, but this time the largely Croat participants were joined by many Muslim students, presumably in sympathy with the wounded Šahinagić, and by sympathetic members of the SDP.[41] They chanted "Down with Cuvaj," "Down with the Hungarians," and "Long Live Social Democracy." They were again dispersed by regular army units and police patrols. This time, the police exercised greater restraint. Bosnian Croat parliamentary delegates, including the ubiquitous Josip Vancaš, helped persuade the demonstrators to disperse. The streets were cleared by 8:30 p.m. When an attempt to reassemble demonstrators on a third evening came to naught, the street movement came to an end.[42]

Most of the youthful demonstrators were Croats and Muslims; Serb and Croat youth were aroused by different provocations, and few were prone to common action. "The Serbs stayed away from these demonstrations," the authorities concluded.[43] But although the slogans and songs were solely Croat and Social Democratic, not all Serbs stayed away. Among those slightly injured on the first evening was Serb student Gavrilo Princip, his clothing torn by a police saber. He subsequently urged other students to join the student action.

In the next several days delegates to the Bosnian Parliament seized upon the demonstrations to denounce the regime for police brutality. The majority Croat-Muslim coalition introduced a resolution calling for a radical overhaul of the police and demanding an investigation of the police violence on the previous two evenings.[44] True to their inclination to frame each controversy in the context of their peoples' political future, both Serb and Croat delegates sought to link their criticism of the police with the question of

Bosnia-Herzegovina's position in the region. Serb delegate Šćepan Grdjić joined in criticizing police behavior, but he reserved his harshest criticism for an unnamed "puppeteer" (presumably a Croat leader) whom he alleged had exploited a demonstration for citizens' rights and freedom of the press by turning it into a manifestation of support for trialism. The majority of Bosnians, he said, want only autonomy for Bosnia-Herzegovina. The Croat delegate Veseličić, who had pleaded on the demonstrators' behalf earlier in the day, evoked Serbs' ire when he accused them of supporting the Croat cause only out of opposition to Vienna.

In addition to revealing sharp differences between Serb and Croat delegates, the parliamentarians made it clear that they would extend only limited support to the youthful demonstrators of their respective nationalities. After a Croat delegate proposed a resolution supporting the Croats in their struggle against the Hungarians, Muslim and Croat delegates pointedly walked out of the chamber. The parliament's president was left almost alone to rule that the proposed resolution exceeded the parliament's jurisdiction. With their strategic withdrawal, the delegates abandoned the students' cause, but they burned no bridges with the authorities and returned the next day to debate other matters.

The February demonstrations revealed the multifaceted relationships among the various political actors in the streets and in parliament. The Croat students did not cooperate closely with their putative allies in parliament, even though Croat delegates shared the same cause with the youthful demonstrators. Many party leaders were delighted to see the students take to the streets to protest Habsburg policies, and some acted as intermediaries between the protestors and imperial officials. But they contorted their denunciations of police violence against the students into rhetorical endorsements of their favored political restructuring of the region. In walking out of parliament, the delegates effectively turned their backs on the protestors once their point had been made, and they quickly resumed a working relationship with the authorities. Such compromising behavior grated on the student ideologues, who sought the strongest possible opposition to the authorities from their elder fellow nationalists in parliament.

A few months later, student discontent turned deadly, this time in the Croatian capital of Zagreb. On June 8, 1912, Luka Jukić, former organizer of student demonstrations in Sarajevo, tried to kill Cuvaj. The circumstances eerily foreshadowed the assassination of Franz Ferdinand in Sarajevo two years later. The count was riding in his car along a Zagreb street with his wife and a government aide when Jukić fired a single shot from beside the street. He missed the count, but the aide was mortally wounded. Pursued for twenty minutes through the streets of Zagreb by police, Jukić succeeded in killing one officer and wounding two others before being subdued. In a swift investigation before the trial, officials uncovered an extensive network of student societies in Croatia and Dalmatia. A dozen coconspirators were arrested and tried along with Jukić. On July 30, 1912, he was sentenced to death by hanging, but the sentence was later commuted to a long prison term.[45] Jukić's assassination attempt was one of many attempts (most of them successful) to kill high-ranking authorities in the early twentieth century. It undoubtedly helped inspire the Sarajevo assassins to take the life of the archduke in 1914.

Underground Serb student organizations

The Bosnian Serb student movement in Sarajevo was coordinated by a cohesive umbrella organization alternately called National Unity (*Narodno jedinstvo*) or National Unification (*Narodno ujedinjenje*).[46] Each chapter had an executive committee whose members recruited new members and informed other students of the organization's purpose—the cultural unification of Serbs and Croats. Students at each school selected representatives to a central board that coordinated all Sarajevo activities, and a "court" was established to resolve "differences and conflicts among members of the organization."[47] Vasa Čubrilović, colleague of the archduke's assassins and later a prolific historian and influential member of the Serbian Academy of Sciences, was a member of the court. Committees held their meetings at members' homes, at public coffeehouses, or in public outdoor locations, often in the heart of Sarajevo. The symbols of membership were rings or a distinctive cap in Serb, Croat, and Slovene national colors.

National Unity's members supported the unity of all South Slavs, but at the same time they embraced Great Serb ideals. "A national culture is unthinkable without national unity," stated their program. "This requires a nationally unified state." According to the government report, the students subscribed to the views expressed in the newspaper *Novi Srbin* (The New Serb) that began publication in Hungary in 1912:

The new Serbs must elevate the belief in the freeing and uniting of the South Slavs to the level of religion. ... If a higher authority commands that we either abandon our desire for freedom or give up our life, we as new Serbs will die, in death still victorious over the enemy, since we cannot be empowered in our lives and will glorify our brief lives with the beautiful gesture of a hero's death.[48]

The youthful Serbs dismissed their elders' participation in the monarchy's parliamentary institutions as futile: "The club condemns the current parliamentary battle of the Slavic tribes and demands transfer of the locus of battle outside parliament to strengthening national consciousness, national strength and national will and activation of national defense by means of work, suffering, and sacrifice."[49]

The government reported that the original intent had been to call this organization "Serb Youth" (*Srpska omladina*) and to use the tenth anniversary of the founding of the Serb cultural society Prosvjeta in Sarajevo to organize chapters in all secondary schools. By 1914, National Unity had counterparts in Banja Luka, Travnik, Tuzla, Mostar, Bijeljina, and probably other towns as well. The overwhelming majority of activists may be judged by their names to have been Serbs, but a few Muslim names were among the leaders. Serbs and Croats in these organizations saw the national recruitment of Muslims as an essential part of their mission. The Serb society in Travnik, according to the government report, sought to "turn Muslims from pan-Islam and win them for the Serb national idea."[50]

The Serb student societies in Bosnia-Herzegovina grew larger and more radical with Serbian victories against the Ottoman Empire and Bulgaria in the Balkan Wars of 1912 and 1913. Nationalist Bosnian Serbs were outraged when Austria-Hungary wielded international influence to force the Serbian kingdom to abandon the port of Scutari (in present-day Albania) in 1913. But more than anything else, the students were galled by the monarchy's imposition of exceptional measures in Bosnia-Herzegovina during 1913.[51] At that time, the civilian head of the Regional Government was removed. His replacement, General Oskar Potiorek, was given the title of Chief (*Poglavar*) of the Regional Government, with powers far beyond those of his civilian predecessors. At the trial of the Sarajevo assassins, the imposition of these measures was singled out by several of the conspirators as motivating them to assassinate the archduke. Their retaliation was part of an escalating cycle of violence. The official symbolic punishments and mild reprimands fueled the flames of radical Serb passions but failed to deter the perpetrators from further agitation. The same ideological impulses that motivated members of National Unity inspired the assassination of Archduke Franz Ferdinand, but Habsburg officials never turned up evidence that the secret society had any role in organizing the archduke's killing. More important were the informal ties that the assassins developed when frequenting the same Belgrade cafés and while participating in earlier protest actions.

Assassination

It fell to Josip Vancaš, as vice mayor, to inform the city council in closed session on April 6, 1914, that the city was to receive a visit on June 28 from Archduke Franz Ferdinand, the designated successor to Franz Joseph as Habsburg emperor. Scheduling the visit for June 28, the Vidovdan holiday, is often ascribed to a malicious desire to provoke Serb sensitivities. Most scholars now agree that the date was selected for convenience rather than symbolism. But the visit itself was an integral part of the empire's strategy to bolster its forces after Serbian victories in the Second Balkan War. In his role as the army's inspector general, the archduke was to observe military maneuvers in which a Habsburg unit repulsed a hypothetical Serbian offensive toward Sarajevo from the southwest. During his visit the archduke was to visit two military bases in the city. By planning a triumphal entry into the capital, Franz Ferdinand was drawing global attention to the monarchy's notable achievements in Bosnia and seeking to demonstrate that the empire enjoyed popularity among most Sarajevans.

When Vancaš announced the impending visit, he was less worried about the visit's symbolism than with a proper reception for the distinguished visitor. Concerned as always about the city's physical appearance, he proposed the emergency paving of Čemaluša Street, where the archduke would pass on his way to the Appel Quay. Mehmed Spaho spoke out against building what he called "Potemkin villages" to show the distinguished guest. His Imperial Highness might not go to some of the other streets in the "upper mahalas," Spaho asserted, but they were in miserable condition and in much need of repair. He particularly urged that Koševo Street be paved, since "the Muslim cemetery at Grlić Woods cannot be reached by vehicles or even pedestrians, especially in bad weather; and here plenty of money has been spent on a road to the cemeteries of other confessions." Spaho was the lone dissenter in three resolutions passed by the council to pave Čemaluša Street and to activate the city's line of credit (approved by the council only two weeks before) to pay for the unanticipated expense.

In mid-morning on June 26, 1914, the archduke arrived by train in Ilidža from the Adriatic Coast and Mostar. He spent the rest of that rainy, foggy day observing a mock battle between two battalions of the Ninth Mountain

Brigade in the hills south and east of Sarajevo. That evening he and his wife Sophie took an hour-long walk in Ilidža, where bear cubs, released especially for the occasion, frolicked in the woods along their path. On June 27, Sophie visited a dozen sites in Sarajevo, most associated with the Catholic or Islamic faith. Serbian Orthodox institutions were kept off her itinerary.

On Sunday June 28, the archduke and his wife were to be honored with a traditional twenty-four cannon shot salute fired from surrounding hills.[52] Their train pulled into the western railway station as cannon fire resounded from the Vraca Hill south of the city. The day was sunny, in contrast to the dismal weather they had encountered on their arrival in Ilidža. After General Potiorek and Sarajevo Mayor Fehim Čurčić greeted him, the archduke briefly inspected the Philippovich military headquarters at the western end of the city, and he then entered an open car with his wife for the drive into town. The chief of the Regional Government, General Potiorek, accompanied them in the first of three cars. The column sped into town along newly paved Čemaluša Street past large welcoming crowds to the Appel Quay. The convoy moved briskly about halfway to the eastern end of the city, then stopped at the post office building, a newly completed Secessionist masterpiece designed by Vancaš. The archduke alighted briefly from the car, took a cursory look at the colorful new structure, shook hands with the head of the post office, and then reentered the car to resume the trip east toward the Sarajevo City Hall. The archduke and his entourage moved more slowly along the Appel Quay so that the heir apparent could take in the sights and bask in the crowd's adulation.

After traveling only a hundred meters to the east, the three-car caravan approached the Čumurija Bridge. Someone in the crowd hurled two bombs at the archduke's car. The first missed the car and fell behind it; the second bounced off the back of the car and exploded under the following vehicle, injuring two passengers. Police on foot pursued the perpetrator, Nedjeljko Čabrinović, along the riverside street to the west. Seeking to avoid capture, he jumped off the riverside wall into the Miljacka River, which was little more than a minor stream at that time of year, and landed on its rocky bed. Hurt in the fall, he was promptly arrested. After a brief delay the archduke's party moved with greater dispatch toward its next scheduled stop at City Hall, where the mayor and vice mayors awaited him.

Franz Ferdinand's last public words were spoken on the steps of Sarajevo City Hall. On being welcomed by the mayor, the archduke stated that he

Above, car bearing Archduke Franz Ferdinand and his wife Sophie traveling along the Appel Quay moments before their assassination, June 28, 1914.

Below, Sarajevo police arrest Gavrilo Princip in the seconds after he assassinated the archduke and his wife. (Both pictures courtesy of Historical Museum, Sarajevo)

appreciated the mayor's welcome but hadn't expected to be greeted by a bomb. He announced his intention to visit the injured passengers in the hospital before departing the city. General Potiorek, chief of the Regional Government, advised him to change the plan and return along the riverside rather than risk parading through the city center's dense, crowd-lined streets. Orders were given to make the change, but the driver of the archduke's car never heard them. When he reached the Latin Bridge, the driver followed the original plan and turned the car to the right, toward the city center. Alerted to his error, he inadvertently brought the car to a stop directly in front of Gavrilo Princip, another of the assassins. Princip fired two shots. One struck the archduke, and the other hit Sophie. She slumped onto the archduke. The driver later reported that they had exchanged a few words, but he was unable to hear what was said. As police arrived at the scene of the killings, the car sped the archduke and Sophie to the nearest medical facilities at the Konak across the river. Both were dead by the time they arrived.

An autopsy was performed and the bodies were embalmed in the Konak on the night of June 28–9. In the afternoon of June 29 the two caskets were moved from the Konak to the Bistrik train station a few hundred meters away. Representatives of the Muslim, Catholic, Sephardic, Ashkenazic, and Protestant religious communities accompanied the funeral bier past an estimated five thousand mourners, as did Josip Vancaš.[53] At 6 p.m. the funeral train set off for Vienna. Sarajevo's public buildings were draped with black flags, and services of mourning were held everywhere in the monarchy.

Aftermath of the assassination

The assassination deeply divided Sarajevans along ethnonational lines. For all the enmity that Franz Ferdinand aroused in Serb nationalists, he was seen by most Croats and many Muslims as the best hope for the creation of a South Slav polity within the Habsburg Monarchy. His assassination led angry Croats and Muslims in Sarajevo to engage in violent anti-Serb demonstrations during the evening of June 28 and much of the day on June 29.[54] The crowd directed its anger principally at Serb shops in the marketplace and at the residences of prominent Serbs.

At 10 p.m. on June 28, only hours after the assassination, a group of about one hundred demonstrators gathered and threw stones through the windows of the café of the Hotel Evropa, owned by the wealthy Serb merchant

Above, Josip Vancaš addresses anti-Serb demonstrators before their violent rampage, June 29, 1914. (Courtesy of Historical Museum, Sarajevo)

Below, debris and destroyed property in the streets after rioting directed at Sarajevo's Serbs in the aftermath of the assassination, June 29, 1914. (Courtesy of Historical Archive, Sarajevo)

Gligorije Jeftanović and known as a gathering place for Serb politicians. The crowd included many from the "better classes," according to the government report, and also a substantial number of military officers. A hastily dispatched unit of ten fully armed security troops on horseback readily dispersed the crowd.

The morning of June 29 began with a rally led by various Muslim and Croat political leaders featuring singing of the monarchy's national anthem and the display of black flags and the emperor's picture. Josip Vancaš was among those addressing the crowd, but after their speeches the leaders melted away, and the police faced fast-moving small groups of Croats and Muslims from all walks of life.[55] In the words of the official report, "The demonstrators virtually launched a small war against Serb shops and residences in the entire city."[56] The mob attacked the cluster of structures near the New Serbian Orthodox Church, threw stones at the metropolitan's residence, and sacked a Serbian Orthodox school. Other small groups stoned the building that housed the Serb cultural society Prosvjeta, sacked a Serb bank, and trashed the offices of the newspaper *Srpska riječ*. They singled out shops of Serb merchants, including the family business of the assassin Nedjeljko Čubrinović, and attacked Serb residences. The personal property of their targets was strewn on the streets and sidewalks in front of their residences and shops.

In those dark days of late June 1914, the two lives snuffed out by the assassins were avenged with the lives of two Serbs killed by crowd violence less than forty-eight hours later.[57] Photos and government reports indicate that the demonstrators commanded widespread support among Sarajevo's non-Serbs. One officer reported that many residents looked on from their windows and applauded the crowd. Vancaš's role, and that of other political leaders, is difficult to determine, but certainly some of them participated in bringing the crowd together and leading participants in the general direction of Serb shops and homes.

Although fewer lives were lost in this sequence of events than in the 1878 uprising against Ottoman rule, the internecine violence was unprecedented in the city's history. In a report from 1920, the assassin Vladimir Čorović alleged that the Habsburg officials could have prevented these riots but instead approached the demonstrations with a "positively disposed passivity."[58] In their reports the officers who commanded the security units offer evidence to refute that interpretation. Their detailed reports, filed a day or two after the events, show that the troops probably saved the new

Serbian Orthodox church and the metropolitan's residence from destruction and dispersed with bayonets a crowd that had invaded Jeftanović's residence. The success of government security forces on the evening of June 28, when the crowd dispersed at the mere appearance of mounted armed troops, gave officials no reason to anticipate widespread attacks by multiple roving groups the next day. It is likely that the security forces saved lives and prevented more widespread destruction. By the time the caskets of Sophie and the archduke were transported to the train station on the evening of June 29, order had been fully restored in the city.

The road from the archduke's assassination to the outbreak of the First World War was long and circuitous. The stern Austro-Hungarian ultimatum delivered to the Kingdom of Serbia on July 23 evoked further rallies by Croats and Muslims elated with the empire's belligerence toward Serbia. These rallies continued for six days.[59] This time, the Habsburg authorities mobilized hundreds of additional soldiers and horses to aid the local security forces, which probably prevented further violence against Serbs and their property.

In the wake of the assassination, an acrimonious internal conflict erupted between the Regional Government and the Vienna-based Joint Finance Ministry, where officials claimed they had never been told of the student radicals. It is true that the government's reports were irregular and incomplete, but the Joint Ministry officials mistook information-gathering for official policy. Much had changed in post-Kállay Bosnia. In legitimizing political parties, permitting elections on a limited franchise, encouraging the formation of student societies chartered by the authorities, and approving the publication of often incendiary writings, the government had relaxed supervision and surveillance since the Kállay years.

Ever since 1914 the assassination has been viewed differently by various ethnonational groups and in the two capital cities most directly affected. Austro-Hungarian and German officials depicted the assassination as a criminal conspiracy hatched in Belgrade, while Serbian official circles portrayed it as a heroic act of national liberation against intolerable Habsburg oppression. Marxist interpreters subsequently sided with the "national liberation" school, and Yugoslav communists joined Serb nationalists in adulating the scruffy Sarajevo assassins as an historical avant-garde. In Vladimir Dedijer's definitive work on the assassination, it is virtually impossible to dissect the author's undisguised Marxist enthusiasm from his more discreet sympathy for Serb nationalism.

Sarajevo at war

The front lines never reached Sarajevo, but the First World War touched every resident of the city. Most males of military age fought for one side or the other. Many enlisted or were drafted into the monarchy's armed forces and fought with the courage and distinction that characterized the empire's forces in the war's first few years. Others, particularly Serbs, volunteered for the Serbian army or joined various paramilitary groups fighting along-side Serbian regulars. The price of participation was heavy. Many Sarajevans never returned, and many others were injured and bore debilitating injuries for the rest of their lives. Those who never left the city endured deprivations in everyday life, and Serbs who stayed were exposed to harsh repression by the Habsburg regime. The monarchy's security officials feared that the assassination was just the tip of the iceberg in the willingness of some Serbs to undertake violence against the monarchy. For the duration of the war, the authorities employed drastic measures in a campaign to destroy the ability of Serbs to organize resistance. Their apprehensions were strengthened by the discovery, ex post facto, of widespread illegal societies among students in every major town of Bosnia-Herzegovina.

But the authorities' correspondence and reports after June 28, 1914, show no desire for vengeance upon Serbs as a people but rather an over-riding concern with the monarchy's security and the perceived continuing threat of violence posed by Bosnian Serbs. One official saw the assassination as an "act of the Great Serb Irredenta, and one of the first needs of the state was to proceed against these (people) with the most firm administrative methods."[60] The government then hunted down those it perceived as the intellectual and political purveyors of subversion among the Bosnian Serbs, executing some, imprisoning many, and shutting down the public life of Bosnian Serb nationalists in its various manifestations. The officials' conduct during their last four years in Sarajevo did little to endear them to the population and contributed to the bitter anti-Habsburg legacy that remained a potent force among many Sarajevans after the war.

Extraordinary measures were introduced in Sarajevo the day after the assassination and remained in effect for most of the war. On June 29, 1914, the government announced its intention to convene a special court for Sarajevo and environs with the authority to impose the death penalty for criminal acts of violence and murder. It published the decree two days later in its official newspaper.[61] Starting on June 28, over a hundred Serbs were arrested on suspicion of supporting the assassins, and many of them were detained for some time. Fifty-eight non-Serbs were also arrested for violent acts against persons and property in the demonstrations of June 29. The Serb nationalist press was put out of business, as was the newspaper *Zvono* (Bell), viewed as the voice of pro-Serb Social Democrats. Police identified and expelled some 4,127 persons who were either citizens of Serbia or Montenegro or who had no identification papers. All political organizations were dissolved by a decree of July 26, 1914. The Serb societies Prosvjeta and Sokol were banned and their property turned over to a government caretaker. The Serb-oriented Muslim society Gajret was also dissolved and its property given to the commission administering vakufs, on the assumption that its Muslim members were loyal to the regime.

In late December 1914 General Potiorek was dismissed from his post after his troops failed to meet their objectives in a major Austro-Hungarian offensive against Serbia. Baron Stjepan Sarkotić, the last person to head Bosnia's Austro-Hungarian government, replaced him on the first day of January 1915. The new chief adopted the position that "no politics is the best politics" in Bosnia-Herzegovina. He formally dissolved the Bosnian Parliament in February 1915 (in any case, it had not met since June 29, 1914) and never reconvened it. The Sarajevo city council, after much debate, bowed to pressure from the authorities and imposed a special "war tax" to defray the extraordinary expenditures of wartime conditions.[62] In November 1915 the city council, too, was dissolved, and the city was governed for the duration of the war by an appointed trustee (*povjerenik*).[63]

In addition to repressive measures, the authorities sought to perpetuate the cult of the House of Habsburg, often with heavy-handed authoritarian measures. The state parades and jubilees continued. In all schools, the day began with the Habsburg national anthem,[64] and inspectors were assigned to ensure it was sung correctly. Each teacher was required to read aloud a special pronouncement before and after noon and to repeat a prayer for children and the success of the imperial armed forces.

Under imminent threat of attack from Montenegrin troops just after Italy joined the Entente powers, the city was partially evacuated by order of military authorities for several weeks in autumn 1915. Observers reported that the marketplace was closed and that whole sections of the city were eerily vacant during this extraordinary measure. The displaced persons took refuge with relatives or friends in nearby communities. Life resumed its drab wartime rhythm when the evacuees returned in late October 1915.

Severe shortages of life's necessities began in late 1914.[65] In January 1915 the city opened a food distribution center, and in May 1915 ration cards for bread were introduced. A public kitchen opened in December 1915 and fed over six hundred persons on its first day of operation. Food service was provided to students and officials in separate facilities. A foundry opened in May 1915 to receive metal items to be melted down in support of the war effort.

Among many Sarajevans' wartime turns of fortune, Milan Srškić's experiences were unique.[66] Conscripted into the Habsburg army, he was deployed with a Hungarian unit to the Russian front. At an opportune moment, he and another Serb soldier deserted to the Russian camp. He put himself at the mercy of Russian soldiers, who were apparently dubious at first of his claims to political prominence. He was delivered to the Serbian embassy in Petrograd and then returned to Serbia, where he was asked to assist in encouraging further defections from the Habsburg side. In Kragujevac, he met Serbia's Crown Prince Aleksandar for the first time. Srškić's wife and small child were able to join him in Serbian-held territory. But in October 1915 the Serbian army was forced into headlong retreat by a joint German, Austro-Hungarian, and Bulgarian offensive. Srškić and his family joined the king, his ministers, and the army in the legendary retreat across northern Albania to the Adriatic coast. There, the survivors of the difficult march were evacuated on British ships to the island of Corfu, where a government-in-exile was established. The Serbian government in Corfu entered into talks with the Yugoslav Committee, a London-based group of prominent Croat and Slovene politicians who hoped to create a unified South Slav state in the event the Habsburg Monarchy was defeated in the war. Srškić was appointed to this committee to represent Serbia, and he "always hewed to the line of the Serbian government," as a colleague put it.[67] In that capacity he participated in the preparation of the Corfu Declaration of July 1917, the document that laid the foundations for the Kingdom of Serbs, Croats, and Slovenes that was created at war's end in December 1918.

Srškić was one of few Sarajevans to have any voice in the order that would follow the Habsburg collapse. In 1918, the vaunted Habsburg Monarchy disappeared from the map with barely a whimper, leaving in its wake the detritus of a fallen empire. Many of its bureaucrats continued to report for work as usual, but they soon took orders from new masters. Many of its soldiers, leaderless and without purpose, left their units and made their way home. In the city where the war began but never saw combat, war-weary residents looked forward to rebuilding their lives in a new, united South Slav polity.

5. Royal Yugoslavia's Forgotten City

During its forty years as the Habsburg showplace in southeast Europe, Sarajevo had become thoroughly integrated into the monarchy's economic, political, and cultural orbit. Those linkages were shattered in 1918. Sarajevo emerged from the First World War an orphan of the defunct Austro-Hungarian monarchy and became part of a new royal South Slav state. Despite Sarajevans' initial enthusiasm for the new polity, almost all facets of life either stagnated or declined during the city's twenty-three years under royal rule. The economy performed erratically, political leaders struggled in vain to win autonomy for the city council, cultural life made only modest advances, and few new buildings were constructed. Although many other cities in the region experienced a similar fate, Sarajevo was unduly disadvantaged by the transfer to Belgrade of many institutions and functions that had previously helped feed its dynamic growth. The new rulers gave preference to Belgrade, Zagreb, and Ljubljana, the major urban centers corresponding to the three groups in the state's formal title, the "Kingdom of the Serbs, Croats, and Slovenes." Neglected because of its diversity and torn by forces emanating from the three favored urban centers with national majorities, Sarajevo became a forgotten city.

Sarajevo in the framework of royal Yugoslavia

Like other postwar southeast European polities, Yugoslavia was structured as a constitutional monarchy. The hybrid creation brought together the Kingdoms of Serbia and Montenegro with the former Habsburg territories of Croatia, Slavonia, Dalmatia, Vojvodina, Slovenia, and Bosnia-Herzegovina under Serbia's ruling Karadjordjević dynasty. Created in some haste because of growing unrest in the South Slav lands and the imminent Italian military threat to the former Habsburg territories,[1] the Kingdom of the Serbs, Croats, and Slovenes was formally proclaimed by the Serbian Prince Regent Aleksandar in Belgrade on December 1, 1918.[2] (The kingdom is

130

referred to here by its informal name of Yugoslavia or the Kingdom of Yugo-
slavia, although it formally acquired the latter title only in January 1929.) As
ruler-in-fact for fifteen of the twenty-three interwar years, Aleksandar
Karadjordjević was the principal architect of royal Yugoslav governance.[3]
Having been designated regent of Serbia in June 1914 by his ailing father
Petar I, Regent Aleksandar of Serbia became Regent Aleksandar of the new
South Slav state upon proclaiming the new kingdom in December 1918. He
assumed the title of king after his father died in August 1921. Aleksandar
ruled as king (first of the Kingdom of Serbs, Croats, and Slovenes until
1929, thereafter of the Kingdom of Yugoslavia) until he was assassinated in
October 1934.

5.1 Formation of the Yugoslav kingdom, 1918.

Most Sarajevans greeted the prospect of life in a new South Slav state with enthusiasm and optimism. When soldiers of the Serbian royal army entered Sarajevo triumphantly on November 6, 1918, marking the city's uncontested passage from Habsburg to South Slav military control, they were hailed as liberators and welcomed with celebratory activities matching any from Habsburg times.[4] Soon Sarajevans were busy preparing new governing institutions, anticipating that the city would continue to be a major administrative center in the new kingdom. Members of the first appointed city council, expecting the imminent dawn of democracy in their land, put forth initiatives for reform and prepared to hold elections based on a broad franchise. But those prospects faded with the regime's unrelenting autocratic centralism and determination to eliminate Bosnia-Herzegovina as an administrative unit, diminishing Sarajevo's role as a regional capital.

Many historical works portray royal Yugoslavia (1918–41) as a Great Serb creation in which Serbs achieved dominance throughout the kingdom through centralization. Andrew Wachtel, in his study of the rise and fall of Yugoslavism, gives a nuanced version of that interpretation: "The issue [was] not merely centralization, but centralization with a strong Serbian accent."[5] Our examination of developments in Sarajevo finds much evidence of such a Serb accent, but it suggests that those who see only a Great Serb polity in interwar Yugoslavia may mistake the means for the end. The core mission of the house of Karadjordjević rulers was autocratic centralism, undertaken to enhance their own stature and authority. Although Great Serb hegemony and autocratic centralization were often promoted by the same political actors, the regime undertook many centralizing measures that did nothing to advance Serb nationalism. Some centralization grated on Serbs as well as Muslims and Croats, and still other measures were resented by members of all groups. Thus autocratic centralism and Great Serb ambitions are best viewed as separate, if related, phenomena,[6] both of which operated against Sarajevo's interests. Sarajevans' quest for greater control over their own affairs was more frequently frustrated by statist, autocratic centralization than by Great Serb interference. Great Serb nationalists inevitably weighed in on the side of centralization, but nationalism was often tangential to the larger struggle for control of city affairs.

In Sarajevo protracted economic stagnation was the overriding problem throughout the period. The government's persistent refusal to grant the city meaningful local self-government rendered the city fathers largely impotent to deal with the problem. In royal Yugoslavia, no less than under Habsburg rule, the city's residents struggled in vain to acquire control over their own destinies. The new rulers offered no grand vision to inspire the growth or reconfiguration of urban space. The house of Karadjordjević replaced the house of Habsburg in the city's memorial culture as the central theme of holidays, statues, memorials, cultural events, and street renaming. But little was altered during the protracted political struggles between the council and the various representatives of royal rule. Many things happened, but few things changed.

New parties and the failure of political Yugoslavism in Sarajevo

The transfer of power from Habsburg to South Slav control began in October 1918, after the defeat of the Central Powers (Germany, Austria-Hungary, Bulgaria, and the Ottoman Empire) on the Salonica front signaled the impending demise of the Habsburg Monarchy. In late October, leading members of the Yugoslav Committee from Bosnia-Herzegovina formed the People's Council of Serbs, Croats, and Slovenes for Bosnia-Herzegovina (*Narodno vijeće Srba Hrvata i Slovenaca za Bosnu i Hercegovinu*), a legislative body that then authorized the formation of the Regional Government of Bosnia-Herzegovina.[7] Among its first acts, the Regional Government directed each city and town in Bosnia-Herzegovina to establish a governing council. At the time the directive was issued, Sarajevo had already organized a postwar council consisting of delegates appointed by the Regional Government.

During its first two years as part of royal Yugoslavia, Sarajevo experienced a vibrant, pluralist political life. Political affiliations in Sarajevo during those formative two years were fluid and often transient. Political life developed along two tracks: the formation of postwar political parties, and the activities of Sarajevo's appointed city council. The city council held its first meeting under royal Yugoslav rule on December 3, 1918, in the meeting chambers of City Hall.[8] In the early months of 1919 politicians hastened to establish political parties, most of them revivals or continuations of prewar organizations.[9] At the same time some members of the Yugoslav Committee, hoping to transcend sectarian politics, sought to consolidate all major political formations in the new state in an all-Yugoslav organization.[10] Svetozar Pribićević, a Serb from Croatia and a leading politician on the Yugoslav Committee, was the prime mover of this initiative. Sarajevo, near the geographic center of the kingdom and home to several nationalities, was chosen as the place to launch the new organization. But the effort proved futile. Although the leaders of the time followed a different path to party formation than had their predecessors under Austro-Hungarian rule, their results were similar. Three national parties, representing the Serbs, Croats, and Bosnian Muslims, dominated Sarajevo's political life throughout the 1920s. The Communist Party, the only supra-national party to gain substantial support in the city, was all but destroyed by government repression, leaving the field open for the three national parties to engage in partisan squabbling.

On February 14 and 15, 1919, Pribićević gathered with like-minded activists in Sarajevo and formed the Yugoslav Democratic Party (*Jugoslovenska demokratska stranka*), commonly called the Democratic Party.[11] The party endorsed the views of the newspaper *Slovenski jug* (Slavic south), which advocated a centralized South Slav polity consisting of "one unified state, one homeland, one society, one social morality, and one state consciousness."[12] Party members favored a kingdom under the Karadjordjević dynasty, radical administrative centralization, abolition of regional autonomy, local self-government, and agrarian reforms giving peasants ownership of the land they cultivated. They respected the national identities of the Serbs, Croats, and Slovenes but hoped that all citizens of the new polity would eventually embrace a transcendent Yugoslav identity. Leading party members—many of whom were Serbs—hoped to reach out to their fellow citizens of all religions, parties, and ethnonational identities.

Leaders of many political factions attended the Democratic Party's founding convocation, but few wanted to see their own groups subsumed in an all-Yugoslav political formation. The Democratic Party program, favoring a unified, centralized Yugoslav polity and promoting Yugoslavism to supersede particular nationalisms, bore the marks of Great Serb nationalism and aroused the suspicion of non-Serbs. The prospect of dynastic centralization was particularly frightening to Croats and Bosnian Muslims, most of whom hoped for a federated kingdom in which the former Habsburg lands of Croatia and Bosnia-Herzegovina enjoyed some autonomy. Great Serb slogans employed at rallies in Sarajevo and Banja Luka during January 1919 reinforced their fears. Even before the Democratic Party was formally founded, leaders of other groups were preemptively organizing parties along ethnoconfessional lines to avoid being engulfed in the all-Yugoslav organization. Pribićević, in his effort to form an umbrella organization, thus helped spawn a revival of the very particularism he had hoped to supersede.

Sarajevo Muslims, led by a Habsburg-era city council member Mehmed Spaho, organized to form a Bosnian Muslim political party. They and other activists convened a gathering of Bosnian Muslims in Sarajevo on February 14, the eve of the planned Democratic Party convocation. The assembled Bosnian Muslims formed the Yugoslav Muslim Organization (JMO; *Jugoslovenska muslimanska organizacija*) and elected Spaho as its first president.[13] Shortly thereafter they established the newspaper *Pravda* (Justice) as the party's official organ. The JMO program supported autonomy for Bosnia-Herzegovina, respect for the sheriat, and compensation for landowners who lost land in agrarian reforms, all of which clashed head-on with Democratic Party objectives. Unsurprisingly, therefore, Pribićević failed to persuade JMO leaders to incorporate their new organization in the Democratic Party. He subsequently denounced the JMO leaders as separatist opponents of the Yugoslav state. But in the November 1920 elections for the kingdom's Constituent Assembly, the first litmus test of party strength, the JMO won 3,409 votes (41.5 percent) in Sarajevo to emerge as the leading party in the city, and it also won the most votes in Bosnia-Herzegovina.

Although avowedly not a nationalist party, the JMO consistently behaved like one, and party leaders jealously guarded their monopoly as the institutional representatives of Bosnia's Muslims. Muslim intellectuals and JMO leaders argued that their group was a religious community rather than a nationality, leaving its members free to identify themselves as Serbs or Croats, but the JMO nonetheless claimed to represent them. In speeches and in newspaper articles, party leaders argued improbably that economic threats to Muslim landowners fundamentally endangered Islam and jeopardized the survival of all Bosnian Muslims.

Not only did Pribićević lose the support of most Bosnian Muslims and Croats, he also failed to gain the support of the largest party in Serbia, the Serb Radical Party, popularly called the Radical Party or the Radicals. The Radicals, led by Serbia's former prime minister, Nikola Pašić, had ruled Serbia since 1903 and had no desire to abandon their preeminence in order to mix with others in a Yugoslav consortium. Instead, they authorized Milan Srškić to form a branch of the Radicals in Bosnia-Hercegovina, formally titled the People's Radical Party (*Narodna radikalna stranka*), to compete head-on with the Democratic Party. Srškić moved with alacrity to do so. The Radicals soon became the leading choice of Serb voters in Bosnia-Herzegovina. During the spring and summer of 1919, Srškić addressed assemblies of Serbs in various towns of Bosnia-Herzegovina as they formed local branches of the Radical Party. With the nationalist slogan "Serbs, assemble!" and a message advocating immediate agrarian reform, he appealed to Serb peasants to elect the party's candidates. He himself became a candidate in the November 1920 elections to the Constituent Assembly and won. In that first test of the party's strength, the Radicals received 1,346 votes (16.4 percent) in Sarajevo. With the Radical Party's successful organizing campaign in Bosnia-Herzegovina, the primary voice of the Bosnian Serbs fell under the guidance of political leaders from Serbia.

The growing strength of the Srškić-led Radicals in Bosnia-Herzegovina ensured that nationalist politics would prevail over the Yugoslav unity advocated by the Democrats. Srškić saw the Yugoslav kingdom as a realization of his political ideals: "That which we so earnestly desired before the war, has indeed happened," he told a Croat colleague.[14] But he was not well disposed toward Bosnian Muslim participation in the new state: "Our Muslims have not identified their nationality, and our state is a national one. That's a state of Serbs, Croats, and Slovenes, and they alone need to be represented. ... I am not an enemy of our Muslims, but their position inflicts damage on us, both Serbs and Croats, and we both must defend ourselves."[15] Srškić, in fact, became known for his pejorative references to Muslims and Islam in both public speeches and private conversations. The Croat sculptor Ivan Meštrović wrote that Srškić once said, "I can't [stand to] look at minarets; they need to disappear."[16] Srškić's disparaging view of the Bosnian Muslims portended a sustained confrontation between the Radicals and the JMO that stymied the work of Sarajevo's city council through most of the interwar era.

While the Bosnian Muslims and Bosnian Serbs each came to be represented by a single dominant party in the immediate postwar years, Bosnian Croats were divided for the first five postwar years between clericals following the tradition of Archbishop Stadler (who had died in 1918) and secular Croat nationalists. On May 2, 1919, supporters of clericism founded the Croat People's Party (*Hrvatska pučka stranka*) in Sarajevo to promote the "principle of positive religion." Secular Croat nationalists, led by Jozo Sunarić, answered by founding the Croat Husbandmen's Party (*Hrvatska težačka stranka*) in August 1919. Like Croat nationalists in neighboring Croatia, the secularists urged that the merger of the three named tribes proceed slowly and naturally through cultural development. "Time has created these differences," opined the party's newspaper. "Only time can clear them away."[17] But the two distinct Bosnian Croat parties survived only until 1923, when the Croat Republican Peasant Party (HSS; *Hrvatska republikanska seljačka stranka*, later renamed the *Hrvatska seljačka stranka*), under the leadership of Stjepan Radić, assumed a leading role among Bosnian Croats.[18] The ascendancy of the HSS strengthened the ties between Bosnian Croats and political leaders in Croatia.

With the formation of the JMO in February 1919, the establishment of the Bosnian branch of the Radical Party in April, and the creation of two Croat parties in May and August, the Democrats lost their original purpose. The vestigial Democratic Party was left in Bosnia-Herzegovina with support only among a relatively few urban Serbs who favored a conciliatory approach to non-Serbs in the kingdom. In Serbia the party devolved into the major opposition party to the Radicals, and it drew well there and in the Serb-inhabited regions of Croatia, Pribićević's home base. But it garnered few votes in Bosnia-Herzegovina or in Sarajevo (280, or 3.4 percent in 1920). With the Democratic Party's failure to become an all-Yugoslav body and the triumph of the Radicals, sectarian identities became the primary determinant of political affiliation in Sarajevo and the royal Yugoslav state.

Social Democrats and the Communist alternatives

The SDP of Bosnia-Herzegovina emerged from the First World War with most of its members committed to revolutionary ideals rather than the evolutionary path favored by social democratic parties in other former Habsburg lands.[19] In its first two years, the party won widespread support and many votes, but it also inculcated fear among powerholders and bolstered the determination of rulers and governments to prevent social upheavals similar to those that occurred in Russia. After a period of legality and unrestricted operations, the party and its activities were banned beginning in late 1920 and forced into a shadowy, clandestine existence. Each phase of its dichotomous interwar life—at first open and legal, then illegal and underground—had a profound influence on life in Sarajevo and helped shape the character of political life for decades to come.

The Bolshevik seizure of power in Russia in October 1917 cast a long shadow over Europe, and the successes of the Russian Bolsheviks emboldened like-minded socialists to challenge the existing order. Party leaders in Bosnia-Herzegovina shared with their counterparts in Serbia the hope of a Bolshevik-style revolution. "The Social Democratic Party of Serbia and the Social Democratic Party of Bosnia-Herzegovina stand on the communist platform," stated their leaders in a salutatory telegram to the founding meeting of the Third International in Moscow in March 1919.[20]

But not all members supported a revolutionary stance. The party's diverse membership at war's end in 1918 included many, referred to here as reformist Social Democrats, who favored an evolutionary course to socialism through participation in parliaments and cooperation with nonsocialists.

As had been the case before the war, Sarajevo was the primary locus of socialist political activity in Bosnia-Herzegovina. Sarajevans regularly accounted for one-third or more of party members and participants in workers' collective actions in Bosnia-Herzegovina. In addition to being the seat of party headquarters and the residence of its most influential leaders, Sarajevo was the principal center of industrial employment and therefore home to more members of the working class, the party's primary constituency, than other towns. In February 1919 the party's Sarajevo branch had around 2,100 members, about 10 percent of the total number of wage-earning workers (19,302 as recorded in the depression year of 1931) and one-third of syndicate (union) members.[21] Reliable statistics about the composition of the Sarajevo party are hard to come by, since party leaders sought blindness rather than balance when it came to the national or religious affiliation of its members. Available information suggests that the party, consistent with its program, drew members from all religious and national groups in Sarajevo, and that Jews (primarily Sephardim) joined the party disproportionately, followed by Serbs.[22] Like the industrial workers who made up its primary constituency, the Sarajevo party was predominantly male, but members included some women, particularly those employed in the tobacco and carpet factories, where they accounted for over half the work force.

Party leaders hastened to set forth their demands as soon as transitional governing institutions were founded in Sarajevo. On November 8, 1918, just two days after the triumphal entry of Serbian troops into Sarajevo, a delegation of Social Democrats presented their views to a meeting of Regional Government officials.[23] The Social Democrats urged the government to endorse sweeping political liberalization and an expanded role for the state in alleviating the desperate plight of industrial workers and the urban poor. They proposed that elections be based on universal suffrage, including, most significantly, the participation of women, and insisted on freedom of the press, speech, and assembly. In response, Regional Government officials promised to consider the proposals and expressed their appreciation for the loyalty shown by the Social Democrats up to that time. The officials' courteous initial reception, however, masked a deep-seated fear of revolutionary communism that they shared with other political leaders in the kingdom, including Regent Aleksandar and his advisers. Those fears were heightened by public manifestations organized by Social Democrats in the first several months of 1919.

The party's commitment to revolutionary change was soon affirmed at higher organizational levels. At a "unity congress" in Belgrade in April 1919, the SDP of Bosnia-Herzegovina joined with similar parties in other Yugoslav regions (except for Slovenia) to become part of the Socialist Workers Party of Yugoslavia (*Socijalistička radnička partija Jugoslavije [komunista]*).[24] Delegates voted to join the Comintern, thereby moving the new party closer to the ideology and strategies of the Russian-led international communist movement. In June 1920, at a second congress in Vukovar, the party again changed its name, this time to the Communist Party (KP; *Komunistička partija*) of Yugoslavia.[25] Revolutionary communist ideology prevailed at both congresses. With the ascendancy of the revolutionaries, most reformists either defected or were expelled in the party's first two formative years. In Sarajevo, reformist Social Democrats led by Jovan Šmitran and identified with the newspaper *Zvono* (Bell) split off to form the Social Patriots' Party in March 1919.[26]

During its legal existence from war's end through late December 1920, the KP was an indigenous organization with a program centered on the immediate needs of workers and impoverished urban dwellers, freely using strikes and demonstrations to advance its aims. Despite their openly expressed admiration for the achievements of Russia's revolutionaries, party leaders in Bosnia-Herzegovina and in Sarajevo were not slavish imitators of the Bolshevik model, and in the early postwar years the party was not under the guidance or control of any foreign party or government. Although its leaders declined to participate in many governing institutions, they entered every possible electoral contest and energetically campaigned for office. As a result, the party developed no underground conspiratorial wing, an omission for which it was severely reprimanded in retrospect by socialist-era historians.

During its two years of legal existence from late 1918 until December 1920, the party organized strikes, demonstrations, lectures, and campaign rallies in preparation for elections. The party's appeals for revolutionary social change drew supporters from a broad spectrum of workers, students, intellectuals, and some peasants. Leaders called on supporters to attend peaceful public rallies and to stage strikes in the manufacturing and transportation sectors. The party sponsored a well-attended public rally in Sarajevo on January 17, 1919, and some thirty thousand workers, twelve thousand in Sarajevo alone, participated in rallies four days later while honoring a general strike called by the party.[27]

Government officials saw the demonstrations as pro-Bolshevik and antimonarchical, and they worried that the movement might grow into general opposition to the regime.[28] Mindful of the impending May Day holiday, the government took stern measures to prevent antigovernment outbursts. The royal government banned all public demonstrations on the May 1 socialist holiday and ordered the gendarmes and regular army units in Sarajevo to prepare for action. Sarajevo party leaders responded with a call for a work stoppage on April 30 that idled many factories and most public transportation. Hundreds of workers gathered in the workers' hall during the night of April 30–May 1, and the government used their gathering as a pretext to move against the party. Gendarmerie and regular army troops stormed the hall, arrested the workers, seized party archives, and sealed off the building. The authorities also banned further publication of the party newspaper *Glas slobode* (Voice of freedom).[29]

The government's precipitate action on May Day 1919 was followed by a public campaign to portray the demonstrators as revolutionary enemies of the state. Sarajevo Mayor Aristotel Petrović accused the demonstrators of "wanting to overthrow the government, to take power and establish a new order."[30] On May 5, 1919, he announced that the Communists had forfeited the nine seats designated for them on the appointed city council and proposed to replace them with socialists "without revolutionary Bolshevist ideas."[31] At the next meeting, a Jewish delegate objected to this proposal, noting that Jews held only four council seats. He proposed that the reformist socialists be given the same. With the council's approval, four reformist delegates led by Jovo Šmitran then joined the city council. In banning the Communists from the council, the Sarajevo city leaders anticipated the comprehensive bans on revolutionary socialism enacted throughout the Yugoslav kingdom in 1920–1.

The repression of workers and party members beginning on May Day 1919 in Sarajevo was the harshest carried out in any Yugoslav city, but it did not last long. In mid-June 1919, at the direction of Yugoslav Prime Minister Pribićević, the government returned the party's archives, permitted *Glas slobode* to resume publication, and allowed activities at the workers' hall to resume.[32] Most detainees were freed immediately, but a few remained jailed until August 1919. The newly released leaders soon again took to the streets. At a public rally in Sarajevo on July 20, 1919, the Communists demanded an end to Western intervention in Russia and the release of the few detainees still in custody from the May Day arrests.[33]

Although their plans were delayed by the unexpected intrusion of government force on May Day, Sarajevo's Communists convened a founding assembly on October 1, 1919, to inaugurate formally their participation in the KP of Yugoslavia.[34] The party's Sarajevo branch had about 1,500 members at that time. The party continued to organize rallies and strikes over the next year. Their slogans and speeches increasingly centered on local concerns but were often coordinated with party-sponsored events elsewhere in Yugoslavia. To capitalize on the party's popularity, the executive committee of the KP of Yugoslavia decided in December 1919 that the party should field candidates at all levels.[35]

The party's decision to contest power at the ballot box led to outright victories in local elections in Zagreb and Belgrade, but the results were overturned by government decree in each case. Anticipating an election for city council seats, Sarajevo KP leaders held a rally attended by 9,000 persons on March 30, 1920.[36] Government officials postponed the Sarajevo election, probably fearing that the KP and the JMO would receive the most votes in a Sarajevo election at that time. Their fears were borne out in November 1920 in the election of delegates for the Constituent Assembly of the kingdom. The KP won 2,101 votes (25.5 percent) in Sarajevo, taking second place behind the JMO's 41.6 percent. The KP's strong showing in Sarajevo was echoed in several other Bosnian cities, but the party had failed in its sporadic efforts to cultivate a following among peasants. As a result the party polled only 5.5 percent of all votes in Bosnia-Herzegovina and 12.4 percent in Yugoslavia, testifying to both its strengths and weaknesses as an urban-based organization in an overwhelmingly agrarian society.

The appointed Sarajevo city council, 1919–20

The appointed Sarajevo city council should have been a willing tool of the new Regional Government. Instead, it became a forum for vigorous democratic debate and protest against many government policies. During its two years of deliberations, the provisional council was a laboratory of effective, open decision making in a state rapidly headed toward centralist autocratic rule. Its members showed a mastery of democratic parliamentary procedures, tolerance for others, and a willingness to hear opposing viewpoints. The council proved to be as much an action committee as a policy-making body, and it pragmatically addressed the city's chronic postwar problems. Its members, most of whom subscribed to the values of the Democratic Party, demonstrated their hopes for a city more secular and unified than before, and they recommended policy changes to make their vision a reality.

Despite widespread contempt for the legacy of Habsburg rule, the council adopted many prewar practices and operated under the same statute that had governed its work in Austro-Hungarian times. In structuring the provisional council, members of the Regional Government implemented a confessional key, dividing seats among the four major religious communities before selecting the prominent, politically active persons of the appropriate confession to fill them. Four seats in the 1918 council were designated for Jews, and nine seats each were designated for Catholics, Orthodox, and Muslims. Additionally, nine seats were awarded to Social Democrats, indicating that the Regional Government intended that all major political groups in the city be represented on the provisional council. As a rule, Social Democrats declined invitations to participate in the provisional bodies of the new royal state, fearing that cooperation with bourgeois ruling institutions would compromise them and their message. Still, some Social Democrats accepted the seats designated for them in the newly formed Sarajevo provisional city council. On December 2, 1918, the Regional Government approved the appointment of council members from all five groups.[37]

The confessional key governed the election of permanent council officers as well, but Jews were not included in the initial allocation of offices. Aristotel Petrović, of Serbian Orthodox religion, was made council president. Ivo Jelinović, a Catholic, and Ibrahim Šarić, a Muslim, were made vice presidents. Vito Alkalaj, a Jewish delegate, protested the absence of Jews among the council's officers and proposed that a Jew be selected as a third vice president. President Petrović, noting that the Regional Government had no objection, endorsed this proposal but deferred the selection until a future meeting when all Jewish delegates could attend. The 1919 council thus responded to the Jewish complaint of underrepresentation just as the 1878 council had responded to the identical complaint from Serbian Orthodox: It simply added another position to the council.

On February 3, 1919, as the council prepared to select a Jewish vice president, delegate Stevo Marković (one of the founders of the Democratic

Party) objected. "In this new life we must finally break away from religious considerations—and from confessional keys," he argued.[38] When other councilmen insisted that the decision to elect a Jewish vice president had already been made, Marković withdrew his objection and the voting proceeded. All councilmen were invited to vote, indicating that selection of officers was not the exclusive prerogative of the group from which the person was to be drawn. However, some councilmen abstained, probably from the belief that Jewish councilmen should select their own vice president. On the second of two secret ballots, Vito Alkalaj was selected over Ašer Alkalaj and Samuel Pinto.

The first order of business was the enactment of a "provisional charter" to establish procedures for electing members to a permanent council.[39] The committee on laws proposed that males over twenty-four be permitted to vote if they had resided in the city for at least five years and could read and write. The committee's proposal "abolished the confessional key," said committee chairman Badovinac, and provided for "equal, direct and secret voting rights, and protected minorities." Women were excluded, he stated, "because of our particular circumstances, especially with regard to Muslim women." But the proposed franchise was not broad enough for Social Democrat delegate Jakšić. He advocated allowing women to vote, establishing the minimum voting age at twenty rather than twenty-four, and setting the residence requirement at six months.

The council debated the proposed franchise requirements and voted on them one by one. Accepting the Social Democrat position, the council voted 16–12 to lower the minimum voting age from twenty-four to twenty. In a gesture of compromise, committee chairman Badovinac offered to lower the minimum residence in the city to three years and to eliminate the literacy requirement. The compromise apparently satisfied everyone and was approved. Following debate, the council deadlocked at fourteen votes each on the proposal to extend the franchise to women. Council President Petrović cast the tiebreaking vote, sending the proposed Social Democrat alternative to defeat. (The Sarajevo city council thereby came within one vote of enfranchising women before the United States did so with the nineteenth amendment to the US Constitution in 1920.[40]) In the debate, council members showed a willingness to compromise and to abide by majority votes. No side got all it wanted, but the final draft law won the support of all councilmen. Social Democrat Jakšić said the new law, "besides some shortcomings, is much more progressive and modern than the previous law. It should be approved immediately so that the city of Sarajevo can hold elections as soon as possible."[41]

Once it was constituted and its officers elected, the provisional council addressed the urgent problems facing the city: feeding the population, enacting public health measures to combat typhus and tuberculosis, providing for basic education, and restoring a host of basic public services. Within the provisional council, delegates worked to maintain good relations among themselves. In March 1919 Simo Stanivuković apologized to fellow delegate Ilija Badovinac, who had headed the drafting committee for the new electoral law.[42] Badovinac had previously announced his intent to resign because of personal attacks from other council members, but a penitent Stanivuković visited him and emphasized that he had intended nothing personal. Badovinac accepted Stanivuković's apologies and agreed to remain in his position.

Most council members shared the position of the Democratic Party that universal public education should replace the existing system of parochial schools. In January 1919 the provisional council approved a recommendation of the education committee to eliminate parochial schools, "so that our children receive a unified basic education in the interest of our common homeland and its future citizens."[43] If enacted, such a measure would have revolutionized elementary education in the city and abolished a major power base of the several conservative religious establishments. The proposal recommended that pupils in the Muslim school in Bembaša "mix with children of other confessions, and that those of other confessions be accepted in this school." Pupils in the Sephardic school were likewise to be reassigned to other schools, "in the interest of the pupils to learn the Serbian or Croatian language, which they typically do not know." The council ordered a newspaper announcement to advise parents of Serbian Orthodox children that their parochial schools would not be opening, because many parents were apparently unaware of the council's decision to unify and secularize the school system.

The councilmen demonstrated enthusiasm for the new Yugoslav state. They supported the idea of a unified Yugoslav nation of three differently named tribes and a predominant role for the Serbo-Croatian language (also referred to as Serbian or Croatian in the council minutes).[44] The council partook of the strong popular antipathy toward the late Habsburg Monarchy and toward Austria and Hungary. As noted above, the council acquiesced in the Regional Government's decision to annul the nine seats allotted to

Communists. They admitted four professed reformist Social Democrats in their place.

Pragmatism prevailed over theoretical issues of group rights or minority protection, but not all issues of group relations could be readily resolved. At a meeting in February 1919, the Croat cultural society Napredak asked for financial assistance to offer adult literacy courses.[45] A subsequent proposal to provide an identical sum to the Serb and Muslim cultural societies Prosvjeta and Gajret set off a protracted debate. Jewish delegates argued that their cultural society, La Benevolencija, was excluded from this equivalent distribution of spoils, and another delegate suggested a four-way division among the cultural societies. Others noted the absurdity of dividing funds according to a confessional key that gave equal allocations to each society regardless of their numbers and needs. In the end, a majority of council members voted to provide the Croat cultural society with the funds it had requested for adult literacy classes, but to leave the question of funds for other cultural societies for a later time.

Despite the council's considerable achievements in the early postwar months, its members confronted strident opposition from nationalists determined to undermine it. Party politics dogged the council's work from the beginning and hobbled its effectiveness. Four Muslims declined appointments to the council, citing their fears that council members were making decisions of lasting import despite not having been democratically elected.[46] The council appointed other Muslims to replace them. In March 1919 JMO leader Mehmed Spaho, protesting the lack of Muslim representation in the Regional Government of Bosnia-Herzegovina, resigned his position as minister in the royal government in Belgrade.[47] The JMO then notified the city council on May 14 that it was withdrawing its support. In a letter to the council president, the Sarajevo board of the JMO denounced the council as "an illegal body, just a result of willfulness and illegalities, with which our organization does not have, and cannot have, anything in common."[48] In May 1919 several Croat councilmen resigned their positions, citing bitter attacks on them by the Serb nationalist newspaper Srpska riječ. Other Croats replaced them.

Already crippled by nationalist attacks, the council suffered further from neglect by officials of the Regional Government, who simply ignored many of the recommendations forwarded to them. Increasingly frustrated with their superiors' procrastination, the council voted unanimously in May 1919 to press the Regional Government to call elections for a new council.[49]

The newly seated reformist Social Democrat, Jovan Šmitran, reiterated his group's opposition to any election held "by the old statute and using a confessional key." Councilmen set a June 1919 deadline and threatened to resign if the Regional Government did not act on its electoral proposal by then. The deadline passed without the threatened resignations being submitted, but the Regional Government's unresponsiveness opened a rift with the provisional city council that never healed.

Despite their impatience with the Regional Government, the councilmen eagerly awaited a visit to Sarajevo by Regent Aleksandar scheduled for September 21, 1920. But as crowds gathered to greet Aleksandar, the councilmen and the mayor found themselves pushed aside by government officials and an army officer arranging the visit. Mayor Petrović was given no role in the celebratory reception, and his car was placed twenty-sixth in the parade of vehicles that accompanied the king through the city.[50] Council members were denied the prime seats they expected to occupy at the military review. The councilmen aired their resentment at the next council meeting on September 23. Petrović noted that he had earlier asked to meet royal government officials in Belgrade but had received no response (in May 1920 he had offered to resign, but instead he accepted a temporary leave

Carriage of the visiting Yugoslav Regent Aleksandar in front of Sarajevo City Hall, September 21, 1920. (From *Milan Srškić (1890–1937)*, Sarajevo, 1938, facing p. 64)

from office). He was exasperated then, he said, but had decided for "reasons of purely patriotic sacrifice" to remain in his post for the regent's visit to town. He announced his intention to resign and added a request that it not be rejected.

Other councilmen echoed his disgust, saying they were tired of attacks on Petrović as the mayor. Out of love for the city, all of them had accepted the duty cast upon them by the legal Regional Government, said councilman Marković, but that same government had failed to enact an electoral law, had refused to approve the city budget, and had provided little of the material assistance it had promised. The councilmen then voted to resign en masse. Only the reformist Social Democrats, fearing that the royal government would simply appoint a commissar to run the town, voted to oppose the mass resignation. But in the end Bogdanović, a reformist Social Democratic councilman, agreed to serve on the committee to write the explanatory memorandum.

Members of the provisional council demonstrated the irrepressible desire of Sarajevans to work together to improve their lot and that of their city. Democracy, flexibility, and cooperation flourished in the Sarajevo city council for the first two postwar years. But the fruits of the council's labors went unrecognized, and its recommendations were never put into practice. Criticized by the nationalist press and ignored by representatives of the new royal government, the council was eventually engulfed by the rising tide of authoritarian centralization in late 1920. The collective resignation of 1920 brought the life of the provisional council to an ignominious end. Muslims, Jews, Croats, and reformist Social Democrats among the former council members soon directed a letter to the Regional Government, expressing regrets for the misunderstandings on the occasion of the regent's visit and voicing hope that there would be no residual bitterness. Only a group of Serb councilmen held fast and declared themselves done with participating in the council's work, revealing that they were among those most deeply offended by the royal snub.

Repression and the consolidation of autocracy

A wave of repressive and centralizing measures to consolidate the regime's authority in Sarajevo followed the elections for the Constituent Assembly in November 1920. The royal government abolished the Regional Government of Bosnia-Herzegovina by stages in the early 1920s, depriving Sarajevo of its role as a regional administrative center.[51] In July 1921 the central authorities reduced the Regional Government from ten ministries to four. Then in April 1922 the national parliament passed a law dividing the country into thirty-three provinces, six of which were in the geographic region of Bosnia-Herzegovina. Four months later Ljubomir Vulović was named regional governor with the exclusive mission of liquidating the Regional Government's remaining institutions. His work was completed in February 1924, when the last three ministries were dissolved and their functions assumed by ministries of the royal government. The Sarajevo area became one of six administrative units in Bosnia-Herzegovina under a grand governor (*veliki župan*).

The royal government also imposed a regimen of stern control on the city of Sarajevo. The city council's role was severely curtailed after the Constituent Assembly elections of November 1920. The reformist Social Democrats, it turned out, had been right in fearing the imposition of a government strongman following the mass resignation of September 1920. The council's next session, convened on December 12, 1920, was presided over by an appointed government commissar, Ljudevit Nowadt, who exercised broad powers. The appointed councilmen became obedient servants of a de facto royal dictatorship imposed on the city. Much as it had in the early years of Habsburg administration, Sarajevo's city council thereafter functioned in royal Yugoslavia as the handmaiden of central administrative rule.

The government's most drastic steps were reserved for the KP. In the aftermath of communist success in the November 1920 elections for Constituent Assembly, the government redoubled its repression and drove the party underground. In December 1920 (provisionally) and again in August 1921 (permanently), the royal regime banned the party, took sweeping repressive measures against its members, and outlawed pro-Communist public demonstrations and publications. The *Obznana* (Proclamation) of December 28, 1920, was promulgated by the royal council of ministers as an interim measure pending legislative approval of a constitution, which occurred on June 28, 1921. Then members of Red Justice, a shadowy group that included members of the KP, made an attempt on the life of Regent Aleksandar on June 29, 1921, and assassinated Milorad Drašković, the former interior minister who had promulgated the Obznana, on July 21. Shortly thereafter, on August 2, 1921, the assembly enacted the "Law on Defense of Public Security and Order in the State," better known as the "Law on Defense of the State," by a vote of 190 to 54, making the ban permanent.[52]

In Sarajevo the crackdown on KP members in 1920–1 was no less harsh than had been the Habsburg repression of Serbs suspected of sympathy with Young Bosnia. Whereas the Habsburg regime had directed its repression against Serb nationalists, the Karadjordjević government took vengeance on its class enemies.[53] When the Obznana was issued in December 1920, Sarajevans learned that all communist organizations in the city would be dissolved, their meeting facilities closed, the party's archives and property seized, and the publication of *Glas slobode* banned. Arrests of violators would follow.[54] Within days, the authorities expelled 318 party activists from the city and confined them to their municipalities of legal residence. Banishment to one's "place of residence" was made possible by restrictive laws governing residency and the fact that many activists were recent immigrants to the city.[55]

Police repression changed both the character of the Communist movement in Sarajevo and the nature of electoral competition in the city. For the next two decades, the KP was reduced to a small conspiratorial group, its effectiveness hobbled by periodic repression and its members watched by police spies. Its numbers were decimated from the 1920 high of about 2,100. Sarajevo historian Budimir Miličić, based on a study of party records, concluded that the number of party members in Sarajevo from 1921–40 never exceeded 120 and fell as low as 26.[56] The Communist youth organization likewise included fewer than one hundred active members at most times during those twenty years. Before the ban, the party had been the primary alternative to single-national parties devoted to nationalist distinctions. By banning and crippling the party, the government effectively disenfranchised over a quarter of the 1920 electorate and allowed the national parties to dominate the city's electoral landscape for the next twenty years.

Autocracy and democracy in the city council, 1920–9

The royal government repeatedly postponed elections for Sarajevo's city council during the 1920s, despite expeditiously holding an election for the Constituent Assembly in November 1920 and three subsequent elections (March 1923, February 1925, and September 1927) for the National Assembly. The reasons for these postponements were political.[57] As noted above, the appointed city council in March 1919 had approved an electoral statute and forwarded it to the Regional Government with the expectation that elections were imminent, but the authorities postponed the election when it became apparent that the JMO and KP would receive the most votes. With the outlawing of the KP in December 1920, the authorities became concerned principally with the prospect of a JMO victory in any election. With the JMO in the opposition in royal Yugoslavia through most of the 1920s, the government appointed mostly councilmen from the Radical Party, knowing that they would faithfully rubber-stamp measures proposed by the government-appointed supervisor. Other appointees were selected from the ranks of the JMO and the HSS, but they, too, were compliant.

JMO leaders complained vehemently of the government's usurpation of power in the council. They campaigned for passage of a measure granting local self-government to cities in Bosnia-Herzegovina, but were met by determined opposition and obstruction. The JMO attributed Sarajevo's economic and political stagnation to the interminable legislative delays and the authoritarian rule of the city commissars. Addressing a party rally in Sarajevo in September 1927, JMO President Mehmed Spaho called the commissars' regime "illegal and unconstitutional" and called for an end to the stagnation and neglect:

[For] seven to eight years nothing has been done here, neither railways nor roads have been built, and here, in our Sarajevo, not a single large building has been erected. The state spends nothing here, but taxes are paid in the same measure, perhaps even greater measure, than in other places. We shall raise our voices against these injustices, which have particularly been directed against Bosnia-Herzegovina, and seek to have them rectified.[58]

The vicissitudes of political alliances finally resulted in late 1927 in passage of a law on municipal self-government for the area of Bosnia-Herzegovina. City council elections were subsequently scheduled (after one additional postponement) for October 1928. With elections imminent, the royal regime realigned the membership of the Sarajevo city council by appointing a majority of delegates from a combination of the JMO and HSS, leaving Radicals in the minority. With these appointments, the government prefigured the probable results of the impending election and prepared a smooth transfer to JMO-HSS rule. The government appointed Edhem Bičakčić, a JMO member considered loyal to the government, as the new city commissar to oversee the transition.

With its new commissar and delegates, the council became for most of 1928 a forum for complaints about neglect, malfeasance, and corruption under the previous leadership. Few new initiatives came forth from this appointed transitional body, but the discussions were lively and infused with hopes for a positive outcome from the impending, oft-postponed elections. When the balloting finally took place as scheduled in October 1928, the voters returned most incumbents to the council. The JMO-HSS coalition emerged with a majority of twenty council members, while the Radicals and a few minor parties controlled a total of fifteen seats. Members of the majority coalition united in electing Bičakčić as mayor, while the Radicals cast blank ballots in protest.

The era of democratic self-government in Sarajevo was distressingly brief (lasting only sixty-two days) and hopelessly contentious. In city council deliberations, delegates of the nationalist parties consistently behaved badly. They largely ignored substantive issues of city management and instead dwelled upon ceremonial and symbolic matters. The outnumbered members of the Radical Party ostentatiously boycotted or protested the actions of the majority Muslim-Croat coalition. Dissatisfied with the appointments they received to the council's working committees, the Radicals cast blank ballots for all committee appointments, which were each passed by twenty-one or twenty-two votes of the majority. Presented with a draft telegram from the council to King Aleksandar, one Radical delegate proposed alternate wording that added the phrases "founder of the Serbian state" to an already loquacious expression of praise and loyalty. And Radical delegates criticized Mayor Bičakčić for failing to make adequate preparations for the two holidays of November 6 (in honor of Serbian troops entering Sarajevo in 1918) and December 1 (the proclamation of the kingdom in 1918).

Furthermore, the shabby, unproductive debates were held in the dark shadow of adverse events elsewhere in the kingdom. In June 1928 the HSS leader Stjepan Radić had been shot on the floor of the National Assembly in the wake of increasingly vitriolic rhetoric between Serb and Croat deputies. He died of his wounds in August. King Aleksandar and his advisors subsequently resolved to put an end to partisan contention by establishing a royal dictatorship and suspending the constitution. The proclamation of the dictatorship on January 6, 1929, spelled an end to the short-lived elected council and the acrimonious deliberations that had characterized its three sessions.

Autocratic centralism, 1929–39

The royal dictatorship was the culmination of the autocratic centralization instituted during the kingdom's first days rather than an abrupt departure from parliamentary democracy. For the Sarajevo city council, the dictatorship restored the autocratic centralist regime that had been in effect from December 1920 until the council elections of 1928. Autocracy was also the hallmark of the king's relations with the National Assembly. In his authoritative analysis of the January dictatorship, Yugoslav historian Nedim Šarac has shown that Regent and King Aleksandar, far from reluctantly imposing authoritarian rule on squabbling parliamentary factions, zealously pursued autocratic centralism from the early months of his regime, bringing his policies to their logical culmination in assuming dictatorial powers in 1929.[59] Throughout the 1920s Aleksandar manipulated, discredited, and marginalized parliamentary institutions, producing, in Šarac's words, a "dysfunctional semi-parliamentary system."[60]

Nevertheless the king acquired unprecedented autocratic authority in the first few years after dictatorship was imposed. The royal ruler suspended the constitution, issued decrees banning political organizations based on nationality or religion, dissolved the National Assembly, and renamed the country the "Kingdom of Yugoslavia" to reflect a more unitary structure. Implementing a variant of a proposal long favored by many Radicals, he abolished administrative units based on historical boundaries and introduced nine new administrative units called *banovinas*, each named after natural features and headed by an appointed governor (*ban*). Sarajevo was part of the Drina Banovina (*Drinska banovina*) and was designated as its administrative center, restoring a modicum of the city's previous status as a regional capital.

In short order the city council that had been elected in October 1928 was dissolved and replaced by an appointed body in February 1929.[61] Under the royal dictatorship, city councils in Belgrade, Zagreb, and Ljubljana were appointed by the king, but members of the Sarajevo council were designated by the governor of the Drina Banovina, signaling the city's second-class stature in the kingdom.[62] The appointed Sarajevo council of 1929 obediently acquiesced to the regime's dictates. In the first few meetings, council delegates scrambled to meet government-imposed deadlines to prepare a budget. Its debates reveal awareness that its conclusions could be overruled at any time by higher authorities.[63]

On the same day that he declared royal dictatorship, the king announced a new hand-picked government headed by General Petar Živković as prime minister. Milan Srškić was appointed minister of justice. From that position, and subsequently as prime minister from July 1932 to January 1934, Srškić became the principal architect of the legal order imposed under the dicta-

torship.[64] In a sweeping overhaul of the legal system, he oversaw the replacement of six different legal systems left over from the prewar political
entities with a comprehensive system of standard laws for all the kingdom.
He oversaw the drafting of a new constitution promulgated by the king in
September 1931, which provided for a cautious return of carefully controlled parliamentary life. The constitution gave a façade of parliamentar-
ianism to the royal dictatorship, but it did not divest the ruler of any real
power.[65] Delegates to the National Assembly could propose and debate legislation, but they could not enact measures independently. Electoral rules
posed insurmountable obstacles to all but candidates of the government-
sponsored Yugoslav National Party, which won all 306 seats at the first
election held under the new constitution.

As minister of justice, Srškić oversaw the drafting of a law that placed
Bosnian Islamic institutions under his ministry. Reis-ul-ulema Džemaludin
Čaušević protested vigorously but in vain to Srškić and the king after seeing
preliminary drafts of the act.[66] The law eliminated the autonomy enjoyed by
the Bosnian Islamic hierarchy as established in the Habsburg-era statute of
1909.[67] The Reis and other Muslim institutions were to relocate to Belgrade
and oversee from there the work of subordinate councils in Sarajevo and the
Macedonian city of Skopje. When the law with its unfavorable provisions
was promulgated on January 31, 1930, the Reis applied to retire from his
position. On June 6 the government approved his request and replaced him
with Ibrahim Maglajlić, a retired mufti who had served in other Bosnian
cities. Maglajlić was installed in an elaborate ceremony in Belgrade in
October 1930 and proceeded to administer Islamic affairs from there. These
changes ended the Bosnian Muslims' treasured religious autonomy and
eliminated several significant institutions in Sarajevo.

In October 1934 King Aleksandar was assassinated while visiting Marseilles. The killing was carried out by a Macedonian, but members of an
extreme Croat national group, the Ustasha, had participated in the planning.
The heir to the throne, Aleksandar's son Petar II, was only eleven years old at
the time, so a three-man regency headed by Aleksandar's cousin Paul was
designated to rule until Petar reached eighteen years of age in 1941.[68]
Although Petar II was to have little impact on policy in royal Yugoslavia
because of his youth, he was frequently honored as "Successor Petar" in the
memorial culture of the time. He fled ahead of the German invasion in 1941
and remained titular head of the government-in-exile in London until the
monarchy was abolished in 1946.

Regent Paul presided over a gradual relaxation of some political controls that Aleksandar had introduced. Many political prisoners were released (including Vladko Maček, leader of the HSS), police repression abated, and censorship was relaxed. The 1931 constitution was retained, but party activity gradually revived with the return of more open and pluralist public political life. Elections for the National Assembly and city councils were held in February 1935. Milan Stojadinović shortly thereafter formed a new government based on a coalition that included the Radicals, the JMO, and the Slovene People's Party. Although Stojadinović brought a measure of stability to the country's political life, his government also moved the country toward dangerous economic dependence on Germany and Italy.

In Sarajevo political relaxation did not undo the consequences of prolonged economic stagnation and pressure on the city's resources. In 1938 the city had an annual budget of 400 dinars per inhabitant, compared to Zagreb's 1,118 dinars, Ljubljana's 1,230 dinars, and Belgrade's 1,300 dinars.[69] The elected city council leaders regularly complained that they lacked the authority to address the city's basic needs. In his assessment of the city's plight in March 1939, Mayor Muhamed Zlatar dismissed the notion of self-government as a fiction. He blamed the twin evils of centralization and economic depression for the city's woes:

The economic depression has left its clearest tracks in the cities, and among [cities] most severely has affected Sarajevo. ... That same economic depression has prevented or hindered an influx of municipal income at a time when that income is so necessary to fight unemployment and to mitigate misery and poverty. ... Rather than the state helping us with our work, we must divert millions from our depressed budget to meet the needs of the state and banovina.[70]

Thus for Sarajevo's elected officials, autocratic centralism continued to impede their ability to conduct basic governing functions.

Memorial culture

Sarajevo's participation in the new Yugoslav state meant the eradication of the memorial culture developed under Habsburg rule. In the first two postwar years, Sarajevans experimented with several holidays and memorials, only to find that the character of memorial culture, like so many other aspects of life in royal Yugoslavia, would be decided for them by the regime. Memorial culture in the interwar era unfolded as a testament to the royals' intent to enshrine the house of Karadjordjević as the centerpiece of a unified, centralized state. Nearly all organized political groups in Sarajevo endorsed the notion of a single Yugoslav nationality consisting of "three named tribes"—the Serbs, Croats, and Slovenes. This was an extraordinary consensus, particularly since the same groups disagreed sharply with one another concerning the political structure the new state should assume. The near consensus on Yugoslavism, however, was all but meaningless, for the trinomial concept left a chasm of ambiguity between ideology and implementation. The elusive concept adroitly sidestepped the questions of whether, when, and how the three tribes might fuse into a single, unified nationality.

In an effort to restructure memorial life in Sarajevo under the new Yugoslav state, political leaders first turned to celebrating separately the heroes of the three named tribes. They also experimented with joint celebrations for heroes from two of the three tribes. But the efforts to promote a common identity consisted mainly of celebrating key events in the life of the Karadjordjević dynasty, an uncanny echo of the imperial cult promoted in Habsburg times. Like its Austro-Hungarian era predecessors, members of the postwar council renamed major streets in their first days in office. The street name changes signified the triumph of South Slav values over memories of Habsburg imperial rule. (Renaming streets became standard practice for each new regime in the twentieth century.) Even before electing permanent officers, the council voted to rename Čemaluša Street as Aleksandar Street and changed Franz Joseph Street to King Petar Street (after Aleksandar's father).[71] The council approved renaming forty-three additional streets on January 10, 1919, so the city could be, in the words of one delegate, "nationalized as much as possible."[72]

Approximately equal numbers of Serb and Croat heroes were honored in the renamed streets, while somewhat fewer Bosnian Muslim figures were honored, among them Husein-kapetan Gradaščević, who led a revolt against Ottoman policies in 1831–2 (see pp. 29–30). No Jews were recognized in the changed street names. Three foreigners were honored for their contributions either to Sarajevo or to the formation of the Yugoslav state: Kállay Walkway, which had honored Benjamin Kállay's twenty years as administrator of Bosnia-Herzegovina, became Wilson Walkway after the US President Woodrow Wilson, who championed national self-determination; the English educator Elizabeth Irby was honored with an eponymous street; and the square in front of Officers' Hall was named after the former French Prime Minister Georges Clemenceau (*Klemantsovjev trg*).

The Social Democratic delegate Krešić opposed renaming Josip Vancaš Street because, even though Vancaš had been his political opponent, he had "done great service for the city of Sarajevo." If Vancaš's offense had been to favor Great Croatia, Krešić asserted, many others were equally guilty of supporting Great Serbia.[73] Krešić's appeal was ignored, and the street named after Sarajevo's master architect assumed the name of Jovan Skerlić, a Sarajevo Serb poet whose program had been adopted by student radicals on the eve of the First World War. The council approved only forty-three changes despite the urging of Social Democrat delegates to change many more names so that Sarajevo would "lose its old feudal character." Most delegates favored changing only those names that "recalled the old regime."

Many events were honored as unofficial holidays in 1919, but not all became enshrined in the official calendar of annual holidays endorsed by the state. January 27 was honored as St. Sava Day, commemorating the Serbian royal family member who procured recognition of an autocephalous Serbian Orthodox Church from the Ecumenical Patriarch in 1219. To demonstrate his support for Croat heroes, Regent Aleksandar traveled to Zagreb for festivities honoring Zrinjski and Frankopan on April 30, 1919. In honoring these two seventeenth-century figures who met death at the hands of a Habsburg duke, the regent both spurned the Habsburg legacy and lionized heroes. Croats in Sarajevo also celebrated that holiday, but non-Croats did not participate, just as non-Serbs had shunned St. Sava Day. The rally on St. Sava Day, organized by the Democratic Party to bring together all nationalities, had erupted into an emotive appeal to join Bosnia-Herzegovina with Serbia, an idea unpopular among both Croats and Muslims in Sarajevo.

With backing from key members of the Regional Government, Sarajevans of Serb and Croat nationality attempted to forge a joint celebration on June 1, 1919, to honor the Croat writer Silvije Kranjčević and the Serb poet Jovan Skerlić.[74] The Croat singing group Trebević and the Serb group Sloga performed side by side, probably for the first time. But the event flopped. Officers' Hall, with seating capacity for several hundred guests, was largely empty except for Regional Government President Atanasije Šola, Sarajevo Mayor Aristotel Petrović, and some royal army officers. Neither Serbs nor Croats appeared inclined to participate in an event that hinted at a possible fusion of the two groups into a single Yugoslav nationality.

The Yugoslav government promoted the Karadjordjević family above all. Celebration of royal birthdays, reminiscent of the cult of the imperial family propagated in Habsburg times, employed many of the same practices, particularly in the prominence given to the confessional communities and the strict schedule of religious services and congratulatory delegations. On December 17, 1920, the celebration of Regent Aleksandar's birthday began before 8:00 a.m. with military formations in front of both the cathedral and the new Serbian Orthodox church.[75] The authorities mandated that religious services be held at specified times throughout the morning. Serbian Orthodox held their service at 8:20 a.m. in the new Serbian Orthodox church, and Catholics followed with a service at 9:00 a.m. in the cathedral. Sephardim, Ashkenazim, and Evangelical Protestants held simultaneous services at 10:00 a.m. in their respective houses of worship. Two hours were allotted for congratulatory delegations to call on Milan Srškić, then the president of the Regional Government. At noon, Muslims gathered for a service led by the Reis-ul-ulema at the Gazi Husrevbeg Mosque. The day concluded with musical events on city streets in the evening and a reception at Officers' Hall at 9:00 p.m.

In December 1920 the royal government's Minister of Religion decreed that five nationwide holidays were to be celebrated.[76] Two holidays were birthdays of the country's monarchs: King Petar I (July 12) and Regent Aleksandar (December 17). A third holiday was the anniversary of the Yugoslav state (December 1), the "day of proclamation of Serbs, Croats, and Slovenes and a single Kingdom of Serbs, Croats, and Slovenes." A fourth holiday, Vidovdan (June 28), attempted to convert an unambiguously Serb event into a memorial for Yugoslav soldiers. That day was described as a "celebratory memorial to all fallen warriors for faith and homeland." In addition, the "first Slavic apostles," Cyril and Methodius, were to be honored on May 24. Sarajevans, not known to insist on working when a holiday was at hand, observed each of these holidays, and some even celebrated them. Sarajevans also acquired a holiday unique to the city: November 6, the day that Serbian troops entered Sarajevo in 1918. That holiday drew little attention in 1919 and 1920, but major festivities were organized by the government in 1921, and it continued to be a major secular holiday during the rest of the interwar period.[77]

The cult of the Karadjordjević family overshadowed all other memorial activities from 1921 onward, culminating in an obsession with the royal house following the proclamation of royal dictatorship in 1929. In 1940 the city council voted to erect a statue of King Petar I, Aleksandar's father, one block south of King Aleksandar Street in King Petar Square between *King* Petar Street and *Successor* Petar Street (named after Aleksandar's son Petar

II).[78] The council allocated 1,285,000 dinars to the project, almost 6 percent of the city's annual budget, at the same meeting at which delegates scrounged for funds to distribute food to the needy in "the poorest city in Yugoslavia—Sarajevo." Owing to the outbreak of war, the statue was never completed.

Despite the many efforts to promote unity of the country and emphasize the common attributes of the three named tribes, ethnoconfessional communities became more distinct in the course of the interwar period. Virtually all Serbs and Croats were aware of their nationality, based on and largely congruent with their religious identity. Jews and Muslims defined their group identities principally by religion, although some Muslims adopted Serb or Croat national identity while participating in public life as Muslims. Their religious identity was respected in the city's public life as the equivalent of Serb or Croat national identity. Capitalist economic relations tended to promote the mixing of peoples and contributed to some integration of the city's associational life so that intermingling was typical among workers in the newer, industrial sector of the economy, as well as in the political groupings that grew out of that sector. Interaction did not lead to assimilation; ethnoconfessional identities remained distinct as they had in previous times. But there was a dearth of violence or overt conflict along ethnic or confessional lines during royal Yugoslav rule.

Social evolution and economic stagnation

In the two decades after the First World War, Sarajevo's population resumed growth at approximately the same annual rate as before the war, increasing from about 58,000 in early 1919 to around 90,000 (an increase of 55 percent) by 1941.[79] Much of the growth came from immigration into the city, principally from villages in Bosnia-Herzegovina.[80] Surveys taken during the 1930s showed that fewer than half of Sarajevo's residents had been born there; 90 percent of those born elsewhere came from other locations within Yugoslavia.[81] Paradoxically the continued immigration into Sarajevo was not occasioned by economic growth but instead coincided with two decades of stagnation and decline. The disparity between the rising needs of a growing population and the city's dwindling capacity to meet them meant economic deprivation and descent into poverty for many Sarajevans.

The root causes of the disparity lay in the countryside. A protracted agrarian crisis in the interwar years was induced by falling agricultural prices, rural overpopulation, and the fragmentation of arable landhold-ings.[82] Yugoslavia's agrarian reforms in many ways aggravated the crisis in Bosnia-Herzegovina.[83] Landholdings of both peasants and former landlords were further fragmented, increasing the number of dwarf holdings that were too small to support a single family.[84] The trends adversely affected Serb, Croat, and Muslim smallholders alike, pressuring many to move to towns and cities. Most immigrants to Sarajevo were driven by desperation rather than drawn by opportunity. They arrived with few skills, no resources, and inflated expectations. Their presence further burdened the city's already strained resources. At times, government officials tried to persuade others not to follow them. In January 1923 the Regional Gov-ernment entreated rural inhabitants, insofar as they had habitable shelter, to stay put rather than succumb to Sarajevo's illusory appeal.[85]

In addition to the legally mandated reallocation of land, many Muslim landowners and peasants were dispossessed in the early years of the new Yugoslav state by peasants, primarily Serbs, who seized land by force in anticipation of radical agrarian reforms. The seizures, sometimes accom-panied by personal violence against Muslims, were concentrated in areas where brigandage and insecurity were common in transitional times. Some Muslims followed a well-trodden path of seeking refuge in Sarajevo from assault by bandits and peasant rebels. Already in February 1920 a Muslim city council delegate complained, "We in Sarajevo especially have masses of indigent."[86] The numbers of indigent in the city would only grow over the years of royal Yugoslav rule.

Overall growth obscured substantial changes in the structure of the city's population, particularly in the first few years after war's end. Many citizens of Austria and Hungary, including some longtime residents of the city, were suddenly considered foreigners. Most found their skills devalued, their prior achievements dismissed, and their citizenship disparaged. The new desiderata for city appointments were summarized in the Sarajevo city council's decision in 1919 to select a doctor who had "complete command of the Serbian language and is our citizen" over a man who had not mastered the language and was not a citizen of the Yugoslav state.[87] Some voluntarily returned to their homelands; others were driven out by discrimination in jobs that had drawn them there in the first place. Josip Vancaš, master architect of the cityscape and resident of the city for almost four decades, was among those who left. He returned to his native Croatia in 1922, having become distinctly unappreciated because of his association with the city's Habsburg past.

The city's economic misfortunes broadly tracked the major crises that befell central and southeastern Europe in the two decades after the First World War. These included the economic damage and dislocations of the war itself; the worldwide fall in agricultural prices that became acute in the mid 1920s; the Great Depression of 1929–34; and a wave of inflation that accompanied closer ties between Yugoslavia and the Axis powers in 1940–1. In addition to these cyclical economic woes, the city's three most important economic sectors—traditional craft production, primary industry, and administrative services—proved vulnerable to two long-term secular changes: the intrusion of capitalist market relations into traditional economic sectors, and the city's relegation to secondary significance by the royal government. Generally speaking, poverty and wealth coexisted in each of the four ethnoconfessional communities. No group monopolized the benefits of the era's meager prosperity, and members of all four groups shared the widespread misery of the urban poor.

The first crises to confront the city were ruinous shortages of basic commodities caused by the disruptions of war. The First World War had extensively damaged the fields, roads, and railroads of Bosnia-Herzegovina, and the new political situation further disrupted the flow of agricultural products into the city. The entire sugar beet crop in northern Bosnia was wiped out, and the number of livestock was reduced by over 50 percent during the war. Owing to archaic regulations, agricultural goods could be shipped from Vojvodina abroad but not to the other parts of Yugoslavia that desperately needed them.[88] The city council's pleas to the royal government evoked a sympathetic response but little concrete assistance.[89] Fortunately sugar was among the goods provided by the American Relief Administration in spring 1919.[90] The shortages persisted, however, and in December 1919 the city council dispatched an emissary to Brod to purchase four wagons of sugar. It considered and rejected a proposal to take the bold step of purchasing twenty-five wagons of sugar directly from merchants in Prague without informing the Yugoslav royal government.[91]

Despite the growth of competitive pressures, life in the Sarajevo marketplace went on much as it had since the sixteenth century. Craftsmen and artisans produced goods and provided services for a market that usually extended no farther than villages near the city. Their shops were scattered over a wide area along both sides of the Miljacka River, principally in the older part of the city east of the Regional Government Building, and many were concentrated in the Baščaršija in the city's eastern end.[92] As a whole, craft producers were religiously heterogeneous, but many trades were monopolized by a single group. Jews, accounting for nearly 20 percent of all shops, were generously overrepresented compared to their percentage of the population. Muslims and Catholics were only slightly overrepresented among the tradesmen, and Serbian Orthodox were underrepresented. Peasants came to the city on market days to trade and mingle, and the Baščaršija remained a colorful combination of social encounters and business transactions. The korzo, practiced since Austro-Hungarian days, continued as the evening outing for many Sarajevans.

Renewed intrusion of capitalist market relations into traditional economic sectors accompanied war's end. Competition continued to ruin the livelihoods of Sarajevo's craftsmen and artisans. The monopolistic *esnafi*, the Ottoman equivalent of medieval guilds, had been abolished by Ottoman reformers in 1851, but some craftsmen continued to enjoy the benefits of government-monitored certifications and concessions. These individual operators largely remained mired in traditional practices and undertook few measures to make their products more competitive. As demand for their products slackened with the influx of cheap mass-produced items, tradesmen found these barriers ineffective to prevent the entry of new, unauthorized competitors into the trades.

Many immigrants to the city, desperate to survive in the troubled economy, tried their hand at craft production. In April 1920 a city council member complained that in Sarajevo, unlike in Serbia, "There are women who have no idea about a craft but nevertheless open shops." Another delegate appealed for a uniform crafts law to apply throughout the kingdom so that "no one without specialist training can receive a concession for any craft."[93] Despite these concerns, the government found no effective way to prevent unauthorized persons from entering the trades. But Budimir Miličić, a historian who has studied the precipitous collapse of crafts production in this period, points out that establishing a shop was a risky venture, and few new shops survived for long.[94] In 1927–33 a total of 1,569 new shops were opened and 944 closed permanently.

Industrial production made up the city's largest economic sector. Most production stopped during the First World War, but because warfare never reached the city, production capacity was little disturbed and remained available when consumers returned to the marketplace. Several large factories were nationalized after the war. A trio of state-owned factories dominated the city's economic output and became key centers of labor unrest:

The varied activity in the Baščaršija
(Main Market), a commercial center
and scene of social outings that drew
men and women of all confessional
communities.

(Photographs from *Sarajevo na bɑščɑršijɑ i po čɑršijskim ulicama*, 1920–40 [Sarajevo in the Baščaršija and on the streets of the čaršija], courtesy of Historical Archive, Sarajevo)

the Main Railway Workshop, the Military Technical Enterprise (which produced military equipment), and the tobacco factory. Many factories were
reactivated in the first half of the 1920s, but the industrial recovery proved
to be short-lived. The erosion of peasant purchasing power occasioned by
the collapse of agricultural prices in the mid-1920s caused demand to level
off and eventually decline. The Great Depression of 1929–34 devastated the
manufacturing sector, and recovery in the latter half of the 1930s was
sporadic and slow. A report from 1938 mentioned a "veritable graveyard" of
factories in Sarajevo's west side.[95]

Amid general economic stagnation, only commercial trade can be said to
have expanded between the two wars, and only the largest, most capital-
intensive enterprises truly thrived. As in craft production, merchants were
organized into individual businesses, from fewer than 1,500 during the
Depression to 2,500 in better times.[96] Serbs and Jews predominated among
owners of the larger mercantile houses. Muslims owned by far the greatest
number of enterprises (43 percent of all firms in 1935), but most were small
family shops. Croats were underrepresented in both large and small mercantile enterprises.

Along with expanded commercial ties, overnight hotel stays in Sarajevo
increased from 21,904 in 1923 to 45,720 in 1939. The hostelry business
was also supported by a small but growing number of tourists. The budget
report for 1940 noted that although Dubrovnik was the leading destination
for European tourists, some were drawn to Sarajevo "not so much for our
new buildings but for our Oriental local color. ... We must jealously preserve it if we want to maintain or increase tourism."[97] The core tourist
attractions were the tiny shops in the Baščaršija, the monumental mosques,
and Habsburg-era neo-Orientalist structures.[98] Archaic shops and traditional craft production held an allure for tourists that they lacked as competitive enterprises.

Only a few major new structures were built during the twenty-three
years of royal Yugoslavia. Among them was the neoclassical new Jewish synagogue, a Sephardic place of worship in the middle of the old city along the
river. Its bold cylindrical design and ornate interior made it an appropriate
statement for a group that had previously worshipped in tiny synagogues on
the periphery of the Baščaršija. Another structure, built as an office building,
still stands. It is called simply the Skyscraper despite being only a dozen
stories tall. It recalls an airport control tower and adds nothing to the skyline
of the central city where it is located. Most other new structures, including

several residential complexes in the city center, were modernist in design. But the interwar era in Sarajevo was principally characterized by the continuation of spatial distribution and land usage inaugurated in the Austro-Hungarian era. The single most significant exception was the new regime's reordering of memorial culture.

Sarajevo and the Cvetković-Maček Agreement (1939–41)

Among the kingdom's Serb leaders, the notion of granting a measure of autonomy to Croats was never completely off the agenda. The idea gained appeal in the late 1930s with the increasingly apparent inadequacies of autocratic centralism and the growing implicit military threat from Germany and Italy. It was no surprise that Mehmed Spaho and Milan Srškić had divergent views about such a prospect. Srškić, unlike many Radical Party members, had long favored seeking a Serb-Croat agreement, and in 1936 he convened in Sarajevo a meeting of Serb politicians prepared to advance the idea. Spaho, on the other hand, was wary that such a pact might come at the expense of the Bosnian Muslims. Both men died, however, before a deal was struck, Srškić in 1937 and Spaho in 1939. The agreement to restructure the state was thus undertaken in the absence of the two most prominent Sarajevo politicians of the interwar era.

In February 1939 Prince Paul dismissed the Stojadinović government and selected Dragiša Cvetković as the new prime minister. Cvetković was asked to seek a compromise with the Croat political leadership. Shortly after taking office, he began talks with Vladko Maček, president of the HSS, who had rejected such a possibility as long as Stojadinović was in office. The lengthy and difficult talks proceeded into the summer of 1939. On June 29, 1939, word arrived in Sarajevo of the death of JMO leader Mehmed Spaho in a Belgrade hotel room. The city council immediately convened a memorial session to honor the revered leader of the Bosnian Muslims. His funeral in Sarajevo on June 30 was attended by a crowd estimated at thirty thousand. In delivering his eulogy, Yugoslav Prime Minister Cvetković singled out a relatively minor episode in Spaho's political life. He praised Spaho for his commitment to the "cooperation of brothers of all religions and all national forces" and specifically credited him with "creating conditions for the revival of Serb-Croat cooperation in the state" in 1928.[99]

Behind Cvetković's accolades lay a desire to invoke Spaho's legacy for an historic Serb-Croat compromise about to be struck. In his last weeks, Spaho had become a thorn in the side of negotiators, insisting on plebiscites and injecting the issue of Bosnian Muslim rights into the talks. Spaho's death removed a major obstacle to reaching a final agreement.[100] Cvetković and Maček subsequently came to terms in late August 1939. Their agreement created a large Croat banovina consisting of historic Croatian lands, parts of Central and Northern Bosnia, Western Herzegovina, and several other areas with substantial Croat populations. The new Croat banovina was to have its own governor and assembly. The agreement also paved the way for a new Yugoslav government to be formed on August 28. Cvetković remained prime minister, Maček became deputy prime minister, the Bosnian Croat HSS leader Juraj Šutej was appointed minister of finance, and Džafer Kulenović, Spaho's successor as president of the JMO, was made minister of forests and mines.

Many Sarajevans hailed the Cvetković-Maček Agreement (also known as the Banovina Plan or simply as the *Sporazum*, or agreement). Šutej received a festive welcome at the railway station upon his return to the city from participation in the talks.[101] The JMO lent more cautious support, referring to the agreement as an interim step toward a definitive resolution. *Pravda*, the party's official newspaper, asserted, "This first level of agreement does not contradict our essential interests."[102] But the party subsequently voiced grave reservations about the agreement, correctly sensing that it divided Bosnia-Herzegovina between Serbs and Croats, with no regard for the Bosnian Muslims. And the new arrangement stilled national strife in the kingdom only briefly. Hundreds of thousands of Croats were left outside the Croat banovina in Serb-dominated areas, including tens of thousands in Sarajevo, which remained in the Drina Banovina. And about 866,000 Serbs were left in areas awarded to the Croats.[103] Some of them demanded revisions of the map to return them to Serb-majority rule.[104] The new arrangement also failed to ameliorate the fundamental economic plight that bedeviled Sarajevo, and its city council continued to be deprived of the tools to control its own destiny.

Along with the rest of Yugoslavia, Sarajevo experienced a modest economic revival as a byproduct of the country's growing integration into the German economic orbit in the late 1930s. Germany's dynamic economy, driven by Hitler's war preparations, consumed many of the raw materials abundantly available in Bosnia-Herzegovina, but wages did not keep up with inflation.[105] Many Sarajevans fell deeper into poverty, and the city continued to struggle with the ballooning fiscal crisis brought on by the "pauperization of the middle class that was the primary basis of communal income: merchants, craftsmen, and the working class," according to Mayor Zlatar.[106] In March 1940 city council delegate Nikola Prnjatović reported that twenty thousand Sarajevans required some form of assistance, and another fifty thousand contributed nothing to the city's coffers. "So ten to fifteen thousand residents, businessmen, and wealthier citizens bear the burden of all municipal obligations. The entire city budget is carried on their shoulders."[107] Further evidence of widespread impoverishment was provided by the city ambulance service. In 1939 it transported 2,046 patients to medical facilities; 1,544 were too poor to pay for the service.[108]

The city council in 1940 resorted to the same desperate financial measures as Habsburg-era councils and the postwar council of the kingdom. Upon pleas by some council members to establish a rationing system, the council created a special agency to distribute provisions similar to the rationing boards that had existed during the First World War under detested Habsburg rule. Faced with chronic revenue shortfalls, the city council in 1940 voted to borrow money rather than to drain the city's pension fund. At the end of 1940, in one of its last acts prior to the beginning of the Second World War, Sarajevo borrowed five million dinars for operating expenses from a Belgrade bank at 5 percent interest over thirty months.[109]

Unlike the advent of the First World War twenty-seven years before, the origins of the Second World War unfolded far from Sarajevo, but the city suffered acutely from the prolonged economic crisis, the drift toward authoritarianism, and the emergence of virulent German and Italian fascism. The interminable and intractable crises of the interwar period left the city ill prepared to cope with a sustained conflict, let alone an occupation. War came in 1941 to a city desperately in need of a return to vitality and a revival of spirit. Its residents were ill prepared for the suffering they would endure, and the sacrifices they would be called upon to make, in the ensuing four years.

6. Occupation and Urban Resistance in the Second World War

Fascism came to Sarajevo in April 1941. Beginning with the German conquest of Yugoslavia, the city endured a combination of harsh German military occupation and malevolent governance by Nazi collaborators. The occupiers and their collaborators wrought immeasurable harm in Sarajevo. They exterminated a significant part of the population, altered the city's demographic balance for the indefinite future, and governed principally through terror and intimidation. Their oppression spurred the growth of opposition movements, some of them peaceful and relatively impotent, others armed and dangerous to the occupiers and their allies. The Communist-led Partisans, the most successful of these movements, undermined and eventually destroyed the forces of the occupiers and their collaborators. Their final victory in April 1945 owed much to an urban-rural lifeline that allowed the KP inside occupied Sarajevo to mount clandestine operations in support of the Partisans in the surrounding hills.

German conquest and occupation
Launching the Axis attack on Yugoslavia, German bombers attacked Belgrade and Sarajevo on April 6, 1941; their raids on Sarajevo struck the airport (then located at Rajlovac) beginning at 6:00 a.m.[1] German, Italian, Hungarian, and Bulgarian forces invaded shortly thereafter. The inept, demoralized Yugoslav royal army offered little effective resistance. Fleeing Belgrade, the royal family, along with top civilian officials and the royal army's high command, sought refuge in Pale, the mountain village northeast of Sarajevo that was to become the headquarters of Radovan Karadžić and the Bosnian Serb leaders during the siege of the 1990s. A week later, on April 12–13, Italian bombers struck Sarajevo in a campaign of apparently indiscriminate bombing, killing civilians and wreaking widespread destruction on the city.[2] With German forces advancing rapidly, Sarajevans

crowded the main train station in the desperate hope of leaving before the occupiers arrived.

Yugoslav royal army units in the vicinity of Sarajevo offered meager resistance. On the night of April 13–14, leaders of the vestigial Yugoslav royal government in Pale decided to flee the country and go into exile. Young King Petar II, his entourage, and government ministers fled southeast through Montenegro and Greece en route to Cairo and their final destination in London. With their leaders having abandoned the country, remaining royal army forces in the vicinity of Sarajevo gave up the fight and dissolved in disarray. Vladimir Dedijer, a young Communist who had fled Belgrade in hopes of joining any armed formation offering resistance, finally located a small royal Yugoslav army antiaircraft unit near Sarajevo on April 15. Dedijer recorded the words of the unit commander: "Get out of here as soon as you can; Yugoslavia is finished. The Germans will soon be here."[3] The first German troops entered the city the same day.

German forces quickly set the tone for their occupation. On their first day in Sarajevo, they removed the plaque commemorating Gavrilo Princip's 1914 assassination of the Habsburg Archduke Franz Ferdinand and sent it to Adolf Hitler. On their second day in town they sacked the recently built (1929) Sephardic synagogue in the heart of the city.[4] With the aid of local vandals, German troops confiscated or burned the invaluable contents of the synagogue's library and archives, tore elaborate ornamentation from the walls, and destroyed much of the roof. German forces also ransacked all other Ashkenazic and Sephardic houses of worship in the city. Their rampage despoiled the city's newest neo-Historicist structure, and their actions ominously portended the destruction of the city's Jewish population a few months later.

The Germans and Italians found much of value in the natural resources and industrial capacity of Bosnia-Herzegovina. Hitler deemed the deposits of bauxite, a mainstay in the production of aluminum required for producing efficient warplanes, to be critical for the German war machine.[5] To secure their military and strategic interests in the land, the two primary Axis allies agreed to divide Bosnia-Herzegovina and Croatia into German and Italian occupation zones defined by a boundary running northwest to southeast. Germany, as the superior Axis power, secured the most important mining, industrial, and agricultural resources for its occupation zone.[6] Within the German zone were coal mines near Tuzla, iron mines in Ljubija near Prijedor in northwestern Bosnia, and the city of Sarajevo with its steel and manufacturing facilities.

Anticipating that local collaborators could provide security in the aftermath of their invasion, the Germans in May 1941 withdrew their main invasion force, the 46th Motorized Corps, and replaced it in Sarajevo with a smaller garrison unit made up of elements of the newly created 15th Division.[7] Within a few weeks, the German component in Sarajevo was reduced to battalion strength that shared garrison duties with several Ustasha and home guard (*Domobran*) units. But the flaws and weakness of the Ustasha regime readily became apparent, and the Germans gradually introduced additional forces into the city. During the war several different German divisions and corps situated their staff headquarters in the former Austro-Hungarian military garrison at Bistrik in the eastern end of Sarajevo.[8] The city thus gained strategic importance as a center of military command, control, communication, and planning for Axis operations. The German army retained broad powers and overriding influence throughout the occupation period.

German soldiers with a swastika flag in the Baščaršija (Courtesy of Historical Museum, Sarajevo)

Ideology and policies of the Ustasha regime

Throughout the Axis-conquered areas of Yugoslavia, the new occupiers wasted no time in replacing the interwar royal government with political structures subservient to the Axis. The Germans turned to their ideological kin, Croat fascists who called themselves *Ustasha* (Rebels), to govern Croatia and Bosnia-Herzegovina. Ante Pavelić, the undisputed Ustasha leader, was born in the Bosnian town of Bradina in 1889 and practiced law in Zagreb, Croatia. Elected to the Zagreb city council in 1920 as a member of the right-wing Croatian Party of Rights, he opposed Croatia's inclusion in royal Yugoslavia. After King Aleksandar proclaimed royal dictatorship in 1929, Pavelić led a small group of followers into exile. He found refuge in Italy and developed a paramilitary force trained in terrorist tactics. The Italian government supported the Ustasha but monitored and restricted their activities. Together with a group of Macedonian terrorists, the Ustasha had planned and carried out the assassination of King Aleksandar at Marseilles in 1934.

The Ustasha traced their ideological origins to nineteenth century Croat nationalist thinkers who sought an independent Croatian state.[9] Echoing Nazi beliefs, Ustasha ideologists asserted that Croats were not Slavs but members of a superior Aryan race. The Ustasha vilified some of the same groups as those considered undesirable by the Nazis: Jews, Roma, Freemasons, and Communists. Additionally, they reviled the Serbs, viewing them as apostates, traitors to the Croat people, and the Croats' primary oppressors in royal Yugoslavia. Central to Ustasha ideology was the belief that Bosnia-Herzegovina was an inalienable part of Croatia and that all its inhabitants were Croats of three different religions. The Ustasha's ideology led them to conclude that Bosnia-Herzegovina should be cleansed of non-Aryan impurities through a process of Croatization.

In Zagreb on April 10, 1941, the Ustasha leader Slavko Kvaternik proclaimed the Independent State of Croatia (NDH; *Nezavisna Država Hrvatska*), an Axis state wholly dependent on German support.[10] Pavelić made his way from Italy to Zagreb and on April 16 assumed the title of *Poglavnik*, the Croatian equivalent of Hitler's title of Führer. He was followed by a group of Ustasha émigrés (numbering between one and two hundred) who returned to Croatia wearing the uniforms of Italian troops who had invaded Ethiopia in 1935.[11] Another group of five to six hundred Ustasha soldiers joined them in late May 1941.[12] At a conference in Vienna on April 21–2, German Foreign Minister Joachim von Ribbentrop secured the agreement of his Italian counterpart, Count Galeazzo Ciano, to incorporate all of Bosnia-Herzegovina in

6.1 Division and occupation of Bosnia-Herzegovina in the Second World War,
1941–5.

the NDH.[13] Their agreement sealed Sarajevo's fate during the Second World
War. For the next four years, Sarajevo endured German military occupation
and remained politically part of the NDH.

Kvaternik and General Horst Glaise von Horstenau, the senior German
military official in Zagreb, headed a delegation to Sarajevo in late April 1941
to introduce the institutions of NDH rule.[14] They designated Jure Francetić
as Trustee for Bosnia-Herzegovina and assigned specific administrative
responsibilities to several other appointed trustees. They further named Atif
Hadžikadić as mayor of Sarajevo and Petar Jurišić as deputy mayor, drawing

these and most other appointees from among Croat Catholic and Bosnian Muslim supporters of the Ustasha in Sarajevo. On June 10, 1941, the Ustasha, employing nomenclature used in medieval Slavic states, established the grand governate (*Velika Župa*) as the unit of local government in the NDH. The city of Sarajevo and its immediate environs, now named Vrhbosna, made up one of the twenty-two grand governates in the NDH.[15] With these decisions, the Germans and Italians turned over Sarajevo and a large part of the central Balkans to a tiny cabal of Croat nationalists with extreme ideological views and a history of terrorist acts.

The Muslims of Bosnia-Herzegovina were idealized by the Ustasha as the "purest of Croats." Even as the Ustasha aspired to eliminate Jews, Serbs, and Roma, they courted the Muslims by designating them as part of the superior Croat nation. Before being summoned by the Axis to lead the NDH, the Ustasha had included only a few Muslim members, but Ustasha leaders generously bestowed key appointments on Muslims who had gained prominence in the interwar years. Some Muslims accepted the cynical flattery inherent in participation in the NDH regime. Most prominent among them was Džafer Kulenović, president of the prewar JMO after Mehmed Spaho's death in August 1939. He would serve as vice president of the NDH throughout Ustasha rule except for the first few months (when the office was held by his brother). All four grand governors of Vrhbosna were Muslims.[16] The Muslim appointees held little real power, but in accepting and holding their positions they implicated the Bosnian Muslims in the formation and operation of the Ustasha state. In return, the Muslim writers and editors of the newspaper *Novi Behar* expressed obsequious admiration for the Ustasha and the NDH.

Pavelić and other Ustasha leaders continued to court Muslims throughout the war, but their largesse was largely a matter of public proclamations and symbolic acts. In August 1941 Pavelić approved the conversion of a Zagreb museum into a mosque. Workers removed the works of Croat sculptor Ivan Meštrović, added three minarets, and reworked the building's interior to accommodate Islamic worship.[17] The project took three years to complete. At the grand opening celebration, held in the twilight of Ustasha power in August 1944, the authorities pointed to the mosque as proof that the Ustasha had embraced Islam, but the Zagreb mosque was too little and too late to appease most Muslims. By that time, many Muslims and Croats had joined Partisan units that were readying the final destruction of the NDH.

While lavishing attention and recruitment efforts on the Bosnian Muslims, the Ustasha set out to destroy perceived enemies. Shortly after taking power, the Ustasha initiated a concerted campaign to kill, imprison, or expel the Jews, Serbs, and Roma living in the NDH. Violence against rural Serbs was widespread, and entire villages were slaughtered. NDH armed forces carried out a large number of deadly raids in Herzegovina in June 1941 and in Bosnian Krajina in July. In Sarajevo and other towns, the Ustasha arrested hundreds of Serbs who had been active in public life and were deemed to have been anti-Croat during royal Yugoslav rule.[18] Metropolitan Petar Zimonjić, head of the Serbian Orthodox Church for Dabrobosna, the extended area around Sarajevo, was tortured in mid-May 1941 and eventually killed.[19] Other Serbian Orthodox clergy were arrested in subsequent days, and on July 11–12, 1942, many of their families were shipped to a concentration camp. The threat of violence led some Sarajevo Serbs to flee to Serbia, where the collaborating regime headed by former Yugoslav Army General Milan Nedić provided relative safety for Serbs.[20]

Dozens of discriminatory laws, directed principally but not exclusively against Jews, were promulgated in the early months of occupation.[21] The Ustasha appear to have maintained a crude hierarchy of groups they held in contempt, as reflected in the varying curfew times imposed on different groups in Sarajevo on July 26, 1941: Jews at 8:00 p.m., Serbs at 9:00 p.m., and Croats and Muslims at midnight. Many laws were directed solely at Jews; other decrees targeted some combination of Jews, Serbs, Roma, Freemasons, and Communists. The laws were designed to identify, isolate, and weaken those groups in preparation for their eventual extermination. While many statutes were replicas of the Nuremburg decrees adopted in Germany by the Nazis and applied throughout the NDH, Ustasha authorities promulgated others that were specific to Sarajevo.

The Ustasha decrees forced Jews and Serbs to identify themselves publicly and to avoid mixing with those of other groups. To prevent Jews and Serbs from obscuring their religious identity, a law annulled conversions to Catholicism—a curious inversion of the Ustasha-sponsored campaign in rural areas to force Serbian Orthodox peasants to convert to Catholicism. Name changes were revoked if they had been adopted after December 1, 1918. Jews and Serbs were forbidden to wear the fez, in an apparent effort to prevent them from passing as Muslims. Jews and Serbs were forbidden from displaying Croat national symbols and the Croat tricolor flag in businesses and institutions. Jews were required to wear a yellow armband with the distinctive black-on-yellow Star of David. The armbands were to bear the word "Jew" in two languages: German (*Jude*) and Croatian (*Žid*).

Other laws authorized Ustasha agents to eradicate the economic foundations of Jewish life in Sarajevo and proscribed Jewish participation in the city's public life.[22] All Jews in government service were dismissed, striking a blow not only at bureaucrats but also at Jews employed in the large state-owned enterprises such as the Main Railway Workshop and the Military Technical Enterprise. Germans were to be given a 20 percent discount in all Jewish-owned shops. Jewish property was confiscated through legal subterfuge. Jews in Sarajevo owned about four hundred mercantile establishments, three hundred craft shops, and three industrial enterprises employing over one hundred workers. These establishments were an inviting source of loot. A decree promulgated on May 11, 1941, provided for trustees (*povjerenci*) to be appointed for Jewish businesses and required that the sign "Jewish Business," either in German or Croatian, be put in all Jewish shops. A total of 303 trustees were appointed to oversee Jewish businesses. When the businesses were confiscated and sold for a fraction of their true value, the purchaser was frequently the trustee himself. The regime also assigned trustees to Jewish religious and cultural societies to monitor their activities and eventually to confiscate their property and financial assets. By the end of 1941 nearly all Jewish-owned buildings, shops, and organizations had been confiscated or disbanded.

Discriminatory measures forced the vast majority of Sarajevo's Jews into abject poverty. Several young Jewish members of the KP enlisted the party's support in providing emergency food and essential supplies in the headquarters of the Jewish community.[23] Led by the revolutionary organizer Vladimir Perić-Valter, the party assisted in appealing to wealthier Sarajevans for money and supplies for the Jewish community. In anticipation of Jews' needs in the winter, party operatives donated a large supply of firewood. Most of it, however, went unused, since most Jews had been removed to camps by the time winter set in. The harsh measures made it increasingly dangerous for Jews and Serbs to be on the streets. They were forbidden from leaving the city. The regime, alarmed that some young people were visiting nearby villages and acquiring food for the city's Jews, warned that anyone importing such goods would be subject to prosecution. All Jewish and Serbian Orthodox organizations were dissolved and banned, and Jews and Serbian Orthodox were forbidden from joining Croat societies. Jews and Serbian Orthodox were not permitted to enter theaters. Esad Čengić, describing the collective impact of these measures, wrote, "Overnight, Sarajevo became for Jews a ghetto from which they could not flee and in which they could not live."[24]

Although the spate of laws promulgated in 1941 marked the first step in the destruction of Sarajevo's Jews, the Ustasha soon reached accommodation with the far more numerous Serb community in the city. Ustasha leaders met with politically prominent Sarajevo Serbs in an unsuccessful bid to gain their public endorsement of the NDH.[25] The authorities, despite having dissolved the Serb cultural society Prosvjeta when the occupation began in 1941, permitted Serbs to form a "Committee for assistance of impoverished Serbs at the Serbian Orthodox Church Commune" (*Odbor za pomaganje srpske širotinje pri Srpskopravoslavnoj crkvenoj opštini*). The regime's organized violence against Serbs abated after the early months of occupation, although Serbs continued to experience discrimination and many became impoverished. Although the Ustasha destroyed comparable churches in Mostar and Banja Luka, both the old and new Serbian Orthodox church buildings in central Sarajevo were preserved. The regime's generosity toward its sworn Serb enemies may have been motivated by the well-founded fear of driving them into the Chetnik or Partisan movements as had happened in many rural areas of the NDH, but it resulted in Sarajevo retaining most of its Serb population throughout the war. In the late winter of 1945, the authority of the NDH began to deteriorate, and Sarajevo's Ustasha authorities came to rely increasingly on the cultural and other societies of the major ethnonational communities to govern the city, feed the population, and educate its children.[26] Tragically, none of the Ustasha's self-interested largesse extended to the city's Jews and Roma.

Holocaust

Srećko Bujas, a judge in Sarajevo's court system and a Croat, witnessed firsthand the destruction of Sarajevo's Jews. In May 1941 Ustasha officials appointed him trustee of the Sephardic community to administer its assets[27] (Branko Milaković was made trustee of the Ashkenazic community, and the two trustees apparently worked closely together). In accepting the appointment, Bujas became entrapped—forced to aid the authorities in some of their extermination activities while protecting as many Jews as possible. Unable to protect all the Jews in the community, he repeatedly called on the authorities to spare small groups of Jews based on special circumstances. He cited laws passed by the Ustasha authorities themselves, argued that employees of the Jewish community were essential to its continued operation, stood up for Jews who had converted to Christianity or Islam, requested exemptions for Jews in mixed marriages, and implored the authorities to take pity on the elderly, infirm, and the very young. All these pleas were in vain, although at times he was able to arrange temporary shelter for some Jews expelled from their apartments to make way for Ustasha officials.

Bujas later wrote of those appalling events in a twenty-page, single-spaced typescript that now rests in the Archive of Bosnia-Herzegovina along with other documents of the postwar commission convened to investigate and report on the occupiers' war crimes.[28] Although he wrote of himself in the third person in the official bureaucratic style required by the commission, Bujas was clearly horrified by the Ustasha's seemingly infinite malevolence and haunted by the futility of his own efforts to intervene. His essay is the most comprehensive and authoritative available account of the annihilation of Sarajevo's Jews. To Bujas, the massive campaign had one final objective: the looting of Jewish apartments and possessions by Ustasha and police authorities. Although he recognized that the ultimate goal was the "final annihilation of all Jews," he noted that their extermination was preceded by "a series of burdensome humiliations of spiritual agony, physical abuse and complete ... plunder of their property." These abuses of Jews before their extermination, according to Bujas, had a purpose: "To humiliate the Jews to the utter limits of the possible and show all other people that they are ... unworthy of being called persons, that they are beyond all legal protection and that their complete annihilation was necessary to save the rest of humanity."[29]

The extermination of Sarajevo's Jews began with chilling efficiency on September 3, 1941.[30] At 3 a.m. on that date, Ustasha officials rousted Jews from their apartments in a quadrangle of urban residences near the destroyed Sephardic synagogue. About five hundred men, women, and children were given half an hour to gather a few possessions and assemble on the street. They were taken to the main railway station under police escort and jammed into cattle cars for shipment to the Krivica "transit camp" near Travnik. Most of them remained at that camp under horrific conditions for the next thirty days.

The Jews' departure set off frenzied looting and seizure of their apartments. Among the perpetrators were German officers and Ustasha officials, most of whom were new to Sarajevo. The residences were emptied so rapidly and thoroughly that NDH troops going through the apartments were able to find fewer than one hundred beds for their military quarters. Five days later, on September 8, similar early morning raids were conducted on the apartments of another five hundred Jews. This group was also sent to the camp at Krivica. The Italian consul wrote with seeming incredulity of the raids and the subsequent separation of the men from women and children. He noted the futility of protest by Sarajevans: "Local Muslims and Catholics would have gone to the grand governor in Travnik, but he told them he was not in a position to do anything about it."[31]

On September 15, 1941, the two trustees of the Jewish communities, Bujas and Milaković, were permitted to visit the Krivica camp. They reported that the camp held three thousand internees, including about three hundred Serbs. The trustees' report did not indicate how the Serbs reached the camp nor whether they were rounded up together with the Jews. Internees told the trustees that they had been given no food until their fourth day in the camp. The trustees reported that a young Jewish student named Asta had been tortured in the basement of a camp building, his screams heard for hours. Later the camp commander was seen wearing his clothes, and the internees concluded that Asta had been killed. In early October the Krivica transit camp was closed down and its male inmates shipped to the infamous Jasenovac death camp across the Sava River in Croatia. Women and children were sent to a separate camp at Loborgrad, north of Zagreb in Croatia.

Throughout the autumn in Sarajevo, more Jews were expelled from their apartments by German and Ustasha officials eager to seize property in advance of further expulsions. Dispossessed Jews were taken to a temporary detention facility at the large army headquarters building in Bistrik. The mass expulsions resumed in October 1941, conducted under the guidance of Ivan Tolj, billed as a "specialist" in resolving the "Jewish question." Over a thousand Jews were assembled and shipped to camps in late October 1941 through the same methods used in September. On Tolj's orders, a few Jews married to Catholics were removed from the assembled deportees and allowed to remain in Sarajevo. Tolj declined to release any Jews married to Serbian Orthodox, saying Serbs were not much different from Jews. The Ustasha security forces targeted Sarajevo's remaining Jews in operations on November 15–17, 1941. The central city was sealed off on November 15, and Ustasha officers went door to door, rounding up Jews from their dwellings. Elderly invalids and small children were included among those taken and put on trucks waiting at specified intersections. Further arrests and deportations continued in smaller numbers through the summer of 1942.

Some Jews, both men and women, succeeded in fleeing by donning the Muslim veil to disguise their identity, but flight from the city was fraught with danger, and most escapes were thwarted by police guarding the train station and others passageways out of the city. Several hundred Jews reached Mostar, in the Italian zone of occupation, where they were at least free from the threat of mass extermination. The best hope for Jews to survive lay with the Partisan resistance movement because Partisans generally welcomed volunteers from all groups. One Partisan unit, however, rejected a group of thirty Jews fleeing Sarajevo in June 1941 and forced them to return to the city to "a certain death," in the words of Partisan commander Danilo Štaka, who later wrote of this episode.[32] More than half the Jews rejected by Partisans fled to Italian-occupied areas and either joined Partisan units there or were interned by Italian forces and eventually released. The others were captured and subsequently perished in Ustasha camps. Štaka characterized the unit's rejection of the Jews as an inexplicable anomaly and denounced it as contrary to the spirit of the national liberation struggle. Another author blamed the decision on Chetnik influence among the Partisans, a factor never suggested by Štaka.[33] In 1988 a third author noted, "It may have been due to the so-called 'left deviation' which emerged here and there in the form of a repulsive and hostile attitude towards the 'class enemy,' 'city slickers,' and the like."[34]

Štaka was correct that this episode was an anomaly. One observer estimated that about 450 Jews joined Partisan units operating in hills around the city, accounting for about 9 percent of those from the city of Sarajevo who joined the Partisans.[35] Once in the Partisan forces, Jews fought bravely. Some of the most decorated Partisans in the region were Sarajevo Jews.[36] But casualties ran high among them, as did casualties among all those who joined the Partisans in 1941. Of approximately 450 Jews who served in the Partisans, 316 perished during the war. Within the city, few Jews remained after the German and Ustasha sweeps of August 1942. Bujas estimated that only 120 Jews avoided the roundups, most by virtue of marriage ties or specialized occupational skills. "They are gone," wrote a German observer, "and those [few] who are still to be found can in no way influence events."[37] Of those who were shipped to camps in 1941–2, only forty returned alive after the war. Another 150 were in German custody until the war's end and were never shipped to camps. Some one thousand evaded death by escaping from Sarajevo to the Italian occupation zone or abroad. Most of them returned after the war to make up the much-reduced Jewish community in Sarajevo.

In exterminating most of Sarajevo's Jews, the Ustasha and Germans wrought inestimable losses on the city. The loss was, above all, an immense human tragedy, albeit a small fraction of the six million human beings exterminated across the continent. The destruction of Sarajevo's Jews removed nearly all members of the group that was most actively engaged in the city's public life, most frequently willing to compromise politically, and most broadly distributed through residences in the city center. It delivered a severe blow to the city's prospects of remaining a pluralist society that welcomed those of all confessions and nationalities.

Origins of the Chetnik and Partisan movements

The initial wave of German and Ustasha brutalities gave rise to the Chetnik and Partisan movements in Bosnia-Herzegovina. Both movements shared an abhorrence of Ustasha atrocities, but they otherwise differed greatly in their ideology, leadership, strategy, and ultimate war aims. The Chetnik movement originated as a gathering of Serb nationalist Yugoslav royal army officers in Serbia, whereas the Partisans were formed by the KP of Yugoslavia. In the early months of occupation, both movements were strongest in rural areas and drew recruits primarily from Serb villagers who feared extermination at the hands of the Ustasha. Leaders of the two movements initially cooperated in some resistance operations, but by the end of 1941 they had become bitter rivals. As each group pursued the extermination of the other, the Chetniks increasingly collaborated with the Axis powers while the Partisans doggedly pursued campaigns of sabotage, harassment, and eventually liberation aimed at defeating the occupiers.

The KP was organizationally well prepared to resist Axis occupation, but its actions were initially hampered by the party's subservience to Soviet foreign policy goals. Having staunchly opposed fascism and sought cooperation with noncommunist parties in a "popular front" strategy through most of the 1930s, the party changed its message after its Soviet mentors signed a nonaggression pact with Germany in August 1939. The KP delicately refrained from advocating armed resistance against Germany, the Soviet Union's new ally. While stopping short of outright pacifism, the party urged the Yugoslav government to avoid war with Germany and seek an alliance with the Soviet Union as the best guarantor of peace. With the German conquest of Yugoslavia, party leaders were torn between the urge to fight fascism and loyalty to their Soviet patrons, who remained bound to an alliance with Germany. The KP at first responded to the Axis occupation with a vague call to resist the occupiers. The KP followed Comintern policy dictates, but it also prepared for the very likely prospect that the German-Soviet alliance would dissolve. Soon the party undertook preparations for a possible armed struggle. In Sarajevo, the KP drew up plans and gathered a considerable cache of arms in anticipation of being ordered into action.

While the KP was dithering, Serb peasants in Eastern Herzegovina and the Bosnian Krajina raised the flag of rebellion and drove Axis forces out of several rural areas.[38] The uprisings took place in areas where peasants had traditionally resisted taxation, conscription, state authority, and landlord abuses. The growing spontaneous resistance was something of an embarrassment to the KP, whose leaders hankered to head up the effort. They were given the green light by an act of Hitler himself. In launching Operation Barbarossa (Germany's massive unannounced attack on the Soviet Union) on June 22, 1941, Hitler abruptly ended the false German-Soviet friendship and removed any objection the Soviet Union might have had to the KP resisting the fascist occupiers. Josip Broz, General Secretary of the KP of Yugoslavia who became known simply as "Tito" during the war, convened a meeting of the KP's central committee. On July 4, 1941, the party called for immediate armed resistance. One Sarajevo KP member later recalled that the decision was "a great relief for Communists and many honorable patriots, for it meant an end to waiting and uncertainty."[39] During the socialist era, July 4, rather than the date of the earlier anemic call for resistance, became a holiday called Soldiers' Day (*Dan borca*).

The Ustasha did not wait for the general uprising to begin. Occupation authorities in Sarajevo, working from a list of KP members, arrested every Communist and sympathizer they could locate in the city on that date. Fortunately for the KP, one of its operatives acquired a copy of the list a week before the arrests were to take place, and all but a few KP members escaped the crackdown by fleeing to the surrounding hills.[40] Still, half a dozen key leaders were arrested, and aggressive police action forced many KP members to remain outside the city for the next few weeks. The repression did not prevent the KP from forming the resistance force that became known as the Partisans. On July 13, 1941, at a meeting in occupied Sarajevo, KP central committee member Svetozar Vukmanović-Tempo relayed the party's call to arms to the KP Committee for Bosnia-Herzegovina. The committee agreed to designate a separate military staff for each of four areas in Bosnia-Herzegovina, including one for the Sarajevo area.[41] The Sarajevo Regional Military Staff, commanded by Slobodan Princip with the aid of Hasan Brkić as political commissar, was charged with organizing armed resistance in the mountainous rural areas around Sarajevo.

The Chetnik movement arose from quite different roots and pursued a radically different strategy. Following the Yugoslav surrender in April 1941, Colonel Draža Mihailović led a small group of Yugoslav royal army officers from their post near Doboj in northern Bosnia to the mountainous redoubt of Ravna Gora in western Serbia, where they arrived on May 13, 1941. There he initiated the Ravna Gora movement, commonly known in the English-language literature as the Chetnik movement.[42] Following the tradition of guerilla bands that fought in Serbia's wars earlier in the century, Mihailović's men adopted the ideology, nomenclature, attire, and telltale full beards of their predecessors. Mihailović declared his loyalty to King Petar II and to the Yugoslav government-in-exile in London, which in turn promoted him to the rank of general and made him its minister of the army, navy and air force. Mihailović and his commanders hoped to seize power after the Germans had been defeated or weakened by Allied military victories. While awaiting the Allied invasion of the Balkan Peninsula (without which, they mistakenly thought, victory over Germany in Europe would not be possible), they planned to avoid armed engagement with the occupiers so that there would be no retaliatory slaughter of Serbs.

Soon the Chetniks' wait-and-see strategy was ruined by relentless Partisan sabotage and harassment operations, which inevitably provoked Axis retaliation against local residents. By early 1942 Mihailović had come to view the Communist-led Partisans as the greatest threat to his strategy and to the Serb people. He favored reconstituting Yugoslavia as a Great Serb state to be achieved by expelling non-Serbs. His wartime pronouncements expounded the Serb nationalist view that non-Serbs were responsible for the country's collapse in 1941 and should be punished. In a report to the government-in-exile in September 1941, Mihailović advocated a plan "of cleansing or moving the village population with the goal of [creating] a homogenous Serb state community."[43] His predilection for violent advancement of Great Serb nationalism was diametrically opposed to the KP-Partisan campaign to unite all nationalities in active resistance to the occupiers under the banner of "Brotherhood and Unity." Chetniks became selective, intermittent collaborators with the Axis occupiers in early 1942, and by 1943 they had become a key component of forces arrayed against the Partisans, particularly in eastern Bosnia and the Sarajevo area.

Chetniks and Partisans competed for recruits among Serb peasants in the hills and mountains surrounding Sarajevo. Chetniks, led by recent arrivals from Serbia, organized a thirty-man unit of local Serbs in the village of

Veliko polje on Mount Igman in January 1942. The newly formed unit billeted on the upper floor of the same building used by a Partisan unit. The soldiers regularly fraternized with one another, and a few switched allegiance simply by exchanging the Chetnik cap (with its cockade) for the Partisan cap (with a five-pointed red star) or vice versa. The caps' insignia were "the visible sign of political differentiation between Partisans and Chetniks, in a time of confusion and ideological vacillation among the fighters," and Partisan leaders worked hard to retain the loyalty of their recruits.[44]

The casual fraternization in Veliko polje came to an end following the arrival of the Partisan First Proletarian Brigade on January 28, 1942. The brigade, including members of the Partisan general staff, passed through the village en route to its destination in Foča in eastern Bosnia, where Tito was to make his headquarters for the next several months. Arriving with hundreds of soldiers and hauling many artillery pieces, the unit gave the impression of being a powerful resistance force. Serb volunteers, including many who had previously served as Partisans, abandoned the Chetnik unit and flocked to join the Partisans. The Serb peasant volunteers thus voted with their feet for the force they believed would offer the staunchest resistance to Ustasha and German rule.

Rivalry for recruits continued unabated for the duration of the war. Partisan units were often targeted for infiltration by Chetniks, and in some instances Partisan commanders were disciplined for suspected pro-Chetnik tendencies. Chetniks sought to win over Serb Partisan leaders and incited Serb Partisans to conduct "putsches" (revolts) by ousting commanders loyal to the Partisan cause. Many Chetnik putsches were directed against Partisans who adopted left-wing communist ideology to justify violence against wealthier peasants, who were characterized as "kulaks" after Stalin's campaign against the same group during the 1930s in the Soviet Union.[45] Putsches were most successful in Herzegovina in the spring of 1942, but they also occasionally took place in the mountainous areas around Sarajevo. Chetnik forces, increasingly allied with the Germans and Ustasha as the war progressed, persistently threatened Partisan control of the area.

On several occasions during the war, Chetnik forces ravaged Muslim settlements in eastern Bosnia and in the Sandžak region in Serbia and Montenegro. They killed many Muslims and terrorized others into fleeing. Many Muslim refugees from eastern Bosnia and the Sandžak fled to Sarajevo in the wake of these attacks.[46] The first of them arrived in the city in July 1941. By the war's end in early April 1945 over fifty thousand refugees, or about half the city's inhabitants, dwelt in camps and private residences. Chetnik atrocities in eastern Bosnia thus became well known to Sarajevans and brought discredit on their claim to be focused on resistance to the occupiers and the NDH.

The Chetnik failure in Sarajevo

In contrast to their successes among Serb peasants early in the war, Chetnik leaders found that most Sarajevo urban Serbs rejected their divisive Great Serb nationalism. Most Serbs and Serbophile Muslims in the city abhorred the Chetnik atrocities in eastern Bosnia, and some were involved in providing humanitarian assistance for Muslim refugees from that area. Colonel Gojko Borota, commander of Chetnik forces in the Sarajevo area, entered the city for a brief visit in summer 1943 and attempted to persuade Hasan Ljubunčić, a KP operative, to join the Chetnik cause. When Ljubunčić asked about atrocities committed a few weeks before against Muslims in the eastern Bosnian town of Foča, he was told that the killing of "Turks" was done because "the people" demanded it, but "the people" had since changed their minds. "These are [now] our brothers," he said.[47]

Chetnik leader Todor Perović, after visiting Sarajevo in September 1943, reported an equally discouraging reception. The city's Serbs "fundamentally sympathize with the Partisans ... the elderly out of fear and caution; the younger, led by the intelligentsia, out of conviction," he wrote to his superior. They "criticize our uncompromising stand against the Partisans and tolerance toward the occupiers," he reported, and "all of them would like us to cooperate with the Partisans."[48] His mission produced a few promises, never fulfilled, of material support for the Chetniks but no Chetnik organization in Sarajevo. Mihailović's passivity toward the Axis occupiers discredited his movement both among potential recruits and Allied leaders. Churchill, Roosevelt, and Stalin, meeting at Teheran from November 28 to December 1, 1943, agreed to direct future aid to the Partisans and terminate their missions to the Chetniks. The shift in Allied assistance hurt the Chetniks and strengthened the Partisans, who had already made substantial gains in the aftermath of the Italian surrender in September 1943. Strategic setbacks thus drove the Chetniks and the Germans to cooperate more closely with one another.[49]

Following the congress of major Chetnik military and civilian leaders at Ba in Serbia in January 1944, Mihailović directed Colonel Borota to seek closer cooperation with the Germans.[50] German Major Rudolf Treu was designated by the German consul in Sarajevo to advance the same cause. Borota and Mihailović harbored the myopic hope the Germans would install the Chetniks as successors to the Ustasha. Treu, on behalf of the Germans, hoped to gain Chetnik cooperation in anti-Partisan operations. The Chetnik command announced formation of a Ravna Gora people's committee for the district and city of Sarajevo,[51] apparently mimicking the Partisan practice of creating embryonic units of government in local areas. The committee, however, proved to be only a propaganda ploy. In a report of August 1944, KP Secretary Vladimir Perić-Valter wrote that "neither specific military nor political organizations exist" and that Chetnik activity was limited to a few Serb businessmen affiliated with the Serb Central Bank or who traded extensively with the Germans.[52]

The Chetniks held out until war's end in northeastern Bosnia and a few areas around Sarajevo, but they were driven from most territory by increasingly successful Partisan offensives. The Chetniks' failure in December 1944 to conquer Tuzla, taken by the Partisans in September 1944, spelled the end of their hopes to expand a stronghold they had established in northeastern Bosnia.[53] But the Partisans refrained from crushing the Chetniks militarily in the hills around Sarajevo, fearful of encountering a strong German force that was protecting the flank of German units retreating from Greece. Not until May 1945, after Sarajevo had been taken by Partisan forces and the Germans had largely abandoned the theater, did the Partisans destroy the remaining Chetnik units. Mihailović, who miraculously escaped the final attacks with a few aides, was eventually captured in March 1946, tried in June and July, sentenced to death, and shot on July 17, 1946. Scattered, small Chetnik units continued to operate in the Sarajevo area for the next three years until they were eradicated in the late 1940s.

The Chetnik failure in the city of Sarajevo was a victory for the city's common life, as many Sarajevo Serbs joined the Partisans and fought for a land of equality for all nationalities. It cost the Chetniks dearly. Chetniks were deprived of the steady flow of recruits, supplies, and guidance that so greatly benefited the Partisans in their efforts to assemble a comprehensive resistance movement. Although the dearth of urban support may not have been decisive in the defeat of the Chetniks, it made them greatly dependent on leadership and matériel from Serbia and rendered dubious their claim to widespread support from Bosnia's Serb population.

The multiple roles of Sarajevo's Muslims

Sarajevo's Muslims were to be found on all sides of the tortuous conflict. "The Bosniak people did not participate in the Second World War," wrote Šaćir Filandra in his comprehensive examination of their role in the twentieth century, explaining that the Muslims "fought for goals determined by their political mentors."[54] Similarly, the historian Enver Redžić wrote of the "tendencies of political diasporization" among the Muslims, resulting in their "participation in Ustasha formations, home guard units, Muslim militias and legions, Partisan units, and in less significant numbers, Chetnik forces."[55] To complicate matters, the sympathies and roles of Sarajevo's Muslims shifted substantially during the war. Many welcomed the Ustasha occupation in its first weeks but became openly critical by summer 1941. By war's end, many had come to sympathize with the Partisans, and Muslim recruits joined its formations in large numbers.

Despite the Sarajevo Muslims' fragmented participation in various wartime formations, their leaders consistently set forth two objectives. They first aimed to protect all Bosnian Muslims from violence and violations of their right to the free exercise of their religion. Secondly, they sought to secure some form of autonomy for Bosnia-Herzegovina under one or another external state sponsor. Both objectives called for political action, and neither was particularly susceptible to a military solution. Thus we find the Sarajevo Muslims articulating their interests in a variety of ways and changing direction as the outcome of the military struggle worked to the disadvantage of some potential allies and to the advantage of others.

Many Sarajevo Muslims premised their support for Ustasha rule on the expectation that the Ustasha would respect Islam and grant autonomy for the Islamic religious community much as the Habsburg regime had in 1909. Mehmed Handžić, president of the society of Islamic religious leaders called *El-Hidaje*, expressed hope for an autonomy statute when he welcomed the NDH in April 1941 as far better than the previous regime of royal Yugoslavia.[56] In July 1941 members of El-Hidaje submitted a memorandum to Mile Budak, minister of religion and education in the NDH, pleading for sweeping religious and cultural autonomy for the Bosnian Muslims.[57] In the memorandum they urged the NDH to avoid "replicating the Belgrade method of decreeing regulations for our religious and cultural autonomy." On August 7, a delegation of Muslims submitted to Poglavnik Ante Pavelić in Zagreb a proposed constitution for the Islamic community. Pavelić gave the proposal to a commission, which duly studied it for the next year but did nothing.

Most Sarajevo Muslims further lost their ardor for the NDH as the Ustasha stepped up their campaign of atrocities, leading to protests by prominent Muslims and open appeals to the Ustasha to halt their killings.[58] In addition to their growing revulsion at Ustasha violence, Muslims worried that they would become the principal victims of retaliatory attacks by Serbs. In autumn 1941 Muslim leaders proclaimed to Andrija Artuković, the visiting NDH Minister of Internal Affairs, their desire "to live peacefully with those of other religions, for rage and revenge would in any case be wrought mainly on Muslims."[59] At the annual meeting of El-Hidaje in Sarajevo on August 14, 1941, over a hundred Sarajevo Muslims appealed to Ustasha authorities to stop the violence:

We condemn all those individual Muslims who have committed any form of assault or violence. We consider that such flaws could only be perpetrated by irresponsible elements and individuals, whose acts are rejected ... by all Muslims. ... We appeal to state authorities to introduce legal security in all areas, not permitting that things be done willfully to cause the suffering of innocent people.[60]

The circumlocutory resolution avoided assigning blame to any person or group. As socialist-era historians have pointed out, the Muslim signatories criticized atrocities as aberrant excesses rather than attacking the Ustasha's core program to eliminate certain groups by force.[61] They did, however, call upon the NDH authorities to establish order and avert further violence. They made clear that the regime's actions in the first few months of the occupation had led them to distance themselves from the Ustasha project. In subsequent months Muslims in other towns of Bosnia-Herzegovina submitted similar protests.

Sarajevo Muslims submitted another protest on December 1, 1941, in which they sharply condemned Ustasha atrocities committed "under the fez as a Muslim symbol," complained of retaliatory attacks on Muslims, and further distanced themselves from Ustasha rule: "Muslims neither participated in creating the Ustasha state nor wanted it. ... Innocent and honorable Muslims cannot be held responsible because some rabble of Muslim religion or a few intellectuals were induced to be included in the Ustasha clique."[62]

While some Sarajevo Muslims served the Ustasha and others voiced their discontent with Ustasha practices through petitions, still others gave up hope that the Ustasha would protect Muslim interests. They turned to outside powers for support of an autonomous Bosnia-Herzegovina. For most this meant appealing to the Germans, although some Muslims harbored anti-German sentiments and myopically contemplated an appeal to

Western nations. Supporters of autonomy harkened back to Austro-Hungarian times, when Bosnia-Herzegovina had been a *corpus separatum* under Habsburg rule, and to the JMO's support for autonomy between the two wars. In August 1942 a group of conservative Sarajevo Muslims formed the Committee of National Salvation to protest the Ustasha failure to protect Muslims from Chetnik atrocities in eastern Bosnia and to put forward the notion of autonomy for Bosnia-Herzegovina as the best guarantee of Muslim security.[63]

Autonomists appealed to the Germans on racial grounds. Contradicting the notion that Muslims were the purest of the Aryan Croats, the petitioners told Hitler,

We are of Gothic origin, and that binds us to the German people. We adhered to our old Gothic Aryan religion under the name of Bogomilism, which we maintained until the arrival of the Turks in 1463, when we converted to Islam. ... During the Austro-Hungarian occupation we had full religious and partial political autonomy. In the First World War we were connected to Germany through our blood relation and with Turkey through Islamic religion and history. For our blood brethren, the Germans, we Muslims were to be a bridge from the West to the Islamic East.[64]

The autonomists asked Hitler to form a "region of Bosnia" under German patronage and to ban the Ustasha within its borders. Furthermore, the petitioners proposed that the Germans organize and provide arms for a Bosnian guard, which they envisioned as an expansion of the already-existing volunteer legion under the command of Uzeir Hadžihasanović (one of the founders of the Committee of National Salvation) and an embryonic army for the "region of Bosnia."

German military and civilian leaders had their hands full with the Partisans and wanted nothing but tranquility in the region, and they were not enthralled with the idea of alienating their Ustasha allies by splitting the NDH into two states. Heinrich Himmler and a group of SS officers were, however, pleased to find that the proposal corresponded with their own idea of creating a separate SS division for Muslims. Over strenuous Ustasha objections, Hitler approved creating the 13th Muslim SS Division in late 1942. Hadžihasanović's Muslim legion was to be the core of the new unit.[65] In consultation with leading Muslims, German officials in Sarajevo advanced plans during March and April 1943 for the new division. They organized recruitment drives and laid plans for the unit's training and deployment. El-Huseini, the mufti of Jerusalem and a supporter of the Third Reich, visited

Jerusalem Mufti El-Huseini and Mile Budak, minister of religion and education of the Independent State of Croatia, in Sarajevo, 1943. (Courtesy of Historical Museum, Sarajevo)

Sarajevo to rally Muslims for the idea. Recruits were promised that the unit would not be deployed outside Bosnia-Herzegovina until security was established for the Muslim population.

The 13th Muslim SS Division was formally established in May 1943 and became known as the Handžar Division (the Dagger Division). Nearly all its enlisted men were Muslims, but most officers were Germans, principally from the indigenous German population (*Volksdeutsche*) in Yugoslavia. It failed to meet the high hopes of the German officers who organized it. The division contributed little to the German war effort, and its brief history was far from illustrious. Its troops pursued a campaign of atrocities and destruction directed against Serbs in eastern Bosnia in 1943 and 1944. As the sole tangible outcome of the Muslim quest for autonomy in wartime, the division was a disgrace to those who helped recruit volunteers to its ranks.

Sarajevo Communists and the Partisan urban-rural lifeline

Unlike the Chetniks, the KP and the Partisans began the war with a strong urban organizational base in Sarajevo.[66] They were quick to exploit it. In the absence of consistent Ustasha and German control of the western approaches to the city, the KP was able to dispatch recruits, food, medicine, and military supplies to strengthen Partisan units in the surrounding hills. Although channels were interrupted numerous times by Axis raids and tightened restrictions, the symbiotic relationship between the Sarajevo KP and the Partisans flourished in the face of the occupiers' inability to seal off the city from its surrounding rural territory. The urban-rural linkage gave the Partisans an advantage over their rivals that only increased with time.

The Central Committee of the KP of Yugoslavia had specified the role of the urban and rural organizations in its call to arms of July 1941.[67] It directed that KP organizations in cities recruit volunteers for Partisan units, provide material support, publicize the ideology and achievements of the resistance movement through propaganda activities, and initiate sabotage and harassment operations. Senior KP leaders were convinced of the value of underground party activities in occupied cities and in 1942 even ordered party organizations to return to towns that had once been liberated but then recaptured by Axis forces.[68] The historian Marko Hoare, in a recent study of the war in Bosnia-Herzegovina, attributes great importance to urban party organizations: "Although the military strength of the Partisan movement lay in its peasant-based armies, its brain and heart lay in the urban-based Communist Party."[69] Nowhere was this more the case than in Sarajevo.

In its embryonic early days, Partisan resistance consisted primarily of sabotage and harassment operations. But notwithstanding occasional short-term compromises with various forces, the Partisans were resolutely committed to resist the occupiers with all the forces they could muster. On July 17, 1941, a group of KP organizers was dispatched from Sarajevo, the first of thousands of fighters who would leave the city to bolster Partisan forces in the surrounding countryside and mountains. The first organizers formed three companies (čete) named Romanija, Trebević, and Semizovac-Srednje after the areas in which they were to operate. Within a few weeks, over a hundred party members and sympathizers had departed the city to join them. The initial deployments reduced the number of KP members in the city from about three hundred on the eve of the war to one hundred or fewer. The KP leaders dispatched as many members and sympathizers as possible into the countryside, keeping only enough party members in the city to carry out successfully the party's key urban tasks.[70] During the war the Sarajevo KP dispatched an estimated 4,300 volunteers from the city to join Partisan units in the surrounding hills, including five hundred in the initial critical period from July 1941 to April 1942.[71]

Party members in Sarajevo transmitted intelligence information to the Partisans, basing their reports on observations of troop movements and an extensive network of agents operating in transportation and communication facilities. The city also contributed to the Partisan leadership cadre, as party leaders frequently moved from the city-based clandestine KP to military commands in the resistance forces. Party officials traveling from one end of Yugoslavia to the other frequently stopped over in Sarajevo, aided by KP escorts in avoiding Ustasha and German patrols. The Partisan movement in the hills served as a refuge for party members who became specific targets of police actions.

Couriers, typically selected from among experienced young party operatives, transmitted vital intelligence information and directives between the KP and Partisan commanders. Leaders often had couriers memorize information and deliver it verbally rather than risk enemy capture of written documents.[72] Couriers also carried messages between occupied cities. The couriers' lives were made particularly treacherous when they were forced to travel by train, where Ustasha and German police were on the alert for false travel documents and disguises. Courier service and communications were interrupted on several occasions by enemy offensives outside the city and police repression of the KP in Sarajevo, but the reciprocal urban-rural lifeline functioned well at most times throughout the war.

Compared to the many thousands who eventually fought in the Partisans, the KP in Sarajevo remained a small group of one hundred or fewer members. They thrived upon the support of many hundreds of sympathizers, but the party's limited membership made it easier for them to engage in clandestine work. Revitalized as an underground organization under Tito's leadership in 1938, the KP retained its basic cellular structure and rigorously adhered to sound principles of clandestine operations. Cells consisting of three to five members operated in residential neighborhoods and industrial enterprises. Cell leaders reported to the KP local committee, made up at most times of four to seven members.

Party members were trained to respond swiftly to the arrest of any of their number. On such occasions they halted operations, assessed the detainee's breadth of contacts, and hastily moved their compromised operatives out of police reach. Those compromised by the arrest of their colleagues were commonly spirited out of town to join the Partisans, and only later did they return to the city for further clandestine work. Party operatives assumed code names, typically based on their physical or personality traits. In postwar literature these became suffixes to their real names. Vaso Miskin Crni (Vaso Miskin Black) was so named after his dark facial features and jet-black hair. Avdo Humo, thought of as educated and well read, was called "Kulturni."[73] Some operatives used several code names, changing them from time to time or when moving from place to place. Code names and proven clandestine techniques limited the damage following many arrests, but the Gestapo and Ustasha police nonetheless arrested hundreds and executed dozens of Communists and their sympathizers during the war.

Few developments in the city went unnoticed by the KP intelligence apparatus. Agents in the main post office intercepted telegrams and monitored phone calls of the occupation authorities.[74] Informants in the state railway organization reported on troop movements and the impact of Partisan sabotage operations on enemy activities. KP clandestine presses, known as the party's "technics," cranked out propaganda pamphlets, broadsides, and a primitive daily newspaper of as many as one thousand copies.[75] At night party loyalists scribbled slogans of revolutionary graffiti on walls in the city, one administering the paint while another stood guard. KP operatives in the city became the eyes and ears of Partisan forces in the surrounding hills. The Sarajevo party organization never possessed the strength to launch an armed uprising without the aid of a Partisan attack from outside the city, but that was not its mission: Partisan leaders never envisioned a self-sustained uprising of the Sarajevo KP, choosing instead to draw on KP members and sympathizers within the city to support the Partisans in the surrounding areas. Even amid the intermittently heavy repression by the Ustasha police and Gestapo, the party maintained effective channels with the rural uprising. Despite erratic but effective harassment from the authorities, the Sarajevo KP successfully performed its assigned tasks at most times throughout the war.

The course of Partisan and KP resistance

The four-year resistance struggle in the Sarajevo area went through three phases. In the first phase, the Partisans and KP made major advancements through late fall 1941. In the second phase, from late 1941 to fall 1943, the Germans and their allies regained control of considerable territory and inflicted damage on the Partisans with several military offensives, followed by the gradual recovery and eventual resurgence of the Communist-led forces. In the final phase, beginning at the time of Italy's surrender to the Allies in September 1943, the KP and Partisans gained strength and confidence in conquering broad swaths of territory. The struggle culminated in a Partisan victory in April 1945.

The first phase began when the KP of Bosnia-Herzegovina and Sarajevo began forming the Partisans and launched an uprising against Axis rule in the final days of July 1941. On the uprising's first day, Partisan forces in the Bosnian Krajina region of northwestern Bosnia liberated the industrial town of Drvar by overwhelming four hundred defenders of the local gendarme station. The beginnings of the uprising in the Sarajevo area were considerably less auspicious.[76] En route to attack a gendarme station near Ilijaš on July 27, masked Partisans inadvertently encountered an Ustasha armed patrol.[77] A firefight ensued, and when German troops came to the aid of the Ustasha, the small Partisan unit broke contact and aborted its plans to attack the gendarmes. On the night of July 31–August 1, several small Partisan units initiated more successful attacks against several gendarme stations and cut telegraph wires on the outskirts of the city. The Ustasha retaliated immediately, hanging thirty peasants taken from several area villages and publicizing the brutal act in widely distributed broadsheets.[78]

The KP's first action within the city of Sarajevo was also inauspicious, but it evoked a furious response. Saboteurs planted explosive devices in machinery at the Main Railway Workshop and set them off on the night of July 29–30, 1941. The explosions caused minimal damage, and the targeted machinery was back in operation in short order. But the occupiers seized on the incident as a pretext to carry out demonstrative retaliation, fulfilling an order issued by their superiors in Zagreb a week before: "[You are to] most urgently imprison all Jews and Orthodox Serbs who were already designated as Communists, regardless of how little they are suspected, who are under the sway of that movement—and take the same measures against Communists of Catholic and Muslim religion."[79]

Police arrested twenty Jews and Serbs on the morning of August 1 and took them to a makeshift detention facility in the former headquarters of Prosvjeta, the Serb cultural society. The suspects were not the perpetrators of the sabotage, but all met the criteria of being Serbs or Jews and suspected Communists. All twenty were then taken to the Vraca Hill south of the city and hanged at 10:00 a.m. in public view. The Ustasha authorities simultaneously put up notices warning against further actions against the state: "In Sarajevo today at 10:00 a.m., twenty Serbs and Jews were hanged for committing sabotage. For each such occurrence of sabotage, regardless of where it is, an appropriate number of hostages already in state custody will be hanged."[80]

With their brutal atrocities against Serbs, Jews, Roma, and Communists, the Axis occupiers proved to be the Partisans' best recruiting agents. The Partisans gained numbers and strength during August 1941 and soon moved beyond sabotage and harassment operations. On August 26, 1941, they liberated the town of Sokolac northeast of Sarajevo. By September 1941 Partisan soldiers in the Sarajevo area numbered over three thousand.[81] Many of the towns (with the notable exception of the village of Pale) and much of the mountainous territory north and east of Sarajevo were in Partisan hands by late fall. In each liberated village and municipality, a people's liberation committee was created for provisional governance. Following an advisory issued after a consultation led by Tito at Stolica (Serbia) in 1941, people's committees became the standard form of interim local government in all territories liberated by the Partisans.[82]

Partisan successes during the first phase of operations led commanders to consider seriously the possibility of conquering Sarajevo. With this in mind, the KP halted the exodus of volunteers to the Partisans while the high command assessed enemy strength in the city and prepared for a possible simultaneous uprising from within and attack from without.[83] Concluding that the attack was certain to be costly and likely to fail, the Partisan high command called off the attack. At no time was the Sarajevo KP strong enough to rise successfully on its own, but KP members were nonetheless disappointed. For their part, the occupying authorities were alarmed by the prospect of an uprising supported by a Partisan attack, and they occasionally issued panicked recommendations that the city be abandoned.[84]

The second phase of the resistance struggle began with several setbacks suffered by the KP and Partisans in the late fall of 1941. Aided by archives inherited from the royal Yugoslav police, the Gestapo carried out a well-prepared wave of arrests in the city during November 1941 that landed ten party members in jail.[85] Outside the city, a joint German-Italian-Ustasha offensive, known to Yugoslav historians as the "second enemy offensive," was launched in January 1942. It brought to a close the first wave of Partisan victories, referred to by one Partisan commander as the "celebrated and successful revolutionary takeoff of Partisan Romanija."[86] The Axis drove the Partisans from much of eastern Bosnia, and Chetniks harassed the Partisans reeling from Axis attacks. The defeats wrought havoc with the channels of transport and communication between the Sarajevo KP and the Partisans. Further arrests in early 1942 brought party activities to a standstill and required an injection of additional party operatives by the regional committee for Bosnia-Herzegovina.

The failure of the second enemy offensive was most apparent northwest of Sarajevo in the protracted struggle for Mount Kozara in the Bosnian Krajina.[87] Despite being completely surrounded by a large German force, the remnants of a sizeable Partisan force escaped from the thickly wooded mountainous area and regrouped. The Partisans' successful escape added to the growing legend of their heroism and invincibility, a legend that would be nourished throughout the socialist period with monuments and cele- brations on the summit of Mount Kozara. In Sarajevo, the Axis forces had neither eliminated a major Partisan unit in battle nor wiped out the KP in the city. The Partisans' ability to evade encirclement and destruction were pivotal to their endurance in the face of defeat. Their hold on the town of Foča, southeast of Sarajevo, was sufficiently strong that Tito and the Partisan general staff relocated there from Serbia in February 1942 and remained until May 1942. The Partisans were also the target of the fourth and fifth enemy offensives (called Operation Weiss and Operation Schwarz, respec- tively, by the Germans) in January and May 1943. The Germans regained lost territory in each offensive, but they failed to annihilate the Partisans. After recovering from their losses in those offensives, Partisan forces in the Sarajevo area continued to grow in numbers, experience, and territory.

The final phase of the resistance struggle began in September 1943 when the Ustasha police and Gestapo carried out further arrests of KP operatives in Sarajevo. Again the party apparatus had to be rebuilt. To undertake that task, regional leaders turned to Vladimir Perić, known by the code name "Valter." Born in the Serbian town of Prijepolje in 1919, he worked in a bank in Belgrade from 1938–40.[88] Shortly after he joined the KP in 1940, his superiors transferred him to the bank's branch in Sarajevo. A youthful twenty-one years old when the war began, he participated in the KP's clan- destine preparations for resistance in the spring of 1941. From 1942–3 he served as deputy political commissar with a Partisan unit in eastern Bosnia. Regional leaders then appointed him secretary of the Sarajevo committee of the KP and charged him with reconstituting the party organization in the city. Valter revitalized the KP's urban-rural link with Partisan forces and reconstructed the KP to resume its support of the Partisan movement with personnel, supplies, and intelligence.

The growing Partisan strength in much of Bosnia-Herzegovina became apparent when the Italians capitulated in September 1943. In the scurry to acquire Italian weapons and territory, the Partisans bested the Germans in much of Herzegovina and western Bosnia. Partisan leaders were sufficiently confident of their position to convene the second major conference to lay foundations for a postwar government. The previous year, in November 1942 in Bihać in northwest Bosnia, fifty-four delegates (out of seventy-two invited) from various areas of Yugoslavia formed the Antifascist Council of People's Liberation of Yugoslavia (AVNOJ; *Antifašističko vijeće narodnog oslobodjenja Jugoslavije*).[89] With their additional battlefield successes, the Communists convened a second meeting of AVNOJ in Jajce in November 1943. A comparable body for Bosnia-Herzegovina, the Regional Antifascist Council for the People's Liberation of Bosnia-Herzegovina (ZAVNOBiH; *Zemaljsko antifašističko vijeće narodnog oslobodjenja Bosne i Hercegovine*), was formed in Mrkonjić grad on November 25–6, 1943, three days before the second AVNOJ session. At the founding session of ZAVNOBiH, 247 delegates from all areas of Bosnia-Herzegovina gathered and elected 173 of their number to the new body.

Sarajevo was to benefit immensely from the political decisions reached at these three meetings. Delegates to the first AVNOJ adopted a plan to create a federal state of several republics, but the precise status of Bosnia-Herzegovina in the future state was unresolved. At the second AVNOJ and first ZAVNOBiH assemblies, delegates affirmed that Bosnia-Herzegovina would become the sixth republic in the federal state rather than acquire some form of special autonomous status within the federation. Since Sarajevo was the presumptive capital of the reconstituted Bosnia-Herzegovina, these two meetings ensured the city a vital role in the postwar Yugoslav state. In postwar times Sarajevans honored ZAVNOBiH for its role in affirming the integrity of Bosnia-Herzegovina by assigning its name to a square at the center of a high-rise housing complex in Novo Sarajevo. November 26, the day that ZAVNOBiH delegates passed the key resolution, was honored as a holiday in Bosnia-Herzegovina after the war.

Occupation and terror

The four years of occupation were the worst of times for the city's residents. Most manufacturing enterprises were shut down or functioned at partial capacity. Food shortages persisted and at times approached critical dimensions. NDH authorities opened public kitchens to feed Sarajevo's poorest residents, but most aid was provided by the various ethnoreligious cultural societies and other volunteer organizations. Visitors to the city frequently remarked on the bleak atmosphere, the large number of persons taken for forced labor each day, and constant police surveillance and arrests.

In the last two years of the war, death unexpectedly came from Anglo-American bombing of the city.[90] Casualties were substantial, but the numbers provided by Ustasha estimates have proven impossible to verify. In the first raid of November 29, 1943, government officials estimated that 132 bombs were dropped, killing 105 and wounding 145 civilians. A raid of July 28, 1944, targeted an antiaircraft installation and a military barracks. On September 8, 1944, an attack on railway links and a military facility at Alipašin Most in Sarajevo Field struck nearby apartment buildings and barracks of a refugee camp, killing three hundred civilians. Two attacks in November killed as many as 173 persons. Damage from these bombings led Sarajevans to appeal to the Allies to spare public historical monuments and the Regional Museum with its priceless collections.

By the fall of 1944 the Germans were reeling from attacks and defeats on several fronts, and they faced likely defeat across much of southeastern Europe. When the Germans retreated from Greece in October 1944, Sarajevo assumed a different and unexpected strategic significance as a key transit point on the only plausible route for German units to withdraw from Greece back to their homeland. Hitler and German commanders, aware of the city's new strategic importance, resolved to hold the city even at substantial cost. They also set out to punish those who had made the occupation miserable for the Germans and Ustasha.

In mid-February 1945 Pavelić dispatched Colonel Vjekoslav Maks Luburić to Sarajevo with instructions to destroy the resistance movement. A sadistically creative specialist in police terror, Luburić announced his intentions in a dinner speech to over one hundred local officials on February 24, 1945.[91] On March 6 he threatened with death anyone who failed to report members of the resistance. He then established the "Criminal War Court of Commander Colonel Luburić" and brought eighty-five persons before the court during March 1945. Thirty-one were condemned to be hanged and the rest were given prison sentences. But the arbitrary killings went beyond those brought before the court. As Partisan forces were closing in on the city, fifty-five persons were hanged from trees in Marindvor on March 27–8 with placards hung around their necks reading, "Long Live the Poglavnik." Many others were tortured and brutally murdered in a villa near the site of the hangings. The postwar commission on war crimes identified 323 victims of Luburić's reign of terror in Sarajevo. The results of his brutality were witnessed by Landrum Bolling, a young American journalist who arrived in the city on April 7 after its liberation by Partisan forces. He was shown a room containing bodies "stacked like cordwood on top of one another. We were told these were Serbs whom the Ustasha had hanged by barbed wire from lamp posts in Sarajevo," he said.[92] Ljuburić's brief reign of terror constituted the Ustasha's final gruesome legacy in Sarajevo. As his last sadistic acts were being carried out, Sarajevo's destiny was being decided on the field of battle in the hills around the city.

The liberation of Sarajevo

By early 1945 the German *Wehrmacht* was on its heels in southeastern Europe. Aided by months of Anglo-American bombing and the Soviet Union's Red Army, the Partisans entered Belgrade on October 20, 1944.[93] Partisan forces took Mostar on February 14, 1945, and in the subsequent three weeks liberated several towns in eastern Bosnia. So swift was the Partisan assault that Hitler approved the German withdrawal from Mostar only after it had taken place. Despite these losses, German armed forces and the NDH remained firmly in control of Sarajevo. The German 21st Mountain Corps, under the command of General Ernest Leyser and headquartered in the Bistrik district of Sarajevo, was a formidable force of at least thirty-five thousand men.[94] Rejecting calls from his commanders for withdrawal from Sarajevo, Hitler on February 20, 1945, declared the city a "stronghold" (*Festung*) to be defended with all available means, and he appointed General Heinz Kathner to the special post of battle commander for Sarajevo (*Kampkommandantur* Sarajevo). The battle-hardened 7th Prinz Eugen SS Division was ordered to break off from the German counteroffensive in Hungary and deploy to Bosnia-Herzegovina as a reserve force under command of the 21st Corps.

Nevertheless the Partisans, by then fully capable of large-scale operations and frontal attacks, made the liberation of Sarajevo the object of the first of several offensives to expel Axis forces from Yugoslavia. Meeting in Belgrade on February 1–3, Partisan commanders laid plans for "Operation Sarajevo" and committed units totaling about fifty thousand troops to the operation. The Partisans designated a special commander and created a unified staff, called the "operational staff of the Sarajevo group of corps of the Yugoslav Army," to lead the operation. Like the Partisans, the Germans prepared thoroughly for the imminent assault. Friedrich von Wedel, chief of staff, coordinated the planning in the headquarters building at Bistrik. He surveyed available military assets and plotted the deployment of German forces in three concentric rings of defense around the city. The plans were well along but not yet finalized by the third week of March 1945.

Sarajevo KP intelligence operatives then carried out their most significant operation of the war. One of their agents stole from German headquarters the master plan for Sarajevo's defense, complete with a detailed map of over one hundred key installations and the forces deployed to defend each of them. Back at German headquarters on the morning of March 23, Colonel Wedel went to retrieve the only copy of the plan in order to make some last-minute adjustments based on the latest reports of troop strength. Despite believing that he had the only key to the cabinet where it was kept, he found the plan had vanished.

The plan's mysterious disappearance touched off panic among German and NDH military leaders. Wedel called in the military police, who launched a massive investigation. In the next few days, they arrested twenty-five German officers and one hundred and fifty members of the NDH armed forces. In the course of their interrogations, they uncovered other Partisan intelligence operatives. Concerned that they had underestimated the reach of the invisible Partisan hand, Axis commanders became convinced they faced an imminent communist uprising in Sarajevo. They had already contemplated the possibility of an uprising in the document stolen by the Partisans, but subsequent interrogations heightened their worries and led them to reformulate their plans.

German commanders soon abandoned their plan for a vigorous defense of the city. Hitler, not wishing to replicate his ex post facto approval to withdraw from Mostar, had already issued approval for withdrawal from Sarajevo in event the defense broke down. His commanders in Sarajevo, taking full advantage of that authorization, advanced their plans for an orderly retreat of the 21st Corps to the northwest as the NDH's 18th Home Army League provided cover for the withdrawal. The change in strategy was greatly advantageous to the Partisans and reduced considerably the intensity of the resistance they were likely to have faced. The success of the KP intelligence operation was capped off a few days later when Colonel Wedel, distraught over the disappearance of the battle plan, committed suicide.

The Sarajevo KP also made significant contributions to the final Partisan victory. The KP was initially overlooked in Partisan military plans to liberate Sarajevo, in part because it received orders from superior party organs rather than through Partisan military channels, but the party organized strike groups, typically consisting of five members and therefore called "fivesomes" (*Petorke*), in enterprises and neighborhoods. Strike groups were envisioned in a party directive of June 1944 as a key element of the city's eventual liberation. Party Secretary Vladimir Perić-Valter directed the formation, training, and deployment of the units. By the final battle, the strike groups numbered some fifteen hundred members. They had amassed considerable quantities of small arms and a sizeable cache of stolen enemy uniforms.

Fivesomes were trained to defend party cadre and other Sarajevans against last-minute German retaliation and to protect essential facilities against anticipated German sabotage. To expand their intelligence-gathering capacity, some strike group members were to don the uniforms of NDH police and conduct patrols in the city. Other units were assigned to coordinate with Partisans entering the city and to arrange quarters for treatment of the wounded. The fivesomes planned postliberation activities such as flying Partisan flags and assembling a chorus to sing the Internationale and Partisan songs to welcome the Partisans. Sarajevo KP leaders, meeting in their last illegal session on April 2 or 3, approved plans to deploy the fivesomes on the evening of April 4, 1945, to coincide with the Partisans' approach to the city and the retreat of most German forces. KP intelligence sources in Sarajevo radioed the Partisan command that a convoy of one thousand German vehicles was headed for Brčko. Partly in response to those reports, the Partisan command ordered its subordinate units on April 4 to conquer the city. Fivesomes successfully defended most key buildings against last-minute Axis sabotage. They repulsed a run toward the Regional Museum by a small Ustasha unit apparently intent on removing the valuable numismatic collection and other treasures from the museum.

Valter personally headed the antisabotage campaign. He visited the main post office and the electrical generating plant to ensure they were safe before heading toward the tobacco factory, which had been set ablaze.[95] In one of the final acts of the German retreat, a German hand grenade killed Valter around midnight between April 5 and 6. He was among the last Sarajevans to lose his life in the city's struggle against fascism, and he would be valorized by Sarajevans for decades, in socialist times as a revolutionary warrior and thereafter as a quintessential Sarajevan. He died as a fighter for the KP and the Yugoslav army—the same Yugoslav army that in 1992 would utterly destroy the post office Valter had successfully secured in 1945.

Wartime losses

Life in Sarajevo during the Second World War was hell in a small place. German soldiers and Ustasha occupation officials were loathed and feared in equal measure. Sarajevans perished from many forms of violence and disease during the war. For Jews, Serbs, and Roma, the occupation meant the considerable likelihood of death and the partial or complete destruction of their respective groups. Others died fighting for various armed formations, from typhus outbreaks in the winters of 1942–3 and 1943–4, malnutrition, and bombing conducted by Axis air forces in 1941 and Allied warplanes in 1943–4. Additionally, thousands fled the city in the war's early days, and some of them never returned. These immense human losses in the Second World War resulted in major changes to the structure of the city's population.[96]

Precise numbers of victims are elusive, but in 1981 a commission created by the city's veterans organization culled a variety of documents to enumerate deaths among Sarajevans during the war.[97] The commission concluded that 10,961 Sarajevans perished from the violence of the Second World War. Some 7,092 Jews perished in the Sarajevo Holocaust, accounting for 65 percent of all war deaths and 68 percent of the prewar Jewish population of Sarajevo. Of the other 1,945 Sarajevans who died as "victims of fascist terror" (a category that excluded deaths in Partisan units and the KP), 1,427 were Serbs, 412 were Muslims, 106 were Croats, and 34 were classified as "other."

The commission identified an additional 1,890 Sarajevans who died as "fallen soldiers" (those who died serving in Partisan units and the KP), including 821 Serbs (43 percent of all fallen soldiers), 499 Muslims (26 percent), 316 Jews (17 percent), 189 Croats (10 percent), and 65 others. Among fallen soldiers, 203 (11 percent) were women. Thus about a third of all Sarajevans who joined the Partisans or served in the KP (estimated variously at 4,300 to 6,000) did not live to see the end of the war. Serb deaths were the greatest numerically among the fallen soldiers, while Jews, with 316 deaths of the approximately 450 who joined the Partisans, suffered deaths at a rate (70 percent) almost equal to that of Jews who died in the Holocaust. The distribution of deaths among ethnonational groups reflects the relative overrepresentation of Serbs and Jews in the KP, as well as the Ustasha determination to exterminate Jews and a large number of Serbs. Equally, the numbers reveal the diversity of those who served and died.

The list of victims reported by the commission in 1981 is almost certainly incomplete, but it is likely the closest approximation to be compiled. As a list of victims in Sarajevo only, it does not include the many thousands of rural Serbs who died in armed attacks and in the same camps to which Jews were sent to a certain death. And it does not include others who died in the battle to drive the Germans from Sarajevo. Operation Sarajevo, which lasted from March 1 to April 15, resulted in the loss of 1,453 lives, many of them Partisans who came from far away to engage in the battle. Another 4,051 were wounded and 303 went missing. In the battle for the city itself, twenty Partisans and another twenty members of the fivesome strike groups were killed.[98]

With so many losses one might expect a significant decline from the city's estimated prewar population of 90,000. But the first postwar estimates put the city's population at 108,000. The difference is accounted for largely by a huge influx of Muslim refugees who fled Chetnik atrocities in eastern Bosnia. Although one calculation put the number of refugees at 54,349, it is doubtful that such a precise numeration was accurate or even possible to determine.[99] Nonetheless, the numbers bespeak a sustained if intermittent Chetnik campaign to kill and expel Muslims from eastern Bosnia and the Sandžak and a resulting substantial immigration to Sarajevo.

The ultimate victor in the struggle for Sarajevo was the KP. The party was not the only group to oppose the occupation and the brutality that accompanied it, but it was the only one to offer effective armed resistance. The KP's elaborate organizational structure, commitment to relentless armed attacks on the enemy, strict adherence to proven operational principles, and fealty to the slogan "Brotherhood and Unity" all contributed to transforming a tiny clandestine organization into a formidable resistance movement. The party's success lay in transcending the sectarian cleavages that the Ustasha and Germans had sought so eagerly to exploit and in transforming common life into unified resistance. To the KP and the Partisans, diversity was not an end in itself but rather a means to achieve the unity of all peoples for the purpose of resisting the fascist occupiers and liberating the land. Like earlier city councils (in 1878 and 1919–20), the KP and the Partisans achieved diverse participation by mobilizing Sarajevans in the service of a greater task. With the aid of the town-to-country lifeline that bound the KP to Partisan units in surrounding areas, party and military leaders overcame rural-urban differences to achieve broad participation from all major nationalities and eventually achieved the liberation of the city and its environs.

War brought out the worst in some Sarajevans, but it brought out the best in most. Tens of thousands committed themselves to the cause of liberation

The Konak, built as the Ottoman seat of government in 1869, guarded by an imperial Habsburg soldier. (Postcard, *c.* 1900, courtesy of Historical Archive, Sarajevo)

The new Serbian Orthodox church, dedicated 1872. (Postcard, *c.* 1900, courtesy of Historical Archive, Sarajevo)

The Catholic cathedral, completed 1889. (Postcard, *c.* 1900, courtesy of Historical Museum, Sarajevo)

Vijećnica (City Hall), completed 1894, exterior from across the Miljacka River. (Postcard, *c.* 1910, courtesy of Historical Archive, Sarajevo)

Palace of Justice (1914), now Faculty of Law and Rectorate of the University, on the north bank of the Miljacka River. (Photograph by the author, 2000)

Evangelical church (1899), now Academy of Fine Arts, on the south bank of the Miljacka River. (Photograph by the author, 1985)

Regional Museum, completed 1910. (Postcard, *c.* 1914, courtesy of Historical Museum, Sarajevo)

Sarajevo's multireligious city center, with Ashkenazic synagogue (1902, foreground), new Serbian Orthodox church (1872), Catholic cathedral (1889), and minarets of several mosques (background). (Photograph by the author, 1994)

Above, panorama of the city from the south. (Postcard, *c.* 1910, courtesy of Historical Archive, Sarajevo)

Left, Baščaršija mosque and its minaret in the eastern end of the city. On the right, the tower of a Catholic church. (Photograph by the author, 1975)

Interior of new Sephardic synagogue, completed
1929, destroyed 1941. (Postcard, *c.* 1929,
courtesy of Historical Archive, Sarajevo)

The Holiday Inn, built in time for the 1984
Winter Olympic Games. (Photograph by the
author, 1985)

Above left, ruins of the reading room, National and University Library (Vijećnica), destroyed by Serb incendiary shells in August 1992. *Above right*, mausoleum of the Jewish cemetry, a key defense position for soldiers of the Army of Bosnia-Herzegovina during the Bosnian war and badly damaged in the fighting. View from a bridge across the Miljacka River. *Below*, damage to lower floors of Associated Military Industry of Sarajevo (UNIS Towers). (All photographs by the author, 1992–6)

Left, flowers adorn the last standing statue of Josip Broz Tito in Sarajevo, in the Marshal Tito Barracks. (Photograph by the author, May 2004)

Below, the Main Post Office Building, designed in Secession style by Josip Vancaš in 1913, destroyed from the inside by Serb nationalist sappers in 1992, and restored to its former condition in 2000. (Photograph by the author, 2000)

and an end to the tyranny and terror. Many of those gave their lives in the cause. Valter epitomized the conviction and determination of many Sarajevans during the war. He mobilized the assistance of those from all groups and devoted himself to aiding the most endangered of them, the Jews. For these qualities he would be valorized as the embodiment of Sarajevans' virtues after the war. The sacrifices of all Sarajevans, and the fact that most were free from any real complicity in the horrific occupation, engendered high expectations of those who would govern after the carnage.

7. Sarajevo under Socialism

Sarajevo underwent an unprecedented transformation during the forty-five years of socialist rule. The city expanded geographically to several times its previous size: to the west into the flatlands of the Sarajevo Field, to the north along the Koševo Stream, and in all directions into the surrounding hills. Its population grew from less than one hundred thousand at war's end to over half a million in 1991. The city's common life expanded greatly into previously separate spheres of political and social life, and segregated residential areas gave way to an array of integrated housing communities. Driving the transformation was a grand vision formulated by a relatively few party members but shared by many Sarajevans who hoped for a more equitable, progressive society and who admired the Partisans' wartime accomplishments.

Foundations of the new order

The victorious Partisans harbored a vision of revolutionary social transformation. In the first postwar years, KP leaders zealously but pragmatically addressed the chronic problems bequeathed to the city by a divisive and destructive war. Relying on spontaneous enthusiasm when possible but invoking authoritarian means when required, they created new institutions to implement revolutionary change and abolished many practices and organizations they viewed as counterrevolutionary. Their diverse undertakings in the first five years after the war left a historical legacy that combined remarkable achievements, radical social change, and intermittent harsh repression. Sarajevo again assumed importance as the capital city of Bosnia-Herzegovina, one of six republics of the Federal People's Republic of Yugoslavia.

Ecstatic Sarajevans began celebrating their liberation even before the Germans had been completely driven from the city. Crowds lined the streets in welcome as the first Partisan unit entered the city at 5:30 p.m. on

7.1 The republics and autonomous provinces of socialist Yugoslavia, 1945–92.

April 5, 1945.[1] Partisan commanders, many of whom had left the city to fight the occupiers, delivered spontaneous speeches to wildly cheering crowds at impromptu gatherings in the city's squares and major intersections. Women offered up freshly baked breads and baklava to the triumphant soldiers and invited them to dine in their homes. The spontaneous celebrations erupted street by street, even as German tanks were firing on Partisans near the Vijećnica to cover the Axis retreat from the city. Partisan commanders, unaccustomed to fighting tanks in an urban environment, ordered the streets cleared of civilians until the city could be secured. By midnight, about the time that Vladimir Perić-Valter died in an effort to

Triumphant Partisans returning to Sarajevo after the city's liberation from German occupation, April 1945. (Courtesy of Historical Museum, Sarajevo)

prevent last-minute German sabotage, the last German soldiers were either rounded up or in retreat. Celebrations began again after midnight, interrupted briefly by a huge explosion as German sappers destroyed an ammunition cache on Mount Hum above the city. Dawn broke on April 6 over a city in jubilation over the end of German occupation and the Partisans' return from the war of liberation.

Benefiting from advance planning and unchallenged control, the KP moved quickly to channel the popular enthusiasm into a mass movement. For weeks after the city's liberation on April 6, 1945, the city's public spaces were filled with organized meetings, rallies, congresses, dedications, and dramatic performances as well as spontaneous celebratory gatherings, all aimed at exploiting the fervor in order to build a new socialist order. On April 8, only two days after liberation, a celebratory rally was held in Sarajevo's main street in front of the National Bank (originally built as the Grand Hotel in 1896), a frequent location of public assemblies in the early socialist years. Under a mammoth portrait of a stern Tito in Partisan uniform, Partisan commanders and KP leaders duly honored the sacrifices of fallen Partisans and victims of fascism, but they sought above all to impart their own enthusiasm for the imminent social transformation. Celebrants were told that the joyous day of liberation meant the beginning of a "magnificent era in the history of this city."[2] Appealing to local pride, Avdo Humo told the crowd that the idea of the uprising in Bosnia-Herzegovina was born in Sarajevo and that a united "people's liberation" front had been created in the heat of battle. In keeping with this national front strategy, speakers from the three major nations who were not KP members addressed the rally: Zaim Šarac as a leading Muslim, Ante Martinović as a Croat leader, and Nedo Zec as a prominent Serb.[3]

A mass funeral was held the next day, April 9, for those who died in the liberation of the city. Some fifteen thousand attended a separate memorial service on April 10 honoring Perić-Valter.[4] Party leaders met on April 13 with representatives of Sarajevo's Serbs, and on April 14 with Muslim and Croat leaders, to express their good intentions and ask for support.[5] On May 1, over forty thousand participated in a May Day rally.[6] Workers from the Main Railway Workshop transported thirteen newly repaired loco- motives on tram tracks to the Marindvor intersection. The repaired loco- motives were festooned with flowers, flags, and slogans, and one irreparable engine was draped with a banner that read, "This is what the occupiers left us."[7] On May 2 a crowd gathered spontaneously in front of the National Bank to celebrate Berlin's fall to Allied forces. Elated Sarajevans again took to the streets on May 8 to celebrate Germany's capitulation to the Allies.[8]

Amid the revelry of the next few months, party leaders radically altered the city's memorial culture. The Partisan warriors who entered the city in early spring had become legends by autumn. The party valorized the Par- tisans, honored Josip Broz Tito as their ultimate embodiment, and promo- ted a forward-looking vision of social change. Hundreds of streets were renamed. The main east-west avenue became the Street of Marshal Tito. Other streets were named after heroes of the revolutionary struggle against Austro-Hungarian and royal Yugoslav overlords and for Partisan heroes, living and dead. The Partisans' keynote slogan—"Brotherhood and Unity"— was invoked to overcome animosity among national groups and to invite the participation of all nationalities in the city's resurgent public life. Sarajevans were repeatedly admonished not to let past antagonisms be carried forward into the new era. Reflecting on the Partisan ideals, two participants wrote, "There is no brotherhood and unity without free expression of national con- sciousness and without a feeling of equality."[9]

These admonitions, like the increasingly organized manifestations of popular euphoria, were directed in part toward those Sarajevans who did

Sarajevans celebrating Germany's surrender to the Allies, May 8, 1945.
(Courtesy of Historical Museum, Sarajevo)

not share the enthusiasm for the Partisans and KP. Some Sarajevans, particularly religious conservatives and those associated with traditional elites,
were wary of rule by the jubilant liberators. A KP report of April 11, 1945,
voiced concern that malcontents "who had not entered our movement"
were gravitating toward the national parties formed in the time of royal

Yugoslavia. "The authority of our officials is well recognized everywhere," the report stated. "The people want to listen to old acquaintances and Serbs from Sarajevo. We should respond there and let them hear our own people, not just reactionaries. ... We should strive politically and be seen as such by the masses."[10]

To channel spontaneous enthusiasm toward specific goals, KP leaders oversaw the revival of some organizations and the formation of many new ones in assemblies and conferences held during May and June of 1945. The United Alliance of Antifascist Youth of Bosnia-Herzegovina (*Ujedinjeni savez antifašističke omladine Bosne i Hercegovine*), held a congress in Sarajevo on May 6–9. The enthusiastic attendees worked and played hard. "Days were for work; evenings were for play, dancing, and love," recalled Jelena Čišić with a fondness suggesting that she had engaged in all four.[11] Youth congress leaders presided over a rally on May 7 to unveil a new plaque honoring Gavrilo Princip at the corner where he assassinated the Habsburg Archduke Franz Ferdinand in 1914.[12] (The Partisans had already cloaked themselves in the mantle of Princip's memory by giving his name to a military unit operating near his birthplace, Bosansko Grahovo.) One speaker drew a dubious parallel between Princip and youth in the Partisan movement, saying that Princip's assassination of the archduke had been intended to liberate "our dear city of Sarajevo, our entire homeland" from oppressive German rule.[13]

An organization for women was created in the first postliberation weeks. Women had participated in the Partisan movement in greater numbers than in any previous social movement in the region, and they had formed organizations of their own during the war. On June 1 over a thousand women participated in the first Sarajevo conference of the Antifascist Women's Front (*Antifašistički front žena*). They elected 120 delegates to a city committee and selected ten women to serve on its executive committee.[14] The group's members organized literacy courses, worked to improve sanitary conditions, and provided care for the many orphans who were relocated to Sarajevo after the war.

Celebrations continued through the spring and summer, prolonged by a series of planned events designed to highlight Partisan achievements and sacrifices. The jubilation reached a climax with Tito's visit to Sarajevo in November 1945. He addressed a crowd estimated at one hundred thousand from the balcony of the National Bank. Denouncing the nationalist extremism of earlier times, Tito called for brotherhood and unity in the Yugoslav heartland of Bosnia-Herzegovina. His visit, which coincided with the beginning of a harsh winter, was the last of the mass public gatherings that had filled the city streets with jubilant Sarajevans in the half year after war's end. Nonetheless, popular enthusiasm continued to fuel many achievements of socialism in the ensuing several years.

Pragmatic problem solving in the city council

The postwar city council was born in the revolutionary euphoria of the Partisan victory. Like other governments established in liberated areas, it was first named the City People's Liberation Committee (*Gradski narodni oslobodolački odbor*, referred to here as the city council). Its members were appointed by the ZAVNOBiH (which had assumed the role of Bosnia-Herzegovina's provisional government) on April 19, 1945, and began work on April 20.[15] Husein Brkić was appointed president of the council, an office referred to as mayor. After his death in 1946 he was succeeded by Ferid Čengić. Three vice presidents were selected, one each from the three largest ethnoconfessional communities, in a tacit admission that the confessional key was still being observed, even if the three were identified in official doc-

Rally of Sarajevans addressed by Yugoslav President Josip Broz Tito, November 1945. (Courtesy of Historical Museum, Sarajevo)

uments only by profession.[16] The council's additional twenty-five members were either members of the KP or sympathizers referred to as "antifascists."

Under the guidance of the KP, the council was the supreme authority in the city, but it did not intrude into areas of jurisdiction designated for the Yugoslav federal government or the Republic of Bosnia-Herzegovina. The city's new rulers drew upon their experience in administering areas liberated by the Partisans in wartime. At first the city was organized into nine neighborhoods (*kvart*, plural *kvartovi*), but in May 1945 the city was reorganized into four districts (*rejon*, plural *rejoni*, a term taken from local governments in the Soviet system). In each district a people's committee was appointed. These bodies functioned mainly as transmission belts to implement the policies and directives of KP leaders in the city.[17] In September the new authorities held the first postwar elections, offering the voters only a single slate of candidates nominated by the people's front. Most nominees were incumbents, so the composition of the elected council was very similar to that of its provisional predecessor.

The KP had only between fifty and sixty members in the city at the time of liberation, since many party members had spent much or all of the wartime years in Partisan formations outside Sarajevo. Many more KP members returned with the liberating Partisans in subsequent weeks. Dane Olbina, a Communist activist in the Main Railway Workshop in the interwar years and a Partisan veteran, took his first airplane flight returning to Sarajevo from Belgrade.[18] KP members, although new to the art of governance, tackled their new challenge with determination, supreme confidence, and unbridled optimism. Council Secretary Milutin Velimir declared myopically that "social problems can be solved in a short time."[19] KP leaders in the city regularly invoked their common vision for a better future, but their decisions in the first three postwar years were governed more by pragmatism than communist ideology. The council's behavior was reminiscent of the approaches used by the council after the First World War.

The new council faced two daunting challenges: provisioning the city and meeting the housing needs of a rapidly expanding population. The city's prewar population of about 90,000 swelled in the weeks after the war to 108,000 as estimated by a preliminary survey in 1945. The influx included thousands of displaced persons who arrived in the city with no means of support. Demobilized Partisans and their families were also largely dependent on the city government for daily sustenance. Food was available and in places even plentiful in the countryside, but transportation and delivery systems had collapsed toward the end of the war, effectively sealing off the city from its usual sources of supply.

The council addressed the short-term emergency by augmenting the existing system of retail distribution. The council provided free food for the needy and made essential items available at below-market prices. As an emergency measure, four food kitchens were opened, ration cards were given to all citizens, and food was given to municipal officials to be distributed either through food communes (*zadrugas*) or existing retail food shops. The council paid special attention to milk for infants, a commodity available but beyond the financial means of many new mothers. Still, the council's reach of authority was insufficient to solve the problem of provisions on its own. At the request of the council, the Yugoslav army and the government of Bosnia-Herzegovina each provided vehicles and fuel to transport much-needed foodstuffs into the city.[20] Only a coordinated effort by the governments of the city and the republic had the capacity to move large quantities of goods from the countryside into the town.

To address the food shortage more permanently, council members turned to collectivist solutions. They placed the system of retail food distribution under city control. Taking their cues from the federal government and drawing on practices in place in Belgrade and Zagreb, they sought to undercut market mechanisms by fixing prices. A special bureau for "supplies and sales" was established in mid-May with a mandate to meet the city's food needs and to "take the initiative in its hands to regulate prices in the Sarajevo market."[21] When the republic government ordered the bureau abolished, the city again turned to precedents in Belgrade and Zagreb. In August 1945 the council authorized establishment of a city-owned enterprise called Granap, and agreed it would operate under a statute modeled on that of the enterprise of the same name in Belgrade.[22] Monopolistic enterprises were established for milk, textiles, meat, and other essential foodstuffs.[23]

In the first postwar days, the council was confronted with thousands of empty dwellings and the need to protect them from usurpation. Many of the vacant apartments had formerly belonged to Jewish victims of the Ustasha and been abandoned by fleeing Germans or Ustasha supporters who had usurped them during the war. The council arranged for such property to be identified and auctioned. The demand for living quarters quickly outstripped the supply owing to the influx of returning Partisans, civilians, war widows and invalids, and displaced persons from rural areas.[24]

Control of the city's housing stock was first vested in the Yugoslav army commander in Sarajevo. Soon returning veterans were found to be occupying empty apartments without authorization, and on June 24 the council was told that housing matters were being transferred to a civilian body, the city's Department of Social Policy.[25] The department director, Mirjana Stanišić-Engel, asked the council to expel all displaced persons from the city and demanded that "no one intervene for whatever kind of individual."[26] The council rejected this extreme proposal and instead passed a resolution saying that "refugee families should not be expelled, nor should those whose providers are in the army, and those who are in any kind of [state] service. Interventions should be made in favor of retaining refugees." The council denounced those who held dual occupancy of apartments and urged those with large flats to share their quarters with others not so fortunate. Despite the jawboning conducted in public manifestations and in the press, party leaders largely failed to convince unauthorized occupants to vacate their dwellings.

To cope with the growing demand, the council directed that existing apartments be subdivided to accommodate more occupants. These actions were pragmatic responses to an acute crisis, but they were sanctioned by an ideology of social ownership. In September 1945 the council created a housing commission to resolve conflicting claims.[27] The city council retained the right to review all the commission's decisions and was soon reviewing nearly every judgment made by the commission. Sarajevans' insatiable hunger for housing collided with the static and diminished supply. By 1948 the council was bogged down in ruling on dozens of appeals at every meeting. With these unprecedented rulings, the council reached intrusively into the homes and daily lives of many Sarajevans. In one case, the council ordered that two residents each take one room in an apartment but share a common kitchen.[28] In another case, a petitioner lost an appeal to divide an apartment because the council deemed him to be ill, but not sufficiently ill to warrant a room of his own. In other decisions, extended families were ordered to crowd into a single dwelling.

The appointees to the 1945 council showed no particular hostility to religion. The council ordered church books and documents returned to appropriate authorities of the Catholic Church in Sarajevo.[29] The council recognized the most important holidays of Sarajevo's major religious communities, including Christmas, Easter, the Muslim Bajram holidays, and the Serbian Orthodox Patron Saints Day.[30] It voted to give civil servants time off to visit their house of worship on other holidays. The council also allowed refugees to move into the Serbian Orthodox seminary building, which the church had been forced to vacate by the Ustasha and was being used as barracks by the Yugoslav army at the time.

The council also saw to the geographic expansion of the city as the building boom got underway in the city's western end. With the authorization of legislative acts passed by the republic assembly, the city boundaries were extended in 1947 to encompass areas several kilometers to the west.[31] Ilidža, at the far western end of the valley, at that time was "almost unpopulated, except for its hotel" built in Austro-Hungarian times, according to one observer in the early 1950s.[32] Ilidža already enjoyed rail service from Sarajevo, with five stops along the way, but the city sought in the 1950s to extend tram service there instead to provide a single transportation system from Sarajevo's center to its western suburbs. The prospect of a costly new tram system was eased when the city received a donation of trams recently taken out of service in Washington, DC. The line was completed in 1961, and the recognizable tram cars were known as "Vašingtonci."[33]

Like the city council of 1919–20, the first socialist-era body sought to address the city's most urgent needs from a practical standpoint. But KP leaders augmented pragmatism with a drive to implement an ideological vision. In the late 1940s most residents shared or at least appreciated that vision, and Sarajevo was in the vanguard of Yugoslav cities implementing revolutionary changes. At war's end the KP had fewer organized rivals than communist parties in most of Eastern Europe, giving it a de facto monopoly on harnessing popular enthusiasm to build the new socialist order. Riding the crest of Tito's popularity and the legend of Partisan liberation in the first three postwar years, the KP did not directly attack those groups that it judged not to pose a threat to the socialist system. Organized religion and cultural societies were permitted and even protected during the early postwar years. The Serb cultural society Prosvjeta was revived, the Croat society Napredak was permitted to continue its activities, and the Muslim societies Gajret and Narodna uzdanica merged into a common organization called *Preporod* (Renaissance).

In the first three postwar years, the KP consolidated control at all levels and concentrated its efforts on prosecuting those believed to have collaborated with the fascist occupiers. Arrests led to several show trials in 1946. The Chetnik leader Draža Mihailović was captured, tried, and executed in Belgrade. In Zagreb the Croat Archbishop Alojzije Stepinac, against whom the case for collaboration was far more dubious, was tried and sentenced to prison along with several prominent Ustasha officials. (Stepinac served five years in detention and was transferred in 1951 to house arrest in his native village in Croatia. He died in 1960, having been made a cardinal by Pope Pius XII in 1953.) The headline-grabbing trials in Belgrade and Zagreb had their counterparts in the less-publicized prosecutions in Sarajevo of twelve members of the group called Young Muslims, who were convicted but given less harsh sentences than Mihailović and Stepinac. Alija Izetbegović, who in 1990 became president of Bosnia-Herzegovina, was sentenced to three years in prison, Nedžib Šaćirbegović to four years, and the remaining defendants to lesser punishments.[34] Other Young Muslim leaders were tried and convicted in September 1947 for "entering into the service of Fascist Germany during the occupation." They were sentenced to jail terms ranging from one to ten years, and some of them were deprived of their property and certain citizenship rights.[35]

The social transformation

Revolutionary communist ideology called for the creation of a new social order inhabited by a new socialist being.[36] Local governments were charged with contributing to this transformation of man and society by eliminating all forms of inequality and achieving mass participation in public life. In a law of 1946 the federal government directed the city council:

To organize and support immediate participation of citizens in the administration of state affairs, particularly to engage them in renewal and construction of the economy; ... and to wipe out all privileges of birth, social position, property holding, education, and national affiliation, and particularly to eliminate the concepts of national and religious hatred and discord.[37]

Sarajevo's party leaders and city council, acting in tandem with republican and federal officials, sought to achieve these goals by organizing work brigades, reordering associational life, building an educational system, and constructing residential settlements following egalitarian principles.

For the first several years of socialist rule, work brigades provided much of the manual labor to build the city. Brigade volunteers were recruited by the people's front, youth and women's organizations, factory syndicates, and various administrative bodies. Participation was voluntary, but the tide of enthusiasm no doubt drew in many who might not otherwise have participated. Volunteers from abroad joined in the effort. Many foreign volunteers returned home inspired by the esprit de corps they had seen, particularly in the youth brigades. Life in the brigades differed from postwar euphoria principally in the addition of many hours of hard labor to the celebratory elan. One observer noted that the volunteers willingly worked such long hours that the republican youth organization had to intervene to limit them.[38] Mornings began with calisthenics. Evenings were filled with singing, dancing, political discussions, spontaneous athletic competitions, and socializing. "They were constantly celebrating. ... They played instruments and danced as though they'd not been hard at work," one observer noted.[39] Productivity contests among brigades brought forth even greater effort to the common cause, but sometimes the leaders' enthusiasm led them to use coercion and quotas to round up recruits.[40] Prisoners of war were put to work alongside youth volunteers in the immediate postwar years. But enthusiasm waned in the latter years of the five-year plan. "Older people were forcibly recruited to work alongside the youthful volunteers for many of these campaigns," according to one youth volunteer who worked in a "well-disciplined brigade" in the summer of 1951.[41]

Among the first structures completed for the entertainment of the working class were two soccer stadiums. At war's end, the city had three stadiums, but only one of them—"Slavija," the home stadium of an interwar Serb team of the same name—held as many as two thousand fans.[42] Two of the stadiums, including Slavija, were sacrificed to lay tracks and build a station for the new standard-gauge rail system. The city council then approved construction of a new stadium north of downtown. Although its location was ideal, the site included a Serbian Orthodox cemetery and considerable private land, and it was dissected by the upper reaches of the Koševo Stream. The organizers exhumed remains from the cemetery and relocated them to a new plot on the Vraca Hill. Private land was expropriated, and the Koševo Stream was diverted into a concrete culvert that led to the Miljacka River.

The new Koševo Stadium was built primarily by seven hundred members of youth brigades, who began work in 1947 in hopes of completing it in time for the first jubilee of physical fitness (*fizička kultura*) of Bosnia-Herzegovina on June 20, 1948. Dane Olbina, as a member of the city council, secured bulldozers and materials for the stadium, arranged to feed and house the volunteers, and worked tirelessly alongside the youth brigades to complete the project on time. Athletic competitions were organized among the brigades; one organizer said the undertaking "represented a unified mass school of physical culture."[43] As in nearly every building project of the time, organizers complained of a chronic shortage of skilled laborers. But the project was completed and dedicated in May 1948 with a great celebration of youth work brigades, led by the volunteers who had worked on it.[44] The stadium seated ten thousand when it was built, and it became the home stadium of the soccer team Sarajevo. Later the facility was completely renovated and expanded to hold many times the spectators, and the opening ceremonies of the Olympic Winter Games were held there in 1984. A second stadium was completed in the Grbavica neighborhood in September 1953.[45] Laborers from the Main Railway Workshop and other railway employees helped build the facility, and it became the home stadium of Željezničar, the soccer club that traced its origins to a workers' club in the interwar years. For decades the greatest cultural divide in the city was between the devoted fans of the Sarajevo and Željezničar teams.

More than any other group, the Muslim women of Sarajevo suffered from traditional barriers to social advancement. Most spent the majority of their time sequestered in their homes, and while in public most wore a veil or a

Youth brigades building Koševo Stadium, 1947. (Courtesy of Historical Museum, Sarajevo)

head-to-foot robe (*feredža*) that included a veil. Their traditional attire was an impediment to employment in many shops and factories. Muslim women had a low literacy rate and endemic health problems, and until 1945 they had not been allowed to vote. The Antifascist Women's Front took aim at each of these problems in the late 1940s.[46] The group organized literacy classes in every quarter of the city and taught thousands of women to read and write in the first several postliberation years. They ran seminars and classes teaching women how to vote and organized massive campaigns to encourage women's voting, efforts that resulted in a near 100 percent turn-out for women, even though the elections offered only a single slate of can-didates. In an effort to reduce communicable diseases (particularly typhus, tuberculosis, and syphilis), the front organized classes and individual instruc-tion for women on prevention and detection. Expectant mothers received instruction in prenatal and postnatal care.

The Antifascist Women's Front of Bosnia-Herzegovina launched a cam-paign at its second congress in 1947 to encourage women to abandon the veil. Removing the veil, in the words of the congress's resolution, began a "life without inequality and without enslavement of one person by another, a life in which there shall be no darkness and backwardness."[47] As soon as the resolution was adopted, Šemsa Kadić, a delegate from Travnik, demonstra-tively removed her veil to the applause of the assembled delegates, and on her urging other Muslim women followed suit.[48] The next three years the organization sponsored rallies and held meetings to encourage other Mus-lim women to shed their veils. The crusading women approached the effort with infectious revolutionary enthusiasm. Prominent male political leaders were enlisted to endorse the effort. Veils were ceremonially removed at rallies held in neighborhoods and enterprises, particularly in the tobacco and textile factories that employed large numbers of women.

The newly-designated Reis-ul-ulema, Ibrahim Fehić, led a group of pro-gressive, progovernment Islamic leaders in endorsing the anti-veiling campaign. In his inaugural address on September 12, 1947, Fehić praised the achievements of the people's liberation war and denied rumors that the new Yugoslav constitution was at odds with Islamic law. "One valuable legacy of the liberation war of our peoples is the proclamation of women's equality," he proclaimed. "But unfortunately women cannot achieve the full express-ion of that equality, as they are inhibited by wearing the veil and gown."[49] On November 1, 1947, the Sarajevo-based Supreme Islamic Council of Yugo-slavia (*Vrhovno islamsko starješinstvo FNRJ*) endorsed the Reis's position and

Gathering of Muslim women, part of the campaign urging them to discontinue wearing the veil, 1947. (Courtesy of Historical Museum, Sarajevo)

A member of the Antifascist Women's Front demonstratively removes her veil at a rally of Muslim women, hoping to encourage others to end the practice, 1947. (Courtesy of Historical Museum, Sarajevo)

assured Muslims that "the veiling of women is not required by religious code. Muslim women, as regards religion, are free to walk about unveiled and tend to their affairs."[50] The council urged Islamic leaders to "spread this message to the broadest levels of our peoples, to approach the topic without spite in a favorable manner without the use of force ... since harmony and brotherhood are most necessary to us." These religious leaders hoped that Muslim women would voluntarily give up wearing their veils and robes, thereby avoiding government-imposed measures: "If possible, this problem [should] be solved by only Muslims as a purely Islamic matter."

Despite the best efforts of progovernment Islamic leaders, the campaign encountered staunch resistance, especially among women outside of Sarajevo and among Muslim men. Statistics compiled by the women's front showed that 95 percent of Sarajevo's Muslim women had abandoned the veil by late 1950, but fewer than 50 percent had done so in other towns of Bosnia-Herzegovina.[51] Faced with widespread resistance to the unveiling campaign, the Bosnian Assembly resorted to compulsion to end the practice completely. Legislation banning the veil was introduced by Džemal Bijedić, who was later to become Yugoslavia's prime minister and emissary to non-aligned nations. Passed on September 28, 1950, the law declared a ban on wearing the veil, "with the goal of ending the centuries old symbol of inferiority and cultural backwardness of Muslim women." Violators were subject to fines and to prison sentences of up to three months. Veils soon disappeared in Sarajevo, and resistance to unveiling elsewhere in the republic was gradually overcome as well.

The second key to improving the status of women, particularly Muslim women, lay in education. In the forty-five years of socialism, Muslim women in Sarajevo achieved approximate educational parity with their male counterparts and with women of other ethnonational groups. They were increasingly represented in all sectors of the work force, but the highest political and economic positions continued to be dominated by men. Because the traditional barriers to women's advancement were stubbornly held, educational parity probably could not have been achieved in the absence of the government's compulsory measures to end the veiling practice.

Party leaders encouraged the formation of hundreds of new organizations and associations in the first postwar years. These groups promoted cultural life, leisure activities, educational advancement, propaganda dissemination, health, fitness, and efforts to build the new socialist order. These organizations were open to members of all ethnonational communities, and none of their names included the designation of a particular religious or ethnonational group. The influence of these organizations was uncontested after the dissolution of secular single-national organizations in the late 1940s, particularly the suppression of the Muslim, Croat, and Serb cultural societies in 1949. The elimination of ethnoreligious segregation in organizations fostered a new form of common life in Sarajevo. Disregarding the religious affiliation and national identity of their members, these groups facilitated mingling in everyday life at work and in leisure time. The new groups caused new bonds to be forged based on collegiality, shared interests, and friendship, augmenting the participation of most Sarajevans in their traditional familial and confessional communities.

The new paradigm of common life was observed in the newsrooms of the city's newspapers and magazines. The world of mononational periodicals, devoted to advancing the interests of a single nation with often harsh polemicizing rhetoric, was superseded by publications devoted to socialist ideals and the notion of "brotherhood and unity." One such publication, the newspaper *Oslobodjenje* (Liberation), had been published from August 1943 to the summer of 1945 in several other locations, but on April 12, 1945, it began publication in Sarajevo. The staffs of other publishing houses were also drawn from various ethnonational groups. Opera, theater, and dance companies were formed or revived in the first postwar months.

The new common life was particularly evident in the organization of athletic teams. Before the war many sports clubs consisted of members of a single ethnonational group and often carried a name that identified them with that group. The ethnonationally based clubs were dissolved after the city's liberation; new clubs were formed on the basis of the city's territorial subdivisions and individual enterprises. "In this manner, sports activities extended the wartime foundation of brotherhood and unity," according to one participant.[52] The prewar workers' teams, banned during the Second World War, were rejuvenated. Physical fitness committees organized group exercise programs and held competitions in local parks, schools, enterprises, and institutions.

During the first decade of socialism in Sarajevo, new institutions were created and others reformulated their roles.[53] The omnibus functions of the Regional Museum were assigned to new institutions, leaving the museum's staff to focus primarily on displays and the maintenance of its invaluable collections, including a substantial library. The State Archive of Bosnia-Herzegovina (later renamed the Archive of Bosnia-Herzegovina) was founded in

1947 as the repository for a huge collection of Austro-Hungarian, royal Yugoslav, wartime, and postwar documents.[54] The Oriental Institute, founded in 1950, became home to the Ottoman-era records previously held by the Regional Museum. It also acquired thousands of manuscripts in Arabic, Turkish, Persian, and other languages of the former Ottoman Empire.[55] The Historical Archive of Sarajevo was established in 1948 as the primary repository for documents, photographs, and publications pertaining to the city's history.[56] The Museum of the Revolution, eventually housed in a modernist building next to the Regional Museum, was established to hold and display the large number of wartime documents and mementoes of the city from the Second World War.

The newly formed National Library was a vanguard institution among those founded in the postwar years. Created by order of the Ministry of Education on May 22, 1945, it first gathered the books left behind by organizations that departed the city as the war ended, collecting eight thousand volumes by July 1945.[57] It then solicited gifts from citizens' private libraries, typically taking in a few hundred volumes at a time. Then in 1949 its holdings increased many times as it received the seized holdings of the Prosvjeta and Napredak national cultural societies after they were closed by the government. The two libraries together housed over forty-five thousand volumes. After a few years in the Regional Museum Building, the library moved to the Vijećnica and became the National and University Library. By 1990 it had acquired over two million volumes, only to lose almost all of them in a fire started by Serb nationalist bombardment in August 1992.

Other research institutes were founded as homes for specialists in a wide range of disciplines in the humanities, physical sciences, and social sciences. Such institutes were founded in the capital cities of each republic as part of the effort to make socialist Yugoslavia into an international center of learning and research. Each of the institutes added to the city's stature as a research center on par with other republican capitals and second only to Belgrade. The most accomplished scholars were honored by membership in the Scientific Society of Bosnia-Herzegovina (*Naučno društvo Bosne i Hercegovine*), created in 1951 and renamed the Academy of Arts and Sciences of Bosnia-Herzegovina (*Akademija nauka i umjetnosti Bosne i Hercegovine*) in 1966.[58] The institution sponsored many scholarly conferences and issued publications to disseminate the work of its members.

The city made great advances in higher education. The University of Sarajevo was founded in 1949. Six faculties were operating by the end of

1950, and the number of students more than tripled from 3,070 in 1952 to 11,683 in 1962.[59] From having a few scattered faculties in the interwar period, the city became a major regional center drawing students from all Yugoslav republics. Other faculties were added in the next two decades, and each faculty either occupied an existing structure or occasioned the design and construction of a new facility. Among these university buildings were the most striking architectural achievements of the socialist era, but some of the efforts were not successful. The economics faculty moved into the former Serbian Orthodox school next to the new Serbian Orthodox church but before the faculty's occupancy, the building was remodeled and its neo-Romanesque features eliminated, replaced by a nondescript modern façade facing the Square of Liberation.

Building up elementary and secondary education was a top priority of all levels of government. Elementary schools were reopened or built in every neighborhood, typically carrying the name of a wartime revolutionary hero. Secondary schools in the city center were operated at first in several structures dating from Austro-Hungarian times, but they proliferated as the city grew in numbers and size, and some moved into new facilities. Technical schools were founded to help meet the expanding demand for skilled workers in the rapidly growing industrial sectors in the first two decades of socialism. The school system countrywide came close to wiping out illiteracy, and Sarajevo schools contributed immensely to the republicwide growth in skilled workers and intellectuals.

Toward a socialist economy

Sarajevo sustained widespread physical damage from several different causes during the war. Greater or lesser damage had been inflicted by Axis bombing in 1941, by German vandalism, by Allied bombing in 1944, by Partisan sabotage, and by sabotage committed by German forces as they withdrew in April 1945. The extensive damage only sharpened Sarajevans' passionate determination to rebuild their town, and rebuilding was just the first step. Under KP direction the recovery campaign extended into the longest and largest economic expansion in the city's history.

In the days after liberation, KP officials urged business leaders and factory managers to return to work. On April 15, one week after liberation, owners of private industrial enterprises and trustees of state-owned factories were brought together, thanked for their contribution to the liberation of the city in a special message from Tito, and urged to renew production as soon as possible.[60] Two days later the city's merchants were addressed by Djuro Pucar, vice president of ZAVNOBiH.[61] They pledged to open their stores immediately, sell goods at prescribed prices, and ration scarce items among their customers. Trade unions were formed or revived in major enterprises in the weeks after the war. Workers' rallies were organized in various enterprises to urge a return to full production as soon as possible. The various appeals brought forth enthused determination. Despite substantial wartime sabotage by the Ustasha and Germans, most enterprises were back in production in a matter of weeks.[62]

Yugoslavia's leaders expeditiously laid the groundwork for widespread nationalization and rapid industrialization of the country.[63] In November 1944, well before Sarajevo was liberated, party leaders issued a decree allowing local authorities to confiscate privately owned properties for specific reasons.[64] Ten months later, the city council in liberated Sarajevo seized the Evropa and Central hotels after officials had rather dubiously linked those establishments to several incidents of sabotage and speculation.[65] Once peace was secured, the new government systematically took over privately owned factories in Sarajevo and appointed trustees (*povjerenici*) to oversee the transition to ownership by the new state. Like the Soviets, Yugoslav Communists divided economic sectors into three categories according to their importance: federal, republican, and local.[66] Heavy industry and producers of military equipment, sectors that included most Sarajevo factories, were deemed of federal importance. Most large factories were seized after the Yugoslav federal assembly passed a law in December 1946 providing for the nationalization of enterprises of federal significance, and most remaining enterprises were nationalized following adoption of a second law in April 1947. At the same time many Sarajevo enterprises were renamed in honor of various revolutionary heroes, making them part of the Partisan revolutionary memorial culture. The Main Railway Workshop took the name of Vaso Miskin-Crni, a Partisan hero who had died unexpectedly in July 1945 just after war's end.

Many operators of small craft shops were brought into the state sector by inclusion in craft producers' collectives that operated much like peasant collectives. The remaining craftspeople accounted for the only significant private-sector production in the city. Craftsmen faced continued competitive pressures from cheaper mass-produced goods, but the city's building boom drove demand for the services of those in the construction trades.

Craft production continued its overall decline dating from the late Austro-Hungarian years. The number of craft shops fell from 1,387 in 1940 (already greatly reduced in the interwar period) to 903 in 1946 and recovered only slightly to 916 in 1951.[67] The number of employees in craft production experienced only a modest increase, from 3,378 in 1946 to 3,832 in 1951.

In April 1947 the Yugoslav federal assembly adopted a five-year plan, and the Assembly of Bosnia-Herzegovina adopted its part of the plan two months later. Designed to run from 1947–51, the plan was broken down into one-year segments. Planning commissions were formed at all levels of government to set goals and monitor performance. The plan was never formally approved by the city council, but the city was deeply involved in the preparation and execution of the plan from the beginning.[68] Under the auspices of the plan, the city's largest expansion in history assumed the specific shape that would substantially alter the use of urban space.

The plan's goals were ambitious in the extreme, mitigated only by the use of low prewar production levels as starting benchmarks in many sectors of the economy. The value of production was expected to increase fourfold over 1939 levels. The federal plan emphasized the development of heavy industry, electrification, transportation, and communications infrastructure. For Sarajevo, the plan foresaw extensive projects in economic sectors of federal and republic significance, including the establishment of new military and metallurgical factories in the western end of the city. Railways were to convert to standard-gauge track, and a new rail station was to be built in Sarajevo to accommodate the larger trains. The city was to extend tram tracks to the western settlement of Ilidža and add bus service to several peripheral neighborhoods. The plan called for the building of a city bakery, a national library, a medical faculty, and a faculty of philosophy. In the third category (economic sectors of only local significance), enterprises were expected to increase employment from 2,608 in 1947 to 7,425 in 1951.

The Tito-Stalin split and socialism in Sarajevo

After months of deteriorating relations between Tito and Soviet leader Joseph Stalin, the Communist Information Bureau (Cominform) voted in June 1948 to expel Yugoslavia from the organization. At the same time, Stalin launched vicious accusations against Tito in an effort to overthrow his regime, and Yugoslavs prepared for a Soviet invasion. After a delay to digest the seriousness of the breach, Tito fought back and accused Stalin of seeking to make Yugoslavia into a puppet of the Soviet Union. The Tito-Stalin power struggle threw the KP throughout Yugoslavia into turmoil.[69] Each party member was forced to choose between loyalty to Tito, whom the Yugoslav Communists admired as the father of their revolution, and Stalin, whom they valorized as the leader of world communism. Most opted for Tito, but a significant number gave their first loyalty to Stalin. The Yugoslav leader responded with a nationwide purge of suspected Stalin sympathizers, called Cominformists. The intraparty split was particularly acute in Sarajevo, where nearly one-half of Bosnia-Herzegovina's Cominformists resided.[70] From late 1948 to 1951 the Sarajevo party and the city council were purged of many of their leading lights.

Just before the purges began, an election was held for city council members, again with only one list of candidates presented to the voters. As in the 1945 election, most incumbents were returned to their posts. The newly selected council first met in late September 1948, with Ferid Čengić as mayor. The new members already felt the heavy hand of central government weighing on their deliberations. As Mayor Čengić explained, "Today's committee is chosen by free will of citizens of Sarajevo ... but at the same time under control of higher authority. That makes our job that much more difficult, for we have two-part control over our work."[71] The council as constituted in September 1948 lasted less than three months. In December 1948 new council members steadfastly loyal to Tito were appointed. Few members were carried over from the previous body. Mayor Čengić lost his post, and Dane Olbina became the new mayor. A new executive committee met on December 10, 1948, and presided over a transition to the new roster of city council members.[72] City offices were shut down for two days while a comparable change in city administrators was implemented.

As mayor, the Partisan veteran Olbina brought decisiveness and a sense of urgency to the council. At his insistence, the council set deadlines for implementing each decision it made. Displaying impatience with the previous council's measured consideration of housing appeals, the new body ordered that unauthorized persons living in Jewish apartments move out immediately or face prosecution. To move the process forward, the council issued certificates to inspectors, granting them the right to enter any apartment in the city at any time. In February 1949 the council formed a department for apartments to hasten the completion of existing apartment buildings and develop proposals for new housing projects.[73] These decisive measures were part of a comprehensive response of the KP throughout Yugoslavia in the aftermath of the Tito-Stalin break. For a few years after the break, the KP consolidated its own power, further centralized the new socialist state, and silenced alternative political views. In May 1949 the city of Sarajevo was elevated in status by being removed from the jurisdiction of the Sarajevo region and assigned the same rank in the governmental hierarchy as the four regions of Bosnia-Herzegovina.[74] Despite the city's enhanced legal status, the council in this time consistently subscribed to the principle of democratic centralism, following the orders and implementing the decisions of higher authorities. Authority in the city was strictly hierarchical and centralized in the hands of the KP.

Subsequent to the Tito-Stalin split, the KP's first reflex was to accelerate the transition to a nationalized command economy and suppress organizations considered potentially counterrevolutionary. This led to the fiercest repression of the socialist era. In 1949 the government closed down the cultural societies in Sarajevo and nationalized their property, including the architecturally distinguished headquarters buildings of the Croat Napredak society and the Serb Prosvjeta. Other suspected leaders of the Young Muslims were tried in 1949 and received harsher sentences than those convicted earlier. Four of them were sentenced to death, although the sentences were never carried out. Many suspected Cominform sympathizers were arrested and sent to Goli otok (Barren Island), a small dot on the map of the Adriatic Sea.

Tito's break with Stalin also dealt a setback to the five-year plan that had been adopted only a year before. Yugoslavia's foreign trade in the postwar period was primarily with Cominform countries. Those developing relations were abruptly terminated and replaced by an economic blockade in 1948. Severe supply shortages forced some Sarajevo projects to be abandoned and others to be completed later than projected. The authorities extended the five-year plan another year, to the end of 1952, and replaced mandatory goals with voluntary guidelines for local enterprises. Despite many unrealistic expectations and unanticipated interruptions, much of the five-year plan was realized, thanks largely to the superior élan of the workers and youth of Sarajevo. Party leaders regularly exhorted everyone to fulfill the plan, and they blamed the Eastern European countries of the Cominform for trying to sabotage its realization. The daily press valorized overachievers who reached their goals ahead of time.[75] Dramatic increases were realized in several sectors during the six years of the five-year plan.

From 1946 to 1951, the value of goods and services produced in Sarajevo increased thirteenfold, albeit from very low starting levels. Many new factories were put into service, transportation facilities were rapidly expanded, and the first major housing projects were undertaken to accommodate the rapidly expanding population of workers and other new inhabitants.

Notwithstanding substantial progress in Sarajevo, the city's advances must be weighed against the catastrophic consequences of collectivization in the countryside. In seeking to out-Stalin the Cominform lands, the KP in 1948 and 1949 conducted intensive campaigns to bring peasants into collectives on the Soviet model.[76] Forced collectivization resulted in falling yields and widespread discontent. The campaign's failure coincided with severe droughts in 1950 and 1952. In 1952–3 many collectives were dissolved and peasants returned to their private holdings. The ill-advised campaign created widespread shortages and hunger in many rural areas and inevitably led to food shortages in the cities.

In addition to intensified repression and harsh collectivization, Stalin's expulsion of Yugoslavia led Tito and his closest associates to rethink the basic character of the socialist society they were seeking to build. Their reassessment in turn led to powerful aftershocks that redirected the transformation already in progress. To distinguish Yugoslav socialism from that of the Soviet Union, Tito and his advisors developed the concept of workers' self-management as an alternative to the bureaucratic centralism of the Soviet system. Under the doctrine of self-management, enterprises were to be managed by elected workers' councils. In contrast to the Soviet system of hierarchical state control, self-management was intended to eliminate the workers' sense of alienation from the system and to lead to the withering of the state—a primary objective in Marxist theory. With the change to self-management, enterprises were no longer owned by the state or a governmental unit but instead became "social property."

Self-management began in December 1949 as a pilot program to be implemented in 215 of the largest state-run enterprises in Yugoslavia.[77] In Sarajevo, the Vaso Miskin Crni enterprise (the former Main Railway Workshop) and the tobacco factory were selected to form workers' councils during the experimental phase.[78] A workers' council was elected in the railway workshop in March 1950 and the tobacco factory in May. The councils met regularly but functioned only as advisory bodies for their first few months. Then in June 1950 workers' self-management councils were mandated by law for all enterprises in the country.[79] By the end of 1950, all large enterprises and most small ones in Sarajevo had elected workers' councils.

Forming the councils was the first and easiest step in turning control over to the workers. A critical assessment of self-management in Sarajevo during its first year revealed that many workers were unqualified and disinclined to run enterprises in the manner the theory had envisioned.[80] Most workers were not able to manage the financial matters of an enterprise, the report found, and some directors were reluctant to disclose financial details, leading to an "administrative-bureaucratic method of resolving things." In some enterprises, strong directors were prone to convert workers' councils into their personal staffs. In others, councils spent many hours resolving the complaints of individual workers and failed to attend to the business of providing overall direction to the enterprise. Relying as it did on worker enthusiasm and commitment, the implementation of self-management was plagued with problems from the outset. It improved only modestly with time.

Physical transformation of the cityscape

Despite some changes to Sarajevo's physical appearance in the first postwar years, the transformation of the cityscape on a large scale began only in the late 1940s. The spatial and physical development of the city under socialism was intended to satisfy the two most pressing needs of a dynamic, expanding working class: employment opportunities and housing for all. Although the city council did not formally adopt a comprehensive urban plan until 1965, industrial and residential development practices were clearly inspired by precedents in other socialist societies.[81] Citizens came to enjoy easy access between factories and homes either by proximity or public transportation, and workers' residences were concentrated in high-rise apartment settlements accessible to shopping, educational institutions, and recreation facilities. As in the Soviet Union and other countries of east and southeast Europe, KP leaders implemented their socialist vision for Sarajevo through a combination of harnessing spontaneous enthusiasm and inaugurating a five-year plan.

Sarajevo's development as a socialist city benefited immensely from a change in economic philosophy proclaimed by Tito ten years after the war. At a rally in June 1955 he announced that economic policy henceforth "should stimulate the development of industrial sectors that directly influence the improvement of living standards."[82] The change was formally adopted in September as policy throughout Yugoslavia. A second five-year plan adopted in 1955 was designed to stimulate consumer spending by boosting personal income, developing light industry, increasing agricultural production, and hastening the transition to self-management. This time the plan achieved most of its specific objectives in four years. The shift in emphasis to higher living standards proved particularly fortuitous. The colossal investment in the industrial base in the late 1940s, coupled with the gradual rise in consumer spending, powered economic growth in the 1950s at a rate unprecedented in Sarajevo's history and unparalleled in most cities of the world. Personal income rose 11 percent annually between 1952 and 1964. In 1948, 72 percent of the population of Bosnia-Herzegovina lived in rural communities; that number fell to 36.6 percent by 1971.[83] The perpetual expansion of the housing stock in Sarajevo and other cities provided a growing supply of comfortable housing for those drawn into urban areas.

As a result, the most conspicuous transformation in the Sarajevo cityscape was the rise of ubiquitous high-rise residential complexes. Drawn by the city's disproportionate economic benefits, better living conditions, and urban cultural life, immigrants came to the city from both the countryside and other towns. Multiple-dwelling structures were built continuously throughout the socialist era. Makeshift structures built in the first few years after the war were gradually replaced by more durable residential buildings. The great expansion of Sarajevo's housing took place westward, into the largely empty spaces of the Sarajevo Field. The first of these were the housing settlements at Grbavica and Čengić Vila, begun in 1949 as part of the five-year plan.[84] The Čengić Vila complex was built by work brigades and domestic prisoners on work detail from a nearby jail. High-rise apartment buildings arose periodically along Vojvoda Putnik Street, which soon became a boulevard with tram tracks between the east and westbound lanes. Many high-rises were built in the spirit of a master design used throughout Yugoslavia, and costs were carefully controlled. Even architects complained of the drab repetitiveness of the new housing structures. Ivan Štraus complained, "The settlements were arranged in rows westwards, and each addition reached the level of mediocrity of its predecessor."[85] One pundit dubbed these structures "Tito Baroque."

Although their uniformity put off some observers, the high-rise housing settlements were redeemed by the convenience they offered their inhabitants, and they fulfilled the socialist vision of making all important services immediately accessible to the working class. Most buildings were grouped in settlements served by cafés, restaurants, shops, one or two schools, a tramway and bus stop, and a small park or central square. With contemporary

utility services, finished interiors, and regular maintenance, the new apartments were valued by those who lived there and coveted by those who did
not. Sarajevans did not stop appreciating their cultural heritage, but they
opted in overwhelming numbers for residence in the new, undistinguished
skyscrapers. The buildings conformed to socialist ideals about the value and
equality of the working class. The buildings' uniformity sent a message of
equality among workers of all professions, and their relatively luxurious
appointments were rewards for the contributions of socialist labor.

Nevertheless, a few housing complexes of distinction were built amid the
monotony of the high-rise settlements. The Ciglane settlement takes its
name from the old brickyard that once occupied the hill on which it was
built. Terraced housing units climb the hill in striking horizontal bands, and
a rail-based tram line moves residents to the higher levels. Other innovative
housing units were built in the first postwar years within the central city
before the rush to large high-rise settlements dominated areas to the west.
Although the high-rise housing complex became the hallmark of socialism
throughout Eastern Europe and the Soviet Union, buildings in Sarajevo were
not slavish imitations of those in other socialist countries. Socialist realism
was the officially endorsed architectural style of the Communist Party of the
Soviet Union, and after coming to power after the war, the KP of Yugoslavia
likewise adopted it.[86] But architects were not held to that style with the same
rigidity as in the Soviet Union and elsewhere in Eastern Europe, and several
projects that deviated from that style were built in the late 1940s.[87]
Architects strictly applied the doctrine in only a few Sarajevo buildings,
most notably the new rail station built to accommodate trains running on
standard-gauge track.

Work brigades had already begun laying standard-gauge track on the
Brod-Sarajevo line, called the "Youth Tracks," when the federal government
approved the new rail station. A team of three Czech architects designed
the station, and project managers and skilled construction workers from
Czechoslovakia and East Germany launched it. In summer 1948 the foreigners were abruptly recalled following Yugoslavia's expulsion from the
Cominform, causing a temporary halt in construction.[88] Work resumed
under the direction of Yugoslav architect Bogdan Stojkov, and the station
was completed by skilled construction workers and volunteer youth brigades from Sarajevo. The new station was dedicated in 1949.

In 1950 the Association of Yugoslav Architects, meeting in Dubrovnik,
unanimously voted to abandon socialist realism as a guiding philosophy for

their work.[89] Thereafter, architects had unimpeded access to contemporary Western architectural concepts, and most buildings were constructed in the spirit of modern architecture prevailing at the time. By the early 1960s it was possible to speak of a "Sarajevo circle" of architects. Their numbers grew with the founding of a faculty of architecture and urban design at the University of Sarajevo. They accounted for most new buildings in Sarajevo and also competed successfully to design projects in other towns and republics.

Sarajevo expanded to several times its prewar size under the general guidance of two comprehensive urban plans.[90] The first was prepared in some haste (under the pressure of the five-year plan) by a team of planners from Czechoslovakia in 1948. It was never formally adopted by the city council, but many of its less controversial provisions were implemented in the succeeding two decades. The planning process was revived in 1951 under the guidance of Mayor Dane Olbina, but it was not finalized until 1963 and was adopted by the city council only in 1965. It was intended to guide development through 1985, and it governed the city's development until the planning for the Olympic Winter Games partially superseded it in the early 1980s.

Both plans foresaw massive spatial expansion. They emphasized longitudinal development to the west and a second corridor of growth to the north along the Koševo Stream. Despite general agreement on the direction and scope of expansion, controversy surrounded plans for areas at the two ends of the historic central city: the Baščaršija to the east and the Marindvor to the west. The Baščaršija conundrum pitted the imperatives of modern urban growth against preservation of the city's historical heritage. Eager to remove reminders of the feudal past from the city, a special commission had ordered the destruction of over two hundred unoccupied craft shops in 1945, resulting in a large unoccupied area in the city center. In 1953 the influential architect Juraj Neidhardt proposed to level all but the most significant historical structures to create a mammoth theme park with a soaring, arched entranceway.[91] In 1955 the city council commissioned the architects Zdravko Kovačević and Alija Bejtić to develop a plan for the area. They proposed to eradicate most of the Ottoman heritage from the area: "The čaršija is essential to the city's needs and contemporary urban functions of city life must develop there. The old čaršija cannot be preserved and must make way for the new. ... [One should] not blindly imitate the old buildings but create organic relations in architecture."[92]

Fortunately, the traditional Baščaršija was saved from the modernizers by the prospect of tourism and by Sarajevans' devotion to their Ottoman · heritage. Critics noted that the 1955 proposal was unlikely to provide the ambience being sought by contemporary tourists. The debate was definitively resolved with final agreement on a Baščaršija plan in 1975. The city fathers preserved the area much in its traditional form and converted many facilities into fashionable restaurants and shops. They even rebuilt in wood the shops that had been torn down in 1945. The area today attracts visitors and is an essential part of the Sarajevo tradition of the korzo.

Marindvor became the modernist counterpoint to Baščaršija traditionalism. Located at the westernmost protrusion of the central city, Marindvor became the starting point for the long Vojvoda Putnik Street and tram tracks that run to Ilidža. On either side of this east-west ribbon of tram tracks and multilane highway, unrestrained modernism reigned in several educational structures and a long progression of high-rise apartment settlements. The faculty of philosophy (1959), the faculty of natural sciences and mathematics (1966), and the stark, imposing façade of the Museum of the Revolution (1963) were built on the flanks of the Habsburg-era Regional Museum Building, making it an isolated, albeit imposing, anachronism in a sea of modernist development. In 1970 a steel and glass high-rise was built on the south side of Marindvor to house the government offices of the Socialist Republic of Bosnia-Herzegovina. A decade later an adjoining building was constructed to house the Assembly of Bosnia-Herzegovina, composed of alternating horizontal windows and panels that offset the vertical thrust of the government office building. The two structures face a plaza with black marble installations and a broad expanse of stone panels. (In the early 1990s the plaza would become the city's new center of public political expression, something not foreseen in the protest-free socialist era.) On the north side of Vojvoda Putnik Boulevard, a Holiday Inn was constructed in the 1980s and twin high-rise towers were built to house the offices of UNIS, the conglomerate of military enterprises.

Like the Baščaršija plan, many designs went through several planning iterations before being constructed. In 1948 the council accepted the design of a Belgrade architect to renovate the seriously damaged Sephardic synagogue and turn it into a cultural center.[93] This project languished on the drawing board for some years. In 1951 the city council's urban council, headed by Mayor Dane Olbina, held an architectural competition to renovate the temple as a concert hall.[94] The winning proposals, elaborate and expensive, went unrealized.[95] In the 1960s an agreement was reached to preserve the structure's shell and turn the interior into a cultural center. The Jewish Community Organization later donated the building to the city, and it has served in recent years as a cultural center for performances and lectures.[96]

The plan to open a new city cemetery was also the subject of protracted community debate. The city had over a hundred cemeteries, the vast majority of them small Muslim graveyards, but most of them had reached capacity by the 1960s.[97] After considering several options, the city council selected a hillside at Bare, north of the central city. All confessional communities reached consensus on the location, but the allocation of land and the permissible size of gravestones remained in dispute for some time. One planner proposed allocating plots regardless of the confession of the deceased. "Since we can live together in the same city," he argued, "we can be together in interment."[98] The religious communities rejected that proposal, but eventually agreement was reached. Separate but adjoining chapels were provided for each religious community in the structure completed in 1965. With the Bare chapel and cemetery prepared to receive new permanent lodgers, most other cemeteries in the city were closed.

The new cemetery created another addition to the succession of burial grounds along the new north-south corridor. The dead in these cemeteries were soon joined by the most vigorous of the living, as the north-south corridor also became home to several facilities for the city's organized sports teams. The Skenderija Sports and Cultural Center, completed in 1969, was a shining star in socialist-era urban design. The multipurpose facility combined a large indoor arena, meeting areas, shops, restaurants, office space, and an art gallery arranged around a large central patio. The mayor at the time considered its completion the highlight of his tenure in office and a major advance in the city's position as a sports, entertainment, and cultural center in Yugoslavia. The Belgrade newspaper *Borba* (Battle) awarded Živorad Janković and Halid Muhasilović, who designed the building, its annual prize for the best architectural achievement in Yugoslavia. It became the primary indoor sports hall and meeting center in the city until the Zetra Sports Center was built adjacent to the Koševo Stadium in preparation for the 1984 Winter Olympics.

Decentralization and local government

After introducing self-management to economic enterprises in 1950, the KP applied the same basic principles to local government and eventually to all sectors of society. The logic of workers' self-management led inexorably to decentralized political power, giving greater authority to lower units of government. If laborers could control the enterprises in which they worked, reasoned party theorists, they should also assume control of the territory on which they lived. Although such thinking might have strengthened Sarajevo's role and stature in the Yugoslav political system, instead it bolstered the position of the city's constituent municipalities, juxtaposing their interests against those of the city government.

Party theorists further concluded that the KP should no longer function as a typical hierarchical Leninist party. In 1953 the party changed its name to the League of Communists (SK; *Savez komunista*) of Yugoslavia to signify its transition from a command organization into a "guiding force" in society. Shortly thereafter, the people's front changed its name to the Socialist Alliance of Working Peoples (*Socijalistički savez radnog naroda*). The philosophy of self-management worked its way through several constitutional changes into the legal system. The basic unit of local government was renamed the municipality (*opština*).[99] Federal and republican constitutions conferred upon municipalities authority that would have been unthinkable in the immediate postwar years of centralized rule. But both in enterprises and in local government, these changes were slow to take hold, and self-management did nothing to dilute the monopolistic position of the SK, which remained for decades a closed and hierarchical organization. But the elevation of municipalities posed a potential challenge to the city of Sarajevo, which was made up of six municipalities as of 1952. Self-management principles threatened to relegate the city government's role to coordinating the work of its constituent municipalities.

Sarajevo's new role in the era of self-management was first spelled out in federal and republican laws promulgated in 1952.[100] Acting in accord with the federal constitution, the republican government reorganized local administration in Bosnia-Herzegovina and designated Sarajevo as a city.[101] But the republic assembly did not carry that designation forward in the law on municipalities and districts passed in 1955, and instead completely eliminated the category of "city" from local government structures. Municipalities, on the other hand, were exalted in the 1955 law as "the fundamental political-territorial organization of self-management of working people and fundamental social-economic unit of the population on its territory."[102] Regional governments were permitted to organize sub-units to function as cities, but only to the extent that those bodies coordinated the activities of selected municipalities. Sarajevo was duly recognized by the Socialist Republic of Bosnia-Herzegovina as such a coordinating body, but the arrangement left the city beholden to its constituent municipalities.

As of 1955 the city was a legal fiction. It functioned as a governing unit only because of the SK, the sinew and muscle that held Yugoslavia together despite cumbersome and unworkable constitutional arrangements. The SK, in turn, was not even mentioned in the early postwar constitutions. That changed in the federal constitution of 1963, which recognized the SK as "the organized leading force of the working class and the working people in building socialism and in creating the solidarity of working people, and of the brotherhood and unity of the people."[103] The same 1963 constitution also reinstated the "city" category of local government, but on the other hand it further enshrined the municipality as a fundamental governing unit. The 1963 federal constitution first used the term "sociopolitical community" to characterize the three most valued governmental bodies: municipalities, republics (along with the two autonomous regions), and the federation. Being absent from this elite list, Sarajevo was again thrust into a second-class legal status. Furthermore, the 1963 Constitution of Bosnia-Herzegovina did not specify Sarajevo as a city, something that it could have done under provisions of the federal constitution that was promulgated simultaneously.

The pendulum began to swing back in favor of the city in 1969. In that year the city council, acting in accord with provisions of federal and republican constitutions, assigned to itself the status of a "sociopolitical community." And the 1974 republican constitution recognized Sarajevo by name as a "separate sociopolitical community of associated municipalities from the territory of the city."[104] With this change, the city government regained some of its earlier stature, but potential conflict between individual municipalities and the city government loomed larger than ever. Since municipalities had been enshrined as the "basic sociopolitical community" of government, the city of Sarajevo, despite its enhanced constitutional position, could expand only by annexing entire municipalities.

In 1977 the city added four municipalities—Hadžici, Pale, Trnovo, and Ilijaš—which together were about three times the size of the six more urbanized municipalities of the city center, Stari grad, Centar, Novo Sarajevo, Novi grad, Vogošća, and Ilidža. The four new municipalities functioned as the aprons of urban sprawl, annexed to the city in anticipation of further growth and already dotted with occasional factories and transportation facilities. Each included small urban settlements that were de facto part of

the city, but each also contained peasant villages, extensive tracts of undeveloped rural land, and mountainous terrain far from the city's urban core.
All ten municipalities exercised considerable political independence from
the city and squabbled amongst themselves for their share (or more) of the
city's services and budget. Residents of the less urbanized municipalities felt
neglected at the expense of the urban core, and those in the older municipalities resented the high cost of extending urban infrastructure to rural
areas. By 1990 the peripheral municipalities enjoyed most services, but the
city was only beginning to extend access to the city's water supply in those
areas.[105]

The city's evolving status revealed the experimental character of economic and political life in Sarajevo after 1948. Tito and the SK, despite adopt-

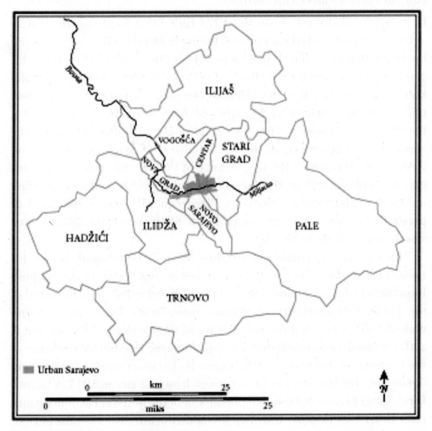

7.2 The ten municipalities of Sarajevo, 1990.

ing many incarnations of self-management in successive constitutions, never successfully created a viable, self-sustaining local government structure for the city of Sarajevo. Their failure would become apparent after Tito's death in 1980 and even more obvious after the SK lost power in the 1990 elections. The relatively powerless constitutional position of the city formed an important backdrop to the discord and fragmentation that developed after power passed to nationalist parties in 1990. With the city's jurisdiction over its constituent municipalities constitutionally limited, the opportunity to weaken the city by taking control of individual municipalities would prove irresistible to aspiring political entrepreneurs during the early 1990s.

Postwar Partisan memorial culture

In an apocryphal scene from the 1972 film *Valter brani Sarajevo* (Valter defends Sarajevo), a German officer, having been relieved of his command for failing to capture the elusive Partisan resistance leader Valter, voices his grudging admiration for the city. "Now that I must leave Sarajevo, I finally know who Valter is," he states. Another German officer orders him, "Then tell me his name right now!" Sweeping his hand across the vista of the city, the first officer answers, "You see this city? *Das ist Walter!*" His last three words have been etched in the consciousness of Sarajevans ever since. Resistance to tyranny is the very essence of the city, according to this cinematic history lesson eagerly embraced by Sarajevans as accurately portraying their fundamental ideals. Valter has frequently been resurrected to personify various causes, most notably during the antinationalist and antiwar demonstrations in March of 1992.

   This socialist-era parable of wartime Sarajevo epitomized the revolutionary spirit. The film was widely viewed in Yugoslavia. In the People's Republic of China, millions watched the film and admired its portrayal of the popular revolutionary resistance movement. *Valter brani Sarajevo* undoubtedly overstated the universality of the Partisan resistance, but it aptly captured the indefatigable determination and remarkable resilience of the Communist-led resistance fighters who harassed Sarajevo's occupiers during the war and aided in driving them from the city in 1945. Vladimir Perić-Valter became Sarajevo's embodiment of the postwar Partisan memorial culture that flourished in Yugoslavia throughout the socialist period. The legend of his life and death fit into a memorial hierarchy that the Communists carefully structured to valorize the Partisans and highlight the sacrifices so many Yugoslavs made during the war.

At the pinnacle of the memorial hierarchy was Josip Broz Tito. It is simply impossible to overstate the stature Tito enjoyed in the minds of most Sarajevans during his lifetime. The respect he enjoyed was derived from his extraordinary Partisan career (undeniably laudatory but carefully manicured for public consumption) and his defiance of Stalin, but he was further admired for his infrequent but thoughtful interventions in political matters. He was the symbolic unifying figure of Yugoslav socialism and the ultimate arbiter of political disputes. Yugoslavs became addicted to Tito.

Tito first visited Sarajevo in November 1945 and returned many times thereafter. Huge crowds greeted him, and banners were hung across major streets along his entry route. During his last visit a few years before his death in 1980, he entered the city from the east in an open-top Mercedes that followed the route Franz Ferdinand had taken in 1914.[106] Aged and corpulent, he sat erect in the car's back seat. Rather than receiving a hearty reception, he was greeted with subdued, reverential applause by the thousands lining his route of entry. Those in the crowd seemed honored just to have laid eyes on him. As he slowly alighted and entered the hotel, a chorus of girls in folk costumes greeted him with flowers and chanted "We are Tito's, Tito is ours." His reception, in short, befitted a saint more than a political leader. Nowhere was Tito more revered than in Sarajevo.

Just below Tito in the postwar memorial hierarchy was a select group of "national heroes," men and a few women, living and dead, honored for "unprecedented heroism in the battle against the people's enemies and for demonstrated heroism and service in the war of people's liberation from 1941–5."[107] Valter was one of sixty-one men and two women from the Sarajevo area who were honored with that designation.[108] National heroes were typically memorialized with life-sized busts placed on modest pedestals. Below them on the hierarchy were "fallen soldiers," those who had perished in battle against the occupiers. Finally there were "victims of fascist terror," noncombatants who died in concentration camps or in other ways perished at the hands of the Germans, Italians, and their collaborators.

It is not true, as many uninformed observers asserted in the 1990s, that the Partisans sought to sweep the victims of violence in the Second World War under the rug of history. National heroes, fallen soldiers, and victims of terror were at the core of postwar memorial culture, honored repeatedly in many different ways during the socialist era. But the party had specific objectives in creating its postwar memorial culture. In particular the party wanted to avoid using wartime victims to inflame nationalist resentment. Party leaders painstakingly avoided categorizing victims in ways that lent credence to allegations of collective national guilt. To that end KP leaders honored victims and demonized perpetrators regardless of their nationality. They made no particular effort to obscure the national identity of victims, but they honored them as victims rather than as Serbs, Jews, Croats, or Muslims. In an effort to enhance the legend of the party's infallibility, its leaders brooked no criticism of the Partisans or the KP. For its insistence on honoring individuals rather than groups, the party endured repeated criticism in the late 1980s and 1990s by nationalists who wanted to bolster claims that their particular group had suffered most during the war.

In the late 1970s, as Tito grew old, the party rejuvenated the Partisan cult with larger and more abstract monuments, in an apparent effort to make his legacy a permanent feature of Yugoslavia's landscape. Each of the six republics and two autonomous provinces was allowed to select a single city that embodied the Partisan struggle to take Tito's name as part of its title. (Bosnia-Herzegovina selected Drvar, famed for the German airborne assault in which Tito was nearly captured, and renamed the city "Tito's Drvar" [*Titov Drvar*]). In Sarajevo city officials made plans for a memorial park on a hill overlooking Sarajevo from the south. Construction of the Vraca Park began in April 1980, just a month before Tito's death, and was completed in November 1981. The Vraca monument was intended to be an enduring memorial to all of Sarajevo's war victims, regardless of nationality. Covering 78,000 square meters, the park's outdoor walkways and stairs ascended gently to an auditorium and a courtyard ringed with oval walls. The walls were covered with white relief letters that spelled the names of over eleven thousand men, women, and children who perished during the Second World War.

Vraca Park was dedicated on November 25, 1981, the "Day of Statehood of Bosnia-Herzegovina" in honor of the first ZAVNOBiH meeting in 1943.[109] The selection of that date signaled the shifting political center from federal Yugoslavia to the Socialist Republic of Bosnia-Herzegovina, even though the ardor of most Sarajevans for Yugoslavia remained undiminished throughout the decade of the 1980s. Dane Olbina, the mayor in 1948–53 and a senior Partisan veteran actively involved in the city's public life, delivered the dedication address. Olbina outlined the history of Sarajevo's contribution to the national liberation struggle. He recalled the first acts of resistance in the city in late July 1941, the formation of Partisan units in the nearby hills, and the role of Sarajevans in supporting the Partisan movement. He noted that some six thousand Sarajevans had participated in the national liberation struggle, and that another nine thousand joined after the city was liberated. Turning to the purpose of establishing the park, Olbina stated, "On these granite surfaces and on the walls of the fortress, one finds information on the fallen soldiers of the national liberation war and the victims of fascist terror in Sarajevo: Jews, Serbs, Muslims, Croats, and others. ... Here are the names of over two thousand fallen soldiers and nine thousand victims of terror."

Aware that over 70 percent of those who perished in Sarajevo were Jews, Olbina highlighted their sacrifice: "[Only] when one reads the names of the murdered children, old people, and particularly information about the horrible fate of our fellow Jewish citizens, does one get a true sense of fascist savagery." In the spirit of Partisan memorial culture at the time, Olbina thus not only named the nationalities of the various victims but also emphasized the disproportionate losses suffered by Jews during the war. His speech refutes the charge that the memorial culture of the time refused to recognize the nationalities of victims of the Second World War.

Vraca Park, with its spectacular view of the city and easy accessibility, became a favorite destination for school excursions and weekend leisure strolls during the last decade of socialism. But it was destroyed during the siege of the 1990s. Bosnian Serb nationalists set up an artillery battery at the site, directing their weapons against Sarajevans and their city in the valley below. They vandalized and burned the small auditorium that once featured presentations about Sarajevo's resistance to Nazi occupation. When I visited the park in 1998, tens of thousands of letters in relief that once spelled the names of fascism's victims had been peeled from the walls and lay on the ground in desecration of the monument to valorize war's victims. Children playing at the site were using some of the letters in a game of dominoes.

The origins of decline

Socialism decayed slowly and painfully in Sarajevo. Not until the early 1990s did Sarajevo succumb to the combined menace of resuscitated nationalism, economic decline, and political impotence, but the crisis of those years was rooted in problems of prior decades. Economic problems originated not with outright decline, but rather with a slowing of the economic boom in the

early 1960s. In an effort to address the slowdown in growth, the SK introduced sweeping economic reforms at the Eighth Party Congress in 1964 to
broaden the market economy and stimulate consumer spending. In an effort
to divert investment into economically productive projects, the building of
new high-rise structures was banned in Sarajevo for several years in the mid-
1960s for most sectors except housing.[110] The key problems stemmed from
the state's continued control over investment dollars and prices. Despite
large investments in political factories in less developed regions, the gap in
the living standards within the country continued to widen and the clamor
for more investment continued unabated.

One source of the economic crisis was the complex and inefficient
system of capital investment in the country. Workers' councils theoretically
controlled their own capital, but the influence of directors and party functionaries remained substantial. Workers' benefits often outweighed in monetary value the wages paid. These constituted expenses to the enterprise but
were considered as entitlements by workers, who viewed them as their
inherent rights under socialist self-management. Since most housing in
urban areas consisted of socially owned apartments in high-rise buildings,
many employees valued their apartments as much or more than the wages
they received. Homebuilding constituted a huge drain on capital, and much
investment potential was diverted into residences that benefited individuals
but made no recurring contribution to economic productivity.

Yugoslavia took loans and credits from western countries and financial
institutions to fund many of its major projects in the 1960s and 1970s. In a
departure from practices in other socialist countries, workers were allowed
to seek employment outside of Yugoslavia. By the early 1970s over a million
Yugoslav "guest workers" were working in Germany, Austria, France, Britain, and other Western European countries. They sent home remittances
that temporarily fed domestic investment, but after the Arab oil embargo of
1972, Western European countries entered an economic recession and
guest workers were often among the first to lose their jobs.

The creeping systemic crisis did not at first diminish the distinctly un-
socialist lifestyle of the average Sarajevan in the 1960s and 1970s. Most
Sarajevans were paid in a combination of salary and entitlements that included an apartment. Leisure time increased and the opportunities to spend it
increased as well. Many Sarajevans built rustic weekend homes known as
vikendicas in the hills around the city. People walked the many paths and skied
the slopes of Mounts Jahorina and Bjelašnica. With the relaxation of cultural

control, Western pop groups gave concerts that drew thousands. Sporting events drew ever larger crowds, particularly for the periodic confrontations between the city's two premier soccer clubs, Sarajevo and Željezničar. Few passed up the opportunity to take an annual vacation on the Adriatic coast, and other Yugoslavs and foreigners reciprocated by visiting Sarajevo, principally on brief trips from Dubrovnik and other coastal towns. Tourism and the rise in household spending propelled growth in the service sector at the expense of industry starting in the 1960s. For many Sarajevans, the last decades of socialism would be remembered as the best of times.

Nationalism, however, loomed as a potentially divisive force in Bosnia-Herzegovina, the only republic in which no nationality commanded an absolute majority, and its capital Sarajevo, in which those of various nationalities and identities mixed and mingled in close proximity. With Yugoslavia's legal recognition of the Bosnian Muslims as a separate nation in the 1960s, national discourse became officially tripartite. In 1964 the Bosnian Muslims, having rejected Croat and Serb identity in socialist-era censuses, finally attained constitutional status comparable to Serbs and Croats.[111] The vast majority of Bosnian Muslims welcomed the official recognition, but Serb and Croat nationalists were affronted that the Muslims rejected an identity as Serbs or Croats of the Islamic faith. Although the nature of Bosnian Muslim identity and its implications for Serb and Croat claims was debated in print and in academic dialogues in the 1960s, it remained for many Bosnians an abstruse theoretical argument in its early years. The nature of Bosnian Muslim identity further raised questions about the relationship of Bosnian Muslims to the Socialist Republic of Bosnia-Herzegovina and to the Yugoslav federation.

Political discourse became increasingly open in the 1970s. A house in the small town of Stojčevac in the Sarajevo suburbs was the site of an extraordinary forum of open discussion among Sarajevo's leading intellectuals.[112] Participants could express their views without attribution and without fear of political consequences, although most or all of the sessions were taped and ended up in the archive of the central committee of the SK of Bosnia-Herzegovina. Beginning in the 1970s, national issues were discussed forthrightly among Serbs, Muslims, and Croats. Since the cadres of intellectuals and party leaders considerably overlapped, those discussions involved both influential academics and leading policymakers. Šaćir Filandra, who reviewed the tapes of these discussions, reported candid exchanges regarding whether the Bosnian Muslims had a genuine literature distinct from that of the Serbs and Croats.[113] Such issues soon made their way into the periodical press, and the limits of tolerance expanded to accommodate vigorous debates about national identity and traditions of all nationalities.

While considering educational reforms in the late 1970s, professors and policy-makers debated issues of nationality and the republic's relationship to the Yugoslav federation. Some professors in the department of literature at the University of Sarajevo felt that the existing teaching curriculum slighted the Bosnian Muslims and the Republic of Bosnia-Herzegovina. In 1979 they argued that the existing program of study, emphasizing Yugoslav literature, highlighted Serb and Croat literature and presented Bosnia-Herzegovina as an artificial communist creation.[114] Members of the history department likewise debated whether to emphasize the history of the peoples of Yugoslavia or that of the peoples of Bosnia-Herzegovina. Most of those who favored recognition of the Bosnian Muslim nationality also supported a shift to republic-level education, but others saw in Yugoslavism the best defense against the threats of other nationalisms. In the end both departments opted to shift their instruction toward the literature and history of the peoples of Bosnia-Herzegovina. With similar intent the Academy of Arts and Sciences in Sarajevo launched an effort in 1968 to prepare a comprehensive synthetic history of Bosnia-Herzegovina. That project never reached fruition because of ongoing disputes over its contents.[115]

In the 1980s Sarajevans were increasingly bedeviled by economic decline and political disagreement. These problems grew progressively worse through a decade that began with Tito's death, taking from socialist Yugoslavia its heroic founder and ultimate arbiter of political discord. Sarajevans found it hard to believe that he really had died on that day of May 4, 1980. The 1980s slogan, "After Tito, Tito," was partly a comment on the durability of his key policies, but it also expressed the hope that his legacy might rejuvenate the moribund socialist Yugoslavia. His successors found themselves unable to achieve a viable solution for any major crisis facing Yugoslavia. Economic problems redoubled after his death. Foreign debt, already $18 billion by 1981, continued to mount,[116] and inflation grew gradually throughout the decade until it reached astronomical levels in 1989.

Under Tito's leadership, Yugoslav socialism had neither denied nor suppressed national identity, although not all groups were accorded equal status at all times during socialist years. At times socialist authorities acted against some nationalists deemed a threat to the socialist order. Party and government leaders in Bosnia-Herzegovina, convinced after Tito's death that nationalism threatened the stability of the republic, led the assault on perceived nationalist excesses. Sarajevo became the center of antinationalist repression in Yugoslavia during the 1980s. Prosecutors in Sarajevo conducted two prosecutions in hopes of discouraging such public expressions. One trial was directed against members of the Young Muslims, the other against Serb nationalist dissident Vojislav Šešelj.

Thirteen members of the Young Muslims were tried and convicted in July and August 1983 of subverting the socialist order.[117] Much of the case centered on *The Islamic Declaration*, a treatise Alija Izetbegović wrote during the late 1960s. The link between that document and the subversion of the socialist order is dubious at best. Izetbegović nowhere mentioned Sarajevo, Bosnia-Herzegovina, or Yugoslavia in his tract. *The Islamic Declaration* is better described as a quest to define a middle path between conservatives and modernizers in global Islam.[118] As with the defendants in the two prosecutions of Young Muslims in the late 1940s, the accused received sentences of varying lengths. Izetbegović was sentenced to fourteen years in prison. He served only six years and emerged from prison as the undisputed leader of the principal Bosnian Muslim political party in 1989.

Six months after the trial of the Young Muslims, prosecutors brought charges against Vojislav Šešelj, a Sarajevo-born Serb and assistant professor of political science at the University of Sarajevo.[119] He had offended party leaders with treatises criticizing single-party rule and the policies of President Tito and Edvard Kardelj, the party's leading theoretician. Šešelj's unpublished manuscripts laid out virulent Serb nationalist themes. He advocated dividing Bosnia-Herzegovina between Serbia and Croatia, and he accused the authorities of promoting Muslim nationalism and persecuting Serbian intellectuals. Some of his writings were seized in February 1984 as he traveled by train from Sarajevo to Belgrade. At his trial in July 1984 he received an eight-year sentence for inciting "hostile propaganda against the constitutional order of Yugoslavia," but his sentence was twice reduced on appeal. He was released in March 1986.

In the long run both prosecutions proved counterproductive. Imprisonment made martyrs of both Šešelj and Izetbegović and in the early 1990s catapulted each into a leadership position at the head of his national group. Šešelj emerged from prison more acerbic than ever, voicing ever harsher criticism of the socialist system, and its alleged persecution of Serbs, at meetings in Belgrade in February 1987 and in Zagreb in March 1987. He moved to Belgrade, became active in fundraising campaigns among émigré

Chetnik organizations, and became a political fixture as a hard-line Serb nationalist. He formed a paramilitary group, recruited volunteers, and deployed it in his native Bosnia to commit some of the worst atrocities against Muslims in the war of 1992–5.

The political and economic problems of the early 1980s began to impact significantly the lives of many Sarajevans. Then, as the city was sinking slowly into the same economic morass that bedeviled the rest of the country, the decline was temporarily stemmed by a single act: The decision of the International Olympic Committee to award the 14th Winter Games to Sarajevo.

The Olympic crescendo

The Winter Olympic Games of 1984 were an appropriate showcase for the city's decades-long shift to tourism, sports, aesthetic allure, and higher living standards. The city drew immediate benefits not only from the games but also from the facilities built in preparation for them. Following the announcement of Sarajevo's selection, the city launched an ambitious building campaign. Many structures were designed to serve the army of Olympic athletes, fans, dignitaries, and reporters that descended on the city. A housing complex for athletes was constructed at Mojmilo, adding to the stock of repetitive high-rise structures in Novo Sarajevo. The Zetra Sports Center was built adjacent to the Koševo Stadium, which was refurbished to become the scene of the spectacular opening ceremony for the games in 1984.

In addition to several hotels constructed near Olympic facilities on the Bjelašnica and Igman mountains, the Holiday Inn was built in the Marindvor area on the near western side of the city. With its bold yellow-and-brown color scheme and cubic composition, it instantly became Sarajevo's most controversial structure. Ivan Štraus, the building's architect, explained that he had "paraphrased a space organization scheme of Sarajevo's Morića Han from the seventeenth century (a famous hotel from those times) in a modern style, as a ten-story cube paneled with surprising yellow aluminum façade square plates."[120] Less charitable was the assessment of Roger Cohen, a *New York Times* journalist who lived in the hotel for months in the early 1990s. Doubtless speaking for the majority, he called it a "hideous mustard-colored block. ... designed, it seemed, with the overriding aim of chilling the soul."[121] Whatever one's judgment of its architectural merits, the hotel remains a conspicuous landmark, an arresting cube of yellow and brown amid the otherwise drab surroundings of Marindvor.

Utility services and structures were modernized in advance of the games. A large new postal-telephone building, consisting of layers of horizontal concrete slabs, was erected amid nondescript high rise housing complexes in western Sarajevo. Natural gas services were extended to the entire city and coal-burning heaters were phased out, alleviating a major cause of visual pollution but rendering the city more vulnerable to energy outages in the war to come. Many Ottoman and Austro-Hungarian structures were repaired and repainted, and some long-neglected facades were restored. A modern airport terminal was completed just in time to serve athletes and passengers arriving for the games.

The 14th Olympic Winter Games opened festively on February 8, 1984, with welcomes by Olympic Committee President Juan Antonio Samaranch and Yugoslav Federation President Mika Špiljak. On the dais with them was the Bosnian Croat politician (and later federal prime minister) Branko Mikulić, whose substantial political influence had led to Sarajevo being chosen to host the 14th Winter Games. The same day, a refurbished Habsburg-era villa overlooking the city was dedicated as the Museum of the 14th Olympic Winter Games by a similar coterie of dignitaries. The museum would hold the mementoes and artifacts of the games for only eight years before being singled out in 1992 as one of the first cultural objects to be destroyed by Bosnian Serb nationalist gunners besieging the city. In 1984, however, it was viewed as an enduring repository to display the achievements of athletes and the city during the games.

One thing was missing from the opening ceremony: snow. While there was adequate snow on the ski runs at higher elevations, the city below was bereft of the winter atmosphere that so many had imagined. Two days after the opening ceremony, the crisis was resolved and another created. Snow fell in such quantities as to create a two-day snow emergency in the city, and downhill ski events were postponed for a day or two.[122] To Sarajevans, most of them thoroughly secularized and far removed from the religious faith of earlier days, it seemed a miracle wrought by an unknown hand to ensure the Games' success. Both the city and the slopes had more than enough snow to win everyone's praises, and another major storm deposited more snow a week later.[123]

The nonsocialist world was introduced to Sarajevo in the best possible light. Since hotel room capacity fell far short of demand, many visitors were accommodated in Sarajevans' private homes and experienced the city's time-honored hospitality. The fifteen hundred competitors and twenty-two thousand visitors included political leaders, Hollywood stars, a bevy of sports figures, and a crush of journalists from around the world. They left with lingering memories of wonderful days passed in an idyllic town surrounded by superb winter recreation facilities. The games and the visitors were remembered no less fondly by Sarajevans, many of whom identify the two weeks of the Olympic Games as the high point of the city's history.

The euphoria could not endure. The Olympic crescendo was an ironic climax that wrung the last benefits from an increasingly obsolete and dysfunctional sociopolitical system. In all sectors except housing, the furious building activity dwindled in the years after the Olympics. A few partly completed construction projects were simply abandoned after the games, leaving such eyesores as the skeletal frames and concrete beams of a never-completed four-lane highway bypassing the Koševo area en route to the city's western end. With fond memories of two weeks in the global spotlight, Sarajevans next turned to face the growing crisis that befell Yugoslavia in the latter half of the 1980s.

8. From Socialist Decline to Sarajevo's National Division

Sarajevo's shift away from socialism, begun in the late 1980s, was interrupted in 1992 by war and a prolonged siege that nearly destroyed the city. Even as late as 1991, as war raged in neighboring Croatia, few Sarajevans anticipated the catastrophe to come. As communism collapsed in the Soviet Union and Eastern Europe, most Sarajevans optimistically anticipated a peaceful transition to democracy, economic improvement, and a continuation of their common life. They shared in the euphoria that accompanied the collapse of communism elsewhere in Eastern Europe, but, aware of the divisive forces that had wrought such destruction half a century earlier, many Sarajevans tempered their enthusiasm with apprehension of separatist nationalisms. Their fears proved justified. Neither Sarajevo nor the Republic of Bosnia-Herzegovina had sufficiently robust political institutions or economies to subdue the forces of separatism that would eventually overwhelm them. Aggressive Serb nationalism in the Republics of Serbia and Montenegro after 1987 and Croat nationalism in the Republic of Croatia after 1989 made it unlikely that Sarajevo could make the transition to pluralist democracy unscathed by intervention from its neighbors.

Weakened government and the erosion of authority

Weakened by economic crisis, nationalism, and the political decentralization enshrined in the 1974 constitution, the Socialist Federal Republic of Yugoslavia lost much of its efficacy and legitimacy in the late 1980s. Owing to similar causes, the city government of Sarajevo also ceded some of its authority to unsanctioned actors in 1990, leaving the city vulnerable to division and the clamorous demands of its competing constituent municipalities. As extralegal economic activities in the city increased, the federal government struggled to impose economic reforms to salvage the Yugoslav economy from its ruinous state. Unfortunately, the best effort to save Yugoslavia's economy was also the last. On taking office in 1989, Yugoslav Federal Prime Minister Ante Marković (born a Bosnian Croat in the Herzegovinian town of Konjic) prescribed drastic measures akin to the "shock therapy" later administered in many countries of Eastern Europe. He pegged the dinar to the German mark, liberalized imports to provide competition for inefficient domestic producers, and began what he foresaw as a four-to-six year process of privatizing socially owned property. The program did indeed produce economic shock. Inflation slowed to near zero in summer 1990 and prices stabilized. At the same time, liquidity evaporated in enterprises of all sizes, and many were unable to pay their suppliers. Wages had lagged behind price increases for some time, and workers sought wage increases rather than girding themselves for further sacrifices.

As Bosnia-Herzegovina's major industrial center and capital city, Sarajevo experienced the rising worker discontent acutely.[1] In the summer and fall of 1990 strikers descended on Sarajevo to press their demands on recalcitrant officials. Workers from the Kreka mining complex in Tuzla (in northeastern Bosnia) arrived in large numbers in Sarajevo on August 19, in the third week of their strike, and held rallies in the Zetra Sports Center. Demanding a 100 percent wage increase, they rejected an offer of a 40 percent raise. The three thousand miners, who had just experienced a catastrophic mining accident that cost 137 lives, also called for more fire and rescue units. All these demands were laid at the feet of republic officials, who had already developed the habit of making promises they could not keep for the sole purpose of pacifying the growing numbers of demonstrators.

Creditors' freezes on companies' bank accounts occasioned some strikes. The huge Elektrobosna plant in Jajce was shut down in November 1990 because it failed to pay its electricity bill to Elektroprivreda Bosnia-Hercegovina, which charged rates that were more than double those in Western Europe. Workers at Elektrobosna blocked the main road to Sarajevo with heavy machinery on December 27, 1990, and threatened to do so again early in January 1991. Shortages of electricity also plagued the sprawling, energy-thirsty Aluminij complex in Mostar. Workers at FAMOS (*Fabrika motora Sarajevo*; Motor Factory Sarajevo) in Ilidža went on strike when that enterprise failed to pay them on time. The liquidity crunch proliferated as one enterprise after another became unable to pay its debts. In addition to causing strikes, the crisis led to higher unemployment, stagnation in the manufacturing sector, and a decline in exports.

The economic pain inflicted by Marković's reforms coincided with domestic and foreign political crises. Iraq's invasion of Kuwait in August

1990 adversely affected many Sarajevans. The construction firm Hidro-gradnja had about 2,400 employees working on projects in Iraq, and the huge energy firm Energoinvest was owed some $34 million by Iraqi contractors. On August 10, 1990, the first contingent of workers returned to Sarajevo from Iraq, and many others followed. Ill-fated projects there cost the economy of Bosnia-Herzegovina an estimated $360 million. Iraq's default on past-due accounts contributed to the liquidity crisis in the city's banks and enterprises. Some companies left skeleton crews at facilities in northern Iraq, but even those were eventually evacuated at the insistence of the Yugoslav Foreign Ministry.

The reform program required, above all, patience. Instead, Marković encountered widespread opposition, most notably from the most powerful politician in Yugoslavia at the time, Slobodan Milošević, president of the Republic of Serbia. The reforms dried up financing for the largest consumer of federal revenues, the Yugoslav People's Army (JNA; *Jugoslavenska narodna armija*). Milošević protégés secured legislation in the assemblies of Serbia and Montenegro to simply print more dinars. This undermined the stability of the currency and sent inflation escalating to unprecedented levels. Inflation rates traced an N-shape, rising throughout the 1980s, steeply declining to virtually zero in summer 1990, then escalating rapidly thereafter. Bosnia-Herzegovina was further victimized by the inflow of dinars from Slovenia and Croatia after those republics adopted their own currencies in 1991. The result was a JNA whose officers received outlandish salaries based on uncontrolled printing of money by the federal Yugoslav government. JNA officers and the Milošević regime were the primary beneficiaries of these changes, which were likely orchestrated personally by Milošević, a former banker who has yet to receive full credit for his unparalleled mastery of economic and monetary policy as a weapon in the wars of Yugoslav succession.

The increasingly severe economic crisis led to an explosion of extralegal commercial activity in Sarajevo and to the erosion of the government's ability to regulate urban space and to collect taxes. Amid rampant illegal construction, the greatest controversy swirled around a gasoline station in Bembaša. Nestled in the narrow passageway along the Miljacka River at the far eastern end of the old city, the station's huge gasoline reserve tanks were installed treacherously close to the ruins of the dervish quarters (*tekija*) built by city founder Isabeg Ishaković around 1462. The oil company Energope-trol began construction of the gasoline station in October 1989, but the enterprise received an "after-the-fact" building permit only in June 1990.[2] The station generated a chorus of protests both from devout Muslims and those with a secular interest in preserving the city's historical legacy. In what could be described as an outright bribe, Energopetrol also paid for a new bridge that crossed the Miljacka to link a small tract on the river's south side with the Baščaršija. "The bridge is a gift of Energopetrol to the citizens of Sarajevo for their understanding in the building of the gas station at Bembaša," said an official.[3] The bridge and the gas station were opened on the same day, July 31, 1990. Despite Energopetrol's largesse, the station continued to draw criticism after its completion.

The Bembaša station was but one instance of disregard for zoning restrictions and building regulations. The building of new structures continued unabated in the period 1989–91, defying the general economic decline. Migration into Sarajevo created continual demand for more housing, and the value of urban land escalated. City inspectors, suspected of cozy financial relationships with builders, gradually lost their power to control new construction.[4] One example of the trouble this caused is the Marksmen's League firing range. Bosnian marksmen, perennial contenders in European competitions, had long practiced at a firing range in Novi grad. Located in what had once been a remote area far from urban activities, the Marksmen's League firing range by 1990 was hemmed in by fifteen new structures, including a private apartment building (constructed without authorization) and a children's hall. The Koševo Center for Sports and Recreation, owner of the league's facilities, protested in vain to Novi grad authorities. The firing range was shortened from three hundred to fifty meters, but the risk of errant shots made the area treacherous for passersby. In November 1990 league members organized a rally, attended by about fifty people, to protest the impotence of city inspectors and to demand that the offending private apartment building be torn down.

Unauthorized encroachment also intruded on traditional uses of the Baščaršija, the main market area. After one house was destroyed by fire, it was rebuilt without city approval. The owner insisted that it was "built in accord with the law," but others believed it violated size restrictions. The first of five planned apartment buildings adjacent to the historical public bath and Catholic seminary, just north of the cathedral, was to be limited to four stories, but the building plans called for a larger structure. According to Dženana Golos, director of the city's Bureau for the Protection of Monuments, the new building would "degrade and devastate" existing cultural monuments. She noted that her department had not been consulted on these revisions. The structure was completed in disregard of the city's restrictions.

In 1990 black marketeers appeared in large numbers and openly sold their wares in small markets that arose spontaneously throughout the city. Sarajevans flocked to these so-called "green plazas." Cigarettes, alcohol, foodstuffs, household items, cosmetics, and car parts were readily available at prices below those in stores because vendors sold their goods without paying taxes. Their merchandise-laden cars bore license plates from Hungary, Romania, and other Eastern European countries. They carried a wide variety of foreign goods, and their prices undercut those in the reform-burdened taxpaying establishments. For many months police shut down such operations or forced them to move, but in summer 1990 the sellers overwhelmed the police and authorities with their large numbers and sheer persistence. City authorities allowed them to establish official booths at Stup, beside the major road to the airport, but commercial activities there soon spilled over into the roadway, interfering with traffic. In late August 1990 the police expelled the itinerants from Stup, and the merchants repaired to other vacant spaces in the city. Most moved to an open area at Ciglane, close to the center of town and across the street from the large housing development of the same name.

Confronted with the competition from the green plazas, many legally operating distributors opened discount shops. Fifteen discount shops opened in Sarajevo in 1990, and new ones continued to open until the first days of war in 1992. Traditional shops were faced with illiquidity, frozen accounts, and reciprocal debt. Their goods turned over more slowly, so they had less cash to pay for supplies. They were caught in a classic liquidity squeeze as freewheeling open marketers threatened the foundations of the socialist system.

In all of these situations Sarajevans expressed frustration with the government's growing incapacity to address the city's problems. They viewed government as distant and its officials as unconcerned and corrupt. In the newer sections of the city such as Novi grad, people protested unauthorized construction and voiced their sense of being crowded by the unrestrained growth. These developments suggest that the government's regulatory capabilities had begun to erode well before the nationalists came to power in November 1990, leading to the widespread disillusionment with socialism that fueled their victory. The state had not withered, as Marxist theory prescribed. It simply lost its grip.

As unsettling as the sudden economic changes, nationalism in neighboring republics posed a growing threat to stability in Bosnia-Herzegovina and Sarajevo. Milošević, having risen to leadership of the Republic of Serbia in 1987, encouraged the intensification of nationalist propaganda attacks against the Bosnian Muslims, Bosnia-Herzegovina, and the city of Sarajevo.[5] Propagandists derided Bosnian Muslims as Serbs of the Islamic faith who had betrayed the Serb nation and who were conspiring to create an Islamic state with Sarajevo as its capital. In these assaults, Bosnian Muslims were portrayed as subhuman, sexually depraved, and morally craven. Sarajevo was characterized as a "dark *vilayet*" (vilayet was an Ottoman administrative unit), suggesting that the city was tainted by vestiges of Ottoman rule and repression of the Serb people and the Serbian Orthodox Church. Serbian popularizers revived the memory of the brutal fate of many Serbs in the Second World War and blamed the Bosnian Muslims who had collaborated with the Ustasha regime. Although these propaganda attacks seemed to have little effect in Bosnia-Herzegovina,[6] they inflamed nationalism among Serbs in the Republics of Serbia, Montenegro, and eventually Croatia, thereby contributing to the outbreak of war in 1992 that would wreak havoc on Sarajevo and its cherished common life.

The dawn of political pluralism

Political pluralism flourished in Sarajevo well ahead of the legislation that authorized it. The Assembly of Bosnia-Herzegovina, caught up in protracted debates over the constitutional structure of the postsocialist republic, failed to approve a package of constitutional changes authorizing multiparty elections until the last day of July 1990.[7] By then elections had already taken place in Slovenia (March 1990) and Croatia (April 1990), and various groups within Bosnia-Herzegovina had been working for many months to organize parties in anticipation of the assembly's approval. Fearful of losing out to competitors, groups of leaders came together and established "organizing committees," the first step toward party organizations that were to be formally proclaimed once the assembly set the terms and date of the multiparty voting.

Multiparty elections were set for November 1990, and the ballot was complicated. Each Bosnian could cast up to seven votes for the seven-person collective presidency of Bosnia-Herzegovina (two votes each for Croat, Serb, and Muslim candidates and one in the category of "other"). In addition, voters could choose among rival slates for members of the Chamber of Citizens of the Assembly of Bosnia-Herzegovina and delegates to the assembly of the municipality in which they lived. Voters in Sarajevo could also choose among slates of candidates for the Sarajevo city council. Dozens of political parties formed in the spring and summer of 1990 to compete in the fall elections. Of these, only six proved to be influential in the interlude between the end of socialism and the beginning of the Bosnian War in April 1992.[8] Three represented multiethnic constituencies, and three were purely nationalist parties. Sarajevans played pivotal roles in all six groups.

The League of Communists (SK) and the Socialist Alliance, the two incumbent political organizations of Bosnia-Herzegovina under socialism, abandoned their claims to monopolistic rule and became social democratic parties. Both parties changed their names and at least tried to change their public images, in preparation for the November elections. In the summer of 1990, the Socialist Alliance adopted the name Democratic Socialist Alliance (*Demokratski socijalistički savez*),[9] and the League of Communists changed its name to the "League of Communists—Social Democratic Party" (*Savez komunista—Socijaldemokratska partija*), a clumsy formulation that revealed the party's own ambivalence about the communist legacy. After losing the election—more on this below—the party changed names again, dropping the League of Communists designation from its name to become simply the Social Democratic Party (*Socijaldemokratska partija*, or SDP, as I will refer to the party from May 1990 to the present).[10] Although the two parties nominated separate slates of candidates, they merged their campaigns. Candidates from each party appeared together at joint rallies, declared strong support for the Partisan tradition, and warned that a victory for nationalist parties would lead to the national division of Bosnia-Herzegovina. At the beginning of the campaign, the two allied parties enjoyed the advantage of large memberships and local organizing committees. Public opinion polls showed the candidates of the social democratic parties in the lead among voters of Bosnia-Herzegovina at all times during the electoral campaign.[11] Leaders of the two parties fully expected to prevail among Sarajevo's voters, believing Sarajevans to be more committed to the ideals of common life and shared values than many voters in Bosnia-Herzegovina.

In May 1990 the SDP of Bosnia-Herzegovina sponsored a rally in downtown Sarajevo, attended by an estimated one hundred thousand people, at the same location where Tito had addressed a similar number of Sarajevans in November 1945. The SDP leaders further modeled their rally on Tito's speech by displaying the same symbols, voicing similar rhetoric, and speaking from the same balcony. Nijaz Duraković, president of the SDP of Bosnia-Herzegovina, repeating Tito's remarks, deplored excessive nationalism emanating from Belgrade and Zagreb. His message was suffused with socialist themes, particularly "brotherhood and unity," and the importance of a united Bosnia-Herzegovina. Urging the crowd to reject nationalist politics as divisive, Duraković led the crowd with the chant, "Say no!," and the rally thereafter was known as the "No meeting."

A new party, the Alliance of Reformist Forces (*Savez reformskih snaga Jugoslavije*; referred to here as the Reformists) shared with the SDP and the Democratic Socialist Alliance a fealty to the Partisan tradition and to Yugoslavism, but its key theme was support for transition to a free market economy. The primary organizer of the Reformists was Yugoslav Federal Prime Minister Marković, architect of the market-oriented economic reforms mentioned above, who hoped that his considerable popularity would extend to the party he created. He chose Mount Kozara in the Bosnian Krajina for the site of the party's founding assembly and scheduled it for July 29, just two days after the forty-ninth anniversary of the beginning of the Partisan uprising (July 27), to underline the nascent party's loyalty to the Partisan legacy. Nenad Kecmanović, a well-regarded Sarajevo political activist in the late socialist years and rector of the University of Sarajevo, became the leading voice of the Reformists in Bosnia-Herzegovina. Throughout the electoral campaign, most polls showed the Reformists running second in voter appeal behind the alliance of the SDP and Democratic Socialist Alliance.

Believing that their strong organization and large constituency presented an irresistible attraction, leaders of the two social democratic parties (the SDP and Democratic Socialist Alliance) offered Marković their support in exchange for him joining their alliance. Marković curtly rejected their offer for fear of being tarred with the brush of socialism's failures. It was a fateful decision. Although social democratic leaders continued to support Reformist ideas and facilitated the registration of local Reformist candidates, the Reformists did not reciprocate, and the two camps undermined each other's appeal during the campaign.[12]

Three major nationalist parties, one each for the Bosnian Muslims, Serbs, and Croats, were formed in 1990 to oppose the social democrats and the Reformists. The three parties had much in common. Each party was led by prominent Sarajevo intellectuals critical of the socialist order, some of whom had spent time in prison or otherwise felt martyred by communist authorities. Each party identified its constituency as members of a single ethnonational group; none sought to draw votes away from either of the other two nationalist parties. Each nationalist party urged voters to cast only two votes for the collective presidency rather than all seven to which each voter was entitled, to assure that each presidency member represented only one nationality. Each party created an exclusive symbolic universe employing signature colors, slogans, symbols, holidays, and a coat of arms distinct to its nationality that did not intrude upon the symbols of the other nationalities. Each held a founding convocation in the summer of 1990 at the Skenderija Sports Center (evidently perceiving no irony in denouncing communism in the halls of Sarajevo's signature socialist-era achievement). Party leaders outlined their program at each founding convocation, and leaders of the other two nationalist parties were given time at the podium to extend their greetings and best wishes. Each party sought to become the monopolistic voice of its nationality group by purging dissidents and marginalizing prospective rivals of their own identity.

The nationalist parties of the 1990s presented themselves as counterparts of one another rather than rivals, emphasizing their opposition to the social democrats and the Reformists. They often cooperated with one another in opposing nonnationalists. Much more than in either Habsburg or royal Yugoslav times, the major parties of the Bosnian Serbs and Bosnian Croats were under the direct influence or control of leading politicians in neighboring Serbia and Croatia. (Croatian President Franjo Tudjman changed the leader of the Bosnian Croat party twice in its first two years in existence.) As in 1906–10 and the 1920s, national parties would emerge dominant over supra-national alternatives in the 1990s.

Notwithstanding their bitter denunciations of communism as a failed political system, leaders of all three parties reflexively adopted most organizational structures and procedures of the Communist regime. All three parties practiced democratic centralism (without calling it that), whereby local leaders could debate party policies but were expected to follow their leaders once a decision was reached. In structure, the parties modeled themselves on the SK in socialist times and on the administrative organization of the Republic of Bosnia-Herzegovina. Each party formed a main board (*glavni odbor* or *izvršni odbor*) as its highest decision making body in Bosnia-Herzegovina, a city board (*gradski odbor*) for Sarajevo, and a municipal board (*opštinski odbor*) for each of Bosnia-Herzegovina's 109 municipalities with a significant number of party members. Each of the lower organs exercised real power, but they were expected to follow the guidance of the main board or the party's principal officers.

The nationalist parties, while adopting socialist-era structures and conduct, departed from Communist precedent in frequently convening ad hoc bodies to make and execute decisions in emergencies. The most common emergency body was called a "crisis staff" (*krizni štab*), convened by party and government officials in dozens of situations and at various party and governmental levels. In existence from a few days to many months, crisis staffs usurped and often exceeded the powers of governmental units and party organs. (Many leaders of Serb crisis staffs were instrumental in perpetrating murders, expulsions, and other ethnic cleansing activities in the spring and summer of 1992.) In addition, the political council of the Serb nationalist party, made up of leading Serb intellectuals from the University of Sarajevo as well as senior party leaders, wielded great influence even though it met infrequently. Advisory councils also played major roles in the other two nationalist parties.

Another ad hoc organization of each political party, the delegate club (*klub poslanika*), consisted of all delegates from that party in a given representative body. The number of delegates comprising the three types of representative bodies—municipal assemblies, the Assembly of Bosnia-Herzegovina, and the Sarajevo city council—had proliferated under socialism, as the doctrine of self-management favored broad participation in legislative bodies over efficiency. Delegate clubs offered an informal venue for discussion. With the advent of multiparty governance in late 1990 and throughout 1991, legislative sessions and council meetings were frequently interrupted by long breaks to allow delegates and party leaders to seek interparty agreements behind the scenes. Delegate clubs often reached decisions that governed delegates' subsequent voting and effectively bound the party to a particular course of action. Such clubs were necessary for political life to function at all in postsocialist Bosnia-Herzegovina.

Leading Muslims held the founding convocation of the Party of Democratic Action (SDA; *Stranka demokratske akcije*) on May 26 in Sarajevo, attended by delegates from 73 of Bosnia-Herzegovina's 109 municipalities.[13] The party elected longtime dissident Alija Izetbegović as its president. Izetbegović had been released from prison in 1989 after serving six years of the fourteen years to which he had been sentenced in 1983. The party supported the preservation of Bosnia-Herzegovina as a unified state of Muslims,

Serbs, and Croats. The SDA's Sarajevo city board held a separate meeting on July 5, 1990, the first day of the Muslim Bajram holiday, at the Zetra Sports Center.[14] Addressing the estimated four thousand people who attended, City Board President Fehim Nametak said the party existed to "return Sarajevo to its true social and cultural identity." Singling out construction of the Bembaša gasoline station as a "barbaric act," he called for the city's historical old town to be returned to its "genuine magnificence" and urged efforts to insure a clean and healthy environment. Not to be mistaken for a mere environmentalist, he went on to call for the restitution of vakuf properties that had been nationalized after the Second World War. Blaming the Communists for "ignoring the national character of the Muslims of Bosnia-Herzegovina," he expressed support for preserving Yugoslavia as a community of sovereign nations and republics. The speech was followed by musical entertainment that included songs ranging from traditional Muslim folk songs (sevdalinke) to contemporary rock and roll.

The Serb Democratic Party (SDS; Srpska demokratska stranka) was established under the guidance of Serb intellectual and political leaders in Belgrade. Early organizers had approached University of Sarajevo Rector Kecmanović to lead the party, but he had declined and instead cast his lot with the Reformists.[15] Radovan Karadžić, despite initially denying any interest in becoming the party's president, was chosen for the office. At a press conference on July 5, 1990, he announced that the Bosnian SDS would model its "program and strategy" after the SDS in Croatia, the leading party representing Serbs living within the Republic of Croatia.[16] About three thousand Serbs attended the founding convocation on July 12 in the Skenderija Sports Center and gave an enthusiastic reception to featured speaker Jovan Rašković, the charismatic leader of the SDS in the Republic of Croatia who was a clinical psychiatrist.[17] But it was Karadžić who set forth the party's guiding principles. He stated that the SDS sought to lure Serbs away from the social democrats and their faulty communist ideology, and he declared that the party would insist on preserving Yugoslavia as a federal state.

In August 1990 a crowd of five thousand flocked to the Romanija soccer stadium in Pale to hear SDS leaders repeat many of the themes proclaimed at the first SDS meeting in central Sarajevo a month earlier. Pale was a special place for Sarajevans of all nationalities. Dotted with ski slopes and pristine woods, Sarajevans took nature walks there on weekends, and many had built weekend cottages. The municipality was home to thriving ski resorts and tourist hotels that provided a livelihood to many of its residents. In 1990

Pale became idealized by SDS leaders as the citadel of Serbdom. To Bosnian Serb nationalist leaders of the SDS, the municipality embodied the Serb ideal of rural self-sufficiency and resistance to urban-centered government authority. Vojislav Milutinović, in evoking the area's appeal, referred to acts allegedly being committed against Serbs elsewhere in Bosnia-Herzegovina: "Here at Pale, at the foot of proud Romanija and the winter beauty of Jahorina, you feel free and comfortable, for here they love Serb children, buses are not stoned, Serb graves are not desecrated, and Serbs are not emigrating under pressure."[18] His idyllic portrait of Pale ominously portended the future of that mountain resort as a Serb Berchtesgaden, and it foreshadowed the actions of SDS nationalists to achieve a Serb ethnic ideal through local domination. Speakers also blamed the socialist government for ending service on the Sarajevo-Višegrad railway line, presumably weakening communication links with Serbia to the east, and for failing to build much-needed roads. Expanding on his espousal of Serbs living peaceably in a federal Yugoslavia, Karadžić said that "others talk about changing borders, and we say peace, and only peace."

The Croat Democratic Union (HDZ; *Hrvatska demokratska zajednica*) of Bosnia-Herzegovina was an offspring of a party of the same name in Croatia headed by the former general, dissident, and historian Franjo Tudjman. When founded in Croatia, the HDZ was conceived as an organization for Croats everywhere, and the Croats of Bosnia-Herzegovina drew the interest of party organizers from the outset. The HDZ of Bosnia-Herzegovina held its founding convocation in the Skenderija Sports Center on August 18, 1990, amid symbols that testified to the party's association with Croatia and its leader. Croat flags with the distinctive *šahovnica* (checkerboard pattern) were prominently displayed, pictures of Croatian President Tudjman adorned the hall, and the meeting opened with the Croat national anthem, '*Lijepa naša domovina*' (Our homeland is beautiful).[19]

Despite profoundly divergent goals, the nationalist parties directed their campaign rhetoric principally against the nationalists' archenemy, the social democrats, and, with somewhat less vitriol, the Reformists. Electoral arithmetic eventually drove them to a three-way truce. Since each voter could potentially vote for seven candidates in polling for the collective presidency, a nationalist party that alienated other nationalists stood to have its own candidates defeated. Party leaders therefore concluded several agreements during the campaign, promising to avoid criticizing one another. To prevent future contention, they further agreed on formulas for sharing key positions at each governmental level based on the ratio of votes garnered by each party.[20] The three parties promised to maintain those ethnonational ratios by granting each party the right to replace any officeholder who died or resigned with a member of the same party.

In the last few weeks of the campaign, the three nationalist parties held joint rallies and told voters that they intended to preserve and strengthen the city's common life.[21] At a meeting in the Sarajevo municipality of Vogošća on November 13, two leaders of the SDA and SDS skillfully turned the rhetoric of the social democrats against them and blamed the socialist regime for the uneasy relations between Muslims and Serbs.[22] Velibor Ostojić, speaking for the SDS, asserted that the Communists "taught us how we must be estranged from our spiritual and national culture, leading to the uncomfortable feeling ... as we seek to be together." Other Serb speakers claimed that the Muslims in Vogošća had "always been good neighbors with the Serbs," and that the SDS wanted to free all people of fear. Muhamed Čengić of the SDA called the joint rally "proof that this people desires to remain and live together." Representatives of the HDZ also addressed the meeting and brought greetings.

In the days immediately before the November elections, each nationalist party held concluding campaign rallies in Sarajevo. In their final appeals for votes, nationalist party leaders emphasized their commitment to good relations between nations. The huge final SDA rally filled the Zetra Sports Center to overflowing and was addressed by the party's three candidates for the seven-person collective presidency: Alija Izetbegović, Fikret Abdić (both in the category of "Muslim") and Ejup Ganić (in the category of "other").[23] Muhamed Kreševljaković the SDA's candidate to head the Sarajevo city council, asked voters to support the SDA so that Sarajevo would become the "most beautiful ... and cleanest city." True to its eclectic cultural legacy, the SDA's rally featured all manner of cultural expression from a fashion show and rock and roll music to the traditional sevdalinka folk music and the choir of the Gazi Husrefbeg medresa. "The sevdalinka is the least that we can do for all peoples of Bosnia-Herzegovina," said Safet Isović in introducing the musicians.

Tellingly, the SDS held its final Sarajevo-area rally in Pale.[24] An overflow crowd came to the House of Culture to hear Karadžić charge that Marković's Reformists were stealing workers' pension money to finance their campaign. He also pleaded for interethnic tolerance, urging attendees to remember the Serbs' "good relations with neighboring Muslims and

Croats with whom they have lived for centuries on this land." He further sought to deflect charges that his cooperation with the other nationalist parties compromised Serb aims. "President Slobodan Milošević has nothing against our cooperation with his greatest opponents in the battle for power," he said, noting that opposition figures in Serbia had charged that the SDS was cooperating with Milošević's Socialist Party of Serbia. As the campaign came to an end, all nationalists used such rhetoric to assuage fears that they would stoke nationalist separatism upon attaining power.

The advent of nationalist rule

On November 18, 1990, Croat, Serb, and Muslim nationalist parties enjoyed convincing victories and superseded the former SK as dominant political formations in Sarajevo and in all municipalities of Bosnia-Herzegovina except Tuzla. The nationalists won all seven seats of the collective presidency, the vast majority of seats in the two houses of the Assembly of Bosnia-Herzegovina, and control of 107 out of 109 municipal assemblies.[25] Either singly or in combination, the nationalist parties received a majority of votes in each of Sarajevo's ten municipalities. Among the ten Sarajevo municipal assemblies, the SDS commanded an absolute majority only in Pale (32 out of 50 seats), while the SDA won an absolute majority in Trnovo (19 of 30 seats) and Stari grad (37 of 70). Only in the municipality of Novo Sarajevo did the nonnationalists come close to victory, winning 49 seats compared to 51 won by the nationalists. Sarajevans also gave nationalists a convincing majority in the Sarajevo city council. The three parties together won 73 of 120 seats: 41 (34 percent) were won by the SDA, 28 (23 percent) by the SDS, and 4 (3 percent) by the HDZ. Together, the two social democratic parties and the Reformists won 42 seats (35 percent), giving those parties combined the largest single bloc of delegates. However, no nationalist party would form a coalition with them, and they remained powerless, though vocal, in the new city council.

Insofar as they remained united, the three nationalist parties were fully in charge. They proved able to remain united on the division of personnel appointments among them at all government levels in accord with the interparty agreements reached during the campaign. In the Sarajevo city council, delegates of the three nationalist parties voted together to select the SDA's Muhamed Kreševljaković as mayor, Maksim Stanišić of the SDS as president of the city's executive committee (the executive organ of the city council), and the HDZ's Aleksandra Balvanović as the city council's vice president.[26] Reformists joined members of the SDP, the Democratic Socialist Alliance, and a few smaller parties to form an opposition coalition known as the Left Bloc. They protested their exclusion from the division of top city offices, but they were ignored. In both the Sarajevo city council and the various municipal assemblies, members of the Left Bloc were marginalized and neglected for the rest of the decade.

The newly elected leaders at all levels of government faced falling tax revenues, rising demands for services, economic stagnation, labor unrest, and, by the summer of 1991, the disintegration of the working partnership among the three nationalist parties. In the Assembly of Bosnia-Herzegovina, SDA and HDZ delegates advocated greater autonomy for the republic within the Yugoslav federal system and considered whether to seek outright independence. SDS delegates, on the other hand, fought any loosening of the republic's links with Yugoslavia, insisted that all Serbs should live in one state (Yugoslavia), and staunchly opposed anything that moved the republic closer to independence. Beyond the Serb nationalist delegates' rhetoric was an implicit threat to form their own breakaway state if the republic became independent.

Sarajevans incessantly debated the issue of Bosnia-Herzegovina's constitutional relationship to Yugoslavia in the first year after the election, but debates in the city council centered on local issues only remotely related to matters of autonomy and independence. For council members, no issue was more acute than the centrifugal force of municipalities seeking greater autonomy from the city. Keeping the city together became Mayor Kreševljaković's biggest challenge. Upon taking office in December 1990, he expressed concern for possible fragmentation of the city. "Sarajevo is in an unenviable political position right now, with many communal problems," he said. "It obviously does not live as a united urban whole, because it consists of many municipalities, and that is divisive."[27] The leaders in every municipality, of all three national affiliations and from all three nationalist parties, felt that their unit received less than its fair share of revenues and services from the city. Officials of the core urban municipalities complained of being shortchanged no less than those on the rural periphery. The Centar municipality even threatened to withdraw from the city's budgetary system.[28] Selim Hadžibajrić, president of the municipal assembly of Stari grad, proclaimed that only those laws approved unanimously by the 120-member city council would be enforced in his municipality.[29] In January 1992 city planners took up the challenge of reorganizing the city so as to satisfy the interests of contending municipalities. One of the three options they proposed was a referendum in the four most rural municipalities on whether to remain a part of the city.[30]

The ten municipalities at first constituted a much more serious threat to the city's unity than did the divergent interests of elected nationalists. The city's top SDA and SDS figures on the council, Kreševljaković and Stanišić, often appeared together in a quest to mollify the discontented municipality leaders. They were occasionally joined by Balvanović. However, Stanišić also participated in creating separate SDS institutions parallel to the legal government. Like some other SDS members, he was apparently torn on the issue of how far and how quickly the party should pursue its separatist program. In contrast, SDA and HDZ leaders in Sarajevo consistently supported the unity of the city and the Republic of Bosnia-Herzegovina during 1991 and early 1992. They were joined in this stance by members of the Left Bloc opposition.

Even as they appeared united in resisting the city's fragmentation into its constituent municipalities, leaders of the three nationalist parties engaged in a systematic division of personnel appointments in every government entity, institution, and enterprise in the city.[31] The kingpins of nationalist party patronage networks spent much of 1991 securing their fair share of jobs at all levels, in some cases running roughshod over professional qualifications and frequently overriding established succession practices. A squabble over the appointment of a school director was one instance in which the division percolated to public attention. As founder of the Ahmet Fetahagić Elementary School, the Centar municipal assembly had the responsibility of appointing a new director. Since delegates could not muster a quorum to make a selection, municipal assembly president and SDS member Radomir Bulatović appointed a retired school director, Rajka Milanović, to the post, evidently to prevent the teacher's professional association from designating a Croat candidate. The situation was resolved by the appointment of an outsider, but only after the parties had tallied up the national identity of all school directors in the municipality and determined that each group was proportionately represented among directors of other schools.

The SDS political encirclement of Sarajevo

Within months after the new city leaders took office, the SDS inaugurated a campaign to remove some municipalities from the city's jurisdiction and encircle the inner city with Serb-controlled areas. The SDS thereby coopted the incipient separatism of the city's constituent municipalities and eventually brought down the tenuous partnership among the three nationalist parties. The city's governing institutions therewith diverged in two directions. In the Sarajevo city council many delegates worked to preserve the city's common life and prevent its fragmentation, but at the next lower level of government—the municipal level—the SDS assault on the city of Sarajevo forced municipal assembly members to choose between loyalty to the city of Sarajevo and support for Serb nationalists seeking to fragment the city. Sarajevo's fate would thus come to depend on the municipalities that made it up. Each of those municipalities was mixed in ethnonational composition (see Table 8.1). Only one (Pale) had an absolute majority of Serb inhabitants. Three (Hadzići, Stari grad, and Trnovo) were over 63 percent Muslim, and three (Centar, Novi grad, and Vogošća) had slim Muslim majorities, between 50 and 51 percent. Only in Trnovo and Stari grad had the SDA been able to secure an absolute majority of delegate seats in the municipal assembly, as the SDS had done in Pale (discussed above, "The Advent of Nationalist Rule.") Thus control of seven of the city's municipalities continued to be contested long after the 1990 elections.

In late April 1991 SDS leaders in Pale, taking advantage of the party's absolute majority in the municipal assembly, announced their intention to secede from the city of Sarajevo and to discontinue forwarding tax revenues to the city.[32] Justifying its decision on economic grounds, the SDS municipal board of Pale accused the Sarajevo city council of neglecting Pale's economic welfare and instead promoting tourism in other municipalities. With this declaration, the Pale municipality became the linchpin in the SDS campaign to weaken the Sarajevo city government and form shadow parallel structures in the Sarajevo area. The SDS action in Pale followed by a week the proclamation in Čelinac (northwestern Bosnia) of the "Community of Municipalities of Bosnian Krajina" (Krajina means "borderland" and refers to the area of northwestern Bosnia that once constituted the Ottoman frontier with the Habsburg Monarchy).[33] The proclamations in Čelinac and Pale were the first steps in what became an extensive effort to secure one-party, single-nationality Serb control in all areas of Bosnia-Herzegovina where Serbs lived.

The SDS campaign for single-party control was euphemistically labeled "regionalization," but with it the party took the first steps on the road to creating a separate Serb state in Bosnia-Herzegovina. Where the party suc-

Table 8.1. POPULATION OF SARAJEVO BY MUNICIPALITY AND NATIONAL IDENTITY, 1991

	Croats	%	Muslims	%	Serbs	%	Yugoslavs	%	Other	%	Total
Centar	5,428	6.8	39,761	50.1	16,631	21.0	13,030	16.4	4,436	5.6	79,286
Hadžići	746	3.1	15,392	63.6	6,362	26.3	841	3.5	859	3.5	24,200
Ilidža	6,934	10.2	29,337	43.2	25,029	36.8	5,181	7.6	1,456	2.1	67,937
Ilijaš	1,736	6.9	10,585	42.0	11,325	45.0	1,167	4.6	371	1.5	25,184
Novi grad	8,889	6.5	69,430	50.8	37,591	27.5	15,580	11.4	5,126	3.8	136,616
Novo Sarajevo	8,798	9.3	33,902	35.7	32,899	34.6	15,099	15.9	4,391	4.6	95,089
Pale	129	0.8	4,364	26.7	11,284	69.0	396	2.4	182	1.1	16,355
Stari grad	1,126	2.2	39,410	77.7	5,150	10.1	3,374	6.6	1,684	3.3	50,744
Trnovo	16	0.2	4,790	68.5	2,059	29.5	72	1.0	54	0.8	6,991
Vogošća	1,071	4.3	12,499	50.7	8,813	35.8	1,730	7.0	534	2.2	24,647
Total	34,873	6.6	259,470	49.2	157,143	29.8	56,470	10.7	19,093	3.6	527,049

Source: Croatia, Državni zavod za statistiku Republike Hrvatske, *Stanovništvo Bosne i Hercegovine: Narodni sastav po naseljima* (The population of Bosnia-Herzegovina. National composition by municipality), Zagreb: Državni zavod za statistiku, 1995, p. 15.

ceeded, regionalization created ethnonational division in Sarajevo and Bosnia-Herzegovina before they were divided militarily and territorially in the spring and summer of 1992. The campaign drew upon proposals for greater regional autonomy that had gained some currency during the late years of socialist rule. The SDS cited associations of municipalities formed in the 1970s as precedents for their own efforts, and party leaders commissioned studies to support their claims that certain areas had been neglected by Bosnia-Herzegovina's government.[34] SDS leaders insisted that the Bosnian Krajina's economic backwardness was the sole motive for forming an association of municipalities there. Karadžić blamed the area's alleged economic stagnation on the concentration of political power in Sarajevo, and SDS leaders consistently denied in public that their aims were political, nationalist, or separatist.[35] "All political connotations of this matter are attributed by others," Karadžić stated.[36] Notwithstanding these denials, the SDS used regionalization to reject the jurisdiction of the government of Bosnia-Herzegovina over Serbs and to create institutions that would subsequently become the administrative structure of a separate Serb state.

In June 1991 the SDS put its regionalization campaign on hold, fearing that its supporters in the Bosnian Krajina region had taken the idea too far in proclaiming a union with Serb-controlled areas in neighboring Croatia. The SDS Main Board (the party's central decision-making body) revived the drive in September 1991 by recommending the formation of several Serb autonomous regions (*Srpske autonomne oblasti*), which together would consist of much of Bosnia-Herzegovina.[37] On September 17, 1991, SDS leaders created a Serb autonomous region in the Sarajevo area under the name "Romanija-Birač," and four others were declared elsewhere in Bosnia-Herzegovina within the next few days.[38] The Sarajevo-area Serb autonomous region was an empty shell when first created, but in proclaiming it the SDS raised an early challenge to the Bosnian government's jurisdiction. It was conceived as the Bosnian Serb nationalist counterpart of Sarajevo's city government. Still, the decisions of various bodies created by the SDS and the speeches of their leaders suggest that the party was groping for a way to extend its jurisdiction in the Sarajevo area rather than following a carefully conceived plan.

The party leaders signaled their indecision by changing the name of the region and deferring certain key decisions on the consolidation of their authority. The Sarajevo-area region bore an awkward name, combining "Romanija," the mountain east of Sarajevo, and "Birač," an area in eastern

Bosnia that was northeast of Sarajevo near the Drina River. Of the municipalities that initially made up the Romanija-Birač Serb Autonomous Region,
only Pale was a municipality of the city of Sarajevo, whereas others were
located in eastern Bosnia.[39] (For the municipalities making up the city of
Sarajevo see map 7.2 on p. 237; for the composition of their populations by
nationality see table 8.1 on p. 266.) During the fall of 1991 leaders moved
to extend the party's authority in the Sarajevo area beyond Pale. On September 25 the Sarajevo city board of the SDS established a committee, consisting of one representative from each of the city's ten municipalities, to
implement the main board's regionalization policy.[40] The same committee
later removed "Birač" from the region's title to indicate their focus on the
Sarajevo area.[41] In municipalities where it succeeded, the SDS regionalization
campaign allowed the party to assert control over territorial defense
(*Teritorijalna odbrana*) units and the police, who were under the jurisdiction
of the Ministry of Internal Affairs (MUP; *Ministarstvo unutrašnjih poslova*).
The police and territorial defense forces each had light weapons at their
disposal, and after acquiring further weapons from the JNA they would
become critical to Bosnian Serb military successes in the spring of 1992.

Serb nationalist consolidation efforts throughout Bosnia-Herzegovina
gained momentum after the tumultuous events on the night of October
14–15, 1991, when Karadžić made an impassioned speech before the
Assembly of Bosnia-Herzegovina, threatening that Muslims might disappear
as a group if Bosnia-Herzegovina were to become independent.[42] Izetbegović responded that Karadžić's threat indicated just why Bosnia-Herzegovina
might no longer be able to remain in federal Yugoslavia. After the assembly
had been adjourned for the day and the Bosnian Serb delegates had departed, HDZ and SDA delegates reconvened the session and passed a "declaration of sovereignty," a measure, bitterly opposed by SDS delegates, that
moved Bosnia-Herzegovina one step closer to independence.[43]

The SDS next moved to consolidate the Serbian autonomous regions into
the single polity that would eventually become the Republika Srpska. On
the evening of October 15, the SDS political council met to discuss strategy
in light of SDA and HDZ approval of the sovereignty declaration. Several
members spoke in favor of uniting the Serb autonomous regions into a single
Bosnian Serb polity.[44] The council also discussed the possibility of establishing a separate assembly of the Serb people of Bosnia-Herzegovina and
holding a plebiscite asking Bosnian Serbs if they wished to remain in federal
Yugoslavia. On October 24, just nine days after the political council put

forth the suggestion, the SDS formed a separate Serb assembly, called here the Bosnian Serb Assembly, consisting of Serb delegates elected to the Assembly of Bosnia-Herzegovina in the elections of November 1990.[45] Further implementing the recommendations of the party's political council, SDS leaders held a plebiscite on November 9 and 10, 1991, asking Bosnian voters whether they wished to remain in federal Yugoslavia. Those who appeared at the polling places in the Bosnian Serb-sponsored plebiscite were required to state their ethnonational identity, and non-Serbs were given yellow ballots to distinguish their votes from those of Bosnian Serbs.[46] Few Bosnian Muslims or Bosnian Croats voted in the plebiscite; Bosnian Serbs voted overwhelmingly to remain in federal Yugoslavia. In addition to indicating whether or not they wished to remain in Yugoslavia, voters in some areas could cast ballots in favor of forming local Bosnian Serb territorial units. Over 99 percent of voters cast ballots in favor of the resolution. After the voting, SDS leaders frequently cited these plebiscite results to justify carving out Serb-inhabited territory from existing municipalities. The Bosnian Serb nationalists indicated their intent to create their own state in a meeting in late December 1991. By creating bodies parallel to those of the individual municipalities and the city of Sarajevo, they thereby replicated the institutions of the government of Bosnia-Herzegovina.

In Sarajevo, SDS leaders launched a campaign to create a separate Bosnian Serb local community (mjesna zajednica) called Rajlovac I to be carved out of the existing local community of Rajlovac in the municipality of Novi grad.[47] Despite months of negotiations, SDS and SDA leaders failed to reach an agreement on the future of Rajlovac. In early May 1992 (after armed hostilities had begun) the Bosnian Serb Assembly declared an expanded Rajlovac to be a municipality and rejected the jurisdiction of the Novi grad municipality over its citizens.[48] The creation of a new Rajlovac municipality brought economic and military benefits to the SDS. In addition to a military housing facility, the new entity contained one-third of the economic organizations of Novi grad, including the Marketi food distribution business.[49] In addition, the new Rajlovac occupied a strategic position just north of the major east-west thoroughfare and tram tracks running from Sarajevo's city center to its western suburbs.

At the third session of the Bosnian Serb Assembly on December 11, 1991, Karadžić and Assembly President Momčilo Krajišnik proposed that such parallel Bosnian Serb institutions be created in municipalities wherever Serbs lived. However, several members objected to creating parallel institutions in all municipalities, arguing that such action would disrupt co-operative relations with other nationalist parties. They were further concerned that Muslims might retaliate by organizing their own parallel bodies in Serb-majority municipalities. The debate revealed widespread recalcitrance on the part of SDS members to move forward with the pro-vocative step of forming parallel Serb institutions. Yielding to these objections, the Bosnian Serb Assembly recommended the formation of local Serb municipal assemblies but added "that the cover letter would specify that this is recommended where necessary, and should in no case be across the board, because the latter would be unnecessary."[50]

Nonetheless, eight days later, on December 19, the SDS main board abandoned the voluntary approach to regionalization and issued a ten-page document entitled "Instructions for the Organization and Activity of the Organs of the Serb People in Bosnia and Herzegovina in Extraordinary Cir-cumstances." With this document, the main board gave local municipal boards a specific blueprint for seizing power by establishing Bosnian Serb single-national institutions wherever the party was organized.[51] Each SDS municipal board was instructed to form two institutions in its munici-pality—a crisis staff and a "Bosnian Serb" municipal assembly—correspond-ing approximately to the executive and legislative functions respectively of municipal governments.[52] Where Bosnian Serbs lacked an absolute majority, the local SDS board was to create a Bosnian Serb municipal assembly as a rival body, consisting only of Serbs, parallel to the existing multiparty assembly. The newly created Serb bodies were to "carry out preparations" to assume power in their respective municipalities.[53]

In the instructions, the main board ordered municipal SDS officials to prepare for a second stage of activities in which they were to seize power and operate in conditions of war. The second stage was to commence only upon receipt of orders from SDS authorities: "The order to carry out the specified tasks, measures, and other activities in these instructions is given exclusively by the Bosnia-Herzegovina SDS president using a secret, preestablished pro-cedure." At that time, local officials were to "establish state organs in the municipality" and "elect or appoint officials and fill management positions." They were told to employ stealth in consolidating control of Serb-inhabited areas: "At approaches to areas inhabited by a Serb population, organize secret patrols and an information system focusing on all possible dangers for the Serb people." In the second stage, SDS municipal boards were to "mobilize all police forces from the ranks of the Serb people and, in cooperation with command posts and headquarters of the JNA, to ensure their gradual subordination," and to "set up secret warehouses and depots to store food."

The main board's instructions of December 19 did not specifically mention Sarajevo, but only two days later Karadžić emphasized that the city was central to SDS plans for single-party rule in Serb-inhabited territory. Speaking to the Bosnian Serb Assembly on December 21, he affirmed that "Serb Sarajevo, that is, the Serb part of Sarajevo, has its continuing existence and it is the center of the Serb autonomous region."[54] Previously, in November 1991, the Bosnian Serb Assembly had sanctioned creation of the Romanija Serb Autonomous Region and resolved that the region would grow to include "parts of other municipalities from this region with a majority [Bosnian] Serb population."[55] At that session, the Bosnian Serb Assembly expressed its intent to exert jurisdiction over the city of Sarajevo, adding that the "status of municipalities in the city of Sarajevo and in parts of the city in which the Serb nation represents a majority will be determined with a separate decision."[56]

The renewed SDS regionalization campaign in the fall of 1991 bore its first fruit in Sarajevo on December 24, 1991, only five days after the SDS main board's instructions to municipal boards. SDS leaders from Sarajevo's constituent municipalities convened a meeting on December 24 and followed the main board's instructions by forming a crisis staff and designating persons responsible for carrying out various duties.[57] On the same day the municipal assembly of Ilijaš, the northernmost Sarajevo suburb, voted to withdraw from the city of Sarajevo and join the Romanija Serb Autonomous Region.[58] The vote was the result of persistent and ultimately successful efforts by SDS leaders to win the votes of Bosnian Serbs from the nonnationalist opposition parties who had been elected to the Ilijaš municipal assembly in November 1990. HDZ and SDA delegates walked out when the item was placed on the agenda, whereupon SDS delegates and their allies from other parties easily passed the resolution.[59] With this vote, the SDS acquired political supremacy in a second large peripheral municipality and led it to reject the jurisdiction of the city of Sarajevo.

In the first few weeks of 1992 the press reported on the proclamation of parallel Serb institutions in most other Sarajevo municipalities. On January 3, 1992, SDS leaders in the Sarajevo suburb of Ilidža decided to create a separate "Serb municipality," but their decision was kept secret for a week and went into effect the day after the Bosnian Serb Assembly proclaimed the "Republic of the Serb People of Bosnia-Herzegovina" on January 9.[60] In the

Stari grad municipality of Sarajevo, in which few Serbs lived, a Serb municipal assembly was formed in the Two Doves café, principally by those living outside the area, on February 22. "Insofar as we can't live together, we can only live beside one another," said Kosta Plakalović, the elected president of the miniscule Serb assembly of the municipality.[61]

In contrast to the rapid response of some local SDS leaders in creating parallel institutions, others in the SDS acted reluctantly or simply refused to form parallel institutions. Since the instructions of December 19 contained no deadline, recalcitrant local leaders could stall for time while arguing against taking the mandated measures. Radomir Bulatović, president of the mixed Centar municipality in the heart of Sarajevo, adamantly opposed creating Serb institutions there. In a rare public rebuke of Karadžić and the SDS separatist program by an SDS member, Bulatović stated on March 19, "I will not permit the division of these municipalities. ... When I said that ...a Serb assembly would not be formed, I was heavily criticized. But I've said it to Karadžić and to the [SDS] political council."[62] His objections were subsequently rendered irrelevant by other SDS members of the municipal assembly, who formed a Serb municipality in his absence and notified him afterward. Nevertheless, the erratic pace of forming parallel institutions in Sarajevo revealed a lack of enthusiasm among many SDS members for such radical political separation. Resistance was strongest in municipalities where the interparty agreement had produced fruitful cooperation between the SDS and SDA. But the SDS leaders promoted parallel institutions insistently and ultimately prevailed in most Sarajevo municipalities.

In early 1992 Pale's SDS leaders began preparing their municipality to become a backup capital for Serb-ruled parts of Bosnia-Herzegovina. In early January 1992 the Sarajevo Olympic Center was notified that the Ski Center at Pale and the Jahorina and Bistrica hotels had separated from their downtown Sarajevo headquarters and established their own, Pale-based enterprise.[63] "That's what started it all," said Deputy Mayor Muhamed Zlatar later in explaining the origins of the Serb breakaway campaign.[64] Pale municipal police established checkpoints on roads leading into the area. A reporter visiting in late January recounted being stopped by the police twice on the road into town. Upon arrival he observed a large sign with "Serbia" written in red letters.[65] Pale's SDS-controlled police force provided security and privacy for military preparations in the months before war began.

During the month following the independence referendum of November 9–10, the SDS further consolidated its authority over key institutions and territory in municipalities under its control. Asserting that the Bosnian Serbs had "lost confidence in the possibility of agreement with the Muslim nation" and had been attacked by militant Bosnian Muslims, the crisis staff of the Romanija Serb Autonomous Region declared on March 3, 1992, that the Bosnian Serbs of Romanija would "undertake all measures to assume full control on the territory of Romanija."[66] The SDS leadership moved its Sarajevo operations to the Holiday Inn (across from the building of the Assembly of Bosnia-Herzegovina), which was then managed by an SDS sympathizer. The hotel's expensive restaurant became the mess hall for SDS paramilitaries, who moved freely about the hotel with their weapons in full view of other guests.[67]

Military preparations

All three nationalist parties in Bosnia-Herzegovina had been preparing for war by creating armed formations, acquiring arms, and recruiting volunteers. Although each group succeeded in raising paramilitary formations, each also vigorously denied having them. Regardless, their successes paled in comparison to the resources of the federal army, which held a monopoly on heavy artillery, planes, helicopters, armored vehicles, and other modern military equipment. That monopoly was to make all the difference in the first few months of the Bosnian War.

The JNA carried proudly the legacy of its origins as a Partisan force in the Second World War. Throughout the socialist period, Tito and his advisors struggled against the dominance of Serbs and Montenegrins in the ranks of the JNA. Despite their considerable successes, the organization succumbed to the control of Serb nationalist officers, first in units stationed in Croatia in 1991 and then in Bosnia-Herzegovina in 1992.[68]

The evolution of the JNA into a Serb-dominated force was manifest on the streets of Sarajevo and its surrounding hills in the last several months of 1991. On November 14, 1991, Mostar-based reservists from the JNA Užice Corps entered Sarajevo in a column of vehicles, fired weapons into the air as they drove through the city from west to east, turned around, and continued firing as they departed.[69] Aleksandra Balvanović, HDZ member and vice president of the Sarajevo city council, denounced the reservists' incursion as part of a broader Serb plan to incite violence, and she warned the council that armed units were being formed in a number of Serb-majority suburbs of Sarajevo.[70]

On November 22, 1991, the Sarajevo weekly *Slobodna Bosna* published a document showing that the SDS had formed a "war staff" and had made detailed plans to besiege Sarajevo in the event of war.[71] The SDS had plans to evacuate Serbs from Sarajevo, the article went on, and to relocate them in "predominantly Serb areas such as Pale, Trebević, Jahorina, Romanija, etc." Sarajevans grew more suspicious of the JNA's intentions in December 1991, when the municipal assembly of Stari grad learned via videotape of preparations for artillery placements in the hills above the municipality.[72] All these reports proved to be accurate accounts of SDS and JNA preparations for the siege of Sarajevo.

The JNA attempted to call up reservists in Sarajevo, but it ran into opposition from local authorities. Nihad Halilović, secretary of defense for the Centar municipality and for the city of Sarajevo, received a call from a JNA representative at 9:00 p.m. on December 24, 1991, asking him to mobilize reservists from the city.[73] Halilović responded that he would follow the orders of the presidency of Bosnia-Herzegovina, not those of the JNA. The presidency, over the objections of its two Bosnian Serb members, had earlier denounced a JNA mobilization in Banja Luka as illegal and told Bosnia-Herzegovina officials that they were free to ignore it. Municipal officials responsible for maintaining the records of JNA reservists declined to turn over documentation to JNA, effectively thwarting the army's mobilization efforts. Nonetheless, JNA troops rounded up known reservists from their homes, and the JNA's military prosecutor interrogated some local municipality officials with the thought of prosecuting them. However, senior JNA officers refrained from further action in order to avoid provoking a confrontation with the authorities of Bosnia-Herzegovina.

With the support of Bosnia-Herzegovina and municipal officials, most of Sarajevo's Bosnian Muslim and Croat reservists declined active service with the JNA. Some Sarajevo Serbs also declined, but many joined and fought under the JNA banner in the war in Croatia. One delegate to the Bosnian Serb Assembly boasted of the role of Sarajevo-area Serbs (using the name Romanija):

The Serb people of Romanija have been mobilized and ready for a long time. ... Our special forces have proved themselves in Vukovar, at Tripinjska Road, and in Borovo Selo. And tomorrow I invite you all to Han pijesak to celebrate the successes of the folk from Romanija in liberating Vukovar.[74]

An agreement known as the Vance Plan, signed in Sarajevo on January 2, 1992, formally ended the war in Croatia. In accord with that agreement, the

JNA withdrew most of its troops from Croatia. Many JNA units relocated to Bosnia-Herzegovina, swelling the total number of JNA troops to around one hundred thousand. Simultaneously the JNA was reorganized to reflect its new role and diminished area of responsibility. Sarajevo was elevated from the headquarters of an army corps to that of the Second Military District with responsibility for almost all of Bosnia-Herzegovina and those areas of Croatia that remained under JNA control.[75] General Milutin Kukanjac, formerly commander of JNA forces in Macedonia, commanded the Second Military District. He and his staff occupied the sprawling military head-quarters building in Bistrik at the eastern end of the city. Other JNA units were stationed in another fifteen locations in Sarajevo. With these organiza-tional changes, the JNA became significantly stronger in Bosnia-Herzego-vina, both in numbers and in command structure.

After the demise of the Communists of Yugoslavia in January 1990 and the SK's subsequent fragmentation into republic-level parties, the JNA was the only significant institution holding Yugoslavia together. Kukanjac, its chief representative in Sarajevo, later complained that he had been left without direction from his superiors in the JNA or the federal presidency. Upon taking command he expressed his desire to improve the JNA's image among members of the various nationalities and to exercise a calming influence on local affairs. For several months he used his position as com-mander to defuse tensions in Sarajevo, to promote political solutions, and to avert the outbreak of war. However, along with believing in the JNA's his-torical mission, he was a devoted Serb nationalist. He later told an inter-viewer, "As far as I am concerned, the enemy were the Muslims and the Croats from the very beginning, along with their leadership and their people."[76]

Besides the willingness of many senior JNA Serbian and Montenegrin officers to cooperate in changing the character of the JNA, the role of Serbian President Milošević was pivotal. Anticipating that Bosnia-Herze-govina would soon become an independent state, he met with a close advisor, federal presidency member Borisav Jović, on December 5, 1991, to convert the JNA in Bosnia into a Bosnian Serb force. He ordered that Bos-nian-born recruits from other republics be transferred to Bosnia-Herzego-vina and that natives of other republics then stationed in Bosnia-Herzegovina be moved out.[77] Jović wrote, "We immediately called [JNA Commander] Veljko Kadijević and included him in the conversation. Slobo told him directly that it would be necessary to execute a swap of troops," ensuring that JNA soldiers born in Bosnia-Herzegovina were deployed there and that those born elsewhere were sent out.[78] On December 25 Kadijević reported to Milošević and Jović that these transfers were 90 percent complete.[79] Jović told BBC journalists Laura Silber and Allan Little that by April 1992 (the month the European Community recognized Bosnia-Herzegovina as an independent state) all but 10 to 15 percent of the ninety thousand JNA troops stationed in Bosna-Herzegovina were native Bosnians.[80] Most, in fact, were Bosnian Serbs.

In addition to the JNA, territorial defense units had been intended to blunt a foreign invasion as part of Yugoslavia's overall defense strategy. Military doctrine in the late socialist period held that a prospective foreign invader should be defeated by main units of the JNA, with territorial defense units resisting in isolation until the full might of the JNA could be brought to bear. The territorial defense units were organized locally, primarily in factories, offices, and other places of work, and each unit received light weapons suitable for mobile guerilla fighters.[81]

Although they were ideally integrated with the JNA in the Yugoslav defense scheme, territorial defense units reported to the ministries of defense of the individual Yugoslav republics as well as to the JNA central command. In September 1990 the JNA ordered that weapons be removed from the territorial defense units and moved to its own armories, citing concerns about the security of the large numbers of weapons under local control.[82] Most units complied with this order, but some either retained some arms or acquired new ones in subsequent months. During 1991 and 1992 most territorial defense units came under the control of the nationalist party that ruled the municipality in which they were located. In a few mixed municipalities, the units split along national lines, members of each group pledging loyalty to the nationalist party leadership in its area.

Meanwhile the Bosnian Muslims centered their organizing efforts in Sarajevo, where, in early May 1991, a small group of leaders met to form the Patriotic League, a paramilitary organization under SDA control.[83] On June 10, 1991, the effort was expanded to include 356 Muslim representatives, and a Council for National Defense of the Muslim People was formed with the Patriotic League as its military arm. A second Muslim paramilitary formation, the Green Berets, was also formed at about the same time. The Patriotic League and Green Berets grew slowly at first, but in the fall of 1991 events in Croatia gave new impetus to their recruiting campaigns.[84] Disillusioned by the JNA's overt support for Serb nationalists in the war in Croatia, many middle-rank officers of Muslim nationality defected from the JNA and joined the embryonic forces loyal to the government of Bosnia-Herzegovina. Among the first to join was Sefer Halilović, later to become the first commander of the Army of the Republic of Bosnia-Herzegovina (ARBiH; *Armija Republike Bosne i Hercegovine*).[85] The SDA's military wing set up shop in the Café Herceg-Bosna, where it gathered weapons and recruited soldiers. The nature of their work was embarrassingly revealed in November 1991 when an antitank weapon (*zolja*) in their growing arsenal caused an explosion, seriously wounding two Muslims in the café.[86] By January 1992 the SDA paramilitary was firmly established in Sarajevo and several other locations, and it periodically brought its volunteers together for inspections.[87] The Green Berets and the Patriotic League each had thousands of volunteers and light infantry weapons by the time the war began in April 1992.

Referendum for independence and the barricade offensive

In weighing whether to recognize Bosnia-Herzegovina as an independent state, the European Community recommended a referendum in early 1992 to determine whether independence was the true wish of the people. The Assembly of Bosnia-Herzegovina, over the objections of SDS delegates, approved the referendum, which was held on February 29 and March 1, 1992. The vast majority of Bosnian Serbs, following orders of the SDS, boycotted the balloting, while Bosnian Croats and Muslims voted overwhelmingly in favor of independence. Citing the nearly unanimous affirmative vote and ignoring the Serb boycott, the European Community agreed to recognize Bosnia-Herzegovina as an independent state effective April 6, 1992—coincidentally, the forty-seventh anniversary of Sarajevo's liberation from Nazi and Ustasha rule.

Within hours after the referendum voting ended on March 1, SDS members and their supporters took up arms, donned masks, and erected barricades at key transit points throughout Sarajevo. Many observers have viewed the SDS barricade campaign as a test of the government's resolve that, if successful, would have delivered the city into the hands of the SDS. This was unlikely. With three key SDS leaders (Karadžić, Krajišnik, and Koljević) in Belgrade consulting with Milošević, the SDS was in no shape to seize power even if the city had fallen into the party's hands. Rather, the available evidence suggests the barricades had a more limited objective—to signal the SDS opposition to Bosnia-Herzegovina's independence and demand the JNA's support in preventing it.

In their public statements, SDS leaders claimed that Serbs erected the barricades in self-defense after the shooting of Serb participants in a wedding outside Sarajevo's old Serbian Orthodox church on March 1. Nikola Gardović, father of the bridegroom, had been killed and a Serbian Orthodox priest wounded in the attack.[88] Serbs alleged that Ramiz Delalić, a Sarajevo gangster, was the gunman, but Sarajevo authorities neither arrested nor charged him for the killing, which suggested to some that he was under the SDA's protection.[89] Delalić later denied that he had killed Gardović, claiming that a videotape shot at the time implicated others at the scene.[90] The killing had all the markings of a gangland hit commissioned by one or another political group, but the full story of the Baščaršija shooting has yet to come to light. SDS leaders and supporters have consistently cited the incident as proof of their exaggerated claim that the Serb nation in Bosnia-Herzegovina was gravely endangered.

The SDS barricades drew a swift response in kind from SDA members and supporters on March 2. Within hours they erected their own barricades in strategic locations. Some were located directly opposite the SDS positions, creating what were called "sandwich" barricades. The battle of the barricades froze transit in the city, and residents had to pass through checkpoints to move about. The crisis drew the immediate attention of General Kukanjac, probably just what the SDS had intended. It also drew a spontaneous response from tens of thousands of Sarajevans, who rallied to demand an end to the obstructions.

Kukanjac summoned key leaders of the SDS, SDA, and HDZ to the Presidency Building for a meeting of what was characterized as the "expanded presidency" of Bosnia-Herzegovina. With Karadžić, Koljević, and Krajišnik in Belgrade, the SDS was represented in Sarajevo by Biljana Plavšić (a member of the presidency) and Rajko Dukić (a key leader of the SDS), who had formed an ad hoc crisis staff on March 2 to act on the party's behalf. According to Dukić, Karadžić called him from Belgrade just before the meeting began to say that he had won a promise that the JNA would not withdraw from Bosnia-Herzegovina. Dukić recalls him saying:

There's no more need for the barricades. They've done what they were intended to do. ... Take down those barricades. ... I was in the presidency with [presidency member] Kostić, and he told me that the presidency of the Socialist Federal Republic of Yugoslavia agreed that the [JNA] will stay in Bosnia-Herzegovina another four years and that there is no problem. And General Kukanjac, in a telephone conversation, repeated the same story to me and assured me that the army will be here and that we don't need to worry.[91]

Dukić's account makes no mention of other factors that may have led the SDS to launch the barricade offensive, but in citing Karadžić's relief at securing the presidency's pledge that the JNA would stay, he probably identified the principal purpose of both the barricades and the three leaders' trip to Belgrade.

After hearing from Karadžić, Dukić reached an agreement with SDA leaders that the barricades should come down. Dukić and SDA Vice President Muhamed Čengić were selected to make a joint appearance on RTV Sarajevo (*Radio Televizija Sarajevo*) to appeal for calm. They set off for the television station, but their route was blocked by the milling crowd, and they made their way instead to a small, private radio station which broadcast their appeal. In the meantime, General Kukanjac had himself begun to visit the barricade locations urging the organizers to take them down.[92] By early morning, the barricades had largely vanished from the city center.

The month of Valter

Sarajevans had poured into the streets to protest the barricades and challenge those who had erected them. Two large crowds assembled, one in front of the Catholic cathedral, the other in Novo Sarajevo. The first demonstrators were responding to a summons from youthful broadcasters at radio station SA3, but thousands more joined as the two crowds marched from opposite directions toward the seat of governmental power, the Assembly Building in Marindvor. A shot was fired in the vicinity of the downtown crowd, evoking the chanted response, "We won't use weapons!" One journalist captured the marchers' buoyant optimism: "There is no general or president who will give the order to fire on fifty or a hundred thousand people, and if someone does order it, he has signed his own condemnation before the world and history."[93] Only a month later, Karadžič's forces fired on just such a crowd in the same location, the opening salvo of a campaign that would earn their leader lasting opprobrium for slaughtering thousands of civilians.

The suburban marchers learned while walking toward the Assembly Building that the expanded presidency had issued the order to dismantle the barricades. Heartened by that news and believing that their Sarajevo neighbors would not use violence against them, the two crowds approached several barricades and shouted for them to be dismantled. Some had already been abandoned, and others were dismantled to cheers of the crowd. Most confrontations remained nonviolent, but in the Pofalići district west of the city, a volley of shots erupted from an SDS barricade, wounding two marchers before the barricade was taken down. Nonetheless, many of the tens of thousands of marchers came away feeling that their nonviolent protests had shattered the will of the nationalists to disrupt life in the city.

The city remained tense on March 3. Rumors swirled of armed formations approaching the city from various directions. That afternoon, barricades again appeared; this time, evidence pointed to SDA members or supporters having initiated them. Karadžić, Krajišnik, and Koljević returned from Belgrade that day, and they were immediately thrust into a revival of the previous day's crisis. Kukanjac convened another emergency meeting of rival leaders, this time at his office. After listening to bickering between the two parties, Kukanjac announced that he would order the creation of "joint patrols" to be conducted by JNA troops and MUP police.[94] Leaders of both the SDS and SDA agreed to support the joint patrols. Again, the barricades disappeared by first light, and on March 4 the first joint patrols began their rounds. Serb officials of the municipality of Pale at first refused to participate, but they relented under pressure and on March 7 agreed to cooperate.[95]

The largely leaderless street gatherings of March 2 were swiftly embraced by the SDP and other nonnationalists with the hope of building momentum for a popular peace movement. The nascent movement was given a unifying symbol—"Valter"—the Partisan resistance leader who had perished in the final hours of Sarajevo's liberation in 1945. The daily newspaper *Oslobodjenje* championed the movement by running a front-page editorial under the German-language headline, "Das ist Walter," reprising the words of the German officer in the film *Valter brani Sarajevo*. Editor Kemal Kurspahić heralded the marchers' success and wrote approvingly of the crowd's gentle demeanor and pacific intentions. The marchers approached the barricades with "songs and lighted candles," he wrote. "Sarajevo dismantled the barricades with its heart." The independence referendum, Kurspahić asserted, showed that this was the most cosmopolitan part of the Balkans, "in which the centuries-long culture of common life, tradition, and tolerance will defeat all challenges of division and conflict."[96]

The SDP organized more rallies over the next several days to support the unity of Bosnia-Herzegovina and to oppose the nationalists' machinations. Like the first "Valter" rallies, most of these were relaxed affairs. At one rally, a "Sex without Borders" placard was raised next to signs saying "We Are

Valter," expressing the good humor of many of those who gathered to oppose national division and war.[97] SDP leader Nijaz Duraković characterized the demonstrations of March 2 as a "magnificent peaceful protest of Sarajevo's citizens" and called for "the preservation of unified vital state organs and institutions that serve the interests of all citizens of Bosnia-Herzegovina, such as RTV Sarajevo and the Ministry of Internal Affairs."

Tens of thousands gathered on March 5 for another rally in front of the Assembly Building. The rally featured the folk rock of popular entertainer Dino Merlin and a hastily assembled musical ensemble called "We Are Valter." On March 6, the Sarajevo city board of the SDP sponsored another rally in front of the National Theater in the city center. "They have begun to divide regions, cities. Tomorrow they will divide villages and streets, factories, apartment buildings, maybe even common beds," Duraković told the crowd. He expressed confidence that the peace movement would dissuade the nationalists from inciting further divisions, but none of the nationalist parties embraced the street demonstrations. Although an SDA spokesman approvingly recognized the contribution of the March 2 marchers in dismantling the barricades, both the SDA and the SDS shunned the subsequent SDP-sponsored rallies and concentrated instead on barking at one another. SDS leaders insisted that the Baščaršija murder of March 1 represented a grave threat to the existence of the Serb nation in Bosnia-Herzegovina. SDA leaders, for their part, denounced the SDS for destroying domestic tranquility and the city's common life.

Notwithstanding Sarajevans' high hopes for peace and their willingness to take to the streets, Kukanjac's policy of joint patrols had only deferred rather than averted armed conflict. Both SDS and SDA leaders used the next two months to prepare for war, but the Serb nationalists gained the most during the interval.[98] No later than the end of March 1992, Kukanjac had achieved a massive transfer of JNA weaponry, equipment, and munitions to SDS members and to facilities located in areas under Bosnian Serb political control.[99] The arming of SDS members was to shift the military balance heavily in their favor once war began. In an interview in 1999, Kukanjac claimed that these transfers had saved Bosnia's Serbs: "For the first time in history, in 1992 Serb lands were encompassed. That was done by the army under my command. If it were not for us, if we hadn't outfitted, trained, and encompassed them, Serbs in these areas would have already probably filled numerous jails and concentration camps."[100] Karadžić, speaking to the Bosnian Serb Assembly in 1995, affirmed Kukanjac's assessment of the

JNA's vital role in arming Bosnian Serb nationalists during the spring of 1992: "Distribution of arms was carried out thanks to the JNA. What could be withdrawn was withdrawn and distributed to the people in Serb areas, but it was the SDS that organized the people and created the army."[101]

With the JNA lending its military advantage to the SDS, the men and women of the Valter movement were doomed to fail in their quest to dissuade political leaders from going to war. In their drive for a separate state, the SDS leaders had nothing but contempt for the defenders of Sarajevo's common life and did not bother to hear them out. On April 1, 1992, the Serb paramilitary forces of Željko Ražnjatović (known as Arkan) assaulted the town of Bijeljina and killed, beat, or expelled most of its non-Serb inhabitants. The attack was followed in the next several days with assaults on several other eastern Bosnian towns.

Recognition weekend and the second death of Valter

April 6, 1992, was a Monday, the third day of a three-day holiday honoring Sarajevo's liberation from German and Ustasha rule in 1945 and the date that the European Community's recognition of Bosnia-Herzegovina's independence took effect. SDA leaders eagerly awaited recognition, hoping that the European Community's endorsement would preserve an integral Bosnia-Herzegovina. SDS leaders just as passionately dreaded it, believing that Bosnia's independence negated their right to be part of Yugoslavia. Hoping to achieve ethnonational separation before the promised recognition took effect, Serb leaders declared their own breakaway state to be independent and initiated attacks on civilians and key institutions in Sarajevo throughout the weekend of April 4–6.

The SDS leaders' creation of a separate Serb police force led to the first violence on this "recognition weekend." They had decided to form such a force many months before. In a telephone conversation with Milošević on September 9, 1991, Karadžić expressed his intention to create a separate Serb MUP.[102] By early 1992 Serb policemen in most municipalities were taking their orders from Serb commanders or SDS political leaders, even though they remained formally part of the MUP of Bosnia-Herzegovina. On March 31, 1992, Momčilo Mandić, a Serb and assistant minister of the MUP of Bosnia-Herzegovina, announced the formation of a separate Serb MUP. He called on all Serb policemen to abandon the unified republican MUP and join the new organization.

Mandić's call for a separate MUP was the culmination of an evolving campaign to form a separate Serb police force. In late March 1992 SDS-appointed police officials abruptly terminated all five non-Serb officers in the Pale municipality and three non-Serb officers in the nearby Sokolac municipality.[103] A three-member commission from the MUP was sent to investigate. "All active and reserve policemen of Muslim nationality were released from their duties," Malko Koroman, chief of police in Pale, told commission members, explaining that he had acted on orders of the "government of the Serb Autonomous Region of Romanija." He justified the firings by noting that Bosnian Serb policemen had left their employment in the SDA-controlled Stari grad municipality.[104] But no one had fired the Serb policemen in Stari grad. They had simply failed to report for work on March 2, leading their superiors to suspect that they had been among those manning the barricades that day. After being reprimanded for their absence, the Serb policemen walked off their jobs. Shortly thereafter they joined the police force in Serb-controlled Pale. These changes removed the last barriers to full SDS control of Pale municipality and its complex of lodging facilities.

In Sarajevo's remaining municipalities, SDS leaders created a separate Serb MUP on the evening of April 4, 1992.[105] Milenko Karišik, deputy commander of the MUP of the Republic of Bosnia-Herzegovina, led police officers of Serb nationality in abandoning their posts to form the new Serb police force. The division touched off a scramble for control of police stations throughout the city. Some fifty masked Serbs seized and plundered the police station at Novo Sarajevo. On April 5, 1992, Bosnian MUP Commander Bakir Alispahić erroneously told RTV Sarajevo that all police stations from Stari grad to Ilidža remained under government control. In a statement issued the same day, officials of the newly formed Serb MUP accused Bosniak Green Berets of orchestrating the expulsion of Serbs from the common police force.[106]

Officers of the Serb MUP then set out to take control of the police academy on Vraca Hill.[107] Serb nationalists valued the academy as the MUP training facility, but its greater strategic significance derived from its location on high ground overlooking the Assembly Building and the affluent high-rise housing complex in Grbavica, which remained under informal Serb paramilitary control. Control of Vraca Hill would be valuable to any Serb aspirations to cut off the city center from its western suburbs. The Serb attack on the academy was also a first strike in the struggle waged by government and Serb forces for control of high ground near the city center.

In the early afternoon of April 5, Serb MUP forces and paramilitary units backed by the JNA approached the school, and Deputy Commander Karišik asked that it be turned over to the Serb MUP. When school officials declined, the Serb forces launched an all-out assault on the school. Karišik later blamed the school's defenders, whom he identified as Green Berets, for starting the battle. "They attacked us," he claimed in a televised debate. "We wanted to take the building peacefully."[108] At 4 p.m. the school director appealed for assistance as the school's lightly armed defenders were being overwhelmed. By the time European Community representatives had negotiated a cease-fire, Serb forces had captured the facility and taken hundreds of police cadets and instructors as prisoners.

On the same afternoon, in a replay of the events of March 2–3, Serb militiamen erected barricades once again at several intersections in the area of the Assembly Building. A huge crowd, the latest incarnation of the Valter movement, had gathered in front of the building. As they had done on March 2, the demonstrators moved toward the barricades in hopes of persuading Serb forces to dismantle them. Unlike on March 2, however, political leaders and JNA commanders had no plan to end the crisis peacefully. Serb forces fired on the demonstrators. They struck and killed Suada Dilberović, a medical student from Dubrovnik. She has been memorialized as Sarajevo's first victim of the Bosnian War, and after the war the Vrbanja Bridge where she perished was renamed the Suada Dilberović Bridge.

The peace demonstrators were at first undeterred by the growing violence directed against them. On the afternoon of April 5, the crowd gained access to the Assembly Building. Through the night, a parade of some 150 speakers urged nationalist leaders from all parties to resign their government positions as a step to avert war. Prime Minister Jure Pelivan reportedly agreed in the early morning hours to submit his resignation. Somehow, from amid the chaos, the crowd designated members of an embryonic "Government of National Salvation" to replace the ruling nationalist parties. Canadian General Lewis MacKenzie, who had arrived in Sarajevo a few weeks prior to command the UN peacekeeping troops being deployed in Croatia, watched the spectacle on television without understanding a word of the speeches, but reported being transfixed by the crowd-driven exercise in populist democracy.[109]

As the exuberant populists were talking of nationalist resignations during the night of April 5–6, Serb paramilitary units and JNA artillery were attacking the central city. Serb militiamen seeking to enter the eastern end of the city from Pale through the Lapišnica Tunnel were repulsed by special police of the government MUP under Dragan Vikić's command. Artillery shells raked several villages on the outskirts of the Stari grad municipality. A team of observers, visiting the village of Jarčedoli the next day, witnessed destroyed homes and smelled recent fires. In the delegation was the deputy commander of the JNA's Second Military District, who extended sympathies and offered to help. The astonished villagers could barely contain their disdain for the JNA, which they believed had been responsible for the attack—no other armed force in the area had the weapons to launch an artillery assault. Local residents claimed that three of their number had been killed in the shelling.

By April 6 the Valter crowd swelled to around fifty thousand, filling much of the expanse from the Assembly Building to Marindvor and across the street to the Holiday Inn. Some carried signs for peace and against the nationalist government leaders. Having previously directed their attention to the Assembly Building and government leaders, part of the crowd surged toward the Holiday Inn at about 2:00 p.m. to confront the Serb nationalists who had some weeks before converted the upper hotel floors into their private billet. Gunmen in the hotel opened fire on the mass of demonstrators below, killing six and wounding over a dozen. Some observers also reported gunfire from an unidentified location to the east in the vicinity of the twin UNIS high-rise towers. A government unit of special police officers commanded by Dragan Vikić entered the hotel and arrested several snipers, but Karadžić and his immediate entourage had already left the city.[110] Later that day, the sniper suspects were exchanged for captives taken at the Vraca police academy.

The Valter movement succumbed to SDS brutality on April 6, forty-seven years to the day after Vladimir Perić-Valter perished fighting the Nazis. The rooftop shootings scattered the crowd and snuffed out the nascent Government of National Salvation. That afternoon the JNA expanded its assault on the city. Artillery fire raked the central tramway depot, marking the first of many times that the primary mover of people in Sarajevo was singled out for attack from the surrounding hills.[111] Mortar and artillery fire rained into the city center. JNA units seized control of Sarajevo's airport in Butmir, claiming they were only seeking to secure the airport and separate the contending factions.[112]

Responsibility for the killing of demonstrators on the afternoon of April 6 remains contested. Serb apologists point to reports of shots coming from buildings to the east, suggesting that Muslim gunmen may have fired on the crowd. The possibility of shooting from other locations cannot be excluded, but, as recorded by television cameras, those in the crowd reacted to gunfire from the Holiday Inn's top floor, which had become a billet for SDS paramilitaries some weeks before.[113] The role of Karadžić in these shootings has not been firmly established, but the culpability of forces under his leadership is beyond doubt. In the words of the Belgrade publication *NIN*, "The Serb side will not admit responsibility for this attack, but it makes sense to assume that this was the first day of sniper terror, which Karadžić's forces carried out in Sarajevo until the end of the war."[114]

Although many Sarajevans were shocked by SDS brutality and came to view recognition weekend as the beginning of Serb nationalist aggression, events in Sarajevo had neither caused nor initiated the war. Serb nationalists had assaulted Bijeljina and expelled its Muslim population several days before their actions in Sarajevo, and they harbored similar intentions for most towns in Bosnia-Herzegovina. It is doubtful that the Valter movement could have halted the Bosnian Serb conquest even if demonstrators had somehow persisted after the killings of April 6. However, the Valter movement's futility does not negate its historical significance. Despite being later vilified by Bosniak nationalists for promoting appeasement in the face of long-planned Serb aggression, the populist demonstrators were perhaps the most eloquent voices for peace in their time. Some paid with their lives as unarmed men and women fighting the armed partition of an indivisible city. But they were too late, too idealistic, and too vulnerable to halt the inexorable drive to war.

9. Death and Life in Sarajevo under Siege

The Bosnian War of 1992–5 horrified and captivated the global human community like no other conflict in half a century.[1] Many were shocked because people were dying and suffering in a part of Europe where most believed ethnic slaughter would never again be countenanced. Bosnian Serb nationalists, benefiting from the superior weaponry they received from the JNA, resurrected the medieval siege in the service of modern nationalism, producing a welter of ironies.[2] The daily violence was conducted under the scrutiny of international civil servants, aid workers, "peacekeepers," journalists, and scholars (including this author) who could travel with relative ease on conveyances not available to the local population. Sarajevo was the lens through which most outsiders viewed the conflict; the agony of Sarajevo became the embodiment of the Bosnian War's savagery and senselessness. At most times, the army of privileged observers could get into and out of the city, stay in relative comfort at the Holiday Inn (the sole hostelry that functioned throughout the war), ride in armored vehicles along the city's most dangerous routes, and send dispatches to the outside world using the latest communications technology.

From the first dispatches to war's end, reports on the Bosnian War emphasized two major themes: the awful plight of the victims, and the utter irrationality of the violence perpetrated upon them. By the end it had become routine for the electronic media to focus exclusively on the violence and its aftermath. Most of these journalists departed once the shooting stopped, but thanks to determined local writers and to the more probing, insightful, and patient among the outsiders, a fuller picture of the war and the Sarajevo siege has emerged. The violence visited upon Sarajevo was indeed senseless, but it arose from the well-considered ideology and calculated strategy of Bosnian Serb nationalists. Sarajevans did not suffer stoically and await the outcome passively; rather, as I hope to show in this chapter, nearly every Sarajevan became part of an epic struggle to preserve a treasured way of life.

Conceiving strangulation

SDS leaders aimed to create a separate, ethnically pure Serbian state, carved from the Republic of Bosnia-Herzegovina. In public statements and by their actions, they implied that goal as early as the fall of 1991, but they most clearly stated their intentions by proclaiming, in a resolution of the Bosnian Serb Assembly on May 12, 1992, that "establishing a state boundary separating (us) from the other two national communities" was the first among six "strategic goals—that is, priorities—of the Serbian people in Bosnia-Herzegovina."[3] Karadžić later explained that the creation of such a state necessitated the expulsion of non-Serbs from Serb-held territory: "We want to achieve the first strategic goal, which is to rid our house of the enemy, that is, the Croats and Muslims, so that we will no longer be together in a state."[4]

The Bosnian Serb nationalists aimed to achieve the division of Sarajevo, the capital city, as a microcosm of Bosnia-Herzegovina. In mid-April 1992, SDS Vice President Koljević, speaking in euphemisms, suggested that the division of the republic should start in Sarajevo and that work on boundaries of "national communities" should start immediately, "so that Sarajevo will be territorialized."[5] On May 12, the Bosnian Serb Assembly adopted as the fifth of six strategic goals "the division of the city of Sarajevo into Serb and Muslim parts and the establishment in each of an effective state authority."[6] (The other four goals enumerated specific Bosnian Serb territorial aspirations elsewhere in Bosnia-Herzegovina.) In seeking the city's ethnonational and political segregation, the Bosnian Serb nationalists set out to destroy Sarajevo's common life.

But how and where should the city be divided? The leaders never adopted a formal resolution on a desired boundary, but the area they foresaw as the "Muslim part" was miniscule. In September 1992 SDS leader and Republika Srpska Vice President Biljana Plavšić suggested that Sarajevo be divided at the Holiday Inn, leaving only the central city from Marindvor to the Baščaršija (often referred to as the "old city" by foreign journalists) outside Serb control.[7] Others suggested an even smaller area, consisting of little more than the Baščaršija. The armored incursion of May 2, discussed below, suggested that some army officers wanted to divide the city at the Presidency Building, even further east than Plavšić proposed.

In addition to seeking the city's political and demographic division, Karadžić and other SDS leaders aimed to use Sarajevo and its citizens as hostages to strengthen their negotiating position. The Bosnian Serb nationalists instituted the siege and promulgated systematic violence as a means of highlighting their own ruthlessness, making their own depravity their greatest lever in negotiating with the timid international community. Since Sarajevo's primary value lay in the vulnerability of its concentrated civilian population, keeping it hostage required that the Bosnian Serb nationalists refrain from conquering the city completely, even before the Bosnian army (ARBiH) and the restraining presence of UN forces took that option away from them. We do not find in the substantial available documentation that the Bosnian Serb nationalists consistently harbored the intent to capture or totally devastate the city. Although they launched many offensives to secure more territory in Sarajevo, the Bosnian Serb nationalists did so to increase pressure on the Bosnian government, tighten the siege, and secure optimum firing positions. Sarajevans suffered death and deprivation from inter-mittent shelling with heavy weapons, sniping, and the cutting off of essential services, not in a stalemated military struggle or stalled conquest by the Bosnian Serb Army (VRS; *Vojska Republike Srpske*), but in a calculated reign of terror.

Karadžić and other Sarajevo-area SDS leaders harbored the intent to besiege the city as early as September 1991. "Romanija has informed me that they are preparing to block Sarajevo," he told Serbian President Milošević in a phone conversation. "No one will be able to leave Sarajevo. It will be a disaster."[8] At the time Karadžić was enraged that Bosniaks (at the time known as Bosnian Muslims) in the northwestern Bosnian town of Bosanska Krupa had detained Milan Martić, interior minister of the Serb autonomous region in Croatia.[9] To Karadžić, Martić's detention was an affront to the Serb people, and Sarajevo would pay the price. In a later conversation with SDS Vice President Nikola Koljević, he repeated the threat: "They'll cut off Sarajevo! Nobody will be able to leave Sarajevo in any direction. Nobody in any direction!"[10]

Karadžić remained deeply offended by the incident in Bosanska Krupa, even though Martić was detained only briefly and released unharmed. "Tonight ... they have brought about some changes within me," he told Milan Babić, president of the Krajina region on September 9.[11] The Bosnian Serb nationalist leadership appears never to have deviated from Karadžić's wrathful formulation. The siege of Sarajevo was conceived and carried out as retaliation for indignities, real or imagined, suffered by the Serb people. Artillery and tank bombardment may have been partly random, but the heaviest assaults followed Serb setbacks on the battlefield or at the nego-tiating table. One finds little evidence of such calculated retaliation in the speeches or documents of the Bosnian Serb nationalist leaders, but the pattern of assaults was clear to UN observers and those in the government of Bosnia-Herzegovina monitoring the shelling.

The sensitivities of the global media and international officials enhanced the city's value as a hostage. When the besieging forces deprived the city of essential services and aid, UN civilian and military officials frequently granted concessions in exchange for Bosnian Serb nationalist promises to permit the resumption of international aid. The Serb nationalists masterfully manipulated the humanitarian concerns of international officials, knowing that the city's dependence on aid delivered under UN escort provided a chokehold to be tightened at any time. In 1994 Karadžić, likening the siege to the Soviet blockade of Berlin in the 1940s, explained to the Bosnian Serb Assembly the value of the siege: "We must preserve the character of this Berlin corridor, so that we force them to definitively divide Sarajevo and consolidate the territories [of each side], and we will give them a square meter of woods [near Sarajevo] for which we will take a square kilometer on the Drina [River]."[12] SDS leaders placed sufficient importance on Sarajevo as a hostage to preempt on occasion the flow of arms under orders of Serb officers. General Djordje Djukić declared in a sworn statement:

Karadžić and Krajišnik interceded in the military matters so far as to use some units and to authorize the usage of some lethal material means on their own. This was distinctly explicit in the zone of the responsibility of the Sarajevo—Romanija corps. ... Krajišnik, using his position, would instruct the director of "Pretis" [a munitions factory], Milorad Motika, to whom and how many artillery grenades and other lethal means he had to give. I was informed about this later through the invoices of the Ministry of Defense to whom we had to justify the payments.[13]

In seeking to divide Sarajevo, Bosnian Serb nationalists also sought the physical segregation of its inhabitants. They killed and imprisoned some Bosniaks and Croats and expelled almost all others from Serb-controlled areas, and at the same time they worked to induce Serbs to leave government-controlled areas, either in a mass exodus or one by one. Before war began, one Bosnian Serb Assembly delegate warned that separation of peoples meant the resettlement of Serbs: "What we must do as of today is to communicate to the Serb people that it must be prepared for territorial exchanges, for relocation of populations."[14] When they commenced their first attacks on the city in early April 1992, SDS leaders made a determined effort to induce all Serbs to emigrate from Sarajevo. Serb officers recognized that the presence of Serbs in the city made it more difficult to justify their military assault on the civilian population. "I'm not horrified by the idea of a Muslim enclave in our territory," General Djukić said in 1993. "A wise state policy in the future will resolve that successfully. ... I just say that which I'm speaking about would be much easier if Serbs left Sarajevo for the most part."[15] The presence of Serbs in Sarajevo and other cities discredited the claim of SDS leaders to speak on behalf of all Bosnian Serbs. Refusing to concede that Serbs had chosen to remain in their homes rather than join the national separatists, SDS leaders portrayed the stay-behind Serbs as hostages of "Muslim" overlords, forced to stay in the cities against their will. One delegate to the Bosnian Serb Assembly charged Bosnian government officials with "manipulation of that part of the Serb people held as ethnic hostages in cities under [Muslim] control."[16] Imbued with the notion that Sarajevo was a collective hostage, Bosnian Serb nationalists wanted government-controlled Sarajevo to be free of Serbs so the city could be thrashed at will.

The road to siege warfare, April–June 1992

At the outbreak of fighting in Sarajevo, both spontaneous groups and well-organized military units came forward to defend the city.[17] Territorial defense units from SDA-controlled municipalities were already preparing for war, albeit with far fewer weapons than those available to the Serb nationalists.[18] The police forces of the MUP were well organized, and an elite unit of special police headed by Dragan Vikić played a major role in the city's defense because of its mobility, well-trained officers, and fighting capabilities. They joined the Patriotic League, the Green Berets, reservists, and a variety of irregular formations that included some of the most unsavory elements in the city. Leaders of several notorious criminal gangs committed their followers to the struggle, typically without abandoning their traditional activities of smuggling, theft, protection, and extortion. These included two gang leaders with the same nickname "Ćelo" (meaning bald man): Ismet Bajramović and Ramiz Delalić (the latter widely presumed to have killed Nikola Gardović, father of the Serb bridegroom discussed in chapter 8). In addition to the more or less organized elements, defense committees formed spontaneously throughout the city. The composition of each defense committee reflected its home neighborhood or housing settlement so that many committees were mixed by nationality, age, and gender. Committee members pooled whatever light weapons they had on hand, and in some cases the committees were able to acquire additional weapons. The combined efforts enabled Sarajevo's citizens to help fend off the first assaults of the JNA and its Serb paramilitary allies.

As the conflict broadened in April 1992, the city's defense was hindered by the very enthusiasm that inspired so many locals to step forward. "Just about every mahala had its own commandant," recalled the chief of the military police, Kerim Lučarević. "The city was covered as if by a spider's web. ... To get from Vratnik to the centre of Sarajevo, one had to go past at least fifty street sentries." A simple trip across the central city area required as much as two hours.[19] *New York Times* correspondent Chuck Sudetic reported, "The streets of the capital have become a maze of barricades, checkpoints and tank traps."[20] Government officials resorted to the threat of armed force to consolidate the local forces under a unified command. Military police dispatched thirty officers with orders to disband unauthorized checkpoints and organize neighborhood defense committees. "Each sentry caved in under persuasion of the police," Lučarević reported.[21]

The Bosnian government faced the challenge of coordinating these diverse forces and placing them under an effective single command structure.[22] On April 15, 1992, the presidency of Bosnia-Herzegovina established a unified territorial defense command and ordered all military forces in the land subordinated to it.[23] Although this event has since been celebrated as the birth of the ARBiH, the consolidation of disparate units into a single army proceeded unevenly over many months and was not complete until the end of the war.[24] The Patriotic League emerged from its thinly veiled clandestine role and became an integral part of the new army. But most criminal gangs and many preexisting groups remained organizationally distinct, and some commanders demonstrated considerable independence from their superiors in the early months of the war. Furthermore, the principal army of the Bosnian Croats, the Croat Council of Defense (*Hrvatsko vijeće obrane*), rejected the authority of the ARBiH throughout the war. Cooperation between the two forces was always limited, and in spring 1993 they went to war with each other.

The city was shelled from the surrounding hills by tank, artillery, and mortar fire. Among the targets were the Koševo Hospital in the central city and the Institute for Physical Therapy and Rehabilitation in Ilidža. United Nations Protection Force (UNPROFOR) troops came under fire while trying to rescue patients from the Ilidža facility.[25] The Sarajevo Radio and Television Center was hit repeatedly, even as SDS officials denounced the alleged bias of RTV Sarajevo and demanded that it be split into three nationally controlled parts. As mentioned above, the Olympic Museum, a Habsburg-era villa that memorialized the city's finest days in 1984, was gutted and its contents destroyed by fire after being hit by artillery shells on April 25, 1992.[26] While Serb nationalist forces were shelling civilian targets in the city, local firefights pitted Serb forces against units loyal to the Bosnian government. Most battles were centered in the city's western and northern suburbs. Serb forces generally fared better in the fighting and gradually took control of Ilidža and much of Novi grad. Serb forces expanded their control of approaches to the city and established roadblocks along key routes. By the end of April, most elements of the Sarajevo siege were in place.

General Kukanjac, commander of the JNA's Second Military District, came to feel that he had been abandoned by Belgrade and had been set up to take the blame for the JNA's failure in Bosnia-Herzegovina.[27] On April 27, 1992, Yugoslav authorities promulgated a new constitution that officially reconstituted the two remaining republics, Montenegro and Serbia (including the once-autonomous areas of Vojvodina and Kosovo) as the Federal Republic of Yugoslavia. In officially recognizing that Bosnia-Herzegovina was no longer part of Yugoslavia, the new constitution left the JNA as an occupying force there. Having failed to persuade Yugoslav officials to transfer authority over JNA units in the republic to Bosnian government control, the presidency of Bosnia-Herzegovina ordered the JNA to withdraw.[28] The Bosnian presidency demanded that the JNA leave behind the arms belonging to Bosnian territorial defense units, and it promised safe passage for the troops as they withdrew. The disposition of the JNA's heavy weapons was to be determined afterward.

At a summit of Serbian civilian and military leaders in Belgrade on April 30, Milošević capitalized on his farsighted order of December 1991 to make the JNA a force of Bosnian-born soldiers. "Slobodan and I expected and foresaw this," wrote his confidant Jović.[29] After much discussion the participants agreed that the JNA should withdraw from Bosnia-Herzegovina within fifteen days. They noted that because of personnel transfers, only ten thousand of the JNA's one hundred thousand soldiers in Bosnia-Herzegovina had not been born there. They would withdraw, leaving another ninety thousand, "largely of Serb nationality, and the Serb leaders in Bosnia-Herzegovina can assume political leadership over them," wrote Jović in summarizing the meeting's decisions. He was pleased with the results of their prescient undertaking: "For us this operation was of preeminent signif-

icance, and for the Serbs in Bosnia-Herzegovina, I think, even more significant. They got their army." The Serbs attending this meeting, however,
had no formal authority to order the JNA's withdrawal. It fell to the federal
presidency, by this time under Milošević's control, to issue the order to
withdraw on May 4. In the hiatus between the summit meeting and the presidency's decision, the JNA in Sarajevo struck what its commander hoped
would be a decisive blow against the government of Bosnia-Herzegovina. It
nearly succeeded.

The JNA's hold on the hills around the city was uncontested, but the
position of JNA units within the city became untenable with the Bosnian
presidency's order to withdraw. JNA units remained in their sixteen military bases in the city, vulnerable (as they had been in Croatia in 1991) to
being surrounded and cut off by their adversaries. Most artillery and mortar
attacks on Sarajevo came from JNA positions in the hills, but some shelling
emanated from bases in the city, adding to the ARBiH's determination to get
the JNA out of town. In the first two days of May 1992, ARBiH units began
surrounding several JNA facilities in Sarajevo, the first step in holding those
troops hostage.

On May 2 the JNA struck back, launching an assault on the city with
armored vehicles and infantry.[30] Some have speculated that the JNA's offensive was intended to force a change in the leadership of the Bosnian government by capturing the Presidency Building and replacing Izetbegović
with Fikret Abdić as president of the presidency.[31] But most observers
believe it was intended to sever the city in two at the Presidency Building,
isolating the old Ottoman city center from its western suburbs and key government facilities.[32] This was consistent with the Bosnian Serb nationalists'
fifth strategic goal of dividing Sarajevo. But the armored columns were
under the command of the JNA rather than Karadžić, and General Kukanjac
had previously shown little enthusiasm for using his forces to dissect the
city.[33] Karadžić, apparently referring to these events, later complained that
the JNA had failed to give tanks to the Bosnian Serbs in order to bring the
battle for Sarajevo to a decisive end, but he did not state what he would have
done with more tanks if the JNA had agreed.[34]

Midday on May 2 two armored columns converged just south of the city
government's headquarters. General Jovan Divjak, deputy commander of
the ARBiH and a Serb opposed to the nationalists' siege, recalled, "Our
worst moment came when they crossed the bridge into the city center. They
were within fifty meters of the Presidency Building."[35] Having apparently

secured a staging area, a unit of sappers moved east along the Miljacka riverbank to the Main Post Office, the structure designed by Vancaš and Valter's final destination on the night of April 5, 1945. The sappers placed explosives in the building, which housed the city's central telephone switching equipment, and blew it up from the inside, gutting the interior and leaving only a skeletal structure of exterior walls. As they fled the structure, JNA soldiers were taken captive by government forces sent to intercept them, but the attack stripped Sarajevo of nearly all telephone service for many months after the attack.

The JNA's armored assault posed a critical early challenge for the nascent ARBiH. Using scarce but highly effective antiarmor weaponry, the ARBiH stopped the armored assault in its tracks.[36] By evening on March 2 JNA tanks and armored personnel carriers were ablaze in the square in front of the Sarajevo city government building. The JNA invasion had been repulsed by lightly equipped but resourceful elements of the ARBiH. Still, damage to the city was extensive, and the JNA's ability to shell the city at will was undiminished.

As the armored vehicles were ablaze in central Sarajevo, JNA officers found a fortuitous opportunity to strike back by arresting Izetbegović in the Sarajevo airport as he returned from peace talks.[37] Before taking him and his daughter to the JNA base at Lukavica for the night, Izetbegović was allowed to speak by phone with his trusted associate, presidency member Ejup Ganić. As in previous conflicts on March 2 and April 6, the discussion between the major actors in the drama was telecast live to Sarajevo viewers. Sarajevans, at least those whose homes were still receiving electricity, watched the tense negotiations between JNA generals and the republic's civilian leaders, and even watched Ganić decline Izetbegović's offer to hand him the reins of power. Ganić, despite rejecting Izetbegović's request to become acting president, assumed control of the situation as Izetbegović passed the night of May 2–3 a hostage of the JNA.

Meanwhile, the ARBiH had Kukanjac, the senior JNA general in Bosnia-Herzegovina, besieged in his headquarters in Bistrik. He and his command group faced the prospect of leaving the city through a gauntlet of angry soldiers in plain view of the destruction that had been wrought by JNA attacks on the city. UNPROFOR Commander General Lewis MacKenzie assumed the role of intermediary. MacKenzie arranged for Izetbegović to be exchanged one-for-one for Kukanjac, but then he was told that Kukanjac wanted his entire entourage to leave the city with him. MacKenzie could not guarantee the safety of such a large group, but Izetbegović blithely assured MacKenzie that he would guarantee the safety of all withdrawing soldiers.

The planned exchange proceeded slowly. Izetbegović and MacKenzie traveled together in a white UN armored personnel carrier to the JNA headquarters, where they picked up Kukanjac. The UN carrier then led a convoy of forty JNA carriers along Dobrovoljačka (Volunteer) Street, bound for the Serb-held base at Lukavica with the plan of dropping Izetbegović off near the Presidency Building along the way. But Izetbegović's guarantee of safe passage proved worthless. Waiting until the convoy was in the narrow confines of the street, ARBiH troops opened fire in accord with orders from Ganić. Their commander described the attack as follows:

Ganić asked us not to open fire until the convoy of vehicles had left the barracks. As I saw it, if the convoy left, they would be free to kill the president; therefore, we had to take Kukanjac prisoner, and exchange him for the president. It would be safer that way. I gave orders for the convoy to be allowed to leave the JNA command headquarters in Bistrik. When they were out in the open, I ordered my men to open fire. We had them surrounded.[38]

Izetbegović, from the top of the vehicle that was taking him to safety, ordered the ARBiH troops to stop firing on the back half of the convoy, and General Divjak, riding with him in the vehicle, repeatedly shouted orders to end the assault. When the shooting subsided, the JNA had sustained six deaths, including a Bosniak woman who had been evacuated with the troops from the headquarters facility. The ARBiH took dozens of JNA prisoners who were later released in a prisoner exchange. The column eventually resumed its westward movement. The Bosnian president was released a few blocks later, in front of the Skenderija Sports Center, whence he returned to the Presidency Building a few hundred meters away. General Kukanjac and his column reached the JNA Lukavica barracks west of the city without further incident, but the bodies of JNA soldiers lay in Sarajevo's streets along with an unknown number of civilian and ARBiH casualties from the fighting.

The failed JNA offensive of May 2 and Kukanjac's battle-scarred withdrawal was to be the last major official act of Kukanjac's command. On May 4 the Yugoslav federal collective presidency ordered JNA forces to withdraw from Bosnia-Herzegovina within fifteen days. Four days later the same body sent some thirty-eight JNA generals into retirement and dismissed Kukanjac from his post, effectively completing the transformation of the JNA from a Yugoslav force into an instrument of Serb nationalism.[39] He left a disputed legacy. There is little doubt that Kukanjac wanted to interject the

JNA as a mediating party between contending forces, and he was somewhat successful in doing that until early April. But on recognition weekend, the JNA's murderous behavior left no doubt of its true disposition, and Kukanjac's continued declarations of JNA impartiality ceased to be credible. Bosniak and Croat leaders derided him as a stalking horse for Great Serb interests. Serb critics, on the other hand, called him a traitor for failing to prosecute their cause more forcefully. In July 1994, in lashing out at his Serb nationalist critics, he revealed his belief that he had conquered much of Sarajevo on their behalf: "When I was in command, not one single cannon, nor a tank, was left to the Muslims, nor did they get one. ... We gave you the arms. ... I must say that I left the Serb part of Sarajevo captured for you.[40]

In accord with a decision reached at a summit of Serbian leaders in Belgrade on April 30, General Ratko Mladić succeeded Kukanjac as commander of the Second Military District in Bosnia-Herzegovina on May 10. Karadžić later claimed that he had requested Mladić for the job.[41] Mladić was known for having ordered the distribution of JNA arms to rebel Serbs in Croatia while commanding the JNA's Knin Corps in 1991. Just two days after his appointment, the VRS superseded the JNA's Second Military District by order of the Bosnian Serb Assembly in its meeting in Banja Luka, and Mladić was appointed the first VRS commander.[42] He changed title but not function, and it became evident that he was appointed commander of the Second Military District on May 10 to provide the Bosnian Serb nationalists with a smooth transition to the VRS on May 12. In the transition from the JNA to the VRS, most units changed names but retained their weaponry, personnel, and commanders. The Sarajevo-based JNA Fourth Corps became the Sarajevo-Romanija Corps of the VRS.[43] Under the command of Major General Tomislav Sipčić, the Sarajevo-Romanija Corps integrated Serb-controlled territorial defense forces into the structure of the former Fourth Corps to bring the unit to a total strength of about thirteen thousand men. With the formation of the VRS and its Sarajevo-Romanija Corps, the Bosnian Serb nationalists formally acquired control of the heavily-armed behemoth that would prosecute the siege of Sarajevo for the next four years. By the time it was formally created on May 12, the VRS possessed enough troops, heavy weapons, ammunition, and supply lines to besiege Sarajevo indefinitely.

Although the JNA's commander and his staff had withdrawn from the city on May 3, hundreds of soldiers remained surrounded in JNA bases in the city. UN sources reported that ARBiH forces had blockaded the military hospital, several barracks housing JNA troops, and a military school with 1,300 teenage pupils.[44] The ARBiH siege of JNA facilities was a desperate effort to wrest some negotiating advantage from a deteriorating situation in the city, which the secretary general described in the following bleak assessment on May 12:

> The city suffers regular heavy shelling and sniper fire nightly, and intermittent shelling at other times, often on a random basis, from Serbian irregulars in the surrounding hills, who use mortars and light artillery allegedly made available to them by JNA. .... Economic life is at a standstill and there are growing shortages of food and other essential supplies owing to the blockade imposed on the city by Serb forces.[45]

With the former Second Military District headquarters at Bistrik in ARBiH hands after Kukanjac's withdrawal, the most valuable remaining asset under JNA control was the Marshal Tito Barracks, a sprawling complex of buildings west of the Holiday Inn. UN sources reported that six hundred to one thousand soldiers were trapped there with nearly two hundred vehicles.[46] The ARBiH covetously eyed the JNA armories, hoping to acquire the weapons and ammunition desperately needed by the republic's armed forces. From the barracks' front gates, JNA riflemen could fire at traffic on the thoroughfare in front of them, making east-west passage a matter of life and death. The base was only a few hundred meters from the Grbavica high-rise neighborhood, which had been occupied by Serb paramilitaries since March. The north-south strip of territory between the barracks and Grbavica remained vulnerable to a Serb effort to partition the central city from its residential suburbs.

Immediately south of the Marshal Tito Barracks was the summit known as Hum, where a giant television transmission tower dominated the landscape. Such transmitters elsewhere in Bosnia-Herzegovina had been favorite targets of Serb paramilitaries, and the Hum tower had been strafed by JNA aircraft on several occasions. On the gentle slopes at the bottom of this hill, just west of the barracks, lay the residential neighborhood of Pofalići. Between May 14 and 16, 1992, various ARBiH units drove Serb nationalist forces from the Hum hill and Pofalići in fierce fighting.[47] In conquering Pofalići, the ARBiH precluded the VRS forces from easily dissecting Sarajevo and secured the route between the central city and the government-held areas to the west. However, in the first salvo of what was to become a routine of revenge, the JNA unleashed tank and artillery fire from the surrounding hills against both the assaulting ARBiH forces and various civilian targets in the city.

Despite the Bosnian government's agreement to allow JNA forces to withdraw from installations in Sarajevo, the departures were not completed until early June. In retaliation for JNA artillery attacks on the city, ARBiH forces mortared JNA installations, provoking even fiercer VRS bombardment of civilian targets from positions in the hills. On the night of May 27–8, 1992, both ARBiH forces *and* Serb irregulars irked at the JNA's departure attacked a column of JNA soldiers withdrawing from the Jusuf Džonlić and Victor Bubanj Barracks under UN escort.[48] On June 6 the JNA withdrew from the Marshal Tito Barracks. As ARBiH forces rushed to retrieve the abandoned stockpiles, JNA pounded its former base with artillery assaults in hopes of destroying arms and ammunitions before they could be retrieved. ARBiH forces, led by Ismet Bajramović Ćelo, won the race.[49] Government forces made off with desperately needed antitank weapons, the key to halting armored assaults on their lines, and a large cache of ammunition. Over the next two days, the JNA unleashed the heaviest artillery barrages to date against civilian targets in the city.[50]

The internationals: UN policy toward Sarajevo

Though the outside world watched Sarajevo intently, no single nation or group of nations was prepared to take the steps necessary to end the killing. Those with the will to break the siege, the soldiers of the ARBiH, lacked the means to do so. Those with the means to break the siege, the major European countries and the United States, lacked the will to employ them, preferring to focus on the humanitarian needs of the conflict's victims. Their inaction cannot be attributed to ignorance or failure to comprehend the enormity of what was taking place. UN officials fully informed member states about the nature and scope of the violence, but the unwillingness of member states to support military action to defend civilians limited the UN's ability to act.

The UN created UNPROFOR to monitor the peace agreement in Croatia, but UN leaders made Sarajevo its headquarters in hopes that its presence would have a calming effect on the city.[51] Beyond urging the cooperation of all "Yugoslav parties" in achieving peace, the UN Security Council at first foresaw no formal role for UNPROFOR in Bosnia-Herzegovina, but the arrival in mid-March of Lieutenant General Satish Nambiar, the first

UNPROFOR commander, had been perceived in Sarajevo as a possible signal of the UN's intention to intervene militarily on behalf of the newly independent Republic of Bosnia-Herzegovina.[52] Even without a specific mandate, UNPROFOR rapidly became a critical factor in the developing military conflict in Sarajevo. The growing violence forced UN officials to make tough policy choices quickly, as can be seen in a series of reports, consultations, and Security Council resolutions in the first three months after the siege began. Developments in Sarajevo, and access to the city through its airport, became the dominant factors in UN decision making, so that policy toward Sarajevo heavily influenced UN policy toward all of Bosnia-Herzegovina. International policy-makers continued to accord the city a primary role throughout the war.

Neither UN nor Western leaders were responsible for the Sarajevo siege. They neither wanted it to happen nor wished for it to continue. But because of a yawning chasm between the UN's quite accurate understanding of the situation and the unwillingness of UN member states to commit resources to address it, UN policies often served to perpetuate the siege and the attendant misery in the city. UN officials spent the entire siege in a no-win dilemma between the notions of peacemaking (using armed force to repel violations of its resolutions) and peacekeeping (monitoring and patrolling an agreement among the parties.) It was a classic case of inadequate means preventing the achievement of admirable ends, and in some cases the damage was made worse by the outright malice of influential individuals in UN organizations.[53]

Following the outbreak of war in early April 1992, the UN Secretary General and Security Council shifted their attention from Croatia and began to monitor carefully the situation in Bosnia-Herzegovina. Security Council Resolution 749 of April 7, 1992, was the first to mention Bosnia-Herzegovina. In it the council "calls upon all parties and others concerned not to resort to violence, particularly in any area where [UNPROFOR] is to be based or deployed."[54] In pronouncements over the next several weeks, both the Security Council and secretary general identified three major sources of the Bosnian conflict: military intervention by the JNA and the Army of the Republic of Croatia (*Hrvatska vojska*); the Bosnian Serbs' wish to create an ethnically pure state; and obstructions to the delivery of humanitarian aid. In a report dated May 12, 1992, the secretary general identified the basic nature of the conflict: "All international observers agree that what is happening is a concerted effort by the Serbs of Bosnia-Herzegovina, with the acquiescence of, and at least some support from, the JNA, to create 'ethnically pure' regions."[55]

In Resolution 752 of May 15, 1992, the council demanded that the JNA and the Army of the Republic of Croatia "either be withdrawn, be subject to the authority of the Government of Bosnia and Herzegovina, or be disbanded and disarmed with their weapons placed under effective international monitoring."[56] The resolution further called upon all parties to "ensure that forcible expulsions of persons from the areas where they live" should "cease immediately." Citing the "urgent need for humanitarian assistance," the council called for "unhindered delivery of humanitarian assistance, including safe and secure access to airports in Bosnia and Herzegovina." The secretary general reported that over 520,000 persons had been displaced as of May 8, 1992.

Recognizing the problems, however, was not the same as resolving them, and council members were actively considering robust measures in May. The secretary general, responding to the council's request, weighed the option of using UNPROFOR to provide "armed protection" for humanitarian convoys.[57] That option, he reported, was fraught with risks.

In assessing the risk of hostile action, it has to be remembered that for some of the parties the infliction of hardship on civilians is actually a war aim, as it leads to the desired movements of population from certain areas. Therefore there appears to be a predisposition to use force to obstruct relief supplies.

To secure Sarajevo airport, he wrote, would "require United Nations troops to secure the surrounding hills from which the airport and its approaches can easily be shelled." He discouraged this option, noting that it would require a "considerable body of troops" and might make it more difficult for UNPROFOR to secure cooperation for its mission in Croatia.

In the absence of a direct UN military commitment, the secretary general put forth a "less ambitious possibility," namely for UNPROFOR to escort humanitarian supplies into the city. "There would need to be an agreement that forces deployed in the surrounding hills would not fire at the airport or its approaches when humanitarian supplies were arriving there." With some refinements, the proposed alternative became the basis for UNPROFOR's rules of engagement in Sarajevo for the next three years. With no permanent member of the Security Council prepared to commit UNPROFOR to a combat role, the council on May 30, 1992, resolved to implement sanctions against the Federal Republic of Yugoslavia (Serbia and Montenegro).[58] Announcement of the sanctions appears to have pushed Belgrade's lead-

ership closer to supporting the reopening the Sarajevo airport, but the proclamation did little to subdue the Serb military rampage. Resolution 757 also
endorsed the secretary general's suggestion that the UN's primary mission
should be the delivery of aid to Sarajevo. It demanded that "all parties
and others concerned create immediately the necessary conditions for unimpeded delivery of humanitarian supplies to Sarajevo and other desti-
nations in Bosnia and Herzegovina, including the establishment of a security
zone encompassing Sarajevo and its airport."

In Resolution 757 the council grouped together the city and its airport.
Within a few days, however, the secretary general assigned first priority to
securing the "reopening of Sarajevo airport for the delivery of humanitarian
supplies and related purposes." The city itself was excluded from the formulation of UNPROFOR's immediate mission, and aid delivery took pre-
cedence over protecting civilians against armed assault. Securing the airport
was described as a "first step in establishing a security zone encompassing
Sarajevo and its airport." With the goal of reopening the airport, Cedric
Thornberry, UNPROFOR's director of civil affairs, brokered an agreement
with the contending parties in Sarajevo on June 5. The agreement pertained
only to the airport and "security corridors between the airport and the city;"
it contained no provisions to reduce attacks on the city itself:

To provide physical guarantees that fire will not be brought to bear against the
airport, flying aircraft, or aircraft on the ground, [the undersigned] agree that:
(a) all antiaircraft weapons systems will be withdrawn from positions from which
they can engage the airport and its air approaches and be placed under UNPRO-
FOR supervision; (b) all artillery, mortar, ground-to-ground missile systems and
tanks within range of the airport will be concentrated in areas agreed by UNPRO-
FOR and subject to UNPROFOR observation at the firing line.[59]

Several days later, in compliance with the UN agreement, the Bosnian Serb
nationalist leaders promised to concentrate their offensive weaponry in five
locations near the airport beginning on June 15, 1992. They took full
advantage of the agreement's specific language and stated, according to UN
observers, "that they would continue to shell the city itself while sparing the
airport."[60] UN officials engaged in "observation at the firing line," in the
words of the initial agreement, as Bosnian Serb gunners targeted the city
with artillery and tank fire. Journalists were stunned by the Kafkaesque
scene of UN monitors calmly taking notes for their reports as murderous
firepower was unleashed on a city with half a million residents.

The agreement to permit unfettered UN operations at the airport was periodically violated, principally but not exclusively by the Bosnian Serb nationalists, who had learned by then that shutting down the airport was a superior method to display displeasure and extract concessions from international negotiators. The Security Council's complaints of interference with free transit through the Sarajevo airport were reiterated in several resolutions during the summer of 1992.[61] The UN effort thus remained narrowly focused on the aid delivery through the Sarajevo airport at the time when the Bosnian Serb nationalists were conducting their widespread initial campaign of conquest and ethnic cleansing. On July 17 the council concurred with the secretary general in rejecting a proposal that the UN supervise heavy weapons throughout Bosnia-Herzegovina.[62]

After receiving reports of ethnic cleansing and a swelling river of refugees, the Security Council finally adopted three resolutions in August 1992 centered on "abuses committed against the civilian population."[63] It expressed "grave alarm" at reports of "mass forcible expulsion and deportation of civilians, imprisonment and abuse of civilians in detention centers, [and] deliberate attacks on noncombatants, hospitals, and ambulances."[64] Also in August, the United Nations Human Rights Commission ordered an investigation of alleged human rights violations. Tadeusz Mazowiecki, special rapporteur of the commission, visited Sarajevo on August 24 to assess the situation. In his report submitted four days later, he concluded, "The greatest threat to life at present comes from the shelling of civilian population centers and the shooting of civilians in besieged towns."[65] He further noted that Sarajevo's city center and airport had been "among the principal targets of the shelling." He was alarmed that the besieging forces were denying essential needs to Sarajevo's residents:

The siege, including the shelling of population centers and the cutting off of supplies of food and other essential goods, is another tactic. ... The city is shelled on a regular basis, in what appears to be a deliberate attempt to spread terror among the population. Snipers shoot innocent civilians. The mission visited the hospital, and was able to see many civilian victims. It was also able to see the damage done to the hospital itself, which has been deliberately shelled on several occasions, despite the proper display of the internationally recognized Red Cross symbol.

Neither Mazowiecki's reports nor the increasingly vivid media accounts of atrocities moved Western nations to take military action. The UN expanded its diplomatic role in late August 1992 by joining the European Community in forming the International Conference on the Former Yugoslavia to advance peace negotiations. But on the ground in Bosnia-Herzegovina, UNPROFOR units gave priority to humanitarian aid and measures required to secure its safe delivery.

In large measure UNPROFOR successfully performed its assigned mission and undoubtedly prevented widespread starvation and malnutrition. Dozens of international aid organizations joined in donating and transporting essential items via the UN "air bridge" or over the "Blue Road" into Sarajevo from the Adriatic coast. These included the UN High Commission for Refugees, international nongovernmental organizations such as the Red Cross, International Rescue Committee, and the Open Society Foundation funded by financier George Soros. Fred Cuny, an international aid worker from Texas, developed and installed an innovative filtration and pumping system within the siege lines to provide water from within the city as an alterative to Serb-controlled water sources.[66] This and other aid endeavors would not have been possible without UNPROFOR support. Some UNPROFOR officers contributed personally to easing the plight of besieged Sarajevans. Many French officers, in particular, supported cultural activities in the city and attended some of the relatively few cultural events that could be organized in times of relative quiet.

Despite the many benefits that various UN bodies brought to Sarajevo, their contributions often entailed costly concessions to the besieging Serbs. UNPROFOR, desperately insistent on the delivery of basic human necessities, itself became hostage to the demands of Bosnian Serb nationalists. In making concessions to secure delivery of aid, UNPROFOR became a part of the siege apparatus by enforcing Serb-dictated limitations on the movement of persons, goods, and services. The UN tightly regulated movement of persons into and out of the city. Regulation was essential to prioritize the limited seats available on UN-controlled flights, but at Serb insistence the UN also declined to support activities that boosted civic pride or expressed Sarajevo's spirit of resistance to armed assault. On July 22, 1992, the UN refused to allow departure of a flight carrying Bosnian athletes and representatives to the Barcelona Summer Olympic Games, saying it could transport only two registered athletes and eight others. An outraged International Olympic Committee extended emergency recognition to all thirty delegates and chartered two planes to transport them to Barcelona, effectively circumventing the UN-enforced blockade.[67]

The UN construed "humanitarian aid" narrowly. When the city of Innsbruck, Austria, offered to provide new uniforms to the beleaguered

Sarajevo Fire Department, the UN refused permission to deliver them because they did not qualify as humanitarian aid.[68] The city's daily newspaper, *Oslobodjenje*, required newsprint to continue publishing, but UNPROFOR Commander General MacKenzie declined UN assistance in getting the needed supplies through Serb lines and charged that the newspaper had inadequately expressed support for peace negotiations.[69]

Mail was excluded from the definition of humanitarian aid, so Sarajevo's residents went for nearly four years with little routine communication with the outside world. Visitors to the city often found themselves flooded with requests to deliver letters and small packages to relatives or friends outside the city. In July 1994 each person boarding a UN flight to Sarajevo was notified of limits on the quantity of cigarettes, alcohol, and coffee to be transported to Sarajevo. Additionally, UN officials restricted each passenger to "six private letters. The letters must be presented to [civilian police] monitors when check takes place. Passengers are fully responsible for the content of the letters."[70] In the contorted world of UN relations with the besieging Serbs, UN officials were put in the position of censoring personal mail. In reality, UN personnel frequently disregarded the restrictions on letters and transported items, although they limited each passenger to baggage that could be personally carried on board.

In September 1994 UN officials intervened to prevent the scheduled visit of Pope John Paul II to Sarajevo. The city had been festooned with posters bearing a picture of the Pope and the words, "You are not abandoned. We are with you."[71] When UN officials informed the Vatican that they could not guarantee the Pope's security, the visit was cancelled,[72] and many of the heartening posters were torn from walls and kiosks by embittered Sarajevans. Three months later UN authorities declined to provide air transportation to the mayors of hundreds of cities across the globe, even though aircraft were regularly landing and taking off at the airport. The mayors had been invited by the Sarajevo city government to attend events marking the 1,000th day of the siege in January 1995. Most mayors eventually arrived in Sarajevo on chartered buses after a long, circuitous trip from Zagreb, and scheduled events went forward, without the participation of UN officials, in the meeting hall of the shell-pocked Holiday Inn.[73]

Some UNPROFOR concessions increased Sarajevans' vulnerability to armed assault, and a few of them led to deaths at key transit points in the city. After the first battles of spring 1992, sniper barriers were erected on the south side of vulnerable intersections and passageways, sometimes with

UNPROFOR assistance. At one intersection, a large blue canvas made a visual shield that obstructed snipers' views, but it did not protect pedestrians against their bullets. The longest sniper barrier in the city was put in place to the east of the Bosnian Assembly Building along Vojvoda Putnik Street in a large open expanse between the city center and the western suburbs under Bosnian control. The UN constructed the barrier by piling cargo containers three high, providing ample protection against snipers only a hundred meters or so away.

Late in 1993, in a concession to the Bosnian Serb nationalists in the interests of building confidence, UNPROFOR officers removed the cargo containers closest to the Assembly Building, leaving an open space of about twenty meters between the first cargo containers and the shelter from sniper fire provided by the Assembly Building. UN officers thus deliberately provided VRS snipers with a corridor of fire where VRS lines were very close to the main east-west thoroughfare. From July 1994 until spring 1995, a French armored personnel carrier was stationed in the middle of this east-west gap. In times of heavy sniper activity, the vehicle shuttled back and forth as civilians crouched and scurried to remain in the vehicle's moving protective shadow. But not all sniping was predictable. The space between the cargo containers and the Assembly Building became a gap of death. Serb sniper hits were sufficiently predictable to induce many photographers from global news organizations to linger behind the French vehicle in hopes of witnessing a shooting of Sarajevo civilians. The gap also left exposed the major east-west tram line, so that many civilians were killed or wounded while riding the tram on those rare occasions when it operated.

In the spring of 1995, as Serb violations of the Carter-negotiated cease-fire multiplied, the new UNPROFOR commander put an end to this inhumane vulnerability. Under the command of General Rupert Smith, the gap of death was closed by extending the row of cargo containers west into the protective shadow of the Assembly Building, providing shelter for passersby from VRS snipers. Sadly, closing the gap of death claimed the life of Eric Hardoin, a French UNPROFOR soldier.[74] He was killed while climbing out of a white UN forklift used to move the cargo containers into place. A video photographer standing nearby recorded the tragic passing of life from the dying soldier's body. It was broadcast worldwide within hours.

UN actions also contributed to killings of Sarajevans on the tarmac of the Sarajevo airport. Crossing the tarmac was the only option available for many

The "gap of death," a narrow corridor protected only by a UN armored personnel carrier, where Serb snipers regularly shot at passing pedestrians and vehicles. The Bosnian Assembly Building, with windows shot out, is on the right. (Photograph by the author, January 1995)

of those seeking to flee the city. Early in the siege, the ARBiH had moved men and matériel across the airport and drawn Serb gunfire, and the besieging Serbs subsequently acquired a UN commitment to shine spotlights on those traversing the airport at night. UNPROFOR soldiers did so regularly, lighting up targets of fleeing women and children to be picked off by Serb snipers in the nearby hills. The UN troops were allowed to pick up the victims and transport them to hospitals in the besieged city.[75] Killings in the gap of death and on the airport tarmac underlined the cruel irony of UN-PROFOR's role in Sarajevo. Its soldiers served the laudable cause of delivering aid to persons in need, but their commanders' compromises often increased civilian exposure to enemy assault. Many UNPROFOR soldiers, drawn from elite units in their home countries, conducted themselves fearlessly and compassionately. In this visitor's experience, many of them were eager to alleviate the plight of Sarajevo's residents but were often restrained from doing so by their rules of engagement. UNPROFOR lacked the mandate, the means, and in some cases the will to challenge militarily the makers of the siege.

Tightening the siege

In the aftermath of Kukanjac's departure from Sarajevo on May 3, Bosnian Serb nationalist leaders and military commanders tightened their hold on the city. Roadblocks were set up on roads leading out of the city, and a system of trenches and bunkers encircled most inhabited areas. At the Bosnian Serb Assembly meeting on May 12 (the day that the VRS was formally constituted and Mladić was made its commander), delegates reported on the situation in their municipalities. Trifko Radić, a member of the Bosnian Serb Assembly representing the western Sarajevo municipality of Ilijaš, boasted that he and his colleagues had sealed off the city:

We are prepared. We hold 50 km of the line of encirclement around Ilijaš. We are organized and I have asked the television to come and record how well organized for the war we are in Ilijaš, how our defense lines are organized. ... We have cut off and mined the railway line and no one can arrive in Sarajevo. We have mined the motorway too. We shall do our best to prevent the enemy from ever getting to Sarajevo from the direction of Zenica, and anyone who tries the upper route will also meet his end.[76]

SDS President Radovan Karadžić joined in praising the Bosnian Serbs' iron grip: "We hold all our areas, all the municipalities, all the settlements around Sarajevo, and we hold our enemies ... in complete encirclement, so that they cannot receive military aid, in manpower or in weapons."[77]

Although they boasted to one another of the siege's effectiveness, Bosnian Serb nationalist leaders publicly denied besieging the city. They characterized their military operations as defensive, intended to fend off ARBiH attacks on Serb-inhabited suburbs. They attributed much of the ordnance falling on the city to ARBiH soldiers attacking their own population. They blamed the breakdowns in vital municipal services on ARBiH forces.[78] As General Mladić explained on May 12, casting blame back upon the victims was critical to Bosnian Serb nationalist strategy:

We should not say we will destroy Sarajevo; we need Sarajevo. We are not going to say that we are going to destroy the power supply pylons or turn off the water supply, no, because that would get America out of its seat, but gentlemen... one day there will be no water at all in Sarajevo. ... Therefore, we have to wisely tell the world, it was they who were shooting, hit the transmission line and the power went off, they were shooting at the water supply facilities, there was a power cut at such and such a place, we are doing our best repairing this... That is what diplomacy is.[79]

The Bosnian Serb nationalists' denials of the siege and bombardment were disingenuous and patently absurd. UN observers and journalists in the city,

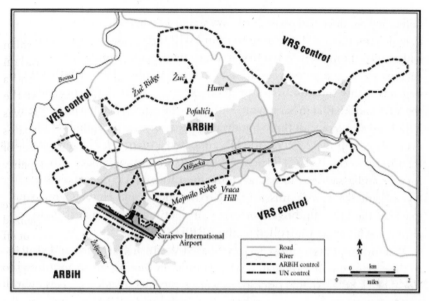

9.1 Front lines in the siege of Sarajevo, June 1992.

themselves often under fire from the surrounding hills, occasionally visited VRS firing positions and could observe the pummeling of the city below. They marveled at the impunity with which VRS artillerymen could take aim at their targets. Bosnian Serb gunners had direct visual access and could identify most of their targets readily with the naked eye. In December 1992 a journalist visited an artillery emplacement on a hill south of the city and recorded his surprise at the view:

Anybody who stops and climbs atop the mud walls can see what the Serbian gunners see, and it is an astonishing sight. Many of the guns are less than one thousand yards from high-rise buildings in the center of the city, and perhaps 500 to 1,000 feet above them. ... It is plain, numbingly so, that the men firing the guns can see exactly what they are hitting.[80]

The war in Sarajevo was a struggle between the well-armed VRS and the well-manned ARBiH. When the war began, the Sarajevo-Romanija Corps had thirteen thousand well-armed troops and six to eight hundred heavy artillery pieces, tanks, and heavy and medium mortars surrounding the city.[81] By contrast, the ARBiH consisted of about 17,300 soldiers, but it had more troops than guns. Some units had one weapon for three or four soldiers, and they were plagued by a paucity of ammunition. The forces defending Sarajevo had no usable heavy weapons when the war began except a single tank that had been used to train MUP forces, and by war's end they had acquired only ten to twenty artillery pieces, one hundred mortars of various sizes, and some recoilless rifles. In October 1992 UNPROFOR began tracking the number of projectiles hitting territories controlled by the VRS and ARBiH in Sarajevo.[82] Until the cease-fire of February 1994, the VRS fired an average of three hundred artillery or mortar rounds at the city every day; on July 22, 1993, the UN reported a record 3,777 impacts.[83] In testimony at the ICTY, Herbert Okun, a US Foreign Service officer and former ambassador who had accompanied former US Secretary of State Cyrus Vance on several missions to Croatia and Bosnia-Herzegovina, summarized the UN's findings: For every projectile fired into Serb-held territory, ten hit areas controlled by the ARBiH.[84]

Wartime reports by most Sarajevo-based Western journalists and visitors to the city frequently relegated ARBiH military operations to an informational black hole. ARBiH operations were typically shrouded in secrecy and conducted in obscurity. Journalists often portrayed ARBiH troops as well-intentioned but hapless soldiers engaged in a futile struggle against overwhelming odds. Bosnian government supporters encouraged this representation during the war to highlight the plight of the city's civilians, but armed defense of the city was much more effective than outsiders frequently portrayed it. After the war, the secrecy surrounding the ARBiH vanished in a rush for public acclaim.[85] In a spate of interviews and memoirs, leading commanders boasted of their roles in military operations, and several commanders competed in claiming primary credit for having saved the city. In contrast to wartime secrecy, the postwar accounts offer a candid, compelling picture of the nature and scope of military operations. In particular, former ARBiH General Nedžad Ajnadžić's detailed analysis provides exceptional insight into the composition and operations of the First Corps, the unit charged with Sarajevo's defense.[86]

Lacking armored units, ARBiH forces relied heavily on antitank weapons to cripple or destroy the armored vehicles deployed against them in VRS offensives. ARBiH units acquired antitank munitions from the stockpiles left behind by JNA units withdrawing from various Sarajevo barracks, but those supplies were exhausted by the end of July 1992.[87] Unit commanders carefully husbanded these prized weapons. Inventive soldiers developed the "Bosnian cocktail," a Coca-Cola can stuffed with explosives capable of disabling tanks and armored personnel carriers.[88] Several ARBiH offensives sputtered to a halt because the troops ran out of ammunition, forcing units to abandon some hard-won territory.[89] Raw determination, ingenuity, guile, and a steady stream of volunteers became the most potent weapons in the ARBiH arsenal. Burdened but undaunted by the lack of arms, ARBiH units launched dozens of offensives during the war with the aim of breaking the siege or driving VRS forces away from the city's most vulnerable areas. They never broke the siege, but they captured key high points in the city and expanded the territory under their control, particularly in the western suburbs.

ARBiH commanders went to extreme lengths to overcome their deficiencies in arms and ammunition. Early in the conflict, they borrowed four cannon used during the Second World War from the permanent collection of the Museum of the Revolution. The cannon, donated to the museum after they were used by Tito's Partisans in the Second World War, were returned at war's end with the report that they had functioned well throughout the conflict.[90] For months, ARBiH operatives hid gunpowder in UN-transported oxygen containers ostensibly bound for city hospitals.[91] This operation, which could not have succeeded without the tacit support of low-ranking UNPROFOR personnel, came to an end when suspicious VRS soldiers stopped and weighed one of the shipments and found the containers were too heavy to contain only compressed gas. UNPROFOR also reported clandestine drops of arms from Iranian aircraft and other Islamic countries, but the extent of such operations is difficult to assess, and they likely did not add substantially to the ARBiH's arsenals.

Unlike the VRS's Romanija Corps, the ARBiH First Corps experienced rapid growth in manpower during 1992, from about 17,300 at the beginning of the war to 33,200 in December 1992, according to Ajnadžić's study. Growth slowed thereafter, with the unit reaching an average of 38,840 soldiers in 1995. The vast majority of Sarajevo's defenders were Bosniaks. Their percentage of the total force varied little from year to year, ranging between 89 percent and 92 percent in the four years of the siege. The number of Serbs declined from 700 to 233 from 1992 to 1995, while the number of Croats gradually increased from 1,010 to 1,822 in the same years. Most First Corps soldiers were defending their home city. Eighty percent were Sarajevo residents, while about 20 percent were refugees, principally from eastern Bosnia. The social composition of the defending force, heavily weighted in favor of the city's working class, would have been the envy of any Marxist revolutionary organizer. About 70 percent of the soldiers had completed technical secondary school, and 80 percent were classified as "work-ers." Twelve percent were "functionaries" and 7 percent were peasants. The fighting force included very few intellectuals, although many fighting-age intellectuals served for brief periods of time in combat units.

The defending forces of the First Corps recorded a total of 436 combat operations during the war.[92] Offensive operations (attacks) outnumbered defensive ones (reactions) 279 to 157. The most combat operations were undertaken in 1992 and early 1993. Although the number of operations declined drastically in 1994 and 1995, the ratio of offensive to defensive operations remained relatively stable in each of the four wartime years. These statistics reinforce the anecdotal evidence in various memoirs and reports suggesting that the ARBiH undertook more initiatives to break the siege than the VRS did to advance its lines.

ARBiH gains in western Sarajevo

Many ARBiH offensives were designed to capture high ground. The com-manding heights around Sarajevo were the key to controlling it, a critical factor recognized by the Bosnian Serbs as early as 1991 in seeking political control of the upland municipalities and in attacking the Vraca police aca-demy. By the beginning of war, the highland overlooks were replete with VRS artillery and snipers. Only by capturing higher ground could the ARBiH effectively challenge their better armed adversaries. Throughout 1992 the exchanges of territory generally favored the ARBiH, but the gains were small and costly.[93]

The conquest of Pofalići and Hum in May 1992 (noted above) was the first modest ARBiH success at conquering high ground. In what became a nearly continuous struggle for control of a few hills in the western suburbs, each side initiated actions to control the hills of Žuč, Mojmilo, and Stup. On June 8, 1992, the ARBiH launched a major offensive designed to seize key hills from the VRS.[94] Some ARBiH actions would be better characterized as clandestine sabotage operations. One unit made five successive assaults on VRS armored vehicles on Mojmilo Hill, each time guided through the encircling minefield by the former JNA soldier who had laid mines there before the war.[95] After initial successes, the ARBiH was driven back by VRS counterattacks, but government forces successfully held on to the Mojmilo Hill, depriving the VRS of a point from which to launch close-in artillery and mortar shelling of the city.

Each ARBiH assault evoked a savage artillery and tank barrage from the surrounding hills, directed against both the attacking units and civilians in the city. The rapid response of VRS artillery led the attackers to withdraw quickly or to bring their own troops so close to enemy trenches that bombardment posed a threat to both sides. The ARBiH finally prevailed in the battle for Žuč in December 1992, sparing some of northwest Sarajevo from further shelling.[96] Even Karadžić later begrudgingly acknowledged the exemplary determination of the ARBiH forces in holding Žuč while asking that his admiration for them not be publicized: "For ninety days we assaulted Žuč—I ask journalists not to write this. We could not drive the Turks from the trenches, nor could they expel us."[97] After the war, Bosniaks in Sarajevo celebrated the Žuč battle as a major victory of the ARBiH.

An epic struggle was waged for Dobrinja, a complex of high-rise residential apartments built as the housing for the 1984 Winter Games. Besides being home to forty thousand Sarajevans (many of whom remained there during the fighting), the Dobrinja settlement was the key to control of the northeastern side of the Sarajevo airport and near the route into town from the JNA barracks at Lukavica. In the early days of the siege, the VRS encircled and cut off Dobrinja, whose residents faced the prospect of starvation or conquest. A battle for Dobrinja erupted just as the airport was scheduled to pass from Serb to UNPROFOR control. On June 16, 1992, VRS units entered part of Dobrinja, killed some residents, and took others prisoner. In subsequent days, elite ARBiH units penetrated Dobrinja and ambushed a VRS unit making its way into one of the courtyards between buildings.[98] In several subsequent days of fighting, ARBiH units secured Dobrinja and established a narrow corridor connecting it with the rest of the besieged city, but it continued to be a prime target for VRS tank and artillery fire.

The quest to eradicate Sarajevo's common life

The Bosnian Serb nationalists' goal of dividing the city mandated that Serb-held areas be rid of Bosniaks and Croats and that Serbs be drawn from what the nationalists called the city's "Muslim part." As noted above, their effort to lure Serbs from the encircled city met with only partial success, but they brutally cleared their conquered territories of non-Serbs, either in the course of Bosnian Serb military campaigns or in separate actions. They murdered some local non-Serbs, imprisoned others, and expelled the vast majority of the rest. One local leader, speaking to the Bosnian Serb

Assembly in July 1992, frankly discussed the brazen ethnic cleansing of Sarajevo's suburbs and attributed it to Karadžić's leadership: "When [Karadžić] walked among us in Ilidža and emboldened us, Serbs in Sarajevo held the required territory under their control and in certain areas extended their territory and drove Muslims from territories where they were effectively a majority."[99]

With their overwhelming advantage in heavy weaponry and visual contact with most buildings in the city, the VRS gunners had their choice of targets. Curiously, in the first months of the siege, they concentrated on a set of targets that represented the signal achievements of the city's secular common life. Their shells and bullets hit virtually every mosque, Catholic church, synagogue, and Serbian Orthodox structure in town, but most major institutions were damaged rather than totally destroyed. In contrast, the VRS destruction left the footprints of a calculated effort in the summer of 1992 to annihilate the city's key institutions of common culture, government, and economy. The assaults were unmistakably directed against the city's chief institutions of collective memory, leading some observers to characterize these attacks as "memoricide." The besieging forces sought to shatter civic pride by wiping out records and physical manifestations of the city's diverse history. On April 25, 1992, they destroyed the Olympic Museum, a converted Habsburg-era villa that housed memorabilia of the city's greatest moments in the 1984 Winter Games. Three weeks later, artillery fire completely destroyed the building and holdings of the Oriental Institute, including a priceless collection of Ottoman-era manuscripts that bore witness to Serb, Croat, and Jewish as well as Bosniak cultural achievements.[100]

VRS artillery gunners directed a barrage of shells at the Vijećnica, the building that housed the National and University Library, on the evening of August 26, 1992. Both the building and its contents held special significance for the city. As the most elaborate neo-Orientalist structure in town, the one-time city hall harked back architecturally to the age of eclectic historicism in the late nineteenth century. Many of the library's volumes were replaceable, but the rich collection of the city's periodical press and many other unique items were completely destroyed.[101] The elegant oak-paneled city council room, used after the Second World War by the Academy of Arts and Sciences of Bosnia-Herzegovina, was a total loss. The library building burned through the night; white ash fell from the sky and accumulated on the ground in some parts of the city.

Bosnian Serb nationalist leaders sought to disrupt the independent pur-veyors of news in the city. Continuing their earlier campaign to divide or disable the city's major news organizations, the Bosnian Serbs targeted the major institutions of broadcast and print news in the city. Attacks in August 1992 devastated the offices of *Oslobodjenje*, housed in a striking high-rise tower in the western party of the city.[102] The Sarajevo Radio and Television Center was hit repeatedly, but the concrete fortress-like structure with-stood many assaults and continued to function throughout the war.

Several key centers of government and commerce were either totally destroyed or rendered unusable, while others sustained only superficial damage from pinpoint strikes or snipers. The high-rise government office building, a skyline-dominating symbol of government authority adjacent to the Bosnian Assembly Building, was pounded for weeks by Bosnian Serb gunners, leaving only a charred skeleton. The twin UNIS Towers, major commercial office buildings, were likewise shelled and burned. The Hotel Evropa, a hostelry built and long owned before the Second World War by the wealthy Serb Jeftanović family, was reduced to a charred ruin but spared total destruction by solid exterior walls as thick as three meters. The Holiday Inn, on the other hand, was never made dysfunctional as a hotel despite receiving many direct hits. After Karadžić's paramilitary troops left the hotel in April 1992, it served guests—mainly journalists, diplomats, and aid workers—throughout the war. Starting in 1993 the US Embassy occupied one suite, which was less than ideally situated on the hotel's vul-nerable southwest corner.

Hospitals were often targeted for attack. Koševo Hospital, the city's primary trauma care center, was singled out for attack by Dragan Kalinić, minister of health of the Republika Srpska, at the Bosnian Serb Assembly meeting on May 12:

Those who will be planning the Sarajevo operation, either of liberating Sarajevo or of destroying the enemy forces in Sarajevo, will have to plan what to do with the medical facilities. And let me tell you this right now, if the military hospital is to end up in the hands of the enemy, I am for the destruction of Koševo Hospital so that the enemy has nowhere to go for medical help.[103]

Since the hospital often lacked electricity during the war and was des-perately short of critical supplies, the artillery and mortar attacks, while never leveling the structures, added to the difficulties of providing basic medical care for the stream of trauma cases that daily entered its doors.

In addition to the physical destruction of major institutions, the Bosnian Serb nationalists sought to deprive Sarajevo's citizens of essential goods and services. Besieging forces targeted the resources of daily life: electricity, water, gas, food, medical supplies, and all means of public transportation. Deprivation increased every citizen's vulnerability and sometimes ended in death. Sarajevans queued up for scarce commodities, particularly bread and water, and came together in public markets to acquire scarce food at outrageous prices. These locations were well known to besieging Serb gunners, and their attacks on these locations caused the siege's worst single-shell casualties. At around 10:00 a.m. on May 27, 1992, the VRS sent three mortar shells into hundreds of Sarajevans waiting in a line to buy bread at a shop on Vaso Miskin Street only a few meters from the Catholic cathedral. The mortars killed sixteen and injured over a hundred.[104] Serb gunners then opened fire on ambulances attempting to reach the wounded, leaving victims crying for help. Television cameras captured their agony as they lay in the street. The bread line massacre, as it became known, was preceded and followed by all-night bombardments from Serb firing positions on the long ridge to the south of the city, killing other civilians and damaging mosques, public buildings, and residences.[105] General Mladić threatened to level the city if the ARBiH did not allow Serb troops, then surrounded by ARBiH forces in several barracks, to leave the city. The unprecedented attacks and threats came as the UN Security Council was considering sanctions against the Republics of Serbia and Montenegro. As described above, the council approved those sanctions on May 30 in an unsuccessful effort to deter further bloody attacks.

Despite the unmistakable pattern of calculated destruction, almost every structure experienced some damage, suggesting that some of the firing was unleashed without a specific target in mind. Random firing spread terror and reminded Sarajevans that no one in the city was out of danger and no structure exempt from destruction. Even structures associated with Serb cultural and religious life were damaged. The offices of the Serb cultural society Prosvjeta were devastated by an attack on the building in which it was housed, and the new Serbian Orthodox church sustained damage to its windows and cupolas. Sniper fire was directed from the hills rising above the city and from many of the high-rise buildings that abounded in the city's western suburbs. Both the VRS and ARBiH used snipers for targeted kills. Many victims of sniper fire were legitimate combatants, but others were civilians shot only because they were available targets in the wrong place at the wrong time.[106]

ARBiH forces succeeded in driving Serb forces from several strongholds in the city, but throughout the war they lacked the tank and artillery support that their infantry needed to break through VRS lines. The result was a protracted military stalemate. In the words of one commander, "The Serb generals failed to conquer Sarajevo with a blitzkrieg, but our units did not have enough fire power to break the siege of the city."[107]

Daily life in Sarajevo under siege

More than an asymmetrical military contest, the Sarajevo siege was an epic struggle of human wills. For those Sarajevans who remained in the city and were fortunate enough to survive the four-year siege, life was both precious and precarious. They steeled themselves against the risk of death and the constant deprivation with the hope of survival and a determination to preserve the trappings of normal urban life.

Boris Nilević was one of the thousands of Serbs who remained in besieged Sarajevo. A historian specializing in the medieval history of the Serbian Orthodox Church in Bosnia-Herzegovina, he served as director of the Institute for History in Sarajevo during the war.[108] No one condemned in stronger terms the Serb nationalist attacks on his city. "This is not a clash of civilizations," he insisted, gesturing at the hills above the city. "This is a barbarian assault *on* civilization."[109] Nilević the historian was dismissing Samuel Huntington's crude explanation for the Bosnian War, but Nilević the Sarajevan was offering to his fellow citizens a rationale for resisting the assaults and preserving a treasured way of life.

Ideological inspiration and mundane motives often came together to reinforce Sarajevans' determination to survive the city's epic siege.[110] Many feared uprooting their lives for an uncertain future in an unfamiliar place. Most had secure jobs. Even if normal employment activity was halted during the war, most jobholders were entitled to an apartment that became familiar and well appointed over years or even decades of residence. Most had family and friends that they did not want to leave. Many valued the city's urban diversity and its economic advantages over the countryside. Relatively few found no way to leave or were deterred by fear of what they might encounter on the way out of the city. And most lived daily with the hope, however unrealistic, that the madness would end shortly .

Whatever the reasons for remaining, those who stayed prized any semblance of normal life. In embattled Sarajevo everyday life itself became a universal form of resistance. Sarajevans survived under siege by adhering to their normal routine and rhythms of everyday life to the greatest possible extent. Social scientists and psychologists have noted that preserving a sense of normalcy is a common response to violence, and this was no doubt the case in besieged Sarajevo.[111] Daily living was for most Sarajevans an affirmation of basic humanity and resistance to the cult of violence that physically surrounded and imprisoned them.

The city in wartime was filled with stories of people taking extraordinary measures to preserve ordinary habits. Thousands of Sarajevans trekked daily to their unlit, unheated workplaces in fulfillment of daily routines, often going without pay for many months and without the prospect of payment anytime soon. As a visitor I heard stories of many individual acts of courage and selflessness. A former Olympic runner who lived on the sixteenth floor of a high-rise apartment building made dozens of daily dashes to the few functioning water sources to supply his elderly neighbors on higher floors. The custodian of a university building dissuaded ARBiH soldiers from taking over a university building, effectively demilitarizing an important educational institution and sparing it from much retaliatory shelling. Acts of bravery bordering on foolhardiness abounded in every walk of urban life. Tom Gjelton has recounted the tale of *Oslobodjenje*'s journalists and workers, who produced and distributed the daily newspaper throughout the war. Teachers and administrators went to great lengths to educate the city's youth, as David Berman has demonstrated in his study of one "war school" in Sarajevo.[112] Many thousands more such everyday acts of human courage passed unrecognized and unrecorded amid the collective urge to survive.

Some organized activities proceeded as planned, often in a spirit of defiance to the ongoing attacks. In September 1992 a long-scheduled academic conference on the Jews of Bosnia-Herzegovina was held in the Holiday Inn as artillery and tank shells pounded the town. Introductory speeches were given by Bosnian President Alija Izetbegović, who compared the city's plight with that of the Jews in the Second World War, and by Ivan Čerešnješ, president of the Jewish community of Bosnia-Herzegovina. Twenty-six papers were delivered at the conference and later published with the aid of the Open Society Foundation.[113] Another conference in March 1993, delayed a year by the start of the war, commemorated the 530th anniversary of Isabeg Ishaković's *vakufnama*, the document considered to have founded Sarajevo. Organizers aimed "to present in a versatile manner the past of Sarajevo as a multicultural urban center" and hailed the conference as a "reflection of spiritual resistance to barbarian destruction of its citizens and all the values of culture created through the centuries."[114] Hosted by the Institute for History and the Oriental Institute, the conference featured more than fifty papers, most of which were published after the war.

Able to monitor the ebb and flow of world events through the news media, Sarajevans maintained hope for foreign intervention to end the savagery. Having faced with disbelief the prospect of war in 1991, they were equally incredulous that the Western democracies they so admired were unwilling to take up arms to end the siege. They universally resorted to black humor, involving many sayings too morbid to be reported here. Periodically deprived of food, water, heating, and electricity, Sarajevans observed that UNPROFOR was a misnomer, because its soldiers offered no protection and were largely prohibited from using force, and because its nations were disunited rather than united. Sarajevans' cynicism also extended to NATO, whose initials were said to stand for "No Action—Talking Only."

Suada Kapić, a journalist and actress, established the "mobile university" to bring guest lecturers into Sarajevo with UN support. She and a group of students and young designers erected a makeshift museum in the courtyard of the National Theater giving voice to the agony of the city's suffering and the determination of its citizens. They produced a mock edition of *Life* magazine, which provoked a mean-spirited threat of legal action from the Time Warner Corporation for copyright violation.[115] They also prepared an ingenious schematic map of Sarajevo (not published until after the war) that highlighted both the brutality of the siege and the absurdity of life in fear and evasion in a twentieth-century European city. A group of writers and photographers produced a survivor's guide to Sarajevo in the familiar green color and tall, slender format of a Michelin travel guide.[116] These creations offered a heartening alternative to the pity evoked in many foreigners' descriptions of life under siege.

The quest for survival stimulated metal craftsmen to develop ingenious but simple devices for cooking and staying warm. A small stove was built to operate on gas (if available), wood, or other flammable materials that might be at hand. More often than not, survival stoves were used to make coffee, the one luxury that Sarajevans indulged whenever the opportunity arose. (Cigarettes, on the other hand, were considered a necessity.) Survival technology was displayed in museum style for visitors on the 1,000th day of the siege in January 1995.

In 1992 the world was on the cusp of the communications revolution ushered in by the Internet, but only a few devotees in Sarajevo were using e-mail when the war began. Sarajevo's telephone capacity was almost wholly destroyed when the JNA annihilated the Main Post Office Building on May 2, 1992, leaving only a few lines linking the city to the outside world. A small group of determined computer gurus, led by Haris Alagić, devised an ingenious if complex solution. The group enlisted assistance from colleagues in France, Switzerland, and the US and received funds from the Open Society Foundation to purchase a computer. The Ministry of Defense gave the group a single telephone line to link their computer with the outside world, and the group set up their central server in a building near the Presidency Building.[117] Runners in Sarajevo collected messages on floppy disks from as many as five thousand Sarajevans a day and brought them to the server, where they were transmitted on the single telephone line to Switzerland twice a day. From there they were disseminated to eleven university centers, principally in Europe. Students then took individual messages and sent them via post to their intended recipients, along with instructions on how to respond. Messages intended for Sarajevans were then brought together in Switzerland and transmitted back into the city. The system was slow and not fully reliable, but it broke the city's communications blockade and linked some of its citizens to the outside world. In autumn 1994 the number of messages was overwhelming the system's capacity. Alagić and his principal colleagues—one Serb, one Croat, and one Jew—traveled to Holland and appealed for support from Dutch universities. With this aid and additional support from the Open Society Foundation, they established Internet access using a satellite link. Their efforts bore fruit but only belatedly. Sarajevo acquired direct Internet access in November 1995—just days before the war ended.

Sarajevans were deeply disturbed by the sheer randomness of death in the city as well as by the mounting number of casualties.[118] No resident of Sarajevo passed those wartime years without mourning the loss of one or several family members, close friends, or neighbors. Grief was deepened by survivor's guilt, the awareness that the sniper might just as well have selected the prior passerby or the artillery shell might have been landed a few feet away or a few minutes earlier or later. Global television coverage transmitted the human agony of the infamous massacres of civilians in the bread line on Miskin Street and at the Markale marketplace, but little notice was taken of most deaths except by those who buried and mourned the victims of the war. Mourning proved as hazardous as life's other life activities. Burial services brought a significant number of people into close proximity, and numerous times gunmen in the surrounding hills shot and killed mourners.

Death mingled with persistent shortages of food and water. The average Sarajevan lost thirty pounds during the siege. With little or no heating gas for weeks at a time, Sarajevans suffered prolonged exposure to cold. Waste disposal became a chronic problem. Toilets went unflushed, and garbage piled high on sidewalks and in the courtyards of apartment buildings. Nonetheless, during years of deprivation and daily threats to their lives, Sarajevans found affirmation in being in the vanguard of a struggle against savagery. Rather than demeaning their lives, siege conditions elevated their sense of purpose. Historian and Sarajevo resident Dževad Juzbašić characterized that period in his life as a "struggle for mere survival, but also for the defense of human dignity."[119]

The national factor

The political leaders of the besieging Serb nationalists went to great lengths to portray the population of besieged Sarajevo as overwhelmingly Bosniak, and they succeeded in persuading some diplomats and reporters that there were few Serbs and Croats left in the city. That characterization was false. Despite some differentiation among major groups in the city, large numbers of Serbs and Croats, and a smaller number of Jews, remained in Sarajevo during the war and suffered with Bosniaks the indiscriminate death, injury, deprivation, and fear created by the Serb nationalist assault on the city. Sarajevo retained its common life throughout the war.

Major religious and cultural institutions continued to function during the war. Although limited by wartime conditions, the Croat cultural society Napredak maintained a program of activities and in 1994 began publishing a monthly journal, *Stećak* (gravemarker, deriving its name from the medieval Bosnian tombstones). Prosvjeta, the Serb cultural society, likewise functioned during the war and beginning in 1994 published *Bosanska vila* (Bosnian nymph, the name of another journal published by Serbs in 1885–1914). Archbishop Vinko Puljić remained in the city during the war, and in November 1994 the Vatican elevated him to the rank of cardinal in a gesture of solidarity with the besieged city. Sarajevo's residents benefited from humanitarian aid delivered by religious humanitarian organizations, including Caritas (Catholic), Dobrotvor (Serbian Orthodox), Merhemet (Muslim), and La Benevolencija (Jewish). None of these organizations had unlimited resources, and some favored recipients belonging to their community, but their aid was undoubtedly critical in supporting the undernourished populace during its protracted time of deprivation.

The Serbs of Sarajevo, in addition to sharing with those of other groups the daily perils of bombardment and sniping, were exposed to the prospect of violence that arose from being identified with their conationalists besieging the city. The lot of those Serbs has also become the one of the most controversial aspects of the siege. According to the 1991 census, 157,193 Serbs lived in the ten municipalities that made up the city, with perhaps half that number living in the area that was besieged during the war. In April and May 1992 SDS leaders undertook a concerted effort to induce Serbs to emigrate from the city, including personal appeals to prominent Serbs to join the exodus and threats against those who refused.[120] In defiance of these calls, most Serbs remained in the city in the first months of the siege, but the campaign yielded some success. When they returned to their places of work on April 7 (the Tuesday after recognition weekend) many Sarajevans discovered that some of their Serb colleagues had fled to Serb-controlled areas outside Sarajevo or to the Republic of Serbia.[121] But in refusing to leave, those Serbs who remained denied the SDS its fundamental goal of separating the national communities. Rizo Selmanagić, a Serb veteran of the Second World War, saw this as a repudiation of SDS leadership: "The real beginning of Karadžić's political defeat lies in the fact that all Serbs did not leave the city in a body, the moment the attack started. Karadžić counted on their leaving Sarajevo."[122]

In the months after the siege began, many other Serbs left the city as shelling and sniping attacks intensified, posing increased hazards to life and limb, and as some of them were brutalized or killed by Croat and Bosniak irregulars operating within the city. In the battle for Pofalići in May 1992, paramilitary forces under the command of the ARBiH killed, detained, or beat some Serbs. Survivors later gave testimony on behalf of the Federal Republic of Yugoslavia in a case before the International Court of Justice. Early in the war, Sarajevo civilian and military police systematically searched Serb homes for weapons, and since many Sarajevo Serbs had routinely kept a weapon in their homes or even had weapons collections, many were detained or imprisoned. "During these checks, people who possessed weapons but were unable to give satisfactory information about their origin were immediately suspected of supporting the SDS," wrote Mirko Pejanović, the most prominent Serb politician to remain in Sarajevo throughout the siege.[123] He reports that hundreds of Serbs died in cities across Bosnia-Herzegovina in the interrogations and detentions that followed these searches and that Serbs were worse off in Sarajevo than elsewhere.[124] Others reported that Bosnian army troops forced Serbs to dig ditches along the city's defensive perimeter.[125]

The situation improved as the disparate paramilitaries and volunteer units were increasingly brought under central control in the summer of 1992. Pejanović writes of a meeting in late spring 1992 in which prominent Serbs pleaded with President Izetbegović to halt mass detention of Serbs at the Koševo Stadium.[126] After Izetbegović ordered an end to such practices, the dangers facing Sarajevo Serbs from paramilitaries and police began to abate. Still, many Serbs died at the hands of paramilitary forces and in prisons. The exact number of Serb civilian deaths in government-held Sarajevo may never be known, but victims are estimated by officials of the Federation of Bosnia-Herzegovina to have numbered at least 150. Although Serb nationalists and officials of the Republika Srpska have claimed that many thousands of Serb civilians were killed by Bosnian government forces, their efforts to substantiate those claims have been unconvincing. Their lists of purported victims have included duplications, hundreds of persons not from Sarajevo, soldiers who died in the ARBiH defending the city against Serb nationalist attacks, and some persons still living.[127] The leaders of the SDA and the Bosnian government had no ideologically inspired plan to erase the Serb presence in Sarajevo comparable to the Serb nationalists' intent to eliminate non-Serbs from the Republika Srpska, but the actions of Bosniak and Croat paramilitary units led many thousands of Serbs to flee the city, particularly in the summer of 1992. By war's end, the number of Serbs in Sarajevo was estimated to be in the low tens of thousands, fewer than twenty percent of those who had lived in the city's ten municipalities in 1991.

Serb Sarajevo

During the war SDS leaders advanced the idea of developing a "Serb Sarajevo" to counterbalance what they called its "Muslim" part. Following their initial territorial seizures in April–June 1992, Bosnian Serb nationalists controlled the periphery of the city, including most territory of the ten municipalities that made up the city in 1990. Many Serbs who fled government-controlled Sarajevo made new homes in Serb-held territory. Various estimates put the total population of the Serb-held areas at 140,000 to 160,000, close to the total number of Serbs in prewar Sarajevo cited above. Serb territory included most of the city's industrial capacity and a significant portion of the housing stock. Karadžić envisioned Serb Sarajevo as a strategically central economic hub of a postwar Serb state:

Sarajevo will be divided and become two cities. ... Everything that is Serb we will retain. For us, Sarajevo integrates eastern Herzegovina, old Herzegovina, and Romanija. ... Romanija has its urban core in Sarajevo, and it will stay that way.... We won't give it away."[128]

International peace negotiations, however, posed a serious threat to ambitions for Serb Sarajevo. Reflecting the reluctance of international negotiators to perpetuate the city's division, most peace plans provided for a demilitarized zone encompassing most or all of Sarajevo in its prewar boundaries. Fearful that Serb Sarajevo would become a peripheral suburb of the city center, Bosnian Serb leaders formally adopted far-reaching plans for a Serb Sarajevo on October 7, 1993.[129] They proposed to disperse governmental functions through several different municipalities and secure the most important industrial facilities in the area. A city council was to be established, and Trifko Radić was designated mayor. Plans were laid to secure facilities for a second university of Sarajevo in the Serb–controlled part of the city. Participants also discussed securing housing for an anticipated mass exodus of Serbs from those areas of Sarajevo not under their control.

The Bosnian Serb nationalists made elaborate plans to ensure their continued control even if the city were reunited and to assure that Serbs benefited from the production of factories in municipalities they controlled. In explaining the plan to the Bosnian Serb Assembly, Karadžić envisioned a dynamic Serb center:

The policy of the SDS is to hold on to Sarajevo. ... We must create a critical mass of intelligentsia here. We will be in contact with a huge world, the aggressive world of Islam. Our capital, our education, our culture, our economy will be in contact here on the Miljacka with this entire world, the exponents of which will be the Bosnian Muslims. We don't dare lose that battle, never or in any way. ... If the Sarajevo theater were to collapse, if [the ARBiH] were to break out to the Drina and cut the [Posavina] corridor, there would be neither a Krajina, nor a Republic of Serb Krajina, nor Herzegovina, nor anything. ... I have already talked to Milošević about this. Serb Sarajevo will be supported by all twelve million Serbs.[130]

Karadžić's grandiose vision was far from being realized. Much like their counterparts in the part of the city under Bosnian government control, residents of Serb Sarajevo endured a gangster-controlled economy, periodic shortages of many essential goods, and an ineffectual security apparatus. The extent of economic criminalization was evident from the opening days of the war. Hundreds of newly manufactured vehicles disappeared from parking lots at the Volkswagen plant in Vogošća, touching off a major scandal that implicated officials from the Republic of Serbia and local authorities. The Bosnian Serb Assembly, after a lengthy investigation, absolved all of the accused and concluded that most vehicles had disappeared into the Republic of Serbia.[131]

Gang control was the major characteristic of the economy in wartime Serb Sarajevo (much as it was in government-controlled territory), as described by its mayor, Trifko Radić:

[In Ilijaš] we have at least 150 mafia guys who drive unregistered Volkswagens. They wear uniforms, carry pistols and the most contemporary weapons, [sun]glasses, walk around, and no one dares engage them. They steal, walk, kill, engage in black market operations, etc. ... No one dares mobilize them. That's linked mafia from Ilidža, Rajlovac, Vogošća, to Ilijaš, and we all fear them."[132]

A black market trade in fuel, cigarettes, and essential foodstuffs thrived along Serb Sarajevo's boundary with Croat-controlled areas to the north and west, and to a lesser extent with the ARBiH-controlled areas of Sarajevo.

When the Dayton peace agreement (formally, the General Framework Agreement for Peace in Bosnia and Herzegovina) returned much of Serb-occupied Sarajevo to the Federation of Bosnia-Herzegovina, aspirations for a dynamic Serb Sarajevo became moot. The dream remained alive for several years, but Serb Sarajevo became a much smaller area of several adjacent municipalities dependent on the economic vitality of the Federation-controlled central city.

Efforts to attenuate the siege

With its gains in Dobrinja in June 1992 (described above), the ARBiH acquired access to the southeastern side of the airport and came within a few hundred yards of breaking the siege. Only the Sarajevo airport lay between Dobrinja and government-controlled territory in Butmir, beyond which lay a treacherous passage over the primitive roads of Mount Igman. Nonetheless, it was unthinkable that the ARBiH would contest UNPROFOR's control of the airport. Early in 1993, compelled by hardships facing civilians and the paucity of their own ammunition and arms, the ARBiH undertook a bold plan to break Sarajevo's isolation by tunneling under the airport. Work began in March 1993 with about two hundred ARBiH troops digging south-westerly from Dobrinja within and northeast from Butmir outside the besieged city.[133]

Most of the digging was done from the Butmir side (800 meters versus 120 meters from Dobrinja). The two tunneling parties met underground on July 30, 1993, in a triumph of engineering prowess and sustained determination. That same night, the army dispatched six hundred soldiers from the besieged city to Mount Igman to reinforce the campaign to break the siege from the outside. The tunnel, called Objekt D-B (for "Object Dobrinja-Butmir"), resembled a kilometer-long horizontal mineshaft. Through it ran electrical cables and a light rail system with wheelbarrow-like trolley cars. A constant inflow of groundwater required a pumping system to keep the tunnel from flooding. Passage through the tunnel was dark, damp, and demanding. The tunnel averaged 1.7 meters in height, but one section was only a meter (39 inches) high, requiring a stooped and swift transit. For the rest of the war, the airport tunnel served as a conduit for arms, munitions, essential supplies, and people.

According to ARBiH estimates, over a million person-passages were made through the tunnel from July 30, 1993, until the end of the war. British Parliamentarian Paddy Ashdown, later the international community's High Representative for Bosnia-Herzegovina, was among the few foreigners to traverse the tunnel. Bosnian President Izetbegović traveled through it numerous times. Government officials of ministerial rank were accorded the courtesy of a trolley ride, although some of them declined and made the journey on foot, stooped over like everyone else. In addition to serving as a human passageway, the tunnel enabled the ARBiH to transport weapons, ammunition, fuel, foodstuffs, and medical supplies. According to its estimates, nearly twenty million tons of food passed through the tunnel into the city. This was less than the thirty-one million tons brought in under UN auspices by air, and it was dwarfed by the 168 tons delivered overland in UN-guarded truck convoys.

Passage through the tunnel led to the next obstacle: the treacherous trip over Mount Igman. The primitive road was under ARBiH control but subject to regular bombardment by VRS artillery. In February 1995 three American diplomats were killed when their armored personnel carrier slid off the road and crashed into the gully below. US diplomat Richard Holbrooke was deeply affected by these first known American casualties of the

Bosnian War. He later dedicated his memoirs to the "three cherished colleagues who did not reach Dayton."[134]

The success of the tunnel inspired the government of Bosnia-Herzegovina to build a second one parallel to the first. Some speculated that this second tunnel, in easing access to the city and therefore alleviating the primary concern of the international community, might contribute to making the siege a permanent feature of Sarajevo's life. Higher, wider, and better equipped than the first tunnel, the second one was completed on November 16, 1995—just five days before the war formally ended.

A damp, cramped tunnel was far from sufficient to break the siege of Sarajevo; after three years of warfare, all parties realized that only foreign military intervention could relieve Sarajevo of its misery. It took a major human tragedy to awaken that possibility in UN leaders and world leaders. It began on Saturday, February 5, 1994, an unusually warm and sunny winter Saturday, a day when few shells fell on the city in the morning hours. Hundreds of Sarajevans, taking advantage of the conditions, visited the Markale marketplace in the city center to buy what food was available from the venders displaying their goods on tables. Suddenly, at 12:37 p.m. the day became the blackest in the four-year siege, as a single shell fell on the market and radiated lethal shrapnel in all directions.[135] Elizabeth Neuffer, correspondent for the *Boston Globe*, arrived on the scene a few minutes later. "A leg, its foot in a boot still attached, lay on the ground. A vast pool of blood, dark and red, washed over the back of the market, coursing around the cabbages and potatoes and shopping bags strewn about the ground. ... Blood-stained rags were draped over unidentified body parts, and men, wailing and crying, hefted bodies into cars doubling as ambulances."[136] Sixty-eight persons were killed and over two hundred wounded in the carnage, the most casualties caused by a single shell during the siege.

World leaders issued unusually harsh condemnations of the Markale massacre and demanded an immediate investigation into the event. UN investigators concluded that the explosion had been caused by a 120-millimeter mortar bomb fired northeast of the market, but they were unable to determine the exact origin of the launch. UNPROFOR commander Lieutenant General Michael Rose reported that it was impossible to determine which side fired the shell based solely on a forensic examination of the impact crater, but he suggested that the VRS was responsible, noting that the same type of mortar had been fired on the Dobrinja neighborhood the day before, killing ten. "The world will certainly draw its own conclusions," he stated.[137] With the Bosnian Serb nationalists identified as the probable per-petrators, Bosnian government officials called for air strikes against VRS positions to end the siege. World leaders called for an immediate cease-fire and intensive negotiations to end the war.

The Bosnian Serb nationalists not only denied responsibility for the single mortar shell, they denied that any such shell could cause the massive casu-alties suffered at Markale and suggested that only a few people had been at the market at the time of the explosion. They asserted instead that shrapnel-laden explosive devices had been laid among the market stalls by the ARBiH and that the widespread carnage was fake. Karadžić gave his explanation: "An explosion took place in the market, killing and injuring a few people. Everything else around this incident has been stage-managed. ... Television footage clearly shows the manipulation of the bodies had taken place in this tragedy. In the footage, one can see the bodies of casualties who had died hours earlier, as well as plastic body parts."[138] He later spun out the fable further, telling the Bosnian Serb Assembly that the bodies "were some sort of mannequins and old corpses from an exchange of Muslim and Croat soldiers a few days before."[139]

The horrific Markale killings galvanized the US to intervene directly to end the attacks on Sarajevo. In February 1994 the US issued an ultimatum to the Serbs to withdraw heavy weapons from a twenty-kilometer "exclusion zone" around Sarajevo, and Russian diplomats brokered a compromise pro-viding for the withdrawal of Bosnian Serb heavy weapons in exchange for deployment of a Russian detachment to UNPROFOR. Although the Bos-nian Serb nationalists complied slowly and reluctantly, they eventually withdrew their heavy weapons beyond effective range of the city, and for the next year Sarajevo was largely free from heavy weapons assault, although small arms fire remained commonplace.

US diplomats also succeeded in bringing together the recalcitrant rival presidents of the Republics of Croatia and Bosnia-Herzegovina, Tudjman and Izetbegović, to end the fighting between Bosniak and Croat forces in central Bosnia that had begun in April 1993. The Framework Agreement for the Federation, known informally as the Washington Agreement, created a Federation of Bosnia-Herzegovina consisting of "territories with a majority of Bosniak and Croat population,"[140] meaning those areas then held by Croat and Bosniak forces. Sarajevo was designated as the capital city of the Fed-eration, even though most of Sarajevo was under VRS control. The agree-ment provided for the Federation legislature to create cantons as internal

administrative units, with each canton to be made up of several municipalities. (In 1996 the Federation legislature created ten cantons, including
the Canton of Sarajevo, and established boundaries for them). In wartime
the Federation and its cantons were little more than conceptual frameworks
for eventual governance, but after the war they gradually assumed many
state functions, and the Federation became one of two entities of Bosnia-
Herzegovina (the other being the Republika Srpska).

In December 1994 former US President Jimmy Carter visited Sarajevo in
the hope of advancing peace negotiations. His visit interrupted the advancing plan of the five-member "contact group" to roll back many Bosnian
Serb gains, but he successfully negotiated a cease-fire scheduled to occur
from January 1 to April 1, 1995. The Carter cease-fire temporarily ended the
shooting in Sarajevo and most places in Bosnia-Herzegovina, but all armed
forces used the respite to regroup and replenish ammunition and supplies.
The cease-fire began to break down late in its second month, and with its
collapse the Bosnian Serb nationalists moved heavy weapons back inside the
thirteen-mile (twenty-kilometer) exclusion zone that they had agreed to
vacate in February 1994. The collapse of the Carter cease-fire was followed
by the most violent attacks on Sarajevo's civilians in the period from April to
August 1995. The renewed heavy shelling signaled the futility of efforts to
end Sarajevo's siege by diplomacy and rapidly forgotten ultimatums.

The end of the siege

The Sarajevo siege ended much as it began, in an agonizingly slow sequence
of diplomatic and military developments. Impetus to end the siege and war
came from developments outside Sarajevo: a change of government in France,
an impending election in the United States, global outrage over Bosnian
Serb atrocities at Srebrenica in July 1995, and the success of Croat and
ARBiH offensives against Serb forces in western Bosnia. Ultimately, the fates
of the city and Bosnia-Herzegovina were decided thousands of miles away, at
a US Air Force base outside Dayton, Ohio.

As the ARBiH initiated several operations throughout Bosnia-Herzegovina in February and March, VRS forces surrounding Sarajevo used the
instruments of siege and assault to highlight their adversary's vulnerabilities.
The VRS's conduct in spring and summer 1995 revealed continuing faith
in the negotiating advantages of atrocities against civilians and indignities
against international actors. Disregarding the exclusion zone agreed to a

year earlier, the VRS moved heavy artillery pieces within striking distance of the city. Mortar, sniper, and artillery attacks against Sarajevans escalated in April and May and led to occasional confrontations between UNPROFOR and the Bosnian Serbs.[141] General Rupert Smith, the British officer who had replaced General Michael Rose as UNPROFOR commander in January 1995, proved more willing than his predecessor to respond with force to Bosnian Serb provocations.

In early April Bosnian Serbs directly challenged UNPROFOR's control of the route from government-controlled Sarajevo to the city's airport. On April 3 they removed two Swiss citizens on a UNESCO mission from a marked UN vehicle and detained them for a month.[142] They also planted mines on the roadside beside the checkpoint controlling access to the airport. When a French UNPROFOR platoon was deployed to restore UN control, VRS troops surrounded the platoon and planted mines around its position. The standoff ended with UN officials conceding the Serbs' right to inspect all vehicles in exchange for a guarantee of safety—the situation extant before the episode began. UNPROFOR and VRS forces exchanged fire on April 7, following VRS shelling of the government-held passage over Mount Igman. Two weeks later the Bosnian Serbs denied airport access to Victor Jackovich, the departing US Ambassador to Bosnia-Herzegovina, forcing him to take the dangerous overland route over Mount Igman.[143] The Bosnian Serbs' behavior in Sarajevo involved far less violence than Croat and Bosniak cease-fire violations elsewhere in the republic, but their ostentatious defiance of UN rules, committed in full view of international media representatives, ratcheted up demands for a more vigorous UN response.

Renewal of hostilities in the spring of 1995 evoked among the British, French, and US a greater willingness to engage the VRS. Jacques Chirac, elected as president of France over the socialist Lionel Jospin in May 1995, pressed for the deployment of more ground troops to end the hostilities, while the Clinton Administration favored air strikes against the VRS.[144] In response to continued Bosnian Serb violations of the weapons exclusion zone, President Clinton won French and British support for NATO bombing strikes against VRS ammunition stores on May 25–6, 1995.[145] The Bosnian Serb nationalists, however, stepped up their attacks and retaliated with more violence against UNPROFOR. On May 25 a Bosnian Serb shell directed at Tuzla killed seventy-one people, most of them teenagers and children, the most casualties caused by a single shell at any time in the war. The VRS also took hundreds of UNPROFOR soldiers hostage, chaining some of them to potential NATO bombing targets as human shields. On June 9 the UN Security Council approved deployment of a British and French rapid reaction force equipped with heavy artillery.[146] Although the Clinton Administration and US public opinion remained reluctant to commit US ground forces to a combat role, President Clinton promised to send a large contingent of troops to aid in the evacuation of UNPROFOR personnel if that became necessary. At the same time, Clinton's special representative, Richard Holbrooke, stepped up American diplomatic efforts to end the Bosnian War.

As UNPROFOR and the VRS were moving toward outright war in Sarajevo, military developments elsewhere were raising the stakes for the Bosnian Serbs. In spring 1995 the steadily rising ARBiH and Croat military prowess, achieved in part with the benefit of undisclosed advice and assistance from the US, finally caught up with and surpassed the VRS's declining capabilities. The VRS's increasing vulnerability was first displayed in western Bosnia and Croatia. On April 8, 1995, Bosnian Croat forces and the Army of the Republic of Croatia launched an offensive to secure part of the Livno Plain in preparation for driving a wedge between Serb forces in Croatia and Bosnia-Herzegovina. Then on May 1 Croat forces stormed into the Serb-controlled area of western Slavonia and subdued token Serb resistance in two days.[147] Croat forces in Bosnia-Herzegovina then resumed their northwestern drive from the Livno Plain on June 4. They arrived within striking distance of Bosansko Grahovo and Glamoč, two Bosnian Krajina towns that controlled access to Knin, the capital of Serb-held territory in Croatia.

With the tide of battle turning against the VRS, Bosnian government forces made a bold attempt to break the siege of Sarajevo, attacking both from within and outside the city.[148] On the early morning of June 15, the ARBiH began a three-pronged assault from inside to drive the VRS back. By initiating attacks on the road from Pale to Lukavica, ARBiH forces attempted to cut a vital VRS supply line from the outside. Their advances continued for two days, accompanied by international admonitions holding the Bosnian government liable for escalating the violence. But on the third day, VRS counterattacks halted the ARBiH advances in most areas, and Mladić's forces gradually recaptured much of the territory they had lost two days earlier. Government forces continued gains in the northern suburbs for another day, but they were also driven back within a few days. On June 28 the ARBiH offensive ended with most territory reconquered by the VRS.

Despite the large but ultimately unsuccessful ARBiH offensive, Bosnian Serb forces completed their release of UNPROFOR hostages on June 18 in exchange for the release of four Serb gunners arrested earlier by UNPRO-FOR. In the aftermath of the exchange and the failed ARBiH breakout attempt, VRS attacks on civilians resumed with unprecedented intensity. Sarajevans and journalists alike remember the shelling of late June and July 1995 as the most severe of the war, accompanied as before by considerable deprivation of everyday goods. Adding to the terror was a new and devastating VRS tactic. An artillery shell hitched to a parachute caused destruction many times that of a conventional delivery system. One such bomb, dropped perilously close to the Presidency Building in June 1995, destroyed an entire building and ruined the electronic infrastructure being used for the city's nascent Internet e-mail system.

In July 1995 the VRS, acting under Karadžić's orders, overwhelmed the UN-declared "safe haven" city of Srebrenica in eastern Bosnia. In several days of systematic slaughter, they killed over seven thousand Bosniak civilians, many of them fleeing for their lives in the aftermath of the city's fall. Global outrage was prompted by the sheer number of victims and by video images of General Mladić personally offering assurances of safety to the victims before they were led off to slaughter. Srebrenica joined Sarajevo as a name evoking vivid images of war crimes by Bosnian Serb nationalists. After annihilating much of Srebrenica's civilian population and entering the nearby town of Žepa, VRS troops were deployed to western Bosnia to reinforce the beleaguered 2nd Krajina Corps in western Bosnia. But the transient military benefits gained by the VRS in western Bosnia were inconsequential compared to the enduring discredit brought to their cause by atrocities against civilians. The reinforced VRS units were unable to stem continuing advances of Croat and Bosniak forces. Croat units took Bosansko Grahovo and Glamoč on July 28, paving the way for "Operation Storm," which crushed the remaining Serb forces in Croatia in just three days in early August.[149]

The Srebrenica slaughter reinforced the determination of Western nations to end the war. In August, Holbrooke issued an ultimatum demanding an end to violence in Sarajevo. As in February 1994, a bloody attack on the Sarajevo marketplace triggered a major escalation in US involvement in Bosnia-Herzegovina. NATO aircraft launched a sustained air assault, called Operation Deliberate Force, on Bosnian Serb targets commencing on the morning of August 30 and continuing, with one four-day hiatus, for two weeks. NATO jets struck military targets throughout the Republika Srpska, and artillery of the British and French rapid reaction force raked Bosnian

Serb heavy weaponry within the exclusion zone. The bombing began on the same day that the Bosnian Serb nationalists agreed to allow Milošević to represent them in peace negotiations. Their acquiescence was a key step on the road to negotiating an end to the war and siege.

An agreement on principles for peace talks was reached in Geneva on September 8, 1995, under the threat of continued NATO bombing and great international pressure.[150] Although the Geneva accord was to serve as the basis for most subsequent talks, the agreement failed to address territorial issues, left the future of Sarajevo unsettled, and did not include a cease-fire commitment. On September 13, as NATO planners worried about finding appropriate targets for a longer campaign, the Bosnian Serbs capitulated and agreed to demands that included withdrawal of their weapons from an exclusion zone around Sarajevo. The bombing campaign ended the same day. The VRS gradually and grudgingly acceded to the agreement they had made, allowing flights in and out of Sarajevo airport and permitting convoys to pass unobstructed on the Blue Route.

During Operation Deliberate Force, Croat and Bosniak forces in western Bosnia capitalized on the VRS setbacks from the bombings and gained additional territory. The ARBiH took the central Bosnian town of Donji Vakuf on September 13; Croat forces conquered Jajce on the same day and Drvar on September 14.[151] Just when the conquest of Prijedor and Banja Luka seemed imminent, the VRS and a detachment of Arkan's paramilitary force launched a four-day counteroffensive on September 18. The counteroffensive probably prevented the fall of Prijedor and may have saved the entire western Republika Srpska for the Bosnian Serb nationalists. Croat-Bosniak offensives resumed shortly thereafter but had largely run out of steam and were superseded by diplomatic developments. During the monthlong military struggles in western Bosnia, boundaries of control within Sarajevo remained essentially unchanged.

Under heavy US and UN pressure, the Bosnian parties reached agreement on a republicwide cease-fire to take effect on October 12, a month after the NATO bombing had ceased. Fighting in western Bosnia sputtered to a halt over the next several days. By the time it was over, the Bosnian Serbs had been reduced to controlling about 49 percent of the land, just what the NATO allies were prepared to give them in a final peace plan. The cease-fire slowly took effect as negotiations were scheduled for Dayton, Ohio, in early November. The war in Bosnia-Herzegovina, and the siege of Sarajevo, was finally headed for a diplomatic resolution.

The siege left thousands of Sarajevans dead and tens of thousands injured. The Bosnia-Herzegovina Department of Public Health, which reported casualties daily, counted 10,615 deaths during the siege, with over 75 percent of all deaths occurring in 1992.[152] Demographers in the Office of the Prosecutor at the ICTY have estimated that a minimum of 4,352 persons (soldiers and civilians) died violent conflict-related deaths in besieged Sarajevo between September 10, 1992, and August 10, 1994, a period that excludes times of the heaviest shelling in 1992 and 1995.[153] They found that the wounded numbered more than three times those who were killed, with civilians accounting for about 37 percent of casualties in the city. Shelling accounted for 66 percent of violent civilian deaths, with sniping blamed for another 18 percent of civilian casualties. These numbers, which remain uncertain and contested, in any case fail to capture the fear, agony, and loss felt by Sarajevans who remained in the city.

The war and siege ended without a victor. Persons on all sides were incredulous that the struggle had gone on for so long and been so utterly destructive. The Bosnian Serb nationalists had come close to accomplishing their goal of separating Sarajevo's peoples, but they had failed to bring the city to its knees. Nationalist forces had been strengthened by the war, and the ubiquitous feelings of resentment and desire for revenge dimmed the prospects for large-scale reconstruction and meaningful reconciliation. The Sarajevo siege wrought great and long-lasting devastation on the city that is still felt today.

10. Sarajevo in the Long Shadow of War

The long siege and war came to an end during the first months of 1996, but the consequences of armed conflict have hung like a pall over the city for years since. In addition to war losses and damage, the city has had to cope with holdovers from the socialist past, including social ownership, powerful syndicate organizations, and a complex legal system that favored the entrenched bureaucracy. Other than the considerable early progress in physical reconstruction, most developments toward a new postwar life for the city gained momentum only with the arrival of the twenty-first century. The city's emergence from the shadow of war has been slow, incremental, and often set back by obstruction from nationalists in both the Republika Srpska and the Federation of Bosnia-Herzegovina. The war dealt a severe blow to the city's common life, notwithstanding the efforts of many brave Sarajevans to keep it alive during the siege.

The contrast with recovery after the Second World War could not have been greater. The triumphant Partisans had given Sarajevans a clear if idealized vision of a new society and a transformed city to be constructed in the aftermath of the war and liberation. In 1996, however, there was no sense of victory, no inspiring vision to compel popular engagement in remaking the city. War was over, but the struggle was not resolved.[1] With international blessing, the Dayton Agreement institutionalized many of the national divisions that had dominated society since 1990. Most Sarajevans were immensely relieved that the war had ended, but a widespread sense of uncertainty about the future fed pervasive lassitude and despair, despite the gradual return of intense activity to the central city.

The Dayton backdrop

The Dayton Agreement had far-reaching consequences for Sarajevo. Most consequentially, it mandated major territorial changes in the Sarajevo area, turning over many of the outlying areas then under VRS control to the Federation. Still, a considerable part of Sarajevo remained in the Republika Srpska; the territory in the Federation was about 61 percent of the ten-municipality prewar city.[2] The reunification of urban areas enabled the city to restore city services and prewar communication and transportation links with the outside world. The new constitution, annex 4 of the Dayton Agreement, specified that Sarajevo would be the capital of Bosnia-Herzegovina,[3] adding to its role as the capital of the Federation as specified in the Washington Agreement. These designations assured Sarajevo's primacy among the cities of Bosnia-Herzegovina, but its significance as the capital city was diminished by the very weak central government defined in the Dayton Agreement.

Sarajevans also suffered, along with others in Bosnia-Herzegovina, from the drawbacks of the Dayton Agreement. Annex 4 bestowed considerable autonomy on the state's two entities, the Republika Srpska and the Federation, and created a complex decisionmaking architecture rife with opportunities for obstruction. The treaty provided for a NATO-led Implementation Force (IFOR) to enforce the military provisions of the agreement.[4] IFOR had only a few vaguely defined obligations, but it received almost unlimited authority to enforce the military provisions of the agreement. It was "authorized to compel the removal, withdrawal, or relocation of specific Forces and weapons from ... any location in Bosnia and Herzegovina,"[5] but instead of full demilitarization, the three armies that fought the war received a constitutional sanction to continue in existence with certain guidelines for force reduction. Annex 10 mandated the designation of a High Representative to monitor compliance with Dayton's civilian provisions. It fell to the High Representative, together with various international agencies and organizations, to determine how to implement the agreement's guarantee that all refugees and displaced persons had the right to return to their prewar homes (annex 7). Annex 11 called for creation of a UN International Police Task Force made up of unarmed officers charged with monitoring local police rather than enforcing the law.

The signatory parties pledged themselves to cooperate fully with the ICTY in The Hague. Radovan Karadžić and Ratko Mladić, the civilian and military leaders of the Bosnian Serb nationalists, had already been indicted by the ICTY at the time the Dayton Agreement was signed, and they were pointedly excluded from representing the Bosnian Serbs in peace talks at Dayton. The Republika Srpska, in signing the agreement, committed itself to turning the two men over to the ICTY, but the fulfillment of the signatories' commitment has been asymmetrical. The Federation, led by its Bosniak officials, has cooperated in turning over indictees and usually produced documentation and witnesses as requested. The Republika Srpska's cooperation has been nominal and grudging. Despite being home to most of those indicted among the lands of the former Yugoslavia, the Republika Srpska has only belatedly, in 2005, turned over to the ICTY a few indictees living in its territory.

Sarajevo has benefited considerably from the presence of organizations that came to the city after the signing of the Dayton Agreement. Postwar Sarajevo became both a ward of the international community and a temporary home to thousands of its administrators, and international officials have consistently supported Sarajevo as the capital of Bosnia-Herzegovina. In the first decade after the war, the capital city benefited more from the influx of international civil servants and their headquarters than from being the domicile of central state institutions.

Transfer of territory to the Federation

Bosnian Serb nationalists received the prospective territorial loss around Sarajevo with vituperative denunciations of those who had agreed to it. Delegates to the Bosnian Serb Assembly were outraged that Milošević had committed them to territorial concessions without their approval.[6] Arguing from the principle that their assembly alone had the right to approve territorial changes in the Republika Srpska, delegates to the Bosnian Serb Assembly refused to accept the Dayton Agreement's territorial adjustments as final. They complained that territory inhabited by 142,700 Serbs (according to one delegate's estimate) would be transferred to Federation jurisdiction, reversing the very separation of nations for which the war had been fought. At their December 17, 1995, session, delegates heaped scorn on Nikola Koljević and Branimir Lukić, who had represented the Republika Srpska in the Dayton negotiations but who had been ignored by Milošević during the talks. Nonetheless, Koljević firmly maintained that the US would not revise the Dayton Agreement, and he promised the delegates only that he would ask the NATO commander to delay for a few weeks the handover of territory.[7]

Grujo Lalović, departing from the Serb leaders' insistence on total ethnic separation, advocated telling the Serbs in Sarajevo's suburbs that they could stay put. At the same time, he demanded that the international community purge from the city *mujahedin* and other armed formations that threatened Serbs.[8] Lalović's proposal was curtly rejected by Assembly President Momčilo Krajišnik, who claimed it violated the very purpose for which the Republika Srpska had been created:

The mission of this republic and its first strategic goal is for us to divide from Muslims and Croats, and no one has the right to create a strategy whereby Serb Sarajevo remains in a common state. ... No one is allowed now to create a new solution to stay together, nor do the folks in Sarajevo want it, namely the people, nor does the leadership of Sarajevo.[9]

He advocated relocating Serbs: "At the end of it all, the best solution is that people leave Sarajevo and locations are found to accommodate them."[10]

Krajišnik's hard-line position prevailed in the assembly and on the ground. The assembly issued a declaration that "disputes the introduction of Croat-Muslim authority in Serb Sarajevo" and other parts of the country. The resolution stated, "The Republika Srpska reserves the right to return to its sovereignty, in peaceful ways and political means, those territories defined in the strategic goals, those territories that belong to the other side on the basis of genocide or brutal conquest by the intervention of foreign powers."[11] However, on the ground Serb gangs used means that were neither peaceful nor political. In the weeks before the scheduled handover, Serb gangs roamed the suburbs of Serb-held Sarajevo, terrorizing the vast majority of Serbs into leaving. Bosnian Serb extremists cleansed several neighborhoods of Serbs, burned apartments, and forcibly expelled those who resisted. Writing of the Ilijaš municipality, Radio Free Europe analyst Patrick Moore wrote, "Most local Serbs were driven out by their own authorities, which withdrew essential services and utilities and contributed to a climate of panic and fear but did not always provide transportation. Armed gangs then looted and intimidated local residents, so that only the old and infirm remained."[12] In the industrial area of Ilidža, said UN spokesperson Alexander Ivanko, "Everything necessary for the life of people in Ilidža and neighboring settlements disappeared—machines, medicine, office equipment, and banks."[13] The vast majority of Serbs, unable to withstand the harassment and devastation, left the areas slated for turnover to the Federation.

In early January IFOR forces were deployed in all Sarajevo districts that were transferred from Serb control to the Federation. The troops were under orders to act only if they themselves came under attack or if lives were threatened, so the roving gangs adroitly avoided attacks on IFOR troops as they ravaged the Serb-inhabited neighborhoods. IFOR troops stood idly by as Serb gangs terrorized their fellow Serbs into fleeing Sarajevo's suburbs. In attacking the Grbavica neighborhood (only a hundred meters from the Bosnian Assembly Building), Serb thugs also destroyed apartments and personal property belonging to Bosniaks and Croats. The gangs removed furniture and stripped luxury apartments of plumbing fixtures, electrical wiring, doors, windows, and parquet floors.[14] Clothing, personal items, and papers of the original Bosniak and Croat occupants, preserved in some cases by Serb occupants through four years of war, were scattered in disarray throughout the apartments. Gangs set fire to individual apartments and entire apartment buildings. Federation fire fighters, dispatched to fight the blazes on March 16, were driven back by Serb grenade assaults. IFOR troops detained twelve arson suspects on the day before Grbavica's scheduled turnover to the Federation and turned them over to Bosnian Serb police as required by their procedures,[15] but the police released them before the day was out. The scorched-earth devastation of Grbavica reinforced the belief of many Sarajevans that the Bosnian Serb leaders wanted to annihilate the possibility of common life in the city, and it exposed the severe constraints on IFOR's actions.

The transfer of Sarajevo's charred suburbs to Federation control took place in late February and March. On February 29, 1996, Federation police officers entered Ilijaš and opened the Sarajevo-Zenica highway, the city's last major access road to civilian traffic. In a ceremony on that date, Federation Interior Minister Avdo Hebib formally declared the Sarajevo siege at an end.[16] On March 19 Grbavica's former residents lined up behind a cordon of Federation police and waited to reclaim their homes. When the police permitted, the crowd surged forward. Sarajevans entered their former homes to find the havoc wrought by the vengeful Serb gangs.

The violence was reciprocated. Although relatively few Serbs remained in the Sarajevo suburbs following the turnover, non-Serbs targeted some of them with violence and the ARBiH singled out others for military mobilization.[17] These actions contributed to a further exodus of Serbs from the neighborhoods. By the summer of 1996, neighborhoods in the Federation were inhabited primarily by Bosniaks. Even after war's end, further ethnic separation took place in the absence of constraints from the authorities and the international community.

Continuing human losses

Armed violence against the civilian population declined only gradually in Sarajevo. Serb snipers continued to fire on pedestrians and trams filled with passengers after the Dayton Agreement was signed in December 1995. These attacks stopped only after IFOR forces suppressed with force the sniper fire emanating from hills south of the city.[18] IFOR troops went about their mission of separating the belligerents and demilitarizing Sarajevo in the early months of 1996. Thousands of ARBiH soldiers were ordered withdrawn from the Marshal Tito Barracks on the near west side. In light of the size of those forces, the ARBiH requested an exception from the IFOR commander, US Admiral Leighton Smith, but he declined. A spokesman outlined the new order of things: "We possess means to force the BiH Army to fulfill its duties. We are prepared to offer even a logistic aid to the BiH Army during the evacuation of its soldiers and arms, and our soldiers will be a guarantee for the full safety of the inhabitants of Sarajevo."[19]

Enforcing provisions of the Dayton Agreement, IFOR dismantled the barricades and checkpoints erected by all military formations, in some cases replacing them with temporary checkpoints of their own. With the Serb-manned roadblocks gone, people and goods were again able to enter the city. Bus service was restored to other towns. Free movement was largely restored along major roads entering the city by June 1996, but dangers continued to linger along less traveled routes between the two entities. Since auto license plates revealed the owner's city of residence, travel outside of one's home entity was treacherous for the first few postwar years. The danger did not recede until after the High Representative, in March 1998, mandated the assignment of random license plate numbers for all vehicles registered in Bosnia-Herzegovina.

The residues of war continued to inflict casualties on the Sarajevo population long after the last shot was fired. Unexploded mines littered the former lines of confrontation. Buried explosive devices often surfaced with the spring thaw, and children at play in the hills and fields near the city were in constant danger of activating them. The city contained hundreds of structures with safety features disabled by war damage. In February 1999 two pedestrians were killed and a third was injured in separate incidents of ice sliding from the roofs of war-damaged buildings.[20] The city began repairs to some 1,500 structures deemed in need of immediate work to meet minimum safety standards. Few elevators in the city were operating at war's end, and when they started functioning again, corroded cables caused several people to plunge to their deaths. Explosions became commonplace as thousands reconnected their stoves and heating appliances to gas lines with improvised arrangements.

According to many observers, Sarajevans experienced elevated rates of cancer, suicide, alcoholism, diabetes, heart disease, and other illnesses in the decade following the war's end. The exact causes of the spike in illness may never be known, but most observers cited rising levels of stress and a general sense of despair in the aftermath of war. Those who endured the city's siege were quick to romanticize their experiences into an idealized time of narrow escapes and great personal sacrifice—views that had substantial basis in their actual experiences but served to darken their perceptions of the postwar environment. A bartered, indecisive peace shattered the dreams that had sustained so many during the war. In the postwar era, the belief in everyday life as a form of resistance turned into a psychological and physical burden, as everyday life turned out to be a letdown.

The political reconstitution of the city of Sarajevo

The Federation's constitution provided for ten cantons, including the Canton of Sarajevo. The constitution vested considerable authority in the cantons at the expense of both the municipalities and the Federation, but it made no provision for the city of Sarajevo. Tarik Kupusović continued to function as the city's mayor in the last two years of the war, but with the delineation of the Sarajevo Canton in 1996, he and the city entered a constitutional black hole. Kupusović gave up his job, and Sarajevo became a city with no mayor and no city government.

The presidents of the Federation's two leading nationalist parties, Alija Izetbegović of the SDA and Krešimir Zubak of the HDZ, reached agreement in October 1996 on a plan to reconstitute the city government. Mediated by Michael Steiner, the first deputy high representative for Bosnia-Herzegovina, the agreement reflected the international community's hope to restore the city's multiethnic composition.[21] The city's formation required a constitutional change approved by the next highest level of government. In September 1997 the assembly of the Canton of Sarajevo unanimously passed amendments to its constitution to create the City of Sarajevo out of the four municipalities of Stari grad, Centar, Novi grad, and Novo Sarajevo.[22] The amendments provided for a city council with twenty-eight members, seven from each of the four municipalities, and it stipulated a minimum of 20 percent of the seats should belong to each group identified in the Federation's constitution—Bosniaks, Croats, and "others."

The council was to elect the mayor and vice mayor (council president and vice president), who could not be of the same nationality. Only days after the

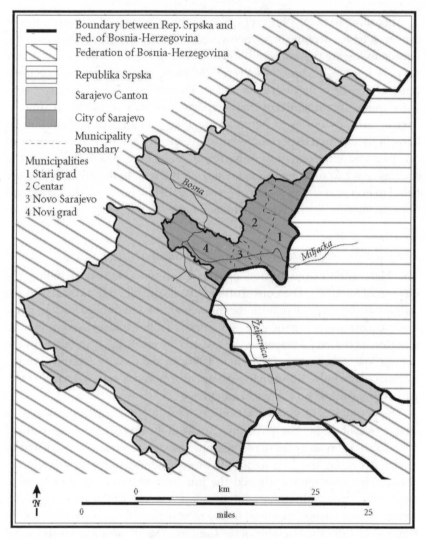

10.1   The city and canton of Sarajevo, 2000.

constitutional changes were enacted, those elected at the September 1997 municipal elections filled the council posts. The city council was formally reestablished in early 1998. Bosnian Serb nationalists continued to tout "Serb Sarajevo" as a single-nation counterpart to the city in the Federation. Little came of this initiative despite much debate and many illusions of grandeur. The financially desperate government of Republika Srpska never allocated funds to build significant new structures, and major governmental institutions were located in Banja Luka in the western part of the entity. The locus of Sarajevo's urban life remained in the Federation.

The Coalition for an Integrated and Democratic Bosnia-Herzegovina, a group of parties led by the SDA, won the municipal elections of September 1997 in Sarajevo. The coalition included the newly formed Party for Bosnia-Herzegovina, headed by wartime Foreign Minister and Prime Minister Haris Silajdžić, who had split from the SDA but continued to share much of its program. The SDS prevailed in the Serb-held municipality of Pale, while moderate nationalist parties fared better than expected in several other parts of Serb Sarajevo. Still, the voting confirmed that much of the Sarajevo electorate remained loyal to nationalist parties. With the exception of the period 2000–2, when social democrats swept into office in most municipalities of Sarajevo Canton, the nationalists dominated postwar politics in Sarajevo.

Reconstruction and the conundrum of economic stagnation

Sarajevo was physically ruined by war and faced a massive cleanup and reconstruction task. Virtually no structure was untouched, and many were badly damaged or destroyed. Gas lines were broken; water supplies were irregular at best; electricity was intermittent; rail lines were not operating; and most roads were in poor condition. Pedestrian walkways were riddled with cavities caused by mortar and artillery strikes; after the war, some of these telltale craters were filled with blood-red plastic as a grotesque memorial to the vast destruction and death during the four-year siege.

The city received more than its share of the $5 billion pledged by the international community to aid the recovery of postwar Bosnia-Herzegovina. International civil servants oversaw the restoration of gas, electric, and telephone services to the city, with most of the work done by local workers and enterprises. (Corruption immediately became an issue, as funds found their way into the pockets of local profiteers with the aid of well-placed political operatives.) Foreign countries remodeled or restored several buildings to accommodate their embassies, and international organizations restored other structures for their headquarters. To accommodate its embassy, the Austrian government spent two million German marks restoring a decrepit and damaged 1888 structure notable for its resemblance to an Alpine country cottage.[23] Embassies of most other countries also occupied existing buildings, and the repair and reconstruction of these buildings was a considerable contribution to the postwar restoration of the city. The US Embassy, a two-bedroom suite in the Holiday Inn during wartime, moved to an area just north of downtown, eventually becoming a sprawling, heavily fortified complex. In addition, many of Sarajevo's landmark structures from the Ottoman and Habsburg eras were restored to their original condition, including the badly-damaged Main Post Office Building on the north side of the Miljacka River.

The service economy in Sarajevo recovered and even expanded in the late 1990s, driven in part by the large presence of international civil servants and nongovernmental organizations. Various agencies of the international community hired local employees as translators, drivers, advisors, and eventually as functionaries to replace departing international civil servants. These organizations paid wages many times those of local employers, and their own employees were even better compensated. Restaurants and hotels opened to cater to expats: The Big Country restaurant became a popular international hangout, serving chicken fried steak and Texas barbecue in a city where local residents preferred roast lamb and sarma. The internationally driven boom in the service industry started to recede in 2000 as donor fatigue led to the decline in aid programs and many aid administrators departed.

The construction industry thrived in Sarajevo during the postwar years. In addition to the thousands of construction workers, engineers, and architects who found employment, business boomed for enterprises and individuals who provided materials such as glass, lumber, bricks, and specialized building materials. The manufacturing sector, however, remained largely moribund. Once the hub of heavy industry in central Yugoslavia, postwar Sarajevo abounded in factories that were destroyed, damaged, or rusting from disuse. Many of the manufacturing facilities were obsolete, and in addition, Bosnian Serbs had dismantled some production facilities in the western part of the city and shipped them off to other parts of the Republika Srpska. Most socially owned enterprises struggled under mismanagement, corruption, and the collapse of their former markets owing to postwar divisions.

Privatization and a sound legal system were prerequisites for foreign investment, but local officials often found reasons and means to impede the implementation of reforms. The barriers to economic growth were well

illustrated by the failure of the Volkswagen plant in Vogošća to become productive despite that firm's investment of hundreds of millions of dollars.[24]
Obstruction by local officials prevented McDonald's Corporation from
opening a franchise in the city. In November 2002 the High Representative
launched the "Bulldozer Initiative," an effort to work with local firms and
businessmen to "identify specific clauses in legislation that prevent companies from expanding their businesses and creating more jobs."[25] Its goal of
passing fifty legislative changes in 150 days was met in 170 days, a remarkable success amidst the glacial advance of most reforms in Bosnia-
Herzegovina. The initiative led to a large number of privatizations.

As was the case throughout Bosnia-Herzegovina, monies were liberally
invested in new religious structures in the Sarajevo area. The King Fahd
Mosque and Cultural Center, a donation of Saudi Arabia in the municipality
of Novi grad, dwarfs most other structures in the city. The Adilbeg Mosque
at Kobilja glava was the personal donation of Adil Zulfikarpašić, a former
Partisan from a prominent Bosniak landowning family who moved to Switzerland after the Second World War and became wealthy from his construction
business in Zurich.[26] The architecture of the monumental structure atop a
hill on the northern approach to the city recalls Middle Eastern motifs.
Along with the King Fahd Mosque, it embodies the heightened presence of
Islamic religious institutions in the city.

Other new construction reflects the changing character of the city's governing elite. Leading SDA members and officers of major industrial enterprises have built large private homes, referred to locally as "villas," that stand
in stark contrast to the modest apartments in which such prominent persons
normally lived during socialist times. The local press has delighted in
headlines contrasting the cost of such structures with their owners' paltry
salaries, insinuating that, as people widely suspect, these homes have been
built (or in some cases rebuilt) with under-the-table money. An underground criminalized economy has flourished in the postwar years, specializing in the trafficking in sex, drugs, weapons, passports, cigarettes, and
gasoline. With the urging of the international community, police made
many arrests and secured some convictions, but the city's role as a transit
point in East-West trafficking remains a major source of economic activity,
protected by some (but not all) officials of the nationalist parties. Police
gradually succeeded in reestablishing government control of the extralegal
marketplaces that sprang up in 1990 (the so-called "green plazas") and
continued to operate during the war, but the operators of the organized

Sarajevo underground are among the wealthiest and best protected of Sarajevo's new elite.

The combination of obsolescence, nationalist obstruction, corruption, legal ambiguity, and political uncertainty has precluded the rejuvenation of Sarajevo's economy. Even though the city has reaped the benefits of the international presence for the past decade, Sarajevans today earn only a small fraction of what they did in 1970 and are correspondingly impoverished. Despite some progress, the dearth of economic prospects inhibits advances in other areas of the city's life.

The return of refugees and displaced persons

The war produced massive human dislocation. In addition to many thousands killed, some two million people became refugees or displaced persons during the war. Through a combination of Bosnian Serb and Croat separatist measures, the vicissitudes of war, and manipulation in the early postwar years, Bosnia-Herzegovina became a segregated country. In a landmark decision extending rights to Bosniaks, Croats, and Serbs in both entities, the Constitutional Court of Bosnia-Herzegovina cited evidence that, as of 1997, 94.88 percent of Federation inhabitants were Bosniaks or Croats and 96.79 percent of Republika Srpska residents were Serbs.[27]

After the Serb-held suburbs were reunited with the core city, the Federation's portion of the city (in effect, the Sarajevo Canton) had a total population of about 349,000.[28] 87 percent of those inhabitants were Bosniaks (8 percent below totals in the Federation, but still an overwhelming majority), their numbers swelled by an estimated 89,000 displaced persons primarily from eastern Bosnia. From 1991 to 1998 the Bosniak population had grown from 252,000 to about 304,000, while the number of Serbs had dropped from 157,193 to about 18,000. The number of Croats declined by 40 percent from 35,000 to 21,000, and the number of "others" (consisting primarily of those who had identified themselves as Yugoslavs before the war, and some Jews and Roma) fell from 75,000 to 7,000.

In Sarajevo, as in all major cities, the national imbalance became more intractable owing to the redistribution of apartments during the war. Many government officials and army officers moved into apartments of Serbs or Croats who left the city. Other apartments were redistributed by the enterprises or institutes that owned them or by the SDA, which assumed control of most of the housing stock in the city. Many longtime Bosniak residents of

Sarajevo upgraded during the war, either taking or being given better apartments while still retaining those from which they moved.[29] This created widespread double occupancy that significantly diminished the available housing stock at war's end.

The international community faced immense challenges in its effort to facilitate a humane return of refugees and displaced persons. The Dayton Agreement guaranteed to all the right to return to their prewar homes. But since many homes were either destroyed or occupied by someone other than their prewar inhabitants, returns would mean expelling recent occupants who themselves were entitled to their dwelling somewhere else in Bosnia-Herzegovina. Equally daunting was the challenge of determining who had the right of occupancy to any given apartment. Almost all dwellings in rural areas were privately owned. Most urban apartments, on the other hand, were social property in which a resident had acquired residency rights that accrued over time and that most Bosnians considered the equivalent of lifetime ownership rights.

The international community sought to link returns to the settlement of property claims and the privatization of socially owned apartments. Returnees were required to submit property claims to authorities where their original home was located, leaving the approval process in the hands of bureaucrats controlled by nationalist parties. Furthermore, residents of socially owned apartments had to purchase them, with the price of purchase reduced for each prewar year of residence. The process was lengthy, complex, costly, and filled with opportunities for obstruction and corruption by local officials. It opened the door to "fictive returns," as they became known locally, in which potential returnees would acquire ownership rights to their apartments but sell them to the current residents. This widespread practice can be seen in the gulf between the percentage of actual returns (estimated at less than one-third of refugees and displaced persons) and the percentage of settled property claims (over 90 percent by the end of 2003).

For the first two years after the Dayton Agreement, many refugees and displaced persons returned to areas in which their nationality ruled. But few who returned were members of "minorities," defined by the international community as "persons who have returned to their preconflict municipalities, currently dominated by (an)other constituent people(s) of BiH."[30] To overcome the logjam in Sarajevo, High Representative Carlos Westendorp launched an initiative in early 1998 to encourage returns to Sarajevo. He brought Bosnian political leaders and international representatives together at a meeting on February 3, 1998, to adopt the "Sarajevo Decla-ration."[31] He appealed to SDA leaders to implement their own rhetorical demands for returns in hopes of making Sarajevo a model for returns throughout Bosnia-Herzegovina.[32] "Returns to Sarajevo today mean returns tomorrow in Banja Luka, Brčko, Drvar and other cities across the country," he declared.[33] He secured the commitment of those present to jump-start the process by returning twenty thousand non-Bosniaks to the city in 1998.

The vast majority of political leaders in Sarajevo publicly endorsed the Sarajevo Declaration. But some felt the city had been unfairly singled out. "Sarajevo didn't expel anyone; Sarajevo doesn't need any kind of decla-ration," one of them said.[34] With only two abstentions, the Sarajevo Canton Assembly passed a plan to implement the declaration's goals, but not before much complaining. "The international community is giving Sarajevans a col-lective guilt complex," said one assembly delegate. Beriz Belkić, coauthor of the plan and a member of the Party for Bosnia-Herzegovina, noted that nowhere were Serbs, Croats, or Bosniaks named in the document, so it was not directed only to encourage the return of non-Bosniaks to Sarajevo. The final resolution rejected the expulsion of any occupant from his or her present location, except for those who had committed crimes or exploited misfortune to end up with two apartments and, by implication, revealed continuing sympathy for Bosniak war victims: "The plan is not directed against those who defended Sarajevo from aggression or who found them-selves in [the city] because of [human] misery, [or] who lost their homes, property, and health," read the resolution.

The Sarajevo Declaration was the most concerted effort after the Dayton Agreement to jump-start the returns process. It did not produce the results in 1998 that the High Representative had hoped, but it signaled the interna-tional community's determination to bring relentless pressure on local officials to process property claims and facilitate returns. The resolution of property claims, along with a secure environment provided by local police, turned out to be the critical preconditions for large-scale returns. Accord-ing to the United Nations High Commission for Refugees, 63,063 non-Bosniaks registered as returnees in the four municipalities of the city of Sarajevo from 1998 to 2005.[35] The annual number of registered returnees reached 20,656 in 2001 and peaked at 26,822 in 2002 before declining pre-cipitously in 2003 and afterward, as most refugees and displaced persons eligible to claim property had done so and decided upon their preferred place of residence. Another 48,563 returned to the other five municipalities in the Sarajevo Canton; non-Bosniak returns to the Sarajevo Canton accounted for almost one quarter of all minority returns to the Federation of Bosnia-Herzegovina. The UNHCR numbers overstate actual returns, since they include many who claimed their property but then reached accommodation with current inhabitants or sold apartments on the slowly-developing real estate market. (The statistics also exclude spontaneous and unregistered returns, of which there were relatively few in the city of Sarajevo.) Most of those who wished to return had largely done so by the end of 2002, and the large-scale process of returns had run its course. The thousands of non-Bosniak returnees to Sarajevo contributed to restoring some of the city's population diversity, but their numbers were insufficient to restore the city's prewar demographic status. As of this writing, observers estimate that about 75 percent of the 400,000 residents of the Sarajevo Canton are Bosniaks, compared with about 50 percent in 1990. The remainder consists principally of Bosnian Serbs and Bosnian Croats, while Jews, Roma, and others are present in fewer numbers.

Institutions and associations: how common the life?

If economic stagnation has led many of Sarajevo's inhabitants and friends to despair, a significant revival of the city's cultural life offers hope. The city's common life has been both resurrected and reinvented in a kaleidoscope of postwar institutions. Among those Serbs and Croats who remained in Sarajevo during the war were some of the most respected intellectual, cultural, and political leaders of prewar Sarajevo. In the aftermath of war, they have joined with many in the Bosniak majority population to continue the tradition of common life in the city. The institutional carriers of postwar common life include several national cultural societies and the political interest groups representing the major nationalities: the Serb Civil Council, the Croat National Council, and the Congress of Bosniak Intellectuals. None of these organizations has been free from contention in the postwar era, and all have come under criticism at one time or another from more extreme nationalists and from those of other nationalities. However, those three interest groups in particular have worked together to promote constitutional changes and encourage the return of displaced persons to the city. They are ethno-nationally separate and in many respects draw the city back to the Austro-Hungarian and interwar eras when cooperation among groups was commonplace but memberships were divided along ethnoconfessional lines.

Some aspects of Sarajevo's common life have flourished in postwar Sarajevo as they did before. The Sarajevo Winter Festival, established as an annual event after the 1984 Olympics, has revived to offer symphony concerts, opera, films, and lectures. The summertime Sarajevo Film Festival, first launched in wartime during the prolonged cease-fire in 1994, expanded its offering after the war and annually shows films in a large outdoor amphitheater. Book promotions take place almost daily. Although few people can afford to buy books, publications flood the market.

The periodical press has been another source of vitality in the preservation and postwar restoration of the city's common life. The newspaper *Oslobodjenje*, which never missed a day of publication during the war, continues to uphold the values of journalistic integrity. Its editorial staff is multiethnic and strongly supports a united Bosnia-Herzegovina. Two weekly news magazines, *Dani* and *Slobodna Bosna*, vie for readers and for sensational headlines. The writers and editorial staffs of both are multiethnic and relish exposing the follies and excesses of politicians regardless of their party affiliation.

The weekly *Ljiljan* began as an unabashed voice of Bosniak national interests but became an independent critic in the late 1990s. *Dnevni avaz* began as a pro-SDA daily newspaper in a format modeled after *USA Today*, but it became independent in the late 1990s. In 2000, in advance of the elections, the paper's editorial direction veered again and it became a vociferous backer of the SDA and a vitriolic critic of social democratic politicians. The pages of *Dnevni avaz* carried highly personal attacks directed against others in the press community, particularly the editor of *Slobodna Bosna*. Distressingly, the paper won, at least temporarily, praise from High Representative Paddy Ashdown during the height of its attacks in autumn 2003. Ashdown's blessing stoked an ongoing assault on various proponents of Sarajevo's common life that particularly centered on Croat intellectuals and those who had remained in Sarajevo during the war.

Despite the city's substantial cultural activity, provisions of the Dayton Agreement impede the continued vitality of many prewar institutions of common life. In the Federation, responsibility for education and culture was given to the ten individual cantons. This provision starved a wide array of educational, cultural, and artistic institutions that had served as prewar custodians of the city's common life. Since most prewar republic institutions were located in Sarajevo, most former state-level organizations had to be financed by the Sarajevo Canton, based on tax receipts from a territory less than two-thirds the size of the prewar city. The Dayton and Federation documents also authorized the nine other cantons and the Republika Srpska to found or develop competing institutions. Sarajevo's status as a leading city was accordingly diminished, and the institutions that sponsored its common life were correspondingly weakened. Hardest hit by these changes were the University of Sarajevo, the Regional Museum, the National and University Library, and the Academy of Arts and Sciences of Bosnia-Herzegovina.

Sarajevo, which has the most tax revenue of the Federation's ten cantons, provides limited budgetary support to these institutions. Competing institutions in the Republika Srpska and Croat-controlled areas of the Federation are unerringly single-ethnic, and some are explicitly committed to undermining the institutions of common life based in Sarajevo. Most of these formerly state-sponsored institutions have come under the leadership of SDA members who reject notions of ethnic purity but who often do little to bolster the number of non-Bosniaks in the organization.

Those organizations that survived the war have been joined by new organizations formed or relocated in the postwar years. The Bosniak Institute was created by Adil Zulfikarpašić in Zurich during the 1970s, and in the late 1990s he moved most of its holdings to Sarajevo. In 2001 he dedicated the institute's Sarajevo home, an edifice that incorporates the Ottoman-era public bath facility near the Catholic cathedral. The building embodies the blend of secular, religious, Western, and Eastern values characteristic of Bosniak national thought. The building's interior is imbued with a sense of traditional Middle Eastern Islamic architecture, yet its exterior is architecturally modern. The edifice obtrudes into a neighborhood of Catholic institutions, but it carefully avoids towering over the more traditional cathedral just across the street to the south.

The city's common life did not die during the war, nor has it perished in the difficult postwar era. However, Sarajevans face many difficult choices in the postsocialist and postwar era, and the future of the city's common life is among them. Some thriving new organizations, such as the Bosniak Institute, are untainted by association with communism but owe much to Bosniak national values. However, many of the city's most venerated institutions and practices have their origins in the dynamic first two decades of the socialist era and were in part designed to overcome national divisiveness. Sarajevans have almost unanimously rejected communism as an ideology, yet they hold fond memories of life before the war, a time when communists ruled the city. Most of them reject national exclusivity in principle, yet they have repeatedly opted to put nationalist political leaders in office. With the city still living in the long shadow of ruinous war and its citizens holding contradictory social values, Sarajevans have yet to discover or invent a full spectrum of cultural, political, and educational institutions that are free from both communist and nationalist authoritarianism. As they endeavor to do so, the future of the city's common life hangs in the balance.

Conclusion

Notwithstanding its natural advantages of location and geology, Sarajevo has been developed primarily by individuals and groups determined to shape its future. The governing authorities of three regimes—Ottoman, Habsburg, and Communist—have facilitated the city's growth. However, Sarajevans themselves have invariably adapted a broader vision to the city's specific circumstances and provided the commitment, resources, and energy to shape their urban environment. The impetus for growth came from three radically different city-building regimes, each of which eventually succumbed to a combination of internal crises and external pressures, but in their days of growth and strength, they each contributed to building a large, diverse urban community. In the early Ottoman period, the city grew from a few hundred residents in scattered villages when it was founded in the 1460s to about 23,500 residents by 1600. The population remained at that level for 280 years. Under Habsburg rule from 1878 to 1910, the city doubled in population to about 51,000. In its third era of expansion under socialist rule, Sarajevo went from about 100,000 residents in 1945 to over half a million in 1991. That number was cut almost in half during the war and siege from 1992–5 and has nearly returned to that number since the Dayton Agreement. The pattern of growth demonstrates that dynamic leaders committed to inclusive values and goals shaped the city's development. Sadly, human malevolence and neglect account for the city's times of stagnation, decline, and near destruction.

From the city's early days, openness to new residents was not just an abstract principle but the key to the city's growth. Sarajevo benefited in all periods of growth from immigration. In the fifteenth and sixteenth centuries, the city drew Slavic-speaking peasant immigrants from the nearby countryside. Many refugees from violence and political oppression found a haven in Sarajevo, including Sephardic Jews fleeing persecution in Spain less than a century after the city was founded. In the era of Ottoman reform, Serb and Jewish merchants enhanced the city's population and added to its diversity. During Habsburg rule, immigrants (including the era's premier architect, Josip Vancaš) boosted the city's growth and brought Western influences to augment the city's Ottoman heritage. At various times in the nineteenth and twentieth centuries, refugees from the eastern Bosnia fled nationalist violence and found a haven in Sarajevo, usually adding to its Muslim (Bosniak) population. Some refugees returned to their homes when the end of violence made it possible to do so, but others remained and made their homes in Sarajevo, taking advantage of the considerable benefits of urban life.

In the last six decades of the twentieth century, the city experienced two horrific wars (1941–5 and 1992–5), each accompanied by widespread killing and immeasurable damage to the city. There seems to be little point in judging which of these campaigns wrought the most destruction. The German-Ustasha occupiers' malign vision of a racially pure society led them to unprecedented destruction of human life, and extreme Serb nationalists with a similarly divisive vision of ethnonational separation attacked the city and its inhabitants five decades later. The leaders in each case carefully planned and systematically implemented the assault, and they preceded and accompanied their attacks with a propaganda campaign to gain Sarajevans' support in conducting the slaughter. Both assaults were intended to destroy Sarajevo's essential historical diversity and cosmopolitanism. But neither ultimately succeeded in achieving an exclusivist vision, thanks in large measure to the resistance that each evoked among Sarajevans determined to preserve what they had created. The highly organized resistance of 1941–5 mutated after the war into an unprecedented campaign of rebuilding and expansion. Not so the resistance of 1992–5, which began to disintegrate with the end of war amid factional disputes about who was responsible for saving the city.

From its foundation, Sarajevo has recognized distinctions among its inhabitants based on their religion, ethnicity, nationality, or some blend of the three. An ethnic key has been in effect as long as the city has existed, even if it has not always been known by that name. Although social democrats and communists indignantly rejected the ethnic key as anachronistic, it guided many of their appointments to key leadership positions and never wholly disappeared from political life. During the decades of socialist rule from 1945–92, national differences became less relevant in public life and were blurred by considerable intermarriage, but the distinctions never vanished. Diversity, rather than assimilation, has been Sarajevo's hallmark for the past five and a half centuries. Common life was a product of reaching across ethnonational boundaries rather than erasing them.

Instances of violence by perpetrators of one group against members of another grew in frequency and intensity as the twentieth century progressed. The killing of the archduke and his wife and the subsequent anti-Serb violence took four lives; violence during the Second World War killed about ten thousand; and around the same number of deaths resulted from the siege of 1992–5 and its attendant population expulsions. One sees in Sarajevo a sad progression in the twentieth century from assassins targeting individual government officials, to leaders employing ideology to mobilize mass movements to exterminate or evict entire groups of human beings. National parties were first established during Austro-Hungarian rule (1906–10), and from the beginning they brought divisiveness to political life in the city and in Bosnia-Herzegovina. In their first incarnation, Serb and Croat parties were only loosely allied with similar formations in neighboring polities. Only a decade later, as parties were again formed to compete in multiparty elections in 1919–20, the national parties were more closely allied with politicians in neighboring areas. The trend toward closer affiliation reached its zenith in the third era of multiparty formation in 1990, as Serb and Croat parties in Bosnia-Herzegovina became de facto extensions of the foreign policies of the republics of Serbia and Croatia.

Common life and tolerance were most at risk in times of political instability, particularly in the early weeks and months after power changed hands in Bosnia-Herzegovina. The Sarajevo Holocaust was carried out in the first months of Axis rule. Most expulsions of Bosniaks and Croats from Serb-controlled territories took place in the first months of war in 1992, and so did the threats and atrocities against Serbs who remained in the city after shelling began in April of that year. Political instability, however, did not always touch off large-scale violence. At no time was life more unsettled, and authority more dispersed, than in the summer of 1878; but Sarajevans engaged in no violence against one another and found common ground in resisting the dreaded Austro-Hungarian occupying forces. Furthermore, violence has not deterred Sarajevans from rebounding and reconstructing a common life in the wake of conflict. The street violence of 1914 and the Austro-Hungarian actions against Serbs did not hinder the reemergence of the city's common life after the First World War. The atrocities of the Second World War were followed by a KP-led effort to bring Sarajevans together in new institutions under a socialist ideology.

Even in the bleak aftermath of the war of the 1990s, the cultural dimensions of the city's common life have advanced even as political life and economic growth have stagnated. Unfortunately, each reconstruction of common life has also involved excesses and instances of revenge: the expulsion of Austro-Hungarian and German citizens (or making them unwelcome, as was the case with Josip Vancaš), the harsh reprisals against perceived Ustasha allies in the 1940s, the violence against Serbs in the city in 1992, and the obstreperous bureaucratic foot-dragging that delayed the return of displaced persons in the late 1990s. Despite these excesses and the losses that violence has cost the city in the past century, Sarajevans have demonstrated the capacity and the will to revitalize the city's common life and preserve its legacy of diversity.

Our historical survey shows that the city's diversity has taken different forms and evolved considerably over the course of its historical development. Diversity has never been unidimensional, and it should never be reduced to an exercise in demographic percentages. Population composition by group has varied widely over the centuries, often with members of a single religious community in the majority. The city did not suddenly change its fundamental character because a group reached 50.1 percent of the population. More important has been the city's common life, openness, response to cultural influences, and receptivity to outsiders. Although at no time have those values completely triumphed, they have distinctively characterized the city over its five centuries of existence. It falls to the city's present-day leaders, residents, and friends to preserve and nourish its historical legacy in the twenty-first century.

Notes

Preface

1. Benedict Anderson, *Imagined Communities: Reflections on the Origin and Spread of Nationalism*, rev. edn, London: Verso, 1998, pp. 5–7.

Introduction

1. Security Council Resolution 824 (1993) (S/RES/824, 6 May 1993), in Daniel Bethlehem and Marc Weller (eds), *The "Yugoslav" Crisis in International Law: General Issues*, Cambridge University Press, 1997, p. 41.
2. The meaning of *komšije* is explained in Ivana Maček, *War Within: Everyday Life in Sarajevo under Siege*, Uppsala Studies in Cultural Anthropology 29, Uppsala: Acta Universitatis Upsaliensis, 2000, pp. 123–38. The terms *višenacionalni* (meaning "of more than one nation" or "multinational") and *suživot* (life together) are used occasionally as alternatives, but the most frequent formulation found in print sources is *zajednički život* (common life, or life together). Variants of *komšije* were, and continue to be, used most frequently in everyday verbal communication.
3. *Random House Webster's College Dictionary*, New York: Random House, 1997.
4. Mark Mazower, *Salonica, City of Ghosts: Christians, Muslims and Jews, 1430–1950*, London: HarperCollins, 2004.
5. Martin Gilbert, *Jerusalem in the Twentieth Century*, New York: John Wiley and Sons, 1996; Eric H. Cline, *Jerusalem Besieged: From Ancient Canaan to Modern Israel*, Ann Arbor: University of Michigan Press, 2004, pp. 11–13 and 201–310; and John Freely, *Istanbul: The Imperial City*, New York: Penguin, 1998, pp. 281–315.
6. Jay Winter, "Paris, London, Berlin 1914–1919: Capital Cities at War," in Jay Winter and Jean-Louis Robert (eds), *Capital Cities at War: Paris, London, Berlin 1914–1919*, Cambridge University Press, 1997, p. 3.

Chapter 1   Sarajevo's Founders and Foundations

1. Most published histories of Sarajevo cover one historical period. If they cover a long range of time, they are written by multiple authors, each author covering a separate period. Among the few works addressing developments over longer periods in a single volume are Alojz Benac and Ljubica Mladenović, *Sarajevo od najstarijih vremena do danas* (Sarajevo from the earliest times to present), Sarajevo: Muzej grada Sarajeva, 1954; Vladislav Skarić, *Sarajevo i njegova okolina od najstarijih vremena do austro-ugarske okupacije* (Sarajevo and its environs from the earliest times to the Austro-Hungarian occupation),

Sarajevo: Opština grada Sarajeva, 1937; Hamdija Kreševljaković, *Esnafi i obrti u starom Sarajevu* (Guilds and crafts in old Sarajevo), Sarajevo: Narodna prosvjeta, 1958; and three illustrated volumes: Muhamed Čurovac (ed), *Sarajevo: Photo-monograph*, Sarajevo: Svjetlost, 1997; Miroslav Prstojević, *Zaboravljeno Sarajevo* (Forgotten Sarajevo), Sarajevo: Ideja, 1992; and Fehim M. Begović, *Staro Sarajevo. Ljudi i dogadjaji* (Old Sarajevo: People and events), Sarajevo: Rabic, 1999. Much may be gleaned about Sarajevo through the centuries from the seminal work of Mustafa Imamović, *Historija Bošnjaka* (The history of the Bosniaks), Sarajevo: Preporod, 1997; and from the multiauthored work, Ibrahim Karabegović *et al.*, *Bosna i Hercegovina od najstarijih vremena do kraja drugog svjetskog rata* (Bosnia-Herzegovina from the earliest times to the end of the Second World War), Sarajevo: Press Centar Armije Republike Bosne i Hercegovine, 1994. For the city's founding and flourishing in Ottoman times, the definitive works are Behija Zlatar, *Zlatna doba Sarajeva* (The golden age of Sarajevo), Sarajevo: Svjetlost, 1996; and Hazim Šabanović, *Bosanski pašaluk* (The territory of the Bosnian pasha), Sarajevo: Svjetlost, 1982.

2. Behija Zlatar, "Bosna i Hercegovina u okvirima Osmanskog Carstva (1463–1593)" (Bosnia-Herzegovina in the framework of the Ottoman Empire), in Karabegović *et al.*, *Bosna i Hercegovina od najstarijih vremena*, p. 82.

3. Zlatar, *Zlatna doba*, pp. 26, 93.

4. Hazim Šabanović, "Postanak i razvoj Sarajeva" (The origins and development of Sarajevo) *Radovi, Odjeljenje istorijsko-filoloških nauka* (Studies of the Department of Historical-Philological Sciences) 5 (1960), pp. 72–6.

5. Zlatar, *Zlatna doba*, p. 26.

6. Ibid., p. 30.

7. Robert J. Donia and John V. A. Fine, Jr., *Bosnia and Herzegovina: A Tradition Betrayed*, London: Hurst, 1994, p. 15. The English historian Noel Malcolm, describing the plethora of medieval states, deems the political history of this era "patchy and confused." Noel Malcolm, *Bosnia: A Short History*, updated edn, New York: New York University Press, 1996, p. 9.

8. Nikolai Todorov, *The Balkan City, 1400–1900*, Seattle: University of Washington Press, 1983, p. 18.

9. Ibid., p. 20.

10. Zlatar, *Zlatna doba*, p. 179.

11. Evlija Čelebi, *Putopis. Odlomci o jugoslovenskim zemljama* (Travelogue: Excerpts regarding the South Slav lands), Sarajevo: Sarajevo Publishing, 1996, pp. 122–3, first published in Turkish as *Evliya Çelebi Seyahatnamesi* in Istanbul in 1896.

12. Zlatar, *Zlatna doba*, p. 77.

13. Ibid., p. 140.

14. Harriet Pass Friedenreich, "Sarajevo: City of Four Faiths," in *The Jews of Yugoslavia: A Quest for Community*, Philadelphia: Jewish Publication Society of America, 1979, pp. 11–25; Moritz Levy, *Die Sephardim in Bosnien. Ein Beitrag zur Geschichte der Juden auf der Balkanhalbinsel* (The Sephardim in Bosnia: A contribution to the history of Jews in the Balkan Peninsula), reproduction of 1911 edn, Klagenfurt: Wieser Verlag, 1996. Levy notes that three court documents from 1565 refer to Jews in the city (pp. 12–13). According to a more recent study, a document from 1557 reported a property dispute

involving a Jew. See Alija Bejtić, "Jevrejske nastambe u Sarajevu" (Jewish residences in Sarajevo), in Samuel Kamhi (ed.), *Spomenica 400 godina od dolaska Jevreja u Bosnu i Hercegovinu* (Commemoration of 400 years of the arrival of Jews in Bosnia and Herzegovina), Sarajevo: Oslobodjenje, 1966, p. 24.

15. Esther Benbassa and Aron Rodrique, *The Jews of the Balkans: The Judeo-Spanish Community, Fifteenth to Twentieth Centuries*, Cambridge, MA: Blackwell, 1995, pp. 8–26.

16. Levy, *Die Sephardim in Bosnien*, p. 16.

17. Čelebi, *Putopis*, p. 118.

18. For Ishaković's role in founding the city, see Zlatar, *Zlatna doba*, pp. 85–90, and Šabanović, *Bosanski pašaluk*, p. 37.

19. The term "governor" is used in this chapter to refer to the highest ranking Ottoman governing official in Bosnia. The names of the administrative unit and of the governor's position changed numerous times during Ottoman rule. The Bosnian *sandžak* (meaning "flag" in its Turkish variant but referring to an administrative territory) was ruled by a *sandžakbeg* from 1453 and in 1580 became an *ejalet*. In 1851 the *sandžak* was transformed into *kajmekamluk*.

20. Zlatar, *Zlatna doba*, p. 223.

21. Early Ottoman censuses counted households and persons with feudal obligations but did not attempt to enumerate the entire population. Nikolai Todorov, a leading authority on Balkan cities, steadfastly refuses to convert households into population estimates, but he quotes favorably a study suggesting an average of five persons per household and an additional 10 percent estimate for the nonproductive population of Ottoman cities other than Istanbul. See Todorov, *The Balkan City*, pp. 27–8, 500 n. 43. Sarajevo had 4,270 households in the late sixteenth century, so the population could be estimated at 23,485, but such a number is at best an approximation. Other estimates and often-overstated guesses in travelers' accounts are discussed in Kreševljaković, *Esnafi i obrti u starom Sarajevu*, pp. 30–2, and Benac and Mladenović, *Sarajevo od najstarijih vremena do danas*, p. 56.

22. Zlatar, *Zlatna doba*, pp. 106, 108.

23. Ibid., p. 200.

24. Ibid., p. 85.

25. Noel Malcolm, *Kosovo: A Short History*, London: Macmillan/New York University Press, 1998, p. 116.

26. Ahmed S. Aličić, *Pokret za autonomiju Bosne od 1831. do 1832. godine.* (The movement for the autonomy of Bosnia, 1831–2), Sarajevo: Orijentalni Institut, 1996, p. 42.

27. Fadil Ademović, *Princ Palikuća u Sarajevu* (Prince Arsonist in Sarajevo), Sarajevo: Rabic, 1997, pp. 11–12, and Skarić, *Sarajevo i njegova okolina*, pp. 110–3.

28. Ademović, *Princ Palikuća u Sarajevu*, p. 194.

29. Imamović, *Historija Bošnjaka*, p. 256.

30. Aličić, *Pokret za autonomiju*, p. 87.

31. Skarić, *Sarajevo i njegova okolina*, pp. 101–2.

32. Michael Robert Hickok, *Ottoman Military Administration in Eighteenth-Century Bosnia*, Leiden: E. J. Brill, 1997.

33. Enes Pelidija, "Bosanski ejalet od 1593. god. to svištovog mira 1791. god." (The Bosnian *Eyalet* from 1593 to the Peace of Sistovo of 1791), in Karabegović *et al., Bosna i Hercegovina od najstarijih vremena*, p. 123.

34. "The Banja Luka battle represents one of the first pages of Bosnian Muslim self-consciousness." Pelidija, "Bosanski ejalet," in Karabegović et al., Bosna i Hercegovina od najstarijih vremena, p. 125. See also Imamović, Historija Bošnjaka, p. 301.

35. Hickok, Ottoman Military Administration in Eighteenth-Century Bosnia, pp. 15–39.

36. Aličić, Pokret za autonomiju, p. 107.

37. Ibid., pp. 159–63.

38. Husnija Kamberović, Husein-kapetan Gradaščević (1802–1834): Biografija uz dvjestotu godišnjicu rodjenja (Husein-kapetan Gradaščević: Biography on the occasion of the two-hundredth anniversary of his birth), Gradačac: Preporod, 2002.

39. Aličić, Pokret za autonomiju, p. 230.

40. Ibrahim Tepić, "Bosna i Hercegovina od kraja XVIII stoljeća do austrougarske okupacije 1878. godine" (Bosnia-Herzegovina from the end of the eighteenth century to the Austro-Hungarian occupation in 1878), in Karabegović et al., Bosna i Hercegovina od najstarijih vremena, p. 149.

41. Galib Šljivo, Omer-paša Latas u Bosni i Hercegovini, 1850–1852 (Omer-Pasha Latas in Bosnia-Herzegovina), Sarajevo: Svjetlost, 1977, p. 12.

42. Tepić, "Bosna i Hercegovina," in Karabegović et al., Bosna i Hercegovina od najstarijih vremena, p. 151.

43. Šljivo, Omer-paša Latas, p. 12.

44. On the role of the Fadilpašić brothers under Austro-Hungarian rule, see Robert Donia, Islam under the Double Eagle: The Muslims of Bosnia and Hercegovina, 1878–1914, Boulder, CO: East European Monographs, 1981, pp. 44–5, 57–9.

45. Berislav Gavranović (ed.), Bosna i Hercegovina u doba austrougarske okupacije 1878. godine (Bosnia-Herzegovina in the period of Austro-Hungarian occupation in 1878), Wassıtsch to Andrássy, July 12, 1878, Sarajevo: Akademija nauka i umjetnosti Bosne i Hercegovine, 1973, p. 186. This volume is a collection of reports from Austro-Hungarian diplomats in Bosnia to the Foreign Ministry in Vienna.

46. Vasa Čubrilović, Bosanski ustanak 1875–1878 (The Bosnian uprising of 1875–8), 2nd edn, Belgrade: Službeni list SRJ, 1996, p. 23.

47. Iljas Hadžibegović, Postanak radničke klase u Bosni i Hercegovini i njen razvoj do 1914. godine (The origins of the working class in Bosnia-Herzegovina and its development to 1914), Sarajevo: Svjetlost, 1980, pp. 42–3.

48. Mitar Papić, Istorija srpskih škola u Bosni i Hercegovini (The history of Serb schools in Bosnia-Herzegovina), Sarajevo: Veselin Masleša, 1978, pp. 18–22.

49. "Saborna crkva Rodjenja Presvete Bogorodice" (The Assembly Church of the Birth of the Most Holy Mother of Christ), flyer distributed at the new Serbian Orthodox church, Sarajevo, n.d. The flyer provides a brief history of the church building compiled by Serbian Orthodox Church officials.

50. Hamdija Kreševljaković, "Sarajevo u doba okupacije Bosne 1878" (Sarajevo in the time of the occupation of Bosnia in 1878), in vol. 4 of Izabrana Djela (Selected works), Sarajevo: Veselin Masleša, 1991, pp. 149–52, first published in 1937.

51. "Kako je osveštena nova srpska crkva u Sarajevu. Iz uspomena g. Petra Budimlića" (How the new Serbian church in Sarajevo was dedicated, according to the recollections of Mr. Petar Budimlić), Jugoslovenska pošta (The Yugoslav Post), Sarajevo, September 20, 1930, p. 9, quoted in flyer from the new Serbian Orthodox church, Sarajevo.

52. Tepić, "Bosna i Hercegovina," in Karabegović *et al.*, *Bosna i Hercegovina od najstarijih vremena*, pp. 158–62, summarizes Osman Topal Pasha's achievements as governor.

53. Todor Kruševac, *Bosansko-hercegovački listovi u xix veku* (Newspapers of Bosnia-Herzegovina in the nineteenth century), Sarajevo: Veselin Masleša, 1978, pp. 27–49.

54. Ahmed S. Aličić, *Uredjenje bosanskog ejaleta od 1789. do 1878. godine* (Organization of the Bosnian ejalet from 1789 to 1878), Sarajevo: Orijentalni Institut, 1983, pp. 82, 103, 121, describes these reforms and their application in Sarajevo.

Chapter 2 The Sarajevo Uprising and the Advent of Habsburg Rule

1. The Habsburg Monarchy became a dual monarchy and was often called Austria-Hungary after 1867, when its Hungarian lands acquired substantial autonomy.

2. The events of 1878 in Sarajevo are discussed in Kreševljaković, *Sarajevo u doba okupacije*, pp. 73–167; Čubrilović, *Bosanski ustanak*, pp. 280–311; Skarić, *Sarajevo i njegova okolina*, pp. 257–90; Enver Imamović, *Historija bosanske vojske* (The history of the Bosnian army), Sarajevo: Art 7, 1999, pp. 237–45; and Mustafa Imamović, *Historija Bošnjaka*, pp. 351–3. Eyewitness accounts are recorded in Grga Martić, *Zapamćenja* (Memoirs), Zagreb: Gjura Trpinac, 1906, pp. 87–103; and Josef Koetschet, *Aus Bosniens letzter Türkenzeit* (From Bosnia's recent Turkish times), Vienna: Georg Grassl, 1905.

3. On the Eastern Crisis and its antecedents, see B. H. Sumner, *Russia and the Balkans 1870–1880*, Hamden, CT: Archon Books, 1962, pp. 137–553; William N. Medlicott, *The Congress of Berlin and After*, London: Methuen, 1938, pp. 2–136; and Charles and Barbara Jelavich, *The Establishment of the Balkan National States, 1804–1920*, Seattle: University of Washington Press, 1977, pp. 141–57.

4. Leopold Neumann and Adolphe Plason (eds), *Recueil des Traités et Conventions conclus par l'Autriche avec les puissances étrangères* (Collection of treaties and conventions concluded by Austria with foreign powers), Vienna: Steyrermühl, 1883, p. 778.

5. The reports of Konrad von Wassitsch, the consul of Austria-Hungary in Sarajevo, are the most informative of the consular documents. His reports, along with other documents from the Austro-Hungarian Foreign Ministry, make up the volume cited previously as Berislav Gavranović (ed.), *Bosna i Hercegovina u doba austrougarske okupacije 1878. godine*, hereafter cited as Gavranović (ed.), along with the sender, recipient, date of the correspondence, and page number. Reports of the British Consul Edward Freeman are summarized in Hamdija Kapidžić, "Sarajevo u avgustu 1878. godine" (Sarajevo in August 1878), *Prilozi za proučavanje istorije Sarajeva* (Contributions to the study of the history of Sarajevo), 1, 1 (1963), pp. 117–31. The Italian consular reports are reviewed in Rade Petrović, "Pokret otpora u Bosni i Hercegovini protiv austrougarske okupacije 1878. godine, prema izvještajima Talijanskog konzulata u Sarajevu" (The movement of resistance in Bosnia-Herzegovina against Austro-Hungarian occupation in 1878, according to the reports of the Italian consulate in Sarajevo), in *Medjunarodni naučni skup povodom 100. godišnjice ustanaka u Bosni i Hercegovini, drugim balkanskim zemljama i istočnoj krizi 1875–1878 godine* (International scholarly conference on the occasion of the hundredth anniversary of the uprising in Bosnia-Herzegovina and other Balkan lands, and the Eastern Crisis of 1875–8), Sarajevo: Akademija nauka i umjetnosti Bosne i Hercegovine, 1977, 2:343–73.

6. Gavranović (ed.), Wassitsch to Andrássy, January 25, 1878, p. 72.

7. Ibid., Foreign Ministry to Wassitsch, Vienna, April 20, 1878, p. 99. This telegram cites a "letter from a good source" in Sarajevo.

8. PRO, Foreign Office 195, 1212: Freeman to Foreign Office, May 27, 1878.

9. Petrović, "Pokret otpora," p. 365.

10. Gavranović (ed.), Wassitsch to Andrássy, June 12, 1878, p. 143.

11. Ibid., Wassitsch to Andrássy, June 28, 1878, p. 155.

12. Ibid.

13. Ibid., Wassitsch to Andrássy, June 6, 1878, p. 137.

14. Ibid., Wassitsch to Andrássy, June 12, 1878, p. 143.

15. Ibid., Wassitsch to Andrássy, July 7, 1878, p. 170.

16. Ibid., Orczy to Andrássy, July 7, 1878, p. 169.

17. Ibid., Wassitsch to Andrássy, July 18, 1878, p. 213.

18. The report of this demonstration came from the Italian consulate. Petrović, "Pokret otpora," p. 362, citing Italian Consul Report 137, July 26, 1878.

19. Among the consuls, Wassitsch prepared the most detailed report of this day's events. Gavranović (ed.), Wassitsch to Andrássy, July 29, 1878, pp. 249–52. Koetschet's account substantially supports the Austro-Hungarian consul and adds some further incidents of less relevance to the general course of events.

20. Ministère des Affaires Étrangères, Paris. Archives Diplomatiques, Correspondence Politique des Consuls: Patin to Foreign Ministry, August 5, 1878.

21. The Italian and French reports of this brief siege are remarkably similar.

22. PRO, Foreign Office 195, 1212: Freeman to Foreign Office, August 3, 1878. With the telegraph wires cut, the consuls were unable to file reports from the evening of July 27 until service was restored on August 3. Their dispatches on that date included several reports written but not sent during their six days without the telegraph.

23. Gavranović (ed.), Wassitsch to Strautz, July 28, 1878, p. 252.

24. Ibid., Wassitsch to Andrássy, July 29, 1878, p. 250.

25. Ibid., Wassitsch to Andrássy, August 4, 1878, p. 277.

26. PRO, Foreign Office 195, 1212: Freeman to Foreign Office, Bosna Serai (Sarajevo), August 3, 1878.

27. The Muslim leaders' ideals and objectives were most clearly laid out in a visit by Vilajetović to Consul Wassitsch at 6.00 a.m. on July 30 and the appeal to all citizens distributed on August 7.

28. Wassitsch reported only that Vilajetović cited Koranic provisions and makes no mention of the sheriat, but the Koran and sheriat appear to have been synonymous in the minds of Muslims advocating a return to an earlier political system. Gavranović (ed.), Wassitsch to Andrássy, August 4, 1878, pp. 273–8. The consul wired this report from Mostar. The appeal, signed by Ismail Haki as "Commander of Bosnia," is found in Kreševljaković, *Sarajevo u doba okupacije*, pp. 102–4.

29. Gavranović (ed.), Wassitsch to Andrássy, July 15, 1878, p. 201.

30. PRO, Foreign Office 195, 1212: Freeman to Foreign Office, Bosna Serai, August 3, 1878.

31. Krešvljaković, *Sarajevo u doba okupacije*, p. 103. Citing a copy in the personal collection of a colleague, Kreševljaković provides the full text of the appeal.

32. Ibid.
33. Milorad Ekmečić, *Ustanak u Bosni, 1875–1878* (Uprising in Bosnia), Sarajevo: Veselin Masleša, 1973, pp. 321–5. Ekmečić states that officially tolerated efforts to create a Serb-Muslim alliance were generally unsuccessful, but he notes that the alliance was more successful and enduring in Sarajevo than elsewhere.
34. Ministère des Affaires Étrangères, Paris. Archives Diplomatiques, Correspondence Politique des Consuls: Patin to Foreign Ministry, Sarajevo, August 17, 1878.
35. Martić, *Zapamćenja*, p. 90.
36. On the battles throughout Bosnia-Herzegovina, see Robert J. Donia, "The Battle for Bosnia: Habsburg Military Strategy in 1878," in Milorad Ekmečić (ed.), *Otpor austrougarskoj okupaciji 1878. godine u Bosni i Hercegovini* (Resistance to Austro-Hungarian occupation in 1878 in Bosnia-Herzegovina), Sarajevo: Akademija nauka i umjetnosti Bosne i Hercegovine, 1979, pp. 109–21, and Mihovil Mandić, *Povijest okupacije Bosne i Hercegovine, 1878* (The history of the occupation of Bosnia-Herzegovina, 1878), Zagreb: Matica hrvatska, 1910, pp. 30–90; and Alfons Falkner von Sonnenburg, *Über Operationen im Gebirgsland, illustrirt durch die Kämpfe der Österreicher bei der Occupation Bosniens, 1878* (On operations in mountainous terrain, illustrated by the battles of the Austrians in the occupation of Bosnia), Munich: F. Straub, 1885, pp. 75–104.
37. Falkner, *Über Operationen im Gebirgsland*, p. 71.
38. Petrović, "Pokret otpora," p. 344.
39. Kreševljaković, *Sarajevo u doba okupacije*, p. 133.
40. Ibid., p. 156.
41. In this I concur with the assessment found in Petrović, "Pokret otpora," p. 365.

Chapter 3 The Making of Fin de Siècle Sarajevo

1. The following are excellent general studies of the city's history in this period: Hamdija Kreševljaković, *Sarajevo za vrijeme austrougarske uprave (1878–1918)* (Sarajevo in the time of Austro-Hungarian administration), Sarajevo: Arhiv grada Sarajeva, 1969; and Todor Kruševac, *Sarajevo pod austro-ugarskom upravom, 1878–1918* (Sarajevo under Austro-Hungarian administration), Sarajevo: Muzej grada Sarajeva, 1960. A thorough, richly documented, and indispensable study of Kállay's life and regime is Tomislav Kraljačić's *Kalajev režim u Bosni i Hercegovini (1882–1903)* (The Kállay regime in Bosnia-Herzegovina), Sarajevo: Veselin Masleša, 1987.
2. Kreševljaković, *Sarajevo za vrijeme austrougarske uprave*, pp. 13–4.
3. Ibid., p. 123.
4. Hamdija Kapidžić, *Hercegovački ustanak 1882. godine* (The Herzegovinian uprising of 1882), Sarajevo: Veselin Masleša, 1973, pp. 75–118.
5. The Habsburg Monarchy's arcane political structure dictated that Bosnia could best be administered by one of three joint ministries with jurisdiction over the entire empire. The task fell to the Joint Ministry of Finance. Administering the province became the primary duty of the joint minister of finance from 1878 until the empire collapsed in 1918.
6. Kraljačić, *Kalajev režim*, pp. 45–61.
7. Benjamin von Kállay, *Geschichte der Serben von den ältesten Zeiten bis 1815* (The history of the Serbs from ancient times to 1815), Budapest: Lauffer, 1878.

8. Neoabsolutism was the name given to the era of conservative rule in the Habsburg Monarchy following suppression of the 1848 revolution under Prince Felix Schwarzenberg and Alexander Bach in Austria from 1849 to 1860. See Robert A. Kann, *A History of the Habsburg Empire 1526–1918*, Berkeley: University of California Press, 1974, pp. 318–26.

9. Kraljačić, *Kalajev režim* pp. 61–6.

10. Iljas Hadžibegović, *Bosanskohercegovački gradovi na razmedju 19. i 20. stoljeća*, Sarajevo: Oslobodjenje, 1991, provides an analysis of population figures for this era.

11. See Dževad Juzbašić, "Nekoliko napomena o Jevrejima u Bosni i Hercegovini u doba austrougarske uprave" (A few remarks on the Jews in Bosnia-Herzegovina in the period of Austro-Hungarian administration), in Dževad Juzbašić, *Politika i privreda u Bosni i Hercegovini pod austrougarskom upravom* (Politics and economy in Bosnia-Hercegovina under Austro-Hungarian administration), Sarajevo: Akademija nauka i umjetnosti Bosne i Hercegovine, 2002, pp. 371–82. Under the category of *Jevreji* (Jews) were two subgroups: *sefardički* (Sephardic) and *drugi* (others). Bosnien und die Hercegovina, Landesregierung, *Die Ergebnisse der Volkszählung in Bosnien und der Hercegovina vom 10. Oktober 1910* (Results of the census in Bosnia-Herzegovina of October 10, 1910), Sarajevo: Landesdruckerie, 1912, 1:5.

12. Todor Kruševac, "Društvene promene kod bosanskih jevreja za austrijskog vremena" (Social change among Bosnian Jews in Austrian times), in Kamhi (ed.), *Spomenica dolaska Jevreja u BiH*, pp. 71–97, discusses the demographic development of the two Jewish communities.

13. *Ergebnisse der Volkszählung 1910*, 1:48.

14. Peter Sugar, *The Industrialization of Bosnia-Herzegovina, 1878–1918*, Seattle: University of Washington Press, 1963, p. 89.

15. Dževad Juzbašić, *Izgradnje železnica u Bosni i Hercegovini u svjetlu austrougarske politike od okupacije do kraja Kállayeve ere* (Railway building in Bosnia-Herzegovina in light of Austro-Hungarian policies from the occupation to the end of the Kállay era), Sarajevo: Akademija nauka i umjetnosti Bosne i Hercegovine, 1974, p. 101.

16. Hadžibegović, *Postanak radničke klase*, pp. 78–9.

17. Kruševac, *Sarajevo pod austro-ugarskom upravom*, pp. 110–16.

18. On the development of industrial facilities, see Kreševljaković, *Sarajevo za vrijeme austrougarske uprave*, pp. 66–71, 78; and Kruševac, *Sarajevo pod austro-ugarskom upravom*, pp. 201–14.

19. Kruševac, *Sarajevo pod austro-ugarskom upravom*, pp. 95–102.

20. Kreševljaković, *Sarajevo za vrijeme austrougarske uprave*, pp. 30–1.

21. Kruševac, *Sarajevo pod austro-ugarskom upravom*, pp. 102–5.

22. Carl E. Schorske, *Fin-de-Siècle Vienna: Politics and Culture*, New York: Knopf, 1980. Schorske's pioneering work established the interconnectedness of comprehensive cultural changes in Vienna around the turn of the century and serves as an inspiration for the analysis undertaken here. His authoritative discussion of the Ringstrasse's intellectual and cultural origins is found in chapter 1, "The Ringstrasse, its Critics, and the Birth of Urban Modernism," pp. 24–115.

23. Ibid., p. 30.

24. For Vancaš's architectural career, see Jela Božić, "Arhitekt Josip Pl. Vancaš" (The architect Josip Vancaš), in Vojka Smiljanić-Djikić (ed.), *Graditelji Sarajeva* (The builders of Sarajevo), Sarajevo: Radio Sarajevo 3, 1988, pp. 379–90; and Boris Spasojević, *Arhitektura stambenih palata austrougarskog perioda u Sarajevu* (The architecture of residential palaces in the Austro-Hungarian period in Sarajevo), 2nd edn, Sarajevo: Rabic, 1999, p. 20.

25. Kreševljaković, *Sarajevo u vrijeme austrougarske uprave*, p. 121 n. 157.

26. Illustrations and brief architectural notes on hundreds of Sarajevo structures may be found in Ibrahim Krzović, *Arhitektura Bosne i Hercegovine, 1878–1918* (The architecture of Bosnia-Herzegovina), Sarajevo: Umjetnička galerija Bosne i Hercegovine, 1987.

27. Another storey was later added, giving the building its present cubic shape.

28. Jela Božić, "Izgradnja i arhitektura Zemaljskog muzeja u Sarajevu" (The construction and architecture of the Regional Museum in Sarajevo), in Almaz Dautbegović (ed.), *Spomenica stogodišnjice rada Zemaljskog muzeja Bosne i Hercegovine 1888–1988* (Commemoration of one hundred years of work of the Regional Museum in Bosnia-Herzegovina), Sarajevo: Zemaljski muzej Bosne i Hercegovine, 1988, p. 419.

29. For the authorities' considerations in constructing the Regional Government Building, see Božo Madžar, "Sto godine Vladine zgrade u Sarajevu (1885–1985)" (A hundred years of the government building in Sarajevo), *Glasnik arhiva i Društva arhivskih radnika Bosne i Hercegovine*, 25 (1985), pp. 249-55.

30. Nedžad Kurto, *Arhitektura Bosne i Hercegovina: razvoj bosanskog stila* (The architecture of Bosnia-Herzegovina: Development of the Bosnian style), Sarajevo: Sarajevo Publishing, 1998, pp. 14, 32.

31. Converted in the 1950s to the University and National Library, this building was attacked in August 1992 with incendiary shells from Serb guns around the city, creating a fire that burned most of the library's contents and flammable components of the interior.

32. Spasojević, *Arhitektura stambenih palata*, p. 22.

33. HHSA, Politisches Archiv, XL, 210, Szlávy to Dahlen, August 24, 1880.

34. Kruševac, *Bosansko-hercegovački listovi*, pp. 187–261, offers a discussion of the papers named here.

35. Kraljačić, *Kalajev režim*, p. 189.

36. Ibid., pp. 385–7.

37. "Provisorisches Status für die Errichtung einer Gemeindevertretung in der Stadt Sarajevo von 22 August 1878" (Provisional statute for establishing a commune representation in the city of Sarajevo of August 22, 1878), in Bosnien und die Hercegovina, Landesregierung, *Sammlung der Gesetze, Verordnungen und Normalweisungen von Bosnien und der Hercegovina* (Collection of laws, ordinances, and instructions of Bosnia-Herzegovina), Sarajevo: Landesdruckerei, 1880, 1:585–6.

38. Kruševac, *Sarajevo pod austro-ugarskom upravom*, pp. 60–1.

39. Berislav Gavranović, *Uspostava redovite katoličke hijerarhije u Bosni i Hercegovini 1881. godine* (Establishment of the Catholic religious hierarchy in Bosnia-Herzegovina), Belgrade: Popović, 1935, pp. 201–2.

40. On the changes in the vakufs, sheriat courts, and religious hierarchy, see Donia, *Islam under the Double Eagle*, pp. 20–4.

41. Kraljačić, *Kalajev režim*, p. 161, citing ABH, GFM, 3542/1888.

42. Ibid., p. 51.

43. The *Ziviladlatus* was the civilian head of Habsburg administration in Bosnia-Herzegovina. He reported to the *Landeschef*, typically a general, who in turn reported to the joint minister of finance.

44. Kruševac, *Sarajevo pod austro-ugarskom upravom*, p. 267, citing *Memoara Protopop Nedeljka* (The memoirs of Protopop Nedeljko), p. 79.

45. Ibid., p. 266, citing *Sarajevski list*, September 6, 1882.

46. Steven Beller, "Kraus's Firework: State Consciousness Raising in the 1908 Jubilee Parade in Vienna and the Problem of Austrian Identity," in Wingfield and Bucur (eds), *Staging the Past: The Politics of Commemoration in Habsburg Central Europe, 1848 to the Present*, West Lafayette, IN: Purdue University Press, 2001, p. 51. Beller notes that a similar "festive illumination of the city" was staged in Vienna in 1898 to commemorate the fortieth anniversary of Franz Joseph's coronation.

47. IAS, SGV, April 3, 1879.

48. IAS, SGV, December 18, 1888.

49. Kraljačić, *Kalajev režim*, pp. 163–4.

50. Ibid., p. 159.

51. Ibid., p. 146.

52. Avram Pinto, *Jevreji Sarajeva i Bosne i Hercegovine*, Sarajevo: Veselin Masleša, 1987, pp. 141–3.

53. Ibid., pp. 166–7.

54. The best contemporary survey of educational change in Habsburg times is Austria-Hungary, k. und k. Gemeinsam Finanzministerium, *Bericht über die Verwaltung von Bosnien und die Hercegovina* (Report on the administration of Bosnia-Herzegovina), Vienna: k.k. Hof- und Staatsdruckerei, 1906, pp. 153–229. See also Kruševac, *Sarajevo pod austro-ugarskom upravom*, pp. 393–409, and Mitar Papić, *Školstvo u Bosni i Hercegovini za vrijeme austro-ugarske okupacije* (Schooling in Bosnia-Herzegovina in the time of Austro-Hungarian occupation), Sarajevo: Veselin Masleša, 1972, pp. 7–19, 41–159, and two other studies by Mitar Papić, *Istorija srpskih škola u Bosni i Hercegovini* (The history of Serb schools in Bosnia-Herzegovina), Sarajevo: Veselin Masleša, 1978, and *Hrvatsko školstvo u Bosni i Hercegovini do 1918. godine* (Croat schooling in Bosnia-Herzegovina until 1918), Sarajevo: Veselin Masleša, 1982.

55. Kruševac, *Sarajevo pod austro-ugarskom upravom*, p. 404.

56. Ibid., p. 406.

57. Austria-Hungary, *Bericht über die Verwaltung*, pp. 172–3.

58. Kruševac, *Sarajevo pod austro-ugarskom upravom*, p. 402.

59. For literacy rates, see Bosnien und die Hercegovina Landesregierung, *Ergebnisse der Volkszählung 1910*, 4:14–43; and Kruševac, *Sarajevo pod austro-ugarskom upravom*, p. 409.

60. Almaz Dautbegović, "Uz stogodišnjicu Zemaljskog muzeja Bosne i Hercegovine u Sarajevu" (On the occasion of the hundredth anniversary of the Regional Museum of Bosnia-Herzegovina in Sarajevo), in Dautbegović (ed.), *Spomenica stogodišnjice rada Zemaljskog muzeja*, pp. 11–13.

61. Risto Besarović, *Iz kulturne prošlosti Bosne i Hercegovine (1878–1918)* (From the cultural past of Bosnia-Herzegovina), Sarajevo: Veselin Masleša, 1987, pp. 10–11. To make the findings of museum researchers more widely known in the rest of Europe, *Wissens-*

chaftliche Mittheilungen aus Bosnien und Hercegovina was published in Vienna from 1893 to 1916. It consisted of selected articles from *Glasnik* in German. Djordje Pejanović, *Bibliografija štampe Bosne i Hercegovine 1850–1941* (Bibliography of the press in Bosnia-Herzegovina), Sarajevo: Veselin Masleša, 1961, pp. 31–2, 34.

62. Kraljačić, *Kalajev režim*, pp. 267–8.
63. Marian Wenzel, *Ukrasni motivi na stećcima* (Oriental Motifs on Tombstones from Medieval Bosnia and Surrounding Regions), Sarajevo: Veselin Masleša, 1965, p. 15; and Marian Wenzel, "Bosnian and Herzegovinian Tombstones: Who Made Them and Why," *Südost Forschungen* (Munich), 21 (1962), pp. 102–43.
64. The case has been made best by John V. A. Fine, Jr., *The Bosnian Church: A New Interpretation*, Boulder, CO: East European Monographs, 1975; Marian Wenzel, "Bosnian History and Austro-Hungarian Policy: Some Medieval Belts, the Bogomil Romance and the King Tvrtko Graves," in Marian Wenzel, *Bosanski stil na stećcima i metalu/Bosnian Style on Tombstones and Metal*, Sarajevo: Sarajevo Publishing, 1999, pp. 169–205; and summarized by Malcolm, *Bosnia: A Short History*, pp. 27–42.

Chapter 4 The New Nationalism, Assassination, and War

1. Kraljačić, *Kalajev režim*, p. 367.
2. Božo Madžar, *Pokret Srba Bosne i Hercegovine za vjersko-prosvjetnu samoupravu* (The movement of the Serbs of Bosnia-Herzegovina for religious and educational autonomy), Sarajevo: Veselin Masleša, 1982, pp. 171–4.
3. Ibid., pp. 343–7.
4. Ibid., p. 419; Mustafa Imamović, *Pravni položaj i unutrašnjo-politički razvitak Bosne i Hercegovine od 1878–1914* (The legal status and internal political development of Bosnia-Herzegovina), 2nd edn, Sarajevo: Bosanski kulturni centar, 1997, p. 95; and *Sarajevski list*, August 19, 1905, p. 1.
5. Donia, *Islam under the Double Eagle*, pp. 55–9; and Zoran Grijak, *Politička djelatnost vrhbosanskog nadbiskupa Josipa Stadlera* (The political activity of Vrhbosna Archbishop Josip Stadler), Zagreb and Sarajevo: Hrvatski institut za povijest and Vrhbosanska nadbiskupija, 2001, pp. 244–8.
6. Grijak, *Politička djelatnost vrhbosanskog nadbiskupa Josipa Stadlera*, p. 224.
7. For the history of the Muslim autonomy movement, see Nusret Šehić, *Autonomni pokret Muslimana za vrijeme austrougarske uprave u Bosni i Hercegovini* (The autonomy movement of Muslims during Austro-Hungarian administration in Bosnia-Herzegovina), Sarajevo: Svjetlost, 1980; the excellent introduction in Ferdo Hauptmann (ed.), *Borba Muslimana Bosne i Hercegovine za vjersku vakufsko-mearifsku autonomiju. Gradja* (The struggle of the Muslims of Bosnia-Herzegovina for religious and cultural autonomy: Sources), Sarajevo: Arhiv Socijalističke Republike Bosne i Hercegovine, 1967, pp. 21–38; and Donia, *Islam under the Double Eagle*, pp. 70–166.
8. Božo Madžar, *Prosvjeta: Srpsko prosvjetno i kulturno društvo 1902–1949* (Prosvjeta: Serb educational and cultural society), Banja Luka and Srpsko Sarajevo: Akademija nauka Republike Srpske, 2001.
9. Ibrahim Kemura, *Uloga "Gajreta" u društvenom životu Muslimana Bosne i Hercegovine 1903–1941* (The role of Gajret in the societal life of the Muslims of Bosnia-Herzegovina, 1903–41), Sarajevo: Veselin Masleša, 1986.

10. Tomislav Išek, *Mjesto i uloga NKD Napredak u kulturnom životu Bosne i Hercegovine (1902– 1918.)* (The place and role of the national cultural society Napredak in the cultural life of Bosnia-Herzegovina, 1902–18), Sarajevo: Institut za istoriju Sarajevo and Hrvatsko kulturno društvo Napredak, 2002.

11. For the formation of political parties, see Mustafa Imamović, *Pravni položaj*, 1997, pp. 134–81; or his summary of the same developments in Mustafa Imamović, *Historija države i prava Bosne i Hercegovine* (The history of the state and laws of Bosnia-Herzegovina), Sarajevo: Magistrat, 2001, pp. 237–41.

12. See Donia, *Islam under the Double Eagle*, pp. 169–71.

13. Imamović, *Pravni položaj*, pp. 174–81.

14. Šaćir Filandra, *Bošnjačka politika u XX. stoljeću* (Bosniak politics in the twentieth century), Sarajevo: Sejtarija, 1998, p. 39.

15. On Serb factions and efforts to bring them into a single organization, see Kruševac, *Sarajevo pod austro-ugarskom upravom*, pp. 338–41, and Imamović, *Pravni položaj*, pp. 149–66.

16. Imamović, *Pravni položaj*, p. 157, citing *Srpska riječ*, May 26, 1907.

17. *Ibid.*, pp. 166–7; Luka Djaković, *Političke organizacije bosanskohercegovačkih katolika Hrvata* (The political organizations of the Catholic Croats of Bosnia-Herzegovina), vol. 1: *Do otvaranja Sabora 1910* (Until the opening of parliament in 1910), Zagreb: Globus, 1985; and Kruševac, *Sarajevo pod austro-ugarskom upravom*, p. 335.

18. Grijak, *Politička djelatnost vrhbosanskog nadbiskupa Josipa Stadlera*, pp. 454–6.

19. Hadžibegović, *Postanak radničke klase*, pp. 135–204, traces the growth of the working class primarily through statistical indicators.

20. Zdravko Antonić (ed.), *Istorija Saveza komunista Bosne i Hercegovine* (History of the League of Communists of Bosnia-Herzegovina), 2 vols, Sarajevo: Institut za istoriju and Oslobodjenje, 1990, 1:29–30, 40–4, describes the founding of the Social Democratic Party and the syndicate organization. This work is hereafter cited as Antonić (ed.), *Istorija SKBiH*.

21. Kruševac, *Sarajevo pod austro-ugarskom upravom*, p. 346, citing *Sarajevski list*, October 9, 1908.

22. Ibid.

23. Ibid., pp. 346–8.

24. Bernadotte Schmitt, *The Annexation of Bosnia, 1908–1909*, London: Cambridge University Press, 1937, pp. 46–7, 119, 226–9.

25. Kruševac, *Sarajevo pod austro-ugarskom upravom*, pp. 349–50.

26. Vojislav Bogićević, "Atentat Bogdana Žerajića 1910 godine" (Bogdan Žerajić's assassination in the year 1910), *Godišnjak Istoriskog društva Bosne i Hercegovine* (Annual of the historical society of Bosnia-Herzegovina), 6 (1954), pp. 87–102; and Vladimir Dedijer, *The Road to Sarajevo*, New York: Simon and Schuster, 1966, pp. 23–50, 177.

27. Odbor za izdavanje Spomenica pok. M. Srškiću (Committee for publication of a memorial to the deceased Milan Srškić), *Milan Srškić*, Sarajevo: Odbora za izdavanje Spomenica pok. M. Srškiću, 1938, p. 110. Hereafter cited as *Milan Srškić*.

28. Kreševljaković, *Sarajevo u vrijeme austrougarske uprave*, pp. 86–7.

29. IAS, SGV, February 16, 17; March, 2, 3, 23; April 6, 27; May 27; June 22—all in 1914.

30. W. A. Dolph Owings, Elizabeth Pribic, and Nikola Pribic (eds and translators), *The Sarajevo Trial*, 2 vols, Chapel Hill, NC: Documentary Publications, 1984. The accused assassins spoke freely during the twelve days of the trial, and their testimony provides detailed information on the manner in which they came together, their rendezvous in Sarajevo, and the passionate convictions that drove them to the deed. See also Martin Pappenheim, *Gavrilo Princips Bekenntnisse. Ein Geschichtlicher Beitrag zur Vorgeschichte des Attentates von Sarajevo* (Gavrilo Princip's confession: An historical contribution to the prehistory of the Sarajevo assassination), Vienna: Rudulf Lechner, 1926, the report of a psychiatrist who interviewed the assassin in his cell in 1916.

31. Veselin Masleša, *Mlada Bosna* (Young Bosnia) 2nd edn, Sarajevo: Veselin Masleša, 1990, pp. 35–7. The press was named after the author.

32. Papić, *Školstvo u Bosni i Hercegovini za vrijeme austro-ugarske okupacije*, pp. 178–9.

33. Dedijer, *The Road to Sarajevo*, chapter 10, "Primitive Rebels of Bosnia."

34. Papić, *Školstvo u Bosni i Hercegovini za vrijeme austro-ugarske okupacije*, pp. 178–9.

35. ABH, 1564/PrBH 1914. "Politička tajna gjačka društva" (Secret student political societies), Director of Sarajevo Teachers' School to Regional Government, November 23, 1910. After the assassination, the authorities reviewed earlier reports that might have made them more attentive to the dangers of student activism. They discovered the extensive report from 1910, and several officials commented upon it. Therefore the 1910 report is included in the folio of documents from 1914.

36. Ibid. The comments quoted here were appended in 1910 by an unidentified official explaining why the school director's recommendations were not implemented.

37. Jaroslav Šidak et al., *Povijest hrvatskog naroda g. 1860–1914* (History of the Croat people, 1860–1914), Zagreb: Školska knjiga, 1968, p. 276.

38. Ibid, p. 280.

39. Dedijer, *The Road to Sarajevo*, p. 264. See also ABH, 423/PrBH 1912: LR to GFM, March 7, 1912.

40. These demonstrations are described in ABH, 310/PrBH 1912: LR to GFM, February 19, 1912; and 423/PrBH 1912: LR to GFM, March 7, 1912.

41. ABH, 314/PrBH 1912: LR to GFM, February 20, 1912.

42. ABH, 322/PrBH 1912: LR to GFM, February 21, 1912.

43. ABH, 423/PrBH 1912: LR to GFM, March 4, 1912.

44. ABH, 325/PrBH 1912: LR to GFM, February 21, 1912.

45. Šidak et al., *Povijest hrvatskog naroda*, p. 283.

46. ABH, 1551/PrBH 1914. "Geheime Schulerorganisation an den b.h. Mittelschulen" (Secret student organization in the middle schools of Bosnia-Herzegovina). This twenty-five-page report, the preliminary result of the government's post-assassination investigation of student organizations, was forwarded to the Joint Finance Ministry on September 23, 1914. It contains reports on the events described here.

47. Ibid., p. 8.

48. Ibid., pp. 14–15.

49. Ibid., pp. 10–11.

50. Ibid., p. 19.

51. Vojislav Bogićević, "'Iznimne mjere' u Bosni i Hercegovini u maju 1913. godine" ("Exceptional measures" in Bosnia-Herzegovina in 1913), *Godišnjak Istoriskog društva Bosne i Hercegovine*, 7 (1955), pp. 209–18.

52. Ninety years after the deed, the most complete account of the archduke's final hours remains the press report in *Sarajevski list*, "Atentati na prijestolonasljednika i suprugu mu" (The assassinations of the successor to the throne and his wife), June 29, 1914, p. 3.

53. The article in *Sarajevski list* makes no mention of officials of the Serbian Orthodox community but states that Danilo Dimović, the Serb vice president of the Bosnian Parliament, was present to accompany the caskets to the train.

54. A preliminary report on these events, along with the reports of eight officers who commanded government security units during the demonstrations, was submitted on July 7, 1914, and contains the most comprehensive description of the attacks. ABH, 1116/PrBH 1914: "Die Unruhen in Sarajevo am 28 und 29. Juni 1914" (The unrest in Sarajevo on June 28 and 29, 1914), July 7, 1914; and enclosures.

55. Second enclosure to ABH, 1116/PrBH 1914, submitted by Political Adjunct v Troyer and Dr. Keller.

56. "Die Unruhen in Sarajevo."

57. A summary report on the demonstrations, including the casualty figures and an estimate of damage, was issued in January 1915 as part of a more comprehensive report. Ibid., pp. 206–42.

58. Vladimir Čorović, *Crna knjiga: Patnje Srba Bosne i Hercegovina za vreme Svetskog rata 1914–1918* (Black book: Agony of the Serbs of Bosnia-Herzegovina at the time of the world war), 3rd edn, Belgrade: Udruženje ratnih dobrovoljaca 1912–18. godine, 1996 (first published in 1920), cited in Božo Madžar (ed.), "Izvještaj vladinog komesara za glavni grad Bosne i Hercegovine Sarajevo o političkoj i privrednoj situaciji u Sarajevu od Sarajevskog atentata do kraja januara 1915. godine" (Report of the government commissar for the capital city of Bosnia-Herzegovina on the political and economic situation in Sarajevo from the Sarajevo assassination to the end of January 1915), *Glasnik arhiva i Društva arhivskih radnika Bosne i Hercegovine* (Journal of the archives and society of archival workers of Bosnia-Herzegovina), 24, 1986, p. 206 n. 2.

59. Ibid., p. 214.

60. Ibid., p. 211.

61. *Sarajevski list*, July 1, 1914.

62. IAS, SGV, January 21, 1915. Spaho used the debate to highlight the misuse of city funds in earlier years. After much speechifying, the tax was approved by a unanimous vote.

63. Kreševljaković, *Sarajevo u vrijeme austrougarske uprave*, p. 90.

64. Papić, *Školstvo u Bosni i Hercegovini za vrijeme austro-ugarske okupacije*, p. 17.

65. Kreševljaković, *Sarajevo u vrijeme austrougarske uprave*, p. 89.

66. On his wartime experiences, see *Milan Srškić*, pp. 5–7.

67. Ibid., p. 7.

Chapter 5 Royal Yugoslavia's Forgotten City

1. Aleksandar Pavković, *The Fragmentation of Yugoslavia: Nationalism in a Multinational State*, London: Macmillan Press, 1997, pp. 22–4, provides a succinct summary of these considerations in the formation of the royal South Slav state.

2. Michael Boro Petrovich, *A History of Modern Serbia, 1804–1918*, New York: Harcourt Brace Jovanovich, 1976, 2:611, 681. For an overview of political developments in Yugo-

slavia between the First and Second World Wars, see Joseph Rothschild, *East Central Europe between the Two World Wars*, Seattle: University of Washington Press, 1974.

3. Branislav Gligorijević's 3-volume *Kralj Aleksandar Karadjordjević*, Belgrade: Zuns, 1996–2003, is the definitive biography of the king.

4. *Narodno jedinstvo*, November 7, 1918, pp. 3–4.

5. Andrew Baruch Wachtel, *Making a Nation, Breaking a Nation: Literature and Cultural Politics in Yugoslavia*, Stanford University Press, 1998, p. 76. Wachtel's observation was a response to Ivo Banac's statement, "The Vidovdan constitution sanctioned the untenable centralist solution of Yugoslavia's national question. Reached without the participation—and against the will—of most of the non-Serb parties, it bore the seeds of further rancor." Wachtel describes Banac's book as "generally considered authoritative ... but not entirely unproblematic." Wachtel cites Banac, *The National Question in Yugoslavia: Origins, History, Politics*, Ithaca, NY: Cornell University Press, 1984, p. 404.

6. For a discussion of the distinction, see Bruce Bigelow, "Centralization Versus Decentralization in Interwar Yugoslavia," *Southeast Europe* 1, 2 (1974), pp. 157–72.

7. Nusret Šehić, *Bosna i Hercegovina 1918–1925: privredni i politički razvoj* (Bosnia-Herzegovina 1918–25: Economic and political development), Sarajevo: Institut za istoriju, 1991, p. 12–13, and Hamdija Kapidžić (ed.), "Rad Narodnog Vijeća SHS Bosne i Hercegovine u novembru i decembru 1918" (The work of the People's Council of the Serbs, Croats, and Slovenes of Bosnia-Herzegovina in November and December 1918), *Glasnik arhiva i Društva arhivista Bosne i Hercegovine* 3 (1963), pp. 148–50. I use the term "Regional Government" here to refer both to the People's Council and the government that it selected. The government consisted at first of a president (Atanasije Šola) and ten ministers.

8. *Narodno jedinstvo*, December 4, 1918, p. 3; and December 6, 1918, p. 3.

9. Banac, *The National Question in Yugoslavia*, especially pp. 169–202 and 359–77, offers a definitive review of party formation and programs during this time.

10. On the movement to unify major parties under a single umbrella Yugoslav organization, see Branislav Gligorijević, *Demokratska stranka i politički odnosi u Kraljevini Srba Hrvata i Slovenaca* (The Democratic Party and political relations in the Kingdom of the Serbs, Croats, and Slovenes), Belgrade: Institut za savremenu istoriju, 1970, pp. 29–44; Nedim Šarac, *Uspostavljanje šestojanuarskog režima 1929. godine sa posebnim osvrtom na Bosnu i Hercegovinu* (Establishment of the regime of January 6, 1929, with particular attention to Bosnia-Herzegovina), Sarajevo: Svjetlost, 1975, pp. 36–7; and Šehić, *Bosna i Hercegovina 1918–1925*, pp. 100–4.

11. Gligorijević, *Demokratska stranka*, pp. 46–56; and Banac, *The National Question*, pp. 169–89.

12. Šehić, *Bosna i Hercegovina 1918–1925*, pp. 100–1, citing the newspaper *Slovenski jug* (Sarajevo), December 3, 1918.

13. On the founding of the JMO and its leaders' negotiations with Pribićević, see Atif Purivatra, *Jugoslovenska muslimanska organizacija u političkom životu Kraljevine Srba Hrvata i Slovenaca* (The Yugoslav Muslim Organization in the political life of the Kingdom of Serbs, Croats, and Slovenes), Sarajevo: Svjetlost, 1974, pp. 75–81; and Banac, *The National Question*, pp. 359–77.

14. *Milan Srškić*, p. 194.

15. Ibid., p. 195.

16. Examples of these pejorative references can be found in Ivan Ribar, *Politički zapisi* (Political observations), Belgrade: Prosveta, 1948, 2:28; and Ivan Meštrović, *Uspomene na političke ljude i dogadjaje* (Memories of political people and events), Zagreb: Matica hrvatska 1969, p. 212.

17. Šehić, *Bosna i Hercegovina 1918–1925*, p. 131, citing the newspaper *Hrvatska sloga* (Croatian unity), October 27, 1919.

18. Tomislav Išek, *Djelatnost Hrvatske seljacke stranke u BiH do zavodjenja diktature* (Activities of the Croatian Peasant Party in Bosnia-Herzegovina until the imposition of dictatorship), Sarajevo: Svjetlost, 1981.

19. The history of the interwar communist and labor movements was exhaustively studied in the socialist period. The most informative studies include Rodoljub Čolaković (ed.), *Pregled istorije Saveza komunista Jugoslavije* (Survey of the history of the League of Communists of Yugoslavia), Belgrade: Institut za izučavanje radničkog pokreta, 1963; Budimir Miličić, *Radnička klasa Sarajeva 1919–1941* (The working class of Sarajevo), Sarajevo: Institut za istoriju, 1985, pp. 301–432; Šehić, *Bosna i Hercegovina 1918–1925*, pp. 73–98; Tomislav Kraljačić, "Razvoj i političke akcije mjesne organizacije KPJ u Sarajevu 1919–1920" (Development and political action of the local organization of the KP of Yugoslavia in Sarajevo), in *Glasnik arhiva i Društva arhivskih radnika Bosne i Hercegovine*, 6 (1966), pp. 181–94 (hereafter cited as "KPJ u Sarajevu"); and an excellent English-language survey, Ivo Banac, "The Communist Party of Yugoslavia during the Period of Legality, 1919–21," in Ivo Banac (ed.), *The Effects of World War I: The Class War after the Great War: The Rise of Communist Parties in East Central Europe, 1918–1921*, Boulder, CO: East European Monographs, 1983, pp. 188–230.

20. Čolaković (ed.), *Pregled istorije SKJ*, p. 38.

21. Miličić, *Radnička klasa Sarajeva*, pp. 100, 302.

22. See the statistics cited in Ibid., pp. 109–10, 335; and Jaša Romano, *Jevreji Jugoslavije 1941–1945. Žrtve genocida i učesnici NOR* (The Jews of Yugoslavia: Victims of genocide and freedom fighters), Belgrade: Savez jevrejskih opština Jugoslavije, 1980, p. 40.

23. "Zapisnik XI sjednice Glavnog odbora narodnog vijeća SHS za BiH, 8 November 1918" (Transcript of the eleventh session of the Main Board of the People's Council of Serbs, Croats, and Slovenes for Bosnia-Herzegovina), in Kapidžić (ed.), "Rad Narodnog Vijeća," pp. 170–3. The text of the Social Democrats' program is found in *Glas slobode*, November 9, 1918.

24. Čolaković (ed.), *Pregled istorije SKJ*, pp. 85–7.

25. I refer to the party as the KP of Yugoslavia from April 1919, when "communist" first appeared in its title, until 1953 when it changed its name to the *Savez Komunista* (SK; League of Communists) of Yugoslavia. It will be called the Social Democratic Party in the period before April 1919. Members inclined to evolutionary views will be called reformist Social Democrats; those seeking revolutionary change will be called Communists.

26. Ibrahim Karabegović, *Reformistički pravac u radničkom pokretu Bosne i Hercegovine 1919–1941. godine* (The reformist direction in the workers' movement of Bosnia-Herzegovina), Sarajevo: Svjetlost, 1979, pp. 20–46.

27. Kraljačić, "KPJ u Sarajevu," p. 184; Miličić, *Radnička klasa Sarajeva*, pp. 340–1; and Ahmed Hadžirović, *Sindikalni pokret u Bosni i Hercegovini 1918–1941* (The syndicate movement in Bosnia-Herzegovina), Belgrade: Rad, 1978, pp. 175–81.
28. Šehic, *Bosna i Hercegovina 1918–1925*, pp. 80–2.
29. Kraljačić, "KPJ u Sarajevu," p. 185.
30. Ibid.
31. IAS, SGV, May 5, 1919.
32. Šehic, *Bosna i Hercegovina 1918–1925*, pp. 92–3, citing letter of Svetozar Pribićević to Atanasije Šola, June 12, 1919.
33. Kraljačić, "KPJ u Sarajevu," pp. 185–6.
34. Miličić, *Radnička klasa Sarajeva*, p. 303.
35. Čolaković (ed.), *Pregled istorije SKJ*, p. 50.
36. Kraljačić, "KPJ u Sarajevu," p. 187.
37. *Narodno jedinstvo*, December 4, 1918, p. 3.
38. IAS, SGV, February 3, 1919.
39. Ibid., February 28 and March 1, 1919.
40. The US Congress approved the amendment and passed the law on June 4, 1919. It was ratified by the required number of states in 1920.
41. IAS, SGV, March 1, 1919.
42. Ibid., March 27, 1919.
43. Ibid., January 13, 1919.
44. Marković, in supporting a donation to the Zrinjski-Frankopan celebration for April 30, observed that Sarajevo "must hold a great cultural celebration, particularly in today's era of centralization and national unity." IAS, SGV, May 7, 1919.
45. Ibid., February 14, 1919.
46. Ibid., January 4, 1919. The four who declined were Asimaga Šabanović, Mehaga Zildžo, Mujaga Baščaušević, and Mujaga Bičakčić.
47. *Pravda*, Sarajevo, March 4, 1919, pp. 1–2.
48. The JMO letter was read by the president. IAS, SGV, May 14, 1919.
49. Ibid., May 14, 1919.
50. Ibid., September 23, 1920.
51. Imamović, *Historija Bošnjaka*, p. 500, provides an account of these successive steps.
52. Banac, "The Communist Party of Yugoslavia," p. 205, and Antonić (ed.), *Istorija SKBiH*, 1:105.
53. Uroš Nedimović, "Komparacije izmedju akcije Mlade Bosne (1914) i Crvene pravde (1921)" (Comparison between the actions of Young Bosnia and Red Justice), *Pregled* 7–8 (1974), pp. 741–8.
54. *Narodno jedinstvo*, December 31, 1920, pp. 1, 2.
55. Miličić, *Radnička klasa Sarajeva*, p. 308.
56. Ibid., p. 336.
57. Seka Brkljača. "Politika prema bosanskohercegovačkim opštinama i opštine prema politici u Kraljevini Srba, Hrvata i Slovenaca" (Policies toward municipalities of Bosnia-Herzegovina and of municipalities toward politics in the Kingdom of Serbs, Croats, and Slovenes), *Prilozi instituta za istoriju Sarajevo*, 33 (2004), pp. 233–51.
58. *Pravda*, September 9, 1927, p. 1.

59. Šarac, *Uspostavljanje šestojanuarskog režima*, pp. 76–110.

60. Ibid., p. 243.

61. IAS, SGV, February 14, 1929.

62. Šarac, *Uspostavljanje šestojanuarskog režima*, pp. 195 n. 7, 213.

63. IAS, SGV, March 21, 1929.

64. See *Milan Srškić*, pp. 129–41, for his role under the dictatorship.

65. Barbara Jelavich, *History of the Balkans: Twentieth Century*, Cambridge University Press, 1983, provides a concise summary of the 1931 constitution and elections.

66. Enes Karić (ed), *Reis Džemaludin Čaušević: prosvjetitelj i reformator* (Reis Džemaludin Čaušević: Enlightener and reformer), 2 vols, Sarajevo: Ljiljan, 2002, 1:316–26.

67. These measures are reported in *Narodno jedinstvo*, February 25, 1930, p. 1; and Šarac, *Uspostavljanje šestojanuarskog režima*, p. 218 n. 42.

68. John Lampe, *Yugoslavia as History: Twice There Was a Country*, New York: Cambridge University Press, 1996, p. 174.

69. Miličić, *Radnička klasa Sarajeva*, p. 93.

70. IAS, SGV, March 8, 1939.

71. *Narodno jedinstvo*, December 6, 1918, p. 3.

72. IAS, SGV, January 10, 1919.

73. Ibid. Delegate Niko Krešić.

74. Reports on this celebration are found in *Narodno jedinstvo*, May 19, 1919, p. 3; May 21, 1919, p. 2; and June 2, 1919, p. 3.

75. *Narodno jedinstvo*, December 15, 1920, p. 2; December 16, 1920, p. 1; and December 18, 1920, p. 2.

76. Ibid., December 21, 1920, p. 1.

77. Ibid., November 6, 1919, p. 3, and November 7, 1921, p. 3.

78. IAS, SGV, April 25, 1940.

79. Censuses were taken in 1921, 1931, and 1939, so population numbers from 1919 to 1941 are conjectural. A survey conducted by the city council in March 1919 concluded that the city had 58,000 residents (IAS, SGV, March 20, 1919). Extrapolating the trends between censuses, various scholars have estimated that the population in 1941 was between 85,000 and 100,000. An estimate of 90,000 has been given by Miličić, *Radnička klasa Sarajeva*, p. 95.

80. Kemal Hrelja, "Pregled društveno-ekonomskih prilika u Sarajevu između dva rata" (Survey of socioeconomic conditions in Sarajevo between the two wars), in Nisam Albahari *et al.* (eds), *Sarajevo u revoluciji* (Sarajevo in revolution), 4 vols, Sarajevo: Istorijski arhiv Sarajevo, 1976–81, 1:63–107. This collection of essays is indispensable for the study of the interwar and wartime periods. Essays will be cited by author, essay title, the abbreviation *SUR*, volume number, and page.

81. Miličić, *Radnička klasa Sarajeva*, p. 95; and Hrelja, "Pregled društveno-ekonomskih prilika," *SUR*, 1:103–4.

82. Wilbert E. Moore, *Economic Demography of Eastern and Southern Europe*, Geneva: League of Nations, 1945, pp. 17–143, discusses the factors common to eastern and southeastern Europe in contrast to the northern and central countries of the continent.

83. The complex issue of agrarian reform between the two wars is beyond the scope of this study. For a succinct summary, see Šehić, *Bosna i Hercegovina 1918–1925*, pp. 45–72.

84. "Owing to agrarian overpopulation the Yugoslav land reform created grave contradictions." Iván T. Berend and György Ránki, *Economic Development in East-Central Europe in the Nineteenth and Twentieth Centuries*, New York: Columbia University Press, 1974, p. 187.

85. Miličić, *Radnička klasa Sarajeva*, p. 96.

86. IAS, SGV, February 26, 1920.

87. Ibid., March 17, 1919.

88. Šehić, *Bosna i Hercegovina 1918–1925*, p. 294.

89. IAS, SGV, January 21, 1920.

90. *Narodno jedinstvo*, May 15, 1919, p. 3.

91. IAS, SGV, December 9 and 22, 1919.

92. Hrelja, "Pregled društveno-ekonomskih prilika," *SUR*, 1:75.

93. IAS, SGV, April 28, 1920.

94. Miličić, *Radnička klasa Sarajeva*, p. 73.

95. Ibid., p. 82.

96. Ibid., pp. 81–8.

97. IAS, SGV, March 17, 1940.

98. Hrelja, "Pregled društveno-ekonomskih prilika," *SUR*, 1:94.

99. *Jugoslovenska pošta*, July 1, 1939, p. 2.

100. Both Spaho's descendants and the Sarajevo press have often speculated that the JMO leader may have been poisoned. Personal communications with the author.

101. *Jugoslovenska pošta*, August 29, 1939, p. 3.

102. *Pravda*, August 26, 1939, p. 1.

103. Lampe, *Yugoslavia as History*, p. 191.

104. Dušan Bataković, *The Serbs of Bosnia and Hercegovina: History and Politics*, Paris: Dialogue, 1996, p. 98.

105. Čolaković (ed.), *Pregled istorije SKJ*, pp. 262–3.

106. IAS, SGV, March 8, 1929.

107. Ibid., March 15, 1940.

108. Ibid., March 17, 1940.

109. Ibid., December 23, 1940.

Chapter 6 Occupation and Urban Resistance in the Second World War

1. Svato Batinica, "Komunisti 'Konstruktive' u Vogošći i bombardovanje Rajlovca" (Communists of "Konstruktiva" in Vogošća and the bombing of Rajlovac), *SUR*, 2:96–7.

2. Božo Madžar, "Ljudske i materijalne žrtve Sarajeva u toku Drugog svjetskog rata" (Human and material damage to Sarajevo in the Second World War), *SUR*, 4:649. The author cites one estimate that three hundred Sarajevans died from bombing attacks in the course of the war.

3. Vladimir Dedijer, *The War Diaries of Vladimir Dedijer*, Ann Arbor: University of Michigan Press, 1990, 1:5–6. Dedijer, together with a small band of Communists and sympathizers, fled Belgrade in search of a resistance force and reached Sarajevo on the night of April 11–12. They remained until April 15, then escaped by jumping onto a train bound for eastern Bosnia.

4. Aleksandar Stajić i Jakov Papo, "Ubistva i drugi zločini izvršeni nad jevrejima u Bosni i Hercegovini u toku neprijateljske okupacije" (Murder and other crimes committed against Jews in Bosnia-Herzegovina during enemy occupation), in Kamhi (ed.), *Spomenica dolaska Jevreja u BiH*, p. 228.

5. Seka Brkljača, "Bosanskohercegovački boksit kao strateška sirovina (1918–1945)" (Bosnian-Herzegovinian bauxite as a strategic raw material), *Časopis za suvremenu povijest* (Journal of contemporary history), 31, 2 (1999), pp. 341–57.

6. Enver Redžić; *Bosnia and Herzegovina in the Second World War*, London: Frank Cass, 2005, p. 9. Redžić points out that the Germans had carefully identified their economic and strategic interests in Bosnia-Herzegovina well before the war began.

7. Muharem Kreso, "Sarajevo-Sjedište okupacionog sistema u Drugom svjetskom ratu" (Sarajevo: Seat of the occupation system in the Second World War), in Dževad Juzbašić (ed.), *Prilozi historiji Sarajeva* (Papers on the history of Sarajevo), Sarajevo: Institut za istoriju and Orijentalni institut, 1997, p. 360.

8. Rafael Brčić, "Okupacioni sistem i ustaška Nezavisna Država Hrvatska u Sarajevu (1941–43)" (The occupation system and Ustasha Independent State of Croatia in Sarajevo), *SUR*, 2:258.

9. Jozo Tomasevich, *War and Revolution in Yugoslavia: Occupation and Collaboration*, Stanford University Press, 2001, pp. 335–40; Redžić; *Bosnia and Herzegovina in the Second World War*, pp. 63–8.

10. On the creation of the NDH and the role of Ante Pavelić, see Fikreta Jelić-Butić, *Ustaše i Nezavisna Država Hrvatska, 1941–1945* (The Ustasha and the Independent State of Croatia), Zagreb: Liber, 1977, pp. 71–82.

11. Matteo J. Milazzo, *The Chetnik Movement and the Yugoslav Resistance*, Baltimore: Johns Hopkins University Press, 1975, p. 6.

12. Tomasevich, *War and Revolution in Yugoslavia*, p. 336.

13. On the delineation of NDH territory, see Tomasevich, *War and Revolution in Yugoslavia*, pp. 83–96; 234–43; and Brčić, "Okupacioni sistem," *SUR*, 2:251–4.

14. Brčić, "Okupacioni sistem," *SUR*, 2:259–62.

15. Sajma Sarić, "Arhivski fond velike župe Vrhbosne" (Archival collection of the grand governor of Vrhbosna [Sarajevo]), *Glasnik arhiva i Društva arhivskih radnika Bosne i Hercegovine*, 14–15, 1974–5, p. 37.

16. Ibid., p. 39. The four Muslim grand governors were Derviš Omerović (June 3–September 26, 1941), Ismetbeg Gavran Kapetanović (September 26, 1941–January 21, 1943), Muhamed Kulenović (January 21, 1943–November 5, 1944), and Ragib Čapljić (November 5, 1944 to April 6, 1945).

17. The building, stripped of its minarets after the Second World War, is still referred to in Zagreb as "the mosque" (*džamija*).

18. Jelić-Butić, *Ustaše i Nezavisna Država Hrvatska*, pp. 165–8.

19. Bataković, *Serbs of Bosnia and Herzegovina*, p. 103, and Madžar, "Ljudske i materijalne žrtve Sarajeva," *SUR*, 4:654.

20. Borivoje Knežić, "Neuspjeli pokušaji četnika da formiraju ravnogorsku organizaciju u Sarajevu" (Unsuccessful attempt by the Chetniks to form a Ravna Gora organization in Sarajevo), SUR, 3:622.

21. On these decrees, see Stajić and Papo, "Ubistva i drugi zločini," in Kamhi (ed.), *Spomenica dolaska Jevreja u BiH*, pp. 218–27.

22. Seka Brkljača, "Uništavanje materijalne osnove jevreja u BiH u Drugom svjetskom ratu" (Annihilation of the material foundations of the Jews in Bosnia-Herzegovina during the Second World War), in Muhamed Nezirović (ed.), *Sefarad 92: Zbornik radova* (Sefarad 92: Collection of works), Sarajevo: Institut za istoriju and Jevrejska zajednica Bosne i Hercegovine, 1995, pp. 201–12. This volume is a collection of papers delivered at a conference in September 1992 while Sarajevo was under siege.

23. Josip Albahari Čučo, "KPJ i pogrom nad Jevrejima" (The KP of Yugoslavia and the pogrom of Jews), *SUR*, 2:677–93.

24. Esad Čengić, "Sarajevski jevreji u II svjetskom ratu" (Sarajevo Jews in the Second World War), in Nezirović (ed.), *Sefarad 92*, p. 174.

25. Knežić, "Neuspjeli pokušaji četnika da formiraju ravnogorsku organizaciju," *SUR*, 3:622–3.

26. Emily Greble Balić, "The Last Months of Wartime: Sarajevo's Experience," paper presented at the conference, "60 godine od završetka drugog svjetskog rata—Kako se sjećati 1945. godine?" (Sixty years since the end of the Second World War: How to remember 1945?), Sarajevo, May 13, 2005.

27. Čučo, "KPJ i pogrom nad Jevrejima," *SUR*, 2:681–2.

28. ABH, Srećko Bujas, "Zločini nad Jevrejima u gradu Sarajevo" (Crimes against Jews in the city of Sarajevo), in fascicle "Gradska komisija za utvrdjivanje zločina okupatora i njihovih pomagača za grad Sarajevo" (City commission for establishing the crimes of the occupiers and their assistants in the city of Sarajevo).

29. Ibid., p. 10.

30. Stajić and Papo, "Ubistva i drugi zločini," in Kamhi (ed.), *Spomenica dolaska Jevreja u BiH*, pp. 235–41.

31. Ibid., pp. 235–6.

32. Danilo Štaka, "Igmanci u Kalinovićkom NOP odredu" (Residents of Igman in the Kalinovik units of the people's liberation movement), SUR 3:259.

33. Jaša Romano, *Jevreji Jugoslavije*, p. 218.

34. Slavko Goldstein, "Jews in the National Liberation War," in Slavko Goldstein (ed), *Jews in Yugoslavia*, Zagreb: Muzejski prostor, 1988, pp. 122–3.

35. Madžar, "Ljudske i materijalne žrtve Sarajeva," *SUR*, 4:660.

36. Čengić, "Sarajevski jevreji," in Nezirović (ed.), *Sefarad 92*, p. 181.

37. Stajić and Papo, "Ubistva i drugi zločini," in Kamhi (ed.), *Spomenica dolaska Jevreja u BiH*, p. 240.

38. Marko Attila Hoare, "The Chetnik-Partisan Conflict and the Origins of Bosnian Statehood," Ph.D. dissertation, Yale University, 2000, p. 246. Under the pressure of the Serb peasant uprising in Herzegovina, the KP organization there proclaimed the uprising on June 24, 1941, well before being ordered to do so by party superiors.

39. Uglješa Danilović, "Sarajevo i sarajevska oblast u ustanku naroda Bosne i Hercegovine (oktobar 1941–maj 1942.)" (Sarajevo and the Sarajevo region in the uprising of the peoples of Bosnia-Herzegovina, October 1941–May 1942), *SUR*, 3:13.

40. Zdravko Antonić, "Sprovodjenje odluka partije o podizanju ustanka u sarajevskoj oblasti" (Implementation of party decisions on raising rebellion in the Sarajevo district), *SUR*, 2:301.

41. Ibid., 3:10.
42. On the origins of the Chetnik movement, see Nusret Šehić, *Četništvo u Bosni i Herce-govini (1918–1941). Politička uloga i oblici djelatnosti četničkih udruženja* (The Chetnik movement in Bosnia-Herzegovina: The political role and forms of activities of Chetnik associations), Sarajevo: Akademija nauka i umjetnosti Bosne i Hercegovine, 1971, pp. 9–54; Milazzo, *The Chetnik Movement*, pp. 14–17; and Jozo Tomasevich, *The Chetniks: War and Revolution in Yugoslavia, 1941–1945*, Stanford University Press, 1975, pp. 122–6.
43. "Program Četničkog pokreta Draža Mihailović od septembra 1941. za vreme i posle završetka Drugog svetskog rata upućen izbegličkoj vladi Kraljevine Jugoslavije" (Program of the Chetnik movement of Draža Mihailović from September 1941 for the time of, and after, the Second World War, directed to the government-in-exile of royal Yugoslavia), in Yugoslavia, Vojnoistoriski institut, *Zbornik dokumenata i podataka o naro-dnooslobodilačkom ratu jugoslovenskih naroda* (Collection of documents and data on the people's liberation war of the Yugoslav peoples), Belgrade: Vojnoistorijski institut Jugoslovenske narodne armije, 1949–86, 14, 1:28. Hereafter cited as *ZNOR*, with document title, volume (*tom*), book (*knjiga*), and page numbers.
44. Štaka, "Igmanci u Kalinovičkom NOP odredu," SUR, 3:259–62.
45. On Chetnik putsches, see Redžić, *Bosnia and Herzegovina in the Second World War*, pp. 138–40; and Danilović, "Sarajevo i sarajevska oblast," *SUR*, 3:52.
46. Hasan Ljubunčić, "Dani nevolja i previranja" (Days of turmoil and turbulence), *SUR*, 3:611.
47. Ibid., 3:617.
48. Todor Perović to Dobroslav Jevdjević, September 29, 1943, Arhiv vojno-istorijski institut, Chetnik archive, k. 223, 32/5–1, Belgrade, cited by Knežić, "Neuspjeli pokušaji četnika da formiraju ravnogorsku organizaciju u Sarajevu," SUR, 3:623.
49. Germans and Chetniks collaborated most frequently at the local level, allowing each side to disclaim widespread cooperation with the other. For an account of the complex process of expanded Chetnik-German collaboration in this period, see Tomasevich, *The Chetniks*, pp. 315–88.
50. On the Chetnik efforts in Sarajevo in 1944–5, see Nedim Šarac, "Uslovi i pravci razvoja narodnooslobodilačkog pokreta u Sarajevu od novembra 1943. do april 1945. godine" (Conditions and directions of development of the people's liberation movement in Sarajevo from November 1943 to April 1945), *SUR*, 4:19, 25–6, 56.
51. Ibid., 4:25.
52. Ibid., citing Arhiv Muzeja revolucije Sarajevo (after 1992 called the Istorijski muzej Sarajevo), no. 5763.
53. Tomasevich, *The Chetniks*, p. 435.
54. Filandra, *Bošnjačka politika*, pp. 157, 165.
55. Enver Redžić, *Muslimansko autonomaštvo i 13. SS divizija: autonomija Bosne i Hercegovine i Hitlerov Treći Rajh* (Muslim autonomism and the 13th SS Division: The autonomy of Bosnia-Herzegovina and Hitler's Third Reich), Sarajevo: Svjetlost, 1987, p. 22.
56. On the quest for autonomy within the NDH, see Filandra, *Bošnjačka politika*, pp. 161–5.
57. Ibid., p. 162.

58. Two able summaries of political diversity among the Muslims of Bosnia-Herzegovina during the war are found in Redžić, *Bosnia and Herzegovina in the Second World War*, pp. 164–92; and Filandra, *Bošnjačka politika*, pp. 157–95.

59. Jelić-Butić, *Ustaše i Nezavisna Država Hrvatska*, p. 200, citing "Glavni stožer domobranstva za drugu polovicu rujna 1941" (Main home guard center for the second half of September 1941).

60. Filandra, *Bošnjačka politika*, p. 184.

61. Ogla Marasović, "Narodnooslobodilački pokret u gradu u prvoj godini ustanka" (The people's liberation movement in the city in the first year of the uprising), *SUR*, 2:488–9.

62. Filandra, *Bošnjačka politika*, p. 163, citing Bošnjački institut, "Zbirka dokumenata o genocidu nad Bošnjacima u Drugom svjetskom ratu" (Collection of documents on genocide against Bosniaks in the Second World War), pp. 160–6.

63. Redžić, *Bosnia and Herzegovina in the Second World War*, p. 175; and Filandra, *Bošnjačka politika*, pp. 163–72.

64. Redžić, *Bosnia and Herzegovina in the Second World War*, p. 178.

65. Ibid.; Redžić, *Muslimansko autonomaštvo*, pp. 84–153.

66. Those serving in units outside the city during the Second World War are referred to in this chapter as the Partisans. These units were first called the People's Liberation Army, then the People's Liberation Yugoslav Army, the Yugoslav Army, and as of March 1, 1945, the Armed Forces of Democratic Federative Yugoslavia (*Oružana sila Demokratske Federativne Jugoslavije*). The army was known for most of the postwar period as the Yugoslav People's Army. See Šarac, "Uslovi i pravci," *SUR*, 4:57. The urban organization, which late in the war designated strike groups but never formally had a military wing, is referred to as the Sarajevo KP.

67. Čolaković (ed.), *Pregled istorije SKJ*, pp. 306, 341.

68. Ibid., pp. 358–9.

69. Hoare, *The Chetnik-Partisan Conflict*, p. 300.

70. Antonić, "Sprovodjenje odluka partije," *SUR*, 2:308.

71. Drago Borovčanin, "Sarajevo u narodnooslobodilačkom pokretu 1941–1945" (Sarajevo in the people's liberation movement), in Juzbašić (ed.), *Prilozi historiji Sarajeva*, p. 383; and Danilović, "Sarajevo i sarajevska oblast," *SUR*, 3:14.

72. Marasović, "Narodnooslobodilački pokret," *UR*, 2:497–503.

73. Author interview with Vladimir Velebit, Zagreb, October 5, 2000.

74. Marasović, "Narodnooslobodilački pokret," *SUR*, 2:476.

75. Ibid., 2:491–2.

76. Danilović, "Sarajevo i sarajevska oblast," *SUR*, 3:10.

77. Antonić, "Sprovodjenje odluka partije," *SUR*, 2:310.

78. Ibid., 2:313.

79. Stajić and Papo, "Ubistva i drugi zločini," in Kamhi (ed.), *Spomenica dolaska Jevreja u BiH*, p. 233.

80. Marasović, "Narodnooslobodilački pokret," *SUR*, 2:475, citing *Službeni list Povjerenstva za Bosnu i Hercegovinu Nezavisne Države Hrvatske* (Official gazette of the Commission for Bosnia-Herzegovina of the Independent State of Croatia), no. 29, p. 3.

81. Danilović, "Sarajevo i sarajevska oblast," *SUR*, 3:14; and Antonić, "Sprovodjenje odluka partije," *SUR*, 2:321.

82. Antonić (ed.), *Istorija SK BiH*, 1:236–7.

83. Marasović, "Narodnooslobodilački pokret," *SUR*, 2:476.

84. Ibid., 2:484.

85. "Izvještaj delegata pokrajinskog komitet KPJ za Bosnu i Hercegovinu od novembra 1941. god. o raspoloženju Muslimana, masovnom hapšenju i proslavi oktobarske revolucije u Sarajevu" (Report of the delegates of the regional committee of the KP for Bosnia-Herzegovina from November 1941 regarding the disposition of Muslims, massive arrests and celebration of the October revolution in Sarajevo), *ZNOR*, 4, 2:157–8.

86. Ratko Jovičić and Dušan Jovanović, "Borbe obnovljenog romanijskog NOP odreda" (Battles of the regenerated Romanija unit of the people's liberation movement), *SUR*, 4:321.

87. After successful operations in eastern Bosnia, the Germans shifted their offensive to northwestern Bosnia in hopes of exterminating the Partisan resistance movement there.

88. "Perić Miloša Vladimir Valter," *SUR*, 4:799.

89. The following review the content and significance of these meetings: Drago Borovčanin, *Izgradnja bosansko-hercegovačke državnosti u uslovima NOR-a* (The building of Bosnian-Herzegovinian statehood in the conditions of the people's liberation war), Sarajevo: Svjetlost, 1979, pp. 144–87; and Redžić, *Bosnia and Herzegovina in the Second World War*, pp. 216–34.

90. Šarac, "Uslovi i pravci," *SUR*, 4:16–17.

91. Ibid., 4:56–7.

92. Interview with Landrum Bolling, May 31, 2002.

93. Lampe, *Yugoslavia as History*, p. 221.

94. Military operations are summarized in Dušan Uzelac and Muharem Kreso, "Sarajevska operacija (1. mart–12. april 1945. godine)" (The Sarajevo Operation, March 1–April 12, 1945), *SUR*, 4:671–712.

95. Šarac, "Uslovi i pravci," *SUR*, 4:60.

96. For a succinct summary of these changes, see Madžar, "Ljudske i materijalne žrtve Sarajeva," *SUR*, 4:653–61; Šarac, "Uslovi i pravci," *SUR*, 4:15–17; Kreso, "Sarajevo–Sjedište okupacionog sistema u Drugom svjetskom ratu," in Juzbašić (ed.), *Prilozi historiji Sarajeva*, pp. 361–2; and David Davidović and Dragutin Kosovac, "Društveno i političko stanje u Sarajevu neposredno poslije oslobodjenja" (The social and political situation in Sarajevo immediately after liberation), in Miodrag Čanković (ed.), *Sarajevo u socijalističkoj Jugoslaviji* (Sarajevo in socialist Yugoslavia), 2 vols, Sarajevo: Istorijski arhiv Sarajevo, 1988–90, 1:11. This two-volume collection of studies and essays is hereafter abbreviated *SUSJ*.

97. Madžar, "Ljudske i materijalne žrtve Sarajeva," *SUR*, 4:653, citing a comprehensive study by a commission of the city's veteran organization, "Izvještaj o radu na provjeravanju spiskova poginulih boraca i zrtava fašističkog terror" (Report on the work of verifying lists of fallen soldiers and victims of fascist terror), Sarajevo: GOSUBNOR-a, 1981.

98. Uzelac and Kreso, "Sarajevska operacija," *SUR*, 4:700.

99. Šarac, "Uslovi i pravci," *SUR*, 4:15.

Chapter 7 Sarajevo under Socialism

1. Ahmet Djonlagić, "Kroz drevne vratničke kapije u Sarajevo" (Through the ancient Vratnik gate into Sarajevo), *SUR*, 4:717–24, describes the triumphal celebrations of April 5 and 6, 1945.

2. Ibid., 1:19.

3. Dragutin Kosovac, "Uspostavljanje narodne vlasti u oslobodjenom gradu" (Establishment of the people's authority in the liberated city), *SUR*, 4:734.

4. Ibid., 4:736.

5. Ibid., 4:740.

6. Ilija Čuk, "Prva prvomajska proslava u slobodnom gradu" (The first of May celebration in the liberated city), *SUSJ*, 1:342–7.

7. Ilija Čuk, "Obnova rada u Glavnoj željezničkoj radionici" (Resumption of work in the Main Railway Workshop), *SUSJ*, 1:429.

8. Davidović and Kosovac, "Društveno i političko stanje," *SUSJ*, 1:32.

9. Ibid., *SUSJ*, 1:21.

10. ABH. Zbirka Narodni oslobodilački rat (people's liberation war collection), Kutija (box) 1, "Zapisnik Okruznog Komiteta KPJ za Sarajevo" (Transcript of the regional committee of the Communist Party of Yugoslavia for Sarajevo), Document # 74: "Stanje na terenu" (The situation on the ground), April 11, 1945, cited in Balić, "The Last Months of Wartime: Sarajevo's Experience," pp. 15–16.

11. Jelena Čišić, "Na prvom kongresu USAOBiH-a" (At the first congress of the United Alliance of Antifascist Youth of Bosnia-Herzegovina), *SUSJ*, 1:261–6.

12. Borko Vukobrat, "Prvi Kongres USAOBiH-a i otkrivanje spomen-ploče Gavrilu Principu" (The first congress of the United Alliance of Antifascist Youth of Bosnia-Herzegovina and the unveiling of the memorial plaque for Gavrilo Princip), *SUSJ*, 1:269.

13. Ibid.

14. Marija Divčić and Senija Milišić, "Organizacija antifašističkog fronta žena" (The organization of the Antifascist Women's Front), *SUSJ*, 1:295–315.

15. IAS, SGV, April 20, 1945. These minutes are entitled, in full, "Zapisnik 1. sjednice Gradskog Narodnog Oslobodilačkog Odbora za grad Sarajevo sastavljen dana 20. aprila 1945. god." (Minutes of the first session of the City People's Liberation Committee for the City of Sarajevo convened on April 20, 1945).

16. "Dušan Vasiljević, *advokat* (attorney); Mate Serka, *trgovac* (merchant); Ferid Čengić, *tipografski radnik* (typesetter)."

17. Dušan Milidragović, "Organizovanje i izgradnja narodne vlasti u Sarajevu" (Organization and founding of the people's authority in Sarajevo), *SUSJ*, 1:75.

18. Dane Olbina, "Povratak u Sarajevo" (Return to Sarajevo), *SUSJ*, 1:40. "For the first time we saw the earth from a bird's perspective and from there we recognized details on the ground."

19. IAS, SGV, September 29, 1945.

20. Ibid., April 20 and 21, 1945.

21. Ibid., September 20, 1945.

22. Ibid., August 17 and 18, 1945.

23. Milidragović, "Organizovanje i izgradnja narodne vlasti," *SUSJ*, 1:82.

24. IAS, SGV, May 4, 1945. A commission was established to provide assistance to everyone in these categories of the victims of war.

25. Ibid., June 24, 1945.

26. Ibid.

27. Ibid., September 20, 1945. In November 1946 the commission was reorganized to include officials of the government of Bosnia-Herzegovina and the Yugoslav Army.

28. Ibid., September 14, 1948.

29. Ibid., April 28, 1945.

30. Ibid., September 20, 1945.

31. Duško Milidragović, "Upravljanje gradom Sarajevom za posljednjih 50 godina" (Administration of the city of Sarajevo in the past fifty years), in Juzbašić (ed.), *Prilozi historiji Sarajeva*, p. 488.

32. Munevera Hadžišehović, *A Muslim Woman in Tito's Yugoslavia*, College Station: Texas AM University Press, 2003, p. 151.

33. Dane Maljković, "Tramvaj do Ilidže" (The tram to Ilidža), *SUSJ*, 2:438–42.

34. Filandra, *Bošnjačka politika u XX stoljeću*, pp. 215–16.

35. Ibid., pp. 212–13.

36. Husnija Kamberović, *Prema modernom društvu; Bosna i Hercegovina od 1945. do 1953. godine*. Tešanj: Centar za kulturu i obrazovanje Tešanj, 2000.

37. Milidragović, "Organizovanje i izgradnja narodne vlasti," *SUSJ*, 1:82–3, citing article 25, "Opšti zakon o narodnim odborima" (General law on people's committees), *Federativne Narodne Republike Jugoslavije, Službeni List* (The official gazette of the Federal Republic of Yugoslavia), 43/45, May 25, 1946.

38. Bogdan Maksimović, "Stadion 'Koševo'" (The Koševo Stadium), *SUSJ*, 1:586.

39. Borivoje Ostojić, "Početak izgradnje stambenog naselja Čengić Vila" (Commencement of building the residential settlement Čengić Vila), *SUSJ*, 1:692.

40. Carol S. Lilly, *Power and Persuasion: Ideology and Rhetoric in Communist Yugoslavia, 1944–1953*, Boulder, CO: Westview, 2001, pp. 120–4, for the problem of coercion in recruiting for the youth brigades.

41. Hadžišehović, *A Muslim Woman in Tito's Yugoslavia*, p. 146.

42. Salko Aljović, "Izgradnja prve faze stadiona 'Koševo'" (Building the first phase of the Koševo Stadium), *SUSJ*, 1:288.

43. Maksimović, "Stadion 'Koševo'," *SUSJ*, 1:587.

44. Ibid., 1:589.

45. Miladin Draškić, "Željezničari grade stadion 'Grbavicu'" (Railway workers build the Grbavica Stadium), *SUSJ*, 1:591–4.

46. Divčić and Milišić, "Organizacija antifašističkog fronta žena," *SUSJ*, 1:302–8.

47. Ibid., 1:311.

48. Senija Milišić, "Emancipacija muslimanske žene u Bosni i Hercegovini nakon oslobodjenja (1947–1952)" (The emancipation of Muslim women in Bosnia-Herzegovina

after liberation), master's thesis, University of Sarajevo, 1987, pp. 47–57, offers an account of the campaign and its results.

49. Gazi Husrevbegova biblioteka (Gazi Husrevbeg Library), Arhiv Rijaseta Islamske Zajednice Bosne i Hercegovine (archive of the headquarters of the Islamic religious community of Bosnia-Herzegovina), Ulema-medžlis (Supreme Islamic religious council): 294/47 (1947). I am indebted to Emily Greble Balić for bringing this document to my attention.

50. Ibid.

51. Milišić, "Emancipacija muslimanske žene," p. 57.

52. Davidović and Kosovac, "Društveno i političko stanje," SUSJ, 1:34.

53. Senija Milišić, "Institucionalizacija nauke u Bosni i Hercegovini (1945–1958)" (The institutionalization of science in Bosnia-Herzegovina), Ph.D. dissertation, University of Sarajevo, 2004.

54. ABH, Arhiv Bosne i Hercegovine 1947–1977. Povodom tridesetogodišnjice osnivanja Arhiva i početka rada arhivske službe u Bosni i Hercegovini (The Archive of Bosnia-Herzegovina, 1947–77, on the occasion of the thirtieth anniversary of founding the archive and the beginning of the work of archival service in Bosnia-Herzegovina), Sarajevo: Svjetlost, 1977, p. 5.

55. Orijentalni institut u Sarajevu 1950–2000 / The Institute for Oriental Studies in Sarajevo 1950–2000, Sarajevo: Orijentalni Institut, 2000, pp. 5–7.

56. Mustafa Dervišević et al., Vodić kroz fondove i zbirke istorijskog arhiva Sarajevo (Guide to the holdings and collections of the Historical Archive of Sarajevo), Sarajevo: Sarajevo: Istorijski arhiv Sarajevo, 2003, p. 5.

57. Džemal Čelić, "Kulturne djelatnosti u našem gradu" (Cultural activity in our city), SUSJ, 1:446.

58. Antonić (ed.), Istorija SK BiH, 2:154.

59. Ibid.

60. Ahmed Tafro, "Industrija" (Industry), SUSJ, 1:397.

61. Kosovac, "Uspostavljanje narodne vlasti," SUR, 4:743.

62. Čuk, "Obnova rada," SUSJ, 1:426, discusses the party's leading role in the Main Railway Workshop's return to productivity in a matter of days.

63. Rudolf Bićanić, Economic Policy in Socialist Yugoslavia. Cambridge: Cambridge University Press, 1973, pp. 22–40; and Susan Woodward, Socialist Unemployment: The Political Economy of Yugoslavia, 1945–1990, Princeton University Press, 1995, pp. 64–97.

64. Dennison Rusinow, The Yugoslav Experiment, 1948–1974, London: Hurst/Berkeley: University of California Press, 1977, p. 20.

65. IAS, SGV, September 20, 1945.

66. Avdo Salčić, "Specifičnosti razvoja privrede u gradu" (The specifics of economic development in the city), SUSJ, 1:385.

67. Ibid., 1:394.

68. Ibid., 1:389–93, summarizes the goals and achievements of the first five-year plan in Sarajevo.

69. The authoritative work on the divisions created within Yugoslavia by the split is Ivo Banac, With Stalin against Tito: Cominformist Splits in Yugoslav Communism, Ithaca, NY: Cornell University Press, 1988.

70. Antonić (ed.), *Istorija SK BiH*, 2:57. Approximately 205 of the 450 suspected Cominformists in Bosnia-Herzegovina were members of the Sarajevo KP. From 1948 to 1950 nearly 2,000 Bosnians, many of them Sarajevans, were purged for sympathizing with the Soviet Union.

71. IAS, SGV, September 29, 1945.

72. Ibid., December 10, 1945.

73. Ostojić, "Početak izgradanje stambenog naselja Čengić Vila," *SUSJ*, 1:688.

74. Milidragović, "Organizovanje i izgradnja narodne vlastu," *SUSJ*, 1:74, 87.

75. *Oslobodjenje*, December 7, 1948, p. 1, offers one of many examples.

76. Antonić (ed.), *Istorija SK BiH*, 1:71, 98.

77. Rusinow, *The Yugoslav Experiment*, p. 56. The pilot project was announced in a joint declaration of the economic council of the federal government and the central committee of the trades union federation on December 23, 1949.

78. Omer Ibrahimagić and Srebrenka Vidjen, "Uvodjenje i razvoj radničkog samoupravljanja i društvenog upravljanja u gradu" (The introduction and development of workers' self-management and social administration in the city), *SUSJ*, 2:31–2.

79. Rusinow, *Yugoslav Experiment*, p. 58. The federal assembly passed the "Basic Law on the Management of State Economic Enterprises and Higher Economic Associations of the Work Collectives" on June 27, 1950.

80. Ibrahimagić and Vidjen, "Uvodjenje i razvoj radničkog samoupravljanja," *SUSJ*, 2:35–6, citing *Oslobodjenje*, August 5, 1951.

81. R. A. French and F. E. Ian Hamilton, "Is There a Socialist City?" in R. A. French and F. E. Ian Hamilton (eds), *The Socialist City: Spatial Structure and Urban Policy*, New York and Chichester John Wiley, 1979, pp. 1–21.

82. Antonić (ed.), *Istorija SK BiH*, 2:129.

83. Ibid., 2:130.

84. Ostojić, "Početak izgradnje stambenog naselja Čengić Vila," *SUSJ*, 1:688. The name of the Čengić Vila neighborhood derives from the name of its one-time owner, Dedaga Čengić, and from the fact that it was the location of Ottoman governor Osman Topal's villa.

85. Ivan Štraus, *Arhitektura Bosne i Hercegovine / The Architecture of Bosnia and Herzegovina, 1945–1995*, Sarajevo: Oko, pp. 121–2.

86. Ibid.

87. Among these was an innovative residential compound of three linked three-story units terraced on a hill on Džidžikovac Street, designed by the brothers Muhamed and Reuf Kadić.

88. Lorenc Eichberger, "Izgradnja nove željezničke stanice" (The building of the new railway station), *SUSJ*, 1:684–7.

89. Štraus, *Arhitektura Bosne i Hercegovine*, p. 28.

90. Mustafa Djumrukčić, "Izrada generalnog urbanističkog plana" (Production of the general urban plan), *SUSJ*, 2:387–409, contains the history of urban planning from liberation through the 1970s.

91. Dijana Alić and Maryam Gusheh, "Reconciling National Narratives in Socialist Bosnia and Herzegovina: The Baščaršija Project, 1948–53," *Journal of the Society of Architectural Historians*, 58, 1 (March 1999), pp. 6–25.

92. Cited in Djumrukčić, "Izrada generalnog urbanističkog plana," *SUSJ*, 2:394.

93. IAS, SGV, July 17, 1948.

94. Djumrukčić, "Izrada generalnog urbanističkog plana," *SUSJ*, 2:396.

95. Štraus, *Arhitektura Bosne i Hercegovine*, p. 31.

96. Kamhi (ed.), *Spomenica dolaska Jevreja u BiH*, p. 5.

97. Djumrukčić, "Izrada generalnog urbanističkog plana," *SUSJ*, 2:405–6.

98. Ibid., 2:406.

99. The translation of *opština* as "municipality" is not wholly apt. Most opštinas consisted of large rural areas named after the largest village or town, so there was little or nothing "municipal" about them. But its translation as "municipality" has become conventional in most scholarly works and at the International Criminal Tribunal for the Former Yugoslavia and is therefore adopted here.

100. Dušan Milidragović, *Komunalno uredjenje grada Sarajeva* (The communal organization of the city of Sarajevo), Sarajevo: Službeni list SRBiH, 1984, pp. 34–98, offers an incisive analysis of the evolution of the city's status in law.

101. Ibid., p. 45.

102. Milidragović, *Komunalno uredjenje grada Sarajeva*, p. 48, citing Federal Republic of Yugoslavia, *Službeni list*, 26, 1955.

103. Vojislav Koštunica and Kosta Čavoški, *Party Pluralism or Monism: Social Movements and the Political System in Yugoslavia, 1944–49*, Boulder, CO: East European Monographs, 1985, p. 209.

104. Bosnia-Herzegovina, *Ustav Socijalističke Republike Bosne i Hercegovine* (Constitution of the Socialist Republic of Bosnia-Herzegovina), adopted February 25, 1974, Article 281, published in *Službeni list Socialističke Republike Bosne i Hercegovine, Službeni list* (The official gazette of the Republic of Bosnia-Herzegovina), 4, 1974.

105. Operation White River (*Bijela rijeka*), a project to bring water to every resident of Sarajevo, was launched in November 1990 but not completed. *Oslobodjenje*, November 8, 1990, p. 10; June 25, 1991, p. 10.

106. Author's personal observation.

107. "Ukazom Predsjednika Federativne Narodne Republike Jugoslavije Josip Broza Tita" (Decree of the president of the Federal People's Republic of Yugoslavia Josip Broz Tito), *SUR*, 4:749.

108. Biographies of those designated "national heroes" from the Sarajevo area can be found in *SUR*, 4:752–814.

109. *Oslobodjenje*, November 26, 1981, p. 3, contains a full report on the ceremony and the texts of some speeches delivered.

110. Štraus, *Arhitektura Bosne i Hercegovine*, p. 55.

111. Francine Friedman describes the process that led to the recognition of the Bosnian Muslims in *The Bosnian Muslims: Denial of a Nation*, Boulder, CO: Westview Press, 1996, pp. 155–68. See also Filandra, *Bošnjačka politika*, pp. 229–39.

112. Filandra, *Bošnjačka politika*, pp. 267–70.

113. Ibid., pp. 268 n. 92.

114. Ibid., pp. 284–96, for the debates regarding the curriculum reform in higher education.

115. Enver Redžić (ed.), *Prilozi za istoriju Bosne i Hercegovine* (Contributions to the history of Bosnia-Herzegovina), 2 vols, Sarajevo: Akademija nauka i umjetnosti Bosne i Hercegovine, 1987. This two-volume set, published nineteen years after the project was initiated, contains only selected "contributions," reflecting the failure of many authors to complete their portions of the synthetic history.

116. Ibid., p. 83.

117. The following contain documents of the charges, trial, and interviews with the defendants: Sead Trhulj, *Mladi Muslimani* (Young Muslims), Sarajevo: Oko, 1994; and Abid Prguda (ed.), *Sarajevski proces. Sudjenje muslimanskim intelektualcima 1983 g.* (Sarajevo trial: The sentencing of Muslim intellectuals in 1983), 2nd edn, Sarajevo: Abid Prguda, 1995.

118. Alija Izetbegović, *Islamska deklaracija* (The Islamic declaration), Sarajevo: Bosna, 1990. The work first appeared in 1970. Izetbegović's detractors, whether Communists, Serb nationalists, or Croat nationalists, have taken isolated quotes out of context to paint him as a promoter of an Islamic Bosnia-Herzegovina governed only by the sheriat.

119. Milan Andrejević, "Vojislav Šešelj under Attack," Radio Free Europe Situation Report, May 4, 1987, pp. 25–9.

120. Štraus, *Arhitektura Bosne i Hercegovine*, p. 102.

121. Roger Cohen, *Hearts Grown Brutal: Sagas of Sarajevo*, New York: Random House, 1998, p. 120.

122. *Oslobodjenje*, February 11, 1984, p. 1; February 12, 1984, p. 2.

123. Ibid., February 19, 1984, p. 18.

Chapter 8 From Socialist Decline to National Division

1. On the economic consequences of the reforms for Sarajevo, see *Oslobodjenje*, August 11, p. 20; August 17, p. 1; August 21, p. 1; and December 28, 1990, pp. 3, 5.

2. Ibid., August 1, 1990, p. 11.

3. Ibid.

4. On the erosion of government authority over building and commerce, see ibid., June 10, 1991, p. 6; July 27, 1990, p. 10; July 31, 1990, p. 9; August 31, 1990, p. 6; November 7, 1990, p. 13; November 25, 1990, p. 3; December 5, 1990, p. 14; and December 30, 1990, p. 5.

5. Norman Cigar, *Genocide in Bosnia: The Policy of Ethnic Cleansing*, College Station: Texas AM University Press, 1995, pp. 23–37; and David Bruce MacDonald, "'Greater Serbia' and 'Greater Croatia': the Moslem Question in Bosnia-Hercegovina," chapter 8 in David Bruce MacDonald, *Balkan Holocausts?: Serbian and Croatian Victim-centred Propaganda and the War in Yugoslavia*, Manchester University Press, 2002.

6. "… things in Bosnia-Herzegovina did not evolve as expected. The 'rallies for truth' organized in the Serb communities there did not yield the desired destabilization and retreat of the Bosnia-Herzegovina leadership. By and large the leaders of the Bosnian Serbs were still not ready to disturb the centuries-old tranquility of coexistence with the Muslims and the Croats." Mihailo Crnobrnja, *The Yugoslav Drama*, 2nd edn, Montreal: McGill-Queens University Press, 1996, p. 142.

7. Republic of Bosnia-Herzegovina, *Sluzbeni list*, July 31, 1990.

8. Neven Andjelic describes the formation of the major political parties in *Bosnia-Herzegovina: The End of a Legacy*, London: Frank Cass, 2003, pp. 159–71.

9. *Oslobodjenje*, July 1, 1990, pp. 1, 2.

10. Ibid., February 24, 1991, p. 2.

11. Suad Arnautović, *Izbori u Bosni i Hercegovini '90. Analiza izbornog procesa* (Elections in Bosnia-Herzegovina, 1990: Analysis of the electoral process), Sarajevo: Promocult, 1996, pp. 52–65.

12. The leaders of the two parties, Nijaz Duraković for the SDP and Kecmanović for the Reformists, reached a deal to cooperate on the eve of the election, but rank-and-file Reformists refused to carry it out, according to Andjelic, *Bosnia-Herzegovina*, p. 180.

13. *Naši Dani* (Our Days), Sarajevo, June 8, 1990, p. 9.

14. *Oslobodjenje*, July 6, 1990, p. 9.

15. Nenad Kecmanović, "Drama sarajevskih Srba" (The drama of Sarajevo's Serbs), *NIN* (*Nedeljne ilustrovane novine*; Weekly illustrated newspaper), Belgrade, September 18, 1992, p. 56.

16. *Oslobodjenje*, July 6, 1990, p. 3, reports on the press conference of July 5.

17. This assembly is reported in Arnautović, *Izbori u Bosni i Hercegovini*, p. 41; *Oslobodjenje*, July 13, 1990, p. 3; *Sedam Dana* (Seven Days), Sarajevo, July 15, 1990, p. 4; and *Naši Dani*, Sarajevo, July 20, 1990, p. 12.

18. *Oslobodjenje*, August 11, 1990, p. 11.

19. Arnautović, *Izbori u Bosni i Hercegovini*, p. 43.

20. Author interview with Stjepan Kljuić, Sarajevo, April 18, 2000.

21. For promises of a peaceful life together and rhetoric at the joint rallies throughout Bosnia-Herzegovina, see Andjelic, *Bosnia-Herzegovina*, p. 179–80, and Kemal Kurspahić, *As Long as Sarajevo Exists*, trans. Colleen London, Stony Creek, CT: Pamphleteer's Press, 1997, pp. 59–60. Andjelic (p. 180) calls the joint rallies "the end of a very wise campaign."

22. *Oslobodjenje*, November 14, 1990, p. 13.

23. Ibid., November 15, 1990, p. 9, and an advertisement for this event, November 14, 1990, p. 19.

24. Ibid., November 15, 1990, p. 9.

25. Election results are found in Arnautović, *Izbori u Bosni i Hercegovini*, pp. 103–27.

26. *Oslobodjenje*, December 21, 1990, p. 10.

27. Ibid.

28. Ibid., November 21, 1991, p. 7; November 24, 1991, p. 5; and January 12, 1992, p. 5.

29. Ibid., October 25, 1991, p. 7.

30. Ibid., January 5, 1992, p. 8.

31. Author interview with Mirko Pejanović, Sarajevo, November 1, 1999. For a discussion of this phenomenon in all of Bosnia-Herzegovina, see Xavier Bougarel, "Bosnia and Hercegovina—State and Communitarianism," in David A. Dyker and Ivan Vejvoda (eds), *Yugoslavia and After: A Study in Fragmentation, Despair and Rebirth*, London: Longman, 1996, pp. 98–102.

32. *Javnost* (The Public), Sarajevo, May 4, 1991, p. 2. *Javnost* was the official biweekly publication of the SDS in Bosnia-Herzegovina; it commenced publication in October 1990.

33. *Glas* (Voice), Banja Luka, April 27–8, 1991, p. 6, provides the best coverage of this event.

34. In March 1991 *Glas* published a series of articles entitled "Regionalizacija i Bosanska krajina: Da li, kako, zašto?" (Regionalization and the Bosnian Krajina: whether, how, and why?), *Glas*, March 6, p. 7; March 15, p. 6; March 28, p. 5; March 29, p. 5; April 2, p. 8; April 8, p. 6; and April 10, p. 7.

35. Examples of such public declarations are found in *Glas*, April 12, p. 7; April 18, p. 4; May 3, p. 5; and May 10, p. 8, all 1991.

36. *Glas*, April 17, 1995, p. 5.

37. International Criminal Tribunal for the Former Yugoslavia (ICTY), "Odluka o imenovanju štaba za regionalizaciju, Srpska demokratska stranka BiH, Gradski odbor, Sarajevo. Broj: 01-37-1/91" (Decision on naming the staff for regionalization, Serb Democratic Party of Bosnia-Herzegovina, City Board, Sarajevo. No 01-37-1/91), September 25, 1991. Prosecutor v. Stanislav Galić, IT-98-29, Exhibit P3683, admitted into evidence on April 22, 2002, pp. 7,657–7,703, as supporting material to the report of Robert J. Donia, "The Siege of Sarajevo: A Background Report," p. 2 n. 9, BCS ERN: SA02-1150. Hereafter each initial citation to a document submitted as evidence in cases before the ICTY is identified by title, case, case number, exhibit number, the document's language, and ERN. (BCS stands for Bosnian-Croatian-Serbian, the tribunal's standard designation for the language formerly called Serbo-Croatian. ERN is the abbreviation for Evidence Registration Number.) Verbal testimony by witnesses before the tribunal is identified by the name of the witness, case and case number, the date of testimony, and page(s) on which it appears in the transcript as found at http://www.un.org/icty/cases/indictindex-e.htm.

38. In mid-September, four Serb autonomous regions were publicly proclaimed: Herzegovina, Romanija-Birač, Semberija, and Northern Bosnia. The decision was subsequently published in *Javnost*, December 7, 1991, p. 10, in an article that simultaneously announced the renaming of the "Community of Municipalities of Bosnian Krajina" created in April 1991 as the "Serb Autonomous Region of Bosnian Krajina."

39. Romanija-Birač consisted of the municipalities of Pale, Han pijesak, Sokolac, Vlasenica, Sekovići, Olovo, and part of Rogatica. *Službeni glasnik srpskog naroda u Bosni i Hercegovini* (Official gazette of the Serb people in Bosnia-Herzegovina), Sarajevo, 1, 1, January 15, 1992, p. 8.

40. ICTY, "Odluka o imenovanju štaba za regionalizaciju," September 25, 1991, BCS ERN: SA02-1150.

41. ICTY, "Skupština srpske autonomne oblasti 'Romanija,' Pale, 11.12.1991. godine. Zapisnik." (Minutes of the meeting of the Serb Autonomous Region of Romanija held in Pale, December 11, 1991), Prosecutor v Galić, IT-98-29, Exhibit P3683, cited in Donia, "The Siege of Sarajevo," p. 3 n. 13. BCS ERN: SA02-3688–SA02-3692. Sarajevo representatives complained that the "Birač" designation was incorporated in the name because SDS representatives from eastern Bosnia had dallied in proclaiming their own autonomous region.

42. *The Death of Yugoslavia*, videotape, London: BBC, part 4. Laura Silber and Allan Little conducted many of the interviews in the BBC documentary, which they used in writing their book *Yugoslavia: Death of a Nation*, New York: Penguin Books, 1997, p. 216. This

event was covered in all media in Bosnia-Herzegovina, and the legality or illegality of the HDZ-SDA maneuver has been debated ever since.

43. *Oslobodjenje*, October 16, 1991, p. 3.

44. ICTY, "SDS Savjet stranke, 18:00 to 21:30. Srpska demokratska stranka Bosne i Hercegovine. Datum: 15.10.1991.godine" (SDS Party Council. Serb Democratic Party of Bosnia and Herzegovina. October 15, 1991), Prosecutor v. Galić, IT-98-29, Exhibit P3683, cited in Donia, "The Siege of Sarajevo," p. 3 n. 17. English ERN: 0304-4271–0304-4274; BCS ERN: SA02-3844–SA02-3848. "English" indicates evidence originating in that language or authorized translations prepared by tribunal translators. The BCS version contains a handwritten note that reads, "The original exists in manuscript" (*Postoji original u rukopisu*).

45. "Decision on establishing the assembly of the Serb people in Bosnia and Herzegovina," Republika Srpska, *Službeni Glasnik*, 1, 1, January 15, 1992, p. 1. See also European Community, "Report of the European Community Arbitration Committee," in *Yugoslav Survey*, 32, 1 (1992), p. 125, and *Oslobodjenje*, November 10, 1991, p. 5. This body was first known as the Assembly of the Serbian People in Bosnia-Herzegovina (*Skupština srpskog naroda u Bosni i Hercegovini*) and was renamed the Assembly of Republika Srpska (*Skupština Republike Srpske*) on August 12, 1992.

46. ICTY, Bosnian Serb Assembly, 2d Session, November 21, 1991, Prosecutor v Slobodan Milošević, IT-02-54, Exhibit 538 ID, English ERN: 0093-0303–0093-0311; BCS ERN: SA01-2012–SA01-2016. Exhibit 531 ID consists of the minutes and transcripts of most sessions of the Bosnian Serb Assembly from its founding session on October 24, 1991, to March 1996. Prosecutors submitted the exhibit on a compact disk to the trial chamber on September 12, 2003, and the court designated it as Exhibit 538 ID, but as of this writing the chamber has not ruled on its admissibility as evidence.

47. In December 1991 a working group from the municipal assembly of Novi grad visited Rajlovac to meet with local leaders and seek a resolution to this dispute. Working group members were told that Serb villagers had suffered economic discrimination and that some 1,600 Serbs had voted in the November 1991 plebiscite to secede from the existing Novi grad municipality and to take with them a JNA military installation. *Oslobodjenje*, December 21, 1991, p. 7.

48. "Zakon o obrazovanju opština Rajlovac sa sjedištem u Rajlovcu. Broj 02-4/92. 11. maja 1992. godine," (Law on the creation of the municipality of Rajlovac with its seat in Rajlovac, no. 2-4/92. May 11, 1992), Republika Srpska, *Službeni glasnik*, 2, 1, February 24, 1993.

49. *Večernje Novine* (The Evening News), Sarajevo, December 19, 1991, p. 12.

50. ICTY, Bosnian Serb Assembly, 3d Session, December 11, 1991, Prosecutor v Slobodan Milošević, IT-02-54, Exhibit 538 ID. English ERN: 0093-3341. The resolution was published as "Preporuka o osnivanju Skupština opština srpskog naroda u Bosni i Hercegovini" (Recommendation on establishing assemblies of municipalities of the Serb people in Bosnia and Herzegovina), Republika Srpska, *Službeni glasnik*, 1, 1, January 15, 1992, p. 9.

51. ICTY, "Srpska demokratska stranka Bosne i Hercegovine. Glavni odbor. Strogo povjerljivo. Uputstvo o organizovanju i djelovanju organa srpskog naroda u Bosni i Hercegovini u vanrednim okolnostima, Sarajevo, 19. decembra 1991. godine" (Serb

Democratic Party of Bosnia and Herzegovina. Main Board. Instructions for the Organization and Activity of the Organs of the Serb People in Bosnia and Herzegovina in Extraordinary Circumstances, Sarajevo, December 19, 1991) (Hereafter ICTY, "Organization and Activity," December 19, 1991) Prosecutor v. Radislav Brdjanin, IT-99–36, Exhibits P25a (BCS) and P25b (English). The office of the prosecutor has acquired several copies of this document from different municipalities, each with a different number handwritten on the cover page that appears to identify the SDS municipal board to which that copy was addressed. The document with a handwritten number 096, admitted in this case, is BCS ERN: 0025-2738–0025-2747; English ERN: 0035-9936–0035-9943.

52. Ibid. The creation of a crisis staff was not without precedent. The presidency of Bosnia-Herzegovina had formed its own crisis staff on September 21, 1991, consisting of three presidency members plus the minister of internal affairs, minister for national defense, and commander of the territorial defense forces. *Oslobodjenje*, December 27, 1991, p. 2. However, the SDS-mandated crisis staffs differed from the presidency staff in being made up of members from one political party (the SDS) and one nationality (Serbs).

53. ICTY, "Organization and Activity," December 19, 1991.

54. ICTY, Bosnian Serb Assembly, 4th Session, December 21, 1991, Prosecutor v Slobodan Milošević, IT-02-54, Exhibit 538 ID. English ERN: 0093-9677–0093-9678. BCS ERN: 0089-8209.

55. ICTY, Bosnian Serb Assembly, 3d Session, November 21, 1991, Prosecutor v Slobodan Milošević, IT-02-54, Exhibit 538 ID. English ERN: 0093-0319; BCS ERN SA0I–2030—SA0I-2031.

56. Ibid., English ERN: 0093-0319–0093-0320; BCS ERN: SA01-2030.

57. The instructions were published in full in *Slobodna Bosna*, March 12, 1992, along with minutes of a meeting of Sarajevo SDS leaders held on December 21, 1991, indicating that the Sarajevo SDS had formed a crisis staff as directed.

58. *Oslobodjenje*, December 25, 1991, p. 7.

59. Ibid., and *Oslobodjenje*, February 5, 1992, p. 10.

60. *Oslobodjenje*, January 11, 1992, p. 12; and *Glas*, January 12, 1992, p. 4. As noted above in the text, the entity first called the "Republic of the Serb People in Bosnia and Herzegovina" (*Republika srpskog naroda u Bosni i Hercegovini*) was renamed on August 12, 1992, the Republika Srpska (meaning the Serb Republic, but never rendered in English translation). I will refer to the new entity by this latter name, Republika Srpska.

61. *Oslobodjenje*, February 23, 1992, p. 5.

62. *Oslobodjenje*, January 15, 1992, p. 8, and March 20, 1992, p. 8.

63. *Oslobodjenje*, January 24, 1992, p. 11. The paper reported that monthly revenues of approximately 50,000 German marks would thenceforth be retained in Pale.

64. Author interview with Muhamed Kreševljaković and Muhamed Zlatar, Sarajevo, October 12, 2000.

65. *Oslobodjenje*, January 29, 1992, p. 4.

66. *Oslobodjenje*, March 5, 1992, p. 4.

67. *Le Monde* journalist Florence Hartman reported arriving at the restaurant at 10.00 p.m. on March 2 and being told she would have to wait three hours for a meal to be

prepared. As she waited, a newly-arrived group of armed Serb gunmen was served immediately and left without paying. *Oslobodjenje*, March 5, 1992, p. 3.

68. Viktor Meier argues convincingly that the transformation of the JNA was completed first in Croatia and only later in Bosnia-Herzegovina in Victor Meier, *Yugoslavia: A History of its Demise*, trans. Sabrina P. Ramet, London: Routledge, 1999, p. 213,

69. *Oslobodjenje*, November 8, 1991, p. 7.

70. *Oslobodjenje*, November 9, 1991, p. 8, and November 15, 1991, p. 3.

71. "Sarajevo na četničkom nišanu" (Sarajevo as the Chetnik target), *Slobodna Bosna*, November 21, 1991, p. 3.

72. *Oslobodjenje*, December 3, 1991, p. 7; December 5, 1991, p. 8; and December 6, 1991, p. 7.

73. *Oslobodjenje*, December 18, 1991, p. 8, and December 28, 1991, p. 8.

74. ICTY, Bosnian Serb Assembly, 4th Session, December 21, 1991, Prosecutor v. Milošević, IT-02-54, Exhibit 538 ID, English ERN: 0093-9663.

75. *Oslobodjenje*, January 5, 1992, p. 4.

76. International Court of Justice, *Bosnia and Herzegovina v. Federal Republic of Yugoslavia*, "Reply of Bosnia and Herzegovina," April 23, 1998. Annex 138: Interview with Milutin Kukanjac, "My Guest—My Truth," Pale TV, July 12, 1994.

77. Borisav Jović, *Poslednji dani SFRJ* (The last days of the Socialist Federal Republic of Yugoslavia), 2nd edn, Kragujevac: Prizma, 1996, p. 420. Milošević anticipated that several Yugoslav republics would shortly be recognized as independent states, according to Jović's notes, and the Serbian president made different plans for Macedonia than for Bosnia-Herzegovina. "If Macedonia wishes to separate, we must reach an agreement with them for a withdrawal of the army and the division of military property."

78. Ibid.

79. Ibid., p. 421.

80. Silber and Little, *Yugoslavia*, New York: Penguin, 1997, p. 218.

81. James Gow, *Legitimacy and the Military: The Yugoslav Crisis*, London: Pinter, 1992, pp. 46–7.

82. ICTY, "Informacija o akciji sigurnijeg obezbjedjenja naoružanja i municije TO SRBiH. … Republički štab teritorijalne odbrane Predsjedništvu SRBiH" (Information on action to achieve greater security for the weapons and munitions of the territorial defense of the Socialist Republic of Bosnia-Herzegovina. From the republic staff of territorial defense to the presidency of Socialist Republic of Bosnia-Herzegovina.), Sarajevo, September 13, 1990. Prosecutor v. Galić, IT-98-29, Exhibit P3683, cited in Donia, "The Siege of Sarajevo," p. 6 n. 44. BCS ERN: 0087-0220–0087-0235.

83. Branka Magaš and Ivo Žanić (eds), *Rat u Hrvatskoj i Bosni i Hercegovini, 1991–1995* (War in Croatia and Bosnia-Herzegovina), Zagreb-Sarajevo: Dani, 1999, p. 378.

84. Šefko Hodžić chronicles the development of the Patriotic League in a series of articles in January 1999 based on interviews with Meho Karišik, head of its military wing. *Oslobodjenje*, January 9, p. 19; January 10, p. 14; January 11, p. 17; January 12, p. 13; January 13, p. 21; January 14, p. 19; January 15, p. 17; January 16, p. 20; and January 17, p. 15.

85. *Oslobodjenje*, January 10, 1999, p. 14.

86. Central Intelligence Agency, *Balkan Battlegrounds: A Military History of the Yugoslav Conflict, 1990–1995* (Washington, DC: CIA, 2002), 1:112, and *Oslobodjenje*, November 9, 1991, p. 8.

87. *Oslobodjenje*, January 12, 1999, p. 13.

88. Victor Meier, then the correspondent for *Frankfurter Allgemeine Zeitung*, was in the area when fatal shooting occurred. Meier, *Yugoslavia*, p. 211. See also *Oslobodjenje*, March 3, 1992, p. 12.

89. Press reports subsequently revealed that the alleged perpetrator, Ramiz Delalić, had been implicated in an earlier shooting and a rape and had received treatment at a Sarajevo psychiatric hospital. *Oslobodjenje*, March 6, 1992, p. 8.

90. Delalić was later convicted of threatening a father and son at a restaurant in Sarajevo and brandishing a pistol in front of restaurant guests on March 1, 1997. In June 1999 he assaulted a policeman by running him over with his car. The postwar international overseer of Bosnia-Herzegovina, High Representative Carlos Westendorp, urged the Sarajevo authorities to investigate thoroughly the past misdeeds of Ramiz Delalić. Bosnia-Herzegovina, Office of the High Representative, press release, June 17, 1999. After Delalić completed his jail sentence, Sarajevo authorities at last launched an investigation of his alleged killing of Gardović in 1992. *Dnevni avaz* (Daily voice), Sarajevo, February 7, 2002, p. 27.

91. Sinan Alić interview with Rajko Dukić, Milići, Bosnia-Herzegovina, March 21, 2000. Alić was the publisher of newspaper *Front Slobode* (Front of Freedom) in Tuzla. Manuscript report on interview, author's personal collection.

92. The agreement and dismantling of the barricades are recounted by the general in Milutin Kukanjac, "Moja istina," *NIN*, January 6, 2000, p. 58, and were reported in *Oslobodjenje*, March 3, 1992, p. 1, and March 4, 1992, p. 2. Kukanjac recalled that he had visited twelve Serb and two Muslim barricades; the Sarajevo newspaper credited him with visiting fourteen Serb and seven Muslim barricades.

93. *Oslobodjenje*, March 4, 1992, p. 2.

94. Kukanjac told an interviewer for the BBC, "They were shaking their fists in each other's faces. I had to break it up!" After the agreement was reached, SDA Party President Izetbegović stated, "We agreed to protect our citizens with joint patrols. They'll be run by the federal army and our Bosnian police." BBC, *The Death of Yugoslavia*, videocassette, part 4.

95. *Oslobodjenje*, March 7, 1992, p. 3, and March 10, 1992, p. 6.

96. *Oslobodjenje*, March 4, 1992, p. 1.

97. For the rallies of the Valter movement in March 1992, see *Oslobodjenje*, March 4, p. 5; and March 7, p. 6; and March 9, p. 12

98. "The patrols postponed some events, and that was in the interest of the Serbs," he recalled. International Court of Justice, *Bosnia and Herzegovina v Federal Republic of Yugoslavia*, "Reply of Bosnia and Herzegovina," April 23, 1998. Annex 138: Interview with Milutin Kukanjac, "My Guest—My Truth," Pale TV, July 12, 1994.

99. ICTY, "Zaključci iz procene stanja na prostoru BiH u zoni odgovornosti 2. VO. Mart 1992. godine" (Conclusions from an assessment of the situation on the territory of Bosnia-Herzegovina in the area of responsibility of the 2d Military District. March 1992), signed by Milutin Kukanjac; illegible stamp, Prosecutor v Galić, IT-98-29,

Exhibit P3683, cited in Donia, "The Siege of Sarajevo," p. 8n60, English ERN: 0300-5185–0300-5194, BCS ERN: 0106-5518–0106-5530. The Bosnian government seized this document among others after Kukanjac and his staff had withdrawn from their Sarajevo headquarters on May 2. It has also been published in Hasan Efendić, *Ko je branio Bosnu* (Who defended Bosnia?), Sarajevo: Oko, 1998, pp. 45–54.

100. Kukanjac, "Moja istina," p. 57.

101. ICTY, Bosnian Serb Assembly, 50th Session, April 16, 1995, Prosecutor v Slobodan Milošević, IT-02-54, Exhibit 538 ID, English ERN: 0096-9865; BCS ERN: 0084-6058.

102. ICTY, Telephone intercept, Karadžić and Milošević, September 9, 1991, Prosecutor v Slobodan Milošević, IT–02–54, Exhibit P613, Tab 48A (English) and 48B (BCS), English ERN: 0092-2914–0092-2917, and BCS ERN: 0206-6173–0206-6176. Security officials of the Republic of Bosnia-Herzegovina monitored and recorded phone conversations of Karadžić and some other SDS officials from mid-1991 onward. These were transcribed and admitted as evidence in trials of Bosnian Serb leaders and former Serbian president Milošević at the ICTY. At the beginning of some calls, Karadžić cautioned the other party that the call was probably being monitored, so he was aware that his phone was tapped.

103. *Oslobodjenje*, March 26, 1992, p. 20.

104. Ibid.

105. On the formation of the Serb MUP, see *Oslobodjenje*, April 1, 1992, p. 1, and April 8, 1992, p. 4.

106. *Oslobodjenje*, April 8, 1992, p. 4.

107. UN, Final Report of the United Nations Commission of Experts established pursuant to Security Council Resolution 780 (1992), Annex 6, "Study of the Battle and Siege of Sarajevo," pt. 1, April 6, 1992, 153–4 (hereafter, *UN Commission of Experts*). The demonstrations and fighting of April 5 and 6 are also discussed in the *New York Times*, April 6, 1992, p. 5, and April 7, 1992, p. 3; CIA, *Balkan Battlegrounds*, 1:152; Silber and Little, *Yugoslavia*, pp. 226–30; and (from a personal angle) Lewis MacKenzie, *Peacekeeper: The Road to Sarajevo* (Vancouver, BC: Douglas and McIntyre, 1993), pp. 135–40. More detailed accounts are provided in numerous articles in *Oslobodjenje*, April 6–8, 1992.

108. *Oslobodjenje*, 8 April 1992, p. 4.

109. MacKenzie, *Peacekeeper*, p. 137.

110. *UN Commission of Experts*, p. 153. For an authoritative account of the killings, see Silber and Little, *Yugoslavia*, p. 229 and *NIN*, December 2, 1999, p. 60.

111. "The first shell to fall on Sarajevo was that which landed on the GRAS (*Gradski saobraćaj*; city transportation) company on April 6, 1992. From this point to the end of the war, GRAS was one of the major targets for the aggressors' attacks." Irfan Mehičić and Muedeta Hadžiabdić (eds), *Privreda u opkoljenom Sarajevu* (The economy in besieged Sarajevo), Sarajevo: Privredna komora regije Sarajevo, 1998, p. 111.

112. *UN Commission of Experts*, April 6, 1992, p. 154.

113. A participant account is summarized by Ed Vulliamy, *Seasons in Hell: Understanding Bosnia's War*, New York: St. Martin's Press, pp. 73–4.

114. *NIN*, December 2, 1999, p. 60.

Chapter 9 Death and Life in Sarajevo under Siege

1. Mary Kaldor, "Bosnia-Herzegovina: A Case Study of a New War," chap. 3 in Mary Kaldor, *New and Old Wars: Organized Violence in a Global Era*, Stanford University Press, 1999.

2. On the irony of using medieval methods in modern warfare, see Cornelia Sorabji, "A Very Modern War: Terror and Territory in Bosnia-Hercegovina," in Robert A. Hinde and Helen E. Watson (eds), *War: A Cruel Necessity? The Bases of Institutionalized Violence*, London: I. B. Tauris, 1995, pp. 81–95.

3. Republika Srpska. *Sluzbeni glasnik Republike Srpske*, "Odluka o strateškim ciljevima srpskog naroda u Bosni i Hercegovina, broj 02-130/92, 12 maja 1992. godine." (Decision on the strategic goals of the Serbian people in Bosnia-Herzegovina, no. 02-130/92, of May 12, 1992), November 26, 1993, no. 22, p. 866. The decision was reached on May 12, 1992, but not published in the official gazette until November 26, 1993.

4. ICTY, Bosnian Serb Assembly, 42nd Session, July 18, 1994, Karadžić, Prosecutor v. Milošević, IT-02-54, Exhibit 538 ID, BCS ERN: 0215-2880–0215-2881.

5. *Oslobodjenje*, April 17, 1992, p. 8, reporting on Dnevnik, RTV Sarajevo.

6. ICTY, Bosnian Serb Assembly, 16th Session, May 12, 1992, Karadžić, Prosecutor v. Milošević, IT-02-54, Exhibit 538 ID, English ERN: 0091-3514.

7. "Sarajevo Siege Deepens, Defying Efforts at Peace," *New York Times*, September 27, 1992, p. 8.

8. ICTY, Telephone intercept, Karadžić and Milošević, 9 September 1991, Prosecutor v. Milošević, IT–02–54, Exhibit P613, Tab 48A (English) and 48B (BCS), English ERN: 0092-2914–0092-2917, and BCS ERN: 0206-6173–0206-6176.

9. *Oslobodjenje* provided an account of this episode in dispatches from its own correspondents and from Belgrade's Tanjug news service, September 10, 1991, pp. 1, 3.

10. ICTY, Telephone intercept, September 9, 1991, Karadžić and Koljević, Prosecutor v. Milošević, IT–02–54, Exhibit P613, Tabs 49A (English) and 49B (BCS), English ERN: 0302-7831–0302-7835, and BCS ERN: 0211-6622–0211-6625.

11. ICTY, Telephone intercept, September 9, 1991, two male voices, probably Karadžić and Milan Babić, Prosecutor v. Milošević, IT–02–54, Exhibit P613, tabs 46A (English) and 46B (BCS), English ERN: 0092-3197 and BCS ERN: 0219-4704–0219-4707 and L006-3297–L006-3300 (each page of Tab 46B bears two BCS designations). The first speaker is certainly Karadžić, as his phone was being tapped and the second speaker begins the conversation by saying "Hello, Radovan." The identity of the second speaker as Milan Babić can be inferred from internal evidence.

12. ICTY, Bosnian Serb Assembly, 40th Session, May 1–11, 1994, Karadžić, Prosecutor v. Milošević, IT-02-54, Exhibit 538 ID, BCS ERN: 0215-2545.

13. International Court of Justice, *Bosnia and Herzegovina v. Federal Republic of Yugoslavia*, Transcript (Zapisnik) of Statement of Djordje Djukić, Annex 140 to "Reply of Bosnia and Herzegovina," April 23, 1998.

14. ICTY, Bosnian Serb Assembly, 8th Session, February 25, 1992, Milutin Najdanović, Prosecutor v. Milošević, IT-02-54, Exhibit 538 ID, English ERN: 0084-0454.

15. ICTY, Bosnian Serb Assembly, 34th Session, September 9, 1993, Djordje Djukić, Prosecutor v. Milošević, IT-02-54, Exhibit 538 ID, BCS ERN: 0215-0636.

16. ICTY, Bosnian Serb Assembly, 39th Session, March 24–5, 1994, Miroslav Toholj, Prosecutor v. Milošević, IT-02-54, Exhibit 538 ID, BCS ERN: 0215-2332.

17. The following deal with the military history of the siege: Zijad Rujanac, *Opsjednuti grad Sarajevo* (The besieged city of Sarajevo), Sarajevo: Bosanski kulturni centar, 2003; and Nedžad Ajnadžić, *Odbrana Sarajeva* (The defense of Sarajevo), Sarajevo: Sedam, 2002. Published diaries of the early months of the siege include Ahmed Džubo, *Zapisi za pamćenje. Ratni dani u Sarajevu i Republici Bosni i Hercegovini, april 1992–april 1993*, Sarajevo: Glavni odbor SUBNOR-a BiH, 2002; and Nusret Šehić, *Dnevni zapisi o životu pod četničkom opsadom tokom 1992. i 1993. god.* (Daily observations on life under Chetnik siege during 1992 and 1993), 2 vols, Sarajevo: Rabic, 2003; and Zlata Filipović, *Zlata's Diary: A Child's Life in Sarajevo*, trans. Christina Pribichevich-Zorić, New York: Viking, 1994. Miroslav Prstojević, *The Wounded City*, trans. Dževahira Arslanagić and Gordana Kisić, Ljubljana: DAG Grafika, 1994, combines photos and eyewitness accounts to tell the story of the siege's first three years.

18. Territorial defense forces came under the leadership of whatever group dominated locally. The Serb territorial defense in Ilidža was organized on April 5, 1992. Its leaders complained of Green Beret paramilitaries shooting at Serb civilians in Dobrinja and elsewhere. SDA and SDS representatives agreed to meet daily there to try to mediate. *Oslobodjenje*, April 16, 1992, p. 3.

19. Kerim Lučarević, *The Battle for Sarajevo: Sentenced to Victory*, Sarajevo: FZV, 2000, p. 53.

20. Chuck Sudetic, "Serbian Militias Overrun a Town: New Concern on U.S. Aid Flights," *New York Times*, April 18, 1992, p. A3, cited in *UN Commission of Experts*, April 17, 1992, p. 161.

21. Lučarević, *The Battle for Sarajevo*, p. 53.

22. "The local base of most military formations meant that, while armies were primarily organized by nationalist parties, some soldiers were of a different national identity, such as the thousands of Bosnian Muslims fighting in the HVO [*Hrvatsko vijeće obrane*, Croat Council of Defense] or the Bosnian Croats and Bosnian Serbs who fought in the Bosnian army." Susan Woodward, *Balkan Tragedy: Chaos and Dissolution after the Cold War*. Washington, DC: Brookings Institution Press, 1995, p. 254.

23. The Bosnian collective presidency (absent its two Serb members, who had resigned on April 6) ordered that all territorial defense forces come under a single command on April 15. At midnight between April 14 and 15, the new official symbol for all members of the territorial defense came into effect (the coat of arms of the medieval Bosnian state) and all units were urged to adopt it. *Oslobodjenje*, April 16, 1992, p. 1.

24. April 15 was celebrated as the "Day of the Army" beginning in 1993, but in 1992 the term *armija* had a pejorative connotation for many Bosnians as shorthand for the JNA. The ARBiH was not formally created until August 1992.

25. "The UN stated that the Swedes were fired upon until the Serbian police chief of Ilidža came out and appealed to the gunmen to hold their fire. … As dusk fell, hillside Serbian forces unleashed intense artillery, mortar and machine gun fire into downtown areas of the city." *UN Commission of Experts*, April 22, 1992, p. 165.

26. *UN Commission of Experts*, April 25, 1992, p. 168.

27. Kukanjac, "Moja istina," *NIN*, January 6, 2000, p. 58.

28. *Oslobodjenje*, April 28, 1992, p. 1.

29. Jović, *Poslednji dani SFRJ*, entry of April 30, 1992, p. 448. Participants were Branko Kostić (president of the federal presidency), Slobodan Milošević, Momir Bulatović (president of Montenegro), General Milan Panić (chief of the JNA General Staff), Radovan Karadžić, Momčilo Krajišnik, Nikola Koljević, and Jović. Kukanjac was conspicuously absent from this meeting.

30. Rujanac, *Opsjednuti grad*, pp. 239–49.

31. Proponents of this explanation note that presidency member Fikret Abdić, believed to be more sympathetic to the Bosnian Serbs than Izetbegović, arrived in Sarajevo on May 2, having passed many checkpoints and barriers in the trip from his home town of Velika Kladuša, and may have been in waiting had the Izetbegović-led government fallen. This interpretation is summarized in Silber and Little, *Yugoslavia*, pp. 237–8.

32. Ibid., pp. 232–3; *Oslobodjenje*, May 3, 1992, p. 3; and CIA, *Balkan Battlegrounds*, 1:152.

33. Silber and Little, *Yugoslavia*, p. 234. The authors refer to the attackers as "Karadžić's forces" while noting that the JNA was "not yet acting wholly on the Serb side."

34. ICTY, Bosnian Serb Assembly, 52nd Session, August 6, 1995, Karadžić, Prosecutor v Milošević, IT-02-54, Exhibit 538 ID, BCS ERN: 0215-4230. "True, the JNA helped us plenty, but in some places they hindered us. In Sarajevo they didn't want to do what we sought. They didn't want to give us a unit of tanks so we could do what we wanted. The war would have concluded had the JNA done that."

35. BBC, *The Death of Yugoslavia*.

36. Lučarević, *The Battle for Sarajevo*, pp. 77–9.

37. Silber and Little provide the most comprehensive account of Izetbegović's kidnapping and eventual exchange, based on interviews with leading participants, in *Yugoslavia*, pp. 232–42, and footage and interviews in the BBC videotape, Brian Lapping Associates (prod.), *The Death of Yugoslavia*. Zlatko Lagumdžija, who arrived with Izetbegović from Rome, recounted his observations in *Oslobodjenje*, May 6, 1992, p. 2.

38. Lučarević, *The Battle for Sarajevo*, p. 82.

39. *Oslobodjenje*, May 9, 1992, citing Tanjug (Belgrade), May 8, 1992.

40. International Court of Justice, *Bosnia and Herzegovina v. Federal Republic of Yugoslavia*, "My Guest—My Truth," Interview on Pale TV, July 12, 1994, Annex 138 to "Reply of Bosnia and Herzegovina," April 23, 1998.

41. "Those officers whom we sought, arrived; I sought Mladić." Bosnian Serb Assembly, 50th Session, April 16, 1995, Karadžić. BCS ERN: 0084-6059.

42. James Gow, *The Serbian Project and its Adversaries: A Strategy of War Crimes*, London: Hurst, 2003, p. 77.

43. CIA, *Balkan Battlegrounds*, 1:153.

44. "Further Report of the Secretary-General Pursuant to Security Council Resolution 749 (1992) (S/23900, 12 May 1992)," in Bethlehem and Weller (eds), *The "Yugoslav" Crisis*, 1:509.

45. Ibid.

46. "Report of the Secretary-General Pursuant to Paragraph 4 of Security Council Resolution 752 (1992) (S/24049, 30 May 1992)," in Bethlehem and Weller (eds), *The "Yugoslav" Crisis*, 1:517.

47. Lučarević, *The Battle for Sarajevo*, pp. 130–5; Murat Kahrović, *Kako smo branili Sarajevo: Prva sandžačka brigada* (How we defended Sarajevo: The First Sandžak Brigade),

Sarajevo: Udruženje gradjana Bošnjaka porijeklom iz Sandžaka, 2001, pp. 93–100; and Rujanac, *Opsjednuti grad Sarajevo*, pp. 256–61.

48. "Report of the Secretary-General Pursuant to Paragraph 4 of Security Council Resolution 752 (1992) (S/24049, 30 May 1992)," in Bethlehem and Weller (eds), *The "Yugoslav"Crisis*, 1:517.

49. Lučarević, *The Battle for Sarajevo*, pp. 128–9.

50. *UN Commission of Experts*, June 6–9, 1992, pp. 202–4.

51. Paragraphs 2–4, "Security Council Resolution 743 (1992) (S/RES/743, 21 February 1992)," in Bethlehem and Weller (eds), *The "Yugoslav"Crisis*, 1:8. In authorizing UN-PROFOR, the Security Council implemented recommendations in a "UN Peace-keeping plan contained in the report of the Secretary General of 11 December 1991 (S/23280), annex III."

52. UN officers took up residence in the newly completed "Pensioners' Home," the award-winning architectural masterpiece next to the headquarters of the newspaper *Oslobodjenje*. The pensioners for which the building was intended would never cross its threshold, as it was destroyed by bombardment during the war.

53. Brendan Simms provides the case for complicity among some British commanders and troops in UNPROFOR in *Unfinest Hour: Britain and the Destruction of Bosnia*, New York: Penguin Books, 2002, pp. 173–222. Among other cases, Simms notes, "Captain Mike Stanley, or Milos Stankovic, a British liaison officer of Serb parentage … was later arrested and released on charges of spying for the Bosnian Serbs," p. 173.

54. Paragraph 5, "Security Council Resolution 749" (1992) (S/RES/749, 7 April 1992), in Bethlehem and Weller (eds), *The "Yugoslav"Crisis*, 1:6.

55. "Further Report of the Secretary-General Pursuant to Security Council Resolution 749 (1992) (S/23900, 12 May 1992)," in Bethlehem and Weller (eds), *The "Yugoslav" Crisis*, 1:509.

56. "Security Council Resolution 752 (1992) (S/RES/752, 15 May 1992)," in Bethlehem and Weller (eds), *The "Yugoslav"Crisis*, 1:7.

57. "Report of the Secretary-General Pursuant to Security Council Resolution 752 (1992) (S/24000, 26 May 1992)," in Bethlehem and Weller (eds), *The "Yugoslav"Crisis*, 1:516.

58. "Security Council Resolution 752 (1992) (S/RES/752, 15 May 1992)," in Bethlehem and Weller (eds), *The "Yugoslav"Crisis*, 1:8.

59. "Agreement of 5 June 1992 on the reopening of Sarajevo airport for humanitarian purposes." Annex to the "Report of the Secretary-General Pursuant to Security Council Resolution 757 (1992) (S/24075, 6 June 1992)," in Bethlehem and Weller (eds), *The "Yugoslav"Crisis*, 1:520.

60. *UN Commission of Experts*, p. 222.

61. Resolutions 761 of 29 June 1992 (1:13), 764 of 13 July 1992 (1:14–15), and Resolution 770 of 13 August 1992 (1:17–18), in *The "Yugoslav"Crisis*.

62. "Statement by the President of the Security Council, 24 July 1992 (S/24346, 24 July 1992)," in *The "Yugoslav"Crisis*, 1:15.

63. "Security Council Resolution 769 (1992) (S/RES/769, 7 August 1992)," in *The "Yugoslav"Crisis*, 1:17.

64. "Security Council Resolution 770 (1992) (S/RES/770, 13 August 1992)," in *The "Yugoslav Crisis"*, 1:17–18.

65. UN, Commission on Human Rights, Economic and Social Council. "Report on the situation of human rights in the territory of the former Yugoslavia submitted by Mr Tadeusz Mazowiecki, Special Rapporteur of the Commission on Human Rights, pursuant to paragraph 14 of Commission resolution 1922/S 1/1 of 14 August 1992," August 28, 1992," New York: UN Economic and Social Council, 1992.

66. Scott Anderson, *The Man Who Tried to Save the World: The Dangerous Life and Mysterious Disappearance of Fred Cuny*, New York: Doubleday, 1999, pp. 132–45.

67. *UN Commission of Experts*, July 22 and 24, 1992, pp. 243, 245.

68. *UN Commission of Experts*, August 29, 1991, p. 289.

69. Tom Gjelton, *Sarajevo Daily: A City and its Newspaper Under Siege*, New York: HarperCollins, 1995, p. 119.

70. Handout given to the author by a UN officer, July 1994.

71. Author's personal observation.

72. The Pope visited Zagreb but cancelled his stopover in Sarajevo.

73. Personal communication from several mayors in attendance, January 1995.

74. "In the minutes before his death, he had been building an anti-sniping barrier of empty cargo containers outside the central Holiday Inn, a place where killing is utterly commonplace." Roger Cohen, "A U.N. Peacekeeper Dies; Bosnia's Pain Does Not," *New York Times*, April 17, 1995, p. A3.

75. Cohen, *Hearts Grown Brutal*, pp. 228–30.

76. ICTY, Bosnian Serb Assembly, 16th Session, May 12, 1992, Trifko Radić (Ilijaš), Prosecutor v Milošević, IT-02-54, Exhibit 538 ID, English ERN: 0091-3520–0091-3521; BCS ERN: 0084-7728.

77. Ibid., Karadžić, English ERN: 0091-3513; BCS ERN: 0084-7722.

78. Leading Bosnian Serb nationalists continued their denial of the siege long after the war had ended. In a trial of Bosnian Serb defendants at the ICTY, Nenad Kecmanović, whose own apartment in Sarajevo had been struck by an artillery shell in the spring of 1992, characterized the siege as a "ring, held by the Serbs to prevent the Muslims from creating a unitary [Bosnia-Herzegovina] at their expense." He blamed the deprivation of municipal services on Izetbegović, stating that he "kept the civilian population in Sarajevo without electric power or water, without heating or sufficient food, with the explanation that 'a city without civilians would become a sort of a military fort and a legitimate military target for the Serbian aggressors.'" ICTY, Prosecutor v. Miroslav Kvocka and others, IT-98-30/1, "Nalaz i Mišljenje Dr Nenad Kecmanović" (Finding and opinion of Dr. Nenad Kecmanović), cited in "Submission of Expert Statement of Dr. Robert J. Donia," March 30, 2001, admitted as prosecution exhibit 3/266.

79. ICTY, Bosnian Serb Assembly, 16th Session, May 12, 1992, Mladić, Prosecutor v. Milošević, IT-02-54, Exhibit 538 ID, English ERN: 00913544; BCS ERN:.

80. *UN Commission of Experts*, December 26, 1992, p. 406, citing the *New York Times*.

81. CIA, *Balkan Battlegrounds*, 1:308.

82. *UN Commission of Experts*, October 12, 1992, p. 343.

83. CIA, *Balkan Battlegrounds*, 1:307.

84. ICTY, Testimony of Herbert Okun, Prosecutor v. Milošević, IT-02-54, February 26, 2003, p. 16,963.

85. *Oslobodjenje*'s treatment of an extended interview with Meho Karišik, the head of the Patriotic League's military wing, illustrates the change in approach. Based on that interview, the paper began a series of articles in April 1993 revealing the full story of the formation of the Muslim paramilitary group (*Oslobodjenje*, April 11, p. 5; April 12, p. 5; April 13, p. 5; April 14, p. 5; and April 15, p. 5). After several articles had appeared, Karišik later recalled, he was told by Rusmir Mahmutćehajić, a vice president in the Bosnian government, that he should "stop publication of the story, for it's not the right time. The war is still going on, and many names are mentioned." Greater openness in postwar times was reflected in *Oslobodjenje*'s decision to run the complete series of articles, including an account of pressure to terminate the 1993 series. *Oslobodjenje*, January 9, 1999, p. 15.

86. Ajnadžić, *Odbrana Sarajeva*.

87. Lučarević, *The Battle for Sarajevo*, p. 184.

88. A UN observer reported on a VRS offensive in February 1993: "The BiH defense of Stup and Azići was reported as complicated by the enormous disparity of firepower between BiH forces and Serbs. Drawing upon stores of the former JNA, the Serbs utilized tanks, heavy machine guns in battle. Although Serb lines were within range of government artillery on nearby Igman Mountain, the BiH forces had only a few tanks and not much ammunition. It was reported that their defense depended mainly upon fighters using small arms and homemade anti-armour grenades." *UN Commission of Experts*, February 17, 1993, p. 450.

89. See, for example, *UN Commission of Experts*, December 5, 1992, p. 387.

90. Author interview with Ahmed Hadžirović, October 2001.

91. Lučarević, *The Battle for Sarajevo*, pp. 201–5.

92. Ibid., pp. 185–203.

93. Speaking of an offensive in Ilidža in August 1992, ARBiH General Jovan Divjak stated that his forces "had decided to continue their costly offensive to break through Serb lines encircling the city." *UN Commission of Experts*, p. 288.

94. CIA, *Balkan Battlegrounds*, 1:153–4, and 2: Map H: "Sarajevo: The Bosnian Army Attempts to Capture Four Key Hilltops, 8 June 1992."

95. Lučarević, *The Battle for Sarajevo*, pp. 67–71, 105–7, 117–19, 139–43.

96. CIA, *Balkan Battlegrounds*, 1:154, and *UN Commission of Experts*, p. 395.

97. ICTY, Bosnian Serb Assembly, 54th Session, October 15–16, 1995, Karadžić, Prosecutor v Milošević, IT-02-54, Exhibit 538 ID, BCS ERN: 0215-4562.

98. Lučarević, provides a participant's account of the battle for Dobrinja in *The Battle for Sarajevo*, pp. 144–74. See also *UN Commission of Experts*, June 17–19, 1992, pp. 209–11.

99. ICTY, Bosnian Serb Assembly, 17th Session, July 24–6, 1992, Nedeljko Prstojević (Ilidža), Prosecutor v. Milošević, IT-02-54, Exhibit 538 ID, BCS ERN: 0214-9561.

100. The Oriental Institute, including its extensive holdings of documents pertaining to all Bosnian religious groups and nationalities, was totally destroyed on May 17, 1992. *Orijentalni institut u Sarajevu 1950–2000 / The Institute for Oriental Studies in Sarajevo*, pp. 12, 17.

101. Tatjana Praštalo, "Death of a Library," *Logos*, 8, 2 (1997), pp. 96–9, and *UN Commission of Experts*, pp. 282–4.

102. *UN Commission of Experts*, pp. 282–3.

103. ICTY, Bosnian Serb Assembly, 16th Session, May 12, 1992, Dragan Kalinić, Prosecutor v. Milošević, IT-02-54, Exhibit 538 ID, English ERN: 0091-3524; BCS ERN: 0084-7731.

104. *Oslobodjenje*, May 28, 1992, p. 1; and May 29, 1992, p. 1; *UN Commission of Experts*, May 27, 1992, pp. 192–3.

105. *UN Commission of Experts*, May 27–9, 1992, pp. 192–5.

106. A vivid description of the impact of random sniper fire on the deaths and lives of Sarajevans is provided by Peter Maass, *Love Thy Neighbor: A Story of War*, New York: Alfred A. Knopf, 1996, pp. 144–8.

107. Kahrović, *Kako smo branili Sarajevo*, p. 310.

108. Before the war he published a book: Boris Nilević, *Srpska pravoslavna crkva u Bosni i Hercegovini do obnove Pećke patrijaršije 1557. godine* (The Serbian Orthodox Church in Bosnia-Herzegovina until the reestablishment of the Peć Patriarchate in 1557), Sarajevo: Veselin Masleša, 1990.

109. Boris Nilević, personal communication with author, Sarajevo, July 1994.

110. David Rieff, *Slaughterhouse: Bosnia and the Failure of the West*, New York: Simon and Schuster, 132–7.

111. Maček, *War Within*, pp. 22–7.

112. David M. Berman, *The Heroes of Treća Gimnazija: A War School in Sarajevo, 1992–1995*, Lanham, MD: Rowman and Littlefield, 2001.

113. Nezirović (ed.), *Sefarad 92*.

114. "Foreword," in Juzbašić (ed.), *Prilozi historiji Sarajeva*, n.p.

115. Suada Kapić (ed.), *Life*, Sarajevo: FAMA, 1995.

116. Maja Razović and Aleksandra Wagner (eds), *Sarajevo Survival Guide*, Sarajevo: FAMA, n.d.

117. Author interview with Haris Alagić, November 1, 2000.

118. For an explanation of what he calls "the Sarajevo feeling—the aura of a sophisticated capital city under siege," see Vulliamy, *Seasons in Hell*, pp. 76–84.

119. Kapić, (ed.), *Life*, Sarajevo, p. 82.

120. Author interview with Rajko Živković, October 9, 1999.

121. Author interview with Kreševljaković and Zlatar, October 12, 2000.

122. Quoted in Mirko Pejanović, *Through Bosnian Eyes: The Political Memoir of a Bosnian Serb*, trans. Marina Bowder, West Lafayette, IN: Purdue University Press, 2004, p. 130.

123. Pejanović, *Through Bosnian Eyes*, p. 132.

124. Ibid., p. 133.

125. ICTY, Testimony of Witness DP1, Prosecutor v. Stanislav Galić, IT-98-29, October 9, 2002, p. 13, 443.

126. Pejanović, *Through Bosnian Eyes*, p. 134.

127. *Dani* (Days), June 5, 2005, pp. 20–3; *Oslobodjenje*, May 21, 2005, pp. 4–5; and "*Preliminarni spiskovi imena Srba ubijenih i nestalih u Sarajevu u periodu od 1992. do 1995. godine*" (Preliminary list of the names of Serbs killed and missing in Sarajevo 1992–5), http://www.mup.vladars.net/, accessed June 20, 2005.

128. ICTY, Bosnian Serb Assembly, 34th Session, August 27, 1993, Karadžić, Prosecutor v Milošević, IT-02-54, Exhibit 538 ID, BCS ERN: 0215-0571.

129. "Zaključci (Conclusions). October 7, 1993, Pale, 02-1166/93, Republika Srpska." Cyrillic typescript. Copy of document in author's possession.

130. ICTY, Bosnian Serb Assembly, 36th Session, December 30–1, 1993, Karadžić, Prosecutor v Milošević, IT-02-54, Exhibit 538 ID, BCS ERN: 0215-1327–0215-1328.

131. ICTY, Bosnian Serb Assembly, 51st Session, June 14–15, 1995, Minutes, Prosecutor v Milošević, IT-02-54, Exhibit 538 ID, BCS ERN: 0215-3923.

132. ICTY, Bosnian Serb Assembly, 32d Session, May 19–20, 1993, Trifko Radić, Prosecutor v Milošević, IT-02-54, Exhibit 538 ID, BCS ERN: 0215-0295.

133. Ajnadžić provides details of the tunnel's construction and dimensions, and the persons and goods transported through it in Odbrana Sarajeva, pp. 257–63.

134. Richard Holbrooke, To End a War, New York: Random House, 1998, p. vii.

135. Oslobodjenje, February 6, 1994, p. 1; and UN Commission of Experts, February 5, 1994, p. 781.

136. Elizabeth Neuffer, The Key to My Neighbor's House: Seeking Justice in Bosnia and Rwanda, New York: Picador, 2001, p. 62.

137. UN Commission of Experts, February 5 and 6, 1994, pp. 782–4.

138. UN Commission of Experts, February 8, 1994, p. 790, citing "Karadžić Says Sarajevo Massacre was a Fraud," Reuters, February 8, 1994.

139. ICTY, Bosnian Serb Assembly, 39th Session, March 24, 1994, Karadžić, Prosecutor v Milošević, IT-02-54, Exhibit 538 ID, BCS ERN: 0215-2273.

140. "Framework Agreement for the Federation," no. I.1–13a, in Snežana Trifunovska (ed.), Former Yugoslavia through Documents: From its dissolution to the peace settlement, The Hague: Martinus Nijhoff, 1999, pp. 83–9; and Burg and Shoup, The War in Bosnia-Herzegovina, pp. 294–8.

141. On April 7 UNPROFOR and VRS forces exchanged artillery fire following VRS shelling of the government-held passage over Mt. Igman. Fort Worth Star Telegram, April 8, 1995, p. A23.

142. New York Times, April 5, 1995, p. A3.

143. New York Times, April 19, 1995, p. A9.

144. On the British, French, and US rising resolve to employ more robust military measures, see Burg and Shoup, The War in Bosnia-Herzegovina, pp. 326, 337–48.

145. "Seesaw Week for U.S. Tactics in Balkans as Hostage Crisis Deepens," New York Times, June 5, 1995, p. A6.

146. Burg and Shoup, The War in Bosnia-Herzegovina, p. 341.

147. CIA, Balkan Battlegrounds, 1:297, and Roger Cohen, "Rebel Serbs Shell Croatian Capital," New York Times, May 3, 1995, p. A6.

148. CIA, Balkan Battlegrounds, 1:309–16.

149. Ibid., 1:374–5.

150. Bosnia-Herzegovina, Office of the High Representative, Bosnia and Herzegovina: Basic Texts, Sarajevo: n.d., front matter, n.p.

151. CIA, Balkan Battlegrounds, 1:381–2.

152. Mirko Petrinić and Milenko Pajić (eds), Raniji gradonačelnici za Sarajevo: 1992–1996 (Former mayors of Sarajevo), Sarajevo: Klub ranijih gradonačelnika Sarajeva, 1997, p. 65, citing the department of public health's bulletin of January 1, 1996.

153. ICTY, Testimony of Ewa Tabeau, Prosecutor v Stanislav Galić, IT–98–29, July 22, 2002, pp. 12,057–12,135.

Chapter 10 Sarajevo in the Long Shadow of War

1. Turning Karl von Clausewitz's adage "War is the continuation of politics by other means" on its head, one observer quipped that in Bosnia-Herzegovina, "Peace is the continuation of conflict without military means." Major Arjen Zwaanswijk, Royal Netherlands Army, personal communication with author, June 2003.

2. "Rebuilding a Multi-ethnic Sarajevo: The Need for Minority Returns," International Crisis Group, Report no. 30, February 3, 1998, p. 2. http://crisisweb.org/home/index.cfm?id=1577&1=1, (accessed March 15, 2005).

3. "General Framework Agreement for Peace in Bosnia and Herzegovina," Annex 4, article 1, para. 5, in Trifunovska (ed.), *Former Yugoslavia through Documents*, no. II–2, p. 441.

4. Ibid., Annex 1A, articles 1 and 6, pp. 443–6 and 449–51. IFOR was renamed the Stabilization Force when its mandate was renewed in summer 1997.

5. Ibid., Annex 1A, article 4, para. 5, section (b), p. 449.

6. For example, ICTY, Bosnian Serb Assembly, 56th Session, December 17, 1995, Ljubo Bosiljčić (Ilidža). BCS ERN: 0215-4778; Miroslav Vještica (Bosanska Krupa), BCS ERN: 0215-4781; and Vojislav Maksimović (Sarajevo), BCS ERN: 0215-4784. Prosecutor v. Milošević, IT-02-54, Exhibit 538 ID.

7. Ibid., Minutes. BCS ERN: 0215-4750.

8. Ibid., Grujo Lalović. BCS ERN: 0215-4790.

9. Ibid., Krajišnik. BCS ERN: 0215-4843.

10. Ibid.

11. Ibid., Minutes. BCS ERN: 0215-4751.

12. *RFE/RL Newsline*, February 29, 1996, http://www.rferl.org/newsline/1996/02/4-see/see-290296.asp

13. Press Agency TWRA, Sarajevo, February 29, 1996, cited in *Open Media Research Institute Daily Digest* (Prague), pt 2, February 29, 1996.

14. Bosnia Action Coalition, "This Week in Bosnia-Herzegovina," February 29, 1996. http://world.std.com/~slm/twib0229.html

15. *Open Media Research Institute Daily Digest*, pt 2, March 18, 1996.

16. *RFE/RL Newsline*, March 1, 1996. http://www.rferl.org/newsline/1996/03/4-SEE/see-010396.asp.

17. Ibid., November 22, 1006, citing *Newsletter of the Helsinki Committee for Human Rights in Bosnia and Herzegovina*.

18. *Open Media Research Institute Daily Digest*, pt 2, March 18, 1996, citing Reuters. Also Press Agency TWRA, Sarajevo, March 18, 1996, e-mail distribution.

19. Press Agency TWRA, Sarajevo, March 19, 1996, e-mail distribution.

20. *Oslobodjenje*, March 8, 1999, p. 8.

21. Nevenko Herceg and Zoran Tomić, *Izbori u Bosni i Hercegovini* (Elections in Bosnia-Herzegovina), West Mostar: Sveučilište u Mostaru, Centar za studije novinarstva, 1998, pp. 173–4.

22. *Dnevni Avaz*, September 5, 1997, p. 6.

23. *Oslobodjenje*, February 24, 1998, p. 9.

24. *Wall Street Journal*, June 16, 1999, p. 1.

25. http://www.ohr.int/ohr-dept/econ/bulldozer-initiative/index.asp, (accessed March 15, 2005).

26. Adil Zulfikarpašić, *The Bosniak*, London: Hurst, 1998. Zulfikarpašić's family history and background are elucidated in a dialogue with Milovan Djilas and Nadežda Gaće.

27. Bosnia-Herzegovina, *Službeni glasnik Bosne i Hercegovine*, "Ustavni sud, Djelimična odluka" (Constitutional Court, partial decision), July 1, 2000, in no. 23 (September 14, 2000), pp. 482, 486. The court ruling cited estimates of the International Crisis Group.

28. "Rebuilding a Multi-ethnic Sarajevo," p. 3. These figures are estimates. Since no official census was taken in the first postwar decade, numbers are approximate. Boundaries of the postwar Sarajevo Canton encompassed 1,277 square kilometers less than the prewar city.

29. Author interview with Alexandra Stiglmayer, Sarajevo, March 19, 1999.

30. "Minority Returns 2003," UN High Commissioner for Refugees. http://www.unhcr.ba/return/T5-min12.pdf, (accessed March 15, 2005).

31. "Sarajevo Return Conference: Sarajevo Declaration," Press Release, Bosnia-Herzegovina, Office of the High Representative, Sarajevo, February 3, 1998.

32. On the educational and textbook revisions initiated as part of the Sarajevo Declaration, see Robert J. Donia, "The Quest for Tolerance in Sarajevo's Textbooks," *Human Rights Review*, 1, 2 (Jan–Mar 2000), pp. 38–55.

33. *Dnevni Avaz*, February 4, 1998, p. 10.

34. *Oslobodjenje*, February 24, 1998, p. 8.

35. United Nations High Commission for Refugees, "Minority Returns from January 1, 1996, to March 31, 2005, in Bosnia and Herzegovina," Sarajevo: UNHCR, 2005.

Bibliography

Archives

Arhiv Bosne i Hercegovina (ABH), Sarajevo.
Archives de Ministère des Affaires Étrangères, Paris.
Gazi Husrevbegova biblioteka, Arhiv Rijaseta Islamske Zajednice Bosne i Herce-
    govine, Sarajevo.
Haus, Hof und Staatsarchiv (HHSA), Vienna.
Historijski muzej Bosne i Hercegovina, Sarajevo.
Istorijski arhiv Sarajevo (IAS).
Public Record Office (PRO), London.

Primary documents and document collections

Austria-Hungary 1906. K. und k. Gemeinsam Finanzministerium, *Bericht über die
    Verwaltung von Bosnien und die Hercegovina*, Vienna: k.k. Hof-und Staatsdruckerei.
Bethlehem, Daniel, and Marc Weller (eds) 1997, *The "Yugoslav"Crisis in International
    Law: General Issues*, Cambridge University Press.
Bosnia-Herzegovina 1880, Landesregierung für Bosnien und die Hercegovina,
    "Provisorisches Status für die Errichtung einer Gemeindevertretung in der Stadt
    Sarajevo von 22 August 1878," in *Sammlung der Gesetze, Verordnungen und Normal-
    weisungen von Bosnien und der Hercegovina*, Sarajevo: Landesdruckerei.
———— 1912, *Die Ergebnisse der Volkszählung in Bosnien und der Hercegovina vom 10.
    Oktober 1910*, Sarajevo: Landesdruckerei.
———— 1945–92, *Službeni glasnik Socialističke Republike Bosne i Hercegovine*. Before
    1963 it was called *Službeni glasnik Federativne Narodne Republike Bosne i Hercegovine*.
———— 1996–2005, *Službeni glasnik Bosne i Hercegovine*.
———— 1998–9, Office of the High Representative, press releases.
———— n.d., Office of the High Representative, *Bosnia and Herzegovina: Basic Texts*,
    Sarajevo: Office of the High Representative.
British Broadcasting Corporation 1995, *The Death of Yugoslavia*, television series
    and videocassettes.
European Community 1992, "Report of the European Community Arbitration
    Committee," *Yugoslav Survey*, 32, 1, pp. 121–34.
Gavranović, Berislav (ed.) 1973, *Bosna i Hercegovina u doba austrougarske okupacije
    1878. god*, Sarajevo: Akademija nauka i umjetnosti Bosne i Hercegovine.

International Court of Justice 1998, *Bosnia and Herzegovina v Federal Republic of Yugoslavia*, "Reply of Bosnia and Herzegovina."

International Criminal Tribunal for the Former Yugoslavia (ICTY) 2001–4, exhibits in cases of Prosecutor v Stanislav Galić (IT-98-29), Prosecutor v. Slobodan Milošević (IT-02-54), Prosecutor v. Radislav Brdjanin (IT-99-36), and Prosecutor v. Miroslav Kvocka *et al.* (IT-98-30/1).

Kapić, Suada (ed.) 1995 *Life*, Sarajevo: FAMA.

Kapidžić, Hamdija (ed.) 1963, "Rad Narodnog Vijeće SHS Bosne i Hercegovine u novembru i decembru 1918," *Glasnik arhiva i Društva arhivista Bosne i Hercegovine*, 3, pp. 147–328.

Madžar, Božo (ed.) 1986, "Izvještaj vladinog komesara za glavni grad Bosne i Hercegovine Sarajevo o političkoj i privrednoj situaciji u Sarajevu od Sarajevskog atentata do kraja januara 1915. godine," *Glasnik arhiva i Društva arhivskih radnika Bosne i Hercegovine*, 26, pp. 205–42.

Neumann, Leopold, and Adolphe Plason (eds) 1883, *Recueil des Traités et Conventions conclus par l'Autriche avec les puissances étrangères*, Vienna: Steyrermühl.

Owings, W. A. Dolph, Elizabeth Pribic, and Nikola Pribic (eds and translators) 1984, *The Sarajevo Trial*, 2 vols. Chapel Hill, NC: Documentary Publications.

Pappenheim, Martin 1926, *Gavrilo Princips Bekenntnisse. Ein Geschichtlicher Beitrag zur Vorgeschichte des Attentates von Sarajevo*, Vienna: Rudulf Lechner.

Prguda, Abid (ed.) 1995, *Sarajevski process. Sudjenje muslimanskim intelektualcima 1983 g.* 2nd edn, Sarajevo: Abid Prguda.

Republika Srpska 1992–3, *Službeni glasnik srpskog naroda u Bosni i Hercegovini*. After August 12, 1992, this publication entity was renamed *Službeni glasnik Republike Srpske*.

Trifunovska, Snežana (ed.) 1999, *Former Yugoslavia through Documents: From its dissolution to the peace settlement*, The Hague: Martinus Nijhoff.

UN, Commission on Human Rights, Economic and Social Council 1992, "Report on the situation of human rights in the territory of the former Yugoslavia submitted by Mr Tadeusz Mazowiecki, Special Rapporteur of the Commission on Human Rights, pursuant to paragraph 14 of Commission Resolution 1922/S1/1 of 14 August 1992," New York: UN Economic and Social Council, 1992.

UN, High Commission for Refugees (UNHCR) 2005, "Minority Returns from January 1, 1996, to March 31, 2005, in Bosnia and Herzegovina," Sarajevo: UNHCR.

UN, United Nations Commission of Experts 1992, *Final Report of the United Nations Commission of Experts established pursuant to Security Council Resolution 780*, Annex 6, "Study of the Battle and Siege of Sarajevo," part 1.

Yugoslavia 1945–9, *Službeni list Federativne Narodne Republike Jugoslavije*.

Yugoslavia 1949–86, Vojnoistoriski institut, *Zbornik dokumenata i podataka o narodnooslobodilačkom ratu jugoslovenskih naroda*, Belgrade: Vojnoistorijski institut Jugoslovenske narodne armije.

Foreign-language periodicals

Dani (Sarajevo).

Dnevni avaz (Sarajevo).

Glas (Banja Luka).

Glas slobode (Sarajevo).

Javnost (Sarajevo).

Jugoslovenska pošta (Sarajevo).

Nada (Sarajevo).

Narodno jedinstvo (Sarajevo).

Naši Dani (Sarajevo).

NIN (Belgrade).

Oslobodjenje (Sarajevo).

Sarajevski list (Sarajevo).

Sedam dani (Sarajevo).

Slobodna Bosna (Sarajevo).

Srpska riječ (Sarajevo).

Večernje novine (Sarajevo).

Wissenschaftliche Mittheilungen aus Bosnien und Hercegovina (Sarajevo).

Books and articles

Ademović, Fadil 1997, *Princ Palikuća u Sarajevu*, Sarajevo: Rabic.

Ajnadžić, Nedžad 2002, *Odbrana Sarajeva*. Sarajevo: Sedam.

Albahari, Nisam *et al.* (eds) 1976–81, *Sarajevo u revoluciji*, 4 vols, Sarajevo: Istorijski arhiv Sarajevo.

Alić, Dijana, and Maryam Gusheh 1999, "Reconciling National Narratives in Socialist Bosnia and Herzegovina: The Baščaršija Project, 1948–1953," *Journal of the Society of Architectural Historians*, 58, 1 (March 1999), pp. 6–25.

Aličić, Ahmed S. 1983, *Uredjenje bosanskog ejaleta od 1789. do 1878. godine*, Sarajevo: Orijentalni institut.

———— 1996, *Pokret za autonomiju Bosne od 1831. do 1832. godine*, Sarajevo: Orijentalni institut.

Anderson, Benedict 1998, *Imagined Communities: Reflections on the Origin and Spread of Nationalism*, rev. edn. London: Verso.

Anderson, Scott 1999, *The Man Who Tried to Save the World: The Dangerous Life and Mysterious Disappearance of Fred Cuny*, New York: Doubleday.

Andjelic, Neven 2003, *Bosnia-Herzegovina: The End of a Legacy*, London: Frank Cass.

Andrejević, Milan 1987, "Vojislav Šešelj under Attack," *Radio Free Europe Situation Report*, May 4, pp. 25–9.

Antonić, Zdravko (ed.) 1990, *Istorija Saveza komunista Bosne i Hercegovine*, 2 vols, Sarajevo: Institut za istoriju and Oslobodjenje.

Arhiv Bosne i Hercegovine 1977, *Arhiv Bosne i Hercegovine 1947–1977. Povodom tridesetogodišnjice osnivanja Arhiva i početka rada arhivske službe u Bosni i Hercegovini*, Sarajevo: Svjetlost.

Arnautović, Suad 1996, *Izbori u Bosni i Hercegovini '90. Analiza izbornog procesa*, Sarajevo: Promocult.

Balić, Emily Greble 2005, "The Last Months of Wartime: Sarajevo's Experience," paper presented at the conference, "60 godine od završetka drugog svjetskog rata—Kako se sjećati 1945. godine?", Sarajevo, May 13.

Banac, Ivo 1983, "The Communist Party of Yugoslavia during the Period of Legality, 1919–1921," in Ivo Banac (ed.), *The Effects of World War I: The Class War after the Great War: The Rise of Communist Parties in East Central Europe, 1918–1921*, pp. 188–230, Boulder, CO: East European Monographs.

———— 1984, *The National Question in Yugoslavia: Origins, History, Politics*, Ithaca, NY: Cornell University Press.

———— 1988, *With Stalin against Tito: Cominformist Splits in Yugoslav Communism*, Ithaca, NY: Cornell University Press.

Bataković, Dušan 1996, *The Serbs of Bosnia and Herzegovina: History and Politics*, Sarajevo: Dialogue.

Begović, Fehim M. 1999, *Staro Sarajevo. Ljudi i dogadjaji*, Sarajevo: Rabic.

Beller, Steven 2001, "Kraus's Firework. State Consciousness Raising in the 1908 Jubilee Parade in Vienna and the Problem of Austrian Identity," in Nancy Wingfield and Maria Bucur (eds), *Staging the Past: The Politics of Commemoration in Habsburg Central Europe, 1848 to the Present*, West Lafayette, IN: Purdue University Press.

Benac, Alojz, and Ljubica Mladenović 1954, *Sarajevo od najstarijih vremena do danas*, Sarajevo: Muzej grada Sarajeva.

Benbassa, Esther, and Aron Rodrique 1995, *The Jews of the Balkans: The Judeo-Spanish Community, Fifteenth to Twentieth Centuries*, Oxford: Blackwell.

Berend, Iván T., and György Ránki 1974, *Economic Development in East-Central Europe in the Nineteenth and Twentieth Centuries*, New York: Columbia University Press.

Berman, David M. 2001, *The Heroes of Treća Gimnazija: A War School in Sarajevo, 1992–1995*, Lanham, MD: Rowman and Littlefield.

Besarović, Risto 1987, *Iz kulturne prošlosti Bosne i Hercegovine (1878–1918)*, Sarajevo: Veselin Masleša.

Bićanić, Rudolf 1973, *Economic Policy in Socialist Yugoslavia*. Cambridge University Press.

Bigelow, Bruce 1974, "Centralization Versus Decentralization in Interwar Yugoslavia," *Southeast Europe* 1, 2, pp. 157–72.

Bogićević, Vojislav 1954, "Atentat Bogdana Žerajića 1910 godine," *Godišnjak Istoriskog društva Bosne i Hercegovine*, 6, pp. 87–102.

———— 1955, "'Iznimne mjere' u Bosni i Hercegovini u maju 1913 godine," *Godišnjak Istoriskog društva Bosne i Hercegovine*, 7, pp. 209–18.

Borovčanin, Drago 1979, *Izgradnja bosansko-hercegovačke državnosti u uslovima NORa*, Sarajevo: Svjetlost.

Bougarel, Xavier 1996, "Bosnia and Hercegovina—State and Communitarianism," in David A. Dyker and Ivan Vejvoda (eds), *Yugoslavia and After: A Study in Fragmentation, Despair and Rebirth*, London: Longman, pp. 87–115.

Božić, Jela 1988, "Arhitekt Josip Pl. Vancaš," in Vojka Smiljanić-Djukić (ed.), *Graditelji Sarajeva*, Sarajevo: Radio Sarajevo 3.

Brkljača, Seka 1999, "Bosanskohercegovački boksit kao strateška sirovina (1918–1945)," *Časopis za suvremenu povijest*, 31, 2, pp. 341–57.

———— 2004, "Politika prema bosanskohercegovačkim opštinama i opštine prema politici u Kraljevini Srba, Hrvata i Slovenaca," *Prilozi instituta za istoriju Sarajevo*, 33, pp. 233–51.

Burg, Steven L., and Paul S. Shoup 1999, *The War in Bosnia-Herzegovina: Ethnic Conflict and International Intervention*, Armonk, NY: M. E. Sharpe.

Čanković, Miodrag (ed.) 1988–90, *Sarajevo u socijalističkoj Jugoslaviji*, 2 vols Sarajevo: Istorijski arhiv Sarajevo.

Čelebi, Evlija 1996, *Putopis; odlomci o jugoslovenskim zemljama*, Sarajevo: Sarajevo Publishing.

Cigar, Norman 1995, *Genocide in Bosnia: The Policy of Ethnic Cleansing*, College Station: Texas A&M University Press.

Cline, Eric H. 2004, *Jerusalem Beseiged: From Ancient Canaan to Modern Israel*, Ann Arbor: University of Michigan Press.

Cohen, Roger 1998, *Hearts Grown Brutal: Sagas of Sarajevo*, New York: Random House.

Čolaković, Rodoljub (ed.) 1963, *Pregled istorije saveza komunista Jugoslavije*, 2 vols, Belgrade: Institut za izučavanje radničkog pokreta.

Čorović, Vladimir 1996, *Crna knjiga: Patnje Srba Bosne i Hercegovina za vreme Svetskog rata 1914–1918*, 3rd edn, Belgrade: Udruženje ratnih dobrovoljaca 1912–1918.

Crnobrnja, Mihailo 1996, *The Yugoslav Drama*, 2nd edn, Montreal: McGill-Queen's University Press.

Čubrilović, Vasa 1996, *Bosanski ustanak 1875–1878*, 2nd edn, Belgrade: Službeni list SRJ.

Čurovac, Muhamed (ed.) 1997, *Sarajevo. Photo-monograph*, Sarajevo: Svjetlost.

Dautbegović, Almaz (ed.) 1988, *Spomenica stogodišnjice rada Zemaljskog muzeja Bosne i Hercegovine 1888–1988*, Sarajevo: Zemaljski muzej Bosne i Hercegovine.

Dedijer, Vladimir 1966, *The Road to Sarajevo*, New York: Simon and Schuster.

———— 1990, *The War Diaries of Vladimir Dedijer*, 3 vols, Ann Arbor: University of Michigan Press.

Derviševič, Mustafa, *et al.* 2003, *Vodič kroz fondove i zbirke istorijskog arhiva Sarajevo*, Sarajevo: Istorijski arhiv Sarajevo.

Djaković, Luka 1985, *Političke organizacije bosanskohercegovačkih katolika Hrvata*, part 1: *Do otvaranja Sabora 1910*. Zagreb: Globus.

Donia, Robert 1979, "The Battle for Bosnia: Habsburg Military Strategy in 1878," in Milorad Ekmečić (ed.), *Otpor austrougarskoj okupaciji 1878. godine u Bosni i Hercegovini*, Sarajevo: Akademija nauka i umjetnosti Bosne i Hercegovine, pp. 109–21.

———— 1981, *Islam under the Double Eagle: The Muslims of Bosnia and Hercegovina, 1878–1914*, Boulder, CO: East European Monographs.

———— 2000, "The Quest for Tolerance in Sarajevo's Textbooks," *Human Rights Review*, 1, 2 (Jan–Mar), pp. 38–55.

———— 2002, "*Fin-de-Siècle* Sarajevo: The Habsburg Transformation of an Ottoman Town," *Austrian History Yearbook*, 32, 43–76.

Donia, Robert, and John V. A. Fine, Jr 1994, *Bosnia and Herzegovina: A Tradition Betrayed*. London: Hurst.

Džubo, Ahmed 2002, *Zapisi za pamćenje. Ratni danu u Sarajevu i Republici Bosni i Hercegovina, april 1992–april 1993*, Sarajevo: Glavni odbor SUBNOR-a BiH.

Efendić, Hasan 1998, *Ko je branio Bosnu*, Sarajevo: Oko.

Ekmečić, Milorad 1973, *Ustanak u Bosni, 1875–1878*, Sarajevo: Veselin Masleša.

Falkner, Alfons von Sonnenburg 1885, *Über Operationen im Gebirgsland, illustrirt durch die Kämpfe der Österreicher bei der Occupation Bosniens, 1878*, Munich: F. Straub.

Filandra, Šaćir 1998, *Bošnjačka politika u XX. stoljeću*, Sarajevo: Sejtarija.

Filipović, Zlata 1994, *Zlata's Diary: A Child's Life in Sarajevo*, trans. Christina Pribichevich-Zorić, New York: Viking.

Fine, John V. A., Jr 1975, *The Bosnian Church: A New Interpretation*, Boulder, CO: East European Monographs.

Freely, John. 1998 *Istanbul: The Imperial City*, New York: Penguin.

French, R. A., and F. E. Ian Hamilton 1979, "Is there a Socialist City?" in R. A. French and F. E. Ian Hamilton (eds), *The Socialist City: Spatial Structure and Urban Policy*, Chichester and New York: John Wiley.

Friedenreich, Harriet Pass 1979, "Sarajevo: City of Four Faiths," chapter 1 of *The Jews of Yugoslavia: A Quest for Community*, Philadelphia, PA: Jewish Publication Society of America.

Friedman, Francine 1996, *The Bosnian Muslims: Denial of a Nation*, Boulder, CO: Westview Press.

Gavranović, Berislav 1935, *Uspostava redovite katoličke hijerarhije u Bosni i Hercegovini 1881. godine*, Belgrade: Popović.

Gilbert, Martin 1996, *Jerusalem in the Twentieth Century*, New York: John Wiley and Sons.

Gjelton, Tom 1995, *Sarajevo Daily: A City and its Newspaper under Siege*, New York: HarperCollins.

Gligorijević, Branislav 1970, *Demokratska stranka i politički odnosi u Kraljevini Srba Hrvata i Slovenaca*, Belgrade: Institut za savremenu istoriju.

——— 1996–2003, *Kralj Aleksandar Karadjordjević*, 3 vols, Belgrade: Zuns.

Goldstein, Slavko, (ed.) 1988, *Jews in Yugoslavia*, Zagreb: Muzejski prostor

Gow, James 1992, *Legitimacy and the Military: The Yugoslav Crisis*, London: Pinter.

——— 2003, *The Serbian Project and its Adversaries: A Strategy of War Crimes*, London: Hurst.

Grijak, Zoran 2001, *Politička djelatnost vrhbosanskog nadbiskupa Josipa Stadlera*, Zagreb and Sarajevo: Hrvatski institut za povijest and Vrhbosanska nadbiskupija.

Hadžibegović, Iljas 1980, *Postanak radničke klase u Bosni i Hercegovini i njen razvoj do 1914. godine*, Sarajevo: Svjetlost.

——— 1991, *Bosanskohercegovački gradovi na razmedju 19. i 20. stoljeća*, Sarajevo: Oslobodjenje.

Hadžirović, Ahmed 1978, *Sindikalni pokret u Bosni i Hercegovini 1918–1941*, Belgrade: Rad.

Hadžišehović, Munevera 2003, *A Muslim Woman in Tito's Yugoslavia*, College Station: Texas A&M University Press.

Hauptmann, Ferdo (ed.) 1967, *Borba Muslimana Bosne i Hercegovine za vjersku vakufsko-mearifsku autonomiju: gradja*, Sarajevo: Arhiv Socijalističke Republike Bosne i Hercegovine.

Herceg, Nevenko, and Zoran Tomić 1998, *Izbori u Bosni i Hercegovini*, West Mostar: Sveučelište u Mostaru, Centar za studije novinarstva.

Hickok, Michael Robert 1997, *Ottoman Military Administration in Eighteenth-Century Bosnia*, Leiden: E. J. Brill.

Hoare, Marko Attila 2000, "The Chetnik-Partisan Conflict and the Origins of Bosnian Statehood", Ph.D. dissertation, Yale University.

Holbrooke, Richard 1998, *To End a War*, New York: Random House.

Imamović, Enver 1999, *Historija bosanske vojske*, Sarajevo: Art 7.

Imamović, Mustafa 1997, *Historija Bošnjaka*, Sarajevo: Preporod.

——— 1997, *Pravni položaj i unutrašnjo-politički razvitak Bosne i Hercegovine od 1878–1914*, 2nd edn, Sarajevo: Bosanski kulturni centar.

——— 2001, *Historija države i prava Bosne i Hercegovina*, Sarajevo: Magistrat.

International Crisis Group 1998, "Rebuilding a Multi-ethnic Sarajevo: The Need for Minority Returns," Report 30, February 3, p. 2.

Išek, Tomislav 1981, *Djelatnost Hrvatske seljacke stranke u BiH do zavodjenja diktature*, Sarajevo: Svjetlost.

——— 2002, *Mjesto i uloga NKD Napredak u kulturnom životu Bosne i Hercegovine (1902–1918)*, Sarajevo: Institut za istoriju Sarajevo and Hrvatsko kulturno društvo Napredak.

Jelavich, Barbara 1983, *History of the Balkans: Twentieth Century*, Cambridge University Press

Jelavich, Charles and Barbara 1977, *The Establishment of the Balkan National States, 1804–1920*, Seattle: University of Washington Press.

Jelić-Butić, Fikreta 1977, *Ustaše i Nezavisna Država Hrvatska, 1941–1945*, Zagreb: Liber.

Jović, Borisav 1996, *Poslednji dani SFRJ*, 2nd edn, Kragujevac: Prizma.

Juzbašić, Dževad 1974, *Izgradnje železnica u Bosni i Hercegovini u svjetlu austrougarske politike od okupacije do kraja Kállayeve era*, Sarajevo: Akademija nauka i umjetnosti Bosne i Hercegovine.

———— (ed.) 1997, *Prilozi historiji Sarajeva*, Sarajevo: Institut za istoriju and Orijentalni institut.

———— 2002, "Nekoliko napomena o Jevrejima u Bosni i Hercegovini u doba austrougarske uprave," in Dževad Juzbašić, *Politika i privreda u Bosni i Hercegovini pod austrougarskom upravom*, Sarajevo: Akademija nauka i umjetnosti Bosne i Hercegovine.

Kahrović, Murat 2001, *Kako smo branili Sarajevo: Prva sandžačka brigada*, Sarajevo: Udruženje gradjana Bošnjaka porijeklom iz Sandžaka.

Kaldor, Mary 1999, "Bosnia-Herzegovina: A Case Study of a New War," chapter 3 of Mary Kaldor, *New and Old Wars: Organized Violence in a Global Era*, Stanford University Press.

Kállay, Benjamin von 1878, *Geschichte der Serben von den ältesten Zeiten bis 1815*, Budapest: Lauffer.

Kamberović, Husnija 2000, *Prema modernom društvu. Bosna i Hercegovina od 1945. do 1953. godine*, Tešanj: Centar za kulturu i obrazovanje Tešanj.

———— 2002, *Husein-kapetan Gradaščević (1802–1834). Biografija uz dvjetostotu godišnjicu rodjenja*, Gradačac: Preporod.

Kamhi, Samuel (ed.) 1966, *Spomenica 400 godina od dolaska Jevreja u Bosnu i Hercegovinu*, Sarajevo: Oslobodjenje.

Kann, Robert A. 1974, *A History of the Habsburg Empire 1526–1918*, Berkeley: University of California Press.

Kapidžić, Hamdija 1963, "Sarajevo u avgustu 1878. godine," *Prilozi za proučavanje istorije Sarajeva* 1, 1, pp. 117–31.

———— 1973, *Hercegovački ustanak 1882. godine*, Sarajevo: Veselin Masleša.

Karabegović, Ibrahim 1979, *Reformistički pravac u radničkom pokretu Bosne i Hercegovine 1919–1941. godine*, Sarajevo: Svjetlost.

Karabegović, Ibrahim *et al.* 1994, *Bosna i Hercegovina od najstarijih vremena do kraja drugog svjetskog rata*, Sarajevo: Press Centar Armije Republike Bosne i Hercegovine.

Karić, Enes (ed.) 2002, *Reis Džemaludin Čaušević. prosvjetitelj i reformator*, 2 vols, Sarajevo: Ljiljan.

Kecmanović, Nenad 1992, "Drama sarajevskih Srba," *NIN*, September 18, pp. 55–8.

Kemura, Ibrahim 1986, *Uloga "Gajreta" u društvenom životu Muslimana Bosne i Hercegovine 1903–1941*, Sarajevo: Veselin Masleša.

Koetschet, Josef 1905, *Aus Bosniens letzter Türkenzeit*, Vienna: Georg Grassl.

Koštunica, Vojislav, and Kosta Čavoški 1985, *Party Pluralism or Monism. Social Movements and the Political System in Yugoslavia, 1944–1949*, Boulder, CO: East European Monographs.

Kraljačić, Tomislav 1966, "Razvoj i političke akcije mjesne organizacije KPJ u Sarajevu 1919–1920," *Glasnik arhiva i Društva arhivskih radnika Bosne i Hercegovine*, 6, pp. 181–94.

———— 1987, *Kalajev režim u Bosni i Hercegovini (1882–1903)*, Sarajevo: Veselin Masleša.

Kreševljaković, Hamdija 1958, *Esnafi i obrti u starom Sarajevu*, Sarajevo: Narodna prosvjeta.

———— 1969, *Sarajevo za vrijeme austrougarkse uprave (1878–1918)*, Sarajevo: Arhiv grada Sarajeva.

———— 1991, *Sarajevo u doba okupacije Bosne 1878*, in Hamdija Kreševljaković, *Izabrana Djela*, vol. 4, Sarajevo: Veselin Masleša.

Kruševac, Todor 1960, *Sarajevo pod austro-ugarskom upravom, 1878–1918*, Sarajevo: Muzej grada Sarajeva. ·

———— 1978, *Bosansko-hercegovački listovi u xix veku*, Sarajevo: Veselin Masleša.

Krzović, Ibrahim 1987, *Arhitektura Bosne i Hercegovine, 1878–1918*, Sarajevo: Umjetnička galerija Bosne i Hercegovine.

Kukanjac, Milutin 2000, "Moja istina," *NIN*, January 6, pp. 56–9.

Kurspahić, Kemal 1997, *As Long As Sarajevo Exists*, trans. Colleen London, Stony Creek, CT: Pamphleteer's Press.

Kurto, Nedžad 1998, *Arhitektura Bosne i Hercegovine: razvoj bosanskog stila*, Sarajevo: Sarajevo Publishing.

Lampe, John 1996, *Yugoslavia as History: Twice There Was a Country*, Cambridge University Press.

Levy, Moritz 1996, *Die Sephardim in Bosnien. Ein Beitrag zur Geschichte der Juden auf der Balkanhalbinsel*, reproduction of 1911 edn, Klagenfurt: Wieser Verlag.

Lilly, Carol S. 2001, *Power and Persuasion: Ideology and Rhetoric in Communist Yugoslavia, 1944–1953*, Boulder, CO: Westview.

Lučarević, Kerim 2000, *The Battle for Sarajevo: Sentenced to Victory*, Sarajevo: FZV.

Maass, Peter 1996, *Love Thy Neighbor: A Story of War*, New York: Alfred A. Knopf.

MacDonald, David Bruce 2002, "'Greater Serbia' and 'Greater Croatia:' the Moslem question in Bosnia-Hercegovina," chapter 8 of David Bruce MacDonald, *Balkan holocausts? Serbian and Croatian victim-centred propaganda and the war in Yugoslavia*, Manchester University Press.

Maček, Ivana 2000, *War Within: Everyday Life in Sarajevo under Siege*, Uppsala Studies in Cultural Anthropology 29. Uppsala: Acta Universitatis Upsaliensis.

MacKenzie, Lewis 1993, *Peacekeeper: The Road to Sarajevo*, Vancouver: Douglas and McIntyre.

Madžar, Božo 1982, *Pokret Srba Bosne i Hercegovine za vjersko-prosvjetnu samoupravu*, Sarajevo: Veselin Masleša.

———— 1985. "Sto godine Vladine zgrade u Sarajevu (1885–1985)," *Glasnik arhiva i Društva arhivskih radnika Bosne i Hercegovine*, 25, pp. 249–55.

———— 2001, *Prosvjeta. Srpsko prosvjetno i kulturno društvo 1902–1949*. Banja Luka and Srpsko Sarajevo: Akademija nauka Republike Srpske.

Magaš, Branka, and Ivo Žanić (eds) 1999, *Rat u Hrvatskoj i Bosni i Hercegovini, 1991–1995*, Zagreb-Sarajevo: Dani.

Malcolm, Noel 1996, *Bosnia: A Short History*, updated edn, New York University Press.

Mandić, Mihovil 1910, *Povijest okupacije Bosne i Hercegovine, 1878*, Zagreb: Matica hrvatska.

Martić, Grga 1906, *Zapamćenja*, Zagreb: Gjura Trpinac.

Masleša, Veselin 1990, *Mlada Bosna*, 2nd edn, Sarajevo: Veselin Masleša.

Mazower, Mark 2004, *Salonica, City of Ghosts: Christians, Muslims and Jews, 1430–1950*, London: HarperCollins.

Medlicott, William N. 1938, *The Congress of Berlin and After*, London: Methuen.

Mehičić, Irfan, and Muedeta Hadžiabdić (eds) 1998, *Privreda u opkoljenom Sarajevu*, Sarajevo: Privredna komora regije Sarajevo

Meier, Viktor 1999, *Yugoslavia: A History of Its Demise*, trans. Sabrina P. Ramet, London: Routledge.

Meštrović, Ivan 1969, *Uspomene na političke ljude i dogadjaje*, Zagreb: Matica hrvatska.

Milazzo, Matteo J. 1975, *The Chetnik Movement and the Yugoslav Resistance*, Baltimore, MD: Johns Hopkins University Press.

Miličić, Budimir 1985, *Radnička klasa Sarajeva 1919–1941. godine*, Sarajevo: Institut za istoriju.

Milidragović, Dušan 1984, *Komunalno uredjenje grada Sarajeva*, Sarajevo: *Službeni list SRBiH*.

Milišić, Senija 1987, "Emancipacija Muslimanske žene u Bosni i Herzegovini nakon osloboboodjenja (1947–52)," master's thesis, University of Sarajevo.

———— 2004, "Institucionalizacija nauke u Bosni i Hercegovini (1945–1958)," Ph.D. dissertation, University of Sarajevo, 2004.

Moore, Wilbert E. 1945, *Economic Demography of Eastern and Southern Europe*, Geneva: League of Nations.

Nedimović, Uroš 1974, "Komparacije izmedju akcije Mlade Bosne (1914) i Crvene pravde (1921)," *Pregled*, 7–8, pp. 741–8.

Neuffer, Elizabeth 2001, *The Key to My Neighbor's House: Seeking Justice in Bosnia and Rwanda*, New York: Picador.

Nezirović, Muhamed (ed.) 1995, *Sefarad 92. Zbornik radova*, Sarajevo: Institut za istoriju and Jevrejska zajednica Bosne i Hercegovine.

Nilević, Boris 1990, *Srpska pravoslavna crkva u Bosni i Hercegovini do obnove Pećke patrijaršije 1557. godine*, Sarajevo: Veselin Masleša.

Odbor za izdavanje Spomenica pok. M. Srškiću 1938, *Milan Srškić*, Sarajevo: Odbora za izdavanje Spomenica pok. M. Srškiću.

Orijentalni Institut 2000, *Orijentalni institut u Sarajevu 1950–2000. / The Institute for Oriental Studies in Sarajevo 1950–2000*, Sarajevo: Orijentalni institut.

Papić, Mitar 1972, *Školstvo u Bosni i Hercegovini za vrijeme austro-ugarske okupacije*, Sarajevo: Veselin Masleša.

———— 1978, *Istorija srpskih škola u Bosni i Hercegovini*, Sarajevo: Veselin Masleša.

———— 1982, *Hrvatsko školstvo u Bosni i Hercegovini do 1918. godine*, Sarajevo: Veselin Masleša.

Pavković, Aleksandar 1997, *The Fragmentation of Yugoslavia: Nationalism in a Multinational State*, London: Macmillan Press.

Pejanović, Djordje 1961, *Bibliografije štampe Bosne i Hercegovine 1850–1941*, Sarajevo: Veselin Masleša.

Pejanović, Mirko 2004, *Through Bosnian Eyes: The Political Memoir of a Bosnian Serb*, trans. Marina Bowder, West Lafayette, IN: Purdue University Press.

Petrinić, Mirko, and Milenko Pajić (eds) 1997, *Raniiji gradonačelnici za Sarajevo, 1992–1996*, Sarajevo: Klub ranijih gradonačelnika Sarajeva.

Petrović, Rade 1977, "Pokret otpora u Bosni i Hercegovini protiv austrougarske okupacije 1878. godine, prema izvještajima Talijanskog konzulata u Sarajevu," volume 3 of *Medjunarodni naučni skup povodom 100. godišnjice ustanaka u Bosni i Hercegovini, drugim balkanskim zemljama i istočnoj krizi 1875–1878 godine*, Sarajevo: Akademija nauka i umjetnosti Bosne i Hercegovine, pp. 343–73.

Petrovich, Michael Boro 1976, *A History of Modern Serbia, 1804–1918*, 2 vols, New York: Harcourt Brace Jovanovich.

Pinto, Avram 1987, *Jevreji Sarajeva i Bosne i Hercegovine*, Sarajevo: Veselin Masleša.

Praštalo, Tatjana 1997, "Death of a Library," *Logos* 8, 2, pp. 96–9.

Prstojević, Miroslav 1992, *Zaboravljeno Sarajevo*, Sarajevo: Ideja.

———— 1994, *The Wounded City*, trans. Dževahira Arslanagić and Gordana Kisić, Ljubljana: DAG Grafika.

Purivatra, Atif 1974, *Jugoslovenska muslimanska organizacija u političkom životu Kraljevine Srba Hrvata i Slovenaca*, Sarajevo: Svjetlost.

Redžić, Enver 1987, *Muslimansko autonomaštvo i 13. SS divizija: autonomija Bosne i Hercegovine i Hitlerov Treći Rajh*, Sarajevo: Svjetlost.

———— (ed.) 1987, *Prilozi za istoriju Bosne i Hercegovine*, 2 vols, Sarajevo: Akademija nauka i umjetnosti Bosne i Hercegovine.

———— 2005, *Bosnia and Herzegovina in the Second World War*, London: Frank Cass.

Ribar, Ivan 1948, *Politički zapisi*, 2 vols, Belgrade: Prosveta.

Rieff, David 1995, *Slaughterhouse: Bosnia and the Failure of the West*, New York: Siimon and Schuster.

Rogel, Carole 1998, *The Breakup of Yugoslavia and the War in Bosnia*, Westport, CT: Greenwood Press.

Romano, Jaša 1980, *Jevreji Jugoslavije 1941–1945; Žrtve genocida i učesnici NOR*, Belgrade: Savez jevrejskih opština Jugoslavije.

Rothschild, Joseph 1974, *East Central Europe between the Two World Wars*, Seattle: University of Washington Press.

Razović, Maja, and Aleksandra Wagner (eds), n.d., *Sarajevo Survival Guide*, Sarajevo: FAMA.

Rujanac, Zijad 2003, *Opsjednuti grad Sarajevo*, Sarajevo: Bosanski kulturni centar.

Rusinow, Dennison 1977, *The Yugoslav Experiment, 1948–1974*, London: Hurst (for Royal Institute of International Affairs).

Šabanović, Hazim 1960, "Postanak i razvoj Sarajeva," *Radovi, Odjeljenje istorijsko-filoloških nauka*, 5, pp. 72–6.

———— 1982, *Bosanski pašaluk*, Sarajevo: Svjetlost.

Šarac, Nedim 1975, *Uspostavljanje šestojanuarskog režima 1929. godine sa posebnim osvrtom na Bosnu i Hercegovinu*, Sarajevo: Svjetlost.

Sarić, Sajma 1974–5, "Arhivski fond velika župe Vrhbosne," *Glasnik arhiva i Društva arhivskih radnika Bosne i Hercegovine*, 14–15, pp. 37–43.

Schmitt, Bernadotte 1937, *The Annexation of Bosnia, 1908–1909*, Cambridge University Press.

Schorske, Carl E. 1980, *Fin-de-Siècle Vienna: Politics and Culture*, New York: Knopf.

Šehić, Nusret 1971, *Četništvo u Bosni i Hercegovini (1918–1941). Politička uloga i oblici djelatnosti četničkih udruženja*, Sarajevo: Akademija nauka i umjetnosti Bosne i Hercegovine.

———— 1980, *Autonomni pokret Muslimana za vrijeme austrougarske uprave u Bosni i Hercegovini*, Sarajevo: Svjetlost.

———— 1991, *Bosna i Hercegovina 1918–1925. privredni i politički razvoj*, Sarajevo: Institut za istoriju.

———— 2003, *Dnevni zapisi o životu pod četničkom opsadom tokom 1992. i 1993. god*, 2 vols, Sarajevo: Rabic.

Šidak, Jaroslav *et al.* 1968, *Povijest hrvatskog naroda g. 1860–1914*, Zagreb: Školska knjiga.

Silber, Laura, and Allan Little 1997, *Yugoslavia: Death of a Nation*, New York: Penguin Books.

Simms, Brendan 2002, *Unfinest Hour: Britain and the Destruction of Bosnia*, New York: Penguin Books.

Skarić, Vladislav 1937, *Sarajevo i njegova okolina od najstarijih vremena do austrougarske okupacije*, Sarajevo: Opština grada Sarajeva.

Šljivo, Galib 1977, *Omer-paša Latas u Bosni i Hercegovini, 1850–1852*, Sarajevo: Svjetlost.

Smiljanić-Djikić, Vojka (ed.), 1988. *Graditelji Sarajeva*, Sarajevo: Radio Sarajevo 3.

Sorabji, Cornelia 1995, "A Very Modern War: Terror and Territory in Bosnia-Hercegovina," in Robert A. Hinde and Helen E. Watson (eds), *War: A Cruel Necessity? The Bases of Institutionalized Violence*, pp. 81–95, London: I. B. Tauris.

Spasojević, Boris 1999, *Arhitektura stambenih palata austrougarskog perioda u Sarajevu*, 2nd edn, Sarajevo: Rabic.

Štraus, Ivan 1998, *Arhitektura Bosne i Hercegovine / The Architecture of Bosnia and Herzegovina, 1945–1995*, Sarajevo: Oko.

Sugar, Peter 1963, *The Industrialization of Bosnia-Herzegovina, 1878–1918*, Seattle: University of Washington Press.

Sumner, B. H. 1962, *Russia and the Balkans 1870–1880*, Hamden, CT: Archon Books.

Trhulj, Sead 1994, *Mladi Muslimani*, Sarajevo: Oko.

Todorov, Nikolai 1983, *The Balkan City, 1400–1900*, Seattle: University of Washington Press.

Tomasevich, Jozo 1975, *The Chetniks: War and Revolution in Yugoslavia, 1941–1945*, Stanford University Press.

——— 2001, *War and Revolution in Yugoslavia: Occupation and Collaboration*, Stanford University Press.

US, Central Intelligence Agency 2002, *Balkan Battlegrounds: A Military History of the Yugoslav Conflict, 1990–1995*, 2 vols, Washington, DC: Central Intelligence Agency.

Vulliamy, Ed 1994, *Seasons in Hell: Understanding Bosnia's War*, New York: St. Martin's Press.

Wachtel, Andrew Baruch 1998, *Making a Nation, Breaking a Nation: Literature and Cultural Politics in Yugoslavia*, Stanford University Press.

Wenzel, Marian 1962, "Bosnian and Herzegovinian Tombstones: Who Made Them and Why," *Südost Forschungen*, 21, pp. 102–43.

——— 1965, *Ukrasni motivi na stećcima. Oriental Motifs on Tombstones from Medieval Bosnia and Surrounding Regions*, Sarajevo: Veselin Masleša.

——— 1999, "Bosnian History and Austro-Hungarian Policy: Some Medieval Belts, the Bogomil Romance and the King Tvrtko Graves," in Marian Wenzel, *Bosanski stil na stećcima i metalu / Bosnian Style on Tombstones and Metal*, pp. 169–205, Sarajevo: Sarajevo Publishing.

Winter, Jay 1997, "Paris, London, Berlin 1914–1919: Capital Cities at War," in Jay Winter and Jean-Louis Robert (eds), *Capital Cities at War: Paris, London, Berlin 1914–1919*, Cambridge University Press.

Woodward, Susan 1995, *Balkan Tragedy: Chaos and Dissolution after the Cold War*, Washington, DC: Brookings Institution Press.

——— 1995, *Socialist Unemployment: The Political Economy of Yugoslavia, 1945–1990*, Princeton University Press.

Zlatar, Behija 1996, *Zlatna doba Sarajeva*, Sarajevo: Svjetlost.

Zulfikarpašić, Adil 1998, *The Bosniak*, London: Hurst.

Index

Abdić, Fikret, 261, 294, 396 n. 31
Academy of Arts and Sciences of Bosnia-
  Herzegovina, 222, 244, 314, 351
Adilbeg Mosque, 345
aerial bombardment: German and Italian, of
  Sarajevo, 168–9, 201, 223; Allied, of
  Sarajevo, 197, 198, 201, 223; NATO, of
  targets in Republika Srpska, 328, 332–3
agrarian crisis, 105, 109, 158–9
agrarian reform, 134–5, 159, 375 n. 84
airport of Sarajevo, see Sarajevo airport
Ajnadžić, Nedžad, 310, 311
Alagić, Haris, 320
Aleksandar I Karadjordjević (Regent and King):
  129, 148, 156–8; assassination of (1934),
  131, 153, 171; memorial culture of, 156–8;
  proclaims dictatorship (1929), 151–2; proclaims Kingdom of Serbs, Croats, and
  Slovenes (1918), 130–1; Sarajevo visit of
  (1920), 146–7
Aličić, Ahmed, 23
Alkalaj, Vito, 142–3
Alliance of Reformist Forces of Yugoslavia, see
  Reformists
American Relief Administration, 160
Anderson, Benedict, xi
annexation of Bosnia-Herzegovina, see Bosnia-
  Herzegovina: annexation of
anniversaries, see holidays
Antifascist Women's Front, 209, 218–20
apartments: 213–4, 226, 346–7; dual
  occupancy of, 213; residential complexes of,
  165, 229–31, 242; Ustasha and NDH expro-
  priation of, 177–8; see also Sarajevo: housing
  policy
ARBiH (*Armija Republike Bosne i Hercegovine*;
  Army of the Republic of Bosnia-
  Herzegovina): 277, 318, 340; sieges of JNA
  installations by, 294, 297–9, 316; casualties

suffered by, 296, 334; Croats in, 311;
  defense of Presidency by, against armored
  JNA incursion (May 1992), 294–5; attack on
  JNA column in Dobrovoljačka Street by,
  296; First Corps of, 310–12; formation of,
  292, 395 n. 24; hides gunpowder in oxygen
  containers, 311; operations of, 296, 298,
  312–13, 329, 331–3, 399 n. 93; outgunned
  by VRS, 281, 309–12, 314, 399 n. 88;
  provisioning of, 326; Serbs in, 311, 323;
  snipers in, 316; strength of, 309–12, 329;
  struggles for high ground by, 283, 311, 312;
  tunnels under airport, 325–6; withdrawal
  from Marshal Tito Barracks of (1996), 340
architectural styles: 1; Middle Eastern, 345,
  351; modern, 1, 165, 232, 233, 246, 351;
  monumental, 1, 16, 79; neo-Baroque, 78;
  neo-Classical, 164; neo-Gothic, 68; neo-
  Historicist, 76, 169; neo-Orientalist, 70–2,
  164, 314; neo-Romanesque, 72, 223; neo-
  Renaissance, 70; romantic historicism, 68,
  70, 72, 92; Secession, 1, 72–3, 78, 92;
  socialist realist, 231–2; Western, 232
Archive of Bosnia-Herzegovina, 91, 177, 221–2
Army of the Republic of Bosnia-Herzegovina,
  see ARBiH
Artuković, Andrija, 187
Ashkenazim, 15, 63, 72, 78–9, 107, 123, 157,
  176; see also Jews, synagogues
Ashdown, Paddy, 326, 350
assassination, see under Franz Ferdinand
Assembly Building, see Bosnian Assembly
  Building
Assembly church, see new Serbian Orthodox
  church
Austria: 343; army of, burns Sarajevo (1697),
  24; see also Habsburg army; Habsburg
  Monarchy
Austria-Hungary, see Habsburg Monarchy

417